What people are s[...]

Science Fiction: The Evolutionary Mythology of the Future

Thomas Lombardo's *Science Fiction: The Evolutionary Mythology of the Future* puts the history of science fiction in the much broader context of the evolution of human future consciousness through the ages. The fresh and inspiring perspective of regarding science fiction as evolutionary mythology of the future opens up new ways to consider its roots and the intellectual developments that fed into it—from ancient myths and Greek philosophy through pivotal medieval thinkers to the nineteenth century. The book is tremendously well researched, based on an intimate knowledge of the history of mythology and philosophy and, last but not least, it breathes the huge enthusiasm of its author for science fiction. Volume One of the planned series is an inspiring read as well for the academic as for the lover of science fiction—with lots of insights into its sources and evolutionary stages, its main tributaries and overarching themes. On the whole the book presents a grand vision of the role of science fiction in the progress of human consciousness.

Dr. Karlheinz Steinmüller, Science Fiction Author and Futurist, Winner of the Kurd Lasswitz Award

Lombardo's book is a brilliant piece of work and I loved reading it. For us who love science fiction, Lombardo's excellent book should not only become a 'must read' but 'obligatory'. The high level of reflections, the many funny examples, the personal approach, and how he succeeds in demonstrating how science fiction, as narratives of the future, is so much more than technological extrapolations and special effects, leave behind a totally different perspective on science fiction than the one

dominating our popular contemporary conception of the field. I simply love the way Lombardo approaches the field!
Dr. Erik F. Øverland, President of the World Futures Studies Federation

Thomas Lombardo's magisterial exploration of science fiction's mythological dimension is meticulously researched but personal and accessible. I wish I'd had this to read when I began writing science fiction, and I know it will be invaluable to futures researchers who want to incorporate science-fictioning as a part of their practice. I eagerly look forward to the next volume.
Karl Schroeder, Science Fiction Author of *Lady of Mazes*, *Ventus*, and *Sun of Suns*

A spectacular read! Informative. Engaging. Insightful. I learned so much from reading it. The book is full of revelations, and gave me a new way to think about Western Civilization. Indeed, the central premise was astonishing—that science fiction—so often trivialized—is in fact a mythology that guides us towards our collective future. An amazing symmetry created with *The War of the Worlds* at the beginning and end of the book. I fully agree with the superlatives by many experts about the depth and quality of Tom's work.
Tim Ward, Author of *Indestructible You* and *The Master Communicator's Handbook*

A rich and enthusiastic account of science fiction's power to help us imagine the future. Tom Lombardo's book is a celebration and inspiration.
Dr. Bryan Alexander, Futurist, Speaker, Writer. Teacher, Consultant, Homesteader, Author of *Gearing Up for Learning Beyond K-12* and *The New Digital Storytelling*

Once again, Dr. Lombardo has taken a subject previously visited by many other writers and brought a new eye and a broader vision in his analysis of the cultural history of science fiction. I heartily endorse his decision to look much earlier for the roots of the genre than is usual and his expansive view of what influences to include in his analysis. It is this sort of rich discussion that has consistently rewarded me as a reader of his work over the years. I look forward to the second volume.

Timothy C. Mack, Esq., Former President World Future Society and Founder of AAI Foresight

For those interested in science fiction, cultural history, or the interplay of myth, science, and literature, Tom Lombardo has given us a veritable cornucopia of fascinating and enlightening information about science fiction and its place in the story of civilization. For those of us interested in the history of ideas and especially the role played by science fiction in the evolution of consciousness and our awareness of the future, Lombardo's work will be the touchstone for many years to come.

Dr. Leslie Combs, CIIS Professor and Director of the Center of Consciousness Studies and President of The Society of Consciousness Studies

Tom Lombardo dives into some of the eternal questions of science fiction, its relationship with tomorrow, with the universe, and with the vastly more complex realm within each human brain and heart.

David Brin, Science Fiction Author of *Startide Rising, The Uplift War, The Postman,* and *Existence*

From the viewpoint of a French social scientist, passionate reader and teacher of science fiction, and an international futurist, I can witness the huge yet mostly undervalued impact of science fiction on the way we create our images of the future. With his new book, Tom Lombardo adds a much needed contribution to the path begun with Berger and Pollack. Too often considered as a literary sub-gender, science fiction is indeed a deep revealer of our worldviews, paradigms, hopes, fears, and blind spots. Digging even deeper, Tom clearly exposes the postmodernity of science fiction as a contemporary myth founder, building the hopes and opening the possibilities for disruptive novelty to happen. The amazingly broad and accurate knowledge Tom displays along with his diachronic brilliant analysis has already made of this first volume a "must-read" and a now necessary reference book in the study both of science fiction and of the future.

Fabienne Goux-Baudiment, Founding member of the French Society for Foresight and Former President of the World Futures Studies Federation

Thomas Lombardo has provided a comprehensive exploration of science fiction as a model for integrating the studies of human evolution, scientific progress, and mythological narratives, ultimately advancing our understanding of and relationship with the future. The dramas (and comedies) that flow through these diverse stories both challenge us to face our fears of the unknown and inspire us to envision possibilities, of which the future—like the imagination—holds multitudes.

Cynthia Wagner, Consulting Editor for AAI Foresight and former Editor of *The Futurist*

Mythology's Scientific Evolution: Tom Lombardo's new history of science fiction seems every bit as comprehensive in scope and meticulous in detail as his last publication, *Future Consciousness*. Beyond scholarly, this first book of his multi-volume series reads like a labor of love. Lombardo views science fiction as a powerful public mythology attuned to our technologically advancing times. He begins with a cogent analysis of how ancient religions, cosmologies, and heroic sagas provided coherent worldviews that embodied shared mythologies, illuminating every aspect of daily life and culture with transcendent meaning. Using numerous examples from philosophy, literature, and emerging sciences, Lombardo then charts a detailed course through the centuries to the more widely creative and speculative scientific mythologies of our own times. This engaging history of science fiction suggests how the most sophisticated and thoughtful works of the genre can create "grand narratives" spanning all of space, time, and human experience, exploring manifold dimensions of inner spirit and outer cosmos. Offering mythological vistas hauntingly familiar yet newly imaginative, the best modern science fiction creates anew what Lombardo terms a "totally immersive" sense of the wondrous possibilities of being alive, in a mysteriously evolving and expansive cosmos awaiting our wise of choice possible futures.

Donald H. Sanborn, Associate Professor Emeritus, Philosophy and Humanities, City Colleges of Chicago

In the endless unrolling of postmodern epistemologies, it is critical to explore the narrative possibilities of alternative formats to objective and abstract reporting. In this regard, science fiction best captures the possibilities of storytelling to reach visions and envision futures way beyond what scientific exposition can do. Who better than Verne, Robida, and Wells, just to name a few, sketched the world as we experience it today in the previous century? In this new work, renowned futurist Tom Lombardo provides an extensive review of the history of the future as it once was in the words of writers, novelists, and talented minds within science fiction (as well as philosophy and science). This makes *Science Fiction: The Evolutionary Mythology of the Future* a must have for both science fiction fans as well as professional futurists.

Dr. Marco Bevolo, Marco Bevolo Consulting, Lecturer and Researcher, NHTV University of Applied Sciences, The Netherlands

In this remarkable book, Tom Lombardo views science fiction as a form of evolutionary mythology for the future. Rather than being juvenile and superficial, it is actually conscious-raising and expansive, enabling its readers to experience their personal connection to the cosmos. In this reader-friendly book, Lombardo uses selections from well-known science fiction authors to exemplify his points. Once readers finish their journey through these pages, I suspect that they will never peruse science fiction stories or novels the same way again!

Stanley Krippner, Ph.D., Professor of Psychology, Saybrook University, Co-author of *Personal Mythology*

As a futurist, it is part of my work to read science fiction. I'm lucky that I love it and always have. I had not previously considered the history of science fiction at any length: Tom Lombardo's book is helpful in this regard. I really enjoyed his introduction and his personal story of how he came to love science fiction — a journey not dissimilar to my own. From there, he examines the genre from a number of different perspectives, including mythology, ancient history to modern history, evolution, science, and extra-terrestrial adventures. In reading Lombardo's book, it is interesting to see how the genre has developed over time and how it links into the human narrative. While not a light read, the book provides excellent food for thought. I look forward to Volume Two!

Patricia Lustig, Fellow of the Royal Society for Arts, Manufacturing and Commerce, CEO of LASA Insight Ltd and Author of *Strategic Foresight: Learning from the Future*

Professor Lombardo's encyclopedic assessment of science fiction as a uniquely evolutionary art form is mind candy of the highest order — must reading for serious fans of the genre.

Oliver Markley, Professor Emeritus, Graduate Studies of the Future, University of Houston-Clear Lake

The future is a contentious topic for many. Literature academics typically deride science fiction as a subpar genre while science academics belittle futures studies as a soft science even below most social sciences. However, as a combined topic, Lombardo explores humanity's perspectives of the future by tracing the history of the art of science fiction and the history of the scientific study of foresight, and shows how these two human endeavors, which often interweave, are noble attempts to intellectually grapple with the unknown and the unknowable while often inspiring human progress. It is a fascinating read for science fiction fans and academics alike.

Dennis Draeger, Futurist and Senior Researcher, *Shaping Tomorrow*

This is an extraordinary labor of love, filled with summaries of stories, following the development of science fiction from the earliest tales to the rise of H. G. Wells. Readers not familiar with some of these stories will wonder at their prescience and in some cases how different from their conventional reputations they can be. In his commentary, Lombardo gives these stories thought-provoking context with respect to progressive versus cyclical views of history, naturalistic versus magical trappings, utopian versus dystopian viewpoints, and other contemporary literary coordinates. With an appropriately large bibliography, this work should become an essential addition to the bookshelves of people interested in the history of science fiction.

Gerald David Nordley, Science Fiction Author of *To Climb a Flat Mountain* and British Interplanetary Society Member and Author of *Mass Beam Propulsion: An Overview*

As a foresight practitioner, science fiction is an important part of my work. Tom Lombardo's book provides foresight practitioners with a great foundation of knowledge about science fiction as mythology and a serious source of future stories and thoughts to inspire the people and organizations they work with. Professionals who concern themselves with the future should read this book to gain more insights into their own myths about the future as well as to broaden their minds. The book provides an overview of important questions about the future of humankind and how we as a society decide how to shape our future. Tom Lombardo's book gives us insight in classic and modern science fiction and best of all points out that there is hope for the future.

Silke den Hartog-de Wilde, *School of Foresight*, Netherlands

I cannot think of anyone better equipped to write on science fiction than Tom Lombardo. He is an excellent researcher and writer. He is also the only person I know who can explain how the dominant themes in science fiction have evolved over time, showing how breakthroughs or crises in science, technology, society, and the human psyche, are reflected in the science fiction of the day. In this book, Tom convincingly shows how science fiction is the new evolutionary mythology of the future; he demonstrates how evolutionary thought has greatly influenced not only science, but all science fiction writing. Also, Tom describes how science fiction writers have creatively explored many alternative future scenarios for humans, helping to clarify the many dangers, challenges, and positive opportunities, as humanity moves at an accelerating rate into the future. As a professional psychologist, he is also able to explore important questions of human consciousness and how humans can evolve their consciousness to deal with accelerative technological change. I recommend this book most wholeheartedly.

Dr. Linda Groff, Emeritus Professor, Political Science & Futures Studies, California State University

Tom first encountered the Martians in the movies when he was six years old and has never left science fiction since. With great knowledge about the most important authors and influential ideas through the centuries, Tom takes us on a journey into the unknown and introduces us to diverse ways of reflection on the deepest issues of existence and human reality, covering areas such as philosophy, mythology, and science along the way. For Tom, the history of science fiction reflects the history of humankind. Although the book delves into human history, its strength lies in the way it highlights an approach about the future for the future. Science fiction is the key to understanding our world, and his comprehensive treatment of the topic is a central virtue of the book. He shows us that we are capable of connecting our greatest ideals and deepest desires through living and feeling possible futures revealed in science fiction. As Tom states, science fiction is about the future of everything and not just about science and technology; it is about the hopes and fears of the human psyche.

Guillermina Baena Paz, Ph.D., Vice-President (Latin America) World Futures Studies Federation

Tom Lombardo knows science fiction—really knows it. I've heard him speak, and the passion and love he brings to the topic is electrifying.

Brenda Cooper, Science Fiction Author of *Wilders*, *Edge of Dark*, and *Spear of Light*

Science Fiction: The Evolutionary Mythology of the Future

Volume One: Prometheus to the Martians

Science Fiction: The Evolutionary Mythology of the Future

Volume One: Prometheus to the Martians

Thomas Lombardo

CHANGE
MAKERS
BOOKS

Winchester, UK
Washington, USA

First published by Changemakers Books, 2018
Changemakers Books is an imprint of John Hunt Publishing Ltd., No. 3 East Street,
Alresford, Hampshire SO24 9EE, UK
office1@jhpbooks.net
www.johnhuntpublishing.com
www.changemakers-books.com

For distributor details and how to order please visit the 'Ordering' section on our website.

ISBN: 978 1 78535 853 1
978 1 78535 854 8 (ebook)
Library of Congress Control Number: 2017954130

A CIP catalogue record for this book is available from the British Library.

Design: Stuart Davies

Printed and bound by CPI Group (UK) Ltd, Croydon, CR0 4YY, UK

We operate a distinctive and ethical publishing philosophy in
all areas of our business, from our global network of authors to
production and worldwide distribution.

Contents

For her receptive and patient ear as I recounted to her a thousand science fiction stories I had read; for her scrupulous and methodical editing and her literary acumen, where I was often the resistant student; and for her unwavering love and support for my life of ideas and scholarship, I dedicate this book to my dear wife, Jeanne Belisle Lombardo.

Chapter 1

Introduction to Science Fiction

Science Fiction as a Way of Life

Yet across the gulf of space, minds that are to our minds as ours are to those beasts that perish, intellects vast and cool and unsympathetic, regarded this earth with envious eyes, and slowly and surely drew their plans against us.
H. G. Wells

It is 1953. Six years old, my young mind completely enthralled, I am mesmerized, sitting with my parents and sister in the *Alhambra Theater* in Waterbury, Connecticut, watching the newly released movie *The War of the Worlds*. Up on the screen the drama unfolds ...

Fear, if not panic in her eyes, the young woman approaches the priest—her uncle—from behind. She puts her hand gently on his arm; but as they talk her grip becomes ever tighter as her anxiety mounts. She is trying to convince him to return to the safety of the army bunker. But the priest's eyes are fixed, gazing toward the mystery—perhaps the miracle—coming into view across the open field. "If they are more advanced than us, they must be closer to the Creator," he says. (Is this true? Do the potential wonders of science and the faith of religion meet in this insight?) The uncle persuades his frightened niece to go back into the bunker.

The priest walks forward across the charred and smoking field, chanting "Though I walk through the valley of the Shadow of Death ..." An eerie melody—spiritual and unearthly in tone—steadily rises in volume, setting a cosmic ambience to the scene. The priest holds up a small Bible with a bright golden image of the Cross on its cover — the image of his God.

Inside the bunker, the army personnel spot the priest walking across the field. The young woman rushes to the narrow lookout opening and seeing her uncle, screams in terror.

In front of the priest, coming into view are three saucer-shaped machines, each floating high above the ground, steadily moving closer. Presumably the machines are from Mars. Without much evidence to go on, that's what the scientists have said.

The machines are black, their two lateral tips and bulbous tops a glowing emerald green; long, curving necks, suggestive of sauropods or plesiosaurs, snake up out of their bodies. At the end of each is something like a head or an eye that pulses in light and sound. The machines seem like some kind of sentient animals. How very strange these things are.

The leader of the triad descends, lowering its great eye toward the priest, as the beating sound from its menacing presence grows louder. The priest thrusts the Bible with its holy image of the Cross upward. (This is the symbolic face-off between earthly religion and transcendent science and technology, a critical archetypal theme in science fiction. Are science and God one? Or are science and God at odds?) The sound from the Martian machine intensifies, reaching a vibratory climax, and out of the Martian eye blasts a stream of scintillating light rays, totally obliterating and vaporizing the priest.

The surrounding army artillery explodes in a tremendous assault of fire power directed at the Martian machines. Tanks, cannons, rockets, machine guns, bazookas all open fire. The sound is colossal. But the Martian machines are impervious, deflecting the army shells with some kind of protective and invisible force. The machines fire back, rays spewing out from their "heads" and pulses of green light-energy shooting outward from their lateral tips. Tanks, cannons, trucks — all forms of human gunnery vaporize in blinding green flashes, as do the humans, their skeletal outlines momentarily visible in the green ghostly glow.

We are powerless against this level of technology, the scientist in the bunker tells the colonel crouched next to him. We are like children against these things, primitive creatures confronting the unfathomable forces of the universe. The retreat begins—a man bursts into flame; a tank glows and disappears; the colonel is vaporized; everyone runs for the hills; the rout of humanity has begun.

Eventually after the Martians decimate most of human civilization, and even stand imperturbable to a direct hit from a hydrogen bomb, they are defeated by God and bacteria, an ending that, as a six year old, I initially found ingenious. (Although I also felt sad that all the Martians died and their wondrous machines collapsed.) As explained in the movie, bacteria on the earth were created by God; the invading Martians were not immune to our germs; and after a sufficient time, the Martians became infected, grew sick, and died. In the end our faith is vindicated, the priest's life is redeemed, and God in His divine benevolence and foresight overcomes the mysterious and malevolent invaders from the great beyond. Yet, at some point after viewing the movie (I can't remember when), I realized that the resolution was lame, since if the Martians were so advanced, why didn't they know that they could be mortally infected by the indigenous microscopic organisms of the Earth? In the final analysis, in the movie The War of the Worlds, the door to wonder—albeit a terrifying wonder—and the transcendent mysteries of the universe was opened, but then slammed shut (Lombardo, 2015a).

* * *

Still, after first watching the movie, my adrenalin was flowing. I repeatedly relived its scenes in my mind. At a gut level, the movie had engaged and charged my psyche—my total being

3

came alive in the experience of viewing *The War of the Worlds*.

I became inspired to write a short story of aliens invading the Earth. I created illustrations for the story (with *Crayola Crayons*). I recruited some of my friends to play the different roles, envisioning that somehow we would do a neighborhood play. I designed costumes (which presumably my friends' mothers would create). Two of my friends volunteered to be the director and producer of the production; others volunteered to build props. We were going to "live the future," a future of spaceships, aliens, and great battles to defend the earth.

My science fiction story though was never brought to the big screen, or even realized as a neighborhood production (for one thing the props and costumes were too elaborate and expensive — my allowance at the time was 25 cents a week), but I saved the illustrated story and still have the original booklet — my first screenplay and second story, created when I was seven years of age. My first illustrated story had been about dinosaurs — a "Lost World" scenario written the year before and also inspired by a movie I had seen, the black and white underground cult-classic, starring Cesar Romero, *Lost Continent* (1951).

Whatever my level of success as a movie producer and writer at the time, the main point of this childhood experience is that the science fiction movie, *The War of the Worlds*, produced by George Pal, and very *loosely* based on the novel by H. G. Wells (which I did not read till years later), totally engaged all the dimensions of my mind and galvanized my behavior. With its intense sights and sounds, the movie stimulated and excited my senses; with its tension and drama, it charged my emotions. It inspired my motivation to act; elevated my intellect, thinking, and imagination into cosmic speculation; seeded my creativity; and provoked in me an urgent desire to share this powerful experience with my friends, leading to collaborative, albeit unrealistic, social action. With its strange and other-worldly realities, it expanded my consciousness, evoking in me a sense of mystery, awe, and wonder. Creating and attempting to play act the story, at least momentarily, gave me a sense of personal identity. I was going to be a writer and producer of science fiction.

In fact, throughout the 1950s, I was an avid movie fan of science fiction, bedazzled and inspired by such early classics as *When Worlds Collide* (1951), *The Thing from Another World* (1951), *The Day the Earth Stood Still* (1951), *Invaders from Mars* (1953), *Them!* (1954), *20 Million Miles to Earth* (1957), *The Mysterians* (1957/1959), *Journey to the Center of the Earth* (1959), *The Time Machine* (1960), and the best of the best of that period, *Forbidden Planet* (1956). These early experiences with science fiction cinema and my enthusiastic efforts in writing and producing science fiction exemplify the *total person immersion* that science fiction can generate in people.

Having watched hundreds of movies—many of them many times over—and read thousands of stories and novels through the years, my fascination and love for science fiction has continued up through the present time. It is, indeed, a common occurrence that science fiction enthusiasts become hooked when they are young and stay devoted fans throughout their lives. And with accomplished science fiction writers—Isaac Asimov as a noteworthy example—the spark to write science fiction was ignited in childhood through reading it. In my case, I have written about science fiction and taught numerous workshops and courses on the topic. And as this book shows, I have created an ever-evolving theory and a vision of science fiction addressing such central questions as: *What is science fiction? How did it develop? What is its value and importance in our lives? How does it fit into the big scheme of things?*

The insight I came to after decades of reading, movie watching, and contemplation—one that serves as the starting point and guiding hypothesis for this book—is:

Science fiction is the most visible, influential, and popular modern form of futurist thinking and imagination in the contemporary world.

So aptly illustrated through my childhood experience with *The War of the Worlds*, science fiction is so popular because, in narrative form, it speaks to the *whole person*: intellect, imagination, emotion, motivation, behavior, the senses, and the self. It resonates with the personal, social, and cosmic; the natural and technological; the secular and the spiritual; and our values, ethics, and aesthetics, stimulating and enhancing *holistic future consciousness*. Readers and moviegoers are drawn into envisioning, feeling, and even acting out possible and often mind-boggling futures. Science fiction engages the total human psyche in the experience of the future.

I define "holistic future consciousness" as the total set of psychological processes and modes of experience and behavior involved in our consciousness of the future. It includes our hopes and fears about the future; our planning, our strategies, and our goals; our images and visions of the future, good and bad, utopian and dystopian; the stories we tell ourselves about where we are heading in the future, and our purposeful behaviors to create desirable and preferable futures and prevent negative possible futures from occurring. It is the total *Gestalt* of our experience and psycho-social engagement with the future (Lombardo, 2006a, 2011a, 2017).

Science fiction taps into all of this. It brings the future alive within our minds and our lives and personally draws us into the fantastical possibilities of tomorrow. Through science fiction, we feel and experience the future along all the dimensions of the human mind, creating "total person immersion" in our holistic consciousness of the future.

For many people science fiction has become a *total way of life*—a way of experiencing and creating reality, and in particular, a colorful and dramatically inspired future (indeed many different futures). In science fiction "fanspeak" the acronym is FIAWOL (Fandom is a way of life). Science fiction fandom and the global science fiction community is an immense, highly diverse, and continuously growing array of associations, groups, clubs, websites, and individuals, immersed in the gadgets, garb, iconic roles, imagery, art, paraphernalia, computer games, virtual realities, cinematic productions, archetypal characters, conventions and conferences, historical traditions, and literary works of science fiction (Clute and Nicholls, 1995; *Encyclopedia of Science Fiction*). This intricate and expansive reality has enthralled and captured a huge population, body and soul.

An excellent example of this global contemporary cultural phenomenon is the "Trekkies," comically and vividly realized in the central characters of the popular TV show *The Big Bang Theory*. Aside from their enthusiastic involvement in the *Star Trek* subculture, the main male characters, Sheldon, Leonard, Howard, and Rajesh, are also active participants in the comic book/super-hero and video gaming subcultures, two other significant groups within the science fiction community. They live science fiction; they cherish it; they dress it. They collect memorabilia, posters, and action figures; they attend conventions; and they regularly socialize through science fiction game-playing, movie-watching, and TV-viewing. They dress in science fiction costumes (vicariously adopting the identities of science fiction characters). Sheldon adopts the garb of both Flash and Mr. Spock, the latter, at times, even haunting him in his dreams. Sheldon's ego-ideal, in fact, is a combination of Flash and Mr. Spock, a synthesis of speed, science, and intellect. It is a standing joke that Sheldon's friends think he is an alien. At times it seems that Sheldon believes so as well. (There is a similar puzzle also raised in the series that perhaps Sheldon is a robot, another science fiction archetype.)

Science Fiction as Futures Narrative
A big part of the psychological power and pull of science fiction can be found in its narrative form. Humans are psychologically

disposed toward making sense of themselves and the world— and the universe as a whole—through stories. Through the narratives we tell ourselves, we give meaning, purpose, and drama to our existence; we create and evolve our personal identities through internal self-narratives (Damasio, 1999, 2010; Wilson, 2011). Societies create a collective sense of identity and vision of the future through shared grand narratives, encompassing and integrating past, present, and future (Polak, 1973; Lombardo, 2006b, 2017). Because science fiction is narrative in form, it naturally resonates with the deep narrative structure and dynamics of the human mind.

When it is done well, science fiction, as narratives of the future, can powerfully and effectively give our lives meaning, drama, color, and a sense of action, direction, and possibilities into the future. At a personal level, science fiction narratives about the future inform and inspire a way of approaching and creating the future. As one key illustration, science fiction has stimulated the inventive imagination of many of its readers, provoking real-life developments in science and technology (Disch, 1998).

A good story about a possible future, with its drama, action, and sensory detail, is psychologically more compelling and realistic than an abstract theory, ideology, depersonalized scenario, or statistical prediction about the future. An engaging and concrete narrative, involving sequential and causative action—a dramatic plot—brings a living presence and propellant energy to a vision of the future. This is how a possible future *feels* and how it *goes*.

Although not all science fiction deals with the future (an important point I consider later on), its primary focus has been on the possibilities of the future. In this regard:

Science fiction can be defined as a literary and narrative approach to the future, involving plots, action sequences, specific settings, dramatic resolutions, and varied and unique characters, human and otherwise. To a significant degree inspired and informed by modern science, technology, and contemporary thought, it involves imaginative and often highly detailed scenario-building and thought experiments about the future (and reality), set in the form of stories.

Science fiction narrative also personally draws us into a rich vicarious experience of the future through its vivid and memorable characters. We live the story through the characters' experiences and actions. Science fiction contains a host of unique and strange characters, admirable, villainous, and enigmatic, concretely realized and at times vividly described. We personally connect with them, or conversely are repelled, if not horrified, by them. The characters at times can provide role models; throughout the history of science fiction we find a rich and diverse assortment of memorable heroes, often possessing superhuman powers and unearthly abilities. Science fiction characters can be godlike, resonating with our highest ideals and deepest desires. Narrative characters give a story an emotional, personal charge, and due to their strange and extravagant qualities science fiction characters can stretch our sense of personal identity and purpose.

All told, through science fiction narrative, involving fantastic and concrete scenarios and settings, dramatic action and sequence, compelling and bizarre characters, and—in its cinematic productions—multimedia simulation of fantastical realities, we are powerfully drawn into imagining and thinking about possible futures, and we are able, at a deep and intimate level, to *live and feel these futures*. This is total person immersion in the future generated through the form, energy, and imagination of the science fiction narrative.

The Future of Everything

A common stereotype, reinforced by the techno razzle-dazzle of science fiction cinema and special effects, is that science fiction is predominately about the future of technology and science.

But this vision of science fiction is way too narrow. Although informed and inspired to varying degrees by modern science and the possibilities of future technologies, science fiction draws from both the physical sciences, as well as social, psychological, and humanistic thought, and is not just *about* the future of physical science and technology. It is about the future of everything.

The name "science fiction" was coined by Hugo Gernsback in the October, 1929 issue of his pulp magazine *Science Wonder Stories*. Gernsback, inspired by the writings of H. G. Wells and Jules Verne, envisioned a new literary genre that was entertaining, but also educational. As he attempted to profusely illustrate in his futurist-techno novel *Ralph 124C 41+: A Romance of the Year 2660* (1911/1925), Gernsback believed the educational purpose of science fiction was to teach about the future possibilities and wonders of science and technology (Clute and Nicholls, 1995). But, both before Gernsback created the name and clearly afterwards, numerous "scientific romance" writers — the encyclopedic Wells being one noteworthy example — and many post-Gernsback "science fiction" authors have explored all dimensions of the future in great depth and detail.

As one excellent opening illustration, "A Rose for Ecclesiastes" (1963) by Roger Zelazny strongly challenges the popular stereotype of science fiction as simply technological extrapolation into the future. Zelazny's story is included in Volume One of the anthology *The Science Fiction Hall of Fame* (Silverberg, 1970), a collection of tales voted by the *Science Fiction Writers of America* as the best science fiction stories ever written, up through 1965. There is some future technology in the story — the biotechnological creation of a rose on the inhospitable surface of Mars — but the narrative's primary focus is psychological, cultural, and religious. The central character is a poet, a linguist, and a classical scholar, rather than a mad scientist or inventor of a new technology. A literary genius, he is assigned to Mars to study the language and culture of its indigenous population and ancient enigmatic civilization.

In the story, our poet and linguist—an emotionally cold, arrogant, and lofty individual—is seduced by a beautiful Martian woman named Braxa, who arouses and entices him through dance, and whom he eventually impregnates. In his romance and sexual intimacy with Braxa, he is unknowingly drawn into an ancient Martian prophecy concerning the renewal of their race. He provides the seed for a new beginning.

In studying the ancient Martian texts, the poet has come to believe that the Martians have given up on life, and have resigned themselves to a philosophy of "nothing new under the sun," as exemplified in the book of Ecclesiastes from the Bible. But he has been fooled by the Martians, misunderstanding them. The Martians are neither passive nor nihilists. While his cold and arrogant heart has been melted by Braxa, to whom he gives the rose as a symbol of his love, he turns into a pawn in the Martian scheme. By the story's end, we can ask: Who is "Ecclesiastes" (the poet or the Martians?) How many different meanings can be given to the word "rose"? And to whom has the rose really been given?

Instead of focusing on the future of technology, "A Rose for Ecclesiastes" delves into the meaning and purpose of life, religious prophecy and fate, love and the weaknesses of the human heart, and the meeting of different cultures from different worlds. It is a mystical and humanistic tale, a character study and a story in anthropological science fiction. And these varied qualities are not unique to this tale within the universe of science fiction. As stated above, we need to significantly broaden the narrow and stereotypical vision of the domain of science fiction as simply technological extrapolation, for much of science fiction goes way beyond such limited confines.

To restate, science fiction is about *the future of everything*. Of course, it delves into future technologies and space travel, but it also explores the future of society, culture, and cities; the future of the human mind, and of crime, madness, and war; and the future of love, sex, and gender. Frequently there are religious and spiritual themes involved. For example, in *The War of the Worlds*, science fiction confronts or *collides* with the issue of God. As I describe below, science fiction can be highly philosophical, stretching the far reaches of human mentality and consciousness, and speculating on the nature of the universe and existence. Science fiction also concerns itself with nature, the environment, and ecology; there are numerous science fiction stories about nature transformed, for better or worse, by human actions, environmental catastrophes, or cosmic events. Science fiction addresses anything that has a future.

Dan Simmons' *Hyperion* (1989) illustrates on a grand scale how science fiction is about the future of everything. Equally so, it demonstrates how science fiction can realize (when it is done well) literary excellence, contradicting the view that the genre is juvenile in plot, characterization, and style. The language of *Hyperion* is rich, poetical, expansive, and colorful. Drawing on the literary classic, Chaucer's *Canterbury Tales*, *Hyperion* tells the story of seven pilgrims who are journeying to the planet Hyperion. They have been called there by enigmatic forces, which seem to include both super-intelligent computers (AI) as well as mysterious personages within a future-transformed Catholic Church. Their mission is to confront the Shrike, a giant metallic being covered in razor-like blades who is killing human settlers by the thousands and seems to come from the future. On the journey, each pilgrim tells their personal story of how they came to this critical juncture in their life; the pilgrims include a poet, a philosopher, a warrior, and a priest. The individual stories are visceral, metaphysical, bizarre, and intricate.

As the first in a series of four novels written by Simmons — collectively referred to as the *Hyperion Cantos*, and spanning three centuries beginning in the twenty-ninth century — we find (as a sample) the following events and themes: The promise of immortality, which involves selling your soul to the "Devil"; a philosophical debate between a future Dali Lama and the Grand Inquisitor; the reincarnation of the poet Keats within cyberspace and the reliving of his death on an alternative virtual earth; bio- and nano-technologically enhanced humans who are aerial beings living untethered and ungrounded in the cold darkness of outer space; a giant tree that is converted into an interstellar spaceship and an even more gargantuan solar ring (surrounding a sun) that is grown out of a tree; the complex and gritty street life of multiple future cities; the fall of human civilization and the rise to power of a corrupt Catholic Church; innumerable alien ecologies and forms of life; and the Second Coming—the mythic narrative of death and resurrection—realized through time travel. Oh, and the Second Coming is a girl.

The *Hyperion Cantos* is an intricate and comprehensive vision of a possible future, covering all dimensions of human life, technological, scientific, psychological, social, ethical, cosmic, spiritual, and religious. It is a grand and rich narrative—a future of everything—informed by classical literature and thought, and yet pointing toward an amazingly strange and mysterious future.

Not only does good science fiction stimulate holistic future consciousness, touching all the psychological dimensions of the human mind, it also facilitates an *integrative* understanding of the future. Good science fiction frequently creates a fully realized, multidimensional vision of the future, in which all the pieces are woven together into an intricate and comprehensive vision. Good science fiction "creates a world." The real future, indeed, will be an interactive synthesis of all dimensions of human existence, and both earthly and cosmic reality, perhaps even including realities we have not even thought about. Aside from the *Hyperion Cantos*, other noteworthy examples of science fiction novels that envision rich and expansive possible future societies (encompassing humans, aliens, and AI) include John

Brunner's *Stand on Zanzibar* (1968), Kim Stanley Robinson's *Red Mars, Green Mars,* and *Blue Mars* trilogy (1991, 1994, 1996), Neal Stephenson's *The Diamond Age* (1995), Ian McDonald's *River of Gods* (2004), and Iain Banks' *Matter* (2008).

But to gain a broader perspective and appreciation of the integrative dimension of science fiction, let's consider H. G. Wells' famous novel, *The Shape of Things to Come* (1933). Grounded in the initial chapters in an extensive historical-political analysis and theoretical exposition on the nature of human society—how did human civilization get to where it is—Wells extrapolates a hypothetical developmental narrative of global humanity over the next two centuries that covers science; technology; education; economics; war and peace; politics and government; and art and social mores. The movie *Things to Come* (1936), although inspired by the book, only scratches the surface of the philosophical and historical depth and futurist detail contained in the book. *The Shape of Things to Come* is a scholarly and inter-disciplinary meditation on humanity, past, present, and future; Wells imaginatively builds a plausible future out of a theoretical analysis of the past. World-building in science fiction has a long history, and the study of history, as an important feature of its integrative nature, has often informed and grounded its futurist extrapolations.

To go back even further in the history of science fiction—before it had its name—Albert Robida's ironic and comical *The Twentieth Century* (1882) is an amazingly animated, prescient, and rich vision of future human society. This novel is the most thoroughly articulated, intricate, and comprehensive fictionalized vision of the future of humanity written in the nineteenth century (of books I have read), integrating numerous extrapolations and predictions on psycho-social, lifestyle, and gender issues; finance and professions; scientific-technological and transportation-communication developments; ethical-political evolution; and entertainment, fashion, cuisine, tourism, and artistic dimensions in the future. Moreover, it is a "slice of life," recounting the escapades and personal challenges of a set of entertaining characters who live in this complex and frenzied, stressful, envisioned future. The integrative complexity of the future world is revealed through the experiences of individual characters. The book also includes hundreds of Robida's drawings (Robida was the first great modern science fiction artist), creating for the reader a multimedia experience of an envisioned multimedia future (news has become orchestrated entertainment).

As stated above, science fiction is often characterized as juvenile. Yet, if this view of science fiction means that its intellectual content is shallow, repetitive, simplistic, and appealing to the immature motives and mindsets of youth, then *Hyperion*, as well as the other novels just cited, by virtue of their intellectual power and scholarly depth, clearly contradict this characterization. As we will see, science fiction is frequently mentally challenging; science fiction is, perhaps more than any other genre, *idea* literature. It involves complex and penetrating experiments in thinking and imagination. The great works of science fiction make the reader delve into the deepest and most philosophically and scientifically profound issues of life and existence. It is the exact opposite of juvenile and dumb.

So, although I proposed above that the psychological impact of science fiction is holistic, engaging all the dimensions of the human mind, including emotion, sensation, and personal identity, I do not intend to minimize the intellectual and imaginative dimensions of the genre. We feel the future through science fiction, but, probably more so than any other form of fictional literature, we are also asked to engage our cognitive, intellectual, and abstract mental capacities within the mind-boggling multiverse of science fiction. Science fiction can be profound—more intellectually demanding than any other form of literature; science fiction can involve penetrating and elevating "thought experiments" about the nature of reality. The world around us can seem very shallow and mundane after a journey through a good science fiction story.

Cosmic Consciousness

To romance of the far future ... is to attempt to see the human race in its cosmic setting, and to mold our hearts to entertain new values.
Olaf Stapledon

Off in the distance, receding away, I can hear the faint voices of my friends heading back to school after our lunch break. I should be heading back as well, but the power of the world of school and friends has lost its force, its substantiality, its necessity. The world around me feels like an ephemeral dream—a momentary blip—in comparison to the much bigger universe in which my mind is immersed. For the last few days, whenever I have had any free time, I have been—in physical space—riveted to my desk in my bedroom. But in the sphere of my consciousness, I have been out roughly eight hundred thousand years into the future. And if this mental jump forward in time wasn't enough to dis-equilibrate my sense of reality, on this particular spring afternoon, I find myself having been pulled further forward, now millions upon millions of years ahead in time, with the sun a swollen red giant sitting motionless on the horizon, snowflakes falling on a deserted beach by a dark wine sea, with gargantuan butterflies fluttering by overhead. The ghostly voices of my friends fade to oblivion, lost somewhere, long dead, in the "dark backward abysm of time." I am with the "Time Traveler" on his journey into the far future in H. G. Wells' *The Time Machine* (published in 1895, three years before *The War of the Worlds*).

Earlier that year I had seen the 1960 movie version of *The Time Machine*, but now I am reading the book, and the book is far more cosmic, strange, and mind expanding than the movie.

(The movie *only* travels out eight hundred thousand years into the future and has an inane Hollywood happy ending.) I have been yanked out of the present, of the relative here and now, into the far reaches of time, and the everyday world has become dramatically transitory and superficial, where before it had seemed so permanent and real. I feel as if I am seeing things the way they actually are, rather than just some momentary glimpse, perspective, or snapshot of existence.

It was not so much that the future scenario explored in the book was strange or unreal; rather it was that the "everyday" world was placed in a much more profound and fundamental context. It lost its obvious and intractable sense of reality and hold on my consciousness. The world around me felt suddenly eclipsed by the deeper and more expansive cosmic reality of *The Time Machine*. As Arthur C. Clarke stated, "Science fiction is an escape into reality."

In what was a more severe case of unconstrained enthusiasm than when I had watched *The War of the Worlds*, after I finished reading *The Time Machine*, I convinced a few of my friends that we should attempt to build a time machine. We were going to construct it out of lumber, with a spinning ring encircling it powered by an electric motor. Heavens knows what I was thinking regarding the technology and physics of time travel (building a space ship to travel to Mars would have been decidedly more realistic), but the spirit of science fiction had grabbed my psyche again. In this case it was the desire to *invent* and in fact science fiction has frequently provoked such creative technological impulses in its readers; for example, the great pioneer of modern rocketry, Robert Goddard, was strongly inspired in his teenage years through reading Wells' *The War of the Worlds*. Science fiction, as part of its psychologically holistic impact, has repeatedly stimulated technological innovations (Disch, 1998). (For guidelines on realistic time machines, grounded in contemporary physics, but also informed and inspired by science fiction scenarios, see Paul Davies' *How to Build a Time Machine,* 2001.)

In spite of my practical foolishness and theoretical naiveté, *The Time Machine* provoked a deep insight, more profound than what I had earlier experienced in viewing *The War of the Worlds*. Reading *The Time Machine* awakened in me a sense of *cosmic consciousness*. In moving into this imagined far distant future, humanity (as a species) and modern human civilization disappear; life on the earth evolves and then slowly vanishes from the scene; the earth stops revolving around the sun; and the sun itself, after blazing yellow hot for countless ages, cools and swells, threatening to envelop the earth. I got a big picture of time and the whole shebang, dramatically and vividly realized in the book. I got a more expansive sense of humanity's place within the big cosmic picture. This cosmic perspective, when convincingly realized as in *The Time Machine*, is one of the most significant and enlightening features of science fiction.

The expression "the future of everything," introduced above, can have two different meanings. On one hand, "everything" can refer to all the different dimensions of a future world: technological, environmental, social, psychological, and religious. A science fiction writer creates a futurist scenario and narrative where all the different pieces and parts of human existence (or an alien world or alternative reality) are described and connected with some level of detail and synthesis.

But "everything" can also mean the "big picture" of it all—of existence and reality as a whole or totality. "Everything" can mean the universe, the cosmos, or the "multi-verse" (if one believes in multiple universes). "Everything" in this sense implies a "cosmic perspective." A science fiction writer may talk about the future of the universe; a science fiction writer may delve into the ultimate nature of reality. And given that science fiction, as narrative, places specific characters within its imaginative settings, we may find ourselves (through the eyes of the characters) contemplating our place (or role) in the big picture of things. Part of the depth of science fiction—of profoundly challenging and engaging our minds—is that it provokes within us states of "cosmic consciousness," of pondering the nature of the universe and our place within it.

Consider, as a second superb example of a narrative-provoking cosmic consciousness, the story "Surface Tension" (1952) by James Blish, another tale voted into the *Science Fiction Hall of Fame* (See also the expanded version in *The Seedling Stars* (1957) by Blish). The setting is a puddle of water on a distant planet, sometime in the future. In this puddle live genetically engineered microscopic water-breathing humans. (Read the novel version to understand how this biological transformation occurred.) As far as these tiny humans can ascertain, who are unaware of their origins, their puddle of water, which is filled with a variety of other microscopic living creatures, is the entire universe. The surface tension of the puddle has prevented them from breaking out of it, to see if anything exists on the other side; the upper boundary of their puddle is their "sky."

A number of these tiny humans have decided to construct a "spaceship" to blast through the surface of their puddle and see what lies beyond. Many of the other humans feel this is a foolhardy idea; the puddle is the universe, and why attempt such a dangerous mission to venture beyond? (Metaphorically, it is like sailing off the presumed edge of the world.) The adventuresome group, though, remain undaunted and tenacious through various setbacks. Finally, propelled by microscopic organisms, they travel in their wooden ship upward from the bottom of the puddle, eventually break through the surface of the water, and find themselves on the surrounding ground encircling the puddle. Looking through the windows of their ship they see a rocky terrain and the sun that their planet orbits in a more distant "new sky" overhead. After their sun sets, they observe the night sky and the brilliant panorama of stars within the heavens. Who would have believed? They are bedazzled—the universe extends vastly beyond anything they had previously believed. They even discover that there are other "universes" around them—other neighboring puddles of water—populated by other tiny humans. They experience the awe and wonder and excitement of expanded cosmic consciousness.

"Surface Tension" is an allegory because *we* are the tiny human creatures living in our metaphorical puddle of water that we incorrectly identify as the entire universe. How far and to what depth does the undiscovered "beyond" reach? Moreover, many of us are comfortable and protected in our limited world and worldview, and have no wish or inclination to extend ourselves, reaching out with our bodies and our minds to what may lie beyond. ("Surface Tension" refers to the constraints within conscious minds, as well as the physical dynamics of puddles of water.) Yet, some of us (the adventuresome ones) develop the necessary courage and imagination and attempt to reach beyond—to transcend the limitations of the normal and the immediate here and now. In breaking through the veil of appearance—what seems like the upper boundary of the "sky"—the courageous and imaginative ones see themselves more accurately and deeply and place themselves in a truer, more encompassing big picture of things. "Surface Tension" is an allegory on the nature of cosmic consciousness—of what prevents us (in thought, feeling, and perception) from realizing it and what it means to achieve it. Science fiction provokes such deep, transformative, and transcendent states of mind. ("Surface Tension" is also a richly drawn depiction of an alternate reality—an aquatic ecology—of alien microscopic life forms, which further amplifies the range of the reader's own consciousness.)

As someone who, in his writing career, championed courage, individual initiative, and self-determination, challenging the status quo, Robert Heinlein (1907-1988)—one of the most popular science fiction writers of all time—wrote a similar kind of story (allegorical in nature) about breaking through the mental constraints of custom, "common sense," and traditional modes of consciousness. In his *Science Fiction Hall of Fame* story "Universe" (Bova, 1973a) which was written a decade earlier than "Surface Tension," we find a colony of humans living within a giant interstellar spaceship, totally unaware of the nature of their confined existence. For almost all of them, the spaceship is the entire universe; they cannot see or travel outside of it, with all pathways running through the ship curving around back on them. It is incomprehensible to them that there is any space beyond the hemispherical space of the ship. They have an ancient creation myth that explains the origin and nature of their world that, although it provides them with meaning and purpose in their lives, locks them into a way of thinking about their reality that they cannot move beyond. They perceive their world as stable and omnipresent, and have no sense whatsoever that they actually are journeying through the vast expanses of outer space. (Little more than five hundred years ago neither did we.) They do not correctly understand their reality. A few mutant humans, though, notably a two-headed one, inhabiting the upper levels of the ship know better, having discovered a viewing portal into outer space and the long-forgotten control room for the ship. "Universe" (1941) and its sequel, ironically titled "Common Sense" (1941) (novelized as *Orphans of the Sky* in 1963), dramatically explore the themes of the struggle for enlightenment, the nature and constraints of tradition and origin stories, courage and fear in the face of the unknown, the rejection of stable security and the pursuit of change, and ultimately, human salvation through the tenacious search for truth.

On the grandest of scales, however, no one surpasses Olaf Stapledon (1886-1950) in taking the reader on colossal visionary adventures that explore the potential future evolution of human and alien minds and societies and cosmic transcendence. With this Oxford philosopher and science fiction writer, we ultimately go on a multi-billion year quest in search of the meaning of the universe and the existence of God. Probably no writer in the West has created such an expansive and in-depth vision of the "cosmic" future of everything.

Olaf Stapledon's novels, *Last and First Men* (1930) and *Star Maker* (1937), propel us on journeys that progressively extend outward, covering billions of years into the future and the entire spatial expanse of the universe. In the former novel we follow the hypothetical evolution of humankind through eighteen different species two billion years into the future. In the later novel, we journey out fifty billion years and watch as biological, stellar, and nebulae forms of intelligence integrate into a cosmic civilization and cosmic mind. Stapledon's fundamental narrative within these novels is the cosmic evolution of intelligence and communal consciousness. We see ourselves within the biggest picture imaginable to the human mind.

In summary, science fiction stimulates holistic future consciousness; we are immersed in the future—we feel it and vicariously participate in it along all the dimensions of the human mind. As futurist narrative, science fiction resonates with our psyche and can stimulate a way of life. Further, contrary to popular stereotypes, science fiction is about the future of everything, facilitating an integrative understanding of future human reality. In particular, science fiction stretches our intellectual and imaginative capacities, affording us the opportunity to experience cosmic consciousness and explore our personal connection with the universe and the totality of existence. Science fiction touches our personal center, but it is equally vast and deep—as vast and deep as it gets.

The Evolutionary Adventure of Science Fiction

A central theme of this book—identified in its subtitle—is that science fiction is the *evolutionary mythology of the future*. One intended meaning to the word "evolutionary" in this subtitle is that science fiction is a transforming and evolving reality through time.

With its numerous roots and tributaries extending far back to the beginnings of recorded human history, science fiction has a deep and multi-faceted heritage. Moreover, science fiction has grown through the ages, continually building upon its past accomplishments. It is still developing, evolving, and diversifying.

As one of its most important features, science fiction is an evolving manifestation of holistic future consciousness; it is an evolving expression, in narrative form, of our ever-expanding and transforming visions of the future of everything, including the future of the cosmos, and all the individual components of and perspectives taken within this developing panorama. The history of science fiction chronicles (among other things) the evolutionary development of our consciousness, understanding, and imaginative visions of possible futures. But as an expression of our evolving holistic future consciousness we should keep in mind that the full multi-dimensional nature of human consciousness, encompassing emotion, motivation and desire, behavioral and social manifestations, ethics and values, and art and perceptual imagery, comes into play in the evolving consciousness of science fiction. The total Gestalt of the human mind, especially in its connection to the future, has been developing with color and dynamism through the history of science fiction.

As a transforming and growing reality, science fiction can be best appreciated through tracing its evolutionary history through time. This evolutionary history is immensely rich and extensive, and connected with numerous philosophical, cultural, and scientific trends in the ongoing development of human consciousness and human society. My approach in this first volume and subsequent volumes is to chronicle this multi-faceted evolutionary history. In this volume I cover:

- The nature and value of myth; the relationship of myth and science fiction; and ways in which science fiction is the evolutionary mythology of the future. (Chapter 2)
- Ancient historical origins of science fiction, including Greek philosophy, science, myth, evolutionary theory, and literature and Lucian's *True History*. (First half of Chapter 3)
- The Middle Ages, including futurist and fantastic visions from *Revelations*, St. Augustine, Roger Bacon, and Dante, as well as scientific, philosophical, artistic, and technological developments in Scholastic and Islamic thought up through the Renaissance circa 1500 CE. (Second half of Chapter 3)
- The rise of modernity, including the Age of Exploration and the associated literary genre of "extraordinary voyages"; the Scientific Revolution, modern astronomy, and early speculations on evolution and alien life, covering Bruno, Kepler, de Fontenelle and others; and early utopian visions and stories of space travel, roughly covering the period of 1500 to 1700. (Chapter 4)
- The eighteenth-century European Enlightenment and the secular theory of progress (a new vision of the future); more stories of space travel, extraordinary voyages, and ideal societies; Romanticism, Romantic science, and Gothic literature, up through the publication of Grainville's *The Last Man* and Mary Shelley's *Frankenstein* at the beginning of the nineteenth century; and the psychological-thematic opposition of fear and apprehension versus hope and wonder within the history of science fiction. (Chapters 5 and 6)
- The nineteenth century, beginning with further Gothic tales; the rise of industrialism, the science of electricity, and mesmerism; the highly influential stories of Edgar Allan Poe and Jules Verne; the development of the theories

of evolution and entropy and the implications of these theories regarding the future; the swelling post-Darwinian wave of tales of robots, future wars, more ideal societies, aliens, and outer space; the pop cultural phenomenon of "Edisonade;" the fantastical and mystical visions of Camille Flammarion; the prescient futurist narratives and amazing futurist artwork of Albert Robida; and finishing with various tales at the end of the century dealing with aliens and in particular, the Martians, with H. G. Wells' *The War of the Worlds* serving as a transition into volume two of this series (Chapters 7 through 10).

As is evident from the above summary of topics covered in this first book, I see science fiction as a complex human reality, with many facets, dimensions, and noteworthy figures. In this first volume and later volumes, I describe the evolution of science fiction literature, science fiction cinema, science fiction art, comics, and graphics, and the science fiction community. As noted earlier, science fiction is a way of life, encompassing multiple dimensions of human experience and social existence.

Beginning in this first volume, I examine the connections between the evolution of science fiction and the evolution of philosophy, science, culture and society in human history. How have trends and developments in society and the world of ideas influenced the growth and direction of science fiction? How has science fiction, in reciprocity, influenced our world? The coming volumes cover relevant ideas in the history of religion; fantasy, and myth; philosophy, science and technology; social theory; and art and culture, that are connected with ongoing developments in the evolution of science fiction.

Throughout the coming volumes, I describe the main themes and topics of science fiction, as well as its breadth and depth and its various strengths and values. I highlight fundamental *narrative themes*, such as space travel, time travel, fantastical adventures, the transcendence of humanity, future wars, and utopian and dystopian sagas, as well as basic *archetypal* concepts and icons, such as the robot, the alien, evolved humans, the rocket ship, and the scientist as either mad villain or heroic adventurer into the unknown. There is though an ever-growing universe of topics and themes within science fiction, which perhaps, in the final analysis, cannot be definitively circumscribed, any more than can the limits of human imagination and possible new discoveries and insights in the future.

One concluding note on history and time: Although my study of science fiction is primarily historical, chronicling in sequential fashion its development over time, I also frequently circle around through time. At points I jump ahead; other times I leap backwards to topics already discussed. Time may be a line moving from past into future, but time is also a Gestalt—a circular whole—in which the future informs, if not reinterprets, the past. In time travel stories, the present can affect and transform the past; in the human mind, in our ongoing interpretations of reality, this is a common occurrence. It is also a common occurrence for our anticipations of the future to affect our experience of the present (Lombardo, 2017). As George Orwell depicted in *1984*, the past is rewritten, and rewritten again, in the ongoing flow of the present. (What did really happen in the past?) In chronicling and interpreting history, such as the history of science fiction, we need to jump back and forth through time to get the big picture, to redraw the big picture, and to see what individual events along the way mean.

Resources on Science Fiction

Before moving to the next chapter, in which I more deeply delve into the meaning of the concept of "the evolutionary mythology of the future," allow me to briefly explain my referencing system and resource bibliography.

As two basic historical streams within science fiction, there are both the fictional narratives of science fiction per se (both print and cinematic modes), and the self-reflective literature and historical-critical studies, both in print and online, *about* science fiction. I've adopted a particular reference system for these two types of sources concerning science fiction.

For the latter category — sources about science fiction — I have created at the end of the book a *Resource Bibliography*. This bibliography includes books, articles, and websites describing and assessing science fiction; numerous histories of the genre; and many illustrated volumes containing book and magazine covers, movie posters and pictures, photos of science fiction authors, and science fiction art. Also included in this bibliography are other historical, scientific, futurist, and philosophical resources that, although not specifically about science fiction, are relevant to the history of science fiction and are cited within this book. Finally, in this *Resource Bibliography* I include specific published anthologies of science fiction stories cited within the text.

Although I primarily address the history of science fiction only to the last decade of the nineteenth century in this first volume, I have taught courses and workshops on science fiction, as well as published a number of articles, that cover the full history of science fiction up to the present. The reader is referred to the *Resource Bibliography* for website links to print, presentation, and video material on these talks, workshops, courses, and publications that cover the entire history of science fiction (See the three-part video, Lombardo, 2014a). Also included in the bibliography are website links to my *Evolving Best Science Fiction Novels* and *Evolving Best Science Fiction Movies* (Lombardo, 2016a, 2016b) that cover classical and contemporary tales and cinematic productions.

In my research and teaching I have frequently consulted a variety of key published studies on science fiction. Many of these publications are cited in this first volume and complete references are included in the *Resource Bibliography*. But for the enthusiastic reader, at the start, listed below are key printed works about science fiction I have drawn upon, many of them beautifully illustrated in color, covering the full breadth of science fiction.

- Aldiss, Brian *Billion Year Spree: The True History of Science Fiction* (1973)
- Aldiss, Brian and Wingrove, David *Trillion Year Spree: The History of Science Fiction* (1986)
- Alkon, Paul *Origins of Futuristic Fiction* (1987)
- Ash, Brian *The Visual Encyclopedia of Science Fiction* (1977)
- Bailey, J. O. *Pilgrims through Space and Time: A History and Analysis of Scientific Fiction* (1947)
- Bleiler, Everett *Science-Fiction: The Early Years* (1991)
- Broderick, Damien and Di Filippo, Paul *Science Fiction: The 101 Best Novels 1985-2010* (2012)
- Clute, John *Science Fiction: The Illustrated Encyclopedia* (1995)
- Clute, John and Nicholls, Peter *The Encyclopedia of Science Fiction* (1995)
- Crossley, Robert *Olaf Stapledon: Speaking for the Future* (1994)
- Disch, Thomas *The Dreams Our Stuff is Made of: How Science Fiction Conquered the World* (1998)
- Gunn, James *Alternate Worlds: An Illustrated History of Science Fiction* (1975)
- Gunn, James (Ed.) *The Road to Science Fiction: From Gilgamesh to Wells.* (1977)
- Gunn, James and Candelaria, Matthew (Ed.) *Speculations on Speculation: Theories of Science Fiction* (2005)
- Holland, Steve *Sci-Fi Art: A Graphic History* (2009)
- Korshak, Stephen (Ed.) *Frank R. Paul: Father of Science Fiction Art* (2010)
- Lundwall, Sam *Science Fiction: What It's All About* (1971)

- Mallory, Michael *The Science Fiction Universe ... and Beyond: Syfy Channel Book on Sci-Fi* (2012)
- Montague, Charlotte *H. P. Lovecraft: The Mysterious Man Behind the Darkness* (2015)
- Moskowitz, Sam *The Immortal Storm: A History of Science Fiction Fandom* (1954)
- Moskowitz, Sam *Explorers of the Infinite: Shapers of Science Fiction* (1963)
- Moskowitz, Sam *Seekers of Tomorrow* (1966)
- Panshin, Alexei and Panshin, Cory *The World Beyond the Hill: Science Fiction and the Quest for Transcendence* (1989)
- Pohl, Frederik *The Way the Future Was: A Memoir* (1978)
- Pringle, David *Science Fiction: The 100 Best Novels* (1985)
- Robb, Brian *Steampunk: An Illustrated History of Fantastical Fiction, Fanciful Film, and Other Victorian Visions* (2012)
- Roberts, Adam *The History of Science Fiction* (2005)
- Robinson, Frank *Science Fiction in the 20th Century: An Illustrated History* (1999)
- Stableford, Brian *New Atlantis: A Narrative History of Scientific Romance* (Four Volumes) (2016)
- Suvin, Darko *Positions and Presuppositions in Science Fiction* (1988)
- Wagar, W. Warren *H. G. Wells: Traversing Time* (2004)
- Wells, H. G. *Experiment in Autobiography* (1934)
- Wuckel, Dieter and Cassiday, Bruce *The Illustrated History of Science Fiction* (1989)

One primary web resource on science fiction, expansive in scope, that is used throughout the entire historical study is *The Encyclopedia of Science Fiction* by John Clute and Peter Nicholls.

The are many other excellent science fiction websites providing big picture overviews, and the reader is referred to the *Resource Bibliography* for a sampling of these sites.

Turning to science fiction narratives, the number of science fiction stories and novels is immense, if not indeterminate and innumerable. (Where is the demarcation line between science fiction and other forms of fiction to be drawn?) I identify and describe hundreds of stories and novels in this volume and subsequent volumes, but I only begin to scratch the surface of the enormous amount of science fiction written through the ages. To get an even bigger picture of the vast amount of science fiction that has been written, the reader is referred to *The Encyclopedia of Science Fiction*, cited above, both print and online versions, as starting points for exploring this colossal universe of imagination. If the reader is interested in a good beginning point for a collection of notable shorter science fiction tales, an excellent place to start is with *The Science Fiction Hall of Fame*, three volumes edited by Robert Silverberg (1970) and Ben Bova (1973a, 1973b).

For science fiction stories and novels identified and discussed within this book and later volumes, I have not created a separate fictional bibliography; there are often multiple publishers and editions for many of these books. The reader is referred to *Amazon* for available in print publications. Instead, for each author I examine in depth (such as Jules Verne and Edgar Allan Poe in the first volume), I create an *Author Bibliography* in the body of the text in the section where the author is discussed, listing "Notable Novels and Stories" by that author.

I describe science fiction as a narrative expression of holistic future consciousness. Explained in more depth in my futurist writings, I see holistic future consciousness as the central evolutionary driving force behind the growth of the human mind and human civilization and, moreover, as a general capacity that humans have been *purposefully* evolving throughout history. In modern times, I see science fiction standing at the forefront in this purposeful evolution of holistic future consciousness. Science fiction, through repeated and ongoing efforts to create narratives of the future, expands and empowers our understanding and our imaginative experience of the future, as well as heightening our desires and abilities to create such envisioned futures.

The reader is referred to my futurist books and articles (frequently cited in this text) and my website (*Center for Future Consciousness*) for a more in-depth analysis of holistic future consciousness and its evolution within human history:

- Lombardo, Thomas *The Evolution of Future Consciousness: The Nature and Historical Development of the Human Capacity to Think about the Future* (2006a)
- Lombardo, Thomas *Contemporary Futurist Thought: Science Fiction, Future Studies, and Theories and Visions of the Future in the Last Century* (2006b)
- Lombardo, Thomas *Wisdom, Consciousness, and the Future: Collected Essays* (2011a)
- Lombardo, Thomas and Lombardo, Jeanne Belisle *Mind Flight: A Journey into the Future* (2011b)
- Lombardo, Thomas *Future Consciousness: The Path to Purposeful Evolution* (2017)

Now, let's go back one thousand years (the time machine of the human mind) to appropriately orient and steer ourselves toward the future.

Chapter 2

Mythology and Science Fiction

Science fiction is a literature of the mythic imagination.
Alexei and Cory Panshin

The Mythic, the Fantastic, the Scientific, and the Real

To understand how science fiction is the evolutionary mythology of the future, we must delve into the history and nature of myth and explore the relationship of myth and science fiction. Myth and science fiction have significant connections and areas of overlap, both thematically and functionally, and through an opening examination of aspects of the history of myth, we can see that science fiction is, in significant ways, an evolutionary outgrowth of ancient fantastical mythology.

There are, of course, relative differences between ancient myth and modern science fiction, in particular the distinctive importance of modern science and technology in science fiction, and how the influence of modern thought helped to separate and emancipate (to a degree) science fiction from earlier mythology. We could reasonably state that science fiction is scientifically informed and inspired myths *about* the future *for* the future.

* * *

Fantastic: Conceived or appearing as if conceived by an unrestrained imagination; imaginary or groundless in not being based on reality; extravagantly fanciful; a sense of deviation from what is normal or expected; marvelous ... incredibly great or extreme.
Dictionary.com

One type of ancient storytelling that today we would identify as myths were narratives of fantastic or extraordinary adventures. Humans have been creating and telling stories of incredible journeys into strange and fantastic places at least since the beginnings of recorded history. Such tales appear in probably all ancient cultures (See, for example, Joseph Campbell's *The Hero with a Thousand Faces,* 1949 and Jim Bloom's *Fantastic Voyages,* 2010). Two of the earliest and most famous and influential tales of fantastical journeys are the Sumerian *Epic of Gilgamesh* (c. 2000 BCE) and Homer's *Odyssey* (c. 800 BCE). Such "extraordinary journeys or adventures," often involving a quest for something of great value (a person, object, and/or deep insight), revealed to the travelers unusual sights, amazing discoveries, mind-expanding revelations, and bizarre realities that transcended the commonplace and the immediate here and now. Such tales were "fantastic" in the sense that what was encountered appeared to significantly go beyond the ordinary and the mundane; what was described in such tales was "extravagantly fanciful" and wondrous, often stretching the boundaries of imagination. Travelers in such adventures encountered outlandish, if not grotesque, beings with supernatural and superhuman powers, hypnotic or sacred objects with magical properties, and astonishing and spectacular lands and locales.

A key recurrent feature in fantastical adventures was the journey into the unknown. What lay beyond the geographical horizon was mysterious and ill defined. This dimension of mystery stimulated human imagination and fueled the drama and the wonder of the tale. We could argue that extraordinary adventure tales contained wild and fantastical sights and imagery because such envisioned journeys transported humans into obscure, exotic, and unexplored realms. Anything becomes conceivable and possible in the darkness and ambiguity of the unknown. As in a psychological Rorschach test, the unknown provided a blank canvas on which human imagination could project whatever thoughts and visions, however extreme, fanciful, and colorful, came into the storyteller's mind (even if the storyteller was simply recounting what they "saw"). Along with imagination, emotion came into play in such tales: both hopes and fears were psychologically projected and miraculously materialized—infused into the epistemological uncertainty—in the form of benevolent spirits, enticing sirens, heinous demons, terrifying sea serpents, and other emotionally charged or unnerving apparitions.

A second type of ancient narrative, which from a contemporary perspective is also generally viewed as myth, is tales of deities, supernatural beings, and the workings of creation. At least as far back in history as stories of extraordinary adventures, humans have also been creating mythic sagas that extended backward to the beginnings of time and upward into higher realms of existence. Such epic visions and tales attempted to explain, through the actions of deities and fantastical beings, the origin, metaphysical framework, and fundamental dramatic themes of life and the universe. Again, as with extraordinary adventures, our ancestors extended their minds beyond local and manifest realities. They created stories, often fantastical in content that recounted the beginnings of the earth, life, and humankind. They envisioned magnificent higher realities (the abode of the gods) and populated these dazzling realms with all manner of powerful beings and great wonders. From the earliest times of recorded history, humans have attempted to explain the grand scheme of things, enveloping themselves and their everyday world within an amazing and highly imaginative transcendent context of primal forces and cosmic personae (Lombardo, 2006a).

All told, for both our earliest tales of fantastic voyages and our cosmic myths of creation and higher realms of existence, human consciousness has never been limited to the commonplace, the familiar, and the immediate here and now. On the wings of our imagination and our ever-evolving thinking processes, our minds have extended outward and upward—inspirited with

34

curiosity, wonder, adventure, and speculation—into the beyond and the extraordinary, however we conceived of such realms. We were capable of conscious and visionary transcendence, even if it often frightened us, as much as it inspired us.

Moreover, the preferred mode of exposition was the narrative. Even with creation myths, descriptions of transcendent realities and supernatural beings were framed in terms of stories, involving drama and the actions and interactions of divine characters. We find conflict and war, love and procreation, sacrifice and courage, and dramatic tension and resolution. In general, our ancient myths, as a mode of understanding and vicariously experiencing the transcendent and the fantastical, were narratives.

A representative sample of fantastic lands and transcendent realms in ancient mythic narratives includes: the "Underworld" (or the "Netherworld") and other versions of Hades and Hell; Tartarus (existing even deeper below); multiple variations on Purgatory; the "Otherworld" (an abode of supernatural beings and the dead); numerous cities and lands existing at the earth's core; Acardia (the pastoral paradise) and other idyllic utopian realms; Atlantis and Lemuria (lost continents); Brahmapura (the abode of Brahma); Elysium or the Elysian Fields (the Isles of the Blessed); the Cedar Forest (from the *Epic of Gilgamesh*); the islands and lands of Sirens, Lotus Eaters, Cyclops, and giant cannibals (from the *Odyssey*); Mount Olympus and other heavenly abodes; Nysa (the land of the nymphs); and the resplendent realms of Shambhala, Shangri-La, Avalon, and El Dorado. (For more examples of fantastical and strange lands, especially those associated with extraordinary adventure tales, both ancient and more modern, again see Bloom's *Fantastic Voyages*, 2010.)

A key dimension of the fantastical content of these narratives was the numerous outlandish creatures and awe-inspiring divine beings. Egyptian, Indian, Zoroastrian, Greek, Babylonian, and Mesopotamian mythologies all contain, as integral to their stories, astounding and powerful characters and personalities, including resplendent deities, hideous monsters, strange human-animal hybrids, colossal giants, and all manner of freakish demons and devils. If humankind, early on, did realize a level of cosmic and expansive consciousness — of the big picture or what was beyond the horizon — their understanding was deeply personified. The universe was an arena in which weird and powerful personae acted out cosmic narrative dramas and themes.

Such transcendent and frequently bizarre beings both reflected typical human traits and qualities — often in exaggerated form — as well as possessing superhuman and transcendent powers. Again from a modern psychological perspective, we can interpret such beliefs in fantastical and multifarious beings populating the cosmos and the realm of the unknown as psychological projections of human character types painted onto the blank canvas of the mysterious universe. We also find among such projected fantastical personae amalgamations of human and non-human animate forms. (Animals often symbolized human ideals and human fears.)

Among the varied fantastical creatures contained in ancient folklore and mythology are: centaurs, combining horse and human; numerous giants and one-eyed Cyclops; sea serpents and a huge array of distinctive dragons; the multi-headed fire-breathing Chimera and the three-headed dog Cerberus (guarding the gates of Hell); gorgons (females with snakes on their head); griffins (the body of a lion and the head and wings of an eagle); harpies (a combination of woman and bird); hydras (many-headed serpents); the Minotaur (the body of a male human and the head of a bull); Ouroboros (the self-eating snake swallowing its tail); satyrs (combining goats and humans); Pegasus, the winged-horse; and unicorns, vampires, werewolves, sirens, and various animated metallic automata. (See for many more examples Jorge Borges's *The Book of Imaginary Beings,* 1969.) And this list does not even include the huge, multifarious array of gods and goddesses, who often also possessed weird and extraordinary qualities.

Such imaginative creatures and personae, most notably ancient deities, possessed an amazing array of incredible powers that far surpassed normal human abilities, including the ability to become invisible; to live forever; to shape-shift into different forms; to instantaneously move from one place to another; to command and control animals; to control the weather, including storms and earthquakes; to create monsters and tremendous weapons; to cast spells; to move the sun and the moon; to build animated machines (automata); to fly through the air and turn water into wine; to induce madness, love, or pregnancy; to foresee the future; to communicate with the dead (the power of necromancy); to posses superhuman muscular strength and intelligence; and in general to have power over both life and death.

Aside from distant lands and higher supernatural realms, the fantastic could also be found in some local haunted forest, dark cave, mystical mountain, and other places within the immediate environment. The supernatural and the fantastic manifested itself in the everyday world.

Indeed our ancestors saw their immediate environment as "enchanted" and filled with gods and spirits and all sorts of unusual creatures. The divine frequently visited the natural world around them, routinely communicating with human minds, molding attitudes and directing behavior. The gods spoke to ancient humans and revealed themselves and their wishes. Demons, monsters, and spirits from the beyond traveled into the everyday world. Our ancestors personified both nature and their local habitats, as well as the cosmos and the skies above (Berman, 1981; Donald, 1991). The mindset of "animism"—that everything in nature is animated and possessed of personified spirits—was perhaps the dominant mode of consciousness and understanding in ancient cultures. Animism, indeed, is an expression of the personification of nature and the universe.

Spirits, deities, and strange mythical creatures that populated nature included dryads (tree nymphs) and assorted other water and wind nymphs; gods and goddesses of flowers, forests, and trees, who often adopted animal forms; fairies, elves, and trolls; gods of air, storm, thunder, volcanoes, marshes, clouds, and rainbows; the great Greek god of the wild, Pan; and permeating all of nature, a great number of different mother earth goddesses across many cultures, including the Egyptian Isis and the Greek Gaea.

All in all, gods and spirits (and other imagined animate beings) were envisioned as both transcendent and beyond the everyday world, and yet also immanent within it, orchestrating physical nature and even entering into and directing conscious human minds. Homer's epochal tales, the *Iliad* and the *Odyssey*, are clear examples describing the presence of gods, goddesses, and other fantastical beings in human life and human consciousness, deities who visited humankind from the higher realm of Mount Olympus and talked to us, often guiding us in our challenges and pursuits in life (Jaynes, 1976; Armstrong, 1994; White, 2003; Wright, 2009).

Human consciousness and imagination in the ancient world also extended into the unknown future, creating fantastic visions and prophesies of what was to come. This capacity of future consciousness was part of our mental ability to transcend the immediate here and now. Although we may associate early religious myths more with stories about the origin and creation of humankind and the world—narratives of the past—ancient myths also delved into the future of the world, indeed, at times the "end of the world." One of the most influential ancient "myths" in the West is the predicted future battle of Armageddon, involving a host of fantastic beings and amazing cataclysmic events. Ancient futurist narratives also described human transformation and ascension to higher or different levels of reality in the future, combining the futuristic with the transcendent, fantastic, and metaphysical. From the Persian Zoroaster and ancient Hindu mythology of the destruction and recreation of the world to St. Augustine and medieval Millennialism, we see stories of great battles in the future, the ongoing physical and spiritual transformative development of future humans, the end of the earth and/or the universe, and the promise of elevated transcendent realities to come (Nisbet, 1994; Noss, 1999; Lombardo, 2006a).

The nineteenth century astronomer and mystical science fiction writer Camille Flammarion extensively recounted, in his book *Omega: The Last Days of the World* (1893-1894), the numerous and varied visions and warnings of the "end of the world" within both ancient and modern times. Does the world end through fire and heat, cold and ice, flood or drought, comets or meteor collisions, or the death of the sun? These different apocalyptic visions informed his science fiction writings and continue to influence modern human consciousness and contemporary science fiction. As Flammarion demonstrated, the end of the world has been a recurrent theme found throughout human history, as diverse and rich in content as the expansive reach of human hope, fear, and imagination. See also John Clute's *The Book of End Times: Grappling with the Millennium* (1999) and Sharan Newman's *The Real History of the End of the World* (2010).

As described in my book *The Evolution of Future Consciousness* (2006a), humans have been thinking about the future (imagining, feeling, and creating it) since before the dawn of recorded history, however primitive and limited their early capacities were in this regard. We are beings of future consciousness, as much as we are beings of imagination and cosmic consciousness; indeed these varied capacities support each other, all of them forms of consciousness that go beyond the immediate here and now, all expressions of the mental capacity for conscious transcendence. And as noted earlier, emotion weaves together with imagination and speculation. In the historical development of future consciousness, we find uplifting, hopeful visions of future utopian and heavenly realms as well as fearful visions of the end of the world and eternal damnation.

The general point to be understood from the above examples is that from ancient times the human mind has embedded the everyday world and ordinary consciousness within an expansive and imaginative framework of ideas, narratives, and diverse personified beings, often bizarre and fantastical in nature that extends far beyond the commonplace and the immediate here and now. Giving meaning and understanding to life and existence, this transcendent and fantastic mode of consciousness is a key dimension of the nature of ancient myths.

* * *

Such imaginative ideas and narratives, however fantastical and strange, were seen as highly credible and believable within the context of the theories of reality adopted by humans at the time. Although there was not one uniform vision (theory) of reality across the diverse cultures around the ancient world (Lombardo, 2006a), ancient mindsets frequently included strange or fantastical realms of existence, populated by supernatural and bizarre beings, as integral to their theories of reality. As indicated above, ancient humans explained nature and existence in terms of spirits and deities. And such ancient theories, more often than not, allowed for the visitation and manifestation of beings from other realms into the everyday here and now, and in many cases, conversely, for human journeys to these exotic or transcendent realms. We made contact with these other realms, and beings from these realms made contact with us. Such contact and communication running in either direction seemed credible and plausible.

Belief in the literal truth of such fantastical realities should not be surprising. As a fundamental feature of the psychology of human consciousness, a person's theory of reality determines what he or she believes is possible and plausible. The credible possibilities of existence are explained and interpreted within the context of the accepted theory of reality. What may seem from a modern point of view as totally implausible if not impossible, within the context of a different theory of reality may seem quite understandable and believable. The ancients believed in a universe of spirits and deities, possessing incredible powers, of personified nature and the cosmos, and of exotic creatures, including animal-animal and animal-human hybrids. Their stories, populated with such realities, seemed credible to them.

Moreover, what a person perceives as real within their everyday world is strongly influenced by what they believe or think is ontologically plausible or possible. A person's interpretations and descriptions of observed facts are framed within the context of their theory of reality (Kuhn, 1962; Feyerabend, 1965, 1969; Lombardo, 2017). Although ancient humans believed in fantastical realities and beings that existed in faraway places or higher realms of existence, these beliefs and underlying theories of reality also influenced their perceptions or observations of the everyday world around them. They believed in gods, spirits, demons, and magical beings and, consequently, routinely observed apparitions, signs, and intimations of these beings in their everyday world. Their world, their perceptions, and their consciousness were "enchanted," animated, and haunted by these entities.

As a self-confirming feedback loop, human thought and imagination extending beyond the immediate here and now circled back on the everyday world, giving it context, substance, structure, and meaning. Cosmic and fantastical consciousness informed the ancients' perceptions and thoughts about their lived reality. They saw what they believed in. Reciprocally, the imaginative theories of reality and associated narratives of the ancients seemed credible because it appeared to them that there was observable evidence, albeit theoretically informed, all around them confirming their beliefs. Because they believed in gods and demons, the gods talked to them and the demons appeared to them in the night, and because of this presumed evidence, their beliefs in this fantastical reality were further reinforced.

This psychological contact between the fantastical and the everyday, the imaginative and the concrete, and the theoretical and the perceptual, also shows up in the fact that ancient visions and stories of transcendent and astonishing beings and realms provided guidance, meaning, and purpose within everyday life. Ancient myths and fantasies provided role models, stories to live by, rituals to partake in, and metaphors of what was of critical value and supreme importance in life. The fantastical narratives inspired, engaging human emotion, motivation, and ethical thinking and action. The fantastical myths and sagas holistically impacted human consciousness and human ways of life. The ancients modeled their lives on their mythic stories, which indeed, is a key aspect of the nature of myth.

* * *

In modern times, ancient beliefs, prophecies, and fantastic tales are viewed by a large segment of the population as without credibility, as "myth" consisting of nothing but wishful thinking or speculative fantasy, rather than being grounded in fact or reality. A common modern meaning associated with the term "myth" is something that isn't true. Typical online definitions of "myth" include: "a fictitious story, person, or thing" (The Free Dictionary); "a widely held but false belief or idea"; and "a misrepresentation of the truth" (Oxford Dictionaries).

To expand, if myths are frequently seen as fantasies, how do we define "fantasy"? Typical online definitions of "fantasy" (my italics) are "imagination unrestricted by reality; [a] genre of fiction that commonly uses *magic* and other *supernatural* elements ... takes place in imaginary worlds where magic and *magical creatures* are common" (*The Free Dictionary; Fantasy – Wikipedia*). A representative definition of magic is "the power of apparently influencing the course of events by using mysterious or *supernatural* forces." And "supernatural" can be defined as "attributed to some force *beyond scientific understanding* or the laws of nature" (*Google Search*: Definition of "magic" and definition of "supernatural").

As evident from the above definitions, magic, the supernatural, and fantasy are dissociated from science. And if we accept modern science as our standard for determining what is realistic or credible, then fantasy, magic, and the supernatural do not align with reality because fantasy is not based on a scientific view of reality. More succinctly, fantasy is whatever does not align with science.

Consequently, because ancient myths are seen as fantasies, often embracing the magical and/or the supernatural, they do not refer to anything true or real (or even realistically possible) since they are not scientifically credible. Also, the creatures and beings described in myths are not scientifically believable. Wizards are not plausible because science says that magic doesn't exist; dragons, cyclops, and minotaurs are not credible because there is no empirical fossil evidence (or evolutionary explanation) for them; spirits, demons, ghosts, and deities are unrealistic fantasies because the universe, in its totality, can be scientifically understood without bringing into the picture such personified supernatural entities influencing reality. We do not need gods to explain thunder, earthquakes, the sun rising in the morning, the direction of human history, or even the origin of life and the universe. *What is a spirit* within a scientific universe? In modern times, science provides our theory and understanding of reality, and ancient mythic beliefs and associated creatures and beings have no credibility within this modern mindset.

We could also argue from a modern scientific point of view that because ancient myths are fantasies and not scientifically credible, they have no psychological or social value, and are even counter-productive and dangerous to human happiness and general well-being. Believing in what is patently false cannot be beneficial to the human mind or society. Being inspired by unrealistic (unscientific) visions and stories is of no practical or adaptive value, and in fact, may be psychologically destructive; it may be a sign of madness and psychosis. People who commune with supernatural or magical beings are often, though not always, put in mental hospitals. Religious belief systems, having ancient and mythic foundations, have been repeatedly critiqued and attacked in modern times, beginning during the Western Enlightenment (c.1750 CE) and up to the present (in the "New Atheism" for example), such antiquated mindsets presumably producing all types of damaging psychological and social effects, including dogmatism, oppression, foolishness, stilted mental growth, neurotic guilt, and self-righteous violence (Lombardo, 2006a; Dawkins, 2006; Hitchens, 2007).

Yet a large percentage of people in our contemporary world still follow the principles and practices of one of the main traditional religions (for example, Judaism, Christianity, Islam, and Hinduism). And they believe in the various fantastical visions and tales contained in ancient myths connected with their particular religion. All these religions contain mythic stories of ancient origin that are fantastical and supernatural; they all embody theories of reality, supporting their respective sagas and tales that do not align with modern science. (Although many followers contend that "metaphorically" their ancient religious and mythical beliefs do align with science.) Moreover, religious individuals following these various traditions also think that their beliefs and practices have beneficial rather than negative effects on the quality of their lives. People who believe in ancient myths and theories of reality associated with their religions also often believe in the possibility, if not the reality, of ghosts, demons, animate spirits, angels, and other fantastical beings who visit and communicate with them (Wright, 2009).

* * *

Human consciousness, in numerous ways, has been evolving across the history of our species, and in particular, there has been a general direction toward increasing vistas of awareness and understanding in both space and time. Our minds have been progressively expanding away from the relative egocentric immediate here and now. Regarding our consciousness of time, our capacities for both historical and future consciousness have progressively extended and enriched through the development of our species; we see and understand a great deal more about the past and the future. Of particular significance, the psychological capacity to envision and purposefully evolve desirable or preferable futures has been progressively evolving and has been the central driving force behind the development of modern human civilization (Lombardo, 2006a, 2017).

Yet, the ancient human mind possessed certain definite powers of thought and imagination. As far back as the beginning of recorded history the human mind demonstrated the capacity to imagine and to think beyond the immediate here and now and the everyday and commonplace. Our capacities for imagination, speculation, future and historical consciousness, and conscious transcendence are evident in ancient myths. All of these capacities are distinguishing strengths of the human mind, and although our minds can reach beyond the immediate here and now, this constellation of abilities has provided meaning to the everyday world. Imagination and our sense of the big picture inform and inspire us. As noted above, ancient fantastical stories and visions provided ethical and motivational direction to human life. There was a pragmatic value in our early capacity for transcendence, even if we think today that the visionary consciousness of the ancients is no longer credible. Insofar as many people worldwide still find credibility in ancient myth, they also see personal and practical relevance in such ancient sagas and stories.

Bringing these two points together, we should look for both continuity and change (evolution) in the history of the powers of the human mind, and in particular in our capacity to transcend the commonplace and the egocentric here and now. Continuity and change are hallmarks of evolution; there is novelty in evolution, but novelty that builds upon what came before. It would be a mistake to think that the ancients were completely stuck in a totally localized and primordial mode of consciousness and that they couldn't imagine wondrous and fantastical realities beyond their local village mentality. Conversely, as we move forward in historical time, it makes sense that our capacities for imagination, historical and future consciousness, cosmic visions, and transcendence have evolved further.

Moreover, although mythic consciousness is usually associated with an early stage in the evolution of the human mind, being more primitive than scientific consciousness (Lombardo, 2016c), it is clear that mythic consciousness has not disappeared in the modern world. One plausible evolutionary view is that more modern forms of consciousness, rather than eliminating more primitive modes of understanding, have layered or built upon earlier forms. Adopting an evolutionary view of continuity and change within human history, perhaps pre-modern fantastical mythology and modern scientific thinking are not unequivocally and totally at odds, and at least along certain lines have realized a level of cumulative integration in contemporary times. Has there perhaps been an evolutionary synthetic process of science and myth that has been ongoing over the last few hundred years since the beginnings of modern science? This ongoing evolving synthesis, encompassing both continuity and change, is what I propose science fiction has been achieving in numerous ways over the last few centuries.

The Value of Myth

... myths are archetypal patterns in human consciousness and where there is consciousness there will be myth.
Rollo May

If we turn to the modern scholar of myth, Joseph Campbell, we find a very positive and sympathetic view of myth and its value and relevance to the modern world. In his book *The Power of Myth*, he asserts that through myth, "... what we're seeking is an *experience of being alive,* so that our life experiences on a purely physical plane will have resonances within our own innermost being and reality, so that we actually feel the *rapture* of being alive" (Campbell, 1988, p. 3). (My *italics* in the above and below quotes from Campbell.) According to Campbell, myth facilitates this heightened level of experience, this rapture of personal existence.

Additionally, he argues that "Mythology is the song. It is the *song of the imagination,* inspired by the energies of the body" (Campbell, 1988, p. 22). Mythology, for Campbell, is aesthetic, lyrical, and expressive, key qualities in the fullest and deepest expression of human consciousness and our experience of life. A song is a celebration, a romance, a revelation and expression of beauty. These experiences are essential to a fully realized life. As I argue in *Future Consciousness* (2017), beauty and vitality are key features in human happiness and a flourishing life.

Campbell further suggests that:

Myth ... serves four functions. The first is the *mystical* function ... realizing what a *wonder* the universe is, and what a wonder you are, and experiencing *awe* before this mystery. Myth opens the world to the dimension of *mystery*, to the realization of the mystery that underlies all forms ... If mystery is manifest through all things, the universe becomes, as it were, a holy picture. You are always addressing the *transcendent* mystery through the conditions of your actual world. (Campbell, 1988, p. 31)

As noted earlier, where there is mystery and the unknown, humans have created various stories and scenarios to make sense of what lies beyond the known; humans have projected meanings onto the unknown. Yet it is part of our expansive awareness of the transcendent that we realize there is something beyond the mundane and the relative here and now that we cannot imagine or grasp. Campbell, in this last quote, is arguing that myth acknowledges, if not highlights, the mystery of existence to be found within the "transcendent," of a higher unknown realm. Myths keep our minds open, through awe and wonder, to the realms of the possible, the undiscovered, the mind-boggling, and the transcendent. The mystery is embraced. For Campbell, myth doesn't aspire to explain it all away.

As one final quote, Campbell argues,

... myths offer *life models*. But the models have to be *appropriate to the time* in which you are living and our time has changed so fast that what was proper fifty years ago is not proper today. ... The old time religion belongs to another age, another people, another set of human values, another universe. By going back you throw yourself out of sync with history (Campbell, 1988, p. 13).

Although Campbell, in great depth and unending fascination, described ancient myths and their meaning and significance to contemporary life and our experience of reality, in this quote, he is arguing that we need myths that are resonant and relevant to our modern times and modern way of thinking. We need myths that tune into the concerns, philosophies, and aspirations of contemporary life and the modern human mind. Where are these new myths to be found? Can we identify myths that embrace, rather than contradict, a modern scientific vision of reality? For Campbell, it is not that myth per se is without value; rather we need to move beyond ancient myths to myths with a contemporary resonance and credibility.

Yet also, in the last quote, Campbell hits upon a key point about myth (or any type of effective narrative): There need to be characters within a story that provide models for us; narratives inform and inspire because there are characters with whom we can resonate. Although ancient myths can be criticized for including personae in explanations of the origin and the workings of nature and the cosmos (animism), such personifications of reality facilitated a psychological resonance between the myth and the human mind. (How well do we personally resonate with the entities of modern science and astronomy, such as quarks, gamma rays, nebulae, black holes, and quasars?) One of the key factors behind the psycho-social power of the narrative is the inclusion of characters within the story; myths, as narratives with characters, possess this inspirational power. Can we therefore somehow combine the credibility of contemporary science and modern thought with the personifications of mythic narrative?

A key concept that Campbell invokes in understanding the meaning and structure of myths is the "archetype." An archetype can be defined as "an original pattern or model represented by some image, persona, or symbol." An archetype is an anchor point of meaning, associated with a recognizable icon. The psychologist Carl Jung, whom Campbell cites in his writings, understood an archetype as a deep, fundamental, and universal idea or theme within the human mind. Archetypes are primordial units of meaning basic to the structure and form of human understanding, existing, according to Jung, in the collective unconscious shared by all human minds. For Jung (1964), the human mind experiences the world and makes sense out of it through archetypes. (Archetypes are fundamental ideas, with associated icons, within a person's theory of reality.) For Campbell, there are common personae, themes, and narrative structures in myths from across the world. These pervasive elements or units of meaning are mythic archetypes. Both Campbell and Jung believed that various common symbols and images show up across human cultures representing the deep archetypal units of meaning and understanding within the human mind.

There can be archetypal themes, archetypal characters, and archetypal narrative structures. As a start, we can list as frequently cited archetypes within the human mind and human narratives the following: death and resurrection, representing both the cycle of life as well as transcendence from one level of existence to a higher level; the sun as the progenitor of life and source of knowledge and wisdom; the earth-mother as protector and/or the giver of life (or the womb from which life springs); light (radiance, illumination) symbolizing wisdom, enlightenment, or a higher spiritual realm; the hero and the heroic journey, involving challenge, courage, and eventual enlightenment; the "shadow," or the dark, destructive monster (demon/devil) symbolizing what our conscious minds reject as evil and/or damaging to our life and spirit; fire or conflagration as symbolic of destruction, purification, or transformation; and the circle or the mandala as a symbol of unity, wholeness, and completion. Both Jung and Campbell were particularly fascinated by the ancient Taoist symbol of the Yin-Yang, which represented unity and harmony enveloping plurality and opposition; good and evil, male and female, and earth and sky are all united within the wholeness and completeness of the archetypal Yin-Yang (Lombardo, 2006a).

For Campbell, who emphatically sees both profound truth

and deep value in myths, a key reason behind his positive view of myth is that he believes that the archetypal patterns in myths express universal and fundamental principles in human understanding and our experience of the world. Myths express something basic about how we think and how we experience our lives. We could argue that ancient myths, although not literally true relative to a modern scientific perspective, have metaphorical, allegorical, or symbolic validity and universal human value that is grounded in their archetypal content and structure. There are fundamental themes and principles by means of which the human mind comprehends the universe and these units of meaning are present within myths, even ancient myths which we may dismiss as non-credible.

We could, though, reject the idea of archetypes—of fundamental structures of meaning in the human mind—that are cross-cultural and universal. Aren't the mindsets of different cultures distinctively unique? Further, isn't the human mind evolving? Aren't the basic units of meaning changing? But, taking a more flexible position, we could argue that archetypes need not be absolutely universal for all humanity, or for all time, but rather are general units of meaning (with appropriate symbols or icons) that repeatedly show up in human life or modes of consciousness. Perhaps there are *degrees* of universality in consciousness across human cultures (Brown, 1991; Pinker, 2002; Lombardo, 2011a). And perhaps archetypes evolve, acquiring new features and nuances; perhaps new archetypes emerge over time (through the combination of older ones). The idea of the archetype brings some level of order and universality to the diverse creations of the human mind; they may not be as universal or absolutely stable as Plato's eternal forms, but they may still exist within human consciousness and thinking.

* * *

Let me introduce another definition of myth that can be synthesized with the above line of thinking found in Campbell. A myth (my italics) is,

> ... a traditional, typically ancient story dealing with supernatural beings, ancestors, or heroes that serves as a *fundamental type in the worldview of a people,* as by explaining aspects of the natural world or delineating the psychology, customs, or ideals of society. (*The Free Dictionary*)

The term "supernatural" (meaning above or beyond nature) can be seen as identifying how the transcendent was understood in ancient theories of reality. But as key to this definition, a myth is a story, involving iconic characters, which expresses fundamental beliefs and values within a society or human mindset. A myth is a narrative revealing what a particular culture or mindset *believes* is most deeply true, important, and valuable. A myth embodies in personified narrative form a theory of reality, ethics, and values for a society or culture.

Relative to current beliefs and values, especially as informed by modern science, we can see ancient myths as not having any validity or life value. But don't we have our own myths (modern in conception), as defined above? The modern world, incorporating various theories of the past, present, and future and the nature of reality, has its grand narratives that express its deepest values and beliefs (Lombardo, 2006a, 2006b, 2015b, 2017). We have stories explaining where we have come from and pointing toward where we are going, and we have various cultural and historical heroes who personify or embody key principles and values expressed through these stories. (The heroes may not be supernatural, although they often have extraordinary abilities or traits.) These grand narratives inspire us into action and guide us toward the future (Polak, 1973). Finally, although our modern narratives may not make reference to the supernatural (spirits, demons, and deities), there are frequently transcendent elements included, especially as ideals, cosmic visions, and envisioned future states to hope for and aspire toward.

We should not minimize the importance of contemporary relevance and credibility in our assessment of the value of various myths, but to whatever degree Campbell and Jung are correct about historically persistent archetypal structures in the human mind (general themes and concepts in our way of thinking), we might find more similarity in meaning and content between ancient and new mythic narratives than, in our modernist arrogance, we would suppose. There may be continuities, and not simply discontinuities, in meaning and visions of reality between ancient myths and modern ones. If archetypes evolve, we may find both continuity and change between old and new myths.

So, pulling together the above definition of a myth—as a fundamental narrative expressing the beliefs and values of a culture or mindset—with Campbell's thinking, we can say that such fundamental narratives identify what is deeply true and good, engender "rapture," "awe and wonder," and an aesthetic experience, especially as it pertains to the transcendent, and provide inspiring and relevant role models for how to live the narrative. The fundamental narratives of different cultures, moreover, may show deep elements of resonance with similar ideas and meanings (cross-temporal and cross-cultural similarities), which Jung and Campbell identify as archetypes, as well as differences that reflect both the distinctive culture and the period of history; myths (and archetypes) may evolve and transform over time.

* * *

One other related view of the nature of myth that is relevant to understanding both the relationship between ancient and modern mythic narratives, as well as the mythic quality of science fiction, can be found in Alexei and Cory Panshin's *Hugo* award-winning *The World Beyond the Hill: Science Fiction and the Quest for Transcendence* (1989); see also Panshin and Panshin, 2005. I discovered the Panshins' book years after first formulating my theory that science fiction is the mythology of the future (Lombardo, 2006b), but their views resonate with and predate some of my own ideas on the topic.

For the Panshins, a myth points toward a transcendent reality (they use the metaphor of "the world beyond the hill"), but a myth is also grounded in a credible (for a particular time and place) theory of reality.

The pointing toward transcendence takes us beyond the mentality of the "village" (another metaphor); that is, in my terminology, beyond the relative here and now and the commonplace toward the fantastic, the extraordinary, and the astounding. "The world beyond the hill"—the transcendent— can be populated with all kinds of wondrous realities. In transcending the reality of the "village" a myth provides something to aspire toward beyond present circumstances and conditions. A myth *takes us* to another place and *draws us* toward that other place; a myth transcends us (our present reality) and provokes us to transcend ourselves (to this new reality).

Yet the envisioned transcendent realm, following from the above discussion, reflects an accepted (credible) fundamental theory of the true and the good for a particular culture. As I argued earlier, and the Panshins think similarly, for ancient humans the fantastical elements in their myths were credible within the context of their theories of reality. For the ancients, the existence of supernatural beings and spirits was highly plausible.

According to the Panshins, myth, whether ancient or modern, is the *credible fantastic* or the *credible transcendent*. For ancient myths it made sense to include reference to supernatural beings, since it was such supernatural beings (as well as other fantastic realities) that served the function of pointing toward transcendence, and given the ancient belief in the reality of a supernatural realm, such myths with supernatural beings provided credible transcendence.

The Panshins note that the myths of ancient times lost their credibility (they were no longer grounded in an acceptable theory of reality) when modern science arose and challenged the spiritualist, mystical, magical, and supernatural mindsets that supported ancient myths. Hence, ancient myths may now seem fanciful and untrue relative to our modern views of reality. (Keeping in mind that there are many people across the globe who still believe in mythic narratives grounded in pre-modern and pre-scientific visions of reality.) For the Panshins, credible and inspiring modern myths need to be on one hand grounded in believable contemporary views of reality and yet within this modern context point toward transcendence beyond the common place. Contemporary myths must make sense to modern consciousness, and yet at the same time generate awe and wonder.

What they propose is that this is exactly what science fiction provides: credible and inspiring modern narratives of transcendence. Science fiction clearly builds on a deep psychological reality going back thousands of years: the aspiration and quest for transcendence—indeed the capacity to imagine and conceptualize the transcendent—but it is modern in form, grounding its narratives within a scientific vision of reality.

In short, a myth provides a fundamental narrative, expressing the beliefs and values of a culture that points toward credible, within that culture and time, transcendence and inspires its believers to reach toward this envisioned transcendent reality. Our ancient myths realized this credible transcendence within the context of a supernatural and spiritual mindset; in contemporary times, this credible transcendence is realized through science fiction.

One other point to highlight in considering the Panshins' view of myth is the central importance and holistic meaning of the "fantastic" in myth. To recall, Campbell used terms like "wonder," "rapture," and "awe" in describing myth, and I pointed out that humans from the beginnings of recorded history, empowered by their imagination, created a huge array of fantastical realms and superhuman beings in their stories of "extraordinary adventures" and higher planes of existence that elevated and *inspired* the human psyche. In developing their argument that science fiction is mythic, the Panshins note that early science fiction magazines used such words as "astounding," "amazing," "astonishing," "marvel," and "wonder" in their titles, all reflecting the transcendent quality of the myths of science fiction. But in understanding how the theme of transcendence connects with such terms, what is noteworthy is the *emotional* dimension of these words. The transcendent jolts us; it can be inspiring, elevating, or unnerving. Indeed, all the above terms are connected in meaning with the term "fantastic," and the term "fantastic" denotes, as part of its meaning, the intense emotions experienced when our consciousness encounters something beyond the accustomed constraints of the commonplace. In reviewing titles, advertisements, and text on the covers of science fiction magazines, we also find that the word "fantastic" is frequently used, which is similar in meaning to "astonishing" or "amazing." All in all, myth (whether ancient or modern) brings to the forefront the fantastical, which involves a *cognitive* apprehension and intense *emotional* reaction to the transcendent and the extraordinary, a psychologically holistic experience. This holistic experience is a key feature in Campbell's conception of myth.

* * *

Building upon the above considerations regarding the nature of myth, as well as ideas from the previous chapter, I propose the following set of characteristic features and values of myth. This list includes psychological, literary, philosophical, and social-cultural functions, as well as the content of myth.

- *Myths are narratives.* The narrative resonates with a fundamental mode of understanding in the human mind — conceptualizing our lives, human society, and the universe as a whole in the form of stories, as opposed to abstract, theoretical, and depersonalized visions of reality. Psycho-socially, the narrative (the story) is more forceful than the theory. Because myths are narratives, myths have deep holistic psychological power and social influence.
- Because of their narrative structure, *myths present a temporalized* or *dynamic vision of reality*, involving sequences of events, to various degrees connecting past, present, and future. Where have we come from; where are we now; where are we heading? Things happen within myths; myths describe some significant transformation or direction within reality.
- *Myths possess a unique type of truth value.* We can argue that the story as a general form for describing reality has more truth value than an abstract theory or static picture. Reality involves events, processes, and interactive forces generating consequences. To quote Muriel Rukeyser, "The universe is made of stories, not of atoms." Also, a compelling myth is intended to have something true to say about reality, at least as presently understood. Moreover, even if a myth may not be literally true, a myth may possess a deep and symbolic truth and meaning; it may capture some fundamental theme regarding human life or the meaning framework of the human mind.
- *Myths contain personifications.* Narratives usually contain

characters that participate in the action of the story. Humans particularly resonate with this dimension of the narrative; we identify with some of the characters and vicariously experience the narrative events through their eyes. We are psychologically repelled by other characters, ones who are villainous, weak, or corrupted. Characters set up the drama and conflict of the narrative, and we resonate with the idea that life contains personal and interpersonal drama and conflict.

- *Myths express archetypal themes.* To various degrees, myths contain general icons and symbols representing fundamental ideas or principles. Myths reach out to the universal, at least as it is experienced or understood by the creators, and penetrate into the deep and most general intuitions and meanings within the human mind.

- Related to the archetypal, myths are frequently *cosmic* in scope. Myths ask and attempt to answer expansive questions about reality; myths aspire to profound truths about life, the universe, and everything. Although *myths educate on the nature of reality*, as Campbell proposed, myths also revel in the *great deep mysteries* of reality and existence, expressing both awe and wonder in the face of the unfathomable beyond-ness of existence.

- Connected to the expansive and cosmic scope of myth, as well as the frequent sense of mystery and the unknown, *myths often postulate fantastical realms and fantastical beings.* Expressive of the creative power and richness of human imagination, myths transcend the commonplace and the mundane, exploring the vast possibilities of existence. Through the cosmic and the fantastical, myths achieve *transcendence.*

- *Myths give personal meaning to life.* Myths connect the cosmic and transcendent to the personal, the former providing meaning for the latter. Characters within myths are frequently situated within cosmic settings, and through such characters we vicariously experience the universe. Myths contextualize our personal lives within the big picture of things.

- Myths engage the heart and stimulate human feelings. *Myths have an emotional dimension.* We fear, we hope, we are thrilled and disappointed in our experiences of mythic narratives. The emotional reactions to myths are a significant part of the *participatory* dimension of myths.

- *Myths are often motivational* and *inspirational*, providing stories that propel us into action and direct us in our lives. As a quality within many narratives, myths do not simply describe and explain reality but rather provoke and motivate us into action.

- Providing direction for our aspirations and actions, *myths often contain ethical guidelines* and values for life. Mythic characters can be either positive ethical exemplars or negative ones. Myths tell us what to seek and what to avoid. Myths often have a prescriptive dimension, as well as a descriptive and explanatory dimension.

- Frequently, *there is an aesthetic dimension to myths*; as Campbell states, myths are "songs." As works of literature, myths have literary beauty, rhythm, harmony, color, energy, and grace. Moreover, mythic narratives are often coupled with aesthetic visualizations (art and sculpture). We can argue that the beauty and truth values of mythic narratives are connected: Beauty is truth and truth is beauty. Part of the engaging, inspirational force of a myth derives from its beauty and aesthetics.

- Through various rites and rituals, *myths provoke personal immersive participation* in the acting out of the myth. The participation may be individual or collective. Invariably, religions and other forms of spirituality and worship that have myths as part of their heritage require participants to act out their key mythic stories as an essential component of their active initiation, identification, and inclusion within the religious or spiritual group. This is part of the behavioral dimension of myths.

- *Numerous icons, totems, images, symbols, and objects of worship,* having deep meaning and significance, *are associated with myths.* The icons can be archetypal. This is part of the sensory-perceptual and symbolic dimensions of myths.

In summary, through its narrative form, myths effectively stimulate emotion, intellect, imagination, and desire; provide personal and social identity; and provoke action and immersive participation. Myths tap into all the major dimensions of human psychology, generating holistic consciousness. Myths give meaning, value, and direction to human life. To various degrees, myths are grounded in the core beliefs and values of a culture (or mindset); myths can be viewed as archetypal, embodying universal themes of human consciousness and culture. Of special note, myths engage human consciousness in the cosmic, fantastical, and transcendent, drawing the mind beyond the ordinary, common place, and immediate here and now.

The Mythic Dimensions of Science Fiction

The myth of the modern Western world has been science fiction.
Alexei and Cory Panshin

I propose that science fiction shares with traditional myths all of the above features and functions. Not all science fiction has all of these mythic qualities, but as a general pattern, all of these features can be regularly found in science fiction. Although not all science fiction is mythic (as described above), it is a distinctive and pervasive feature of science fiction that it is mythic. Science fiction is mythology.

Science fiction is narrative, temporal-dynamic in form, and filled with a distinctive and colorful assortment of characters. One of the key qualities that make for good science fiction is the exciting and engaging nature of its stories. Exemplified in its greatest and most popular writers, some excellent examples of highly engaging stories include: *The Island of Dr. Moreau* (1896) and *The Invisible Man* (1897) by H. G. Wells; *The Princess of Mars* (1912) and *The Land that Time Forgot* (1918) by Edgar Rice Burroughs; *Methuselah's Children* (1941) — among other stories in the "Future History" saga, *The Past through Tomorrow* (1967) — and *The Moon is a Harsh Mistress* (1966) by Robert Heinlein; *The Demolished Man* (1953) and *The Stars, My Destination* (1956) by Alfred Bester; and more recently, the Hugo Award-winning novels, *A Fire Upon the Deep* (1992) by Vernor Vinge; *Hominids* (2002) by Robert Sawyer; *Spin* (2005) by Robert Charles Wilson; and *The Three-Body Problem* (2014) by Cixin Liu.

Guided by imaginative extrapolations of science, together with other forms of creative inspiration, science fiction has produced the most head-spinning assortment of amazing creatures and characters within the history of human thought. The characters in science fiction, even if they are human, are frequently fantastical and often superhuman in their powers. Aside from the central protagonists (an obsessed murderer, telepathic cop, and tiger-faced teleporting human) in Bester's two novels cited above, and Simmons' Shrike in *Hyperion*, other bizarre and memorable science fiction characters (including alien beings) include the geometrically transformative, shape-shifting *The Metal Monster* (1920) by Abraham Merritt; the ostrich-like Martian "Tweel" in Stanley Weinbaum's "A Martian Odyssey" (1932); the octopusian intellect "Old Faithful" by Raymond Gallun (1934); A. E. van Vogt's carnivorous cat-like "Black Destroyer" (1939); the galaxy-disrupting, mental mutant "The Mule" from Isaac Asimov's *Foundation Trilogy* (1951, 1952,

1953); the free-loving messiah from Mars, Valentine Michael Smith, from Heinlein's *Stranger in a Strange Land* (1961); the Morlock cosmic scientist Nebogipfel in Stephen Baxter's *The Time Ships* (1995); the "wolf-like pack-minds" in Vernor Vinge's *A Fire Upon the Deep* (1992); the intelligent and endearing giant spiders, notably Sherkaner Underhill, in Vinge's *A Deepness in the Sky* (1999); and the thaumatological scientist Isaac Dan der Grimnebulin and his insect-human lover, the artist Lin, in China Miéville's *Perdido Street Station* (2000).

As literature, science fiction often aspires toward aesthetic standards of beauty and literary color and style. The stylistic grace, lyricism, and poetic qualities of Ray Bradbury's novels, such as *The Martian Chronicles* (1950) and *Fahrenheit 451* (1953), are noteworthy examples in this regard, as well as Stapledon's *Star Maker* (1937), and more recently Wilson's *Spin* (2005), Jo Walton's *Among Others* (2010), and *Annihilation* (2014) by Jeff Vandermeer.

The artistic dimension of science fiction (both in art and cinema), in its unique and imaginative fashion, strives for sensory beauty, mesmerizing cosmic effects, and brilliant, thought-provoking visualizations. The art of science fiction is at the creative cutting edge of contemporary art (Roberts, 2005; Fenner and Fenner, 1993-2015). Some of the most well-known science fiction artists, who have realized unique expressions of beauty and imaginative visualization in their works, include the surrealistic Richard Powers, the astronomic and heavenly Chesley Bonestell, the luminous dream-like Hannes Bok, the starry and erotic Virgil Finlay, the nightmarish H.R. Giger, the visceral, animated, and colorful Frank Frazetta, and the most highly awarded contemporary science fiction painter, the vibrant and other-worldly Michael Whelan.

Moreover, science fiction is filled with icons, symbols, images, and totems, which include, as archetypal examples, the robot, the rocket ship, the ray gun, the alien, and towering futuristic cities. Science fiction art is filled with these images; for many science fans, the various icons are idealized as objects of beauty and worship. Some of the most famous iconic images in science fiction include the memorable robots in *Metropolis*, *The Day the Earth Stood Still*, and *Forbidden Planet*; both Frankenstein (the mad scientist hovering over his operating table) and his creature (in different incarnations); various visions of *The Time Machine*; "Big Brother" from *1984* (1949); the menacing metallic *Terminator* with its glowing red eyes; the giant towering worms of *Dune* (1965); the half-buried *Statue of Liberty* from *The Planet of the Apes*; the Martian machines (several versions, hovering or walking) from *The War of the Worlds*; the monolith, the Star Child, and the eye of Hal from *2001*; the star ship *Enterprise* from *Star Trek*; the hideous creature of the *Alien* series; the light saber from *Star Wars* (a double-icon if held by Darth Vader); the gargantuan mother-ship of *Close Encounters*; the Shrike from *Hyperion* (1989); the tiger-faced protagonist of *The Stars, My Destination* (1956); and for those familiar with the early history of science fiction magazines, C. L. Moore's Medusa "Shambleau" (1933); the utterly bizarre other-worldly beings of H. P. Lovecraft's "The Shadow Out of Time" (1936); and the contemplative robot (Jenkins), together with shadowed figures of dog and rabbit, from Clifford Simak's tale of "Aesop" included in his novel *City* (1952). And this list does not include all the iconic super-hero characters (and the imagery of their colorful costumes) that serve as role models and alter-egos for science fiction and comic book enthusiasts of all ages. Especially in the last hundred years, with the emergence of cinema, the comics, and book and magazine cover art, science fiction has become strongly associated with an ever-evolving and highly dramatic and vibrant visual dimension, filled with a host of memorable images and iconic objects.

As two of its strongest qualities, science fiction is frequently cosmic, generating wonder and a sense of mystery, and science fiction is clearly populated with fantastical settings and mind-expansive scenarios. Science fiction continually pushes and stretches the imaginative limits on both these dimensions, often creating a sense of mental vertigo. It engages the transcendent. In science fiction we explore the immense reaches of the universe, the entire past and future history of the cosmos, and through alternate realities the possibility space of existence. Insofar as we vicariously experience the cosmos through characters in its stories, we are personally connected with the universe and all its vast wonders. We become children of the cosmos; we connect with the big picture of things. And in this transcendent space, our minds often sparkle and scintillate in the ambience of the fantastical. Aside from the cosmic mind-expanding novels of Camille Flammarion and Olaf Stapledon, already noted, other more recent science fiction novels that dramatically realize cosmic consciousness include Stephen Baxter's *Xeelee* (1997, 2010) and *Manifold* (2000, 2001, 2002) series; Greg Egan's *Permutation City* (1994) and *Diaspora* (1997); MacDonald's *River of Gods* (2004); and for a comic excursion into the farthest reaches of space, time, and artificial intelligence, Cory Doctorow's and Charles Stross's post-Singularity novel, *The Rapture of the Nerds* (2012).

As noted earlier, science fiction can create total person immersion for its fans. First as children and then as adults, devotees of the genre actively play out science fiction scenarios and narratives through science fiction toys, action figures, and video games. Whatever may be the inspirational themes and anchor points, science fiction stimulates action in its fans and readers. Through all its various fandom activities, modes of engagement, icons and paraphernalia, and storylines and philosophies, science fiction affords the props, social support, and existential themes for active participation in a total way of life.

Science fiction is especially motivational insofar as it provides both ideals and preferable visions of the future to aspire toward, and warnings and negative scenarios to avoid or fight against.

The good versus evil polarity, to whatever degree it is clearly identified within science fiction stories and scenarios, provides a dramatic opposition that can be visualized, internalized, and vicariously played out in life. Consider as examples the classic (archetypal) confrontation of the fight for freedom against forces of oppression in the *Terminator* series, *The Matrix* trilogy, the Federation versus the Borg in *Star Trek*, and the Jedi versus the Dark Side in *Star Wars*. Inspired by such stories and others, science fiction fans often see the world as an ongoing struggle for individuality and freedom (the spirit of science fiction) against conformity, groupthink, and "the system" (the ordinary and mundane), and act upon the world through such dramatized mindsets.

The utopian-dystopian polarity in science fiction clearly taps into the ethical dimension of myth, identifying hopeful and good futures for human society as well as fearful and bad futures. The above cinematic series provide dramatized illustrations of the struggle for the good future against dystopian forces. Yet science fiction often also gets us to ponder over what is good and what is bad, for it is not always so clear once we step out of the constraints of the commonplace. Although there is a good deal of simplistic "black and white" and "good guys versus bad guys" thinking in science fiction—especially popular science fiction cinema—in contemplating the future, science fiction can get us into rethinking our ethical philosophies and assumptions. We are transported to futurist and alien cultures where values, norms, and modes of thinking and behaving may be very different than in present day, jolting us out of our moral assumptions and ethical complacency.

Beginning with Bacon's *New Atlantis* (1627), which has both a social-ethical dimension as well as a plethora of scientific-technological extrapolations, some of the most noteworthy utopian novels in the history of science fiction include *Vril, The Power of the Coming Race* (1871) by Sir Edward Bulwer-Lytton;

Looking Backward 2000-1887 (1888) by Edward Bellamy; *A Modern Utopia* (1905) and *Men Like Gods* (1923) by H. G. Wells; *Brain Wave* (1954) by Poul Anderson; *Permutation City* (1994) by Greg Egan; *The Diamond Age* (1995) by Neal Stephenson (a utopian-dystopian mix); and the *Red Mars/Green Mars/Blue Mars* trilogy (1991, 1994, 1996) by Kim Stanley Robinson, as well as Robinson's *2312* (2012).

Some of the best known dystopias include *Paris in the Twentieth Century* (1863) by Jules Verne; *The Sleeper Awakes* (1899/1910) by H. G. Wells; "The Machine Stops" (1909) by E. M. Forster; *City of Endless Night* (1920) by Milo Hastings; *We* (1921) by Yevgeny Zamyatin; *Metropolis* (1926) by Fritz Lang and Thea von Harbou; *Brave New World* (1932) by Aldous Huxley; *1984* (1949) by George Orwell; *The Space Merchants* (1952/1953) by Frederik Pohl and C.M. Kornbluth; *The Handmaid's Tale* (1986) by Margaret Atwood; and *Parable of the Talents* (1999) by Octavia Butler.

Various novels within the utopian-dystopian continuum are ambiguous, getting us to question our ethics and values. Is the envisioned society good or bad? Sometimes we can see it either way. Although *We* and *Brave New World*, for example, are popularly viewed as dystopian, if we question certain basic beliefs we have about what the good life is—which these novels explicitly challenge—then both novels can be read as psychologically jolting utopian visions. (They transcend our ethical mindsets.) Other classic novels that also have uncertain or complex double meanings include *Erewhon: or, Over the Range* (1872) by Samuel Butler; *The Twentieth Century* (1882) by Albert Robida; *The Humanoids* (1949) by Jack Williamson; *The Dispossessed: An Ambiguous Utopia* (1974) by Ursula LeGuin; and *Accelerando* (2005) by Charles Stross. All told, science fiction, as expressed through utopian-dystopian novels, powerfully demonstrates, as does traditional myth, an ethical dimension, and perhaps goes one step further by challenging traditional or contemporary beliefs regarding what good and evil are.

Next on the list of shared qualities with myth, science fiction embodies a plethora of archetypes. Even if the genre points toward the future, it is filled with universal themes and ideas expressing basic units of meaning within the human mind that have a deep history in storytelling and myth. We find in science fiction the themes of death, resurrection, and immortality; the hero's journey toward enlightenment; the promise and temptation of great power; multiple versions of paradise and damnation; the interweaving and struggle of order and chaos; both mother and father archetypal figures; beings that are both angel and demon-like; the battle of good and evil and war versus peace; ignorance and dogmatism versus enlightenment and the liberation of the mind; and evolution and transcendence. What gets conceptually transformed in these science fiction tales is that the classic archetypal themes are frequently anchored to futurist visions and scientific and technological wonders. A key question, though, regarding archetypes in science fiction, as noted earlier, is to what degree such basic themes reflect traditional archetypes of early myth, and to what degree the archetypes in science fiction are diversifying, evolving, and going beyond what came before.

Next, consider what "truth value" can be found in science fiction. Many science fiction writers and commentators have argued that the purpose of science fiction is not to predict the future (Pohl, 1996). Historically this argument fails, for predicting the future is exactly what many science fiction writers have attempted to do. As a prime example, H. G. Wells in his utopian and dystopian novels, such as *The Sleeper Awakes* (1899/1910), *The World Set Free* (1914), and *The Shape of Things to Come* (1933) engage in complex and detailed predictions about the future; in *The War in the Air* (1908) he predicts World War I and the ascendency of aerial warfare.

Prediction does not have to be exact; rather, a plausible narrative about the future is presented, highlighting credible consequences of key developments that the author observes occurring within the contemporary world. The story presents a possible narrative scenario for what may transpire in the future if such trends continue. A good example of this general predictive mindset is Frederik Pohl and C. M. Kornbluth's *The Space Merchants* written in the early 1950s, which envisions a future—very suggestive of our present world—that is dominated by big business, commercialism, marketing, and advertisement. (Verne's *Paris in the Twentieth Century* (1863) and Robida's *The Twentieth Century* (1882) were also prescient in this regard.) Pohl also correctly anticipates the rise of "virtual romance" in his short story "Day Million" (1966). It is undoubtedly true that futurist science fiction misses the target more than it hits it, for the future is inextricably uncertain and humans are fallible. But to use some more recent illustrations, in reading William Gibson's *Neuromancer* (1984), Neal Stephenson's *Snow Crash* (1992) and *The Diamond Age* (1995), and Charles Stross' *Accelerando* (2005), there is a clear sense that such novels *ring true*—including the *feel* of it all—about the way human society is heading and what is coming to pass in a high-tech, computerized, "Internet of everything" world.

Modern science fiction was kick started in the progressive futurist expectations of the Age of Enlightenment (c. 1700-1800 CE), and the fearful anticipations of the future in the Romantic movement (c. 1800-1850 CE). Science fiction is filled with the hopes and fears associated with anticipated future developments in modern techno-industrial civilization. Science fiction looks ahead, realistically extrapolating from the present to the future in many ways, offering both wonders and warnings. We can have multiple predictions and alternative plausible future realities, from different philosophical perspectives, covering the possibility space of thoughtfully considered futures.

To further explore the truth dimension of science fiction, consider the following quote of the great science fiction writer

Arthur C. Clarke (partially cited earlier):

> ... science fiction is often very far from escapism, in fact you might say that science fiction is escape into reality ... It's a fiction which does concern itself with real issues: the origin of man; our future. In fact I can't think of any form of literature which is more concerned with real issues, reality.

Clarke contends that science fiction, more than any other form of literature, grapples with the most basic questions of reality; it frequently penetrates beyond the surface to deep and more expansive truths, even if the "truth" turns out to elicit new profound questions, rather than simplistic and shallow answers.

Just as a traditional myth expressed something fundamental about human existence, science fiction can articulate deep truths about human life and the universe. As noted earlier, novels like *The Time Machine* (1895) and *Star Maker* (1937), in realizing cosmic consciousness, help us to take in the big picture of things and see more deeply into reality. Clarke's *Childhood's End* (1953), *2001: A Space Odyssey* (1968), and his multiple award-winning *Rendezvous with Rama* (1973), all place humanity within the context of vastly superior forms of alien intelligence, providing us with cosmic perspectives on present limitations and future possibilities of humanity (and the human mind) within our vast and evolutionary universe. Just as there is insightful and revealing truth to be found in fictional literature, science fiction literature, in broadening the scope of the universe of drama and action, can discover and express even deeper and more encompassing insights about humanity and existence than traditional literature. We live in a cosmic arena of space, time, and existential possibilities, and this is the territory explored in science fiction. Science fiction explores the domain of *deep and more universal truth*.

As a final mythic quality of science fiction, ancient myths at times pointed toward the future, and insofar as myth engages holistic consciousness, such ancient tales provoked *holistic future consciousness*. Science fiction also generates holistic future consciousness, engaging the intellect, imagination, emotion, motivation, and immersive participation and action. Moreover, science fiction works toward further evolving holistic future consciousness, since it both expands our imagination about the future (and the possibilities of existence) and provokes us into thinking about preferable and non-preferable futures, about which directions to take and which directions to avoid. All in all, science fiction generates *mythic holistic future consciousness*.

* * *

As a start, these significant commonalities in structure and function between science fiction and myth explain a big part of why science fiction can be seen as mythological. But there is even more to be said on the connections between myth and science fiction.

Significant similarities exist in the imagery and the narrative content of ancient myth and modern science fiction. First consider common imagery: spirits ascending into the heavens versus rocket ships (or self-propelled spacesuits) ascending into outer space; benevolent wizards versus genius scientists and inventors; evil wizards versus mad scientists and sinister intelligent aliens; angels versus good aliens; demons, dragons, and monsters versus evil and hideous aliens. Visions of alien landscapes and ecologies (as well as futuristic cities) often call to mind the heavenly worlds or visions of hell from ancient myth and fantasy, while images of magical devices and supernatural forces often resemble images of super-technologies and bedazzling scientific effects.

The common, underlying archetypes in these above examples, inclusive of both ancient myth and modern science fiction, are: movement into a higher or transcendent realm as a literal or metaphorical ascension in consciousness or physical embodiment; benevolent and malevolent super-humans or trans-humans as ideals, threats, or wish-fulfillments; realms of paradise and hell as expressions of our deepest hopes and fears; icons and instruments possessing extraordinary powers as symbols of transcendent empowerment; and evil personifications representing mystery and the dark unknown. In science fiction, the imagery and archetypal meanings of these examples are visualized and conceptualized in the dressings of contemporary science and technology, rather than in terms of ancient fantasies and magical-supernatural belief systems of reality. Yet to highlight the similarity even stronger, as Arthur C. Clarke once noted, "Any sufficiently advanced technology is indistinguishable from magic." I would add that any sufficiently evolved alien is indistinguishable from an angel (or a demon).

At the level of narrative content, a good example of the mythic (and archetypal) shining through in a science fiction setting is the wondrous and inspiring movie *Close Encounters of the Third Kind*. The movie contains the following mythic narrative themes: Beings from a *higher realm* communicate with humans, transmitting a *mysterious* message and *psychically implanting* various *enigmatic symbols* in human consciousness; the human characters are drawn (almost pulled against their conscious will such as in a magical spell) into a challenging *journey of adventure* and *discovery* that eventually leads to *enlightenment* and *transcendence into the heavens*. Metaphorically, God calls out to humans asking us to follow Him—with a good deal of mystery and faith thrown in—promising cosmic awareness and ascension into a celestial realm. At the end of the saga, we see heaven (the spacious illuminant interior of the resplendent alien spaceship), and gazing in *emotional rapture* upon such magnificent and overpowering beauty, we experience *awe* and *wonder*.

A second excellent example is *2001: A Space Odyssey* (1968).

71

Both the book and the movie, released the same year, embody the mythic narrative theme of death and resurrection. Through the use of mysterious monoliths (iconic objects of worship), godlike alien beings from outer space guide humanity forward in technological and psychological evolution. As a symbol of this evolutionary process, in one scene the animal bone used as a weapon by our ape-like ancestors morphs into a spaceship. Eventually humanity is led on a journey to the farther reaches of the universe through a streaming and bedazzling optical array, and we observe the accelerated aging and death of the central human character, who is then "resurrected" as a celestial and illuminant Starchild, the next step in human evolution. The transformation, at the story's end, is from a physical being to an ethereal being of light, symbolizing the spiritual. The gods raise us from the dead and make us anew — such has been the mythic hope of humanity through the ages — except in *2001* it is realized through advanced technology, space travel, and hyper-evolved aliens.

At times, science fiction writers self-consciously create their stories using ancient myths and mythic characters within the content of their narratives. They retell, re-mix, reconsider, and transpose mythic content and archetypes in science fiction settings. Consider the following illustrative examples:

Roger Zelazny, in his Hugo award-winning novel *Lord of Light* (1967), envisions a distant world in the future, presumably one that in the past was settled by space faring humans. Here the main characters are techno-empowered humans who have adopted the identities of the deities of Hindu religion, including Shiva, Vishnu, Brahma, and, as the central protagonist, one who seems to have taken on the identity of the Buddha. These Hindu and Eastern personae possess various miraculous and superhuman capacities, similar to the supernatural powers associated with the ancient mythic characters. Moreover, the basic dramatic plot revolves around the conflict between the hierarchal system of Hinduism and the individualist, egalitarian philosophy of Buddhism—suggestive of the actual historical conflict between the philosophies of Hinduism and Buddhism.

Harlan Ellison, in his Hugo award-winning short-story "The Deathbird" (1974), retells part of the book of *Genesis*, of Adam and Eve and their temptation in the Garden of Eden, shifting the roles of God and Satan (the snake), where the "bad guy" turns out to be the good guy, and the presumed "good guy" turns out to be mad. The story questions whether it is obedience or self-determination (the key theme in the original Biblical story) that is the pathway to meaning and value in life.

In Dan Simmons' novel *Ilium* (2003) and its sequel *Olympos* (2005), we find ourselves on the surface of Mars in the future. And yet, what is transpiring on the surface is the mythic siege of Troy, complete with the city, the Greek army and defending Trojans—all the main characters recounted in Homer's *Iliad*—and most baffling of all, the Olympian gods and goddesses (who live on Mount Olympus). We find Zeus, Athena, and Aphrodite, among other deities, apparently possessing godlike powers, watching and guiding the conflict, as well as communicating (as Homer had recounted) with humans, such as Achilles, who are engaged in the battle. How can such a reality exist? What does all of this mean?

Simmons is superb at describing the mode of human consciousness that is enchanted, haunted, and guided by the voices and the presence of gods and goddesses, possibly reflecting how all humans experienced life thousands of years ago (Jaynes, 1976). But just as fascinating, in this science fiction narrative there is a human historian from the future (relative to our now), somehow placed in the middle of this great human epic, and knowing the ancient story of the siege of Troy as recounted in the *Iliad*. This character decides to interfere with the plans of the gods and goddesses and change the course of events, saving Troy. The humans (led by this future historian) rebel against the gods, a significant archetypal theme we find in both ancient Greek myth and modern "individualistic" inspired science fiction.

Finally, in Robert Silverberg's short story "Breckenridge and the Continuum" (1974), we observe a modern man (from our present day), unable to find meaning or purpose in his life, miraculously thrust into a strange and distant future. While journeying across a barren landscape with a small group of fellow travelers, presumably in search of some mysterious city, he finds himself telling ancient mythic tales to the group over campfires every night. Yet, in his nightly tales, he keeps mixing up different elements from different stories, concocting a whole new array of myths out of the inventive blending and recombination of previous myths. In this ongoing creative process, as our modern man journeys across the unknown toward the equally unknown, he finds renewed purpose and meaning in his life, and eventually is transported back into his own time where he sees everything afresh.

In "Breckenridge and the Continuum" Silverberg proposes that it is through storytelling and myth-making that we find meaning and purpose in our lives. He also suggests that new myths get created by synthetically mixing together old myths, reflecting the general theory of creativity that what is new consists of novel combinations of the old (Lombardo, 2011c).

I would suggest that Silverberg in "Breckenridge and the Continuum" presents a science fiction story about the mythic nature of science fiction. Science fiction, as the mythology of the future, is creatively developed through the use and recombination of mythologies and archetypes from the past. As such, it provides meaning and purpose to our journey into the future.

Science Fiction versus Myth and Fantasy
Having described a number of important similarities and points

of resonance between science fiction and traditional mythology, are there significant differences as well? As introduced above, science fiction is informed and inspired by contemporary thought and, in particular, modern science and technology and the scientific theory of reality. Yet, on this difference and others, the contrast between science fiction and ancient myth turns out to be approximate and rough, rather than absolute and unambiguous.

First, let us describe in more depth the purported differences between science fiction and ancient myth:

Clute, in his *Science Fiction: The Illustrated Encyclopedia* (1995), distinguishes "proto science fiction" (early tales that had distinguishing science fiction elements, such as Bacon's *New Atlantis*, 1627) and traditional stories of fantasy because the former tales offered arguments and explanations for the realistic plausibility of the fantastic scenarios included in the story. On the other hand, according to Clute, pure fantasy tales from earlier times provided no such arguments, clearly being stories of "make believe," having no plausible connection with reality and truth. Proto-science fiction made rational and empirical sense; fantasy did not.

Of special importance for Clute, with the rise of modern science and the secular theory of progress (c. 1600-1800), the strange, fantastical, or different could now be set in a hypothetical future that plausibly could arise as a consequence of scientific and secular progress. Clute argues that modern science and the secular theory of progress, followed by evolutionary theory in the nineteenth century, all pointed to the idea that the future, due to natural forces and human efforts, could be very different from the present or the past. The strange, fantastical, and even cosmic, once the domain of fantasy and ancient myth, could now arguably be set in the context of a secular and scientifically inspired future. According to Clute, the ancients generally did not believe that the future would be significantly different from the present, but modern science, secular thinking, and the theory of evolution all seemed to imply that strange and wondrous new things *could* emerge in the years ahead. This different reality foreseen in the future could be rationally and empirically justified and explained in terms of principles of science and secular thinking. (As the Panshins would put it, science provided a modern mode of thought that allowed for credible transcendence in the future.) Speculative yet plausible stories grounded in science could be written about strange future possibilities. Modern science fiction, for Clute, was born in this insight.

But at a more fundamental level, I propose that modern science challenged the validity and credibility of theories of reality found in ancient myth, providing a new vision of what was plausible and real (now or in the future), and "proto science fiction" (or science fiction in general) adopted this new theory of reality—that of modern science—in the creation of its strange or fantastic scenarios (Lombardo, 2006b). Science fiction is informed and inspired by a scientific vision of reality— a reality of natural transformation and progressive human change— whereas ancient myth reflected unscientific and archaic theories of reality. As a general formula, science fiction is scientifically plausible; ancient myth is not. Building on Clute's ideas, I propose that it was this new scientific theory of reality that supported the idea of a future significantly different from the present (that could be justified in terms of scientific-secular concepts), and opened the way for the emergence of strange, yet plausible tales of envisioned futures. Hence, science fiction was born with the emergence of the new scientific vision of reality that supported a new vision of the future.

Although there is a degree of truth in the above argued distinctions between ancient myth and fantasy and science fiction, the separation of the two domains is not so simple or clear-cut. As just a couple general points, although Clute in his *Illustrated Encyclopedia* presents what seems to be a clear dividing line, in Clute and Nicholls' more substantive and in-depth *Encyclopedia of Science Fiction* (1995), they acknowledge that it is impossible to make an absolute distinction between science fiction and fantasy. Further, as they also acknowledge, the historical point at which "proto science fiction" emerges in history is open to debate, with various perspectives taken by different writers and historians of science fiction. Nicholls takes the view that there is no clear historical dividing line at all demarcating early fantastical tales, such as the mythic *Odyssey* of Homer, from modern science fiction. One flows out of the other.

To throw further doubt on an absolute and unambiguous demarcation between ancient fantasy and myth and modern science and science fiction, consider the following additional arguments:

As already noted, ancient fantastical myths were not simply expressions of unbridled imagination, or without any possible perceived truth value. Within the context of prevalent theories of reality in ancient times, the myths of the past were intended to be credible and true, and people of the time saw plenty of evidence around them (albeit interpreted through their mindsets) to support their fantastical beliefs. Contrary to Clute, at least to a significant degree, the ancients did not believe that their tales of fantasy and myth were simply make-believe. (Do contemporary followers of traditional religions think their sacred mythic stories are make-believe?) In resonance with Panshin, the myths were (and by some still are) viewed as credible.

Moreover, although informed by pre-modern theories of reality, there were credible visions of the future, where the future was viewed as clearly different from the present, including such notable and highly influential pre-modern writings, as in St. Augustine's *City of God* (426 CE) and the Biblical Book of Revelation (c. 70-95 CE). Within Hindu mythology, as a cosmic vision of time and sequential universes, inclusive of the future of our own universe, Shiva destroys each consecutive universe roughly every two billion years. As noted earlier, visions of the end of times, which have permeated throughout human history, foresaw both great cataclysms and monumental positive transformations in the years ahead. It is simply a mistake to think that the ancients were locked into the unchanging present and saw no possibility of fundamental transformation in the future (Lombardo, 2006a).

We could argue, though, that modern humanity, especially over the last few centuries, is more acutely aware of ongoing change within the world, given the apparent accelerative advances occurring in industry, technology, and science. Consequently, the modern mind is more sympathetic with the idea that the future will be different from the present or the past (Gunn, 1975). Therefore, science fiction, as a modern phenomenon, reflects this alteration in worldview, emphasizing change over stability and continuity.

But this change in mindset from ancient to modern is a matter of degree rather than an absolute dividing line. (There are still many contemporary people and cultures that embrace the truth of stability and continuity in life.) The ancients may have been more inclined to believe in a cyclical and repetitive theory of time rather than a linear, transformative theory (Lombardo, 2006a, 2017), but even Socrates (469-399 BCE), who lived over two thousand years ago, complained about fundamental transformations in human life occurring around him, including, notably, the shift from an oral to a written culture (Nisbet, 1994). For some ancient Greeks, change was a fact of life; the philosopher Heraclitus (535-470 BCE) presumably proclaimed, "The only thing that stays the same is that nothing stays the same." And change was not simply perceived as chaotic or degenerative, as in Plato (424-348 BCE), but progressive and even evolutionary, as within the writings of the ancient philosophers Democritus (460-370 BCE) and Lucretius (99-55 BCE) (Lombardo, 2006a).

We could argue that science fiction, informed and inspired by the dynamic and transformative vision of secular progress tends to be oriented toward the new, the innovative, and the futuristic, whereas traditional myth and fantasy are more oriented toward origins and the past, but this again is also only relatively true. Science fiction does delve into the past (for example through time travel and cosmic histories), and at times into alternative histories of the past, and ancient myth, as noted earlier, did delve into the future. As some noteworthy contemporary examples, Stephen Baxter's *The Time Ships* (1995), *Vacuum Diagrams* (1997), *Manifold Origin (2001)*, and *Evolution* (2002) all journey millions, if not billions, of years into the distant past. Although science fiction may focus on the future, in a broader sense, science fiction takes in all of time—past, present, and future—for science fiction explores all the possibilities of existence. (Again, similarly, ancient cosmic myths take in all of time as well.)

It does seem to be a basic characteristic of human psychology and society that there are opposing dispositions of mind toward embracing the new and the different versus holding onto tradition and the past (Nisbet, 1994; Lombardo, 2006b; 2017)— an opposition in mindsets though that extends back thousands of years in human history—and in this context, science fiction more strongly embraces the first mindset and disposition than the second. But this opposition in thinking has been part of human societies and mindsets long before the emergence of science fiction or the secular theory of progress. As long as we keep in mind these qualifications, we can legitimately state that science fiction is oriented toward the new and the different and the possibilities of the future.

Perhaps the most fundamental question in determining the conceptual and historical dividing lines separating traditional myth and fantasy and science fiction is how sharply we can distinguish between stories informed by contemporary science and stories that are not grounded in a modern scientific worldview. How clearly can we distinguish between the scientifically plausible and implausible in fantastical tales?

First we should note that during the ongoing history of modern science, within a specific time, there is usually a significant level of consensus regarding the official scientific vision of reality. Yet with ongoing developments in science, the consensual view often dramatically changes. What is scientifically credible does not stay put. Scientific truth is dynamic rather than static (Kuhn, 1962).

Moreover, within science fiction often the distinction between the scientifically plausible versus implausible rests upon the perspective and reasoning of the particular writer. Science fiction writers have repeatedly attempted to demonstrate in their stories, with great ingenuity, inventiveness, and unusual lines of reasoning, that their strange and far-out ideas were scientifically plausible or possible, *even if* the scientific establishment of the time rejected their proposed ideas as ridiculous. See, for example, Jules Verne's efforts in *A Journey to the Center of the Earth* (1864) to validate the implausible hypothesis (for his time) that the inner earth was hollow and open to human exploration. It has often been noted that science fiction writers invent hypothetical futures or strange realities that at the time seem way out, or totally implausible relative to present scientific thinking, and yet often come to pass as the future unfolds. Science fiction writers repeatedly venture into the territory of the implausible, challenging what is scientifically plausible.

Indeed, in spite of the relative level of consensus in a scientific discipline for a given period, even scientists have a hard time totally agreeing on all the fundamentals of their scientific view of reality. Some philosophers of science have argued that a key feature of science—a healthy, growth-promoting feature—is a level of theoretical conflict regarding the nature of reality being studied (Feyerabend, 1965, 1969, 1970). There is a certain amount of fuzziness separating the scientifically plausible and implausible—a territory of debate and multiple interpretations—and this area of ambiguity especially shows up in science fiction.

Like ancient myth and fantasy, science fiction extends the arena of human imagination and postulates innumerable fantastical scenarios, characters, and realms of existence. Science fiction exists in that outlying territory of human thinking, at the boundaries of the mysterious and unknown, where what is plausible and what is real are to degrees uncertain and open to debate and transformation. Indeed, part of the appeal of science fiction is to explore the "far out" expanses of existence and human imagination. Isn't pushing the envelope of plausibility a strength of science fiction? As the great early pioneer in rocketry, Robert Goddard stated, "It is difficult to say what is impossible, for the dream of yesterday is the hope of today and the reality of tomorrow."

As Adam Roberts contends in his *The History of Science Fiction* (2005), if we adopt a Feyerabend pluralistic perspective on science, where at any given point in time there are multiple competing views of reality, and agree that this quality is a valuable, growth-promoting feature of science, then science fiction, through its diverse speculative visions, contributes into this dynamic and pluralistic quality of science (Feyerabend, 1965, 1969, 1970). In this sense, science fiction, with its far-out diverse visions at the borderland of the credible, is part of the scientific endeavor. Science fiction is not only inspired by science, but may contribute to the ongoing evolution of science, even if this means at times challenging the established views within science.

To go further, science fiction writers do not always *even attempt* to make their stories (sound) scientifically plausible. Two of the most popular and influential science fiction writers of the twentieth century were Edgar Rice Burroughs and E. E. "Doc" Smith. Edgar Rice Burroughs' science fiction (or as some would describe as "science fantasy") was filled with numerous scientifically implausible, if not mystical and magical, ideas.

Sometimes Burroughs tries to give his inventive ideas some level of scientific credibility—his *Land that Time Forgot* series (1918/1919) has a provocative twist on evolutionary theory—but often he does not. John Carter, the hero of Burroughs' Mars novels, such as *The Princess of Mars* (1912) and *The Gods of Mars* (1913), magically teleports (body and mind) back and forth between the earth and Mars. There is no scientific explanation given for this process, and in essence it appears magical. The seminal space operas of "Doc" Smith, as he explicitly acknowledged, contained numerous outlandish and scientifically implausible technologies in which he let his imagination "run wild." At one level, Smith sounds scientific—using a colorful assortment of scientific sounding words—as he is describing razzle-dazzle technologies (colossal spaceships, stupendous engines, wondrous machines, atom-splitting weapons, super-luminal space travel and communication, and amazing mind-controlled gadgetry) in the *Lensmen* and *Skylark* space opera series (primarily published in the 1930s and 1940s), but the scientific clarity and credibility is much more apparent than real. Smith's space operas bedazzle the mind with often the same level of scientific clarity and credibility as many contemporary science fiction movies that are big on special effects and devoid of plausible scientific explanation.

As one noteworthy example of going beyond the scientifically credible, although modern science (since Einstein) states that it is physically impossible for objects traveling through space to exceed the speed of light, science fiction writers (including "Doc" Smith) have envisioned numerous ways (hypothetical technological devices depicted with various degrees of fuzziness) for getting around this fundamental scientific law. To hell with scientific plausibility; we have to get to the stars in some reasonable period of time, and traveling under the speed of light will take way too long. So let's concoct some scientific sounding way to move faster, including jumping across space through some "higher dimension." Science fiction is filled with "faster-than-light" spaceships, the *Star Trek Enterprise* with its warp-drive being a well-known contemporary example.

Also numerous science fiction novels, such as Alfred Bester's *The Demolished Man* (1953) and *The Stars, My Destination* (1956), two of the most engaging and highly regarded science fiction books of the twentieth century, postulate various psychic powers, including telepathy, psychokinesis, and psychic teleportation, and yet there is little, if any, scientific evidence or plausible scientific explanation for such abilities. (Advanced aliens also frequently have such powers.) L. Frank Baum could get away with having Dorothy click the heels of her ruby slippers to transport herself back to Kansas, and we accept that this is not scientifically plausible. Yet, in *The Stars, My Destination* something similar happens repeatedly, referred to in the novel as "jaunting." Perhaps, someday and somehow, we will possess such mental powers, but at this time, there is no plausible scientific foundation for such phenomena, or the construction of a technological device to facilitate such abilities.

As science and technology have advanced over the last four centuries, to different degrees many scientists and secular philosophers, while embracing the new, have maintained and supported ideas inspired by ancient myth, fantasy, and religion. Although many advocates of the new scientific worldview believed science represented a clear advance over traditional religious and mythic thought—contradicting these earlier ideas and rendering them scientifically implausible—many other advocates of science combined the new scientific ideas with religious and mythic thought (Lombardo, 2006a). God and evolution, for example, have continually mixed together in the mindsets of many notable scientists, both in the past and in the present. God was not thrown out the window with the emergence of Copernican astronomy and Newtonian mechanics. As a general point, the separation of worldviews between science, on one hand, and religion, myth, and fantasy on the other, has not been entirely clean or simple (Barbour, 1997). So, how clearly can the separation be made within science fiction?

Various notable early science fiction writers, such as Johannes Kepler (*Somnium*, 1634) and Francis Bacon (*New Atlantis*, 1627), mixed scientific and religious/mystical/supernatural ideas. Another important early example, the popular astronomer and science fiction writer Camille Flammarion (*Lumen* 1872/1897, *Omega* 1893-1894) combined contemporary scientific thinking on biological evolution, physical optics, environmental science, and astronomy with immaterial spirits, reincarnation, and mental teleportation through the cosmos. Olaf Stapledon in *Star Maker* (1937) synthesized a scientific and naturalistic theory of the evolution of cosmic intelligence with a vision of a transcendent Creator/God. More recently, in *River of Gods* (2004) by Ian MacDonald—a magnificent "future of everything" novel set in India—the actual existence of Hindu deities is explained and assimilated into a time travel/quantum physics/super AI scenario, uniting religious beliefs in supernatural beings with modern science.

As two noteworthy contemporary illustrations from the cinema, the *Star Wars* and *The Matrix* series combine a plethora of scientific-looking technologies with mystical-spiritual-supernatural theories of reality. What scientific sense can we make out of the "force" or the capacity to control matter with the mind? Can the dead rise again in a scientific universe? In both of these popular science fiction movie series, scientific technologies and theories of reality cohabit a universe with mystical and spiritual forces, the latter suggestive of (if not directly derived from) ancient religions, spiritual traditions, and mythologies.

In all these examples modern science significantly informs and inspires the various narratives, providing language, concepts, and imagery derived from science and modern technologies, but the narratives are not completely constrained by the "official" scientific worldview; nonscientific ideas on reality, derived from fantasy, mysticism, spiritualism, pseudo-science, psychic concepts, religion, and unconstrained speculation, are often included as well.

Still, as an approximate general historical truth, as we move into modern times, scientific thinking attempted to distinguish itself from classical mythology, religion, and fantasy by embracing a new theory of reality and a new epistemology in opposition to what was perceived as the archaic, supernatural, superstitious, and metaphysical ideas and methods that supported ancient religious and mythic beliefs and narratives. Throughout the growth of modern science, scientifically minded writers repeatedly critiqued the religious and mythological past. This was the emancipating spirit of the European Enlightenment, which gave birth to the modern secular theory of progress. A different type of universe and a host of new ideas and technologies emerged as science blossomed and attempted to shake itself free of the past.

This new scientific vision of reality informed and inspired the birth and growth of modern science fiction. For example, with the emergence of modern scientific astronomy, replacing the geocentric vision of the heavens, a vastly more expansive and richly detailed vision of reality opened up to human consciousness, stimulating human imagination and storytelling. The new scientific universe of outer space, populated with myriad stars—now recognized as suns at vast distances, and presumably, myriad planets circling these stars existing beyond our solar system—became the new cosmic reality. There were other diverse worlds in the universe. Could we travel to such worlds? By what means could we do it? Were there inhabitants and strange civilizations on these worlds? Perhaps they would visit (or invade) us?

Further, with each significant subsequent advance in either science or scientifically grounded new technologies—such as in the fields of electricity and magnetism, chemistry, geology, evolutionary biology, genetics, rocketry, quantum physics, relativity theory, communication technologies, ecology, and computer science—writers of science fiction were provided with wave upon wave of new scientifically grounded ideas, terms, and possibilities for their narratives. Such ongoing scientific and technological developments, of course, provoked both, anticipatory hope and wonder, as well as fear and apprehension, but the ever-evolving scientific universe and array of scientific technologies continually fueled the human imagination. Even when the extrapolations from science were highly questionable, such as in "Doc" Smith, it was science and modern technologies that provided the vocabulary and territory of ideas in which Smith's imagination, among others, could "run wild."

Within science fiction, as Roberts (2005) argues, there has existed in modern times a tension and ambiguity between fantasy, inclusive of magic and the mystical, the metaphysical and supernatural, the sacred and divine, and ancient mythological ideas—as found, for example, in J. R. R. Tolkien's *The Lord of the Rings*—and "hard science fiction" that emphasizes the physical and technological and is "rigorously" attentive to the principles and restrictions of empirical and mathematical science; a good contemporary example is the science fiction of Stephen Baxter in numerous books cited above. This tension creates a polarity and a continuum within science fiction literature; there seem to be clear cases of pure fantasy, clear cases of pure high-tech science fiction, and then many cases falling somewhere along the continuum, where science fiction writers blend ideas that are techno-scientific with ideas that seem mystical and unscientific, and where they may either stretch or ignore the limits of the scientifically credible or intelligible, or in some manner or form, attempt to make the mystical and spiritual compatible or coexistent with a scientific universe.

It follows then that the content and form of science fiction is complex and diversified, as opposed to simple and uniform.

Both fantasy and myth, as well as modern science and secular thinking, have contributed into the content, style, and ongoing development of science fiction, producing a variety of different blends of theories of reality and modes of consciousness. Sometimes it is more scientific; sometimes it is less; sometimes it is a smorgasbord. But keeping this continuum in mind, as well as the relative ambiguity pertaining to scientific plausibility, science fiction literature is informed and inspired by ideas derived from modern science, or at the very least, ideas reflective of contemporary thinking about reality and the human condition.

In this regard, to return to my earlier point, science fiction is a mixture of continuity and change, with its origins extending far into the distant past, yet repeatedly being enriched and expanded upon through modern science and secular thinking, as new influences have an impact on the genre. With myth and fantasy as its historical starting point, tales of "extraordinary adventures," utopian visions, scientific astronomy, Enlightenment and Romantic philosophies, Gothic literature, horror, and modern mysticism, evolutionary theory, modern technology, computer science and techno-culture, and contemporary social and political thought have all contributed into the evolution and complex composition of science fiction. Some of these influences are more scientific; in other cases, such as Romanticism and the Gothic, less so. These varied roots and contributing tributaries intermix and cross-fertilize, with new branches emerging out of the mix.

Although it is a mistake to think that science fiction is simply a modern phenomenon, as an ongoing evolutionary process, science fiction continually absorbs new ideas and perspectives, giving it an overall contemporary and forward-looking quality. Although science fiction brings with it numerous qualities, functions, and even content associated with ancient myth, fantasy, and religion, it is strongly informed and influenced by modern science, technology, and ongoing developments in contemporary thinking. Science fiction can therefore be described as a diverse and complex mythology of the future, with a forward-looking orientation, embracing the new, informed and guided, to various degrees, by science and contemporary thought, as interpreted and liberally experimented with in different imaginative and speculative ways by different authors. It does not so much totally separate itself from ancient myth and fantasy as to assimilate and transcend it.

The Evolutionary Mythology of Science Fiction

The activity we are undertaking is not science, but art ... Yet our aim is not merely to create aesthetically admirable fiction. We must achieve neither mere history, nor mere fiction, but myth. A true myth is one which, within the universe of a certain culture ... expresses richly, and often perhaps tragically, the highest aspirations possible within a culture.
Olaf Stapledon

Science fiction is myth about the future for the future.

To recall, Campbell argued that our modern myths and role models within such myths need to be grounded and inspired by contemporary themes and issues. We need myths and mythic characters within our lives, but ones infused with ideas and values taken from the modern world. Following the Panshins, we need myths that are credible within a modern mindset.

Along similar lines, in an article in *The Futurist*, "New Myths for a New Millennium," Stanley Krippner and his co-authors (1998) argued that myths are necessary and valuable for the human mind and human society and we should not do away with them, but we need "new myths" for the future—rather than sticking with the old myths—that inspire us and make sense within a modern mindset and philosophy.

This is where science fiction comes in. It is mythic, along the various dimensions described in the previous sections, as well as being informed by contemporary thinking, including modern science. The new myths for modern times are to be found in science fiction, building upon and yet transcending the myths of old.

Following the above definition of myth by Olaf Stapledon from his book *Last and First Men* (1930), a myth embodies the dreams and visions of a mind set, a culture, and a time period set in the form of a story. But note that Stapledon's definition of myth as the ideals and aspirations of a culture and mindset inherently reaches toward the future.

Science fiction, at least to a significant degree, is *about* the future, inclusive of possibilities, predictabilities, and both preferable and dystopian alternatives. The great majority of the science fiction novels and stories mentioned thus far have been set in different hypothetical futures; for example, Simmons's *Hyperion Cantos*, "Doc" Smith's space operas, Alfred Bester's psycho-techno novels, Flammarion's mystical cosmic visions— including "end of the world" scenarios—contemporary "future of everything" novels by Robinson, McDonald, Baxter, Egan, and Stephenson, and of course, the writings of Wells and Stapledon.

Informed and inspired by modern ideas and themes, inclusive of modern scientific thought, science fiction creates narratives about the future (both possibilities and aspirations). It is modern myths—containing all the distinctive qualities of traditional myth—about the future. Science fiction provides a possibility space for imagining and thinking about the future in engaging mythic narrative form.

But science fiction does more than just provide myths *about* the future; it provides myths *for the future*, insofar as it inspires and facilitates the creation of the future.

In resonance with the long standing evolutionary trend toward increasing expansiveness of consciousness in space and time that runs back to prehistoric times (Lombardo, 2006a, 2009), science fiction expresses and propels the cosmic and fantastical limits of imagination, creativity, and speculation. Informed by ongoing developments in contemporary thought and science, science fiction keeps expanding and enriching human consciousness, exploring the possibility space of imagination and existence, especially with respect to the possibilities of the future.

This evolving possibility space in human consciousness and, in particular, future consciousness, generated within science fiction, serves as a foundation for the ongoing *creation of the future*. Science fiction stimulates us into thinking more deeply, more imaginatively, and more expansively about the future (and existence in general). By expanding the arena of consciousness, we extend the possibility space within which human creation can take place. Through stories, or myths, about the future and the possibilities of existence, the mental working space for creating the future is extended.

Moreover, given its inspirational and psychologically holistic nature, science fiction provokes engagement, participation, and empowerment, as well as prescriptions and warnings about preferable and undesirable futures. The heightened awareness produced in science fiction touches us personally and emotionally, and this energized and heightened consciousness is directed toward ourselves and our future lives. Science fiction generates emotionally charged purposeful action. Indeed, out of science fiction, especially through its warnings and positive dreams, comes an ethical and goal directed dimension. What should we strive for? How should we live? What should we avoid? As I noted early on in this book, science fiction inspires a total way of life, a way of life that, although it is enacted in the present, points toward envisioned futures. Through science fiction we create and live the future.

Furthermore, following Roberts' argument for a scientific function within science fiction, science fiction clearly has repeatedly stimulated and provoked scientists, technologists, and even social visionaries in the creation of new theories, technologies, and social experiments in living. As Thomas Disch (1998) has argued, science fiction has influenced cultural, scientific, and technological development in multifarious ways throughout modern history.

The expression "for the future" underscores the practical relevance of science fiction for our personal and collective lives and actions in the future. Since humans need myths— in particular, contemporary humanity needs new myths relevant to contemporary times—science fiction fits the bill. Science fiction is the form of modern future consciousness that is most influential within our contemporary world, and I expect that in the future it will continue to wield this influence. Its holistic, narrative, and multimedia dimensions clearly resonate with the full psychological dimensionality of the human mind. Moreover, it *should* be leading the way into the future, for in its ideal form, as psychologically efficacious narrative, it synthesizes past and future, intellect and emotion, the humanistic-ethical and the scientific-technological, and art and science, rightly placing humanity within a cosmic context.

At this point it is appropriate to introduce some of the narrative territories in which science fiction does not directly deal with the future, and consider how even within these non-futurist areas of storytelling, science fiction helps in the creation of the future.

The sub-genre of alternative histories has been particularly popular within science fiction. Imagine some critical event in the past, where if that specific event had gone differently, the whole of history would have unfolded in a totally different way. In science fiction, such an event is referred to as a "Jonbar Point," inspired by Jack Williamson's time travel story "The Legion of Time" (1938/1952) in which the entire future history of humanity hinges upon whether a character named John Barr picks up a rusty discarded magnet off the ground. Picking up the magnet leads to a flourishing and positive future for humankind; not picking up the magnet leads to a dark and terrible future. "The Legion of Time" explores both possibilities in our history and our future; it explores in narrative form multiple timelines and creates a dramatic plot around the struggle over which timeline will become our permanent reality.

Science fiction frequently speculates on various "Jonbar Points" in our past, where some critical event is changed that totally transforms our present reality. What if the South had secured the Little Round Top, won the Battle of Gettysburg, and been victorious in the Civil War? What if the Axis powers had won the Second World War? What if a functional computer had been built by Charles Babbage—who had created designs for functional computers but never succeeded in building one—in the nineteenth century? In such hypothetical realities (alternative histories), the world would be much different from what it is today. All three of these alternative histories have been the subject of well-known science fiction novels, respectively, Ward Moore's *Bring the Jubilee* (1955), Philip K. Dick's *The Man in the High Castle* (1962), and William Gibson and Bruce Sterling's *The Difference Engine* (1990).

Alternative histories provide possibility spaces of imagination, transcending the constraints of normal consciousness and worldviews, and thus expanding our awareness. (Our minds and our perspectives of reality are locked and constrained by our stories and understanding of the past.) This stretching of the possible facilitates creativity. Moreover, such narratives engage the reader in thinking about historical causality and the sequential flow of time; why do events proceed in the way they do? Can we imagine alternative historical sequences? Such thinking about history and time facilitates a deeper grasp of how history connects with the future.

Indeed, alternative histories can significantly impact the ongoing creation of the future in our present world. (As a general psychological principle, our understanding and interpretation of the past affects both our experiences and actions in the present and our visions of the future, Lombardo, 2017.) A case in point is Steampunk, a sub-genre of science fiction, which in numerous and varied narratives creates alternative histories of the nineteenth century and early twentieth century. *The Difference Engine*, for example, is a Steampunk novel, which envisions a late nineteenth-century world populated with functional, steam-powered computers, as well as other advanced steam-powered technologies. Imagine combining nineteenth-century customs, garb, language, and design with contemporary technological contraptions that were "in reality" (our reality) never invented within that period. Through its novels—other well-known ones including K. W. Jeter's *Morlock Night* (1979), Tim Powers' *The Anubis Gates* (1983), and James Blaylock's *Homunculus* (1986)— and its universe of graphics, art, music, costumes, paraphernalia, and assorted websites and conventions, Steampunk has emerged in the last twenty years as a vibrant subculture. Inspired by a number of alternative histories of the nineteenth century written in the 1980s and 1990s (Robb, 2012), Steampunk has created a set of unique pathways into the future by reconfiguring the past.

Pushing the boundaries of imagination even further, instead of simply envisioning an alternative history, we can envision an alternative reality. This alternative reality can reside within a "different dimension" (however we make scientific sense of that concept), an alternative universe (perhaps following contemporary scientific cosmology and the "many worlds" interpretation of quantum physics), or it may simply float in possibility space, without any explanation of the why or how of its existence. Science fiction stories involving different dimensions (which can bleed into the idea of alternative universes) include such classics as Murray Leinster's "The Fifth-Dimension Catapult" (1931), "Doc" Smith's *Skylark of Valeron* (1935), Clifford Simak's *City* (1952), and the Hugo and Nebula award winning *The Gods Themselves* (1972) by Isaac Asimov. Tales of alternative universes include, again by Murray Leinster, "Sidewise in Time" (1934), "Doc" Smith's *Lensmen* series, and clearly inspired by the "many worlds" hypothesis of quantum physics, both Stephen Baxter's *The Time Ships* (1995) and Robert Sawyer's *Neanderthal Parallax* trilogy, published in the first decade of the new millennium.

Perhaps the most notable alternative reality novel in recent times that is not "localized" anywhere but within human imagination is China Miéville's *Perdido Street Station* (2000). Aside from the stupendous inventiveness of the novel—the events described in the book take place in a bizarre, immensely grungy, gargantuan city named New Crobuzon, populated with mobile cactus beings, human-insect amalgams, birdlike people, gargoyles, a higher dimension giant spider, mind-eating hypnotic moths, intelligent appliances and concatenated junk, etc.—what the book achieves is a blending of elements of Gothic-Romantic, Steampunk, mystical-magical, and scientific-technological extrapolation. Satanic agents from Hell even make an appearance in the story. The novel's alternative reality is informed by almost all the tributaries of thought that have fed into the evolution of science fiction. *Perdido Street Station* illustrates how the modern human imagination, informed and inspired by diverse influences in the history of science fiction, can realize amazing new heights of creativity, further opening up the possibility space of human consciousness.

Finally, science fiction can also be about the present. As one frequent scenario, the twist is that something extraordinary or bizarre happens which totally upsets the normalcy and human complacency of our everyday world. The classic example is *The War of the Worlds*, in which, as we go about our day-to-day routines our world is attacked by aliens and suddenly thrown into complete disarray. Numerous subsequent science fiction movies (for example, *Invasion of the Body Snatchers* and *Independence Day*) have dramatically portrayed such catastrophes. Along similar lines, meteoroids and comets may come out of the blue and collide with the earth causing vast, if not worldwide, destruction. (See Wells' "The Star," 1897, Philip Wylie and Edwin Balmer's *When Worlds Collide*, 1932, Larry Niven and Jerry Pournelle's *Lucifer's Hammer*, 1977, and the movies *Deep Impact* and *Armageddon*.) Time machines may get invented in the present and unsettle time, both past and present (see Ward Moore's *Bring the Jubilee*, 1953). Or, bringing alternative universes into the plot, a techno-advanced Neanderthal man pops into existence in our present-day reality, causing worldwide cultural repercussions (see Robert Sawyer's *Hominids*, 2002).

Taking a different imaginative perspective on the present, as is suggested in the movie *The Matrix*, the present may not be what it appears to be; our world and our personal lives may *actually* be virtual reality simulations within an immense computer; the conceivable far-out possibilities of technology can throw everything around us (including our consciousness of reality) into question. (Could our conscious lives be hallucinogenic fabrications created by highly advanced aliens?) Although the science fiction writer Philip K. Dick wrote primarily about the future, his working strategy was to question the nature of reality — including the human self — and our normal understanding of things. Just as the fantastical and the supernatural permeated into the everyday world of the ancients, the strange and disconcerting possibilities suggested by science, advancing technologies, and contemporary philosophical speculation can penetrate into our normal world. (See, for example, Dick's *The Three Stigmata of Palmer Eldritch*, 1965, *Ubik*, 1969, and *Valis*, 1981.) Understandably, if we dramatically change our perspective on the present, we change our attitude and our orientation to the future.

Science fiction, whether about the future, the past, or the present — or even some totally strange alternative reality — can feed and inspire the creation of the future. As part of the draw and appeal of science fiction, the history of science fiction reveals a perpetual and ever transcending push toward stretching the imagination and empowering the human mind. How inventive can we get? How realistic and convincing can we make our flights of imagination? It seems to me that this imaginative thrust is an evolutionary process, without determinable end or boundary, perpetually enriching and inspiring our consciousness as we flow and navigate into the future; indeed as we create it.

* * *

The future ain't what it used to be, and it never was.
Anonymous

On what basis do I define science fiction as the "evolutionary mythology of the future"?

As noted earlier, science fiction is a continually evolving genre of futurist themes, scenarios, and thought experiments, where new writers build upon the heritage of great works of the past. We could say that science fiction has its own evolutionary history, integrating continuity and change. Informed by its evolving heritage of consciousness-expanding possibilities, as well as continually emerging new developments in science and contemporary thought, science fiction involves the ongoing cumulative evolution of holistic future consciousness. Science fiction can be viewed as a dynamic, self-reflective, and perpetually deepening think tank about the future, if not reality in general. Taking into account alternative histories and realities, science fiction involves the ongoing evolution of imagination regarding the possibilities of existence.

Let us consider three novels involving visions of the evolution of humanity in the future: H. G. Wells' *The Time Machine* (1895), where future humanity (c. 800,000 CE) is divided between the beautiful, idyllic, and fragile Eloi and the dark, subterranean, and cannibalistic Morlock, who feed on the Eloi; Olaf Stapledon's *Last and First Men* (1931), which stretches two billion years into the future and chronicles the rise and fall of eighteen different species of humans, many of them intentionally technologically facilitated creations of the previous species of humans; and Greg Egan's *Diaspora* (1997), where human consciousness is realized in both robotic bodies and virtual minds of immense power and intellect, the latter going in search of the riddles of the cosmos through enveloping and ever-ascending multiverses. Across these novels, we find ever-evolving visions of humanity's future as successive generations of science fiction writers purposefully incorporate new ideas from science and philosophical thought into their narratives. Self-reflectively, each generation *purposefully evolves* humanity's visions of its own future. This ongoing development illustrates the cumulative evolutionary process in science fiction thought.

But not only does humanity's sense of its future possibilities historically transform and evolve across these three illustrative novels, we also find in all cases the future of humanity conceived in evolutionary terms. All three writers apply the scientific theory of evolution to "predicting" the future of humanity. For Wells, Stapledon, and Egan, our future is evolution.

Yet to go one step further, our understanding of evolution and how it applies to ourselves has been evolving; that is, the scientific theory of evolution has been growing and transforming over time (Lombardo, 2002a, 2006a, 2017). This transforming scientific picture of evolutionary reality has fed into the ongoing development of science fiction, for example, regarding how we understand the future evolution of our species. We see this evolution in evolutionary thinking in the above-cited novels. In Wells' story, social stratification and differential environmental adaptation generate diversity — indeed a fundamental bifurcation in future human evolution;

in Stapledon, environmental adaptation, purposefully applied biological and scientific techniques, chaos and chance, and the intentional selection of philosophical ideals drive the evolution of humanity through multiple successive species; and finally, in Egan's novel, artificial intelligence, robotic engineering, and enhanced virtual realities (super realities)—including minds that exist in virtual reality—now enter into the universe of imagined processes facilitating future human evolution.

From early on, in the eighteenth and nineteenth centuries, science fiction has grappled with understanding the nature of evolution, progress, and change. Both Enlightenment philosophy, with its vision of secular progress, and the Romantic recoil, with its apprehensions over industrial and technological change, laid the modern seeds of science fiction. Together they express the double-edged sword of fear and hope regarding human progress and change in the future. The theory of evolution, building on the vision of progressive change from the Enlightenment, expanded the vistas and ongoing debates within science fiction over where natural and social change are heading in the future, and in what ways we should attempt to guide the process (Nisbet, 1994). For example, Wells was especially concerned with secular progress and evolution, and how these concepts inform and inspire us in the ongoing guidance of humanity's future (Wells, 1934; Wagar, 2004).

As we move through the second half of the nineteenth century and into the twentieth century, evolution became an increasingly influential and all-encompassing way of thinking about reality (Lombardo, 2002b; 2002c; 2002d; 2006a). The central scientific narrative to emerge in contemporary times is cosmic evolution: The universe as a totality, including humanity, is a result of evolutionary processes (Chaisson, 2005, 2009; Lombardo, 2017). Cosmic evolution lays out a "story of us all" (Watson, 2001, 2005). Moreover, evolution and progress have been woven together in modern philosophy and futurist thinking (Lombardo, 2006a; 2006b; Kelley, 2010; Phipps, 2012). Within the contemporary scientific framework, as well as within much of modern philosophy and futurist thinking, humans are seen as evolutionary beings living in an evolutionary universe.

Insofar as science fiction deals with the scientifically plausible, evolution provides the foundational scientific framework in which contemporary science fiction is written. Science fiction writers, since the time of H. G. Wells, if not before, have pondered the meaning and message of evolution as a framework for understanding both the past and the future. As exemplified in the writings of Wells, Stapledon, and Egan, among many others, evolution in numerous ways has informed and structured the ongoing development of science fiction. Insofar as modern science fiction assumes a scientific theory of reality as it is presently articulated, it embraces an evolutionary vision of nature, humanity, and the universe.

It's noteworthy that evolution as a scientific framework lends itself to science fiction drama. Evolution is a double-edged sword; there is becoming and passing away; emergence and extinction; order and chaos; creation and destruction; and competition and cooperation, all enveloped in a sea of both natural law and irreducible uncertainties (hence a combination of predictability and unpredictability). These dualities and tensions in the cosmic evolutionary narrative provide a dynamic context for creating drama and adventure within science fiction stories. The risks, uncertainties, potential catastrophes, and varied possibilities within the evolutionary saga give great narrative energy to futurist science fiction. Instead of a universe of divine providence and guidance and guarantees from above, as conceived by the ancients, the evolutionary universe is a contingent and chancy (Tarnas, 1991). Wells was concerned, especially later in his career, that humanity may not make it into the far future, and in Stapledon's *Last and First Men*, humanity in the future repeatedly hovers on the edge of annihilation. Undeniably, evolution brings tension and unavoidable adventure to the future.

Since the emergence of the scientific theory of evolution in the mid-nineteenth century, aside from Wells, Stapledon, and Egan, (and as just a representative sample), science fiction writers such as Sir Edward Bulwer-Lytton in *Vril, The Power of the Coming Race* (1871); Camille Flammarion in *Omega: The End of the World* (1893/1894); J. D. Beresford in *The Hampdenshire Wonder* (1911); S. Fowler Wright in *The Amphibians: A Romance of 500,000 Years Hence* (1924); A.E. van Vogt in *Slan* (1940); Theodore Sturgeon in *More than Human* (1953); Arthur C. Clarke in *Childhood's End* (1953); Stephen Baxter in *The Time Ships* (1995) and *Evolution* (2003); Greg Bear in *Darwin's Radio* (1999); Robert Sawyer in *Hominids* (2002); Charles Stross in *Accelerando* (2005); and Robert Silverberg, in his psychedelic trip in human evolution, *Son of Man* (1971), have explored humankind's future evolutionary journey and potentialities within an evolutionary universe.

As a final important way in which science fiction is evolutionary mythology, science fiction is a significant developmental expression, in mythic narrative form, of the *purposeful evolution of evolution* specifically regarding our ongoing enhancement of our mental capacities for facilitating evolution. Science fiction, through imaginative and thoughtful narratives, is a purposeful evolution of holistic future consciousness: Science fiction intentionally strives to expand our multidimensional experience and understanding of the future and empower us in thoughtfully and imaginatively guiding evolution in the creation of our future.

Humans reflect and amplify through their conscious minds the evolutionary process of the cosmos (Lombardo, 2009, 2011c, 2014b, 2017). Humans build upon the evolutionary process within the universe, introducing purposeful change guided through the acquisition of knowledge and higher cognitive processes, such as thinking and imagination. Humans engage in *purposeful evolution*, throughout history attempting to advance and improve upon their nature and their conditions of existence.

Of special note, humans continually attempt to "evolve" their minds and capacities, and in so doing, improve their abilities to more effectively and wisely steer reality toward desirable ends. We are purposefully evolving our minds as instruments of evolution.

Humans realize purposeful evolution (an evolution of evolution) through future consciousness, creating goals, plans, visions, and future-directional action, which we often apply to ourselves. Future consciousness and consequently purposeful evolution are self-consciously enhanced through science fiction. As a narrative think tank about the future, integrative in scope, science fiction advances our own efforts to evolve ourselves in preferable directions. Through the heightening and development of our holistic future consciousness within science fiction, we become more informed, energized, and capable of purposefully guiding, creating, or evolving our future. We expand our consciousness of the future and our power regarding the future. Through science fiction, we purposefully evolve our future consciousness (or our imaginative consciousness taken as a whole) to more intentionally and efficaciously evolve our future. And, because science fiction is mythic, it resonates with the holistic dimensions of the human mind—generating total person immersion in the future—and informs and inspires us toward the transcendent, wondrous, cosmic, and fantastical.

To recap, the mythology of the future created within science fiction is evolutionary because:

- Science fiction has a deep heritage, going back to ancient myths, with many tributaries and a rich historical foundation. Science fiction did not just "pop into existence" at some narrowly circumscribed point in time, and its present reality is an accumulation of ideas and themes derived from the past.
- Science fiction continually and self-reflectively builds

upon this heritage, integrating new developments in science, technology, and contemporary thought, an ever-evolving "think tank" about the future, and indeed about the nature of reality and the possibilities of imagination.

- Science fiction, insofar as it is informed by contemporary science, conceptualizes reality in evolutionary terms. The most scientifically plausible all-encompassing explanation of reality at this time in human history is contemporary evolutionary theory; scientifically informed science fiction sets its scenarios and narratives in an evolutionary universe. Scientifically informed visions of the future of humanity are evolutionary, and as the theory of evolution itself evolves, our evolutionary understanding of the future of humanity, as evidenced within science fiction, evolves.

- Science fiction, being both self-reflective and a mode of mythic future consciousness, is engaged in the purposeful evolution of holistic future consciousness. Throughout human history, future consciousness has evolved (Lombardo, 2006a) and in our present times science fiction is significantly contributing to this ongoing developmental process, empowering our capacities for purposefully guiding evolution and creating the future.

Science fiction evolves; science fiction is informed by evolutionary theory (which itself is evolving); and science fiction purposefully facilitates the further evolution of humanity by empowering the human mind to guide its own evolution. It enhances our holistic future consciousness to purposefully evolve ourselves.

Chapter 3

Ancient History through the Middle Ages

Those who are now renowned have taken over as if in a relay race (from hand to hand, relieving one another) from many many predecessors who on their part progress, and thus have themselves made possible progress.
Aristotle

The historical development of science fiction is part of the evolutionary growth of the total sphere of human consciousness (Lombardo, 2014, 2016c). This chronicle of its evolution aims to demonstrate that the spirit and main themes of science fiction reflect core intellectual, imaginative, and emotional features as well as developmental directions within the history of the conscious human mind. Although science fiction has distinctive features, it is embedded within and intimately connected with the evolving content and dynamics of human consciousness. Science fiction is not a modern or quirky aberration within human consciousness; it ties in with the dynamical core and growth of human mentality.

As such, science fiction did not suddenly emerge fully formed in contemporary times. The ideas that have contributed to the growth of science fiction go back thousands of years. As explained in the previous chapter, one key connection between ancient thought and modern science fiction is mythology and all those qualities associated with mythic consciousness. The roots and developmental tributaries of science fiction extend into the ancient past and derive from primordial forms of human experience.

Accordingly, the evolution of science fiction is connected with the broad and complex history of the human mind and human society. In tracing out the evolution of science fiction, the tributaries that feed into its growth extend outward across a wide expanse of areas of inquiry, speculation, and social-intellectual trends within human history. In this chapter, we delve into ancient and Medieval mythology; philosophy, culture, science and technology; theology and metaphysics; and literature and art.

The Apollonian and the Dionysian and Ancient Greek Mythology

> *But Zeus in the anger of his heart hid it, because Prometheus the crafty deceived him; therefore he planned sorrow and mischief against men. He hid fire; but that the noble son of Iapetus stole again for men from Zeus the counsellor in a hollow fennel-stalk, so that Zeus who delights in thunder did not see it. But afterwards Zeus who gathers the clouds said to him in anger ... `Son of Iapetus, surpassing all in cunning, you are glad that you have outwitted me and stolen fire — a great plague to you yourself and to men that shall be. But I will give men as the price for fire an evil thing in which they may all be glad of heart while they embrace their own destruction.'*

Hesiod

In describing the early historical roots of science fiction, an appropriate place to begin is ancient Greek thought, the intellectual and literary fountainhead of Western Civilization. Their science, philosophy, mythology, and literature provided a host of different concepts, perspectives, and attitudes that fed into the evolution of science fiction. Western science fiction (at least) can be viewed as a natural outgrowth of fundamental psychological, philosophical, and scientific themes within the evolution of Western human consciousness that developed, if not originated, with the ancient Greeks.

An important first theme, associated with the ancient Greeks, is the mythologically personified contrast between the *Apollonian* and the *Dionysian* mindsets and ways of life. The nineteenth-century philosopher, Friedrich Nietzsche, in *The Birth of Tragedy* (1872), highlighted this distinction in describing a basic duality within ancient Greek literature, as have numerous other writers, before and since (*Apollonian and Dionysian*).

In Greek mythology, Apollo is the god of reason, light, and order; Dionysius is the god of revelry, sensation, intoxication, and abandonment. The contrast between these two gods, as personifications of modes of human existence, represents the polarity of reason and logic versus emotion and sensation in human psychology. As an ontological-philosophical distinction it represents the contrast of order (reason) versus chaos (emotion) in the world at large. The Apollonian mindset is also associated with ordered human civilization, whereas the Dionysian mindset reflects exuberant and unconstrained nature and the primordial within human reality. The Apollonian is calm and elevated; the Dionysian is energetic and immersive, the latter trait connected with rituals often associated with blood, wine, eroticism, and the earth. From a modern psychological perspective, the ancient Greeks expressed a fundamental insight into the dual nature of the human mind through this mythic personification in Apollo and Dionysius.

This duality of the Apollonian and Dionysian can be seen as an expression of a deep archetypal theme in human consciousness that extends even further back in time than the Greeks. Ancient Egyptian and Babylonian thought, both of which strongly influenced the early Greeks, identified a fundamental polarity in existence between the forces of order and chaos. The cosmos, including human existence, involved an interplay between these two primordial forces or principles. Chaos was often (though not always) identified as more fundamental (see Hesiod's mythology below), with the drama of life conceptualized as the struggle to realize, maintain, and even advance order in opposition to the destructive forces of chaos (Lombardo, 2006a).

In more modern times the Apollonian-Dionysian polarity finds expression in European Enlightenment philosophy (c. eighteenth century), emphasizing order, science, and reason versus the philosophy of Romanticism (c. nineteenth century), highlighting emotion, art, immersion in nature, and the senses. Moreover, the archetypal contrast of order and chaos continues to be significant in contemporary human thought, for example as discussed in a later chapter on modern scientific theories of evolution and entropy (Lombardo, 2002a).

All in all, as expressed and personified in Greek mythology with Apollo and Dionysius, there has existed a fundamental polarity in modes of human experience, philosophies, and ways of life that extends through Western history up to the present. Various historians, philosophers, and scholars have labeled and described this polarity along very similar lines—circling around the contrast of intellect and reason versus emotion and sensation—identifying what seems to be an archetypal feature of the human (at least Western) mind (Pirsig, 1974; Tarnas, 1991; Watson, 2005).

This fundamental duality in consciousness across the ages has significantly influenced the nature and evolution of science fiction. On one hand, modern science fiction emerged (c. nineteenth century) as a literature of thoughtful and rational extrapolations of science and technology, as inspired by the philosophy of the European Enlightenment. But during these formative years, there were science fiction stories that expressed the deep apprehensions of Romantic philosophy regarding a world ruled by reason and science; further there were stories that highlighted emotional-sensory engagement and intense exhilaration, reflective of Dionysian and Romantic consciousness. Also, modern science fiction, from its beginnings, was influenced by a mixture (often contentious) of different values and visions of preferable futures associated with Enlightenment and Romantic philosophies.

As a literature of speculative exploration on scientific thinking, science fiction has aspired toward the qualities of the "fantastic," "amazing," and "astonishing" within its consciousness-expanding cosmic narratives. Through the intellectual mind we can experience "awe and wonder." But, science fiction has also realized such qualities through a Dionysian mode of consciousness. Science fiction has often been highly sensationalistic, thrilling, visceral, and electrifying, if not even psychedelic in its content, especially so within contemporary science fiction cinema and its exaggerated, hyper-stimulating, phantasmagoric special effects.

Greek culture also pursued balance and harmony as a central principle in life, encompassing music and art, ethics, philosophy, science and mathematics, politics, and the psychology of the human mind. In this regard Apollo (and the Apollonian mode of being) and Dionysius (and the Dionysian mode of being) were identified as necessary and complementary dimensions in human life. The good life was achieved through a balance and integration of the two mindsets or principles.

Analogously, modern science fiction in the nineteenth century can be seen to arise as a creative fusion, rather than an oppositional polarity, of Western Enlightenment and Romantic ideas and philosophies. There are novels, past and present, more in resonance with rationalistic Enlightenment and others more in resonance with the philosophy of Romanticism, but most noteworthy modern science fiction stories synthesize science and reason with passion and adventure (and often Dionysian sensationalism). Thus in line with the Greek principle of balance, good science fiction (as argued in the opening chapter) is psychologically holistic, clearly expressing and yet pulling together the Apollonian/rational Enlightenment and Dionysian/Romantic modes of consciousness. As Gernsbach proposed, science fiction should be both educational and entertaining, both intellectually enlightening and personally captivating.

As distinctive approaches to understanding reality and pursuing the good life, a second key polarity found in ancient Greek culture is the naturalistic, abstract, and rational mindset versus the supernatural, personified, and mythic-narrative mindset. This second basic dichotomy, although in some ways related to the Apollonian-Dionysian distinction, is somewhat different: Instead of the contrast of thought versus emotion/ sensation, this second contrast is between abstract theory and naturalism versus personified narratives and supernaturalism. Insofar as there is a parallel between these two polarities, it is that the Apollonian is associated with the rational (abstract thought), and the Dionysian—with its emphasis on emotional-sensory immersive experience— with the personal and personified.

The supernatural-personified mindset is strongly connected with traditional religion and myth, whereas the naturalistic-rational mindset is the foundation of modern science. Both mindsets have fed into and influenced the evolution of science fiction.

*　*　*

In this section, I examine the supernatural-personified mindset in Greek thought, beginning with two of the most famous mythic narratives of ancient Greece: Homer's *Iliad* and *Odyssey* and the story of *Jason and the Argonauts*, recounted in various ancient Greek writings, including those of Homer. (Greek mythology is an immense area of human study and inquiry. Classic and representative works include *Bulfinch's Mythology* (1855); Edith Hamilton's *Mythology* (1942); and *The Complete World of Greek Mythology* (2004) by Richard Buxton.)

The *Iliad* and the *Odyssey* are the two oldest extant works of Western literature, presumably written by Homer toward the end of the eighth century BCE, although the epic tales almost certainly describe events that took place centuries before Homer lived. Among the most influential books ever written in the West, the *Iliad* tells part of the story of the siege of Troy—the saga of Helen, Paris, Agamemnon, Achilles, Hector, and a host of other Greek and Trojan characters—while the *Odyssey* describes the journey and return of Odysseus to his home in the city of Ithaca in Greece after the battle of Troy.

The Homeric legacy, as created in these two literary works, was an enchanted and animated world, filled with personified deities, such as Zeus, Poseidon, and Athena, and fantastical beings, such as lotus-eaters, Cyclops, ghosts, witches, sirens, and assorted monsters that Odysseus encountered on his travels back from Troy to his home in Ithaca. Moreover, in both tales the Greek gods and goddesses frequently interact, directly or indirectly, with the humans. Most of the major events in both tales are initiated and orchestrated by Greek deities. For example, the attack on Troy by the Greeks was presumably instigated by a personal conflict among the Greek goddesses Hera, Athena, and Aphrodite.

For Homer, the cosmos and creation itself was personified, and the story of it all, which includes the siege of Troy and the journey of Odysseus as pivotal events in human history, was filled with conflict and drama among personified divinities, often with humans dragged into the maelstrom. The numerous mythic tales of the Greek gods and goddesses are especially noteworthy in that these imagined deities exhibited a full range of human personality traits and types of behavior, both virtuous and flawed. The full dimensionality of human psychology was projected into these "higher" beings.

The *Odyssey* is particularly important among the historical tributaries feeding into science fiction. For one thing, it is one of the most influential "extraordinary adventures" written in the West, a model for numerous similar tales (including science fiction tales) in the centuries to follow. The term "odyssey" derives its meaning from this classic story: "a long journey full of adventures, involving a series of experiences that give knowledge or understanding to someone." This definition reads like the archetypal narrative behind numerous science fiction tales of exploration and enlightenment; it aligns with key features in Joseph Campbell's (1949) concept of the "Hero's Journey."

As we follow Odysseus on his ten-year quest to find his way home to his wife Penelope, we travel through many different lands, full of surprises and obstacles, in which the variety of fantastical beings noted above either hinder or help him on his dangerous journey, at times capturing him, seducing him, mesmerizing him, and even threatening his life.

A unique combination of both human strengths and weaknesses, Odysseus is one of the earliest heroic figures in Western literature and myth, who after many tribulations, and at times ready to give up his quest, realizes success in the end, reuniting with his wife after slaying all of her would-be suitors.

Of special note, as a heroic figure on a fantastical adventure, Odysseus represents the emerging Greek ideal of self-determination. Buffeted by the forces of both fate and chance, and the whims of the gods, Odysseus tenaciously presses forward to achieve his personal goal. This self-assertive challenge of a human against both nature and supernatural deities is metaphorically an expression of humanity's abandonment of a god-centered mindset for making sense of the universe and finding guidance and empowerment in life. Rather, the world can be understood and successfully mastered by individual human efforts without supernatural deities; humans can move from children, needing direction and support, to adults. The philosophy of self-determination is a key idea contributing to the emergence of Western modernist thinking, the theory of secular progress, and the modern origins of science fiction.

References to the story of *Jason and the Argonauts* and the quest for the "Golden Fleece" can be found in both the *Iliad* and the *Odyssey*, as well as other ancient Greek poetic writings going back to the seventh century BCE. Probably the most well-known version of the tale, the epic poem *Argonautica*, was created by Apollonius of Rhodes (third century BCE) and would provide a literary model for various later well-known sagas, including Virgil's *Aeneid (Argonautica)*.

The story recounts the "extraordinary adventures" of Jason and the crew of his ship, the *Argo*, to numerous strange lands in search of the mythical and symbolic "Golden Fleece." Included in the tale are various Greek deities (Athena, Aphrodite, and Hera); mythic figures (Heracles, the giant automata Talos, and the enchantress Circe); and countless fantastical realities (dragons' teeth that turn into warriors, animated "Clashing Rocks," and fire-breathing oxen), all woven around a romantic element involving Jason and the sorceress Medea, who helps Jason on his quest and eventually marries him. Again, as in Homer, the world is animated and enchanted, and Jason must make his way through currents and forces that are initiated and directed by the Greek gods. Moreover, in this tale, there are various earthly characters possessing superhuman and magical powers as well. (In the *Iliad* the almost indestructible Achilles can be seen as superhuman.) *Jason and the Argonauts* is one of the greatest works of Western fantasy, in contemporary times inspiring movie adaptations filled with incredible special effects, including the famous version containing the amazing visualizations of Ray Harryhausen, one of the key influential figures in the development of science fiction and fantasy special effects.

Both *The Odyssey* and *Jason and the Argonauts* provided seminal and archetypal visions for later space travel adventure tales involving spaceships, courageous captains, and intrepid crews venturing into the unknown and having to confront bizarre and dangerous creatures and unexpected and inexplicable cosmic forces. Finding themselves variously lost, captured, and mentally incapacitated by strange and powerful beings, explorers in outer space (or other mysterious realms) in modern science fiction followed similar journeys and encountered similar challenges as those described in ancient Greek extraordinary adventures, such as in *The Odyssey* and *Jason and the Argonauts.* Moreover, as in both these ancient tales, there were frequently romantic "love stories" woven into the adventure: the hero in such tales, after confronting and overcoming tremendous adversaries, had to find his way back to the love of his heart or rescue her from sinister beings.

Another key work in ancient Greek mythology is Hesiod's *Theogony*. Indeed, Hesiod's *Theogony* can be seen as the foundational document underlying and supporting ancient Greek mythic consciousness. The poet Hesiod lived between 750 and 650 BCE. In his *Theogony* he describes "the genealogy of the gods" and includes the various personal dramas associated with these deities that led to present human life. It is the first Greek mythical "cosmogony," a story and explanation of the beginning of the universe.

The *Theogony* identifies the origin of the cosmos as Chaos, or a formless primordial void out of which everything else emerged. This starting point in the story of creation probably reflects other popular mythological theories of ancient times—similar ideas of the world emerging out of chaos can be found in Vedic, Hindu, Babylonian, and Judaic creation mythologies. It is likely that Hesiod's creation story had Middle Eastern and Babylonian origins (Kirk and Raven, 1966; Lombardo, 2006a; *Hesiod*).

According to Hesiod, in the beginning was Chaos, and from Chaos came Gaia (the earth), Tartarus (the abyss), and Eros (love). Chaos also produced Night and Darkness, which mated with the help of Eros to produce the Day. Earth brought forth the Ocean, the Mountains, and Heaven (Ouranos). Earth and sky—Gaia and Ouranos—then mated producing the Titans, the first gods and goddesses of ancient Greece. Cronos—a son of Ouranos and the ruler of the Titans, who would also become the god of time—usurped the power of his father but in turn was overthrown by his son, Zeus. Zeus thereupon became the supreme ruler of all the later Greek gods and goddesses. Most of the gods and goddesses in Homer's tales are either children of Cronos (brothers and sisters of Zeus), or children of Zeus and one of his goddess mates.

Beginning in Chaos (perhaps appropriately so), the Greek pantheon of gods and goddesses, consumed by internal rivalry, tumultuous romances, jealousies, and personal conflicts, emerged as an all-encompassing patriarchy with Zeus reigning on high from his thrown on mythical Mount Olympus. In Hesiod's mythic tale of creation the two fundamental cosmic forces at work generating the universe are sexual reproduction and violent war, and Zeus, personifying both forces, is immensely powerful on both counts. Essentially, a dominance hierarchy of control is achieved by a male deity through conquest, sexual and otherwise.

This pivotal coupling of the powers of sexual reproduction and violent destructiveness represents in the personified form of Zeus a historically ancient and yet equally modern vision of the primary forces involved in both creation and creativity in nature. Note for example the ancient Greek Empedocles' philosophy of love and hate as primal cosmic forces; Freud's Eros and Thanatos as key bio-psychological motives; and integration/reciprocity and competition/war in Bloom's theory of social and bio-physical evolution (Lombardo, 2011c, 2017). Although from a modern scientific point of view, we would not hypothesize a personal being that embodies such qualities, somehow ruling over and shaping the dynamics of existence, the personal qualities possessed by Zeus represent a psychological projection of a deep and insightful understanding on the part of the ancient Greeks regarding the dynamics of the universe. Indeed, for those modern believers in the supernatural metaphysics of Christianity, the twin forces of love (although not sexual) and hate align with God and Satan.

As the psychologist Julian Jaynes argues in his book *The Origin of Consciousness in the Breakdown of the Bicameral Mind* (1976), and Dan Simmons so effectively describes in his science fiction novels *Ilium* and *Olympos*, which were inspired by the *Iliad* and *Odyssey*, the conscious minds of Hesiodic-Homeric-period Greeks were populated by the voices and apparitions of their personified deities; as described in the previous chapter, humans spoke to the gods and the gods spoke to them. The historian of religion, Karen Armstrong (1994), makes a similar point for the ancient world at large: The gods were not only in the world, they were often in our minds, appearing and speaking to us and guiding our actions. The gods were imminent and yet also transcendent.

What we think of as "ancient myths" featured personified and supernatural beings (representing cosmic forces and psychological archetypes) who engaged in various interactions, both supportive and combative, with each other, as well as with humans. These myths were presented in narrative form, recounting both the creation of the world and the ongoing influence of deities or other personified beings within the world. Ancient myths were attempts to explain the world in narrative form, and given the colossal forces perceived in nature, the characters in the narrative were supernatural and superhuman, both "above" nature, ruling over it, and above humanity, superior to us in their powers. As such, both the realms and powers of supernatural beings were transcendent to those of humans.

Using the stories associated with the Greek god Dionysius as a case in point, humans, through participatory rites and rituals, attempted to get into psychological resonance with the gods and their associated dramas. Ancient myths provided a way to act out and personally understand the saga of creation and the drama of life. I have already introduced the idea that science fiction is a participatory and engaging reality in which people find meaning and purpose in life, and in this regard, among others, science fiction shares a deep similarity with ancient myths. Indeed, just as ancient people attempted to immerse themselves in and ascend into transcendent states or realms, modern science fiction fans and devotees vicariously transport themselves into the transcendent realms of outer space, alien worlds, time travel, alternate timelines, and the minds of more evolved forms of intelligence, whether it be aliens, or humans in the future.

Greek Science, Technology, and Philosophy

... But Aristarchus of Samos brought out a book consisting of certain hypotheses, in which the premises lead to the result that the universe is many times greater than that now so called. His hypotheses are that the fixed stars and the Sun remain unmoved, that the Earth revolves about the Sun in the circumference of a circle, the Sun lying in the middle of the orbit, and that the sphere of the fixed stars, situated about the same centre as the Sun, is so great that the circle in which he supposes the Earth to revolve bears such a proportion to the distance of the fixed stars as the centre of the sphere bears to its surface.
Archimedes (*The Sand Reckoner*)

The human mind is an evolutionary phenomenon, and throughout its ongoing development there have been significant progressive steps forward in our capacities to understand ourselves and the world around us. Across history, human consciousness has expanded outward in space and time and reached upwards toward more abstract forms of intelligence. It is a frequently argued hypothesis that beginning around the seventh century BCE, across the world, an important evolutionary transformation occurred in the growth of the human mind that would move humanity beyond personified mythic narratives as an explanation of reality.

From approximately 700 to 400 BCE, a period generally referred to as the "Axial Age," (for human history seems to pivot on this age), a number of influential religious and philosophical figures emerged across Asia and Europe. These thinkers produced a rich variety of new ideas and teachings on reality, knowledge, God, and the meaning of life. They were responsible for the creation of many new religions, spiritual practices, and theories of philosophy. They emphasized self-responsibility, abstraction, literacy, and a rejection of the authority of royalty. They expressed a movement away from polytheism and animism toward inner development, morality, and an enhanced sense of individuality. This group of religious and philosophical leaders and figureheads included Isaiah, Socrates, Zoroaster, Lao-tzu, Confucius, and Siddhartha Gautama, or as he is more popularly known, the Buddha (Lombardo, 2006a).

As one representative exponent of this historical and evolutionary theory, Merlin Donald (1991) argues that the dominant mode of understanding in the human mind before the seventh century BCE was "mythic," but that thereafter the human mind developed the capacity for "theoretic" understanding. It was this new mode of understanding that spawned the abstract-scientific perspective on reality and fueled the philosophy of self-determination that emancipated the human mind from the influence of mythic gods and the mindset of supernatural personification. Yet even if we assume that this theory of human cognitive evolution is true, the "mythic" mode of understanding did not disappear; rather the "theoretic" mindset was layered on top of it (Lombardo, 2016c). An uneasy and complex coupling emerged in the ancient human mind circa seventh century BCE that is still with us today.

Beginning in that period, in the writings of such naturalistic philosophers as Thales, Anaximander, and Empedocles, we see the emergence of a mindset different from the mythic regarding our understanding of nature, the cosmos, and reality. What if we can understand the world in terms of forces, substances, mathematical laws, and properties within the natural world without resorting to otherworldly or supernatural factors? What if we can understand the world in abstract principles as opposed to personified entities? What if we can approach life from a rational (logical) mindset where we reason out the nature of the cosmos rather than gain knowledge and inspiration through prophecies, revelations, soothsayers, sacred religious texts, religious rites, rituals, and visions? This emerging alternative way of knowing and thinking—which in ancient Greece reached its asymptote in the writings of Parmenides, Plato, and Aristotle, as well as various Greek "scientists,"—represented the beginnings of naturalism, empiricism, rationalism, and theoretical abstraction in Western history, and would feed into the genesis of modern science and philosophy in the seventeenth century (Lombardo, 2006a, Chapters 3 and 4), which in turn would feed into the beginnings of modern science fiction.

Adopting a naturalistic and abstract perspective on reality, Thales (620-546 BCE) proposed that the primary substance out of which everything in nature is composed is water, its fluidity suggesting the capacity to form and transform into diverse configurations. Anaximander (611-547 BCE), another "scientific" and naturalistic philosopher, argued that the primary material substance or principle was "apeíron," which meant the "infinite" or "limitless" (in both space and time) out of which everything is made. The "aperíon," which is the "arche" of all things, suggests the idea of chaos (the formless) out of which all order arises. Anaximenes (585-528 BCE), on the other hand, proposed that the primary substance was "air," all physical things "condensing" out of this rarified reality. Bringing to the forefront in his theory of reality the primacy of abstract principles, Pythagoras (570-495 BCE) believed that the universe was mathematical in its organization and dynamic form. As a key component of his general cosmology, Empedocles (490-435 BCE) developed the historically influential theory that the four "roots" (or elements) out of which everything is created are earth, air, fire, and water. Yet, although Empedocles' theory of four primary elements sounds naturalistic and materialistic, he "metaphorically" identified each of these physical substances with a Greek deity and described the interaction of the two fundamental forces of the universe as the ongoing dialectic of the Greek gods, Aphrodite (representing love) and Ares (representing war and strife). As one final striking example of the naturalistic perspective, Democritus (460-370 BCE), sounding very modernist and scientific in his thinking, argued that the universe in its entirety consists of an infinite number of physical atoms moving through the spatial void, mechanistically interacting with each other, and that all perceptible objects are composed of conglomerations of these atoms. Even if gods and goddesses crept into these different theories of reality and the cosmos, it is notable that naturalistic and abstract explanations were coming to the forefront in explaining the make-up and dynamics of the totality of reality. By the time we come to Lucretius (99-55 BCE), a later follower of Democritus, the gods and goddesses appear to have been completely jettisoned in favor of a materialistic and evolutionary theory of reality.

Cosmology and astronomy have especially informed and inspired the evolution of science fiction; the emergence of the modern science of astronomy circa 1600-1800 CE would be a key stimulus in the first writings of modern science fiction. Astronomy was one of the significant areas of inquiry in which the Greeks (c. 600 to 400 BCE) began to move away from the personified and supernatural toward the abstract and naturalistic. Ancient Greek astronomy was originally built upon observations and theories of Mesopotamian, Babylonian, Egyptian, and Zoroastrian astronomers and astrologers (*Greek*

Astronomy; Ancient Greek Astronomy). In resonance with these varied historical influences, Greek theories of the heavens frequently included, besides empirical observations, theological and philosophical ideas (for example, the presumed perfection of the heavens). As such, early Greek astronomy, although moving in a modernist direction, was a combination of both empirical science and mathematics and theological ideas. As cosmic thinkers, taking in the totality of everything, Greek astronomers attempted to explain the observable heavens and the universe, entertaining and combining a variety of different hypotheses— abstract-naturalistic and personified-supernatural—coupled with mathematical methods.

On the empirical end, the ancient Greeks possessed basic observational knowledge of stars and planets and their positions in the sky for purposes of navigation and agriculture. The word "planet" derives from the Greek word for "wanderer," since the observable planets did not move across the night sky in unison with the stars. Also, as basic empirical contributions to astronomy, Thales discovered the seasonal solstice and equinox, and presumably predicted an eclipse, perhaps based upon his knowledge of Babylonian astronomy. Anaximander created perhaps the first European map of the known world (the region surrounding the Mediterranean Sea).

On the more theoretical end, Anaximander thought that the sun, moon, and stars moved around the earth, and that the earth was suspended in empty space (a revolutionary idea at the time). Further he proposed that these heavenly bodies were at different distances away from the earth in a vast three-dimensional space.

The mystical-mathematical philosopher Pythagoras argued that the earth and the heavenly bodies were spheres, the sphere being the perfect shape. This is possibly the first recorded instance of the idea that the earth is a sphere, but the reason for his hypothesis was mystical. (The heavens are perfect, and the sphere is the perfect form; hence the earth must be a sphere.)

As a key theoretical-mathematical concept, also with mystical overtones, Pythagoras presumably argued that there existed a "harmony or music of the spheres," an idea that would influence later cosmology and astronomy. The motions of heavenly bodies exist in a mathematical proportionality—a harmony—creating a cosmic music. Pythagoras also realized that the morning and evening star was the same object, namely Venus. Further, he believed that the earth and the seas were not stable, that existing land may have been under the sea in earlier eras, and that present seas may have once been dry land, thus anticipating later evolutionary and dynamic theories of natural reality.

The philosopher Anaxagoras (500-428 BCE) attempted to provide scientific (naturalistic) explanations for meteors, eclipses, rainbows, and the sun and stars. For example, he believed that the sun and the stars were fiery stones. Further, he thought that the moon was a world like the earth—he presumably observed mountains and valleys on the moon—and he believed that it might be inhabited. Here we see the beginnings of two related ideas that would become very popular in science fiction, providing both setting and dramatic encounters for extraordinary space adventures: 1) There are other worlds in the universe (to be explored); and 2) these worlds may contain "aliens" that, possessing bizarre qualities and strange powers, could be a source of both promise and threat.

Both Plato (424-348 BCE) and Aristotle (384-322 BCE), the two most influential of the ancient Greek philosophers, thought that the earth was at the center of the universe, an idea that would dominate the West for the next two thousand years. Plato proposed that the stars, sun, and moon rotate around a spherical earth on concentric crystalline spheres. Inspired by this hypothesis, Eudoxus (c. 400-350 BCE) developed a mathematical-geometrical model of concentric rotating spheres to explain the varied motions of the observable planets, an immensely influential geometrical-dynamic model expressing a geocentric vision of the universe.

Yet, with Aristarchus (310-230 BCE) and Eratosthenes (276-195 BCE) the idea emerged that it was not that the stars and sun moved through the sky but that the earth rotates. For Aristarchus the sun is at the center of the universe. Moreover, Aristarchus mathematically calculated that the stars, which he believed were suns, were at much vaster distances than commonly supposed, and that the earth was tiny in comparison with the size of the universe. Eratosthenes produced an estimate of the size of the earth that was fairly accurate by modern standards.

It was this kind of vision of the universe that, once it had gained popular support and credibility in modern times, became the fantastical reality of space adventures for modern science fiction. Yet, for the ancient Greeks (as well as other early cultures) and up through the Middle Ages, the size of the universe (and outer space) was colossally underestimated; both "deep space" and "deep time," the vast arenas for modern science fiction adventure, would not be revealed until the eighteenth century.

Moreover, the view that the earth was at the center of the universe remained dominant in ancient times. Human minds persisted in their egocentricity. Hipparchus (190-120 BCE), one of the greatest Greek astronomers, developed a vast and detailed star catalogue. His astronomy included extensive mathematical reasoning and efforts to make exact astronomical predictions, serving as one key source of information for later astronomers, including Ptolemy. Presumably based on his mathematical and observational studies, Hipparchus argued for the predictive superiority of the geocentric theory (the earth at the center of the universe) over the heliocentric theory (the sun at the center of the universe).

Completing this brief survey of ancient astronomy, the Roman Ptolemy (100 CE-170 CE), building on the work of astronomical observations and geometrical-mathematical concepts of the ancient Greeks, developed in his book *Almagest* (originally titled

"Mathematical Treatise") the theory of epicycles to explain the movement of the stars, planets, moons, and sun through the sky, with the earth at the center of the universe. Ptolemy's theory would dominate European astronomy for close to 1500 years. It was within this universe that Dante's visionary *Divine Comedy* takes place. Ptolemy included an extensive list of the constellations in his studies, and wrote profusely on the geography of the earth, and yet he also believed in the principles of astrology, a reflection of a personified perspective of the heavens.

All in all, the dominant geocentric theory of the heavens (with additional Biblical ideas on creation), which in essence was a highly egocentric mindset, constrained the ancient and Medieval Western minds to a very limited vision of the universe of space and time, generally precluding the possibility of other worlds, other forms of intelligent life, and imagined grand adventures into the cosmos.

Greek thinking on technology is another sphere in which the supernatural-personified gets blended with the scientific and naturalistic. Technology in modern times is strongly associated with science, and its potential future wonders with science fiction. Yet with the ancient Greeks, technology and its origins are understood (to a significant degree) within the framework of personified mythology.

On the practical and scientific side of things, the ancient Greeks were responsible for a host of technological inventions, including the creation of the water mill, odometer, alarm clock, and techniques of cartography and natural medicine (*Ancient History*). Of special note, perhaps the greatest of the Greek mathematical scientists, Archimedes (287-212 BCE), is credited not only with numerous achievements in mathematics and geometry but also various scientific discoveries and technological creations, including the screw pump ("Archimedes Screw"), compound pulleys, and various war machines. There is also the famous story of Archimedes discovering the scientific principle of displacement while taking a bath and running into the street shouting "Eureka!" ("I have found it!"). This classic story of sudden creative insight became an archetypal narrative informing Western thinking on scientific discovery (Koestler, 1964) and served as the inspiration for numerous tales of fantastical inventions in science fiction. Amazingly, Archimedes also calculated the number of grains of sand needed to fill the universe.

Yet, behind the practical, hands-on intelligence and mathematical genius involved in developing new technologies, naturalistic principles, and astronomic calculations, the Greeks also created a mythology of technology.

Perhaps the most well-known mythic tale connected with technology is the story of Prometheus, who steals the secret of fire from the gods—a symbol of technological power over nature—bringing it to humanity and presumably seeding the rise of human civilization.

Moreover, the ancient Greeks had what we might call a "god of technology," Hephaestus, who was more specifically the god of metallurgy, sculpture, arts and crafts, blacksmiths, fire, and volcanoes. In one mythic version of his origins, he is the son of Zeus and Hera. He made all the weapons and created all the marvelous techno-magical devices of the Greek gods, including Hermes's winged helmet and sandals and the chariot of the sun-god Helios. He also created metallic *automatons* that walked about Mount Olympus. Hephaestus had the power to instill animate motion in his constructed devices; he made animated gold and silver lions and dogs that protected the palace of Alkinoos and would attack any would-be invaders. In some mythic stories of Hephaestus, he is a cripple and invents an automaton to help him move about (he is the first "cyborg"). It is from Hephaestus that Prometheus obtains the gift of fire for humanity (*Hephaestus*).

One of the most famous of the technological inventions of

Hephaestus is Talos, often identified as the first imagined "robot" in human history. Directed by Zeus, Hephaestus creates a giant animated human-like android (also described as a bull) made of bronze, to protect Europa (a love interest of Zeus) on the island of Crete. A "life fluid" ("ichor") flowed through a single artery of Talos's body, giving him the power of motion. Unfortunately, in defending the island of Crete against Jason and the Argonauts, Talos is tricked by Medea (the sorceress) into removing the nail in his ankle, thus allowing all the "ichor" to flow out of his body. Consequently, Talos "died" (lost his power of animate motion) (*Talos*).

Although there is a magical dimension to Hephaestus and his powers of invention, there is also a mechanistic and naturalistic dimension. Hephaestus forges amazing devices and animate creatures out of the raw materials of nature; he is a craftsman and an engineer who can construct various mechanisms that both mimic living things and transcend the powers of the mundane. He is an archetypal and inspirational figure of the scientific inventor who possesses powers to create miraculous machines and technologies.

In considering the myths of Hephaestus, it is worth noting that the ancient Greeks were psychologically predisposed to see statues and artifacts as possessing inner animate spirits. The Greeks, as well as other ancient peoples around the world, not only viewed nature as personified and alive but, within this mindset of animism, saw statues—created in the likeness of deities and living creatures, imagined or real—as possessing consciousness and other animate capacities. From deep within our history, we have been psychologically disposed to personify our surrounding reality, including our sculptures and our gadgets, especially those that were modeled on human or other living forms.

Even in modern times, children naturally see their dolls, play-animals, and other toys as being alive and possessing personalities; adults personify their automobiles and computers. Many of us still pray to statues of religious and spiritual figures, as if the spirit of the deity was somehow embodied in the statue. Many of us talk to our machines. We can argue that animism and the personification of nature psychologically seeded our modern vision of intelligent animate machines, a mainstay of modern science fiction.

Likewise, the modern aspiration to create animate mechanisms is an expression of our desire to become equal to the gods, to those presumed beings who first breathed life and intelligence into the world and into us. This was the dream and the obsession—as well as the undoing—of Mary Shelley's mad scientist Frankenstein. All in all, the science fiction narrative theme of creating animate, living, or even conscious beings out of the raw materials of nature goes back to the ancient Greeks (at the very least). This envisioned power, both divine and mechanical, is personified in the Greek god Hephaestus.

Another significant figure in the Greek mythology of technology is Daedalus, a mythic artist and craftsman first mentioned by Homer. Daedalus is credited with creating the famous "labyrinth," constructed to contain the Minotaur (half man/half bull), a maze so complex that Daedalus, the inventor, is barely able to find his way out of it—a metaphorical warning on how ingenious inventions can transcend and backfire on the inventor.

Probably the most famous story connected with Daedalus concerns the fatal flight of his son, Icarus. Entrapped with his son in a tower, Daedalus creates wings (out of feathers, strings, and melted wax) for both himself and his son—the dream of creating the power of flight through naturalistic technology. After teaching Icarus to use the wings properly, Daedalus tells his son not to fly too high (a metaphorical warning on grandiose personal aspiration) or the sun's heat (a metaphorical symbol of the superhuman transcendent reality of the gods) will melt the wax holding the wings together. The son, thoughtlessly enraptured by the sun's brilliance (the power of the gods), foolishly ignores the warning. The wax melts, the wings fall off, and Icarus plummets into the sea below and drowns.

In this story, Daedalus also symbolizes a philosophical caveat: humans must use foresight and consider the potential consequences and dangers of innovation and we should show caution in our aspirations to attain godlike powers through our devices. Technology may empower, but this cautionary archetypal narrative theme running back to the ancient Greeks has influenced modern science fiction, which has repeatedly addressed the issues of risk and uncertainty, hubris and vanity, and wisdom and ethics regarding our drive toward technological advancement and transcendence. Do we really have what it takes to be equal to the gods?

In other mythic tales, Daedalus is given wings (by the goddess Athena) and he does achieve successful flight, traveling to various locations throughout the ancient world. He is also credited in other stories with having created various wondrous technological inventions, including animate bronze sculptures possessing the capacity to speak (hence intelligence)—creative powers also attributed to Hephaestus.

Overall, the cognitive emancipation from a deified and personified mindset was far from complete with Greek philosophy, technological thinking, and science. The mythic and theoretical mindsets (to use Donald's terms), and the naturalistic and supernatural, continued to blend together in numerous ways. Yet, it was through the naturalistic and rationalistic philosophers and scientists of ancient Greece that an opposition to and shift away from the gods and personified myths began to manifest itself.

* * *

We must make a distinction and ask, what is that which always is and has no becoming; and what is that which is always becoming and never is? That which is apprehended by intelligence and reason is always in the same state; but that which is conceived by opinion with the help of sensation and without reason, is always in a process of becoming and perishing and never really is.
Plato

I now turn to the philosopher Plato and his multi-faceted significance in the history of science fiction. Plato, in many respects, is the paradigm case of the Apollonian, theoretic, and rationalistic perspectives in ancient Greece. And yet in his philosophical *Dialogues*, which highlight the skills and values associated with logical and critical thinking, he repeatedly referred to the gods and other personified spirits, paying homage to his mythic cultural heritage. Plato was also clearly "mystical," describing the intuitive rapture of eternal truths, the mode of understanding that Donald identifies as *preceding* the "mythological" in human evolution. Pythagoras, with his mathematical and musical mysticism, was one of the key influences instigating Plato's epistemic mysticism, as well as inspiring Plato's professed love of the beauty of geometry and music. In sum, Plato was a complex mixture of the rational, the intuitive, the ethereal and eternal, and the aesthetic.

Along with Aristotle, Plato was one of the two most influential ancient Greek philosophers, by some assessments perhaps the most significant Western philosopher of all time (Lombardo, 2006a, Chapter 3). Because of his immense overall influence on Western thought, in a number of important respects Plato had a powerful impact—both contributory and inhibitory—on the future evolution of science fiction.

Although seen as the archetypal starting point for Western rationalism—the idea that true knowledge is gained through abstract reason—Plato was also unequivocally an ontological dualist, believing in two different realms of existence: There was the eternal and mental/spiritual realm and the temporal and perceptual/material realm, with the former thought by Plato to be on a higher plane of existence and more absolutely real than the latter.

Early Christianity (for example, as exemplified in St. Augustine) would embrace Plato's dualism. Within Plato's supposedly higher realm of spirit and mind, Christianity located its supernatural deities and heavenly spirits. In addition, for Plato and later for Christianity, it was the immaterial spirit (mind or soul) that was immortal, and not the transitory physical body. Perhaps the Christian divine realm (heaven) was not as agitated and sensationalistic an arena of action as the Olympian realm envisioned by the ancient Greeks, yet the general mindset that the cosmos was a drama orchestrated by personified and powerful spiritual deities dominated Christian thinking through the Middle Ages. In this regard, Christianity continued the mythic-personified framework of understanding expressed by the earliest Greeks and other ancient cultures, but now grounded in a post-Platonic/Augustinian metaphysics.

Plato's immensely influential dualistic theory of mind/spirit versus physical matter provided a distinctive metaphysical arena in which all manner of immaterial and transcendent beings could be placed. In like manner, as we will see, science fiction writers have repeatedly invented "mental forces," disembodied minds, and ethereal nonmaterial entities that in some manner or form are distinct, if not transcendent to the physical world. Although we may not popularly associate science fiction (or science for that matter) with narratives about mental or spiritual realities, the historical fact is that many science fiction writers have included these types of transcendent nonphysical mental realities, and Plato, more than anyone else in the philosophical history of the West, shaped this idea of a nonphysical, higher realm of mind and spirit.

Yet, the Platonic-Christian emphasis on the spiritual and nonphysical worked against the development of the physical sciences throughout the Middle Ages. Accordingly, insofar as modern science fiction was built upon a scientific vision of reality, and science (at least in its early period) predominately dealt with the workings of the physical world, the Platonic-Christian vision of reality also worked against the emergence of modern science fiction. Additionally, insofar as visions of a future better than the present were "located" in the heavenly spiritual afterlife, the Christian mindset worked against envisioning transformed and better futures—utopian science fiction—within the naturalistic and temporal world.

Nonetheless, Plato can be seen as the philosophical beginning of utopian thinking, a significant tributary that feeds into the evolution of science fiction; modern science fiction, indeed, has frequently and deeply explored the nature of the ideal society. Plato, in *The Republic,* envisioned an ideal human society ruled by "Philosopher Kings." Following from his tripartite theory of the human psyche—Reason, Appetite, and Spirit—he saw his ideal society as consisting of three classes: the rulers (who operate according to reason); the soldiers or guardians (who operate according to spirit in the sense of cultural conscience); and the common people (whose lives are primarily influenced by appetite, in essence, the desires and impulses of the body). For Plato, an ideal society (as well as an ideal mind) involves a harmony and balance of all three dimensions, but with reason (the ruler Philosopher King) in charge and determining the balance and harmony of the whole. Plato, in his normative psychology and his normative theory of society, was a rationalist; reason should rule.

Plato did not approve of the liberal and democratic practices of Athens, where he lived. Instead he was attracted to the more authoritarian system of Sparta (Bloom, 2000). Athens had become in Plato's time a web of commercial exchange, with many subcultures and a definite international flavor. Sparta, on the other hand, was more isolated, less materialistic, and based on a rigid system of conformity and control. In Plato's mind, Sparta was order; Athens was chaos. And insofar as Plato in his cosmic ontology saw order and harmony as supreme, existing at the apex of existence, he saw the well-ordered society ruled from the top down as ideal.

In *The Republic*, Plato argues against democracy as a viable form of government and instead supports the idea of a "Philosopher King" who would rule with wisdom, benevolence, and a sense of justice. Not just anyone or everyone can rule in Plato's ideal society and Philosopher Kings must be educated and trained from youth to rule wisely and competently. Philosopher Kings must gain an understanding of the eternal principles of truth, beauty, the good, and justice, and not be overpowered by the flux and corruption of popular opinion, the senses, materialism, and time. In essence, for Plato, the determination of society and its operations cannot be left up to the uneducated masses who are motivated by bodily desires and the agitations of the senses—an ideal society must be ruled by rational thinkers from above.

The Republic is probably the most influential utopian vision in the history of Western civilization. In *The Republic* we find numerous important themes emblematic of Plato's general philosophy, including his theory of "eternal forms" (as the ultimate constituents of knowledge and reality); his "Allegory of the Cave" (illustrating the limited and shallow perspective of the everyday world); his critique of democracy; and his views on the nature of justice as the central virtue and value of an ideal society. Plato's *Republic* is an ideal society deeply informed by a grand philosophical scheme concerning reality, knowledge, psychology, and ethics.

Plato's ideal society, though, is not envisioned as existing in the future. It is presented as an ideal model of how a just society should be organized, existing in abstract philosophical space.

Moreover, given Plato's elevation of the eternal and timeless above the temporal and transforming, his utopia is static and unchanging; numerous later utopias (at least in the early modern period) would take the same form. Here is the ideal, here is perfection, and any change would be a corruption. Indeed, change *is* corruption. Eventually, though, utopian narratives envisioned ideal hypothetical futures, once the modern philosophy of secular progress popularized the view that the future could be better than the past. By the time we get to H. G. Wells' utopian writings (c. 1905), a viable utopia is described as dynamic and evolving, rather than static, and hypothetically existing in the future. Yet still, as Wells acknowledged, Plato's *The Republic* had a big impact on Wells' novel *A Modern Utopia* (1905), and more generally, Plato's rationalistic philosophical *Dialogues* impressed the young Wells, providing him with a model for clear, organized, and self-reflective thinking.

Although Plato saw his utopian vision as an expression of his ethical and social ideals, later writers would argue that Plato's ideal society was dystopian, since it was authoritarian, tyrannical, and highly repressive compared to our modern individualist and democratic ideals. The guardians in *The Republic* physically enforce the rules of the Philosopher Kings on the masses. Relative to modern standards of human freedom and individualism, *The Republic* is more of a dystopia (a bad society) than a utopia (a good society) (Lombardo, 2010). We could argue that the historical archetype of modern dystopias, which invariably involve the repressive control of the population by some centralized and authoritarian absolute source of power (for example, in *We*, *City of Endless Night*, *Brave New World*, and *1984*), finds its origins in Plato's *The Republic*.

Still, who is right and who is wrong on this fundamental issue regarding the ideal human society? Plato presents a variety of thoughtful considerations in arguing for his point of view: Democracy is unruly, chaotic, and conflicting and reflects the unenlightened and lowest common denominator of popular opinion. His society may be rigid, controlled by centralized authority, and enforced by a warrior class (the guardians), yet he argues that this social arrangement is ethically ideal and psychologically sane, bringing justice, order, and enlightened understanding to society. On what grounds do we dismiss his vision and arguments as unsound and leading to a bad society?

In envisioning ideal versus dystopian future human societies, it has been an ongoing challenge to unambiguously separate the good and the bad. Are our modern democratic judgments of an ideal society temporally and culturally relative, and hence no better or worse than Plato's? Are we all that certain that Plato's vision is ethically flawed and humanistically undesirable? We will see, for example, in H. G. Wells' utopian thinking—which is clearly informed and inspired by modernist evolutionary ideas—that his visions of ideal societies align in many respects with a top-down authoritarian model of government envisioned in Plato's *The Republic*. The ongoing historical evolution of visions of ideal societies (whether placed in the future or not) has reflected various significant differences of view in social and political philosophy—for example, should we emphasize the importance of social order or conversely individual freedom—that have been debated and continue to be debated in our time (Nisbet, 1994; Lombardo, 2006b, Chapter 4).

Prometheus, Progress, and Self-Determination

Hesiod set before men the first idea of progress: the idea that the good life is attainable; that this attainment is dependent upon the thought and activity of men themselves; that the essential requisite is the actualization of the members of the community by a common regard for justice.
Frederick Teggert

Plato elevated the eternal and timeless above the temporal and change, and his ideal society is envisioned as a stable, unchanging reality. Plato saw change as chaotic and generating corruption. The popular historical view is that the ancient world, which includes ancient Greece, did not view time (or change) as having a progressive direction; presumably the ancients did not believe that things would or could get better in the future. As is generally argued, the most influential view of time in the ancient world was the cyclical view (time is a circle, such as in the cycle of the seasons), which clearly does not generate progressive change but only repetition. If any direction to time was identified it was decline; once there was a "Golden Age," once there was a paradise on earth, but something went wrong (sin or stupidity), and things have gone downhill ever since (Franz, 1978; Lombardo, 2006a, Chapter 3).

One writer who strongly disputes this popular interpretation of ancient thinking about time is Robert Nisbet in *History of the Idea of Progress* (1994). For Nisbet, the concept of directional progress across historical time and potentially into the future goes back to the ancient Greeks. As introduced earlier, the theme of progress (and change) in the future is one of the most important ideas contributing to the emergence of modern science fiction. Clearly in a history of science fiction it is important to ascertain when and how this key idea first appeared in Western thinking, and Nisbet's answer is that it began with the ancient Greeks.

Interestingly, Nisbet anchors his historical study of the idea of progress in ancient Greece to two individuals, who are not generally seen as supporting the idea of temporal progress, but rather supporting the ideas of temporal decline and eternal perfectionism—respectively, Hesiod and Plato.

Hesiod, in his *Works and Days*, presented his famous "Five Ages of Man" historical theory. In what sounds much like a theory of human decline, Hesiod states that human history began in a Golden Age (the first humans) and was successively followed by the Silver, Bronze, Heroic (the age of Homer's *Iliad* and *Odyssey*), and, finally, the Iron Age, in which Hesiod locates his present. But according to Nisbet, as one reads through Hesiod's descriptions of these successive eras, rather than suffering a universal and steady decline, each era is clearly described as having both positive and negative features. In fact, the message comes across that through human effort the good life can be realized; a positive future is a potentiality open to human achievement; and we are not hopelessly doomed to decline.

Perhaps the most convincing illustration of the idea of progress in Hesiod is the story of Prometheus, found in the *Theogony*. As the tale is presented, Prometheus brings to primitive humankind the gift of fire (the ability to control fire) which, as a critical stimulus (the beginning of technology), initiates the road to civilization. Also, as another beneficent action attributed to Prometheus, humankind acquired reason, after having been first created on the earth without it. These stories of Prometheus seem to imply that early humankind was at a much lower level of development than present human civilization, and hence there has been progress from a more primitive past to a more advanced present. According to Nisbet, alongside cyclical and decline theories of time in ancient Greece, there was the opposing idea, as expressed in Hesiod's stories of Prometheus, that humans in earlier eras had been brutish, primitive, animal-like, and lacking in the skills and intellectual accomplishments of present Greek civilization. See also, for example, the view of human history put forth by Xenophanes (570-475 BCE), another notable ancient Greek: "The gods have not, of course, revealed all things to mortals from the beginning; but rather, seeking in the course of time, they discover what is better."

Turning to Plato, Nisbet points out that in the dialogues *The Laws*, *The Statesman*, and *Protagoras*, the first two written after *The Republic*, Plato presents the idea that there has been a progressive development of human civilization through history, involving advances in technology, knowledge, culture, and government. Hence, although Plato in *The Republic* presents a timeless, perfect vision of an ideal society, especially in his later writings, he presents a progressive vision of the ongoing improvement of human society across time.

Nisbet proposes that the key idea to be found in ancient Greek philosophical thought is *growth* and *development*, to be found in their cosmologies, histories, theories of life, and visions of humankind. Of special note, among the ancient Greek philosophers, the one thinker who is most strongly associated with the developmental vision of nature is Aristotle.

Aristotle, who was Plato's greatest student, downplayed the transcendent and dualistic. Aristotle was the great naturalistic Greek philosopher and the founding father of empiricist epistemology (knowledge is to be gained through perceptual observation and thinking based on observation). Aristotle saw both "form" and "matter" and the psychological and physical united in observable reality. (For Aristotle, the "psyche" or "soul" is the form of the body.) Aristotle, although anticipated by the pre-Socratic naturalist philosophers, can be seen as the most influential inspirational starting point for the rise of empirical and naturalistic science, and hence in resonance with the modern spirit of scientific thought and science fiction. Aristotle created an extensive zoological classification system and theory of the nature of life. Theophrastus (371-287 BCE), Aristotle's student and philosophical successor, created a complementary botanical classification system and is often referred to as "the father of botany," as Aristotle is referred to as "the father of zoology." All in all, Aristotle and his students were enthralled with the study of nature.

Aristotle was a "developmentalist" in his dynamic theory of reality, where "form" was the functional activity of a thing, and natural entities were teleologically driven toward self-actualization (or self-realization) of their forms. Form is dynamic. What something is, is what it does, and what it does is to develop toward self-actualization. (Randall, 1960; Lombardo, 1987, 2006a, Chapter 3).

One philosophical figure who influenced both Aristotle and Plato, and is most closely associated with a philosophy of change, is Heraclitus (535-475 BCE). Heraclitus is remembered for his central emphasis on the ubiquity of change in the world. According to Heraclitus, "You can't step into the same river twice"—not only because the river perpetually flows and transforms, but also because you are not the same person stepping into it the second time. For Heraclitus, all is change. "The only thing that stays the same is that nothing stays the same." Also, presumably from Heraclitus, "The father of all things is war" (conflict is the source of creation) and fire is the underlying "substance" of nature.

As historians of science fiction such as Clute (1995) and Gunn (1975) have argued, modern science fiction was born in the realization that the future could be different from the past—that change was a very real and essential fact within the world and within human existence. Following upon the dynamic philosophies of Heraclitus and Aristotle, and anticipating the presumed modern insight of potential change for humanity in the future, the philosophical line of thinkers from Democritus (460-370 BCE) and Leucippus (fifth century BCE), to the Roman writer Lucretius (99-55 BCE) clearly brought together the themes of change, historical progress, and even evolution in their theories of reality, long before the modern Western Enlightenment vision of secular progress.

Democritus, the creator of the theory of atoms, believed that all complex realities within the world had arisen out of the ongoing concatenation of physical atoms. Democritus was a naturalist and a thoroughgoing materialist. In his vision there is a general movement in time within the physical world from the simple to the complex. In this sense, there is a progressive direction to time within the physical world.

Lucretius, adopting this progressive theory of change, created an exceedingly prescient and "scientific" vision of reality. Although written in poetic form, his *On the Nature of Things* proposed that existence is evolutionary and human civilization is progressive (moving from the simple and primitive to the complex and more civilized). He also strongly argued that naturalistic explanations are sufficient to account for everything. Indeed, he rejected supernatural and deistic speculations as empirically groundless and superstitious; according to him, "Fear created the first gods in the world" (Lombardo, 2006a, Chapter 3).

Lucretius describes the cosmos as beginning in chance, with physical forms coming together through collision and "conformation of atoms" (the order emerging out of chaos theme), which eventually brings forth life. For Lucretius, different living forms arose in the primitive beginnings of nature; some survived and some became extinct, depending on their capacity to secure food and protect themselves. Those forms that survived reproduced and passed on their traits to their offspring, a process that sounds similar to Darwin's notion of natural selection. When Lucretius comes to the development of humanity, he describes early humans as existing in a hunter-gatherer state without clothes, weapons, fire, huts, or communities, generally not possessing any social constraints on their behavior. Slowly, through ingenuity and natural intelligence, humans developed all the different aspects of organized society, technology, and the crafts. For Lucretius, progress did not derive from the gods; it is a creation of humanity. Lucretius' history is speculative, but it is striking how close it comes to the modern scientific view of the evolution of humanity as we understand it today.

In the tradition of the Greek naturalist philosophers, Lucretius saw change as due to natural rather than supernatural forces or the will of the gods. What Lucretius adds to this naturalist viewpoint is that *progressive* change in history is also due to inherent forces and principles in physical nature. In fact, he turns the question of the relationship of God, nature, and humanity on its head. Instead of gods having created the world and humankind, the physical world is the origin of humankind, and it is humanity that, in fear of nature and attempting to comprehend the causes of things, invents gods as an explanation. Thus, in Lucretius we see the psychological emancipation and triumph of the Greek ideal that humans have been, and can be even more so in the future, the masters of their own fate. The gods are jettisoned as an explanation of human existence and human civilization. Moreover, we see the Greek ideal of self-determination applied both to the past and to the potential future.

If two key stimuli for the emergence of modern science fiction were the belief in the future progress of humankind and the theory of evolution as a scientific explanation of natural change— Wells for one embraced both of these ideas—then Lucretius articulates the Western beginnings of both these ideas. Further, if science fiction attempted to embrace (to whatever degree it is successful and consistent in this endeavor) a scientific vision of reality (as opposed to otherworldly, supernatural personified deities pulling the strings), then Lucretius is an early important spokesperson of this naturalistic vision of reality. And, in adopting a naturalistic perspective on change, which includes the actions and efforts of humans, Lucretius also anticipates the philosophy of self-determination central to the Western Enlightenment philosophy of progress, a key idea, with its risks, as well as hopes, in the emergence of modern science fiction. Again we find this idea also in Wells.

The ideas of naturalistic progress and self-determination espoused in Lucretius lead us back to Homer's mythic narrative epics. Although the *Iliad* and the *Odyssey* brim with gods and goddesses who attempt to orchestrate human affairs, as argued earlier, the saga of Odysseus attempting to return to his beloved wife Penelope, and suffering various challenges along the way (frequently a consequence of actions taken by the gods), also embodies the emerging Greek ideal of self-determination in the face of the gods and the forces of fate and chance. Are we the masters of our own fate? Or are we helpless pawns amidst more powerful forces, which include supernatural beings attempting to control our lives? Who or what determines our future (Polak, 1973; Watson, 2005)?

Often our efforts toward self-determination may fail and lead to tragedy (a basic dramatic theme in science fiction, as well as ancient Greek literature). But with the ancient Greeks there emerged the modernist ideal that our future and our fate was in our hands, however flawed we were as creators of our own destiny (Lombardo, 2006a). The Greeks are the Western source of the democratic ideal, of governance through self-determination rather than authoritarian rule (whether by gods or kings). Given the struggles encountered and human failings revealed, Greek literature presents both heroic and tragic themes, often combined; we confront the gods and the forces of the world, often failing in our efforts, but at least we have attempted to personally realize our goals and control our lives.

As Lucretius rejected the supernatural as an explanation for the nature of the world, Odysseus opposes the supernatural as the determining factor behind the control of his life. The futurist Frederik Polak (1973) contends that with Odysseus we find the beginnings of the Greek idea that through self-determination and human effort, an improved or better future can be achieved.

As a general developmental psychological process in humans, children exhibit opposition to and a desire for emancipation from both the dictates and the support of their parents. Leaving the comfort and protective security of the parents opens the door to the possibility of self-accomplishment, but also personal risk and failure. It is noteworthy that within Greek mythology the archetypal act of the child rebelling against the parent is central to the mythic explanation of the rise of the Olympian gods. As children of the Titans, the Olympians overthrow their progenitors and banish them to the heavens above—perhaps to be revered, but definitely to be removed and prevented from interfering with the ongoing saga of life.

In review: Modern science fiction was born within the context of the Enlightenment theory of secular progress. The future could be very different than the present and the cause behind this transformation through time, as the Enlightenment philosophers envisioned it, would be humans applying principles of science and reason for the betterment of humankind. The concept of secular progress was built upon the dual principles of self-determination and a scientific/naturalistic foundation of knowledge that would inform and empower humanity's progressive transformation of the world. When modern science fiction emerged in the nineteenth century, it looked toward the future as an arena of great potential changes fueled by human efforts to use science and reason to improve the world, expressing both hope and fear regarding where it would all go.

As the historical origins of this modern way of thinking, the rational and naturalistic outlook, the philosophy of self-determination, and the ideas of natural change, and even progress and evolution, all can be found within ancient Greek thinking. We could even suggest that the dramatic opposition between humans and parental-figure gods in Greek myth and literature is a metaphorical symbol—a psychological expression—of the philosophical idea that the gods are not necessary to understand or explain the universe and humans (without divine revelation or guidance from above) can figure it all out.

* * *

It is possible that the overthrow and transcendence of a particular way of thinking and living—a mode of consciousness—can be envisioned within that very mindset.

As introduced earlier, within Greek mythology one of the most well-known stories concerns Prometheus, one of the Titans, who steals the secret of fire (symbolic of power, self-determination, and human civilization) from the gods and brings it to earth, giving the secret to humans. As described by Hesiod, Zeus, enraged by this action, punishes Prometheus by chaining him to a rock, where a giant bird pecks and eats away at his internal organs (in particular his liver).

Notably, the name Prometheus means "forethought" or "foresight." Prometheus is the "god" of or for the future. In a very powerful and dramatic sense, the ancient Greeks created a god-like personification (a psychological projection) of the capacity of future consciousness, in particular to anticipate and direct the future. And moreover, this personification and what it represented was seen as the source of Greek civilization. Prometheus is often described as the creator and great benefactor of humanity.

As described in Hesiod and other ancient Greek writings, Prometheus stole the secret of fire from Hephaestus, the Greek god of technology. In enacting punishment upon humans (for Prometheus' gift of fire to humans) Zeus ordered Hephaestus to create Pandora, the first human woman, out of mud and clay. Pandora is brought to earth with a jar (later referred to as "Pandora's Box") containing all the woes and miseries of human life, and out of foolish curiosity, once on earth, she opens the jar, and in an act of divine retribution, releases innumerable dark forces on humankind. Through power over fire, we may have taken a big step forward, but we will have to pay for it, and life from now on won't be so easy. The story of Prometheus and Pandora is a story of the end of childlike innocence for humanity.

Perhaps it is better to stay children, innocent and incompetent. As implied in this tale, in gaining the power of self-determination, and perhaps becoming equal to the gods (our archetypal parents), we incur a great cost. Yet, the icon of Prometheus, expressing the promise of emancipation from the gods, has been an influential and inspirational archetypal idea throughout human history. There is a risk in personal power and freedom, but perhaps it is worth it.

One of the key starting points of Greek tragedy can be found in Aeschylus' plays on Prometheus. "Prometheus Bound", and the lost versions of "Prometheus Unbound" and "Prometheus the Fire Bringer", provide a dramatic telling of Prometheus stealing fire and his punishment by Zeus, but in the second play, Prometheus is freed from his chains and torture by Heracles. Within Aeschylus' stories, Prometheus emerges as a heroic figure, opposing Zeus, suffering for it, but then realizing freedom in the end.

Aeschylus sees Prometheus not only bringing the gift of fire to humanity, but as the great benefactor, giving humanity all the arts of civilization, including writing, science, and medicine. For example, within Aeschylus's narration, Prometheus states: "But harken to the miseries that afflicted mankind—how they were witless and I made them to have sense and be endowed with reason..."

Nisbet argues that faith in future progress through human effort and creativity—what I would identify as key features of future consciousness—can be found in Aeschylus' plays. Nisbet, quoting the historian W. K. C. Guthrie,

How hard it is to enter fully into the minds of men to whom personification comes so naturally as it did the Greeks! If the spirit of Forethought—Prometheus—is not a living, divine person, suffering the torments of having defied the tyranny of Zeus, the whole tragedy has no importance. Yet I find it difficult to believe that in writing this speech Aeschylus had not thought of the meaning of the word, no consciousness that he was really describing a technical revolution brought about historically by human ingenuity alone.

Hence, Greek myth, with its personified narratives and godly beings orchestrating human affairs, contains a story and symbolic character expressing the aspiration to break free of this way of thinking and living. And this mythic narrative of Prometheus, embodying various archetypal themes, is one of the key defining core narratives within the history of science fiction: Humanity aspiring toward and realizing (or perhaps being given) greater knowledge, power, and self-determination (to become like gods) opens the door to both great risk and great opportunity, including disaster, self-annihilation, yet also possibly transcendence. Mary Shelley's *Frankenstein* is, as she described it, the "modern Prometheus," but Shelley's *Frankenstein* is anti-Promethean (we fail) and only one among many modern versions and variations on Prometheus in science fiction. Sometimes these Promethean tales are dark and tragic, as with *Frankenstein*, and sometimes the stories are uplifting, hopeful, and positive.

Also of note in this early Greek myth, the secret of fire, promising increased human power and control over life, is stolen from the god of technology. Is it through technology that we will become equal to the gods? This belief captures one core contention of the modern European Enlightenment, as well as resonating with more contemporary messages within our techno-enthused modern world, for example as expressed in both futurist technological speculation (Kurzweil, 1999, 2005; Diamandis and Kotler, 2012) and high-tech science fiction, such as in Greg Egan's *Diaspora* (1997) and Ian McDonald's *River of Gods* (2004).

Yet perhaps we need something more than technological power to realize a "god-like" or human-transcendent state, such as wisdom or mental evolution? Clearly, the Enlightenment philosophers also believed in the critical importance of the evolution of the mind and wisdom in realizing progress. This view is a frequent and counter-balancing theme in modern science fiction; as critical to human self-empowerment, mind needs to evolve as well as technology. Panshin and Panshin (1989) bring up this point in describing the limitations of the techno-inspired science fiction of the *Golden Age* (1938-1950). This alternative vision of human empowerment aligns with the Greek ideal, as epitomized in Plato and Aristotle, that humankind needs to develop its mental capacities and its wisdom and character virtues in order to realize the good life, if not the good future. As Wells stated, "History (or civilization) becomes more and more a race between catastrophe and education," and the education he is speaking of is the principled development of the human mind.

Lucian's *True History*

> *I'm writing about things I have neither seen nor experienced nor heard tell of from anybody else; things, what is more, that do not in fact exist and could not ever exist at all. So my readers must not believe a word I say.*
> Lucian *True History*

Histories of science fiction often begin with the Roman writer Lucian of Samosata (modern Turkey) (c. 125-180 CE) and his famous fictional work *True History* or *True Story* (Gunn, 1977). The above quote is from the opening of this multifaceted tale which includes, among its numerous extraordinary adventures, journeys to strange lands ("rivers of wine"), encounters with bizarre creatures ("vine women" with roots implanted in the ground), and a story of interplanetary flight and war between humans and aliens in outer space. The title is paradoxical, if not comical, since Lucian states right at the beginning of the tale that everything depicted within the story is fictitious and realistically impossible.

Lucian's *True History* is the most famous of ancient tales in ancient Greek and Roman literature describing travels to the moon, sun, and other celestial regions (Roberts, 2005). As such, the story is part of the "extraordinary voyages" tradition expressive of the deep human desire for adventure and exploration. As with other ancient stories of far adventures, Lucian's story introduces the reader to fantastical settings and beings—in this case "outer space" and other-worldly aliens.

Ironically, Lucian's stated purpose in *True History* was to satirize and critique the fantastical tales of other writers, such as Diogenes, Homer, and Herodotus. According to Lucian, these writers appeared to believe (or pretended to believe) in the bizarre realities and characters described in their stories. In Lucian's mind such "tall tales" filled with "tomfoolery" could not possibly be true, but since numerous other writers were concocting such ludicrous flights of fantasy, Lucian saw no reason why he shouldn't invent an outrageous story as well—even, perhaps, outdoing other such tales in imaginative scope and blatant ridiculousness, gaining even greater literary notoriety. But he would not pretend, as he accused other writers of doing, that his stories were true.

The reasoning behind Lucian's judgment that the fantastical tales of other writers could not conceivably be true derived from his theory of reality. Embracing, to a degree, the modern scientific spirit, Lucian was both knowledgeable and highly sympathetic with the Greek philosopher Epicurus (341-270 BCE), a famous advocate of the naturalistic, materialistic, and anti-supernaturalism of Democritus. Lucian's critique of the credibility of other fantastical tales appears based upon a naturalist perspective of reality derived from the ancient Greeks—gods, personified celestial beings, bizarre monsters, and magical lands could not possibly exist within a naturalistic, fact-based framework. Influenced by the naturalistic philosophy of Democritus, Lucretius, and Epicurus, Lucian argued for the philosophical emancipation and superiority of naturalistic thought over supernatural and magical ways of thinking.

Paradoxically, given his disclaimer and philosophical starting point, Lucian invented a tale that in several regards began to map out the future territory of both science fiction and scientific imagination. In Lucian's *True History* a group of voyagers in a sailing ship on the open sea are pulled upward into a great storm and propelled all the way to the surface of the moon (a naturalistic explanation for space flight). On the moon they encounter lunar inhabitants different, in both physiology and habits of behavior, from earthly humans. There are only males, who have artificial penises of wood or ivory, a fur-lined pouch in their bellies, and give birth to offspring out of their calves. As the story unfolds various other alien life forms from numerous different worlds or astral regions (the Big Dipper, Sirius, and the Milky Way) come on the scene. These beings, some of them amalgamations of animals and vegetables, are both strange and, in some cases, gigantic.

The plot involves an interplanetary war that emerges between beings of the moon and beings of the sun, along with various alien allies, over the conquest and colonization of the "morning star" (Venus). The battle takes place on a colossal scale (Lucian frequently used exaggeration and gigantism in his fantastical imagery) involving millions of combatants with various inventive types of weaponry and defense (for example, weapons consisting of mushrooms and asparagus). The beings of the sun eventually prevail, a peace is negotiated, and Venus is settled with inhabitants from both the moon and the sun.

The fantastic imagery in Lucian's tale is a blending of outlandish naturalistic speculation and mythic and theological themes from ancient Greek thought. There are tree men who give birth through acorns, giant fleas and ants, and centaur warriors (half man/half horse) who fly through outer space. His technical imagination is no less impressive. We find an apparatus that functions like a telescope, detachable eyeballs, clothing made of flexible glass, and spider creatures that spin giant networked walking surfaces through space.

It is ironic and provocative, given the intentional craziness of his literary creations and his opening statement that his tale could not possibly be true, that these speculations actually align with many later ideas put forth in naturalistic extrapolative science fiction and modern scientific-technological thinking; for example, aliens and alien worlds; military and transportation space technologies; astronomical equipment; and interplanetary war and colonization. In letting his "imagination run wild" (a phrase that "Doc" Smith would use 2000 years later), Lucian envisioned a variety of totally implausible realities for his time that in more modern forms would come to be seen as plausible possibilities within a scientific mindset.

Although, Lucian was not the only one of his time to write of journeys into the heavens, we can identify him as a critical starting point for several fundamental narrative themes within the history of science fiction: space travel; exploration of other worlds; aliens; communication with aliens; and interplanetary war, with battles among aerial aliens zooming about through outer space.

Lucian's understanding of the vast and complex nature of the heavens was certainly limited. His saga only encompasses three highly visible objects in the sky—the sun, the moon, and Venus. Although there are other participants who come from more distant realms, he did not venture farther out in his imaginative tale. Still, Lucian provides an illustrative example, of how science fiction outer space adventures can be seen as a natural outgrowth and expression of the "extraordinary voyages" tradition, while aliens in space trace their heritage to the fantastical beings encountered on such voyages.

As noted, centuries prior to Lucian, human imagination frequently extended into the heavens populating them with all kinds of personified beings. Within diverse ancient cultures (Babylonian, Egyptian, Hindu, and Chinese) observable constellations were seen as the heavenly embodiments of various mythic and godly personalities and creatures (Orion, Taurus, Leo, and the Pleiades or Seven Sisters, as notable examples); the sun, the moon, and visible planets were also seen as manifestations of personified gods or spirits: The sun was the god Ra (Egyptian), or the chariot of Apollo (Greek) journeying across the sky; Mars or Ares was the god of war; and the planet Saturn was Cronos, the ruler of the Titans and the father of Zeus. But all told, while the heavenly bodies were personified, they were not seen as worlds on which there existed beings with personhood.

Contrary to the argument above that Lucian embraced a theory of reality consistent with the Greek naturalistic philosophers, Roberts argues that Lucian, as revealed in other imaginative tales, was actually more sympathetic with the personified mythic vision of reality and the heavens. For example, in another of his space travel stories (*Ikaromenippos*), Lucian personifies the moon as a goddess who watches over the earth lamenting the way "philosophers" have abused and degraded her personhood— naturalistic thought taking the magic out of her being and identity.

What can be granted on this point is that Lucian, in line with other ancient writers and thinkers, combines both the mythic-personified-supernatural and the scientific-naturalistic in his writings. As Roberts notes there is a great deal of naturalistic extrapolation within *True History*, and as I argued above, Lucian's criticism and parody on the fantastical tales of previous writers appeared to be based on the naturalistic philosophy that arose out of Democritus and his followers. As introduced earlier, science fiction throughout its history frequently mixes together the scientific with the mythic and scientifically implausible. In Lucian's *True History*, the heavenly bodies become other worlds, but he then repopulates the heavens with various imaginative aliens, which are suggestive of the fantastic beings of personified mythology.

Although Roberts (2005) argues that Lucian has no real conception of "outer space" in his saga, and his adventurous travelers are really just journeying into the visible and not very distant abode of the "sky," what is noteworthy in Lucian is that in his *True History* instead of "objects in the sky" being manifestations of personified beings—at least for the sun, moon, and Venus—the objects were seen as "other worlds." This is a fundamental theme in the history of science fiction that emerged out of modern astronomy: There are other worlds in the universe beyond the earth to be explored, and these other worlds may contain inhabitants and alternative civilizations much different from those of earth. Within modern science fiction outer space stories, we stand back from ourselves, our culture, and our world and contemplate other types of minds, cultures, and worlds. To some degree, Lucian achieved this modern perspective in *True History*.

Roberts contends that if Greek philosophy and natural science had maintained a dominant and central position in the West after the fall of the Roman Empire, modern science fiction might have arisen much sooner in Western civilization. Although in the years after the fall of Rome, the emerging Islamic Empire attempted to synthesize the scientific spirit—the rational and empirical—with religious thinking—the mythic and mystical— European culture and philosophy came under the pervasive control of Christian religion and theology in the Middle Ages. Dualistic in its Platonic metaphysical framework, Christianity focused on ethics, spiritual salvation, and the afterlife, with visions of heavenly reward and hellish damnation thrown in. The scientific spirit—naturalistic, empirical, and rationalistic— slumbered in the West for one thousand years. It was only with the rediscovery of the ancient Greeks in the later Middle Ages, facilitated through contact with the writings of Islamic scientists and philosophers, and the opening up of a new age of discovery and exploration, that the pathway toward modern science fiction was reignited in the West. And yet, the European Middle Ages is not without relevance to the historical evolution of science fiction.

The Fantastical and Futuristic

The education of the human race, represented by the people of God, has advanced, like that of an individual, through certain epochs or, as it were, ages, so that it might gradually rise from earthly to heavenly things, and from the visible to the invisible.

And by this universal conflagration, the qualities of the corruptible elements which suited our corruptible bodies shall utterly perish, and our substance shall receive such qualities as shall, by a wonderful transmutation, harmonize with our immortal bodies so that, as the world itself is renewed to some better thing, it is fitly accommodated to men, themselves renewed in their flesh to some better thing.
St. Augustine

In my book *The Evolution of Future Consciousness* (Lombardo, 2006a) I argue that it is totally wrongheaded to think that humans, prior to the beginnings of the modern era (circa the eighteenth century), had no sense of the future. Future consciousness, understood as a holistic psychological and social phenomenon involving thinking, imagination, purpose, goal setting, planning, emotion, and a developmental sense of self, evolved within humans across an extended period of time that stretches back millions of years into the past.

The evolution of future consciousness drove the evolution of human civilization: tool making and technology; bonding and partnerships; collaborative hunting and trade; agriculture and urbanization; religious rites, ethics, and law; and even war and conflict, are all expressions of the capacities of future consciousness. It is the significant amplification of temporal consciousness in humans—of both memory and anticipation—that more than anything else gives us our distinctive and more advanced capacities relative to the rest of the animal kingdom. This is not to deny that animals do not have some level of memory and foresight; it is simply not anywhere near as developed as in humans (Lombardo, 2006a, 2017). Moreover, this argument does not imply that there wasn't a good deal of "accidental" or unintentional evolution and progress going on as well in the history of humanity, but thoughtful, memory-informed (learning and culture), purposeful consciousness and behavior distinguished and elevated humanity, creating the unique and complex reality of human civilization.

As I proposed in the opening chapters, science fiction is an evolutionary expression of holistic future consciousness. Before we further explore how medieval future-oriented narratives, visions, and myths are historical tributaries, in content and philosophy, feeding into the development of modern science fiction, let's review the development of the concept of time in ancient times.

Even if we acknowledge that the cyclic theory was the most influential and pervasive mindset in the ancient world regarding the nature of time (Franz, 1978), it is not true that the ancients did not understand or express the alternative vision of time—the linear or transformative vision—where the future is seen as more than just a repetition of the past. First with Hesiod and Heraclitus, and then later with Democritus and Lucretius, we see the emergence of the idea that reality involves change and that change is directional rather than simply cyclic and repetitious (Nisbet, 1994). The origins of the progressive and evolutionary visions of time, critical to the emergence of science fiction, can be found within human history thousands of years ago. Further, the progressive vision of time (and the future) repeatedly shows up in the Middle Ages.

To set the stage and expand further the argument that the ancients understood linear and progressive time, let's consider the pivotal significance of the Persian figure of Zoroaster (660-583 BCE), one of the most important thinkers of the Axial Age. The teachings and influence of Zoroaster provide a critical connecting link between ancient philosophy and religion and visions of the future in the Middle Ages. Zoroaster believed that human history involved an ongoing conflict between the cosmic forces of good and evil—personified in the supreme god *Ahura Mazda* ("Wise Lord") and *Angra Mainyu* ("the Bad Spirit"). This conflict would eventually lead to the coming of a Messiah who would lead the forces of good against the forces of evil in a great final battle, "Armageddon," resulting in the defeat of evil, and the "Apocalypse," where the ultimate truth of things is revealed. Those humans who follow the forces of good will be rewarded with eternal life in heaven; those who side with evil will be punished eternally in hell (Noss, 1999).

This vision of time—of the saga of human and cosmic history—is decidedly linear and progressive and future directional. History moves along a path of war and conflict that leads to a positive and progressive ending in the future—the defeat of cosmic evil and the reward of eternal life. The vision is also dualistic, both ethically and ontologically: There are two opposing moral forces, good and evil, and it is the spiritual or immaterial souls of humans (rather than their physical bodies) that are "transported" to either Heaven or Hell after the final battle. It is also teleological and mythic, in that the coming of the Messiah and the eventual triumph of good over evil at the end of time is foreordained and orchestrated by the supreme god of good. It is a progressive narrative where the upward flow of time, and indeed the "plot," moves in a positive direction, and this plot is guided by personified cosmic forces (Lombardo,

2006a, Chapter 3).

Zoroaster's visionary narrative of a progressive future is highly resonant with the mindsets of many people in our contemporary world. In all probability the Jewish, Christian, and Islamic visions of the future, which contain many of the same elements and themes, derive from Zoroaster's philosophical and religious influence in the ancient Middle East, particularly around what was then the ancient empire of Babylon. The futurist mindset of Christian and Islamic thinking in the Middle Ages developed out of Zoroaster's cosmic narrative of human history and the future. Some version, derivative from Zoroaster's narrative myth, was the story of the future taught by medieval Christian theologians and priests and accepted by the "common folk" throughout the European Middle Ages; it is the archetypal tale informing modern Christian-Islamic visions of the future.

Expressed within Zoroaster's cosmic saga we find a narrative of the future that even within secular thinking has been highly influential. The Zoroastrian story of the future is progressive and involves a fundamental conflict of good versus evil that is eventually resolved with the triumph of good over evil. There is a great battle and conflagration to come (chaos within the world), but out of this colossal and violent struggle will emerge some higher level of human existence. Modern science fiction tales are filled with stories involving versions of Armageddon, the Apocalypse, and transcendence out of the worldwide conflagration. Innumerable modern science fiction stories embody various elements of Zoroaster's cosmic vision even to the point of including godlike aliens (our Messiah) who will guide or help us in the defeat of some powerful sinister force within the universe. This is the fundamental plot line in "Doc" Smith's *Lensmen* series. And many of Wells' stories of future utopias involve as a necessary prelude a highly destructive worldwide war (an Armageddon) that wipes out the old to make room for the new.

In *Origins of Futuristic Fiction* (1987), Paul Alkon asserts that in pre-modern times there were no real narratives of the future, either predictive or fictional, but rather prophetic visions that focused on the end of times (end of the world scenarios) without saying much about what led up to the final cataclysm or containing anything like a story set in the future. However, the Zoroastrian vision providing a foundation for Christian thinking about the future, did contain an archetypal narrative for the fundamental drama of human life (the battle of good and evil), as well as a vision of how the world, as we know it, would come to an end and what would follow afterwards in the future. As pointed out above, this general narrative—involving a cataclysmic battle of good versus evil, a Messiah, and victory and reward—would provide a basic skeleton for numerous more specific tales of the future, as variations on a general theme. We see this general narrative plot—of dramatic tension, cosmic conflict, and transcendent resolution—in both modern and in medieval times. Even if we admit that this archetypal narrative was not a detailed and personalized story of either moving toward the future or the "shape of things to come," it provided a general narrative framework for innumerable subsequent stories, with characters and more specific plots, dealing with the future.

There are clear features of the Zoroastrian vision of the future expressed in the Book of Revelation in the New Testament, the final book in the Christian Bible. Probably written toward the end of the first century CE, due to its controversial and bizarre content it was not officially accepted into the New Testament until centuries later. Mystic, prophetic, apocalyptic, and richly visionary in its strange and fantastical imagery, the central plot in Revelation is the war of good and evil and of God versus Satan, culminating in a great battle and "Last Judgment," and the subsequent establishment of a new and better world (the "New Jerusalem") ruled by Christ after his "Second Coming," which will presumably last one thousand years.

One noteworthy feature of Revelation is its fantastical imagery, of hideous and terrifying beings and incredible catastrophic events: a seven-headed dragon; hail and fire raining down from the heavens; the seas turning to blood; a seven-headed leopard-like beast from the sea; the sun scorching the earth; angels galore; the Four Horsemen of the Apocalypse; earthquakes, lightning and thunder, lakes of fire, and burning sulfur; and the death and destruction of the metaphorical "Whore of Babylon." The intensity of the narrative provokes fear, terror, and an agitated, foreboding about the future. (We could suggest that the intense imagery is a psychological projection of deep and powerful fear over the uncertainty of the future.)

The various bizarre and obscure beings have been variously interpreted over the centuries; the saga seems to strike archetypal chords within the human psyche that are strongly unsettling and yet possess a magnetic draw. From a modernist secular point of view, the whole narrative reads like a psychedelic nightmare or a psychotic hallucination. The Book of Revelation, which came to dominate Christian thinking on the future during the Middle Ages, epitomizes both the fantastical imagery earlier humanity could conjure as well as the emotional charge that could be generated in such narratives about the future. In Revelation, the fantastical, the catastrophic, the terrifying, and the futuristic are synthesized.

People in the modern Western world are much more familiar with the Book of Revelation and its prophecy of Armageddon and the Last Judgment than Zoroaster's earlier visions of similar events. Indeed, many people in modern times still believe in at least the metaphorical, if not literal, truth of the Christian version of this futurist narrative. Yet, regardless of whether we see this tale as Persian or Judeo-Christian, as a metaphorical or literal truth, or as possessing any kind of truth or value at all, I suggest that this story is a fundamental mythic narrative, highly influential and in some manner or form seen as credible, in the modern Western mind and specifically in visions of the future, both religious and secular.

There are many archetypal themes within it: of chaos and renewed order; of condemnation and redemption; of sin and evil and a Savior; and of a great cleansing of the human spirit. How deeply this archetypal myth penetrates into the mindset of Western humanity is perhaps open to debate, but it keeps resurfacing in the tales we tell about the future. In fact, the story (the myth) is so powerful and recurrent in human imagination that we should consider whether it even propels our own behavior and thinking as a self-fulfilling prophecy. Although modern science fiction and the secular mind may have (to a degree) transcended ancient mythic and religious theories of reality, this narrative has informed and influenced numerous science fiction stories, as well as other futurist visions, in contemporary times. We keep telling stories (or predicting scenarios) involving a great battle that will lead, after great destruction, to a new and better world. We keep waiting for a messiah, of some sort, who will lead us through the battle to the better world. Our minds and our behavior seem to gravitate in this imagined direction.

* * *

At the beginning of the European Middle Ages we find a key figure—writer, philosopher, and confessor—who, adopting a Zoroastrian narrative of the future embraced a linear and progressive vision of time and added further thematic elements to this futurist perspective. This figure is St. Augustine (354-430 CE), who, according to Karen Armstrong (1994), is the most influential architect of Christian doctrine after Paul the Apostle. St. Augustine is also a central influential figure in the evolution of the utopian narrative—after Plato—one of the important tributaries of thought that would feed into the evolution of science fiction.

Modeling his narrative vision of the history and future of humanity on his understanding of the developmental stages in the life of individual humans, in *City of God*, St. Augustine saw humankind as progressing through a series of steps, from the most primitive and infantile—and equally most corrupt and imperfect after the biblical "Fall of Man,"—toward higher and higher levels of maturity, godliness, and perfection. This developmental process would culminate in a "transmutation" of the flesh and renewal in more perfect human bodies, coinciding with a millennial-long utopian paradise after Armageddon and the Second Coming of Christ.

St. Augustine saw the ongoing historical conflict of good and evil reflective of two distinctive and opposing ways of human life, which he represented in his dual model of a "City of Man" (the evil way of life) and a "City of God" (the good way of life). Augustine believed that within his own time most of humankind lived in the "City of Man." But with the anticipated thousand-year reign of Christ after the Second Coming, the earth itself would be renewed and all godly persons would live in peace, harmony, and love of God in the "City of God." Although still possessing physical bodies—now perfected—humanity would have ascended to a level in which spiritual and godly concerns ("the invisible") take precedence over more bodily ("the visible") interests. On this last point, clearly dualistic, he aligns himself with Plato, elevating the mental/spiritual above the physical. Of particular note, St. Augustine identified physical lust (sexuality) as a key feature of the more lowly physical concerns of humans. After the thousand-year paradise on earth, human souls in the utopian "City of God" would become disembodied and ascend into eternal life in heaven. For Augustine, this whole saga, teleological in its plot and dynamics, was being orchestrated by God (Nisbet, 1994; Lombardo, 2006a).

Such an incredible, metaphysical vision of the future! There is no question that St. Augustine firmly believed in the linear directionality of time and that he saw this temporal direction (this transformation) as progressive. Of course, his concept of progress was founded on his Christian theory of reality and ethics, being God-centered and dualistic, with progress the result of transcendent forces rather than human efforts. But St. Augustine definitely saw the future as promising something both very different and much better than the present. Our modern Western secular concept of progress would directly evolve out of St. Augustine's Christian-inspired vision of the directionality of time (Lombardo, 2006a).

Between St. Augustine and modernity (c. 1500 CE), Christians devoutly believed in both the imminent Second Coming of Christ and the promise of the paradisiacal Millennium to follow. This narrative and psychologically holistic mindset (of anticipation, hope, joy, good work, and personal salvation) provided the cosmic framework and motivational energy of human future consciousness throughout Europe during the Middle Ages. Moreover, following from the prophecies of the Book of Revelation and derivative sources, people anticipated the great battle of Armageddon and the "end of the world" with great trepidation.

As with Zoroaster before him, we can identify significant narrative themes in St. Augustine's "mythic" vision of the future that contributed into the evolution of science fiction. For one thing, the future promises an ongoing perfection and elevation of the human character and mind. Second, the future promises some kind of transformation ("transmutation") of our bodies toward something better. Third, St. Augustine locates a social utopia — an ideal human society — in the future. Fourth, he sees us moving beyond our animal and biological nature into something higher and more ethereal. Finally, there is a cosmic dimension to the whole narrative: Cosmic forces are moving us forward; we are participants within a cosmic saga; and we will eventually realize greater cosmic understanding and a more cosmic level of existence in the future. All these elements of the narrative pointed toward a credible and plausible transcendence of the now being realized in the future. There is no doubt that in *City of God* Augustine provides a personally inspiring, cosmically informed fantastical vision.

All of these narrative themes are informed by St. Augustine's Christian-Platonic mindset and theory of reality, but nevertheless we find similar themes and stories set within secular and scientific mindsets in modern science fiction. Through science, technology, and secular thinking we will improve and perfect our bodies and minds; we will create a better form of society; we will perhaps evolve into beings of pure energy transcending our bodies of physical matter; and through advanced scientific understanding and the exploration of space, we will gain cosmic awareness and become beings of the cosmos. We can reasonably argue that modernists (post Middle Ages) took from the Greeks the philosophy of self-determination and, combining it with secular and scientific thinking, envisioned how humans could elevate themselves through their own efforts and advanced understanding in ways very similar to the visions and ideals of St. Augustine. Moreover, as for example with Wells, modernist secular and science fiction narratives of progress often envision some great war that must be passed through in order to realize all of our higher dreams.

It should be highlighted that St. Augustine's utopian vision posited an ideal human society situated in the future and as a result of progressive forces operating through human history. Although these forces have a supernatural origin, what is happening in the temporal and observable world is a notable movement forward, in stages, toward higher social, psychological, ethical, and spiritual levels. It has been argued, for example, in Clute (1995) and other historians of science fiction, that early utopias were neither envisioned as existing in the future nor viewed as a consequence of ongoing progressive forces. Such arguments are clearly not valid regarding St. Augustine's utopian vision. Indeed, for all those later Christian thinkers who embraced St. Augustine's vision of the earthly paradisiacal *Millennium* (a powerful and diverse social wave of thinking up through modern times), there was a strong sense that, through the positive and benevolent forces of Providence, the future would bring about some higher and more ideal state of human existence and society. As Nisbet (1994) points out, from the time of St. Augustine up to the beginnings of modernity with the Scientific Revolution (circa the sixteenth and seventeenth centuries), there were various philosophical and theological expressions of the concept of progress, involving the belief that human society had progressed through the past and was continuing to progress, eventually leading to some kind of ideal society in the future.

As noted, one of the main historical tributaries of science fiction is utopian thinking. Utopian thinking is social, psychological, and ethical speculation on a better or more ideal human reality. Although it may include such factors, utopian visions do not have to contain advanced technologies. *The Republic*, for example, exclusively focuses on psychological, social, and philosophical ideals, to the exclusion of anything technological. But beginning with St. Augustine, utopian thinking gets wedded with futurist thinking, where the envisioned ideal society exists in the future. This fundamental narrative connection of utopia and the future would be explored in great depth in modern science fiction; it would also be explored in equal depth within modern nonfictional extrapolations and projections on the future; Wells did both (Manuel and Manual, 1979; Lombardo, J. B., 2010).

Dropping the supernatural and theological metaphysics, can we envision a better social reality that results from natural forces and the efforts of human self-determination? Of course, along with the secular utopian comes the secular dystopian: What can go wrong that would lead to negative human societies in the future? If we abandon the security of believing that God (our source of absolute moral guarantees and ontological power) is orchestrating the progression toward a better world, leaving the creation of that forward ascent to our own devices, then it becomes both open and uncertain whether we can realize our positive social dreams. Indeed, the possibility of future dystopias is the social version of Frankenstein's monster, where human efforts (supplanting God) take over the role of creation and due to our limitations and failings bring forth social nightmares and disasters rather than heavenly dreams.

"Millennialism," expressed in both the Book of Revelation and St. Augustine's writings, would be a highly influential vision of the future throughout both the Middle Ages and into modern times. Another noteworthy and influential expression of futurist thinking in the Middle Ages—one that finds inspirational roots in both millennialism and the Book of Revelation—is the visionary philosophy of the mystic prophet Joachim of Fiore (1135-1202). Based on his reading of the Book of Revelation, as well as "deep reflection" on the meaning of the "Holy Trinity," Joachim proposed a grand theory of history and the future that also clearly contained a dimension of progress and credible transcendence (Nisbet, 1994).

Inspired by the Christian "Trinity," Joachim outlined three distinct stages of humanity: the "Era of the Father"—recounted in the Old Testament—or the "Age of Flesh"; the "Era of the Son"—recounted in the New Testament and up to Joachim's time—an "Age of both Flesh and Spirit"; and finally, the future "Age of the Holy Spirit," an "Era of Pure Spirit" that, according to Joachim, would begin in the year 1260 (his near future). The new "Age of the Holy Spirit," which would last one thousand years, would bring fundamental changes to the world, including the end of the hierarchical domination of the Church, which, in

Joachim's mind, would no longer be necessary, since humanity would realize a level of ethical and spiritual self-determination and the Church and its hierarchy of control would no longer be needed.

In Joachim's dualistic theory of progress we again see humanity moving (evolving) from a life of the flesh (the material world) to a life of the spirit. Seen as a heretic in his time—he saw the Pope as the Anti-Christ and the Vatican as the modern Babylon as described in the Book of Revelation—Joachim's vision was both highly controversial in his time and a source of inspiration for many. St. Thomas Aquinas strongly criticized Joachim's ideas, but Dante placed Joachim in paradise in the *Divine Comedy*.

Before turning to Dante's *Divine Comedy*, let me say some more about the nature of future consciousness and how this general human capacity relates to the themes in the above discussion. At the most basic level, future consciousness manifests itself in innumerable and mundane aspects of human life: When we set goals; make plans; create instruments, tools, and constructed habitats; negotiate trades and agreements; and take actions to achieve desired ends, we are engaging our future consciousness. In this sense, humans, even prior to recorded history, exhibited future consciousness in mundane, everyday matters of life.

When we come to recorded history, beginning approximately six thousand years ago, we find stories and myths about both the past and our origins, and about the envisioned future. It may be that the ancient masses did not think in any detail or depth about the future, insofar as they actively and thoughtfully considered visions of the big future and various possibilities ahead of them. And given the monotony and regularity of everyday life, people may not have expected big changes to occur in their own lives. But there were theories and narratives of the big picture (as noted in both Greek and medieval times). If anything, given the ubiquity and dominance of a particular vision within a culture, such as the Christian vision of a Second Coming, imaginatively thinking about the long term or big future and its possibilities was undoubtedly discouraged and repressed. People in medieval Europe were simply obediently waiting for the Messiah to come. Moreover, given the slower pace of change, once a dominant narrative was established, people looked toward the revered authoritative architects of the story for insight and guidance—which is a form of future consciousness locked into a mindset established in the past—and did not, as a rule, entertain other possibilities for the future.

Still, all told, there were visions and theories of the future that took narrative forms. Indeed, as illustrated with Zoroaster, the Book of Revelation, and Augustine's *City of God*, the narrative content and major ideas within these early visions articulated generative and archetypal themes, anticipating if not strongly influencing later stories of the future (and hence modern future consciousness) in science fiction.

The *Divine Comedy*

Dante's *Divine Comedy* is a seminal and powerful work in the history of fantastical imagination, cosmological visions, and Western ethical thinking.

The *Divine Comedy*, written by Dante Alighieri (1265-1321) during the years 1308 to 1321, is generally considered the apex of Western literature during the Middle Ages. Divided into three parts: *Inferno*, *Purgatoria*, and *Paradiso*, and drawing upon the Christian theology and philosophy of St. Thomas Aquinas, as well as numerous mythic elements often taken from the Greeks, the story tells of Dante's journey, first guided by the Roman poet Virgil, and then Beatrice (a real love of his life), through Hell, Purgatory, and finally Heaven. Although on the surface the *Divine Comedy* describes a "physical" journey through hell, purgatory, and heaven, it is generally considered an allegory in which the deeper meaning concerns itself with the journey of the human soul toward God. Having lost his way in life, the journey—decidedly extraordinary and fantastical— allows Dante to see and understand better what is good and what is bad in human affairs; observe and contemplate the grand scheme of things; and ultimately find a renewed sense of enlightened spiritual direction. It is a mythic story of enlightenment realized through transcendence.

It might seem out of place to discuss Dante's *Divine Comedy* within a history of science fiction, and Roberts (2005), for one, sees this great work of literature as clearly falling outside of the historical spirit of science fiction. For Roberts the story is religious, supernatural, and allegorical. But there are many important features to Dante's adventure that are of great relevance to science fiction. For one thing, Dante's story connects the personal with the cosmic; his journey, which reveals the fundamental make-up of the cosmos as he understood it, provides a meaningful framework for interpreting the meaning and purpose of his life. As noted earlier, one of the features of ancient myth and modern science fiction is creating this cosmic-personal connection: How does my life fit within and reflect the grand scheme of things? What is the grand scheme—both moral and ontological—of things? This is a central archetypal theme in both ancient myths and modern science fiction. Indeed, informed by the dominant vision of reality in the Christian Middle Ages, Dante's *Divine Comedy* can be seen as the final great expression of this mythic theme in pre-modern times.

Keeping in mind that the narrative has an allegorical dimension (but then so does science fiction in many cases), Dante created a detailed picture of the universe—of heaven and earth— as he understood reality during his time. Hell, the first domain explored on the journey, lies in the underworld or the interior of the earth; hell consists of nine concentric circles, beginning with Limbo and reaching its center in the lake of ice where Satan is trapped. After leaving hell, Dante and Virgil travel through the center of the earth (where gravity reverses) and they come out on the opposite side from which they entered, where they find Mount Purgatory in the southern hemisphere. Although living in the late Middle Ages, Dante believed that the earth was not flat but rather a sphere; still, in line with the geocentric mindset, he kept our planet at the center of the cosmos. After ascending through the levels of Mount Purgatory, where at the top he and Virgil enter the Garden of Eden, he journeys, now with Beatrice as his guide, into the nine celestial spheres of heaven that surround the earth (drawn from Ptolemy's geocentric model of the universe). He travels to the moon and the spheres of the sun and the planets. After passing through the *Primum Mobile,* the abode of the angels, in the outermost sphere, he enters the *Empyrean* and gazes upon God, who appears as three concentric circles of light—the Father, the Son, and the Holy Spirit. In this conclusion to the saga he "sees God" and achieves enlightenment.

As a general point regarding this depiction of the grand scheme of things, Dante attempted to synthesize various naturalistic concepts (such as Ptolemy's astronomy) with the Christian vision of reality. Although we might find, from a modern point of view, Dante's vision of the earth, hell, purgatory, and the heavens as archaic and scientifically flawed, Dante was presenting a vision of reality—resonant with the thinking of his time—that wove together a credible combination of the naturalistic/observational and the religious, spiritual, and theological. Even if the "physical journey" is allegorical—where the "deep meaning" of the tale is a spiritual and moral journey toward enlightenment—the general description of the territories through which he traveled represented a highly credible vision of the universe as he understood it, embodying both naturalistic and theological components. His depiction of the earth, sun, and planets is Ptolemaic, integrated and enveloped within a Christian vision of the heavens, which includes the abodes of angels and God. In this scheme, Heaven was a supernatural realm above the earthly naturalistic realm, both ontologically (a higher state of reality) and physically.

So, as a mythic narrative theme, in the *Divine Comedy*, we find a traveler who (in journeying across the known universe) encounters at the end of the adventure some ultimate being or great revelation about existence; in essence, this is what happens in Stapledon's *Star Maker*. In fact, as a core narrative theme in science fiction, space travel frequently involves journeys to the infinite, the ultimate, and eventual cosmic revelation. What, then, is so different in narrative structure and meaning about Dante's *Divine Comedy*? As allegory, Beatrice, who joins Dante in purgatory, symbolizes benevolent guidance on the journey to God (both psychologically and physically); analogously, in science fiction we often have benevolent and advanced aliens from the "heavens above" who guide humanity toward further evolution and a deeper understanding of existence.

Reflecting the Christian mindset of his time, Dante saw the cosmos as having a moral order and purpose. Recall Zoroaster and St. Augustine's idea, adopted in Christian theology, that the central narrative of the cosmos is a moral struggle. We can see this moral vision of reality as a grand example of personification of the universe, where the human mind projects human qualities onto the world, in this case, moral qualities and ethical purpose. It is also fascinating that the nine circles of hell align with specific human vices (lust, gluttony, greed, anger, and heresy, for example) where appropriate punishment is tailored to the specific sin; in Purgatory we find again a concentric structure with different vices being addressed within successive levels; and finally, in the outer spheres of heaven, which astronomically are identified with the moving spheres of the moon, sun, planets, and stars, we find that each sphere aligns with specific human virtues, such as wisdom, justice, faith, hope, and love. As one immense multifaceted personification, as we travel through the cosmos we simultaneously travel through a moral and psychological universe. This moral universe and the moral lessons of the journey are conceptualized within a Christian mindset; enlightenment at the end of the tale involves contact with the Christian God. Interestingly, we will see in modern science fiction stories of space exploration that aliens encountered on different planets often get associated with particular moral and psychological qualities, such as Martians being demonic and war-like, and Venusians being loving and angelic. Moreover, as illustrated in Camille Flammarion, journeying out into deeper regions of space gets associated with progressively higher levels of moral, spiritual, and intellectual development.

More generally, even if we reject Dante's moral-ontological scheme as human-centric, personified cosmology, we can still ask if the modern mind has abandoned the ancient notion that there is a moral dimension to the grand scheme of things. Although a common answer has been that science sees no moral order in the universe, this view of things is by no means universally accepted, even within the scientific community. For example, the scientific theory of evolution has been and continues to be used as a naturalistic framework for grounding a theory of morality (or ethics) in nature and the universe. More recently conservationists and environmentalists have proposed ethical principles and practices derived from holistic ecological science (Lombardo, 2002d, 2006a, 2006b, 2017). Science fiction writers have, in various ways, attempted to work ethical and moral dimensions into their grand cosmic visions of reality. "Doc" Smith created his whole *Lensmen* series around a hypothetical cosmic moral struggle spanning thousands of years.

We may find Dante's scheme both pedantic and ridiculous, but Dante in the *Divine Comedy* provides an intricate, highly organized and comprehensive vision of reality. As noted above, he was inspired by the writings of St. Thomas Aquinas in various ways, who he in fact meets in the "wisdom" sphere in heaven. Aquinas is generally regarded as the philosophical culmination of European Scholasticism, in which all of existence (human, natural, and spiritual) is integrated in a grand unified theory of reality. Even if we suppose that the Middle Ages in Europe was a time of philosophical and scientific stagnation, in coming to the end of this era, we find in St. Thomas Aquinas and Dante grand and imposing big pictures of high intellectual achievement in which everything is accounted for and makes sense.

We can, in fact, view the coming of the modern era as a rupture of the unified and comprehensive vision of reality realized in the last centuries of the Middle Ages. There was more to the universe than what we thought—a beyond-ness, a mystery, a vastness yet to be understood or explored. And who is to say what the existential journey of humanity is really all about? This is part of the spirit of the modern era and unequivocally central to the spirit of science fiction, a reopening of the mind to other possibilities of thought and imagination. Just as Aquinas' great philosophical system lost its dominance and centrality, Dante's ultimate narrative of the human journey lost its unchallenged preeminence in Western consciousness. (This is not to imply that these great writers and their works are not still revered and studied in modern times.)

In highlighting the comprehensive scope of the *Divine Comedy*, I should note that Dante's intellect and literary imagination were not limited to Christian or medieval ideas. As a mythic fantasy, with a moral and spiritual message, the *Divine Comedy* is populated with a vast array of fantastical creatures and scenarios drawn from earlier myth and fantasy. The developmental historical lines of tales of extraordinary adventures—and what Campbell refers to as "Hero's Journey" narratives—are continued and magnificently expressed in Dante's *Divine Comedy*.

On Dante's mythic journey, we encounter from Greek myth the three-headed dog Cerberus; the Minotaur (man and bull); the Griffin, a combination of lion and eagle; the River Styx, which borders the earth and the underworld; the Furies and the monster Geryon, combining human and animal qualities; as well as all manner of grotesque and nightmarish scenes and forms of punishment bordering on the surrealistic. In the *Inferno*, reaching a frightening and hideous apex of imagination, appears the three-headed, six-winged Satan, who chews on the bodies of the great traitors, Brutus, Cassius, and Judas.

To complete this rich, imaginative, and often graphic, vision of things—attempting to take all of human history into account—Dante includes along the journey hundreds, if not thousands, of famous people of the past, who now, as souls in the afterlife, are either being appropriately punished or rewarded for their vices and virtues in their former life on earth. It is very clear to Dante what the future holds for all of us: punishment, penance, or heavenly reward. In his grand phantasmagoria, Dante observes and contemplates "life, the universe, and everything" on his journey toward enlightenment and salvation. Moreover, he frequently talks to many of the human souls in the afterlife, including St. Peter and Mary, who reside in the celestial sphere of fixed stars in the heavens, right next to the angels. Whether metaphorically or literally, our destiny is either in the stars above or in the bowels of hell below.

Medieval Thought and *The Garden of Earthly Delights*

Although in the thirteenth and early fourteenth century, European medieval philosophy and literature (Christian at its core) was reaching its apex of development in the *Summa Theologica* (written 1265-1274) of St. Thomas Aquinas (1225-1274) and Dante's *Divine Comedy*, concurrently another line of thinking was gaining force in Europe that would eventually challenge the dominance of the Christian belief system. This emerging new mindset involved a naturalistic approach to reality; a scientific and experimental philosophy of knowledge acquisition; and a spirit of technological inventiveness.

At the core of many modern science fiction stories are one or more envisioned hypothetical technologies that do not presently exist. We can go back at least as far as the thirteenth century to see powerful expressions of technological visioning and creativity. Many "futuristic" technologies (such as airplanes, submarines, and helicopters), were imagined, if not actually designed and created, during this period or soon thereafter. Just as importantly, and having been dormant during most of the Middle Ages, the scientific spirit, so critical to modern science fiction, began to reassert itself in Europe toward the end of the Middle Ages.

A key factor instigating the rise of naturalistic scientific thinking and technological inventiveness in Europe came from outside of the Christian West. While Europe slumbered through the "Dark Ages," Greek philosophy, mathematics, and naturalistic writings were the subject of great interest and study in the spreading Islamic Empire. A great number of Islamic scholars assimilated naturalistic Greek philosophy, science, and mathematics and significantly further advanced its lines of thinking and inquiry. When Europe rediscovered Greek thought, such as the philosophy of Aristotle, in the eleventh and twelfth centuries, it was primarily through contact with Islamic scholarship (Lombardo, 2006a).

In the centuries after Mohammed (c. 570-632 CE), as Islam spread across the Middle East and eastward through northern Africa and into Spain, it encountered the teachings and ideas of many different cultures. Through trade and conquest, Islam created a thriving economic and intellectual network across the Middle East during the time when Christian Europe had sunk into the relatively illiterate, chaotic, and unproductive Dark Ages. The city of Baghdad became one of the great cities of the world and, at first, was very open and tolerant to the ideas and practices of non-Islamic people.

In the ninth century CE, Islam discovered the ancient Greeks. Through the study of ancient Greek philosophy, science, medicine, and mathematics, coupled with their own genius and inventiveness, Islamic thinkers created one of the great intellectual cultures in human history. Armstrong (1994) describes this period as having features of both the European Renaissance and European Enlightenment. During this time, Islam produced a series of great scholars, philosophers, and scientists, including Alkindi (813-880); Alhazen (965-1038); Avicenna (980-1037); Al-Ghazzali (1058-1111); and Averroës (1126-1198). Such philosophical thinkers and scientific investigators of nature greatly contributed to the ongoing advancement of knowledge. While medieval Europe had, to a large degree, closed its mind to pre-Christian traditions and culture, Islam opened itself to the multicultural heritage and intellectual wealth of the past and, building upon it, flourished.

Of special note, during its apex, Islam was a culture of both faith and reason—of science and religion—attempting to synthesize these seemingly disparate perspectives in its philosophy and way of life. Yet, it was the religious confidence and enthusiasm of Islamic culture—the conviction that it possessed the all-enveloping truth—that propelled its efforts to bring all human learning, including naturalistic science, under the umbrella of its monotheistic belief system; in the final analysis, faith in Allah and the teachings of Mohammed reigned supreme (Armstrong, 1994; Watson, 2005). Although cosmopolitan and synthetic in its creations, Islam was cultural-centric and religious in its underlying philosophy. In this regard, in the thirteenth century Aquinas was no different, believing that Christian religious thought could be integrated with Greek philosophy and science, in particular, the ideas of Aristotle.

Still, as Armstrong (1994) notes, after contact with ancient Greek ideas, an intellectual movement developed in Islam, referred to as "Falsafab," which was an attempted synthesis of abstract science and philosophy and practical guidance in life; the purpose of this movement was to understand how to live a philosophically enlightened life. In encountering the ideas of Plato and Aristotle, Islamic thinkers strove to integrate their religion with the rationalist and naturalistic principles of the Greeks, and find a scheme for life.

Avicenna took the view that the universe was a rational and orderly system, and although mystical revelation was important as a road to the truth, so was reason. In particular, Avicenna attempted to reconcile the ideas of Plato and Aristotle with Islamic religion by developing *rational* proofs of the existence of God. Likewise, in attempting to synthesize Plato and Aristotle with the *Qur'an*, Averroës went even further, articulating a highly rationalistic philosophy and theology in which he argued that Greek reason and Islamic revelation were entirely compatible with each other. Following this trend and incorporating ideas from the Greek atomists, Alhazen created one of the great scientific works in the early history of the study of optics—one that would later have a great impact on European science— presenting his ideas in a highly analytical, mathematical, and naturalistic format (Lombardo, 1987).

In general, Islamic philosophers of this period worked toward bringing the rational-empirical and the mystical-revelatory approaches to life together into a synthetic whole. For many of the great Islamic thinkers of the *Falsafab* movement, the scientific-rational and mystical-revelatory, which constitute two of the most influential approaches to the future in human history and are often seen, from a modernist perspective, as totally incompatible with each other, could be synthesized into a coherent whole. As I have noted on several occasions, one developmental line in the evolution of science fiction has been to incorporate spiritual and theistic ideas into the scientific mindset; the *Falsafab* movement attempted to realize this synthesis during the Middle Ages.

Influenced by the writings of Avicenna, the prolific Arab physician Ibn al-Nafis (1213-1288) reputedly wrote over one hundred medical textbooks and studied and wrote on law, literature, and theology as well. He is most famous for being the first person in history to correctly describe the pulmonary circulation of the blood between the heart and lungs (*al-Nafis*). His *Theologus Autodidactus* (probably written sometime between 1268 and 1277) is considered the first theological novel in history (using a personalized narrative as a vehicle for presenting a theological theory), but the book has also been viewed as a science fiction novel, synthesizing futurist and scientific ideas with Islamic religious thinking (*Theologus Autodidactus*). The novel shows the influence of both Islamic theological writings and ancient Greek philosophical ideas on the nature of the mind and soul.

A "coming of age" and "desert island" tale (a thematic setting that Al-Nafis derived from previous Islamic writers), the basic plot of the novel involves a feral child (Kāmil, "the perfect one"), born through spontaneous generation, growing up on an island and self-educating himself, and then coming in contact with other humans and being taken back to civilization. While living alone on the island, through self-directed learning and thinking, Kāmil develops a great deal of knowledge about the natural world, but he only achieves a complete cosmic understanding of things (inclusive of the nature of God, the soul, and the resurrection of the dead) after religious revelations instigated through contact with human civilization.

The novel culminates in a futurist vision of the end of the world, integrating into the story ideas from science, philosophy, cosmology, history, theology, and eschatology. One main intent within the novel is to demonstrate the compatibility between scientific-philosophical thinking and Islamic prophecy and religious ideas, which includes as one important issue (for the history of science fiction)—predicting the future. The futurist vision of the end of the world that he presents follows from a synthesis of Islamic revelation and scientific historical determinism; the future can be predicted through understanding the forces of nature and human history, yet this future can also be grasped through religious revelation.

Because of its theological/religious vision of humankind, the universe, and the future, Al-Nafis' futurist "end of the world" scenario could be seen as more religious prophecy than science fiction (along the lines of the Book of Revelations). Yet for Ibn al-Nafis, who was strongly influenced by *Falsafab* thinking, the rational-empiricist mindset of science and the prophetic-revelatory visions of religion were not incompatible, but mutually supportive and connected; that is a main argument within the story. This attitude of the harmonious relationship between scientific and religious ideas, of particular note about the future, would continue in early modern science, and accordingly in many modern science fiction novels. A noteworthy early example of a vision of the end of the world that pulled together theological futurism and scientific naturalistic ideas is Jean-Baptiste De Grainville's *The Last Man* (1805), followed by Flammarion's *Omega* (1894), and even more recently, Walter Miller's Hugo award-winning *A Canticle of Leibowitz* (1960).

* * *

Turning to the late Middle Ages in Europe, Robert Grosseteste (1168-1253), who was strongly influenced by both Islamic (notably Alhazen) and Aristotelian writings, produced a series of "scientific" books involving expositions on light, mathematics, and physical cosmogony that contained early formulations of the principles of induction, deduction, and experimental methodology, including the ideas of scientific falsification and verification. As with all early expressions of scientific thinking in medieval and early modern Europe, Grosseteste attempted to synthesize the scientific and the theological in his overall philosophy of knowledge and existence.

Roger Bacon (1214-1294) — or "Doctor Mirabilis" ("the

wonderful teacher") as he came to be known—studied and incorporated in his writings many of Grosseteste's ideas on scientific inquiry, as well as Islamic thinking (notably Alhazen) on the study of optics. Although obsessed with alchemy and astrology, combining the mystical-magical with the scientific, Bacon came to be seen as one of the great early prophets of modern science and technology. Indeed, the science fiction writer James Blish wrote a historical fiction novel featuring Bacon titled *Doctor Mirabilis* (1984) that portrays Bacon as a visionary futurist, struggling against the intellectual and cultural constraints of his time.

Although perhaps less of a heretic and iconoclast and more conformist than popular scholarship has portrayed him, Bacon is still a superb example of the high level of technological speculation and futurist visioning that emerged in the late Middle Ages (the thirteenth century). Within his writings can be found clear anticipations of aircraft, submarines, helicopters, suspension bridges, and automobile-like transportation. He seems to have speculated on the possibility of "antigravity" devices and presents a clear description of the chemical composition and explosive properties of gunpowder. Fueling some of the mystique associated with Bacon, historical legend says that he possessed an automaton, a mechanical "talking head" that could answer any verbal question communicated to it.

It is a popular view that the break with the Middle Ages and the rise of Modernism begins with the European Renaissance in the fifteenth century. And although known as a time of great efflorescence in the arts, technological advance is another key dimension of the Renaissance (Watson, 2005). Two of the central values of the Renaissance were invention and imagination, and the period produced considerable technological innovation. The compass, mechanical clock, gunpowder, and the printing press all emerged as significant technological innovations in European life during the Renaissance (although many of these inventions were originally produced by the Chinese). The creation (or discovery) of the principles of perspective (geometrical projection) was another noteworthy achievement, uniting art with mathematics and science. The first printed book in Europe that can be dated was produced in the year 1457, after which mass printing caught on very quickly (Lombardo, 2006a).

The Renaissance produced one of the greatest creative geniuses in Western history, Leonardo da Vinci (1452-1519). Engineer, artist, and naturalist, Leonardo produced an amazing array of prescient and prophetic technological designs (*Leonardo da Vinci,* 1956). Among his most noteworthy machines and mechanical devices were a helicopter, calculator, armored fighting machine (an armored tank), solar power technology, ball bearings, parachute, machine gun, diving suit, self-propelling cart, and robotic knight. He also outlined and speculated on a redesigned "futurist" city, incorporating many innovative engineering principles and mechanisms. If Leonardo had had a strong literary inclination, synthesizing his technological inventiveness with the narrative form, he easily could have been the first modern science fiction writer. He had a huge assortment of innovative technological visions in his mind to work with to create futurist scenarios and dramas.

The study of optics and perspective in the thirteenth and fourteenth centuries would be one of the seeds of the coming Scientific Revolution. Bacon and Grosseteste wrote books on optics and light as key expressions of their scientific approach to reality. As one of the central artistic figures of the Renaissance, Leonardo da Vinci intensively contemplated, researched, and incorporated into his great works of art the principles of perspective and optical projection. Understanding the geometry of perspective was one of the key developments in Renaissance art, transforming art from rather flat pictorial scenes — representative of medieval art — into perspectival simulations of the three-dimensional world. Aside from the study of optical perspective, Leonardo was also deeply involved in the study of the physics of light and the physiology of vision, and designed various optical instruments, including a telescope (Lombardo, 1987). The telescope would be a key new technology connected with the rise of modern science, opening a vast new universe for contemplation and study.

Coupled with Leonardo's technological inventiveness, scientific acumen, and great artistry, he possessed a deep fascination with nature and life. Indeed, all these facets of his genius form a whole. Leonardo produced a huge number of intricate drawings of the human body (including internal organs) and numerous other living forms—both animal and botanical—as well as natural landscapes. Clearly it was his detailed observations of the forms and patterns of nature that both informed and inspired him in his paintings and grounded his scientific thinking. Leonardo synthesized the artistic, technological, and naturalistic, all key dimensions of the Renaissance. Not only did he advance and integrate various key features of holistic human consciousness, with his visionary eye he channeled and applied this holistic intelligence to the future.

Leonardo da Vinci is an archetypal icon in subsequent visions of the creative genius and technological innovator. (Roger Bacon would be another such inspirational figure.) An exemplar of the visionary mind able to transcend the imaginative constraints of a particular culture and time, Leonardo could see ahead and see beyond. The scientific and technological genius, as epitomized in Leonardo, would become a pivotal character in modern science fiction.

Even though Greek philosophy and naturalistic themes became increasingly influential in the fifteenth century, medieval and Renaissance art was steeped in the imagery of Christian narrative and theology. It is within this historical context of theology and art, and yet mixed together with a bizarre and hallucinogenic naturalism, that we find one of the most provocative and visually arresting paintings of the Renaissance, if not within all of Western art: *The Garden of Earthly Delights* (created between 1490 and 1510) by Hieronymus Bosch (1450-1516).

The Garden of Earthly Delights is one among many paintings containing weird and astonishing imagery created by Hieronymus Bosch (see for example, also *The Last Judgment*, *The Haywain*, and *The Temptation of St. Anthony*), but it is by far the most inventive and famous (Siegel, 2016). *The Garden of Earthly Delights* is an ideal anchor point for the modern history of fantastical art that would feed into and stimulate the evolution of modern science fiction and fantasy art—the visual-aesthetic dimension of holistic future consciousness in science fiction.

The *Garden* is a triptych consisting of three foldable panels. From left to right are depictions of Adam and Eve in the Garden of Eden (where Adam, in spite of the presence of Christ in the scene, lustily gazes upon the naked Eve); a center fantastical scene of nude figures engaging in dubious and highly erotic activities (with a host of animals and pieces of fruit involved); and a right side depicting a dark and fiery scene of damnation in Hell (with various demons, nightmarish constructions, and perverse forms of human torture). When folded, the outer cover appears to show a vision of God creating the earth. (There is a cosmic envelopment represented in the construction of the painting.)

Larger than the flanking panels, the center interior panel visually dominates the composition, and throughout history has been the subject of great controversy regarding its meaning. The whole triptych, and especially the center panel, is decidedly surrealistic and filled with fantastical creatures; bizarre amalgamations of different animals and body parts; numerous carnal contortions of naked figures; an assortment of symbolic birds and ruby-red pieces of fruit; and along the top of the panels, in pinks and blues (symbolic of earthly and heavenly realms), evocative and dreamlike castles and fountain-like structures. (Such castles appear in other paintings by Bosch, along with other depictions of the Garden of Eden as well.)

From a depth psychology perspective (Freudian or Jungian), the *Garden* (again, notably the center panel) can be seen as a powerful, uninhibited, and graphic expression of the unconscious—of desires, fantasies, pleasures, and bizarre imagery from deep within the human psyche. The right panel of Hell, filled with demons and forms of torture, can be seen as a visual expression of the monsters and fears of the unconscious let loose. Using Freudian terms, the center panel is Eros—the sexual, life instinct let loose—and the right panel is Thanatos— the death instinct—crazed, grotesque, and unshackled. In this sense, the *Garden* is Dionysian; it is a breaking free of the mental constraints of the conscious mind, the intellect, and the super-ego expressed in creative and energetic visual form.

Art historians have debated whether the central panel is a "warning," depicting the unabashed abandonment into carnal sin that will be punished, as depicted in the right panel showing the punishments and pains of Hell. Or perhaps it is a reverie—an uninhibited celebration of life, the flesh, and pleasure. Perhaps it is both, for as Freud argued, the human mind can embody contradictions; we are both excited by the Dionysian and yet anxious and fearful over suffering damnation for our sensuality and bodily impulses.

There are a number of reasons for including *The Garden of Earthly Delights* in this history of the evolution of science fiction. First, it superbly illustrates the incredible heights of fantastical imagery the human mind can realize; in particular, this painting, which stands at the transition between the Middle Ages and modern times, brings together fantastical thematic elements of both mindsets: In it we have God, Paradise and Damnation; naturalistic yet bizarre fauna; strange forms of play and frolic;

and wild sex (including bestiality). It is a gold mine of material for the speculative imagination, easily imagined as the basis for a modern fantasy or science fiction story.

Second, *The Garden* is a symbolic visualization of what may come in modern times. The architects of the Scientific Revolution and the European Enlightenment promised, through advances in technology and the abandonment of superstitious and repressive religious beliefs, a future "Garden of Earthly Delights." The *Garden* is a Renaissance visual expression of a secular garden and utopia — coupled with the guilt of the Middle Ages (the right panel). The middle panel, in particular, has a futuristic quality.

Third, the evolution of science fiction as a literary and artistic expression of human consciousness embodies a visual dimension that would become increasingly important moving into the twentieth century. Evolutionary tributaries of science fiction, futuristic, and fantasy art (perhaps also astronomical-cosmic art) complement and amplify the literary traditions. *The Garden of Earthly Delights* is one of the most significant creations of fantastical — and surrealistic — art feeding into the visual dimension of contemporary science fiction. Any deep history of science fiction and fantasy art would have to include the *Garden*. It is unequivocally the most famous piece of fantastical art from the beginning of the modern era.

If nothing else, Bosch's castles show up again in Richard Power's (one of the great modern science fiction artists) surrealistic twentieth-century science fiction paintings. Moreover, various creatures in the *Garden* — as well as other surrealistic paintings of Bosch, including the triptych *The Temptation of St. Anthony* — could easily pass as aliens from some other world.

Finally, my intuition tells me that there is "something" critically important and provocative — if not prescient — about *The Garden*, such that to exclude it from a psychologically holistic history of science fiction would be to miss a very important piece of the story of the genre. *The Garden of Earthly Delights* calls across the ages; it ignites the imagination; it titillates the senses; it challenges the intellect; it visualizes in its center panel some kind of erotic fantastical utopian reality; it ascends into the world of dreams, of both heaven and hell. It pushes against the boundaries of consciousness.

* * *

You're the chief communications officer and central character aboard the *Santa Maria*, responsible for sending and receiving messages through the hypothetical ether extending to the Spanish shore. The miracle of distal communication through the air is achieved, so you believe, via the resonant vibrations of countless tiny cherubs and angels clustered and aligned between your transmitter/receiver and the one in Spain. The giant red moon though, ascending in the Western sky, seems to be creating interference, disrupting the harmonic oscillations of the angels and cherubs, and breaking up the incoming and outgoing signals.

Columbus is leading you, along with his other two ships, the *Niña* and the *Pinta*, across the ocean in search of India. Although enlightened people of the era believe that the earth is a sphere and that India lies on the western end of the Atlantic, there are those, including members of the crew, who fear that the ships will come to the edge of the world and fall off into the abyss. You, though, educated in the holy sciences of the great saint Roger Bacon, who had opened the Western mind to the possibilities of technological progress and scientific understanding two centuries earlier, do not have such superstitious beliefs; the world is a globe and there is no great waterfall into the oblivion beyond the horizon.

Then one day, just when Columbus is ready to turn back under pressure from his anxious crew, birds are sighted in the sky, igniting hope that land may be near. But as the birds come closer you see that they have no feet. The currents below suddenly increase in force and velocity, irresistibly pulling your tiny ship forward with the others. To the sound of a thunderous waterfall that shakes the air, the *Niña*, *Pinta*, and the *Santa Maria*, with you and Columbus and the whole crew aboard, fall off the edge of the world.

This entertaining story, "Sail On! Sail On!," published by the science fiction writer Philip José Farmer in 1952, is an alternative history in which the twelfth-century scholar Roger Bacon instigates the Scientific Revolution three centuries earlier than in our own timeline. In this alternative reality, Columbus fails to "discover" the New World because the earth is not round after all but flat with a surrounding edge. We could ask if this story is science fiction or just fantasy, but for me it clearly falls in the former category. Fantastical as the alternative reality of cherubs vibrating with each other through the ether may seem, this and the imagined technological devices humans use to pick up their transmission seem grounded in a scientific understanding of natural reality, albeit a different one than our own.

I include this story at this point in my history for a couple of reasons: It deals with a significant historical event—Columbus' epic journey of discovery as part of the Age of Exploration—that symbolized the transition from the medieval mindset, with its closed and limited universe, to the Modern Age, when people confronted the discovery of a new world and a greatly expanded universe. Although written in the twentieth century, it is a fitting tale for concluding this chapter.

But in this story, the opening of new vistas of exploration and enlightenment does not happen; we remained trapped and circumscribed by a bounded earth. Perhaps, as a metaphor on the medieval mind, in this story we are trapped by our fears and our mindset on reality.

I see Farmer's "Sail On! Sail On!" as an allegory. The

medieval mind, wanting to keep science within the metaphysical framework and philosophical dominion of Christian theology, interpreted radio transmissions in this tale as the work of cherubs and angels. (Or were the cherubs and angels actually "real" in this alternative reality?) Yet, in our reality, the mindset of Christian theology would, in the early centuries of the Modern era, suffer repeated assaults upon its validity and compatibility with the newly emerging scientific and secular philosophy of reality. For many secular and scientific thinkers, the medieval vision of reality, because of its confined circumference of thought, did sail off the edge of the world and plummet into oblivion.

Looking toward the future, as we did in the time of Columbus, who knows what lies beyond the horizon? We could have fallen off the edge into the unknown then; we still might fall off some proverbial edge tomorrow. Fears of the unknown and the future still haunt us. As an alternative reality story, "Sail on Sail on!" stimulates us into thinking about our own interpretations of reality and whether we might fall off a precipice into the void due to our own limitations in understanding. The story forces us into questioning our own scientifically informed mindset. This story, and the subgenre of the alternative history in general, compels us to entertain multiple views of history and reality, bringing us into the minds of characters whose beliefs are as firm as our own.

Chapter Four

The Rise of Modernity

When the Heavens appeared to me as only a blue vault ... the Universe appeared little, and confined within narrow bounds, I seemed oppressed; presently, they give an infinite extent and profundity to this blue vault ... it now seems to me that I breathe with more liberty, that I am in a much greater extent of Air, and that the Universe is far more magnificent.
Bernard le Bovier de Fontenelle

The Age of Exploration

Although many Europeans in the thirteenth and fourteenth centuries did not believe that the world was flat and bounded by a surrounding edge, it was not until the great wave of European exploration of the globe, that it was conclusively demonstrated, first by the expedition of Magellan in 1519-1521, that the earth could be circumnavigated without falling off some hypothetical edge.

The "Age of Exploration" (also referred to as the "Age of Discovery"), stretching from the fifteenth through the seventeenth centuries, was an influential era within the evolutionary history of science fiction for a number of reasons. By venturing into the unknown (*terra incognito*), its leading explorers and adventurers were challenging the constricting beliefs, fears, and superstitions of their time. Along with the Italian Renaissance (c. fifteenth century) and the Protestant Reformation (c. sixteenth century), the Age of Exploration was a key emancipatory expression against the restrictive mindset and beliefs of the Middle Ages (Lombardo, 2006a). This increased freedom of thought—of transcending boundaries and mental constraints—was a central feature in the rise of modernity. The courageous and adventuresome navigations to the far reaches of the globe can be seen as a metaphor, symbolic of the growing desire to venture beyond the mental prisons of the Middle Ages. Modern science fiction is an expression of the freedom of thought and imagination that arises out of this spirit of exploration and adventure to go beyond the confines and security of familiar mental and physical spaces in our lives.

Second, the new wave of global exploration fueled human imagination with colorful and provocative stories of strange new lands, new sights, new peoples and cultures, and exotic new creatures, sometimes more imagined than real. As noted earlier, one of the historical tributaries of science fiction is tales of adventure into strange and unexplored lands; such tales go back to the beginnings of recorded history. With the coming of the Age of Exploration, many new tales, often rivaling the older ones in fantastical color and detail, were added into the ever-evolving array of stories of adventure. Science fiction and fantasy tales of exploration and discovery in the coming centuries, often involving encounters with previously unknown cultures, cities, animal life, and types of humanity across the globe—let alone in outer space—would be inspired by the chronicles of the Age of Exploration. In essence, the discoveries of the Age of Exploration opened up a much larger sphere of the possibilities of nature and even forms of humanity to be explored within the realm of imagination and storytelling.

To recall, ancient stories of adventure often included fantastical realities and beings, and at times ventured outward into cosmic arenas. But up to the time of the Age of Exploration, such fantastical and imaginative tales were fundamentally anchored to a Euro-Centric mindset. As part of the emancipatory thrust of modernity, the numerous and diverse encounters with non-Western cultures and peoples helped to push Western consciousness beyond its limiting cultural prejudices and forms of perception. Yet even such new chronicled encounters were invariably interpreted in terms of Western beliefs and values; the process of the opening of the Western mind through contact with other cultures was (and still is) a slow and difficult process. For all humans, including Westerners, culture strongly influences perception, understanding, and the "factual" descriptions we create, especially of realities never previously encountered (Feyerabend, 1965, 1969; Best and Kellner, 1997; Holmes, 2008).

Still, chronicled journeys into the strange and unknown, both real and imagined, that emerged within the literature of the Age of Exploration would contribute new ideas and stimulate and stretch the human imagination. Aside from contributing to new fictional stories of earthly adventures, chronicles of the Age of Exploration also influenced the creation of later imagined journeys into outer space. Contact with non-Western cultures and new species of life during this period would provide starting points for envisioned alien beings and cultures encountered in later fictional journeys into outer space.

All in all, the Age of Exploration opened up the human mind (for indigenous peoples across the globe as well) to strange and novel possibilities of life, humanity, nature, and types of societies, clearly providing fuel for the development of science fiction adventures.

The Scientific Transformation of Nature and the Heavens

Copernicus, Kepler, and Galileo put in place the dynamite that would blow up the theology and metaphysics of the medieval world. Newton lit the fuse.
Neil Postman

The Reformation, the Renaissance, and the Age of Exploration contributed to the European emancipation from the authoritarian shackles of Christian medieval thinking and to the emergence of modernist philosophy and modes of thinking, but the key development in this cultural transformation (especially relevant to science fiction) was the Scientific Revolution, running from the sixteenth through the seventeenth centuries.

First, let's describe a simplified "black and white" version of this transformation. The Scientific Revolution involved the contributions of many different individuals, notably Copernicus, Galileo, Kepler, Descartes, Francis Bacon, and Isaac Newton. Usurping the principles of medieval theology, the Revolution involved a set of interconnected ideas and principles, including rationalism, abstract theory, empirical observation, naturalism, mathematics, experimentation, systematic doubt, and hypothesis testing taking precedence over and replacing faith, revelation, supernaturalism, sacred texts, authoritarian mentality, and a personified universe. The early years of the Scientific Revolution revealed many new discoveries and laws of nature, including a modern heliocentric model of the solar system (replacing Ptolemy's geocentric model); various principles of telescopy, microscopy, and optics that facilitated a deeper and more expansive study of nature; the mathematical laws of planetary motion; principles of magnetism; the circulation of blood through the pumping of the heart; microscopic life; analytic geometry and calculus; the moons of Jupiter and Saturn; the accumulation of prehistoric fossils; and laws of gravity, motion, and mechanics.

All these new discoveries and uncovered laws of nature both explained and more intricately described the universe without the need for personified deities, magic and miracles, and purposeful spirits and forces.

In general, the Scientific Revolution entailed both an openness to new ideas and a questioning of the religious and philosophical authority and specific doctrines of the Christian church; the replacement of one theory (epistemology) of knowledge acquisition and confirmation—faith, revelation, and sacred texts—with a new one—logic, experimentation, and observation; and an emerging new theory of reality—of matter, energy, mechanistic causality, and motion—replacing the old theory of spirits and spiritual forces, deities, magic, teleology, animated nature, and angels dancing on the head of a pin (Panshin and Panshin, 1989; Lombardo, 2006a).

Of particular note, with the rejection of the geocentric theory of the cosmos (Dante's Ptolemaic model), the dualist division of the earthly realm and the higher (surrounding) heavenly realm became untenable. Galileo—in discovering the bigger moons of Jupiter—opened up the plausibility, soon embraced by many scientifically minded thinkers, that there were multiple worlds out there in "outer space." Indeed, the Scientific Revolution led to the "naturalization of the heavens." As Newton seemed to demonstrate, the same natural laws of gravity and mechanics that apply on the earth apply to the heavens above. Kepler had earlier created a set of naturalistic laws of planetary motion that mathematically and comprehensively described the orbits of the earth, Mars, Jupiter, and all the other known planets. In fact, as scientists gazed outward into the night sky with evermore powerful telescopes, observing more and pondering the meaning of their new discoveries, the "heavens" changed from a divine and eternal realm into "outer space," the natural and colossally expansive realm within which both the earth and the solar system, as a totality, exist, all spinning like tops, through the vastness of the cosmos (Holmes, 2008).

We could say that the vision of the cosmos and its creation in Dante's *Divine Comedy*—grounded in the Christian Bible—steadily lost credibility with the onset of the Scientific Revolution. A new vision of reality progressively replaced an older vision, with numerous challenges, counter-reactions, and attempted compromises along the way. As noted earlier, the ancients believed (by and large) in the plausibility of their fantastical sagas, stories, and myths within the context of theories of reality that they thought were true. Angels, demons, human-animal hybrids, visitations from the gods, and supernatural deities made sense within an animated, inspirited, god-centered reality. Within the new vision of reality articulated by science, such sagas and myths turned into "fantasy;" they no longer seemed credible (Panshin and Panshin, 1989).

Science fiction historians and scholars have argued that science fiction could only emerge once modern science had first developed. Although this point might seem obvious, I believe that there is a more accurate way to describe what happened historically. What we call modern science fiction is basically informed by an evolving theory of reality (and a new epistemology) that finds its modern origins in the Scientific Revolution. This evolving modern theory of reality seems notably at odds with earlier more ancient theories of reality. There were always tales of fantastical, mind-expanding adventures involving fantastic beings, but such stories, grounded in earlier theories of reality, lost credibility in the face of the modern scientific theory of reality. The new scientific view of reality provided a transformed framework for judging the plausibility for such tales. The new view provided, to use Panshin's expression, a new and different theory of the "credible transcendent."

In presenting the imaginative and the fantastical within a scientifically plausible context, it is important to note that with the coming of science there was a vastly expanded arena of imaginative possibilities. As science would steadily uncover in the coming centuries, the size, age, depth, intricacy, order, and complexity of the universe far exceeded the egocentric and narrow visions of ancient myth, classical religion, and the European medieval mindset. Early scientists experienced an intensified sense of awe and wonder in the face of a much-expanded universe; the possibilities of the utterly different opened up considerably, both at the microscopic and macrocosmic levels; the possibilities of alien worlds became a plausible, understandable, and mind-boggling reality. As expressed in the opening quote in this chapter by the popular science writer Bernard le Bovier de Fontenelle (1686), the universe, as it was understood and could be provocatively explored in imagination, was colossally inflated with the emergence of modern science.

Moreover, when we bring in the modern theory of secular progress — inspired by and following on the heels of the Scientific Revolution — the universe of fantastical possibilities that could be achieved in the future was nothing short of the miraculous and infinite. It is amazing that a new mode of thinking and method of inquiry motivated by the conscientious intent to strictly observe and study nature, depend on reason, and eradicate superstitious assumptions and groundless speculation, would generate a universe of vastly expanded possibilities and incredible, mind-boggling depth, intricacy, and immensity.

* * *

This most beautiful system of the Sun, planets, and comets, could only proceed from the counsel and dominion of an intelligent and powerful Being.
Isaac Newton

But that history was so simple! Let's now complicate the picture of the Scientific Revolution.

First, consider Giordano Bruno (1548-1600), the great martyr of the Scientific Revolution, whom Roberts (2005) considers a central figure in the emergence of the scientific vision of reality and modern science fiction. In Bruno's *On the Infinite Universe and Worlds* (1584), inspired by the early revelations of modern astronomy, he argued that the universe (i.e., outer space) was infinite in size and must contain an infinite number of inhabited worlds. He boldly and controversially contended that the sun was really just a star, of the same kind that we observe by the thousands in the night sky. The sun was just much closer than any other star. Around all these other suns or stars, he reasoned, must orbit planets like those in our solar system. And there must be living, intelligent beings on these worlds. But Bruno believed that this infinite universe of infinite worlds and multitudinous life forms clearly demonstrated the infinite and amazing power of God, the Creator. God did not make just one inhabited world—ours—but an infinite number of worlds.

Bruno possessed a highly creative mind, proposing a host of speculative ideas, both scientific and religious throughout his numerous books and writings, and he seems to have been a person of significant intellectual independence, refusing to abandon or recant his numerous controversial beliefs. He challenged the geocentric mindset of the Middle Ages that saw the world of humanity at the center stage of the universe, but he also appears to have challenged accepted Catholic doctrines regarding the Holy Trinity, the divinity of Christ, the virginity of Mary, and the relationship of God and the universe. Probably as a result of all these iconoclastic cosmic and theological beliefs, he was burned at the stake by the Church and became one of the great martyrs of the Scientific Revolution.

Roberts sees Bruno as the central iconic figure in the emergence of modern science and science fiction due to his challenging the dominant vision of a divine cosmos, replacing it with a naturalistic vision of the universe. Although Bruno's theory of an infinite universe of infinite worlds opened the heavens to infinite possibilities beyond the highly circumscribed vision of the Middle Ages—a liberation of the modern mind and human speculation—Bruno did not believe that he was abandoning the idea that God created or orchestrated the universe. Bruno believed that he was synthesizing Christian religion with the newest revelations and implications of science. In essence, he did not reject a "God-centered" universe and theory of reality in the face of a growing scientific vision of nature and the cosmos; he simply modified the former to accommodate the latter, believing that he was actually reinforcing and amplifying ideas on God and the universe through the new discoveries and implications of science.

Later in the seventeenth century, Galileo (1564-1642) ran into similar difficulties with the Church. In his scientific writings Galileo supported the heliocentric theory of Copernicus over the Church-sanctioned geocentric theory and was consequently accused of heresy. Unlike Bruno, when push came to shove, Galileo finally agreed to publicly recant his views; although one of the great architects of the Scientific Revolution, Galileo ultimately balked at openly opposing the authority of the Christian Church and its vision of the universe. Although it appeared (to Galileo) that the new ideas and discoveries of astronomical science were at odds with orthodox religious ideas, Galileo was unwilling to lead the way forward, publicly championing an open antagonism between Western science and religion.

As science continued to develop through the seventeenth century, with new discoveries, new theories, and an increasingly novel and distinctive view of reality, a clear and open confrontation between science and religion still took considerable time to manifest itself. Consider these other significant figures of the Scientific Revolution:

Isaac Newton (1642-1726), who is popularly seen as the theoretical culmination of the Scientific Revolution, believed that the universe he described in his laws of mechanics and gravity was created by God at the beginning of time. For Newton, the stable and harmonious physical universe of matter and motion, governed by physical causality and mathematical natural laws, was not incompatible with a religious vision of an eternally existing Creator. Indeed, the lawfulness of the universe (which Newton discovered) reflected a God of order and law; the universe was a reflection of the orderly "mind of God."

Following the later philosopher Alfred North Whitehead (1925), we could argue that the scientific pursuit of discovering order in nature reflected the earlier religious belief in a God that gave order to the universe. That is indeed how many early scientists conceptualized their endeavors.

The French rationalist philosopher and mathematician, Rene Descartes (1596-1650), inventor of analytic geometry and another key figure in the rise of modern science, advocated that all dogma and habitual beliefs grounded in the past be subjected to systematic doubt. To start afresh—and this was central to Descartes' modernist and scientific agenda—everything must be examined in the light of reason and clear thinking. (Again we see the argument for the "opening of the mind," transcending the constraints and biases of tradition and conformity.) Yet, after presumably starting out on this new road to an improved understanding of the universe, Descartes brought God back into the picture (through reasoning rather than faith, revelation, or sacred text), and ended up arguing for a dualistic universe of mind and matter, where the latter was subject to the laws and principles of science but the former remained within the province of religion. Moreover, after having earlier proposed that the universe was evolutionary, not having been created in its present form at the beginning of time, he later decided to publicly abandon this view because it appeared to conflict with *Genesis*. Although one of the great early spokespersons of science, Descartes was very careful not to say anything that would ruffle the feathers of the Church, as it had in the cases of Galileo and Bruno. Descartes realized the potential conflict of religious and scientific thinking but created a dualistic theory of reality (of mind and matter) and a practical strategy for avoiding having to publicly acknowledge this conflict of worldviews and face the dire consequences.

* * *

Behold a universe so immense that I am lost in it. I no longer know
where I am. I am just nothing at all. Our world is terrifying in its
insignificance.
Bernard le Bovier de Fontenelle

By the late seventeenth century, though, the heliocentric theory
of the solar system, as a central idea in the emerging modern
scientific vision, had become less controversial and heretical
in the eyes of the Church. Greatly contributing to this general
shift in mindset, was the author Bernard le Bovier de Fontenelle
(1657-1757), the most influential person in popularizing the
theory of Copernicus. In his *Conversations on the Plurality of*
Worlds (1686) — a series of dialogues between a philosopher and a
woman friend set in the context of a walk under the night sky and
the stars — Fontenelle explains with great clarity and simplicity
the general theory of Copernicus. Moreover, he presents various
ideas concerning other worlds and extraterrestrial life. The
philosopher details the possibilities of life on the moon, as well
as those for each planet in the known solar system, and then
delves into the theory that the stars are really distant suns, each
of which has its own orbiting planets. Fontenelle and Kepler
(discussed below) were most responsible in the early years of
the Scientific Revolution for the idea that alien intelligence and
life could be much different from earthly forms of life and mind.

For Fountenelle, "All philosophy is based on two things
only: curiosity and poor eyesight," a clear and humble
acknowledgement of humankind's limitations in the quest to
understand the cosmos. Although Fontenelle did not significantly
upset Church authorities with his *Conversations*, in the same year
he also published *History of Oracles,* which did create a degree
of controversy. In the *Oracles* he argued that there was a general
trend in our ongoing and improving understanding of nature,
which involved the progressive elimination of supernatural
and magical explanations. This point hits at a deeper level than

simply the geocentric versus heliocentric theories of the solar system, for it raises the question of the nature of reality and how best to know and understand it.

Another example of the commingling of science and religion in spite of ongoing scientific advances was Christian Huygens' *Cosmotheros: The Celestial Worlds Discovered: Or, Conjectures Concerning the Inhabitants, Plants, and Productions of the Worlds in the Planets* (1698). Here, in unparalleled intellectual depth and detail, the author combines alien life forms and other worlds; God; rationalist philosophy; and scientific astronomy. A great early astronomer and scientist, Huygens (1646-1716), who studied and graphically modeled the rings of Saturn and discovered Titan, Saturn's largest moon, argued that there must exist numerous other planets in the universe (beyond the solar system), none of which God could have made for no purpose. It followed, then, that such other worlds must be inhabited. For Huygens, such "scientific" conclusions followed from the "uniformity of nature" principle.

What is perhaps most noteworthy about Huygens' *Cosmotheros*, especially within the history of science fiction, is that for its time it contained the most thorough, detailed, and scientifically informed discussion of the varied conditions of other planets in the solar system and the possibilities of life and intelligence commensurate with such different worlds. Yet, even acknowledging diverse planetary conditions necessitating different forms of life, Huygens also attempted to demonstrate that certain uniform qualities of life and mind exist across inhabitants in different worlds, such as animal and plant forms; the need for water; perceptual senses in animals; functional hands; fundamental types of appendages and modes of locomotion; societies; protective habitations; and even higher capacities of reason, at least in some of each planets' inhabitants. Huygens did recognize the elements of uncertainty and speculation in his discussion of extraterrestrial life, but within this context, he lays out in broad strokes what he believed was a rational and scientifically informed zoology (and psychology, ethics, and sociology) of other worlds. Indeed, Huygens created perhaps the first comprehensive scientific theory of aliens.

Moreover, Huygens advocated that humanity should venture outward and colonize other planets and moons. According to him, as our scientific and technological capacities increase in the future, we should take advantage of these new powers and explore the planets and stars. Thus, on two important counts— the possibilities of alien environments and life forms and the technologically empowered future exploration of outer space— Huygens outlined and anticipated the narrative territory of science fiction journeys into outer space and to other worlds.

Nonetheless, and notably, this great scientist and astronomer who significantly contributed to the emerging new vision of the cosmos and the possibilities of extraterrestrial life did not abandon his belief in a spiritual and creator God. Indeed, as one reads through *Cosmotheros*, the arguments presented repeatedly weave together astronomy and scientific and rational considerations with references to the wisdom and divine purpose of God the Creator. He does not see the new astronomy and science as contradicting the Bible or the Christian God. Indeed, his speculative explorations are continually guided by the fundamental consideration: What must the universe and its multitudinous worlds and inhabitants be like, if we assume (which he never questions) a benevolent, omnipotent, and wise Creator?

Another important figure in the early history of Western science, Gottfried Leibnitz (1646-1716), co-inventor with Newton of calculus, developed a scientific philosophy that in several significant ways anticipated future scientific ideas in the centuries to come. Yet, Leibnitz too maintained a strong belief in the Christian God and many of its associated doctrines, attempting to work out a philosophy in which the scientific and the religious could co-exist.

The great adversary of Newton, Leibnitz rejected Newton's ideas on absolute space and time, instead proposing that both space and time were relative; without events, objects, and motions anchoring our measurements, there is no space or time. Contemporary scientists have frequently argued that Leibnitz's theory of relativity, much more so than Newton's physics, significantly anticipates and aligns with Einstein's twentieth-century ideas on space and time (Smolin, 1997).

Additionally, Leibnitz rejected the "static creationism" of Newton. The universe in its beginning was not as it exists today. Instead, Leibnitz proposed a dynamic and evolutionary universe that he believed was compatible with the idea of God. (The story of creation though in *Genesis* clearly seemed to be at odds with an evolutionary view of the cosmos.) To quote from his *The Ultimate Origination of Things* (1697):

> To realize in its completeness the universal beauty and perfection of the works of God, we must recognize a certain perpetual and very free progress of the whole universe, such that it is always going forward to greater perfection. ... And ... no end of progress is ever reached.

The related ideas of evolution and progress—of a dynamic, developmental, and directional reality—provided an expansive sense of possibilities for the future, perhaps infinite in scope. These ideas would come full force into the Western mind in the centuries ahead, but Leibnitz clearly anticipated this progressive and developmental vision of reality and the future. To recall, Descartes had pulled back on defending a similar view half a century earlier. But the tide was turning, as it already had on the controversy surrounding the heliocentric theory of the solar system. Static creationism and static perfectionism (for example, that the universe and humanity were created in a perfect state) were losing their hold on the Western mind; a new all-encompassing dynamic and progressive vision of reality was beginning to emerge, starting in the seventeenth century (Green, 1959).

As the above examples illustrate, then, even though early scientists were working out and applying a new methodology and theory of knowledge for uncovering the structure and dynamics of nature, and even though early scientific discoveries and theories appeared to contradict ideas about reality within the Bible, almost all early Western scientists and scientifically inspired philosophers continued to accept (at least publicly) the teachings of the Christian Church. In fact, scientists went out of their way to demonstrate how the two worldviews could be made compatible. Many early scientists saw their work as demonstrating the glory and power of God; they saw science as a way to understand the "mind of God," even if what was in the mind of God did not seem to be what it had been before.

In short, the modern scientific framework provided a new theory of reality for judging the plausibility of beliefs and knowledge claims; the older theories, religiously inspired, increasingly lost their credibility as a framework for judging realistic plausibility. Yet, this transition in philosophical perspective was neither sudden nor absolute. Although science and modern science fiction presumably transcended religious visions of reality, as noted in the opening chapters, even modern science fiction writers, who were inspired and informed by science, frequently included ideas that harkened back to religious spiritualism, mysticism, mythology, and theism. The absolute "either-or" vision of science versus religion, even up through contemporary times, has never completely congealed and differentiated in either science or science fiction (Barbour, 1997).

The Synthetic Genius of Kepler—Journeys to the Moon

Let us create vessels and sails adjusted to the heavenly ether and there will be plenty of people unafraid of the empty wastes. In the meantime, we shall prepare for the brave sky-travelers maps of the celestial bodies.
Kepler (Writing to Galileo)

The one significant early figure in the Scientific Revolution not yet discussed in any depth is Johannes Kepler (1571-1630). We could argue that it was Kepler more than either Copernicus or Galileo who started the Scientific Revolution, for Kepler's three laws of planetary motion were the first mathematically formulated and empirically grounded (data-based) laws of nature to emerge within the new science. Newton's laws were derived off of Kepler's laws. Just as importantly, Kepler was the first to accurately understand and describe the optics of the eye, and his understanding of light, led him to correctly grasp the optics of the telescope (Lombardo, 1987).

Yet, Kepler was a true mystic, as much as a mathematical genius and empirical scientist, and his laws of planetary motion derived from his creative inspiration that the solar system operated in a way similar to the Christian Holy Trinity. (See Arthur Koestler's *The Act of Creation* (1964) for an enthralling discussion of Kepler's creative genius.) In many ways Platonic and Pythagorean in his philosophy, in search of the ideal mathematical forms manifested within the world of nature, Kepler believed that there was a mathematical-geometrical harmony within the heavens. He is a superb example of how early science did not reject the religious and the mystical, but rather found ways to synthesize the two theories of reality.

Kepler is especially significant in the history of science fiction since his *Somnium* ("The Dream"), written circa 1600 but not published till 1634, after Kepler's death, can rightfully be considered the first modern Western science fiction story. While various scientists or scientifically minded philosophers speculated on journeying to other inhabited worlds, and as we saw running back to Lucian's time, numerous fantastical stories were written about traveling to the moon (Roberts, 2005), it was Kepler who wrote the first such story to contain a wealth of scientifically grounded ideas on the moon and its possible inhabitants. Yet, in spite of the scientific dimensions to his tale, Kepler also included within it various mystical and supernatural elements.

Kepler's mother had been accused of being a witch, and in *Somnium* we find a "witch-mother" figure who, securing the help of other "wise spirits" or daemons that move through the ether, transports the protagonist through the "cold and rarified" space from the earth to the moon. In arriving on the moon, our protagonist finds two very different realities, which Kepler describes in great scientific and astronomical detail. He calls the side of the moon always facing the earth "Subvolva" (under the earth) and the side always facing away "Privolva" (deprived of earth). Describing the length of days, months, and years; the motion and varying positions of the sun and the earth in the lunar sky; and the atmospheric and temperature conditions on each side—all of which Kepler derives from his understanding of astronomy and basic science—he goes on to explain how the inhabitants of the two sides are very different, psychologically and socially, given the differences in their physical environment. The Subvolva side of the moon always has the large and luminous globe of the earth—which goes through phases—somewhere in the sky, thus giving its inhabitants more positive and stable ways of life and states of mind. The Privolva side is missing this luminous beacon, and when the sun sets, the sky is plunged into darkness. The inhabitants who live on the Privolva side are nomadic and much stranger—even grotesque—than the inhabitants of the Subvolva side. In essence, in this tale Kepler attempts to think out and predict the nature of alien life and intelligence based upon a scientifically grounded understanding of the physical world of these inhabitants (Gunn, 1977).

Further, giving the story an aura of the spooky and mystical, the journey to the moon turns out to be a dream which the protagonist had after conversing with his "witch mother." Did she plant the whole experience in his mind? Was he actually whisked off to the moon while he was asleep? Was the journey real or imagined?

Either way, and even taking into account that the journey to the moon is accomplished through the help of spirits, Kepler did believe that in the future, with "vessels" suited for the "heavenly ether" and "empty wastes," we would travel into outer space and explore the cosmos. Space travel (and adventures in the unknown) was connected in his mind with the future and the great promises and visions of the new science. And yet Kepler also thought of this great future adventure into the cosmos as a spiritual journey as much as a physical one. Through both science and the anticipated exploration of the heavens, reading the "Book of Nature," we are in search of the mind of God and the "harmony of the spheres." Thus envisioned, for Kepler the exploration of outer space is a mythic quest for enlightenment.

Even though the skies above and outer space were demystified and naturalized with the beginnings of modern astronomy—the dualistic theory of heaven and earth breaking down—the planets and the stars would continue to hold an elevated and mysterious allure for the modern mind. Are not the secrets to our true nature, our place in the world, and the nature, origin, and destiny of the grand scheme of things to be found in the exploration of outer space? Within the medieval dualist perspective, the "heavens" promised revelation of the true and the ultimate; for the modern mind, adopting a naturalistic perspective, the "heavens" promised the same thing. Arguments in modern science for the value and deep meaning of space flight frequently include (among other elements) references to cosmic enlightenment and even "spiritual" purpose (Wachhorst, 2000; Lombardo, 2002e). When we look at modern science fiction journeys into outer space, we frequently see the same mythic theme of cosmic enlightenment.

Kepler's science and philosophy provides an excellent illustration of a key historical and conceptual connection between the theology and metaphysics of the Middle Ages and the emergence of modern science. Although the ancient Greeks believed in a fundamental order underlying the cosmos, it was the Christian notion of an ordered universe, as an expression of the "mind of God," that directly inspired the early scientists to go in search of this presumed order within nature. With Kepler and Newton and others, science emerged as a quest to understand, through rational, empirical, and mathematical means, the "mind of God," an envisioned journey toward cosmic enlightenment.

* * *

As the sun was personified and worshipped as the giver of light and life in ancient mythologies, the moon — the ruler of the night — was also invested with numerous mystical, personified, and divine qualities. The moon was hypnotic, spooky, mysterious, and magnetic, beckoning the human spirit. The bright full moon in the night sky seemed to be watching us, guiding us, providing a portal into some higher realm; moonlight shadows suggested ghostly and dreamlike apparitions. Demonic spirits were connected with the moon, but so was romantic love. Since the beginnings of recorded history the moon has been a powerful "psychic" object — with mystical powers — and we have dreamed of traveling to its shores throughout the ages.

Beginning with Kepler in the early seventeenth century, we find a wave of numerous speculative stories of journeys to the moon. Inspired by the new astronomy and the new sciences, we even find stories that present scientifically plausible (in the very loose sense) mechanisms and explanations for how to travel to the moon. In retrospect, the naturalistic explanations of space flight offered at the time may now seem naïve and ridiculous (but then in retrospect the same can often be said for the credibility of the ideas of any age), but at least travelers to the moon were not being transported by angels, daemons, or witch-spirits, as was the case with Kepler.

Some of the most noteworthy books in the seventeenth century that involved journeys to the moon included: Francis Goodwin's (1562-1633) *The Man in the Moone* (1638); John Wilkins' (1614-1672) *The Discovery of a World in the Moone* (1638); and Cyrano de Bergerac's (1619-1655) *Comical History of the States and Empires of the Moon* (1657). Cyrano de Bergerac also wrote a tale of journeying to the sun: *The States and Empires of the Sun* (1662). In all these books we find speculative visions of lunar inhabitants (in de Bergerac's journey to the sun we also find solar inhabitants), and there appear not only cultural comparisons of alien inhabitants with human society but, as with de Bergerac, satire on human society as well. Perhaps most significantly we find the juxtaposition of scientific, astronomical, and technological ideas with religious and spiritual themes grounded in Christian theology.

In Goodwin's book, the traveler is carried to the moon by birds (giant swans) tied to a raft. Once the traveler arrives and encounters the moon's inhabitants, he raises the question of whether they believe in Christ, to which they respond affirmatively. (This seemed an important opening question to ask of aliens.) As described in the story, the lunar inhabitants speak in a language of "tunes and strange sounds" and live in a pastoral paradise. Following from Kepler's hypothesis, there are seas on the moon as well. After visiting for six months, the traveler returns to the earth. In Wilkins' story, similar theological themes are brought to the forefront: Do the inhabitants suffer, as we do, from "original sin," and have they achieved salvation? For Wilkins, the moon turns out to be a paradise without sinners.

Cyrano de Bergerac considers a host of different possibilities, naturalistic and spiritual, for traveling into space: hot gases, magnets, springs, giant mechanical grasshoppers, dew captured in bottles, the pull of the moon goddess, "rockets," and mirrors powered by the rays of the sun. It is through the solar powered rockets that the protagonist in de Bergerac's story first successfully reaches the lunar surface. Once he arrives, the traveler encounters the Biblical prophet Elijah and is informed that the Garden of Eden was moved from the earth because of the "Flood" and now is on the moon. Indeed, as is revealed, our traveler has landed in the Garden of Eden. In his conversation with Elijah, the traveler repeatedly pokes fun at his religious views and is expelled from the Garden of Eden. In journeying across the rest of the moon, the traveler meets lunar inhabitants that resemble giant horses and beings that communicate through music, live in mobile cities, and inhale their food. Eventually he is jailed and put on trial for his dubious claim that there *really are* inhabitants living on the earth. But he is ultimately released and, clinging to an aerial lunar creature flying upward into the sky—a being presumably possessed by a devil—he finds his way back to the earth.

In de Bergerac's tale of journeying to the sun, the protagonist meets a race of intelligent birds who live in a utopian society. Again, the protagonist finds himself in hot water with the local inhabitants after engaging in theological and cosmological debate, and he is put on trial for being a human. As in the moon story, he is freed and finds his way back to earth. Here too, the satire targets human beliefs and behaviors. And yet, underneath the fantastical imagery and free-spirited dialogue, de Bergerac addresses serious questions: Do there really exist innumerable, if not infinite, inhabited worlds in the cosmos? If so, what are the theological implications of this creative plentitude?

Another recurrent early issue regarding alien worlds was whether Christ had visited them. A related question was whether aliens were born into original sin and required salvation. But how many worlds (if there were an infinite number) could Christ have visited? Did Christ die and resurrect on an infinite number of worlds? Through such speculative astronomy and storytelling, not only is Christianity being debated and tested, but outer space and aliens are being assimilated into the Christian mindset as well. Naturally these stories reveal both human arrogance and deep anxiety: We assume the whole universe can be made sense of within our earth-centric religious stories, and we are apprehensive and frightened that our most cherished beliefs will fail in the face of infinity.

Aside from the theological, there are also the roles aliens and alien societies play in both understanding ourselves and in providing a projective space in which to concretely imagine ideal social realities. In de Bergerac, the aliens and their worlds provide comical mirrors on human mores. In many of the early moon tales (and innumerable later stories of aliens), the alien setting provides an imaginative space to think through what exactly would constitute a "paradise" and what ideal intelligent minds would be like. Clearly stories of space travel and alien encounters served psychological, social, and ethical inquiry and speculation. Outer space and aliens provided a canvas for creating utopias, dystopias, and both evolved and impaired minds.

* * *

Grounded in the theories and discoveries of Bruno, Galileo, and Kepler, among others, a universe of myriad, if not infinite worlds becomes the new cosmic arena to be explored through astronomy, as well as within stories of human imagination. With Kepler we find a serious effort to apply science to understanding the environmental and physical conditions on other worlds, notably the moon. And from there the question arises—one that Kepler addresses as well—regarding what types of life or intelligence could exist upon alien worlds, given differences between the physical conditions of those worlds and the earth. Thinking out scientifically what alien worlds would be like, and what kinds of life could exist upon such worlds, would become significant areas of imaginative exploration in modern science fiction. We can say that Kepler, followed by Fontenelle and Huygens, constitutes the modern starting point for all of this, synthesizing the science of astronomy with biology, psychology, and human imagination.

Still, as we see above, early stories of space travel mixed science with spiritual, mystical, and religious themes. As Roberts (2005) notes, using Bruno as a paradigm illustrative case, the idea of multiple worlds created great anxiety in the religious mind of the seventeenth century. Had aliens experienced salvation? Did Christ appear on alien worlds as well? Was the earth special or not? Modern astronomy seemed to challenge the human-centric vision of reality in more ways than one, and early writers of fictional space exploration grappled with the compatibility of religious doctrine and modern astronomy, often coming up with ways to bring the two perspectives into alignment.

Regardless of how one mixes together science, myth, and religion, tales of space exploration and other worlds would become the natural and modern evolutionary extension of earlier tales of great adventure into the unknown. Space became the arena of the "extraordinary journey." Moreover, given the diverse conditions that could be encountered in journeys to other planets, stories of outer space provided a fertile arena in which to imagine all kinds of bizarre and fantastical realities and beings, another key feature of earlier voyages of adventure. To varying degrees, depending upon the science fiction writer, the strange and the different was constrained and guided in its imaginative creation by the principles of science. Still, the reality and inherent possibilities within a scientifically framed universe vastly expanded in scope and richness the possibilities envisioned within classical myth and religion.

While these early tales of traveling to the moon generally took place in the hypothetical present, in the coming centuries, visions and stories of space travel became strongly connected with the future. As technology advanced we came to believe that we would acquire the technological powers needed to travel into outer space. Kepler (and Huygens after him) did contemplate the realistic possibility of space travel in the future, contributing to the secular-scientific vision of progress. Kepler the astronomer was not simply charting the stars for science; he was providing for *"the brave sky-travelers maps of the celestial bodies"* to help guide them on the grand adventure to come.

Utopian Visions and Technological Dreams

A truly golden little book, no less beneficial than entertaining, of a republic's best state and of the new island Utopia.
Thomas More

Besides tales of extraordinary adventures, another evolutionary tributary that feeds into modern science fiction is utopian thought. To recall, Plato created a philosophically grounded utopia within his *The Republic* and St. Augustine envisioned a Christian inspired and God-centered utopia in his *City of God*. In more modern times, existing at the transition between the Renaissance and the Scientific Revolution, are three noteworthy utopias (among many others of the era) that are worth examining in the context of the evolution of science fiction: Sir Thomas More's (1478–1535) *Utopia* (1516); Tommaso Campanella's (1568-1639) *The City of the Sun* (1623); and Francis Bacon's (1561-1626) *New Atlantis* (1627).

More took as the title for his book the term "utopia," which, derived from Greek, literally means "no place" or "not a place." This meaning of the word would seem to imply that the island society of "Utopia" he describes in the book could not really exist; the word does not represent anything that is real. But More also states in the addendum to his book that the intended meaning of the title is more in line with the Greek "eutopia," indicating a "good place" — a place of bliss and happiness. If we combine the two meanings, we have an envisioned society that does not in reality exist, at least not in present times, but is rather an imagined or hypothetical ideal society (perhaps that could exist).

As Clute (1995) and other science fiction historians, such as Roberts, (2005) argue — and as was also the case with Plato — More did not envision his ideal society as something possibly existing in the future. For one thing, in *Utopia* the author turns his gaze toward an idealized past, citing Plato as a significant point of inspiration. Also, More's *Utopia* describes an imagined island society discovered by travelers somewhere in the New World, hypothetically existing in his present day. Furthermore, More uses this hypothetical ideal society to provide a preferable alternative to the social injustices of his own time. *Utopia* serves the function of social criticism.

But this perspective on More and other early utopias is at best incomplete. Although early (pre-modern) utopian writers, as the frequent argument goes, presumably did not see their ideal societies as something that could be achieved in the future, St. Augustine and the whole line of Millennial thinking to follow provide a strong counter-example to this view (Nisbet, 1994). Millennialism did envision an ideal state of humanity to be realized in the future. And even if early modern utopias such as More's were not imagined as existing in some hypothetical, more advanced future — and this point is even open to debate — these various early idealistic visions provided the intellectual seeds of

futurist thought—including science fiction futurist narratives—
on the social, political, ethical, and psychological possibilities
and preferable directions for humanity in the future (Manuel
and Manuel, 1979; Lombardo, 2010).

Indeed, when ideals are postulated regarding human behavior
and society there is an implicit, if not explicit, prescriptive
element to such proposals. An ideal entails a "should." More's
utopian vision, then, serves as a prescriptive call to action: We
should attempt to transform our presently flawed society into
one more in line with the envisioned utopia in his book. In
essence, More's *Utopia* may not be a predicted future, but it is a
preferable future to strive for.

Throughout recorded history humans have created
philosophies and systems of value and belief that identify
preferable or ideal states for human existence. Such values
and beliefs have provided guidance and direction for human
behavior. Ideals point toward preferable futures and guide
human improvement, short or long term. This is critical to our
capacity for future consciousness and purposeful evolution. Our
ethical systems provide normative goals for our purposeful,
future-directional behavior (Lombardo, 2017). Utopias, past and
present, fit within this general mode of human consciousness.

Within this context, we can see why utopias (as well as
dystopias) are an integral and important historical tributary in
the evolution of science fiction. Utopias are expressions of social
ideals (which may include psychological, political, and even
ecological considerations as well), and as such they map out
preferable directions for the future of humans. Dystopias map
out undesirable future directions. When science fiction envisions
the future, the human side of this vision, even if contextualized in
scientific-technological developments, is essential to its narrative
realism. Utopias and dystopias (whether or not explicitly set in
the future) have provided numerous maps of the hopes and fears
to be considered in creating the psycho-social features of science

fiction narratives of the future.

As introduced above, More's *Utopia* can be interpreted as a comparative critique and satire on the failings of the European social reality in which the author lived. The first part of *Utopia* presents the flaws and evils—in particular the greed, injustice, and excessive pride—in the structures and governance of contemporary Europe. The second part describes the society of Utopia. (The isolated geographical setting symbolizes the promise of freedom and new beginnings in a human colony beyond the influence of the corrupt Old World.) Most of the social ills described in the first part of the book are addressed and rectified with different social practices in his imagined Utopia. In this sense, More's *Utopia* does set up a model and ideal for improvement over the presently existing flawed and undesirable social reality of his time.

As was the case in Plato's *The Republic*, in many ways *Utopia* describes a highly ordered society. The size of the population is controlled with the citizens evenly distributed throughout the cities on the island. There is no private property or personal privacy, nor is there unemployment. Everyone wears the same type of clothing and meals are a communal affair. Vocations are controlled, and individual travel between cities across the island is closely monitored. On the other hand, there is some limited degree of religious freedom, although atheists are despised and most members of the society adhere to a monotheism and personal God. As with other religious utopias, God is the source of all values and the ultimate authority. And indicative of contemporary biases, not only is slavery a universal practice in all households but the society is also clearly sexist: wives must confess their sins to their husbands once a month. The society is decidedly patriarchal and hierarchal in its power structure.

Moderation and tranquility are other key qualities in More's *Utopia*, as well as general freedom from fear and anxiety; the members of the society are, by and large, content. The inhabitants pursue ethical and healthful pleasures—moderation is a key guiding principle—and engage in good work that produces positive contributions to the society as a whole. Moreover, citizens are concerned with each other's well-being—part of the benevolent watchfulness of the society—and for the most part enjoy good physical health. In stark contrast with contemporary Europe, More's *Utopia* is a peaceful society of social harmony with calm and contented citizens.

From our modern Western individualist point of view, More's *Utopia* may seem oppressive and suffocating. But given the aggressive, competitive, self-serving, and power-hungry forms of human behavior—all expressive of the negative side of individualism—what More supports and adopts in his ideal society is social uniformity and over-arching control, along with the elimination of greed and personal aggrandizement (there is no private property) and pride. As prescriptions for how to counteract the chaos, conflict, and selfishness in modern life, later utopias often took the form of authoritarian societies (see Bellamy and Wells for example). Yet for those who cherish freedom and individuality, it is highly questionable whether such a society of extreme social control and diminished individuality is a utopia to strive toward. Indeed it seems more a dystopia to fear and avoid (But see also Zamyatin's *We*).

As Nisbet (1994) observes, in the modern West we find two very different visions of social progress. One vision identifies increased individuality and freedom as criteria of human progress; the second identifies increased social order. Both visions of progress assume particular ideals and values that would rectify identified flaws or limitations in contemporary society. But the envisioned utopias of the future, created over the last few centuries, that follow from these two value systems highlight different social problems and postulate contradictory preferable directions: To prevent chaos and conflict in the present we need increased social order and centralized control; to fight against tyranny and injustice and protect our individuality and freedom, we need to eliminate authoritarian and totalitarian governments, and perhaps even embrace some form of political anarchy (Nisbet, 1994). How are we to decide what type of society to aspire toward, and which type to avoid? What types of negative or positive narratives of the future can we create on either end of this ideological dichotomy? Modern science fiction is filled with examples from across the ideological spectrum.

Perhaps the critical problem we find in More's *Utopia*, as well as many other early utopian visions, is that the imagined ideal society is static. Because of this unending sameness, it is stiflingly monotonous; nothing changes, nothing happens; there is no drama or excitement. This static perfectionism goes back to Plato; indeed, we could argue that it is implicit in any vision that involves some absolute ideal form of existence (including a heavenly one—what happens in heaven?). Perhaps change implies a fall from perfection? Whatever the reason for this stasis, More's perfect, Platonic, Christian utopia, one where all individuality is squashed, is, to put it simply, boring.

In anticipation of coming chapters, within the eighteenth-century Western Enlightenment and the theory of secular progress, the future holds the promise for something different, something better, and the future extends without end. As Condorcet stated, "... the perfectibility of man is absolutely indefinite." There is always room for improvement and time for adventure. For the dynamic philosophy of evolution, which emerged in the nineteenth century, all systems, natural or social, undergo inevitable change. A perfect and static system of life or human society is unnatural, as viewed through evolutionary thinking (Lombardo, 2010; Lombardo, 2017). To envision a scientifically informed utopia, in our present day and age, we need transformation and evolution. Moreover, an engaging and realistic narrative of a better future world requires action, drama, and human striving. From a contemporary perspective, the ultimate dystopia—either lived or vicariously experienced—may be a society that resists change because it thinks it's perfect. It would be excruciatingly monotonous and destructive to the human spirit.

* * *

I shall make the heavens a temple and the stars an altar.
Tommaso Campanella

Although not as well known as More's *Utopia*, Campanella's *The City of the Sun* (written in 1602 and published in 1623) contains a number of fascinating and prescient ideas in the evolution of science fiction and utopian thought. As in More's *Utopia*, *The City of the Sun* hypothetically exists in present times in a remote corner of the earth. And as in More, the tale combines the theme of a journey to a strange land with the utopian vision of an ideal society.

Campanella's city consists of a set of seven-walled concentric circles (symbolizing the seven known planets, including the moon) encircling an elevated temple on a central hill. Within the temple are an altar and two large globes depicting the earth and the seven planets. On the temple dome above are painted the major stars of the heavens. Within the temple, people pray to the stars—in particular the sun, which symbolizes the beneficent and creative powers of God. The whole structural scheme of the city, cosmic in vision, symbolizes the perceived unity and compatibility of astronomy and theology, of the sciences and religion. The design of the city facilitates cosmic consciousness, of God and the universe.

On the concentric walls are represented in verse and graphics the sum of human knowledge as determined by the city's scholars. There are no "closed books" hidden away. All knowledge—of the arts, sciences, mathematics, and history—

is available and on display, and the people of the city acquire their education by repeatedly passing around the rings of the city and viewing the contents of these walls of knowledge. Thus, *The City of the Sun* has a centrally coordinated and universally accessible repository of all knowledge. The acquisition of knowledge—universal education—is a key feature of this utopian city, anticipating the value placed on knowledge and education in Western Enlightenment philosophy and modernity. Notably, one wall contains all new discoveries and technological innovations of the time; staying abreast of new inventions and developments across the globe is integral to the philosophy of the city. Although Campanella colossally underestimates the need for space to record new knowledge in the coming centuries, his model clearly reflects an expectation of continued progress in the growth of human knowledge.

As with More, there is no private property, since it is connected with self-love and provokes self-centered interests and greed, among other vices. The citizens of *The City of the Sun* work, instead, toward the common good. Indeed, as in More's vision, the city is ruled and governed through an articulated set of central virtues that all citizens are expected to live by. The central ruler of the city is a priest, otherwise referred to as "Metaphysic," who has three princes, respectively responsible for Power, Wisdom, and Love. Power is responsible for all things connected with war. Wisdom is responsible for the content of knowledge represented on the walls. Moreover there is a set of "magistrates," each responsible for the teaching and enforcement of a particular virtue, such as fortitude, chastity, truth, and kindness.

Also of special note, human reproduction is selectively controlled. Instead of leaving it up to the capricious fortunes of individual choice, lust, and chance, the prince of Love determines how couples are paired and when—guided by science, good sense, and astrology—they will reproduce.

The physical characteristics of *The City of the Sun* exemplify an overarching unity and integration of purpose and design, with individuality and individual sentiments taking a back seat to order and community. The structural design of the city, modeled on the solar system, is expressive or symbolic of this philosophy of the centralized coordination of everything. If we see the sun as God, then the city is literally and architecturally "god-centered," with everything and everyone actively revolving around and guided by a central power determining what is good.

Although his utopia is set in a remote and contemporary "other place," toward the end of his book, Campanella gets futuristic and prophetic. Through the words of the traveler who narrates the story, we learn that the city's system of belief and governance is intended to eventually spread across the globe, creating a single world culture and government. *The City of the Sun* is a vision of a preferable global future built upon order—the ultimate value and center of gravity around which all individuals move in resonance. Although his ideal society is one that fits into a God-centered grand scheme of things, Campanella's highly progressive approach to human life and society, including his emphasis on education, the ongoing growth of knowledge and the human mind, and an architectural design modeled on an astronomical vision of the cosmos, mark him as one of the great philosophers of his time.

* * *

Human knowledge and human power meet in one; for where the cause is not known the effect cannot be produced. Nature to be commanded must be obeyed ...
Francis Bacon

As one of the key thinkers of the Scientific Revolution, Francis Bacon's *New Atlantis* was the most scientific and technological in spirit of the early utopias, and the closest to modern science fiction. Describing both an idealized and systematic way to replace the archaic practices and beliefs of the day with new knowledge, and a host of hypothetical new discoveries and inventions following from his new methods of research that would benefit humankind, the novel has a decidedly futurist spirit. Yet in spite of his naturalistic and empiricist philosophy, Bacon keeps the Christian God in center stage of his ideal and prescient hypothetical society.

Within his philosophy of knowledge as described in his book *Novum Organum Scientiarum* (1620), Bacon proposed that all past beliefs which were ungrounded in fact or reason should be rejected. He referred to these unsubstantiated beliefs as "idols of knowledge." He proposed a "new method" that would liberate humanity from these idols, a method that was rational and based upon fact. Specifically, he is credited with formulating the modern principle of empirical induction, by which knowledge should be based upon the careful and repeated observation and analysis of facts and phenomena within nature, often leading to experimentation and consequent generalizations based upon these observable facts. Instead of consulting religious authority or basing our beliefs on faith, we should directly investigate the natural world, collect facts, and draw empirical generalizations as the method for gaining accurate and true knowledge.

Bacon did not see science and scientific knowledge as an end in itself, though. Rather, science should serve as a foundation for the improvement of humanity; knowledge serves progress. Through understanding nature, we can control nature, and through the control of nature we can improve human life in the future. This pivotal insight that humanity can control and improve natural reality—as well as human society—through the application of scientific knowledge was at the core of the theory of secular progress that would emerge in the coming century. In essence, we find in Bacon the connecting link between the goals and ideals of the Scientific Revolution and the subsequent Western Enlightenment. This insight was also key to the emergence of modern science fiction, in which narratives were frequently set in a world intentionally transformed through advances in scientific knowledge and the application of technology, presumably for the betterment of humankind.

Given this philosophy of knowledge and naturalistic power, we see in Bacon's *New Atlantis* an imaginatively conceived hypothetical society that puts into practice not only this new philosophy of knowledge but its practical applications as well, with all the benefits that accrue as a consequence. His scientific philosophy served as a basis for his utopian thinking and narrative visioning.

At the beginning of the narrative we find a group of sailors lost in the Pacific Ocean who come upon an unknown land. Coming close to shore, the sailors are met by representatives from this land who, before allowing them to disembark, require that they profess their belief in the Christian God and a variety of associated Christian moral virtues; clearly the core belief system and ethical practices of this newly discovered society are God-centered and Christian based. (The implicit message is that only by reverence to God can we enter into the potential wonders of modern science and technology.) The sailors profess their Christian faith and are taken into the city.

In their initial encounters with the inhabitants of this new land, the sailors observe an amazing and highly admirable level of character and moral excellence. Showing both Christian benevolence and startling medical skill, the citizens of *New Atlantis* tend to the sailors, who have become ill from the arduous journey across the ocean, and applying various medical treatments, quickly return them to good health. In demonstrating moral and technological levels of development far beyond that of common humanity, these characters give us a preview of Bacon's ideal society, one where science and Christian ethics are synthesized in a vision of human betterment.

The most often cited and fascinating part of *New Atlantis* is the rich and provocative description provided of the state-sponsored scientific institution "Salomon's (or Solomon's) House." An organized college and research institute based on Bacon's principles of scientific inquiry and scientific application, Salomon's House is identified as "the very eye of the kingdom." The central purpose of the institute is "... the knowledge of causes, and secret motions of things; and the enlarging of the bounds of human empire, to the effecting of all things possible." (A futurist vision if ever there was one.) In Bacon's *New Atlantis* the scientific laboratory becomes the engine driving advancement and discovery, one that will open up the wonders of nature; it is an instrument of enlightenment and power. Yet, while the scientific laboratory and the scientists who work in them would become key and recurrent elements in later science fiction, Bacon attributes the existence and successful operation of this scientific research institute to God granting "the grace to know the works of Creation, and the secrets of them." God, not humankind, empowers science and the scientific laboratory.

After explaining the religious and spiritual foundation of the institute, Bacon gives us a "tour," describing research in such diverse areas as: refrigeration; insulation; weather (including lightning and thunder); cements and building materials; human diseases; desalination; numerous chemical processes; air purification; food and nutrition; botany and anatomy; light and sound; wind; and medicine, among numerous other areas of inquiry. The comprehensive breadth of scientific study and technological applications envisioned by Bacon is impressive.

And none of this is science simply for science's sake. As just an illustrative sample, Bacon describes the following purposes and accomplishments of the scientific and technological research done at Salomon's House:

- The prolongation of life
- The restitution of youth and the retardation of age
- Curing diseases thought to be incurable
- The reduction of pain and the enhancement of sensory pleasures
- Increasing or modifying strength, stature, or features of the body
- Increasing intellectual powers
- Combining body parts and making new species
- Creating new foods and new materials of apparel
- The creation of virtual reality (deception of the senses)

What is especially noteworthy in this list is that Bacon embraces the idea and positive possibilities of biotechnology and the purposeful (science-informed) improvement of the human species. We will not just make better gadgets or journey into outer space in the future; we will also create better humans with our new science and technology; we will (like gods) gain power over life and the capacities of the mind. In essence, Bacon envisions the future purposeful evolution of humans, both psychological and biological, through the application of science.

Bacon does not—as would his philosophical successors in the Age of Enlightenment—connect his ideal society's theological beliefs with his "idols of knowledge." (On what grounds can he justify his theology given his scientific epistemology of empirical observation, experimentation, and inductive generalization?) Rather, instead of replacing the spiritual and theistic vision of reality with the scientific vision of reality, Bacon layers the former on top of the latter; the former makes possible and guides the latter. In this, he follows the early architects of the Scientific Revolution, who did not see an incompatibility between the religious and scientific. Bacon's aim in the *New Atlantis* is to open the floodgates to the future possibilities of scientific and technological power that he, quite correctly, realized could transform the world, create new forms of life, and alter society and humanity. What he didn't see was that this coming transformation and the mode of human consciousness empowering it would call into question, if not undermine, his most fundamental beliefs about the ultimate God-centered nature of reality.

Although early utopian visions such as *Utopia*, *The City of the Sun*, and the *New Atlantis* are not explicitly set in the future they all begin with a journey to some strange and unexplored land. All three were written during the Age of Exploration. There is a sense of adventure not only into the physical *terra incognito* but also into unknown social, psychological, and ethical realms that is associated with the Age of Exploration and the long-standing tradition of tales of extraordinary voyages.

As has been argued, the only realistic way to imagine an alternative human society was to place it in some isolated and unknown location, disconnected from contemporary human society. Instead of encountering bizarre beasts and fantastical mythic realities, utopian voyagers encountered cultures different from those of European society. These new and diverse isolated societies provided food for thought and speculation about the possibilities of human existence, untarnished by the influence and corruption of the modern world.

In the coming centuries, numerous other journeys to strange and unusual societies would be envisioned (often combined with strange flora and fauna); sometimes these societies existed in unexplored regions on the earth (or below its surface); sometimes they existed in outer space on other planets. The story of adventure into the unknown and encounters with "the other" — psycho-social, technological, and biological — would become a fundamental theme in science fiction.

Sometimes these new lands, societies, and beings are inspiring and utopian; sometimes the new realities are terrifying, dangerous, or dystopian; sometimes they border on the incomprehensible. In many cases, through such narratives we experience enlightenment on our journeys into the vast possibility space beyond the ordinary and the relative here and now. Utopias (and dystopias), earth-bound or celestial, going back to their earliest expressions support transcendence into the beyond.

Chapter 5

The Age of Enlightenment

Western Enlightenment and the Theory of Progress

Thus we surpass all the times that have been before us; and it is highly probable that those that will succeed, will far surpass us.
John Edwards

The eighteenth-century Western (or European) Enlightenment followed and built upon the Scientific Revolution. Inspired by the ideals of the new scientific approach to knowledge and reality—of reason and empirical observation—it took these principles and ideals to their logical and practical conclusions. The central spokesmen of the Western Enlightenment included, in its earliest years, Francis Bacon and the philosopher Baruch Spinoza (1633-1677). The philosophy of the Enlightenment in subsequent years was then further developed and articulated through the influential writings of John Locke (1632-1704), Voltaire (1694-1778), David Hume (1711-1776), and Denis Diderot (1713-1784), culminating with the Marquis de Condorcet (1743-1794), whom Wendell Bell (1997) refers to as the first "modern futurist." The great German philosopher, Immanuel Kant (1724-1804), is often included at the developmental apex of the Enlightenment, but Kant actually tried to save a place for faith and religion in his philosophical system, which runs counter to the strong emphasis on secular thought that emerged in the Enlightenment. The core philosophical message of the Enlightenment, both abstract and practical, was the rejection of the worldview of Western religion in favor of the principle of *self-determined secular progress* grounded in science and reason (Lombardo, 2006a). This principle and all of its implications

222

(including worries, self-doubts, and nightmares over it) was a key instigating idea in the birth of modern science fiction.

Notably, in the philosophical writings of Locke, Spinoza, and Hume, we find ever-stronger and more comprehensive arguments that knowledge claims must be grounded in reason (inclusive of mathematics) and empirical observation (which would include experimentation), and if our beliefs cannot be supported in this fashion, the beliefs have no validity, meaning, or authority. They are nothing more than Bacon's "idols of knowledge." By the time we arrive at the great empiricist skeptic Hume, and his *Enquiry Concerning Human Understanding* (1748), we find a thoroughgoing and devastating critique of religious and metaphysical beliefs, since, according to Hume, such beliefs are not grounded in either rational argument or empirical observation; as various Enlightenment philosophers came to believe, such archaic, superstitious, and often dogmatic beliefs are incompatible with the rational and empirical philosophy of knowledge that emerged in the Scientific Revolution.

The word "enlightenment" means to wake up, to become conscious of, to gain knowledge. It can mean to come out of the darkness—of mental confinement, obscurity, and error. The philosophers of the Enlightenment came to believe that religious doctrine—indeed even the pronouncements and presumed authority of royalty—were mental and behavioral shackles, without any epistemological justification, that constrained the conscious mind. It is better to break free of such oppression and open our minds to a world without superstition and authoritarian straightjackets. Both Bacon and Descartes laid the foundations for this emancipation of the human mind— the former critiquing the idols of the knowledge and the latter subjecting all beliefs to systematic doubt—but neither of them could (or would) critically apply their new philosophies of knowledge to their own religious beliefs. Even Locke, though critical of the authoritarianism of royalty, failed to question

God and Western religious belief. Only when we get to Hume, Voltaire, and Condorcet does the spirit of total epistemological freedom from unjustified knowledge claims reach its inevitable conclusion.

It follows then that if religious doctrine and its associated institutions are associated with mental oppression, it is preferable that an enlightened humanity, free from subservience to religious authority, take responsibility for its own understanding and quality of life. This is the philosophy of self-determination that formed the foundation for the great democratic revolutions of the late eighteenth century; it is better to give individuals the right—the freedom and liberty—to pursue their own happiness and well-being than to be subject to the dictates of unjustified authority.

Moreover, with the rise of science and modern technology it appeared that a method existed that, if conscientiously applied by self-directed humans, would lead to a better world. Instead of bowing to authority and asking through prayer for guidance and assistance from God, let us study nature and the workings of the world and applying this knowledge, invent and innovate new technologies that will improve our world. It is clear that Bacon understood the pragmatic power and benefits of the new science, for the *New Atlantis* was built upon the systematic scientific investigation of nature and applications of this growing body of knowledge to the betterment of humankind.

It was out of this philosophy of self-determination through the application of science and technology that the concept of secular progress arose in the eighteenth century in the West. To recall, the idea of progress has a long history in Western civilization, going back to Zoroaster, Lucretius, and St. Augustine. With the exception of Lucretius, who was naturalistic in his philosophy, the concept of progress was grounded in the belief that divine Providence guided the saga of humanity toward a better world. Secular progress, as formulated in modern times, embraced both self-determination (individual freedom) and science (naturalism) as an alternative mindset and methodology for realizing positive change or progress in life and in the future.

The concept of secular progress can be defined as follows: Beginning from Nisbet's (1994) general definition "... the idea of progress holds that mankind has advanced in the past — from some aboriginal condition of primitiveness, barbarism, or even nullity — is now advancing, and will continue to advance through the foreseeable future," we should add that not only are the methods of advancement secular (reason and observation) but that that the criteria for achieving successful advancement are secular as well (improvements in the natural world and human society). Through worldly (scientific, rational, and empirical) means we progressively create an increasingly better world. There is no need to invoke the help of heaven, or worry about heavenly reward.

Aside from the perceived mental and existential oppression that religion and royalty imposed on the world around them, Enlightenment philosophers also saw the material life for common humanity as impoverished, brutish, and difficult. Had the religion-dominated life of the last millennium given humanity, as a whole, a better world? It seemed that this traditional and archaic way of life was based on nothing but a promissory note for a better life in the hereafter, while humanity suffered material deprivation, ill health, and poverty in this one.

It was the French economist Jacques Turgot (1727-1781) who, in his "A Philosophical Review of the Successive Advances of the Human Mind" (1750), put forth the first clear formulation of a purely secular concept of progress. Comprehensive in scope, covering all aspects of human life, Turgot's concept of progress pivoted on three major objectives for the future: increasing knowledge, freedom, and economic growth. For Turgot, these three future-focused objectives were mutually reinforcing. As Bacon had posited, the application of scientific knowledge should lead to increased material well-being and physical health. Critical to the ideal of secular progress was the hope and belief that through science and technology the physical conditions of human life could be steadily and vastly improved. Moreover, through intellectual freedom, knowledge would grow, breaking free of the dogmatic religious shackles of the past. In the mid-eighteenth century, Turgot enthusiastically led the way in this new vision of the future, inspiring Condorcet, Adam Smith, and other later prophets of secular progress and the perpetual improvement of the human condition.

As the eighteenth century unfolded, this vision of technological advance and material improvement gained increasing public credibility. Beginning with the invention of the printing press in Europe in 1450, the speed of technological innovation began to accelerate in modern times. In the eighteenth and early nineteenth centuries, among many other inventions, the steam engine, the steamboat, the first balloon flights, the threshing machine, the weaving machine, the power loom, the circular saw, the sewing machine, the cotton gin, and the electric battery first appeared. By 1750 the Industrial Revolution had begun. It seemed clear to the "naked eye" — the test of empiricism — that human society was being significantly transformed, in many cases for the better, through the advances of science and technology.

It is a common argument that our increasing dependency on technology and science has made modern humanity excessively materialistic, especially insofar as how we define and measure improvement in quality of life (Lombardo, 2017). But the philosophy of the Enlightenment was not inherently a materialistic vision. We could say that the Enlightenment rejected the metaphysical, supernatural, and the spiritual (in the sense of disembodied spirits); but it did not ignore or minimize the psychological, social, humanistic, or ethical dimensions of human reality. (Locke, Hume, and Kant were all great explorers of the intricacies of the conscious human mind.) Still, since the earliest advances in science dealt with the physical world, the consequent technological applications were physical realities as well. Within such a mindset of technological development and possible future inventions based on physical science, we are inclined to envision a better future reality as consisting primarily of great new gadgets. Moreover, since it was a common belief of the Enlightenment that human happiness suffered as a consequence of material and economic impoverishment, positive visions of the future would naturally include a world of material plenty and physical technological advances that presumably would support greater human comfort and happiness (Lombardo, 2006a).

All told, the Enlightenment embraced the idea of secular progress and ignited in the modern Western mind the general expectation that the future would be different from the present and that this process of change would be positive in its direction. The great economic theorist, Adam Smith (1723-1790), who, inspired by the ideas of Turgot, went so far as to propose that there was a "natural law of progress" at work within human history. Recall that Descartes and Leibnitz had already proposed "progressive" or evolutionary theories of nature—nature moves forward. Other philosophers and social scientists in the century ahead, such as Spencer and Comte, would further develop this idea of natural progress, weaving it together with the nineteenth-century theory of evolution. Hence, in the eighteenth and nineteenth centuries secular progress within human society came to be justified as an expression and full flowering of a process occurring within the natural world, if not the cosmos as a whole (Lombardo, 2006a).

Although Smith is primarily remembered for his theory of economics, as outlined in his famous book *The Wealth of Nations* (1776), he saw the possibilities of economic and material improvement as part of a general progressive motion within human history that also included the social and the ethical; indeed, he saw material and psycho-social progress as connected, each supporting the growth of the other. And if we look at the quintessential spokesmen of the Enlightenment, Voltaire and Condorcet, we see a comprehensive and integrative vision of human progress covering all the fundamental dimensions of human existence.

It has been argued that if humanity abandons religion, it eliminates any kind of foundation for ethics and morality. Voltaire, for one, did not agree with this argument. A great admirer of Newton, Voltaire proposed reconstructing human society based on science, reason, and observation. He attacked all forms of absolute authority and dogma, religious and secular, and defended various civil liberties including freedom of religion. He did not believe that God determined human destiny, and he came to totally reject religion as a structure that could provide beneficial guidance in life. Yet, in spite of such expressions of confidence in a secular vision of progress and the human capacity to morally direct the future, a key theme within later science fiction would be apprehensions and fears regarding humanity attempting to "play God" and morally guide the future.

In his classic philosophical statement of the Enlightenment *Sketch for a Historical Picture of the Progress of the Human Mind* (1795), Marquis de Condorcet (Marie-Jean-Antoine Nicolas de Caritat) clearly set science and progress in opposition to religion. He declared himself to be the adversary of all forms of tyranny, which in his mind included royalty, nobility, political monarchies, and the priesthood. Religion, he believed, was based on superstition and an ignorance of nature, and thus was the enemy of progress, which, critically for Condorcet, meant increasing human freedom. Rather than supporting a moral life, religion had led to immorality, including war, persecution, corruption, greed, and the suppression of the rights of human beings. Instead, Condorcet envisioned the ideal society of the future, inclusive of ethical ideals, as one ruled by science and reason.

A key figure in the French Revolution, Condorcet's vision of secular progress was comprehensive in scope and, in particular, highlighted progress in the human mind and character. Once unshackled from the dogmas and constraints of superstition and the religious mindset, the perfectibility of humanity faced no limit. Developing a secular theory of history to support his secular theory of the future, Condorcet argued that there had been ten stages thus far in human history, with the French Revolution (1789-1799) ushering in the beginning of the newest and potentially most "glorious" period in human advancement. He hoped and expected that there would be improvements in the arts, morality, human intelligence, physical health and abilities, and of course science. Given the opportunity for universally accessible and "enlightened" education, human society and human nature would rise to greater and greater heights in the future. Condorcet envisioned a secular, dynamic, and ever-progressive future utopia for humankind. Hence, in Condorcet we see an early expression of the idea that part of the coming transformation of reality in the future would involve the transformation of human nature and the human mind. Part of the vision of modern science fiction, insofar as it involves the future of everything, includes narratives of transformed or evolved humans in the future and not just super-technologies to come.

So, what is the significance of this self-empowering and transformative mindset within the history and development of science fiction? First, we should note that the Enlightenment embraced the emerging new worldview of modern science. Modern science provided a new theory of reality regarding which ideas about reality were credible or plausible. But second, finding its beginnings in Bacon's *New Atlantis*, the application of science to the improvement of life provided a new theory of the future. This new theory of the future was secular progress.

Secular progress, based upon the principles of science and rationality, provided both a vision of material transformation as well as social-economic-political-psychological transformation in the future. The future could be envisioned as different from and better than the present. Indeed, the concept of secular progress provided a mindset for conceptualizing utopian societies; through secular progress a utopian society could be realized in the future. No longer was the utopian society in "another place"; now it was clearly in "another time," specifically the future. Furthermore, utopian visions would become more secularized, based on science and reason rather than the God and Providence (as in St. Augustine and Millennialism for example).

More generally, by taking a transformative and progressive vision of reality, as the Enlightenment philosophers did, the future opened up as an arena of wondrous possibilities. As Clute (1995) argues, modern science fiction begins with the idea that the strange and the different could be placed within the context of the future. In particular, the future will be different due to the application of science and technology to human life. Where before the wondrous, bizarre, and fantastical was located in strange lands or divine places, informed by the theory of reality of ancient myth and religions, now we could imagine future human realities empowered by future science and technology. The idea of secular progress provided a plausible process at work in the world that should generate over time unusual and highly different conditions than those in the present. If the theory of progress is true and humans are beginning to more effectively facilitate progress through reason, self-determination, and science, then we should naturally expect the world of the future to be significantly transformed in its make-up. We should expect transcendence.

Alien Visitations and Extraordinary Adventures

The famous Planetarey Caravan, which I spoke of before, being now entire finish'd and render'd convenient for all such Persons who have any Desire to visit the Moon, Venus, Mercury, or any other of the Planets ...
Advertisement in the *Country Gentleman*, London, 1726

In Isaac Newton's laws of motion, when one body exerts a force upon a second body, the second body simultaneously exerts a force equal in magnitude and opposite in direction on the first body. In Georg Wilhelm Friedrich Hegel's (1770-1831) Idealist philosophy, a thesis will by necessity provoke its antithesis. As we will see in the next few sections, the optimistic scientific philosophy of secular progress and the future would provoke philosophical and literary counter-reactions that would also contribute to the evolution of modern science fiction. Science fiction evolved in both hope and fear of what the human mind imagined.

One significant early counter-reaction to the scientism and rationalism of the Enlightenment can be found in Jonathan Swift's (1667-1745) *Gulliver's Travels* (originally titled *Travels into Several Remote Nations of the World. In Four Parts. By Lemuel Gulliver, First a Surgeon, and then a Captain of Several Ships*) (1726/1735). One of the most popular and highly esteemed works of English literature, *Gulliver's Travels* might seem to be more a novel of intentional fantasy and social satire than an important book in the development of science fiction, yet, it often appears in histories of early science fiction, and within its series of imaginative stories we find a number of significant themes and ideas integral to the genre.

Gulliver's Travels is divided into four parts, each of which covers a journey to strange lands where a variety of bizarre societies and inhabitants are encountered. In essence, it is a series of "extraordinary voyages," but it is also a parody on this whole literary genre, with comical and exaggerated characters and situations. The four parts or main voyages include:

- *A Voyage to Lilliput,* a land inhabited by tiny Lilliputians (one-twelfth the size of humans)
- *A Voyage to Brobdingnag,* a land inhabited by giant Brobdingnagians (twelve times as big as humans)
- *A Voyage to Laputa* (an aerial city) and *Balnibarbi* (a land controlled by the Laputans); *Luggnagg* (a society of aged immortals); *Glubbdubdrib* (a land of magicians and ghosts of famous people of the past); and Japan
- *A Voyage to the Country of the Houyhnhnms* (intelligent horses), but also inhabited by Yahoos, who are primitive and bestial humanoids

The entire saga is highly imaginative, entertaining, and frequently very comical, and, throughout, the tales can be seen as an ongoing satire on human nature and the customs of modern society. Instead of finding some utopian society (as in other extraordinary voyage tales), Gulliver encounters a variety of mindsets and ways of life, all of which have obvious flaws, stupidities, and weaknesses. Swift undoubtedly meant his work to be a parody on adventures into *terra incognito* by which he could examine, through his extremist or fantastically imagined lands and characters, the failings of humankind and contemporary European society.

One of the many targets of *Gulliver's Travels* was the Scientific Revolution and the European Enlightenment. Part three, describing the aerial city of Laputa, provides a colorful and comical critique of scientism and rationalism. "La puta" in Spanish means "the whore," and in Laputa we find a society ruled by totally impractical male scientists enthralled with math, astronomy, music, and technology. The city floats in the clouds, suspended and moved about by a giant magnet. The scientists themselves are "lost in the clouds," not even able to design properly fitting clothes for themselves. Laputa is blatantly a satire on Bacon's *New Atlantis*, with its world ruled by scientists presumably working out all the technological applications and implications of science. Yet, the efforts of the scientists are devoted to such preposterous and ludicrous endeavors as extracting sunbeams from cucumbers and learning how to mix paint by smell. Moreover, the scientists fail miserly in matters of the heart. The women of Laputa, portrayed as highly erotic and totally dissatisfied with the romantic skills of their scientist husbands, secretly travel to the land below, Balnibarbi, where they engage in adultery with its male inhabitants, whom they much prefer to their husbands. Lost in their ethereal pursuits, the male scientists in Laputa are oblivious to the unfaithfulness of their wives. The message: There is something inherently flawed and incomplete, both humanistically and practically, about a society ruled by science and reason.

Swift continues in his satire and critique on excessive rationalism in part four of the book, where Gulliver finds himself in the country of Houyhnhnms and Yahoos. Houyhnhnms are verbal, intelligent, and rational horses with whom Gulliver converses at length. In the horses' language, the word "Houyhnhnms" means "perfection of nature," and indeed Gulliver finds the civilized Houyhnhnms vastly superior to the crude and brutish Yahoo, who spend a great deal of time digging in the mud for "pretty stones." The Yahoo can be seen as symbolizing the deep brutish nature of humans, who, despite the overlay of civilized habits and morals, are inherently stupid and crude beasts. Indeed, Gulliver finds in the Yahoo too many qualities disquietingly suggestive of humans. After returning to human civilization, Gulliver finds himself repelled by human contact (they remind him too much of the Yahoo) and he spends a great deal of time attempting to communicate with the "normal" horses in his stables, in the process becoming mad. Again, this can be seen as symbolic of the inherent failings of a life of reason, for it was the Houyhnhnms who were presumably the paragons of rationality and civilized refinement.

Satires on the present were a common form of literature during Swift's time, serving, through intentional humor, as critiques of current mores. Up through contemporary times, frequently through the exaggeration of present customs and behaviors, satires make their critical observations especially visible to the reader. The fantastical makes the real more conspicuous and vivid. The fantastical and the preposterous become magnifying mirrors for highlighting deficiencies and flaws in contemporary human reality. As further illustrated in this section below, other notable tales and fantastical adventures of the eighteenth century, with an even more pronounced science fiction dimension than *Gulliver's Travels*, would critically and humorously lampoon contemporary "modern" beliefs and behaviors.

In the centuries to come science fiction would frequently provide critiques of the present modern world through exaggerated settings and characters, for example, including bizarre aliens, transformative technologies, great catastrophes, or extraordinary futurist settings. Although we might not associate science fiction with satire and comedy, later classic tales, such as Philip Jose Farmer's libidinous *Flesh* (1960/1968), Frederik Pohl and C. M. Kornbluth's prescient satire on modern marketing and commercialism *The Space Merchants* (1952/1953), and Karel Čapek's deep and hilarious *The Absolute at Large* (1922) and *The War with the Newts* (1937), are all comical and critical tales on humanity that exaggerate human flaws, desires, and attitudes to make their points.

Although satire, the tale of Laputa is a dystopia as well, where the philosophy of reason and science, embraced by Bacon and others as a utopian ideal, when carried to an extreme leads to disaster and the impoverishment of the human soul. Serious or comical-satirical, dystopias have served a critical function in science fiction in assessing our contemporary world and its values and goals. In a dystopia, we consider how some set of beliefs and modes of behavior, if wholeheartedly embraced by some society (hypothetical or in the future), would lead to undesirable, if not terrifying, consequences. Dystopias are the opposite of utopias. In later times, novels such as Milo Hastings' *City of Endless Night* (1920) and Yevgeny Zamyatin's *We* (1921) presented dystopian critiques through particular exaggeration of the scientific-rational mindset as a philosophy for totally orchestrating human life and human society.

Yet, bear in mind that *both* utopias and dystopias invariably make negative points about the contemporary world. For example, in More's *Utopia*, the narrative begins by describing contemporary social and ethical problems, and then, through a depiction of an ideal society, by contrast attempts to show how things could be better. Indeed, utopias invariably define their ideals relative to the perceived problems of the day. Plato's *The Republic* and St. Augustine's *City of God* defined their ideals relative to the perceived weaknesses and difficulties of humankind and human society. A comparison of the real and the ideal is set up. Utopias first critique and then solve the problems raised in the critique. In more modern times, H. G. Wells in *The Food of the Gods* (1904), *Men Like Gods* (1923), and *The Shape of Things to Come* (1933) and Olaf Stapledon in *Last and First Men* (1931) define their utopian ideals and visions relative to critical analyses (and at times satires) of present humanity.

* * *

Among its many notable qualities, *Gulliver's Travels* masterfully delves into the issue of human arrogance: How vain are we about ourselves and our "modern" civilization given our deeper brutish nature? Can we really transcend our animal nature?

How pretentious is it to believe that through science and reason we can jettison a personal God and create a vastly superior world on our own, indeed a true utopia? These are questions science fiction would address at length and from many diverse perspectives in the centuries to come.

Voltaire, one of the central spokesmen of the Enlightenment, provided just such a lesson in humility—in fact, cosmic humility—in his short work of fiction, *Micromégas*, a devastating fantastical satire on the arrogance and frivolity of humankind in the face of the mysteries of the universe. According to science fiction historians, *Micromégas* (written in 1730 and published in 1750) is the first alien visitation story (Roberts, 2005). As reviewed earlier, stories had been written of humans going to the moon, but in this story, aliens—one from Saturn and one from the star system of Sirius—travel to the earth, where they encounter a group of humans and have a conversation with them. The conversation is decidedly philosophical, for the visitors are alien philosophers and scientists, and the upshot of the dialogue is a comical indictment on the intellectual vanity and egocentricity of humankind.

The central protagonist of the story, Micromégas, is a giant (approximately 20,000 feet in height) who lives on a proportionately immense planet orbiting the star Sirius. Commensurate with his immense size, his ten million-year lifespan far exceeds that of humans. He sets out on an exploration of the Milky Way after a dispute with fellow Sirians over his study of the hundred-foot-long insects that live on his planet. He transverses the galaxy without much effort, with the help of sunbeams and comets, never once noticing the vault of the "empyreal heaven" (is there really such a thing?) and eventually comes upon our star system. He visits Saturn, where he finds a race of intelligent beings and befriends one of them, who becomes his fellow traveler on further explorations through our solar system. The Saturnian is a giant as well, but at 6,000 feet in height still significantly smaller than Micromégas. In their initial conversations, they discuss how many senses each possesses; how many substances in the universe they are knowledgeable of; the respective lengths of their lives; and how, no matter how intelligent, capable, or long-lived a form of life may be, desire and need always exceed capacity—life is always too short. Regarding their knowledge of diverse senses and forms of substance, the numbers they quote far exceed the number that humans recognize: Micromégas possesses a thousand different senses and knows of three hundred distinct substances.

Their initial survey of the surface of the earth seems to indicate a complete absence of intelligent life. Of course, these two aliens are so much bigger than any living earthly creature that they do not look closely enough to see any of the animals, which of course include humans. (They have such an expansive perspective that we are too minuscule and inconsequential to notice.) Undaunted, Micromégas constructs a makeshift microscope and discovers a whale in the ocean, and soon thereafter a sailing ship filled with human philosophers. The traveler from Saturn does not believe that anything so small (whale or human)—which appears to the giant aliens like tiny insects—could possess either a soul or intelligence. Micromégas then constructs a communication device (and quickly learns human speech) allowing him to converse with the humans. It is only after the humans answer some scientific and mathematical questions posed by Micromégas, that he and his fellow traveler from Saturn, conclude that humans, despite their microscopic size, possess intelligence.

So far so good. But then Micromégas and the Saturnian ask the humans what they know about their inner nature and the soul, upon which a succession of these human philosophers spout a series of different and often contradictory answers, each citing some great philosophical authority, such as Aristotle, Descartes, and Leibnitz, in support of their particular view.

Finally, one of the human philosophers cites Locke, expressing perhaps the most humble and open-minded opinion on things, but he is thereupon followed by another human philosopher, citing St. Thomas Aquinas as providing the definitive answers for all the great questions, concluding his speech with the assertion that God created the entire universe as a stage for the human drama. This final bombastic expression of intellectual vanity and human-centric thinking sends the alien travelers into uncontrollable laughter. In the story's conclusion, Micromégas and the Saturnian promise to provide the humans with a book that will contain all the answers to the universe, yet when the humans open the book later, they find it is filled with blank pages—the *tabula rasa* (blank tablet) metaphor used by John Locke to describe the original condition of the human mind before experience and learning.

The universe is vast in both space and time; the mysteries, depths, and complexities of nature extend far beyond present human knowledge and imagination. We are dwarfed, physically and mentally, by the cosmos. We are tiny beings that live such very short lives, disagreeing and fighting among ourselves over the most insignificant of matters. Yet, we believe, quite comically and childishly, that it was *all* made for us by some Supreme Being, who revealed Himself to us and has allowed us to figure it all out. Yet, as Micromégas well understands, for all intelligence and life within the universe, visions and aspirations always far exceed understanding and grasp. This is the basic message Voltaire—great skeptic, free thinker, and leader of the Enlightenment—delivers in *Micromégas*. Various elements and variations on this message form many of the essential themes in science fiction, especially when science fiction gets cosmic in its narrative visions. Possessing fleeting and limiting perspectives, we are tiny specks within the cosmos, yet we think we have been given the big answers to the biggest questions.

The conclusion of *Micromégas* leaves us with several questions:

What is the meaning of the blank pages found in the book that presumably contained the answers to everything? That there are no ultimate answers? That we are too feeble and primitive to understand them? That the answers have yet to be found? That the profundity of the human mind amounts to nothing?

* * *

Throughout the eighteenth century, other fictitious aliens would visit the earth. A well-known tale of alien visitation, with some new twists, was *The Philosopher Without Pretension or the Rare Man* (1775) written by Louis-Guillaume De La Folie (1739-1780). What is noteworthy about this tale is that the alien spaceship that crashes on the earth is powered by electricity, recent scientific research into the phenomenon of electricity informing the technological contrivances in the story. Indeed, *The Philosopher* contains the first imagined alien spaceship of any kind in Western literature. The alien visitors, in this case from the planet Mercury, repair their damaged space ship with the help of humans. At least in this story, humans and aliens can cooperate.

Technological inventiveness also shows up in *The Invisible Spy* (1755) by Eliza Haywood (1693-1756), in which the central protagonist possesses a belt that makes him invisible (Wells did not invent the "invisible man"). Perhaps of more interest from a futurist point of view, he also possesses what he refers to as a "wonderful tablet" that records and provides printed records of everything that he says to it—a speech recognition device with a technologically empowered memory storage capacity.

Still, the most popular form of literature of the era, which would contribute into the evolution of science fiction, were the continuing tales of "extraordinary adventures," such as *Gulliver's Travels*, taking human protagonists on journeys to the farthest reaches of the globe and even into the interior of the earth, as well as to the moon and the known planets of the solar system.

Consider journeys into the interior of the earth, a popular theme of adventure stories throughout the eighteenth and nineteenth centuries (Roberts, 2005). Although by our contemporary scientific understanding of the structure and dynamics of the earth, it seems highly implausible that any kind of habitable interior realm could exist, this "scientific fact" was far from obvious to writers of previous centuries. Even if we see Dante's journey as allegorical, as a famous early subterranean explorer he did go "down there" and consistent with popular imagination (then and even now), he found a fiery and hot interior: a Hell populated with monsters. In fact, the earth's interior was open to considerable debate and speculation even into the twentieth century. See, for example, Edgar Rice Burroughs' rousing subterranean adventure tales, *At the Earth's Core* (1914) and *Pellucidar* (1915) and Abraham Merritt's amazing psychedelic journey *The Moon Pool* (1919). Rather, the interior of the earth presented an ideal *terra incognito* in which all kinds of imaginative adventures could take place.

In *The Life and Adventures of Peter Wilkins* (1750) by Robert Paltock (1697-1767) we find the protagonist entering a subterranean world below the South Pole (the poles of the earth as unexplored regions being popular places to descend into the interior of the earth), where he finds a population of naked flying humanlike beings, the Glums and the Gawrys, who live in an Eden-like reality. The inhabitants view Wilkins as the prophesied savior of their world, and he teaches them about the "one God," but also about modern technology. Expressive of Western colonial vanity, our protagonist brings true religion and true science to the indigenous natives.

Perhaps the most well-known of fictionalized journeys into the interior of the earth during the eighteenth century was *Niels Klim's Underground Travels* (1741) by Ludvig Holberg (1684-1754). Holberg's book describes the protagonist, Niels Klim, descending into an underground cave and falling into a "hollow earth," where he finds himself orbiting within an interior solar system around an interior sun. In his adventures within this subterranean realm, he visits a planet populated by intelligent trees that have heads, are able to speak, and walk around on detachable roots that serve as legs. In the story Klim also journeys to various other lands on the "firmament" (the spherical interior surface of the hollow earth that surrounds the interior solar system) where he encounters a country of intelligent monkeys and other societies of diverse animals, including sentient lions, pigs, tigers, and wolves, all of which talk and create technologies. After twelve years in the interior he finds his way back to the surface of the earth.

The "most eminent writer among the Danes in the eighteenth century," Holberg created books of poetry, fictional comedy, history, satire, and cultural studies of contemporary European affairs. He was especially interested in the "vices and follies" and superstitions of the modern European populace. In this regard, his *Underground Travels* can be read as a critical satire on Western customs and behavior, in which the various non-human inhabitants of the hollow earth exhibit a wide range of foolish human-like behaviors carried to extremes. Again, the fantastic serves to highlight the real.

But the book is also a provocative and stimulating expression of human imagination. In the "Apologetic Preface" to the book, presumably written by Niels Klim's grandsons, the argument is made for the credibility of the bizarre tale recounted in the book. Who is to say what is possible or plausible? Similar in ludicrous inventiveness to both Lucian's *True History* and Swift's *Gulliver's Travels*, after the tongue-in-cheek opening argument for the possible truth of the tale, the story dives into a fantastical and often comical adventure containing a wide assortment of astounding creatures and unusual societies. Of particular note, and even if intended as satire, Holberg explores a host of strange cultures and forms of perverse psychology, contributing to the ongoing evolution of imaginative and conceivable possibilities of "alien" (non-human) minds and societies.

In the story, after falling into the open cave, Niels Klim descends into a subterranean solar system on the back of a giant eagle. He lands on the inner planet of Nazar in the Kingdom of Potu, which is ruled by intelligent trees. At first mistaken for a new "comet" by the Potuans, on closer inspection, they decide that he is some kind of strange monkey. He meets the king of Potu and, learning the language of the tree people, begins to record observations on the Potuans' various customs and beliefs. He is particularly fascinated with Potuan religion. The Potuans are forbidden to talk about God or discuss theology; anyone who does is sent to the madhouse, bled, and eventually banished to the firmament above. The Potuans have an "inconceivable-God's day" annual festival when all the trees remain silent and motionless, praying all day.

Niels eventually travels across the entire surface of Nazar, which measures six hundred miles in circumference, and meets different "races" of tree, including oak, cypress, and juniper. One race, he observes, becomes more childish, impulsive, and lustful as they age, forcing the youth to do all the important work, while the elders are all put into cages. In another race and culture of tree, the male trees do all the physical work (including domestic) and serve as prostitutes for the female trees. Another culture of philosophical trees lives among filth and squalor, failing to practice whatever highfalutin ideals they preach. Another race of seven-headed tree geniuses comes up with so many different ideas that they cause chaos and confusion in the culture. In his cross-cultural studies, Klim notes that the social status of trees in a culture is determined by the number of branches a tree possesses and the number of offspring the tree has germinated.

When Niels returns from his journey around the planet, he proposes to the king of Potua that female trees be denied any positions of public power. This suggestion upsets and offends the Potuans and he is straightaway expelled from Nazar. From there he travels to the firmament where he first encounters a country ("Martinia") of intelligent monkeys, who find him stupid and slow-witted. As Niels notes, the monkeys abhor anything that is simple to understand; they revel in complicated, frenetic thinking and useless babble. Taking advantage of this cultural mindset, Niels introduces the totally pointless invention of "wigs" (unknown to the monkeys) which the King of the monkeys and his court love. He becomes rich in the process, but must flee the land by boat when the monkey queen falls in love with him. He travels across the seas of the firmament to the "Land-of-Wonders," encountering and recording in his tale new forms of intelligence, which now include mermaids; verbal-technological animals who have hands and fingers; and mobile, communicative musical instruments (in "Music-land").

Eventually he discovers a barbaric race of humans living like dogs in the land of Quama, who believe Niels to be an emissary from the sun. Niels advances their civilization by teaching the Quamites many new skills, including horseback riding and the creation and use of rifles. The humans are now able, in great battles on land and sea, to conquer their surrounding enemies (various intelligent animals). Establishing the "Fifth Monarchy," Niels is crowned "Niels the Great, Ambassador of Sun, and King of Quama." But power goes to his head, and he becomes paranoid, ruthless, and cruel, igniting an uprising against him. Again he runs away, and in his wanderings, falls down into a deep cavern that turns out to be the same hollow passageway through which he had first descended into the hollow earth. For some reason, he falls upward (relative to the outer surface of the earth) and lands back in the same cave where his journey began twelve years earlier.

Even if Holberg saw his imaginative inner solar system as fanciful rather than plausible, in the mid-eighteenth century it was far from obvious that the earth was solid rather than hollow. The illustrious astronomer and scientist Edmund Halley (1656-1742) had proposed a scientifically grounded hollow earth theory in the late seventeenth century. Into the next century and a half, a number of famous stories would be written recounting journeys into the earth's interior, with accompanying scientific arguments and naturalistic detail supporting the plausibility of such scenarios.

The scientific credibility of a tale should be judged relative to the contemporary scientific understanding of nature. For his time, Holberg's notion of an interior solar system is ingenious; it is unclear who in human history first suggested this provocative idea. Moreover, Holberg's idea of intelligent plants would continue as a popular speculative theme in later science fiction, even into the twenty-first century. Are intelligent plants or trees scientifically plausible? Have we even yet to decide?

Holberg was more of a social-historical thinker than a naturalist or physical scientist, though, and his tale of *Niels Klim* focuses more on issues of society, morals, and mind than physical speculations on the interior of the earth. The main substance of the book deals with alternative societies and forms of mentality, even if the various speculations are primarily exaggerations of human qualities and forms of social order. Yet all in all he does use a science fiction-like adventure into a strange reality with strange inhabitants to frame his humanistic commentary. And the story overall is highly entertaining and engaging with its bizarre imagery and comical depictions of its characters, including Niels Klim.

In the eighteenth century there were also numerous fictitious journeys to the moon (Roberts, 2005). As with Cyrano de Bergerac's lunar tale, the function of these stories was often satire on human society. In fact, as the century moved along it became increasingly scientifically implausible that the moon had inhabitants, since through ongoing astronomical observations it became apparent that the moon did not possess an atmosphere. Could a story of traveling to the moon and meeting lunar inhabitants any longer be considered a real possibility? Still, scientific implausibility did not prevent "science fiction-like" stories about the moon and its inhabitants from being written, in the eighteenth and nineteenth centuries.

In 1793, for example, we find the tale *A Voyage to the Moon* (anonymous) that introduces the idea of traveling there in a balloon. In the "real world" we had created and successfully tested a variety of manned balloons by the end of the eighteenth century (Holmes, 2008), and such real-world technological achievements provided a plausible mechanism for getting to the moon. The protagonist in *A Voyage to the Moon* finds upon arrival on the lunar surface serpentine aliens.

We also have Thomas Gray's science fiction poem, "The Inhabitable Moon" (1737). Here we find hypothetical lunar inhabitants who are "cyborg-like" (the coupling of the biological and mechanical), as well as the ideas of eventual lunar conquest by humans and the establishment of a human lunar colony.

But in the eighteenth century the moon was no longer the outer limits of human imagination and space exploration. The emerging science of astronomy, with improvements in telescopy, was progressively revealing more and more about the solar system and even what lies beyond it. In his 1750 political satire, *An Account of the Planet Mercury*, Chevalier Bethune imagined a Mercurian society of winged creatures who were ruled by beings of the sun.

The first untethered, manned, hot air balloon flight was achieved in 1783, proving that humanity was not bound to the earth (see the next chapter). Yet long before this technological achievement, or the imaginative balloon flight in *A Voyage to the Moon*, Eberhard Kindermann published his *The Rapid Journey by Airship to the Upper World* (1744) in which five humans go to Mars in a balloon.

One other noteworthy journey into outer space in this period was *The Voyage of Lord Ceton to the Seven Planets* (1765) by a woman author, Marie-Anne de Roumier. In this tale two human space travelers are transported by an angel to all the known planets of the solar system—including the sun—finding distinctive forms of life and intelligence on each world. Aside from the angel—a spiritual being—providing the mode of transportation, Roumeir's story blends astronomical science with theological concepts in proposing that alien worlds are inhabited by reincarnated human souls from earth. Reflecting ancient spiritualist and religious thinking, outer space is seen as a heavenly realm where human souls realize an afterlife (or another life). The famous nineteenth-century astronomer, mystic, and science fiction writer Camille Flammarion was influenced by Roumier's vision, working reincarnation of souls into his grand narrative sagas of the cosmos, for example, in *Lumen* (1872/1897). Similarly, in his *Journey in Other Worlds* (1894), John Jacob Astor populates Saturn with the souls of dead humans. Even if outer space in modern times was becoming increasingly a scientific concept and naturalistic territory of exploration, replacing the idea that the heavens were a spiritual and eternal realm, outer space would still frequently be associated with some higher level of reality, one inhabited by ethereal sages and providing cosmic insight and existential elevation.

Utopian Visions and Futuristic Fiction

Other generations will come to fill the space that we now occupy. They will appear on the same stage, behold the same sun, and push us so far back into antiquity that there will remain of us neither trace, nor vestige, nor memory.
Louis-Sébastien Mercier

One of the most fascinating explorers of imagination in the late eighteenth century was Nicolas-Edme Restif de la Bretonne (1734-1806). Writing madly and profusely in a rambling and disorganized fashion, and synthesizing elements of utopian thought, mental telepathy, reincarnation, extraordinary adventures (across the globe and beyond), technological extrapolation, fantastical art, evolution, and eroticized cosmology, he penned at least two noteworthy tales that are significant in the history of science fiction: *The Discovery of Australia by a Flying Man, or the French Daedalus* (1781) and *The Posthumous Ones* (1802).

Restif—referred to by some as the "Rousseau of the gutter"— was obsessed with sex: in his lifestyle and reminiscences; his artwork; his utopian writings; and his philosophical speculations. According to Roberts (2005), Restif de la Bretonne was a believer in free love, who wrote numerous amorous tales reveling in promiscuity and eroticism that were notable for their titillating and highly explicit illustrations. His pornographic tales frequently involved his own highly graphic and intimate personal recollections of sexual affairs and encounters (perhaps fanciful, perhaps real), and he was an outspoken advocate for fundamental moral-social changes in human sexual behavior. As a utopian writer, he "took it upon himself nothing less than the total reform of society," and illustrating his obsession with sex, he wrote numerous books specifically dealing with new social directions and norms on sexual behavior, including the regulation of prostitution.

Yet he also went beyond earthly affairs in his sexual-erotic imagery and thinking, developing a visionary and romantic cosmology of the solar system grounded in sexual ideation. As he explains in his *The Discovery of Australia,* all matter is alive and the sun and the planets emit seminal fluids, engaging in a kind of astronomical copulation. The sun fertilizes the earth through light.

The Discovery of Australia is on the surface an extraordinary adventure tale, where the protagonist invents a flying apparatus (with mechanical wings and an umbrella on the head) and, taking his wife on the journey, travels around the world, with a notable visit to the wilds of Australia. There they observe, among other strange sights, a variety of human-animal hybrids (suggesting some kind of pre-human evolutionary heritage). What is especially interesting about this dimension of the story is that Restif, an engraver and illustrator, provides in the book a wondrous assortment of drawings of these fantastical half-human, half-animal creatures. In many cases there are clear sexual elements to the imagery as well. (Is this some kind of envisioned innocent and primitive Eden-like utopia?) His illustrations for the book, which can be found on *Amazing Illustrations,* provide a benchmark for the evolution of fantastic art within the late eighteenth century.

In *The Posthumous Ones,* we again find a flying apparatus and recorded travels across the globe, but now we also have a mysterious old man encountered on the global journey, who, with his heightened mental powers, can penetrate into other human minds. The protagonist provides the old man "with wings," whereupon they initially travel further around the globe, establishing an earthly utopia. They then take flight for the vast reaches of the solar system. Journeying across the solar system they meet various aliens and, using the old man's psychic powers, enter into their minds. As they move toward the sun on their solar adventure, the protagonist experiences a great cosmic insight: "Life is the product of the ineffable copulation of God."

As quoted in *Amazing Illustrations,* Restif de la Bretonne "... was inordinately vain, of extremely relaxed morals, and perhaps not entirely sane. His books ... and their license of subject and language renders them 'quite unfit for general perusal'." All the more reason for enjoying his wild, uncensored, and imaginative writings and artwork, and pondering the significance of it all. For mad though he may have been, Restif de la Bretonne decidedly contributed into the creative, evolving stream of the fantastical within the history of science fiction.

* * *

Restif de la Bretonne can be viewed as a utopian thinker (Manuel and Manuel, 1979), both a critic of contemporary European society and a vocal advocate for social and ethical change. To recall, progressive social ideals and social criticism are frequently coupled together, the criticisms serving as a foundation and justification for presenting a different and preferable vision of society—the utopia is the solution to the identified social problems. The Enlightenment theory of secular progress, including both social-political and rational-scientific ideals, was a utopian vision in this bipolar sense, identifying both the problems of the day (superstition, authoritarianism, elitism, poverty, and dogmatism) as well as the solution (science, reason, and freedom) to such problems.

Enlightenment writers such as Turgot and Condorcet provide a clear vision of a future, built on secular progress that will be both different from and better than the present. In this sense they were, among others, utopian thinkers who located their ideal visions of society in the future. In the present we find numerous social problems and failings; but in the future we will create and live within a much better world. Moreover, writers like Turgot and Condorcet did not envision static utopias in the future; based on ideas such as a historical law of progress; the hypothesized human drive toward ongoing innovation; the continued acquisition of new knowledge; and the "infinite perfectibility of man," there would be no end or final stage to human perfection. The promise of the future was unending progressive change; stasis was anathema to a utopian reality (Lombardo, 2010).

It is a small but significant step from such a futurist utopian philosophy to creating a futurist utopian narrative. Especially in the latter part of the eighteenth century, on the heels of the European Enlightenment, there was a growing popularity in "futuristic fictions," where utopias were set in an imagined future, not only providing ideal visions of human society but critiques as well of present society. These "futuristic fictions" explored, to various degrees, both social and scientific-technological possibilities. Although invariably limited in imaginative freedom, depicting future human society through the eyes of the present, the futurist narrative, however constrained by the assumptions of the present, at least was spreading its wings in the era of the Enlightenment (Manuel and Manuel, 1979; Alkon, 1987; Roberts, 2005).

We should note at this point that the first notable secular futuristic fiction appeared prior to the Enlightenment in the seventeenth century. According to Paul Alkon, in his *Origins of Futuristic Fiction* (1987), the French writer, Jacques Guttin, attempted to create a narrative of the future in his *Epigone: The History of the Future Century*, published in 1659. As mentioned earlier, Alkon argues that prior to modern times the future was a realm reserved for prophets, poets, astrologers, and practitioners of deliberative rhetoric. Nonetheless, according to Alkon, Guttin did at least attempt to write an actual *story* with specific characters and settings set in the future.

Still, as both Alkon and Roberts note, although secular and futuristic in its intent, *Epigone*, an "extraordinary voyage" tale to exotic lands and strange civilizations—including an Amazonian culture "devoted to sensual pleasure"—is filled with mythic, chivalric, and medieval romantic themes, including elements highly derivative from Virgil's *Aeneid* and Homer's *Odyssey*. Steeped in the past, it is not really a tale of a future in any significant way that is different from the present or the past. Yet, we should keep in mind that stories of the future frequently derive content and themes from the past, including religious and mythic elements. *Epigone,* though, never gets beyond this mindset grounded in the past.

More to the point, as Alkon repeatedly illustrates, the future envisioned in *Epigone* is actually an "alternative reality" future, with a past that is notably different from our own actual past. Therefore, the story is not a possible or hypothetical future for our own world. Yet, this envisioning of an alternative reality, both past and future, is an historically significant feature of the story, since the sub-genre of alternative realities (as explained earlier) is an important arena of imagination in science fiction; it opens up possibility spaces of speculation along many different fronts. Indeed, alternative pasts have been a noteworthy area of speculative narratives in works such as Philip Dick's *The Man in the High Castle* (1962) and Ward Moore's *Bring the Jubilee* (1955). Carried to the extreme in Stephen Baxter's *The Time Ships* (1995), we have innumerable different pasts *and* different futures. As Alkon notes, alternative histories became a distinctive literary genre as early as the nineteenth century with Louis Geoffroy's *Napoleon and the Conquest of the World* (1856) and Charles Renouvier's *Uchronia (Utopia in History)* (1876). Alternative realities (including alternative pasts) are part of the "what if" mind space of science fiction; it is a way to transcend accepted reality and thinking, rejecting (at least in speculation) the idea that the past is a definitively set reality.

Alkon next cites Samuel Madden's *Memoirs of the Twentieth Century* (1733) as a notable book in the modern evolution of futuristic fiction, as well as science fiction. For one thing, and distinguishing it from Guttin's *Epigone*, although *Memoirs* is a satire (on ponderous history books of the period), the content of the book clearly pertains to a possible, if not a plausible, future emerging from the reality of the present time. Second, the story involves time travel from the future to the present, with a hypothetical guardian angel traveling back from the twentieth century (the late 1990s) and delivering to the narrator of the book in the present (the 1730s) a set of "letters" and "reports" purportedly written by government officials living in this future reality. The future is revealed through time travel. As far as Alkon is aware, this tale is the first instance of a story containing a supposed document from the future. The various letters not only describe contemporary affairs in the late twentieth century, but also include "historical" passages that explain how "earlier" events in the twentieth century led to this "future present." Hence, Madden, to some degree at least, presents a "future history" describing a causally connected series of events leading to a hypothetical future.

Even if Madden's envisioned future is severely constrained by the mentality and culture of his time—it is Eurocentric, with England still a dominant power and the Pope still a significant figure in world affairs—through the exposition of his fictitious narrator, Madden does emphasize that the future will be much different from the present, especially due to the ongoing advances of science. As the narrator notes, modern science is generating a host of new discoveries and ideas that seem amazing and incredible, if not fantastic and implausible (relative to traditional thinking). If anything, what is most probable in the future is that, relative to our present mindset, it will seem impossible and totally surprising. (The narrator also notes that for any era in history, even prior to the emergence of modern science, what was to come in subsequent periods would seem impossible and totally unexpected relative to the present.) In essence, Madden realizes that, especially due to the expected continued growth of science, the future is a reality space in which the unanticipated, the fantastical, and the amazing will occur. This recognition of fundamental change and transcendence in the future through science is a key theme in the Age of Enlightenment.

Another frequently cited eighteenth-century example of a "futuristic fiction," the *Reign of King George VI, 1900-1925* (1763) by an anonymous author, describes a future England set in the twentieth century. The novel depicts successive future wars between England and, successively, France, Russia, and Spain, where the British Empire, through military victories, expands across Europe while continuing to maintain its control over great swaths of North America. (The author does not anticipate the American Revolution.) The British monarchy persists as an authoritarian form of government; indeed, the King of England becomes the King of France as well. Although the spirit of progress and change, both technological and social, was intensifying in the mid-eighteenth century, this "futuristic fiction" is another illustration of linear and time-bound thinking. The author envisions a future English society (its politics and culture) that is fundamentally no different from the present. The King still rules in the future and the Empire continues to grow through military conquest. What has yet to be adequately understood—and in fact is very difficult to imagine—is that not only will technology change (or be transformed), but society, morals, and the human mind will also be transformed in the future.

On the other hand, the work most frequently cited as the first clear example of a futurist utopian narrative—where fundamental progressive change, both social and technological, is predicted in the future—is Louis-Sébastien Mercier's (1740-1814) *The Year 2440: A Dream If Ever There Was One* (1771). Highly imaginative for its time—it was banned and labeled as blasphemous—it was an extremely popular book, going through twenty-five editions and numerous translations, selling tens of thousands of copies, and eliciting a host of utopian imitations across Europe in the decades to follow. It also has been described as highly bombastic and moralizing, weak in narrative strength, and excessive in its preachiness.

Louis-Sébastien Mercier was very active in the French Revolution and highly critical, in his many writings, of contemporary French society, a society of social and economic inequality and injustice ruled by dictatorial royalty, the wealthy elite, and authoritarian religious figureheads that the

Revolution attempted to eradicate and replace with a more egalitarian society. The French Revolution championed the Enlightenment ideals of human freedom and equality (as did the American Revolution) and Mercier believed that his book greatly contributed to igniting this social revolt in France against tyranny and inequality. (Fiction influences fact.) *The Year 2440* reflects this new emerging modernist ideological stance; Mercier's world of the future is founded on liberty and equality, freedom of thought, and universal education.

The book begins in present times with a heated dialogue between the central character and an Englishman concerning various flaws and failings in contemporary French society. Then the central character falls into a deep sleep (a Rip Van Winkle scenario) and wakes up in Paris in the twenty-fifth century. What the protagonist finds upon awakening is a society wondrously transformed, shaped by the ideals of reason and science as espoused within the philosophy of the Enlightenment.

Paris is clean, peaceful, and in general highly ordered in its ways of life. The city atmosphere is "airy and clement." Streets are broad and brilliantly illuminated, and the city architecture has been reconstructed and beautified. There is ample housing and comfortable hospitals. City traffic has been significantly reduced. Overall, urban reality has been vastly improved.

All people walk, depending on their destination, on the prescribed correct side of the streets. There are no beggars or prostitutes on the streets, and no longer is there crowding or boisterous mobs of people. Everyone, in fact, that the protagonist meets seems cheerful, polite, and happy. Human psychology seems transformed.

Moreover, religion has been drastically altered; there is no formal religion anymore at all. The Catholic Church has been abolished (hence there are no monks or priests) with a philosophy of Deism (belief in a Creator God without supernatural intervention) taking its place. Education is grounded in the study of physics and algebra (the youth should learn what is relevant to the modern age, namely science and mathematics) rather than the archaic and useless subjects of Greek and Latin. In essence, religion and education have been aligned with modernist and scientific ideals.

In the spirit of liberty and equality, slavery and colonialism have been eliminated. Also, there is no longer any standing army for the world is at peace. Kings govern wisely, having given up on the "frenzied ambition of ruling over desolate countries filled with aching hearts." Social oppression has been eliminated and human rights have come to the forefront.

Our time traveler finds further surprising changes in Paris: Gone are "dancing masters" and "pastry chefs." Taxes, guilds, foreign trade, and arbitrary arrests have also disappeared. Perhaps reaching the heights of excessive moral purity and constraint, "coffee, tea, and tobacco, and all useless and immoral previously-written literature has been destroyed." There is moral evolution in the future.

Having become aware of the first successful manned balloon trips in the early 1780s, Mercier published a revised edition to his book (1786). Adding more to his earlier technological extrapolations, he envisioned his future utopian reality globally united in peace and enhanced communication through "aeronauts" and their incredible flying machines. Balloon empowered flying machines would become a common feature in later futurist fiction; within one hundred years, Albert Robida, in his seminal work *The Twentieth Century* (1883), would describe a future Paris in which the predominant mode of transportation, even at a personal level, was the balloon.

As Manuel and Manuel (1979) state, Mercier created a "terrestrial urban paradise where reason and utility reigned supreme." But perhaps Mercier's utopian paradise of the future is too clean, orderly, and peaceful. Although he champions the central value of freedom, where are the individuality, flux, and innovation in his ideal vision of the future? Although peaceful, his ideal future seems more controlled and uniform (totalitarian) than diverse and unconstrained (democratic and/or anarchistic). A highly structured, and we could say, "rational society" might seem a desirable direction to pursue; More and Bacon had such kinds of highly organized social systems. But would such a stable and peaceful society be consistent with the ideals of freedom and secular progress, and would it psychologically be desirable?

Here then are the paradoxes: Both the French and American Revolutions championed the ideals of the Enlightenment. In both cases there was a revolt against perceived tyranny, inequality, oppression, the ruthless pursuit of power, and injustice. The right of individuals to be masters of their own fate was central to these social upheavals. Ironically, a highly ordered, uniform, and even peaceful society envisioned as a result of these revolutions seems anathema to individualistic ideals. (Are individualism and rational order compatible?) Further, as expressions of the Enlightenment, both revolutions supported reason and science as the road to truth and progress, and yet the actual pathway in human history taken to realize these new ideals involved conflict, war, and violence. Neither the Americans nor the French "reasoned" existing authority figures out of their positions of power; indeed, what is most common in human history, if not universal, is that those in power have never willingly given up their positions of power without a fight (physically or ideologically).

As Alkon argues, Mercier's future utopia is not so much a prediction about the future (he may have been realistically pessimistic about the future) as a proposed preferable future, an ideal to hope for and aspire toward. If so, even if his professed philosophy reflected the Enlightenment, his ideal vision (in a long line running back to Plato) seems too rigid, orderly, uniform and inconsistent with the Enlightenment philosophy of individualism and freedom. In the coming centuries, images of future societies that were rationally ordered, stable, and peaceful (such as Mercier's) would become paragon cases of dystopias, rather than utopias. That is, once the philosophy of individualism, freedom, and unending change and progress really sank in, those ideal images of reason, peace, and order transformed in people's minds from utopias into perceived dystopias.

We can return now to the question of how the evolution of utopias feeds into the growth of science fiction. In this context, we can also address how utopian thinking is relevant to my thesis that science fiction is the evolutionary mythology of the future. If science fiction encompasses the future of everything, than as utopias in modern times provided integrative ideal visions of the future, pulling in both the social-humanistic and the scientific-technological, then these utopias of the future provided the foundation for generating integrative visions of the future in science fiction. Indeed, integrative dystopias (social-technological) also provided rich and diverse comprehensive settings from which to draw in the creation of science fiction narratives.

Regarding the question of myth, both utopias and dystopias of the future are powerfully mythic, for such narratives, at the very least, realize transcendence (going beyond existing conditions); engage the full range of human emotion; frequently inspire and provoke action (consider Mercier's opinion of the impact of his book); and address the question of the meaning and purpose of human life: What is the good life and what isn't?

Myths can be either heavenly or nightmarish in their imagery and psychological impact. Narrative utopias are myths based on hope; dystopian stories are myths of fear. But the latter also reveals to us what we want by showing us (often in exaggerated form) what we don't want. And as stated above, what we once viewed as heaven may have been transformed in our present perspective into hell, and perhaps vice versa. Myths evolve; how we interpret myths evolve. The history of utopias and dystopias, including the huge array of them in science fiction, provides a mental space of possibilities and narrative experiments in which to imagine and thoughtfully consider what are preferable and non-preferable directions for the future, and ponder why we think what we do about our values and preferences.

Chapter Six

Romanticism and the Gothic

Romanticism and Romantic Science

... a new and restless spirit, seeking violently to burst through old and cramping forms, a nervous preoccupation with perpetually changing inner states of consciousness, a longing for the unbounded and the indefinable, for perpetual movement and change, an effort to return to the forgotten sources of life, a passionate effort at self-assertion both individual and collective ...
Isaiah Berlin

As we move into the latter decades of the eighteenth century two connected ways of thinking and artistic expression—of energetic modes of consciousness—would emerge that were both highly influential in the ongoing evolution of science fiction. These two movements were Gothic literature and the philosophy of Romanticism, both of which would impact Western literature, poetry, philosophy, art, music, and even science. Romanticism is the broader and more powerful cultural movement, encompassing the Gothic, but each in its own way represents a reaction against different aspects of modernity, in particular, the scientism and rationalism of the philosophy of the Enlightenment. Let's begin with Romanticism.

Romanticism was a complex, many-faceted movement. As with my views on the Scientific Revolution—one more extreme and black and white; one more complicated and nuanced—here I present first, a more standard view, and then a more recent interpretation of this philosophical-artistic movement. Both perspectives contain important elements of truth, and both provide enlightening insights into the roots of science fiction in the nineteenth century (*Romanticism*).

Starting with the more traditional or standard view of Romanticism:

The strongest attack in the eighteenth century on the modern theory of scientific truth and secular progress arose in Romanticism. As a movement in philosophy, art, and literature, Romanticism can be approximately dated from 1750 to 1810, but its influence continues up to the present day. Some of the central literary figures of Romanticism included the poets Lord Byron (1788-1824), Samuel Coleridge (1772-1834), William Wordsworth (1770-1850), Percy Shelley (1792-1822), and John Keats (1795-1821), all pursuing beauty, lyricism, and intuitive insight as the pathways to understanding and meaning within the human condition. In many cases they were colorful "personalities," which is part of the Romantic aura. Romanticism also extended into the visual arts; Romantic art was exuberant, emotional, and vibrant, breaking free of the formal constraints of previous artistic periods. Combining both modes of artistic expression, the English Romantic poet and painter William Blake (1757-1827) created mystical, dynamic, and luminous works in both word and image. Blake's art is archetypal, cosmic, and highly visionary, drawing upon biblical and mythological themes. (Romanticism frequently found inspiration in the past.) Extending into musical art, in the compositions of Berlioz, Beethoven, Liszt, Verdi, and numerous other nineteenth-century composers, Romantic music realized an intense, passionate, colorful, flamboyant, and exuberant style, transcending the Classical focus on form. Romanticism, in art, music, and literature, sang from the heart, reveled in the senses, and danced to the melodies of reality.

Recall the distinction between the Apollonian and Dionysian modes of consciousness. Enlightenment philosophy, with its emphasis on reason, falls within the Apollonian mindset, whereas Romanticism can be seen as the modern evolutionary expression of the Dionysian mindset of ancient Greece. As the contemporary scientist E. O. Wilson notes, many people of the time found Enlightenment philosophy "bloodless," with its focus on rationality, objectivity, science, and utility; this cold philosophical vision seemed to destroy the human element. In contrast, Romanticism—as a Dionysian mode of consciousness, reveling in the senses, emotion, and human subjectivity—recoiled against the rationalistic, orderly, abstract, and "bloodless" philosophy of the Enlightenment (Wilson, 1998a, 1998b).

In essence, modern Romanticism set out to dethrone rational Enlightenment and everything associated with it from its position of growing cultural power, providing an alternative and competing approach and attitude toward life and the future. This critique and existential opposition—this antithesis to reason and secular progress—created a deep cultural schism in modern Western society, or as Watson (2005) refers to it, the "modern incoherence," which is still with us up to the present day. Is the meaning of life found through emotion, art, and the senses, or through science, reason, and techno-industrial progress? This was the existential opposition the Romantic revolution set up against the Enlightenment.

Whereas the Enlightenment emphasized reason and science, Romanticism embraced emotion, passion, "sensibility", and the a-rational or irrational. Indeed, Romanticism reveled in intense emotionality, in horror, terror, agony, eros, and ecstasy. One of the historical roots of Romanticism was the German "Sturm und Drang" (storm and urge, or storm and stress) literary movement of the 1760s through the 1780s. In place of cool reason, we have hot emotion; we have chaos instead of order. Further, Romanticists examined the "dark side" of humanity—of violence, conflict, and fear—which we also find in "Sturm and Drang". In Romanticism we see the exploration of unconscious—beyond the veil of reason—desires and feelings (Watson, 2005).

Moreover, Newton's scientific vision of an orderly "clockwork universe" inspired a mechanistic and machine model of nature (and in fact a mechanistic model of human society) (Goerner, 1999). Reacting against the modern "scientific rationalization of nature," Romanticist philosophers, artists, and writers saw nature as alive, inspirited, enchanted, spontaneous, and organic. Romanticists understood nature through poetry and art, rather than through scientific abstraction. Romanticists often reveled in raw nature, in opposition to the constraints, refinements, and excessive order of modern civilization. Instead of Bacon's notion of conquering nature through science and technology, many Romanticists wanted to return to a purer harmony and unity with nature. If science wanted to detach itself from nature, adopting an objectivist stance on reality, Romanticists wanted to immerse themselves, personally and subjectively, in nature. Romanticists *felt* nature.

Further, whereas Western science searched for grand abstractions and universal knowledge, the Romanticists valued uniqueness and diversity. Whereas the Enlightenment searched for scientific certainty, the Romanticists embraced uncertainty and wonder. Philosophers of secular progress frequently championed the importance of order; Romanticist philosophers embraced chaos, turbulence, the strange, and the macabre (Lombardo, 2006a).

Romanticism can also be seen as a regressive movement, a recoil into the past, expressing a desire to "return to nature," to see nature as "animated" and "enchanted," and rejecting the technology, urbanization, and burgeoning industry of modern times. In this regard, whereas the Enlightenment wished to rid humanity of superstition and the supernatural, the Romanticists reasserted the value and truth of ancient myths and the mystical. Romanticism, especially in its Gothic offspring, embraced the visions, ideals, and ghosts of medieval times.

For Romanticists, it was far from obvious whether the great thrust forward of science and secular progress was producing a better world. Romanticists saw modern civilization as dehumanizing and alienating. Modern humanity was cut off from nature through urbanization. Secular progress and urbanized civilization were creating increasing oppression and regimentation within the human spirit. The individual was being suffocated in the name of secular progress. Although philosophers of the Enlightenment often championed the ideals of freedom and self-expression, the Romanticists saw the results of increasing modernization as producing the opposite effect. The Romanticists firmly believed in the values of individualism and freedom, which they thought were being undercut in the new modern world order. If Enlightenment philosophers and advocates of modern science and technology saw humanity moving toward a heaven or paradise on earth, Romanticists saw a nightmare unfolding, a progressive death of the human spirit. In this contrary interpretation of the utopia of the Enlightenment, we again see the ambiguity of the utopian-dystopian opposition.

For the Romanticists, capitalism, industrialism, and consumerism were turning humans into machines—cogs in the wheel of progress and production—who lose themselves in things at the expense of human feeling and human intimacy. In short, to the Romanticists, a philosophy of progress built on rationality, objectivity, mechanization, and efficiency is not progress at all; it is regressive and a dive into death. It ignores the human heart, destroys spontaneity, kills individualism, and isolates humans in the unnatural constructions of technology, industry, and urbanization. As Max Weber, the late nineteenth-century sociologist and economist stated, modernity created a "bureaucratization of the human spirit" and placed the human being in an "Iron Cage" (Lombardo, 2006a). All of these key ideas within the Romantic critique of modernism would feed into the imagination and storytelling of modern science fiction.

As another important theme, the First Industrial Revolution (1760-1820) and the accelerative growth of modern technology, following on the heels of the Scientific Revolution, emphasized transforming the external world. Further, modern science brought with it an emphasis on objectivity, and its early successes dealt primarily with the physical world. In opposition, the Romanticists turned inward, delving into the subjective, personal, and the deep inner self. Romanticism emphasized the subjective and inner side of human existence and rejected the Enlightenment ideal of a single objective truth. In general, Romanticism brought back into the human equation, in great force, the subjective and personalized dimensions of humanity that, in their minds, had been repressed or minimized in objective science and the techno-industrialized modern world.

Although the Romanticists were critical of the secular theory of progress and valued the mythical traditions of the past, they were not so much dismissive of the future as simply offering an alternative vision of tomorrow. They feared that science and the rational secular ideal of progress were more Faustian (a deal with the devil motivated by human ego and vanity) than Promethean. Rationality, objectivity, and techno-industrialism were leading to a very undesirable future. Emotion rather than reason needed to guide the future. Through the novel, poetry, and the visual and musical arts, the Romanticists created an alternative interpretation of the world to that of science, and defined a different set of ideals to strive toward in creating a better world in the future. The Romanticists presented a different approach to heightened future consciousness, one that highlighted sensory and aesthetic experience, intuition, and emotion.

In this regard, the artist replaced the scientist as the guiding personal archetype and beacon for the future. The Romantic poet Lord Byron elevated the artist as hero to the central position in Romantic philosophy. If objective truth was the ultimate goal of science, Romanticists elevated beauty to center stage instead, and it was the artist that most centrally pursued beauty. Just as the search for truth had been for many early scientists an effort to read the "mind of God," the creation of beauty became the central spiritual quest for the Romanticists and the most important human ideal. Moreover, beauty and the aesthetic, for the Romanticists, took precedence over the utilitarian values of capitalism, industrialism, and technology. The modern world was dehumanizing and destructive; the modern world was ugly; its efficiency and utilitarian value were not enough. Hence, it was the artist who, with passion and true humanity, focused on the pursuit of beauty, must lead the way into the future. Artistic future consciousness transcends rational and utilitarian future consciousness.

Another key theme in Romanticism was creativity. Romanticists valued inspiration, intuition, revelation, and mystery; they valued freedom in both imagination and emotional expression. In his discussion of Romanticism, which he describes as "the great reversal of values," Peter Watson (2005) identifies the elevation of creativity as pivotal to Romantic philosophy and art. For the Romanticists, "man" is fundamentally a creative being, who invents both the individual self and human values. There is no true self or definitive set of values. Ultimately what is central in human life is created rather than discovered, and thus lies outside the scope of science. Life is art; life is will; life is an act of creation. It is the creative artist, often solitary and alienated from mass conformist human society (as Byron envisioned and lived the archetype), struggling to realize his or her unique vision, that epitomizes the Romantic ideal. In essence, the creativity (and creation) of the unique replaces the discovery of objective and universal truth as the fundamental human ideal.

All in all, the rise of Romanticism set the stage for one of the central ongoing debates in the subsequent development of science fiction. Are science, techno-industrial development, and secular progress good things? Are we moving toward a better future by embracing these ideals? Or, are we losing our connection with nature, our humanity, our sense of beauty, and our inner emotional selves in the process? Is a rational, scientific, and technological future something to hope for and aspire toward, or something to fear? What constitutes a viable utopia of the future? What makes for a dystopia? As will become apparent, many science fiction dystopias of the future were basically variations on the Romantic critique of scientific-rationalistic-techno-industrialized visions of the future.

Moreover, as a literary, narrative mode of consciousness and expression, science fiction aligns with the Romantic spirit. Although informed by scientific theory, the genre as a form of art that employs personification and drama stands in opposition to the abstract formulations of science. In an essential sense, the future is felt. Indeed, when science fiction focuses on scientific and technological exposition to the exclusion of personalized characters and emotionally engaging stories, it becomes wooden and dry. The spirit of Romanticism is a deep and essential part of modern science fiction.

As one final point, even if there are, as described above, some clear differences between Enlightenment philosophy and Romanticism, it is noteworthy that the modern Western ideal of individualism finds strong expression in both philosophies. Within the Western Enlightenment, individual self-determination and freedom are pivotal values set in opposition to governmental and religious tyranny and dogmatism; in Romanticism the spirit of individualism, including the creative spirit, is set in opposition to the conformist, rationalistic, mechanized, and orderly modern society. Clearly there is an element of resonance between these two philosophies. Yet, as noted earlier, an envisioned future society ruled by reason and science seems to yield a highly ordered world that suppresses human freedom and individuality. As the Romanticists argued, a modern world as a product of advancing rational science, technology, and industry is one that, in fact, destroys individuality and freedom, rather than enhancing it.

* * *

*My opinion is this — that deep Thinking is only attainable by a man
of deep Feeling, and that all Truth is a species of Revelation.*
Samuel Coleridge

Now consider an alternative view: Romanticism was not
necessarily opposed to science, but rather, to a significant
degree, both energized it and was energized by it.

Although standard accounts of Romanticism usually portray
it as anti-scientific, Richard Holmes, in *The Age of Wonder: How
the Romantic Generation Discovered the Beauty and Terror of Science*
(2008), paints an alternative picture. As Holmes notes, Samuel
Coleridge, one of the central spokesmen of Romanticism,
describes turn-of-the century science as constituting a "Second
Scientific Revolution" (an expression he probably coined in
1819), a time when a host of new discoveries and technological
inventions were emerging, generating great excitement in the
Western world. Holmes' book, which focuses on this period (1770-
1830) and its second wave of scientific discoveries, contradicts
the stereotypical image of the rational, dispassionate, and
objectivist (that is "bloodless") scientist, substituting a vision of
"wonder driven figures" who immersed themselves in the study
of nature with fascination, great passion, deep appreciation,
awe, cosmic wonder, and an exuberant sense of adventure. In
essence, capturing the spirit and influence of philosophical
Romanticism, these scientists of the Second Scientific Revolution
were Romantic scientists, "driven by a common ideal of intense,
even reckless, personal commitment to discovery." For Holmes,
the rapture felt by the Romanticists toward nature permeated
into the scientific quest circa 1800; scientists of the era came at
the study of nature with the heart of Romanticists. Rather than
Romanticism *in toto* contradicting the scientific quest, to some
significant degree it empowered and energized it.

And to complete the circle of influence, Holmes also argues that the great Romantic poets, such as Coleridge and Shelley, were greatly informed and inspired by the new discoveries and visions of science, especially those of the Second Scientific Revolution. Science brought wonder and astonishment over nature into the Romantic mind. Indeed, to cement even further the intimate and positive connection of Romanticism and the Second Scientific Revolution, two of the greatest scientists of that era, William Herschel and Humphry Davy, were also devoted and accomplished artists (musical composer and poet respectively); science and art were synthesized and mutually reinforcing in their psyches.

Holmes' book attempts to demonstrate a strong, if not necessary, connection between the scientific quest and both human emotion and a personal, subjective engagement with nature. Our popular stereotype of the cerebral and "bloodless" scientist misses the dimension of passion and personal investment that more often than not infuses scientific consciousness.

Moreover, these dimensions of emotionality and subjectivity have a positive impact on scientific research and discovery. The scientific way of life is one of awe, wonder, dedication, and personal sacrifice; these qualities benefit the scientific quest and the search for truth. Instead of cold dehumanizing objectivity, it is a deeply experienced humanity that drives the spirit of science. Such a mode of consciousness—one I term "holistic consciousness" rather than simply rational or cognitive consciousness—empowers rather than hinders the scientist.

In addition, the discovery of truth, of nature and the cosmos, is not some abstract ideation simply contemplated by a detached scientific mind, but a jolting and powerful revelation that penetrates deeply into the mind of the scientist. Truth as experienced by the scientific mind is not simply cognitive, but emotional and often aesthetic as well.

In agreement with Holmes, we can argue that the popular

vision of science and scientists as "bloodless" — objective, impersonal, and rational — is historically inaccurate and psychologically impossible. Scientists have always brought personal and emotional qualities into their work, and all science is subjective and theoretically biased (Kuhn, 1962; Feyerabend, 1965, 1969; Lombardo, 2017). Equally, we can argue that there is a sense of the mystical in the scientific quest; consider, for example, Bruno and Kepler. Furthermore, we can also state that the philosophers of the Enlightenment, such as Voltaire and Condorcet, though dedicated to a life of reason, were filled with emotion and passion. If anything, their visions of a future guided by reason and science were filled with positive emotionality, of hope, excitement, and awe toward the future. As Coleridge states in the opening quote, deep thinking is always accompanied by deep feeling.

All in all, Holmes describes the period of 1770-1830 as "The Age of Wonder" and the "Age of Romantic Science." As he demonstrates, quoting Plato, "In Wonder all Philosophy began ..." And for Holmes, what unites turn-of-the-nineteenth-century science and art is the experience of wonder. Both scientists and artists of the time saw a mysterious and potentially infinite universe that provoked both wonder and terror. Moreover, just as Byron championed the archetype of the solitary artistic genius, out of this era comes the image of the "solitary genius scientist" in the passionate pursuit of knowledge through strange and unknown territories. The scientist is on a metaphorical journey, an exploratory voyage of discovery in the scientific quest. Further, during this period in history, discovery as an intuitive flash of revelation — a "Eureka moment" — became a popular way of viewing advances in scientific understanding (Lombardo, 2011c), bringing an a-rational and emotionally energizing dimension to the apprehension of new truths.

Holmes' description of Romantic scientists as "wonder driven figures" with a "personal commitment to discovery" captures a fundamental, if not archetypal, narrative theme in the evolution of science fiction, especially as it unfolded in the later nineteenth century. Stories such as those written by Jules Verne and H. G. Wells that we would today identify as "science fiction" were frequently labeled as "scientific romances," pulling together scientific and technological ideas (and speculations) with dramatic adventure, and clearly engaging the reader at an emotional, as well as cognitive level; the two dimensions were intertwined. These stories often combined strong elements of mystery with deep and surprising revelations about the nature of reality; further, the protagonists were often scientifically minded individuals on passionate quests of discovery and innovation. There was a sense of wonder and awe (and often risk) in the face of the profound depths and majesty of the universe and nature.

Scientific discovery and mind-boggling technological innovation are central narrative themes in science fiction, where often the central protagonist, filled with passion and personal commitment, goes on an "adventure" into the farther reaches of reality and its possibilities. With courage and conviction, the scientist further opens up reality. In essence, this is Holmes' image of the Romantic scientist, one he illustrates with a series of non-fictional "scientific romances" that describe the lives of many of the great scientists of the Age of Wonder. These dramatic and inspiring narratives clearly refute the view of science and scientists as damaging to the human spirit, leading to disaster and the impoverishment of the human soul. The scientist can be (and has been) heroic, impassioned, and elevating, contributing to the evolution and expansion of human consciousness.

It is valuable to highlight some of the key historical figures and their accomplishments that Holmes describes in his book. These individuals made important contributions to the Second Scientific Revolution, ushering in a new wave of discoveries that built upon the First Scientific Revolution of the previous two centuries. As with the first revolution, ideas and themes emerging in this second revolution in science would also have a strong impact in multiple ways upon the evolution of science fiction.

Holmes contends that the "Age of Wonder" (of Romantic science) was launched with Captain James Cook's (1728-1779) voyage of the *Endeavour* (1768-1771) to the south Pacific, involving exploration, mapping, and anthropological-naturalistic studies of Tahiti, New Zealand, and Australia. Still, this first voyage and later ones by Cook, was also a natural continuation of the Age of Exploration, in which European adventurers journeyed to unknown regions and observed and recorded discoveries of a vast array of new botanical and animal species and indigenous cultures and peoples. In line with Holmes' theme of "wonder-inspired science," Cook enthusiastically undertook the journey with a sense of adventure and fascination to further the scientific study of the diverse and marvelous forms of nature, as well as contribute astronomical observations from the other side of the globe.

Holmes' subject in this first of the chapters of his book is not Cook, however, but Joseph Banks (1743-1820), who, sailing on the *Endeavour* and later serving as President of the Royal Society of London, epitomized this spirit of scientific adventure. Supplied with a great assortment of scientific instruments and supported by assistants for nature drawings and record keeping, Banks embraced the opportunity to travel around the world, studying first-hand the wonders of nature. Although his primary task was to record and collect botanical specimens, on the three-year journey he also involved himself in zoological studies—in particular anthropological investigation—personally immersing himself in the ways of life of various Tahitian cultures. Holmes describes the young Banks as a "confident child of the Enlightenment," but also possessing the "dreamy inwardness" of a Romanticist. Tahiti was particularly fascinating and mysterious to Banks, and as Holmes suggests, Banks probably saw in the Tahitians the "noble savage" uncorrupted by modern civilization (both a literary and science fiction archetype); indeed, through his emphatic and enthusiastic participation in Tahitian life, Banks came to realize the artificiality and arbitrariness of modern European civilization. Upon his return to England, Banks leveraged his new-found celebrity to publicly educate and expand European consciousness on the diverse and eye-opening possibilities of human values and ways of life. As discussed earlier, a key contribution of the Age of Exploration to the evolution of science fiction was providing new and colorful perspectives on the "other" and the "different," at biological, psychological, and socio-cultural levels. As a highly influential popularizer of science and its values, Banks significantly reinforced and added to this growing awareness of the fascinating diversity in nature and culture. As President of the Royal Society, a position he held for over forty years, he did much to promote other famous adventures into the unknown, such as Mongo Park's (1771-1806) daring journeys of exploration—that eventually led to the explorer's tragic death—chronicled in Park's *Travels in the Interior of Africa* (1799). Holmes sees Banks as a key architect of Romantic science, one who, as described below, would be a great supporter of both Humphry Davy and William Herschel, two of the most significant scientific minds of the Romantic period.

Capturing the spirit of adventure, wonder, and even transcendence, the great balloon craze of 1783-1800 was another important expression of Romantic science. The brothers Joseph-Michel Montgolfier (1740–1810) and Jacques-Étienne Montgolfier (1745–1799) launched the first successful manned hot-air balloon flight in 1783, soon to be followed by Alexandre Charles' (1746-1823) first "lighter than air" (hydrogen) balloon flight later that same year. The dream of human flight and leaving the bounds of the earth goes back at least to the myth of Icarus, which greatly inspired these first balloonists and the many enthusiasts soon to follow; in ascending into the sky they aspired to turn myth into reality. Almost immediately after the first successful flights, different writers and commentators examined both the positive benefits and negative uses of this new invention (the English came to fear that France would use balloons to invade England). As many saw it, the balloons were a "road into the air" opening up a "new epoch" in the advancement of human civilization. The poet Percy Shelley saw this breaking free of earthly bounds, made possible by these manned balloons, as a symbol of freedom and transcendence. And just as the first moon landings would later give humanity its first real vision of the earth from outer space, the manned balloon flights gave the first "aeronauts" (a term coined at the time) spectacular views of the earth—of rivers, mountains, fields and cities—as never seen before. Not that earlier visionaries had not imagined it; recall that Cyrano de Bergerac had envisioned balloon flight to the moon centuries earlier. Moreover, balloon travel would figure significantly in later science fiction visions of both the future (Robido's *The Twentieth Century*) and, in particular, future war (Wells' *The War in the Air*). Clearly carrying humanity off the surface of the earth in balloons was the first in a series of technological modes of aerial ascension, including airplanes and rockets that would repeatedly stimulate science fiction imagination in its variously conceived journeys away from the terrestrial hold of our planet.

Lighter than air manned balloon flight was a product of science-empowered technological invention (one of the central aspirations of the Age of Enlightenment). The science that empowered these flights was chemistry, which, with its rapid advances toward the end of the eighteenth century, was one of the most important emerging scientific disciplines of the period. Hydrogen, which was used in Charles' balloons and others, was only first isolated and discovered by the chemist Henry Cavendish (1731-1810) in 1766. Other individuals, such as Joseph Priestly (1733-1804)—theologian, educator, philosopher, scientist, and political theorist—further contributed to the growing understanding of diverse chemical gases, including oxygen and nitrous oxide (laughing gas). In the same period Antoine-Laurent de Lavoisier (1743-1794) (the "father of modern chemistry") and John Dalton (1766-1844) identified additional new "atomic" elements and brought systematic order to the world of chemistry through the construction of the "Table of Elements" by Dalton in 1808. The old theory of air, water, earth, and fire (from Empedocles) as the primary substances of nature was totally overturned with the rise of modern chemistry during this time; reality was transformed. (Yet, Priestley for one, embraced both the old and the new, of past and futurist vision, attempting to combine Christian religion and Enlightenment science, proposing that through science humanity would achieve the new Millennium.) All in all, the forward march of science, including the rapid growth of chemistry, permeated the popular imagination of the era. As Holmes notes, balloon flights drew immense audiences, enthralling the crowds with the spectacle and thrill of it all. As a provocative observation of the time put it: "Chemistry plus showmanship equals crowds plus wonder plus money." Through advances in modern chemistry (and good marketing) everyone could participate in the astonishing discoveries and achievements of science; the pump was being primed for the astounding adventures of science fiction to come.

More than anyone else in this era, Sir William Herschel (1738-1822) opened the universe—of both discovery and imagination—much further than before. Herschel follows in the line of Copernicus, Galileo, and Kepler (perhaps transcending them) in expanding human awareness and understanding of the vast depth of the cosmos, in both space and time. As a youth, Herschel became a proficient performer on various different musical instruments and studied musical composition, but he also studied philosophy, pondered the existence of God, and debated with his family members the respective ideas of Leibnitz and Newton. He was interested in cosmology from his early years and would eventually write about the deep Pythagorean-Platonic issue of the relationship of music, mathematics, and the universe. Hershel possessed a cosmic mind, and eventually in his astronomical studies he would profoundly extend human cosmic consciousness.

As Herschel matured into adulthood, his ever-growing fascination with astronomy motivated him to construct a series of ever larger, more powerful "reflecting" telescopes. In fact, Herschel eventually constructed the most powerful telescopes built by anyone up to that time. Assisted by his devoted and amazingly diligent sister Caroline Herschel (1750-1848), Herschel, using one of his earlier telescopes, began a systematic study and survey of "nebulae"—the fuzzy, ill-defined patches of light in the night sky. These nebulae would become highly significant in our growing understanding of the universe. Also, through this rigorous and methodical study of the night sky, Herschel discovered a point of light with an anomalous pattern of motion, which, after careful calculation and repeated observations (with no clear Eureka moment), he concluded was a previously unknown planet in our solar system orbiting the sun far beyond Saturn. Called "Uranus," the discovery of this new planet brought Herschel worldwide fame. In this one discovery, the size of the known solar system doubled, and Herschel came to symbolize the new expanding vision of the universe emerging through the science of astronomy. But this discovery was just the beginning, a relatively minor cosmological first step in what was to come.

For one thing, Herschel would eventually discover previously undetected moons orbiting Saturn, and find that Uranus had moons orbiting it as well. Moreover, when, upon closer telescopic resolution, he discovered that the fuzzy nebulae were often immense clusters of stars, he began to seriously consider the possibility that many of these nebulae actually existed outside the Milky Way. As he stated in "An Investigation of the

Construction of the Heavens" (1784), in contradiction to popular opinion, the Milky Way was not the entire universe (a possibility Kant had proposed in his "Universal Natural History of the Heavens" (1755), positing that there might be "island universes" outside the Milky Way). Eventually cataloguing over two thousand nebulae, Herschel came to believe that many of these nebulae were other galaxies beyond the Milky Way. And he was right. He first clearly observed and correctly drew the shape of the Andromeda galaxy, one of our closest galactic neighbors, a mere two-and-a-half million light years away. Moreover, he was the first person to realize that the sun was moving through space and that our solar system was orbiting around the center of the Milky Way. He also determined that the Milky Way was disc shaped. Not realizing at the time the nature and significance of what he had uncovered, he is also credited with having discovered infrared radiation.

When all was said and done, Herschel transformed our notions of space and time in the universe, noting, for example, in "On the Construction of the Heavens" (1785), that a three-dimensional form (rather than a dome shaped diagram) would best represent the surrounding universe. He conducted his astronomical studies with increasingly powerful telescopes, penetrating ever farther into "deep space" and progressively extending the visible boundaries of the universe. For Hershel, galaxies outside the Milky Way must be immensely far away. Further, by 1802 he realized that "deep space" implied "deep time," for if other galaxies were at colossal distances from us, then the time necessary for light to reach us and for us to see these distal objects implied that universe must be much older than previously supposed. And not only were space and time deep; the cosmos was dynamic. Contradicting the prevalent and ancient view that the heavens were stable, Herschel proposed that nebulae were the birth places of stars, and that stars came into existence and eventually died. There was continual "becoming and passing away" of stars within nebulae, which he described as "laboratories of the universe." And just as the solar system moves around the center of the Milky Way, the Milky Way is moving relative to other galaxies. Furthermore, just as stars eventually die, so will the Milky Way. We exist in a transformative universe—a universe that seems alive. Putting humanity in our proper cosmic place, Herschel pushed beyond the human-centric, the geo-centric, the solar-centric, and even the galactic-centric (our Milky Way) in reconceptualizing the nature of the universe.

In the spirit of popular opinion at the time, Herschel firmly believed in the existence of life and intelligence on other planets. From early in his astronomical studies, he believed there was life on the moon; confirming this belief was one main reason behind his construction of bigger and bigger telescopes. In fact, he claimed to have observed forests on the moon and, in his publication "On the Nature and Construction of the Sun" (1795), he suggested not only that the sun had a cool interior but that it was also inhabited by intelligent beings. Herschel was fascinated all his life by the idea of extraterrestrial intelligence, and believed—again putting humanity in more expansive cosmic perspective—that there were various levels of civilization in the universe, some lower and some higher than human civilization. Again, such ideas provided fertile ground for later science fiction.

Herschel's new vision of a vast, generative, and transformative universe—built upon naturalistic processes and laws, and scientifically grounded in a huge number of new observations and data accumulated through his intensive astronomical studies with the most powerful telescopes ever constructed— inspired the development of naturalistic and even atheistic explanations of the universe. For example, in *The System of the World* (1809) and *Celestial Mechanics* (1829-1839), the scientist and mathematician Pierre-Simon Laplace (1749-1827) developed a deterministic explanation of the entire universe built on natural laws and principles, without the apparent need for a Creator God. Laplace's astronomy included a "nebular" explanation for our sun and solar system, the sun and the planets presumably having condensed out of gas. And Erasmus Darwin (1731-1802) (the grandfather of Charles Darwin), in part inspired by Herschel's life metaphor of the cosmos (of birth, change, and death within galaxies and stars), proposed in his popular and influential book *The Botanic Garden* (1791) that all the stars would eventually collapse into a universal cosmic death, but that metaphorically, like "Phoenix" arising from the ashes, a new universe would be born out of this cosmic collapse. We will return to such cosmic ideas in the nineteenth-century theory of entropy and the heat death of the universe, and in Flammarion's vision of the birth and death of cosmos without end.

All told, the universe that Herschel first revealed (and later astronomers would both further corroborate and expand upon) became the universe in which science fiction writers would create their space operas and narratives of space exploration and discovery. It was a universe vastly different and incredibly greater in scope and inherent dynamism than anything envisioned in the Middle Ages. As Herschel stated, "I have looked further into space than ever human being did before me."

The connection between Herschel and the Romantic spirit is at least twofold. First, Herschel clearly recognized and reinforced in his writings the psychologically holistic nature of the scientific endeavor and the artistic dimension of scientific study. He frequently compared astronomy with art. The scientist brings passion, as well as reason and careful observation, into scientific work. Herschel was amazingly disciplined, but equally he was powerfully inspired and enthralled with the wonders and possibilities of the universe. Moreover, he described learning to proficiently use astronomical instruments as similar to learning to play a musical instrument. There is an "art of seeing" through a telescope. Science is not simply the passive, detached, and objective observation of data.

Second, contrary to the more traditional view that the Romanticists rejected the value of science, it is clear that at the very least, the Romantic poets, such as Coleridge, Byron, Shelley, and Keats, were inspired by the cosmic imagery of modern science and especially Hershel's discoveries and his new, expansive ideas on the cosmos. From his youth Coleridge was enthralled by the immense, mysterious, and wondrous universe being revealed through science. He was strongly influenced by both Herschel and Davy, and his poetry and essays are infused with astronomical imagery and metaphors (as was the poetry of Byron and Keats). As Holmes recounts, Coleridge attempted to unite and reconcile science with art and poetry.

Percy Shelley's strong interest in science is reflected in his essay, "The Necessity of Atheism" (1811), in which he invoked science and modern astronomy in his criticisms and rejection of human-centric (and earth-centric) Christian religion and the idea of an afterlife. And his lyrical drama *Prometheus Unbound* (1820) is not only informed and infused with scientific ideas, but raises Prometheus to a heroic and victorious figure who is freed from his bondage and triumphs over the archetypal father figure of Zeus. Prometheus—a Romantic rebellious figure, like Shelley and Byron—symbolizing the rise of humanity through self-determination and the acquisition of knowledge, transcends the authority and rule of the sky God, which of course represents the tyranny and oppressiveness of traditional Western religion. Romanticism, science, mythology, and individualism are synthesized in Shelley's Promethean drama. There will be a much different take on the "Promethean" image and the value of science in Mary Shelley's *Frankenstein*, a novel which expresses a much more conservative and reactionary Romantic spirit.

One way to portray the antagonism between Romanticism and science is that at least some Romantic writers (as Holmes chronicles) saw scientific rationality, when carried to an extreme, as destructive and impoverished; a satisfactory experience and understanding of reality requires imagination and creativity as well. Also critiqued was the mathematical mindset, strongly associated with science, which can be seen as simply abstract form and equations, empty of color and feeling. But the emotionally detached, rationalistic scientist (or mathematician for that matter), without feeling or a creative imagination, is an extreme and unrealistic caricature—a straw man—and Herschel, for one, clearly did not fit this stereotype.

Another way to describe the presumed Romantic antagonism toward science, also touched upon by Holmes, is that it actually reflected a concern over the presumed materialism of modern science, which not only seemed to rob humanity of both spirit and soul, but robbed the universe of a spiritual (non-material) God. Where do art, passion, emotion, imagination, and the self fit within a materialistic universe? As the nineteenth century progressed, there was an increasing popular concern that science—often associated with physical materialism— was challenging Christianity and more generally a belief in a spiritual God. Wasn't it apparent that modern science and its technological creations were turning human society into a materialistically-driven world, infused with industry and gadgetry, to the exclusion of the human spirit? Again, as we will see in Shelley's *Frankenstein*, the question is raised whether the Creature, a product of science and technology, possesses a soul. (Presumably physical science cannot create a soul.)

But the idea that science is exclusively or necessarily materialistic—to whatever degree the public and Romanticists accepted it—is historically and conceptually flawed. From as early as Descartes, scientists delved into the realms of consciousness, mind, and human emotions; the Enlightenment philosophers Locke and Hume, for example, inspired by the principles of science, developed elaborate and highly influential empiricist theories of the conscious human mind, as a prelude to the emergence of a scientific approach to consciousness in the late nineteenth century (Boring, 1950; Watson, 1971; Lombardo, 1987).

Sir Humphry Davy (1778-1829), who became President of the Royal Society after Banks, transcended all these unrealistic stereotypes of science and scientists. Both a poet and Romantic essayist, as well as a world-renowned scientist, Davy delved into a broad range of scientific studies with passion and imagination, including: states of consciousness; chemistry; electricity and galvanism; scientific methodology; and cosmology, brilliantly pulling them all together into a cohesive scheme. He also wrote on alien intelligence in the universe and even engaged in science fiction narrative. Davy was one of the great "personalities" and "showmen" of Romantic science, a synthesis of emotion and passion, intellect and reason, and even Dionysian sensationalism.

In his youth Davy wrote poetry, a pursuit he continued throughout his life, and in 1796 penned an essay "On Consciousness," in which he attempted to disprove the existence of an eternal and unchangeable human soul based on the insight that everything in nature is dynamic and transformative. The conscious human mind was part of nature, and nature in totality was dynamic. As part of his dynamic philosophy of reality, from early on he embraced the hopeful philosophy of ongoing progress, both for humanity and science, stating that humankind was "capable of an infinite degree of happiness" and that "the perfectibility of science is absolutely indefinite."

In 1797 he became fascinated with chemistry—eventually heralding the emergence of modern chemistry—isolating and discovering various fundamental atomic elements, including potassium, sodium, and calcium. Coincident with his experimental work, he began developing universal theories of the physical universe, encompassing chemistry, light, and gravity. He also began to investigate in 1798 (regularly using himself as an experimental subject) the conscious effects and medical benefits of the inhalation of gases, including nitrous oxide. Although he described his work in this direction as empirical, involving careful and unbiased observation of facts, he often described his gas-induced conscious states using poetry. Moreover, he believed that such drug-induced states enhanced or elevated human consciousness, and he was particularly interested in the hallucinatory effects of gases. (Davy also believed that science elevated consciousness.) Based on this work he was described as an "aerial flying" chemist, in pursuit of "ecstatic, lunatic, and Liputatic sensations." Davy, was indeed attempting through the science of chemistry to "open the doors of perception," a clear effort to unite the physical realm with consciousness and the mind.

Such research and thinking, with accompanying states of "elevated" and "hallucinogenic" consciousness, epitomizes (perhaps in an extreme form) the Romantic scientist. In Davy's mind, the perception of truth and the perception of beauty were related, imagination being required in each, and the love of nature (a necessary element in scientific consciousness) was the same as the love of the sublime and the beautiful—a key psychological dimension of the artist. Moreover, hope was an essential factor in the scientific pursuit; Davy believed that through science we could create a better world. Hope empowered the scientific intellect. In science, strong feelings were connected with powerful ideas and visionary imagination; science involved the aspiration toward excellence and the good.

By the turn of the century Davy had developed a new scientific passion, the study of "galvanism" (named after its discoverer Luigi Aloisio Galvani 1737-1798). Galvanism referred to the observed phenomenon of the production of muscular contractions in an animal body through the application of an electrical current. Sounding like the fictional character Frankenstein, Davy wrote: "I have made some important galvanic discoveries which seem to lead to the door of the temple of life."

Using various dramatic on-stage scientific demonstrations, he gave his first public lecture on galvanism in 1801. It was a spectacular success. One year later at the Royal Institution of London, he began his highly popular lectures on science and chemistry, which Coleridge attended. Coleridge was deeply impressed and inspired by Davy's hopeful vision of the promises of science. Coleridge, the poet, and Davy, the evangelist of science: In deep resonance, the two became lifelong friends and intellectual colleagues. By this time, Banks also recognized that Davy was a new rising star in science, one who entertained and mesmerized his audiences with his charismatic personality, his magnetism, and his amazingly energetic mind.

Davy's scientific romanticism—his passionate embrace of scientific inquiry and education and his sense of personal mission—was coupled with a futuristic and evolutionary understanding of science and humanity. As noted above, Davy saw science as empowering realistic hope for a better future. In fact, Davy had a clear sense of the ongoing evolution of future consciousness in humanity and the way science fit into this developmental process. He argued that primitive humans were creatures of sensation and immediate wants and desires with no sense of "futurity." But with the emergence of science, humans had been able to connect desires with a host of new empowering ideas, fueling hope with a clear sense of how to improve the human condition. With his development of the "safety lamp" for miners—one of his most noteworthy inventions—Davy believed he powerfully demonstrated how the scientific method could be used to solve practical human problems. When Davy became President of the Royal Society in 1820 after the death of Banks, his inaugural presentation was titled "The Prospects and Progress of Science." In this talk, he argued for the great promise of science in the future, highlighting both the rational and rigorous methods of induction and the element of passion in the scientific quest. All in all, Davy synthesized the future-oriented Enlightenment vision of secular progress through science and the passionate energy and personalized vision of humanity of the Romantic spirit.

Also of relevance to the history of science fiction is Davy's cosmic *Consolations in Travel, or the Last Days of a Philosopher* (1830), written at the end of his life. Here was a personal travel narrative—one that traversed both the earth and the solar system—integrating science, history, evolution, the future of humanity, and elements of science fiction. He includes a scientific theory of the creation of the universe and critically discusses the theory that humans evolved from more primitive life forms. He proposes a vision of the spiritual evolution of humans on the earth over time. As in earlier writings, he again argues that science is a positive force in the advancement of human civilization, not only providing practical benefits but also expanding (enlightening) the conscious human mind. For Davy, scientists are of greater value than artists, religious leaders, and statesmen. In line with a Romantic vision of scientists, he describes the pursuit of science as a dramatic endeavor (rather than a passionless pursuit) and a dangerous one at that. Science is a personal adventure. All these ideas anticipate key themes and articulate important values within modern science fiction.

In the sections that sound most like science fiction, Davy explains and supports Herschel's idea of evolving stars and a dynamic universe populated with alien life forms. Guided by a disembodied female voice through some of his narrated cosmic travels (suggestive of Dante's *Divine Comedy*), Davy meets super-intelligent aliens in our solar system. He proposes that there are "angelic intelligences" in the heavens that are "ministers of the eternal mind," connecting outer space and aliens with theistic and spiritual themes. He also meets the spirit of Newton in his astronomical travels, and puts forth the theory that humans upon death rise to various levels in our planetary system, contingent upon how well they have developed their minds in their earthly life (how much knowledge they have acquired) and how great their desire for heavenly ascension was. Combining the poetic and the theoretic, and spiritual mysticism and scientific astronomy in a personal narrative form, Davy's *Consolations in Travel* was a very popular book in its time. It would influence Victorian scientists in later decades, and it is notable that the French edition was edited by Camille Flammarion—about whom we shall learn more—who, in his fantastical writings of the cosmos included various ideas similar to those of Davy.

As one final note on Davy, although he championed the central importance of chemistry within science, highlighting its rapid advances in his time to which he contributed, Davy's scientific interests were broad and interdisciplinary. In his *Travels* he wrote about electricity and its significance in understanding the animated quality of life. The scientific study of electricity, through Volta, Galvani, and Benjamin Franklin, among others, was already underway in Davy's time, but in the subsequent decades it would emerge as perhaps the most influential discipline of scientific inquiry of the Second Scientific Revolution. As such, it greatly stimulated speculation about the potential wonders of the future and the imagination (both fears and hopes) of science fiction writers. Mary Shelley, Edgar Allen Poe, and Albert Robida, for example, would find the new scientific ideas pertaining to electricity and magnetism (including galvanism), as provocative stimuli for their writings.

Holmes' book has a chapter titled "The Sorcerer and the Apprentice" in which he describes the relationship between Davy—teacher and mentor—and his most famous student and laboratory assistant, Michael Faraday (1791-1867). After the death of Davy, Faraday would become the most important figure in the scientific study of electricity. Indeed Faraday would become much more famous and historically significant than Davy, considered by historians of science to be one of the greatest scientists of all time. In later sections, I continue the chronicle of the Second Scientific Revolution, beyond the "Age of Wonder," and its impact on science fiction, bringing in more about the study of electricity and Michael Faraday, a story that will continue through the remaining decades of the nineteenth century.

* * *

In summary, pulling together the standard view of Romanticism with Holmes' vision of Romantic Science and the Second Scientific Revolution, on one hand there were various negative reactions to the emergence of modern science and the philosophy of the Enlightenment. Modern science appeared to threaten religious and spiritual thinking; it appeared too materialistic; it appeared too abstract, rationalistic, and mathematical, disregarding the personal and the emotional side of human life. Its technological inventions leading to increasing industrialization seemed dehumanizing, cutting humanity off from nature. Efficiency seemed to be replacing beauty; order seemed to be suppressing spontaneity and creativity. And perhaps it appeared that humans were attempting to "play God" with their destiny. In counter-reaction to all these presumed negative qualities of science, technology, and rationality, humanity needed to reassert the importance of emotion, passion, personality, nature, subjectivity, spirit, beauty, and art.

Yet, as Holmes demonstrates, the scientists of the "Age of Wonder" were not dehumanized and emotionless minds; passion, wonder, and inspiration were powerfully present within their scientific consciousness. Moreover, many of the poets and writers of the Romantic era found uplifting imagery and exciting visions in the new ideas of science. The future envisioned by Coleridge and Davy was not mechanized and depressing, but emotionally stimulating and consciously elevating. Beauty is truth and truth is beauty, and science with its new discoveries and technological creations is on a journey of awe and wonder toward the sublime. Given the psychologically holistic nature of the human mind (involving intellect, emotion, desire, and sensation), both the scientist and the artist are on a conscious-expanding Romantic adventure of insight and revelation; both the artist and the scientist are heroic in very similar ways. While the Age of Romanticism was flourishing, the Second Scientific Revolution was equally in full swing; one did not seem to suppress the other. And as has been noted on several occasions before, the great scientists of the First and now the Second Scientific Revolution frequently combined their scientific ideas with both spiritual and mystical visions.

What seems a more accurate assessment of this period (1770-1830) is that there were two divergent emotional responses, coupled with two respective and distinctive cognitive frameworks, regarding science, the Enlightenment, and the vision of secular progress. On one hand, there was fear and apprehension, supported by a pre-scientific mindset, leading to a recoil from modernity and science. On the other hand, there was hope, wonder, and enthusiasm (just as Romantic a response), supported by a vision of science as consciousness expanding and enlightening, and technology as a form of human empowerment and advancement. In the former case, with a fear of a God hovering over our heads, the scientist is portrayed as vain, mad, heartless, foolish, and power-hungry, if not evil; in the latter case, the scientist is seen as heroic, courageous, rational, and hopeful. These two Romantic-infused attitudes to science and secular progress capture two of the fundamental narrative and character archetypes in science fiction. Science fiction is a romantic adventure—an emotionally charged journey—into the unknown, approached either with fear or hope by either flawed or heroic characters. We will see that Mary Shelley adopts the "fear mindset" version of Romanticism, with a flawed central character, although her husband Percy, with Prometheus and Herschel as his heroes, stood decidedly on the other side of the divide.

These two attitudes can be further clarified through the theory of the dialectic, introduced earlier, and the associated oscillatory theory of history espoused by the great German philosopher Georg Wilhelm Friedrich Hegel (1770-1831). For Hegel, history moves through a process of thesis, antithesis, and synthesis—the dialectic—and in this process popular trends and attitudes move back and forth in an oppositional and oscillatory fashion. The theme of oscillatory change through oppositional states can be traced in history back to the Taoist Yin-Yang and the Greek philosophers Heraclitus and Empedocles. In more modern times, but prior to Hegel, it can be found in the theories of human history in Giambattista Vico (1668-1744) and Jacques Turgot. With Vico and Turgot human history moves through alternating periods of order and chaos (creation and destruction); with Hegel, any mindset characterizing an era in history eventually provokes its opposite or counter-reaction. Of special note, when we arrive at H. G. Wells and Olaf Stapledon, the dialectical theory of human history—of order and chaos and creation and destruction—would profoundly inform their science fiction visions of the future.

Within such a theoretical framework for understanding human history, the rationalism of the Enlightenment provoked its opposite in the emotionalism-sensualism of Romanticism; the Enlightenment hope of secular progress provoked fear among at least some Romantic writers and artists; the Enlightenment embrace of change and the future provoked a counter-reaction toward preserving stability (old ways of life) and the past (a recurrent theme in human history); and the growth of technology, civilization, and industrialization ignited a desire to return to nature (another feature of Romanticism). Finally, the presumed objectivism of science and rationalism in the Enlightenment provoked a Romantic counter-reaction embracing subjectivism and inner consciousness.

Yet, as Hegel argued, after thesis and antithesis comes synthesis, and with the Romantic scientists and science-inspired Romantic poets, emotion and reason, subjectivism and objectivism, art and science, and science and nature were integrated into holistic experiences and descriptions of reality. Similarly, as a scientifically inspired form of literature influenced by both Romanticism and the Enlightenment, science fiction would fuse these various polarities—the model of the Romantic scientist, such as exemplified in Hershel and Davy, providing a positive archetypal character leading the extraordinary adventure into the unexplored regions of the cosmos. Moreover, the emotions of hope and fear in the face of the mysterious unknown were often dramatically coupled in the exciting "edge of your seat" fictional adventures and "scientific romances" of the nineteenth century, a main tributary of science fiction. Even when the narrative theme was anti-scientific and the central character was flawed, modern science fiction wove together the artistic values and literary style of Romanticism with the ideas and suggested possibilities of science and secular progress. In the coming century, science fiction, as holistic narratives, stimulating both emotion and the intellect, would in various ways synthesize or juxtapose the themes and attitudes of the Enlightenment and Romanticism.

The Gothic: Horror, Mystery, Madness, and the Supernatural

Gothic literature can be seen as an extreme expression of Romanticism, with its emphasis on dark and powerful human emotions, the twists and turns of inner consciousness, the rejection of a purely scientific vision of reality (bringing in mysticism, supernaturalism, and the occult), and a shifting backwards in time, especially to medieval-like settings and scenarios. What is especially noteworthy in Gothic literature is the dimension of horror, madness, fear, and dread (as opposed to wondrous mystery). Science fiction writers in the early nineteenth century strongly influenced by Gothic themes included Mary Shelley, E. T. A. Hoffman, and Edgar Allen Poe. Also of note, beginning with John William Polidori's (1795-1821)*The Vampyre* (1819), written contemporaneously with Shelley's *Frankenstein*, and reaching its defining modern expression in Bram Stoker's (1847-1912) *Dracula* (1897), the "vampire" sub-genre became one of the most long-lived and popular expressions of Gothic literature.

The origin of Gothic literature in modern times is usually identified as Horace Walpole's (1717-1797) *The Castle of Otranto* (1763). The story describes dramatic, and at times inexplicable and terrifying events surrounding a family that inhabits a haunted castle during the Middle Ages. There is the avenging and powerful ghost Alfonso (of a man poisoned during the Crusades), who appears responsible at the beginning of the story for the death of one of the family members (a son); a nefarious and licentious human character (the father in the family), who is haunted by the ghost; and a beautiful young heroine pursued by the evil father, a man who is married but willing to abandon his faithful wife to maintain control of the castle. In the story's climax the evil father is defeated and the rightful heir, the young male hero of the story, secures both the castle and the young woman with the assistance of the ghost. Worldly evil is vanquished and the pure of heart rewarded by supernatural forces of justice.

There are several features to *The Castle of Otranto* that are significant in the evolution of gothic literature and science fiction. The medieval architectural setting (from which the term Gothic derives), often in the form of a dark and labyrinthine castle (or abbey or monastery), and filled with secret passageways, is a central feature in much of Gothic literature. The setting—gloomy, mysterious, and frightening—is created to prime the emotional pump and provoke feelings of apprehension, uncertainty, dread, and terror in the reader. The castle or monastery holds secrets originating from deep in its past—for example ancestral curses—and in one manner or form, the spirits of the dead may haunt its rooms and passageways. Ghosts and other supernatural beings inhabit the old building and there are bizarre and spooking happenings within it. Gothic writers frequently connected such medieval structures with a "dark and terrifying period" in human history; the evil of the past permeates into the present. Overall, the Gothic setting was critical to the ambience created in the story, the medieval building itself serving as a main "character" in the narrative. The Gothic medieval structure often seemed intentionally malevolent and almost alive or conscious; the castle seemed to possess a spirit.

Gothic literature can also be connected with the Gothic Revival Architecture movement begun in the late 1740s in England. As part of the Romantic counter-reaction to the rise of modernism, Gothic Revival Architecture harkened back to the designs and aesthetics of the past—notably Gothic art and architecture of the Middle Ages—and as such, can be seen as regressive and opposed to modernist design and connected ways of life. Gothic literature was appropriately set within Gothic architectural structures and populated with medieval elements and themes associated with that earlier time. Walpole, who was a nostalgist and antiquarian, actually constructed and lived in a mini-castle—Strawberry Hill House—that served as the model for his castle of Otranto. He surrounded himself with a Gothic ambience, as a key expression of his fascination with the past, which in turn fed his imagination.

Yet, although the Gothic movement, in both architecture and literature, involved a return to the past, the past as portrayed in Gothic literature was not a pleasant or sane place. Gothic writers connected their imagined medieval buildings and settings with "a dark and terrifying period" in human history, with torture, sorcery, demonic rituals, and superstitious cruelty. And if the narrative took place in the present within some old medieval castle or religious edifice, then the building became a source of mystery and threat due to its age or unknown origins; the deep past was dark and terrifying. Indeed, we can argue that as science revealed more of the world, eliminating the mystery of things, Gothic literature attempted to resurrect or rediscover mystery in the past, even if the mysteries encountered were unnerving and horrific. This is perhaps the central appeal of Gothic literature (at least Gothic horror such as *The Castle of Otranto*): It generates anxiety, fear, and terror.

What is it that motivates people *toward* experiencing fear of the unknown? What motivates people toward the suspenseful anticipation of the horrific? At times, we go looking for monsters, if not create them. What fascinates us about madness and evil, two other key features in Gothic literature? What internal darkness in us makes us gravitate towards the whirlpool of mental chaos? In proposing that science fiction is our modern mythology, and that in particular science fiction aspires toward transcendence beyond the commonplace and here and now, it's clear that our modern myth-making often creates objects of fear, including hideous monsters. Throughout the evolution of science fiction such elements of Gothic horror frequently occupy center stage, and are powerful motivational draws into the science fiction experience. What is transcendent and fantastical may be bone-chilling and horrendous, yet we are pulled toward it. Is it simply that we need to be stimulated and titillated, and shocked out of our dull conscious complacency, even if the stimuli are frightening and ugly?

Sparked by Walpole's literary recoil against scientific rationalism and modernism, the Gothic fascination with supernatural mystery and horror, as well as spiritualism and mysticism, would continue into the nineteenth century. Other notable novels in the Gothic tradition (or showing strong Gothic features) include *The Mysteries of Udolpho* by Ann Radcliffe (1794);

The Monk: A Romance by Matthew Gregory Lewis (1796); *The Devil's Elixirs* by E. T. A. Hoffman (1815); Shelley's *Frankenstein* (1818); Polidori's *The Vampyre* (1819); many of the well-known stories of Edgar Allen Poe in the 1830s and 1840s; Robert Lewis Stephenson's famous *Strange Case of Dr Jekyll and Mr Hyde* (1886); and Stoker's *Dracula* (1897). Spiritualism and mysticism would be particularly popular in Victorian England throughout most of the nineteenth century, again as a reaction against the scientific mindset (but perhaps also in response to the excessive moral rigidity of the era). Spiritualism and mysticism would find its supreme cosmic expression in the nineteenth-century work and writings of Camille Flammarion in France in the 1880s. And the mysterious horrific, coupled with the cosmic and the mystical, would continue full-force into the twentieth century in the writings of William Hope Hodgson and H. P. Lovecraft, the latter in particular bringing into his stories numerous other Gothic elements.

The science fiction writer and historian Brian Aldiss (1973) has gone so far as to argue that modern science fiction is an evolutionary outgrowth of Gothic literature, citing Shelley's *Frankenstein* as the seminal work of the genre. (Does this mean that science fiction begins in fear?) Panshin and Panshin (1989) also highlight the importance of Gothic literature in the emergence of science fiction, but locate as a key starting point Walpole's novel. Their argument is that Walpole's novel is the first modern *attempt* to "reshape traditional myth" to align with the modern Western mindset. Walpole wanted to combine the fantastical imagination of ancient mythic stories and medieval romance literature with a modern depiction of human characters as expressed in the popular realistic novels of his time. In Walpole's mind, the former types of stories were excessively fanciful whereas the latter were too realistically constrained. As he states in the introduction to *The Castle of Otranto*, in wanting to strike a balance, Walpole strove to synthesize characters that were realistic and modern in tone with fantastical and supernatural features that hearkened back to the mindset of the Middle Ages. To recall, for the Panshins, myth involves plausible transcendence, and Walpole does pull together the transcendent mystery of ancient romance with plausible modern human characters. Yet, as the Panshins acknowledge, Walpole failed in his overall effort to synthesize the fantastic and transcendent with the plausible, for the most fantastical feature in the novel is a ghost, which is inexplicable within the modern scientific mindset. The characters may be modern and plausible, but the ghost isn't.

Indeed, and agreeing with Roberts (2005), there is an important sense in which Gothic literature is anathema to science fiction, at least in so far as Gothic literature embraces the supernatural. The supernatural is scientifically implausible, and strictly speaking should lie outside of science fiction. But of course this argument by Roberts only goes so far. The supernatural and the spiritual frequently creep into science fiction. What is scientifically plausible turns out to be a point of contention (at least to some degree) among science fiction authors.

Even acknowledging various points of contention, the Panshins propose that *The Castle of Otranto* can be viewed as a key origin point for not only Gothic literature, the supernatural horror story, and science fiction, but also for the mystery novel, the historical novel, and the romantic spiritualist revival of the nineteenth century.

Although Walpole may have attempted to create realistically grounded characters in his novel, one of the most distinctive features of Gothic literature to emerge in the subsequent century was the incredible imaginative array of characters, human and otherwise, in its stories. We find werewolves and vampires; witches and warlocks; ghosts and zombies; demons, goblins, trolls, and devils; and other monstrous creatures of the supernatural populating Gothic tales. There are indefinable "things that go bump in the night." At times, there are characters, human or otherwise, such as in *The Monk*, who engage in debauchery and sadism; who are diabolic; or who practice black magic or other forms of dark wizardry. On the human end of the spectrum of characters we frequently find damsels in distress, reluctant or foolish heroes, and individuals obsessed, possessed, or clearly mad. As noted earlier, one of the noteworthy features of science fiction is the colorful and diverse array of characters created in its stories. The Gothic imagination—infused with the supernatural, magical, demonic, lecherous, hysterical, and psychopathological—significantly contributed into the evolution of bizarre characters in science fiction. Although perhaps not supernatural, science fiction characters possessed all of the perversions, eccentricities, and macabre qualities of Gothic characters.

The frequent inclusion of madness, mental aberration, and extreme and unsettling emotionality in Gothic characters is especially interesting. For one thing, the Romantic impulse to venture into the rich and energetic sphere of inner consciousness is bolstered and amplified by diving into the pathological turmoil and terror of frightened and obsessed human minds. Fear and madness are intense psychological states. But also, adding uncertainty and mystery to a Gothic story, it may be that the monsters and evil beings within the narrative are, in actuality, manifestations of madness and anxiety in the minds of the characters within the tale. The monsters, ghosts, and other objects of terror are perhaps psychological projections of the human characters. As Ann Radcliffe routinely reveals in the climaxes of her numerous popular Gothic novels, such as *The Mysteries of Udolpho*, it only appears that there is something supernatural at work; in actuality, it is the darkness and torment of one or more characters that gives the stories their frightening and evil qualities. In general, the supernatural dimension in Gothic literature often gets associated with the psychopathological. Moreover, the borderland between madness and the supernatural can be fuzzy and permeable. Is the evil within us, or outside of us? Can we be sure either way? If the human mind, in its powers of imagination, reaches toward transcendence beyond the common place and the "normal," the universe discovered is filled with both angelic hopes and monsters created out of our fears.

One particular archetypal character found in Gothic literature is the Romantic "Byronic Hero." Lord Byron provided a realistic exemplar of the Romantic figure of the solitary creative artist, rebellious and estranged from normal society. The "Byronic Hero" served as the character model for the central protagonist, Lord Ruthven, in Polidori's *The Vampyre*. A solitary, mysterious, and brooding figure, the Bryonic Hero was "proud, moody, cynical, with defiance on his brow, and misery in his heart." This character archetype would not only appear in Gothic literature, but science fiction literature as well, where the creative scientist or inventor was often described as aloof and isolated, dark and mysterious, and in extreme cases obsessed, if not mad. Such a character archetype was much different from the inspiring and uplifting Romantic scientist described by Holmes. Although we do find positive visions of scientific heroes in science fiction, the Gothic crept into science fiction, and we find gradations from the sane, socially conscious, and heroic to Byronic types that at the opposite extreme become the mad scientist isolated away on a remote island or castle—as much a moody alchemist and withdrawn artist as a rational scientist. Hearts either hang heavy in Gothic literature and Gothic-inspired science fiction, or soar upward in egomaniacal and psychotic rhapsody.

In short, we can argue that the spirit of Gothic literature diametrically opposed the rational, realistic, and scientific philosophy that would fertilize the imagination of science fiction writers in modern times. Gothic was, and still is, supernatural and regressive, anchoring its themes and ideas to a medieval mindset. Yet, just as mythic themes and mystical inclinations have informed and inspired science fiction down through the ages, the Gothic elements of horror, suspense, and terror; of madness and monsters; of dark passageways and things that go bump in the night, have repeatedly worked their way into science fiction. Journeys into the transcendent and unknown, a common narrative in science fiction, can provoke fear and terrifying images. Further, in science fiction cinema especially, horror, madness, and science fiction often get strongly connected, and the scientist-inventor in the tale may be a tormented or evil individual hell-bent on creating monsters.

Grainville's *The Last Man* and Shelley's *Frankenstein*

I had a dream, which was not all a dream.
The bright sun was extinguish'd, and the stars
Did wander darkling in the eternal space,
Rayless, and pathless, and the icy earth
Swung blind and blackening in the moonless air ...
Lord Byron

Lord Byron's famous poem "Darkness" (1816), quoted above, expressed an "end of the world" vision of human existence. Written during the "summer of darkness," when volcanic eruptions in the East Indies from the previous year literally darkened the sky with ash, and giant sun spots appeared, perhaps signaling the death of the sun, there was an apocalyptic and fearful social consciousness pervasive throughout Europe. In stark contrast to the bright vision of the future, as embodied in the Enlightenment theory of progress and the ever-expanding, consciousness raising discoveries of modern science, in this poem Byron conveys a totally antithetical mood toward the future of human existence, one that is bleak and depressing. The world ends. Humanity expires. The forces of the heavens, of nature, of the gods, trump our vanity and optimism. The poem expresses the "dark side" of the Romantic movement, bringing to the forefront all those anxious, unsettling, and brooding emotions within the human psyche over the tenuousness of human existence and our impotence in face of the cosmic forces of nature.

The early nineteenth-century literary work that most deeply and powerfully expresses a dark and depressing consciousness of the future of humanity is Jean Baptiste Grainville's (1746-1805) *The Last Man* (1805). (First translated and published in English in 1806 as *The Last Man, or Omegarus and Syderia, a Romance of Futurity.*) Although the book would gain ever-increasing fame and influence in the decades after its publication, initially it attracted no attention at all. Indeed, less than a year after its publication, Grainville committed suicide, perhaps in large part due to the abysmal reception given to his book. From a psychological point of view, it is understandable that the utterly bleak and dispirited nature of its themes and its ultimate fatalistic resolution would pull the mind of its author into self-annihilation and existential oblivion. *The Last Man* is very possibly the most depressing novel—infuriatingly so—that I have ever read.

Described as the "first modern novel to depict the end of the world" and "the death of all human beings," *The Last Man* is a combination of biblical mythology, in particular the Book of Revelation, and modern social and scientific thought. The story chronicles the life, and especially the final period of earthly existence of Omegarus, the "last man." The story is set in a vaguely defined far future, where human civilization has run its course and is within its final decline. Indeed, both the earth and the sun are close to complete exhaustion. The novel is decidedly dark Romantic in its tone, in a way very similar to Shelley's *Frankenstein* (to be discussed below), with an incessant descriptive emphasis on painful, depressing, and negative conscious emotions in both the central protagonist, Omegarus, as well as in other major characters. The central emotional tone of the book, repeatedly highlighted throughout, is human disappointment and resignation. Moreover, descriptions of the dying earth and its eroded landscape, decaying human habitations, ruined and crumbling cities, and even events in the sky are equally gloomy and dismal. The novel is incredibly bleak, both psychologically and atmospherically.

The basic plot begins with the efforts of Omegarus, the last fertile man on earth, to find the last fertile woman, Syderia, hopefully to procreate together, bringing a renewal of life and re-energized growth to humanity. Humanity in this far future has been steadily dwindling in population, no longer able to biologically reproduce. As part of the overall decline of things, after numerous scientific and technological advances and achievements in earlier periods, humanity has exhausted the natural resources of the earth. The great cities of the past have emptied and crumbled. Assisted by various other characters in the story—some human and some more spiritual and mythic (for example, a personified Spirit of the Earth)—Omegarus, who lives in France, goes on a transoceanic journey, searching for and eventually finding Syderia, who lives in Brazil.

But as the story progresses what is revealed to Omegarus is that if he and Sideria wed and reproduce, becoming the new Adam and Eve and thus starting a whole new wave of human civilization, the final apocalypse will be prevented from occurring, at least for the present. Omegarus learns that he and Sideria must make the ultimate sacrifice, forgoing an earthly life together in love, partnership, and carnal intimacy in order to allow for the realization of God's ultimate plan of the universal resurrection of the dead, the ascension of Godly souls into eternal happiness and peace in Heaven, and the end of the world. Omegarus is haunted throughout the story by the Father of Humankind, Adam, who first communicates to him this existential dilemma, and Omegarus psychologically struggles with his choice, torn between the desire for love and the moral-spiritual obligation to acquiesce to God.

What may seem bizarre, if not pathologically neurotic, about *The Last Man* is how romantic love, personal happiness, and self-determination get usurped in favor of a vaguely defined metaphysical promise and "moral" obligation. The state of eternal bliss in the afterlife in heaven, delivered as a promissory note, is barely imagined within the story; the story focuses instead on the real world misery and anguish that is endured for a presumably higher good in the hereafter. A great part of this suffering is a result of characters begrudgingly coming to accept this higher good. Moreover, the human quest for self-empowerment and the aspiration toward the betterment of the human condition are trivialized in the novel—as self-centered vanity and selfishness—overshadowed by the cosmic forces and higher purposes of God. Who are we to believe that we have a right to determine our own destiny? Who are we to put value in our creations? The psychological and philosophical feel of the novel is totally at odds with the optimistic and humanistic values of the modern European Enlightenment. Indeed, the values of *The Last Man* seem perverse and upside-down. Indeed we can see the novel, intentional or not, as a *reductio ad absurdum* expression of a god-centered value system. The ideals of human autonomy and romantic love are negated in the face of God's plans.

Strong Gothic and mystical elements appear in *The Last Man* as well, with its inclusion of dark and frightening scenarios and scenes, and ghosts and spirits, including the Spirit of Death, whose final duty it is to kill the last woman and man. There are prophecies, signs, premonitions, and spooky dreams throughout the tale. We descend into the bowels of Hell and into the mysterious subterranean laboratories of the Spirit of the Earth (the "Terrestrial Genius" who has been assigned by God to watch over and protect the Earth through science). *The Last Man* is filled with the fantastical, supernatural, and spiritual, most of which brings with it an eerie and unnerving aura.

Yet aside from its religious and mystical dark side, Grainville also brings into play in his degenerative vision of the future the scientific-secular idea that everything in the natural world, inclusive of the earth, the sun, and human civilization, has a finite lifespan; there is birth and becoming, and death and passing away within all natural forms. Indeed, the universe has a finite lifespan. Our protagonist, Omegarus, needs to accept this fundamental fact of nature; the future will not go on forever. Grainville also connects the theme of humanity exhausting the resources of earth with human greed and excessive neediness that has accelerated the process of decay. The ruined earth in this far future is a consequence of humanity's disregard for the earth and our lack of foresight. At least in part we are doomed because of our sins and mental limitations. All told, Grainville appears to reject, on ontological grounds, both naturalistic and supernaturalistic, the ideology of progress and the unending continuation of humankind: Civilization and its advancement require resources and resources are finite. Everything must come to an end. Both God and nature conspire against us.

Given the abysmally fatalistic quality of this dark and moody novel, what possible value and importance can it have within the evolution of science fiction? In *Origins of Futuristic Fiction* (1987) Paul Alkon devotes a lengthy chapter to Grainville's book, highlighting a number of significant features and explaining how it represented a unique step forward in futurist fiction. For one thing, as Alkon describes it, the novel embodies a "secularization of the apocalypse," bringing a variety of naturalistic considerations into an end-of-the-world scenario. Grainville's book is the modern starting point for numerous other novels, many of them science fiction, that imagined the end of humanity and the earth due not simply to God's will but to naturalistic or social factors.

This line of thought was beginning to circulate at the time.

Contemporary with Grainville's novel, Thomas Malthus published his highly influential *An Essay on the Principle of Population* (Six editions from 1798 to 1826). Skeptical of the optimistic visions of progress that Condorcet and others had promoted, Malthus argued that there were naturalistic constraints on human advancement. He proposed that human population increases faster than food production (that population growth stretches beyond available resources), and that naturalistic forces routinely come into play—war, famine, and disease in particular—that hold the growth of civilization in check. There may be scientifically solid reasons why human civilization will not keep moving forward, and indeed may collapse. Numerous and influential lines of secular thought and speculation, both fictional and non-fictional, followed in the wake of Malthus and Grainville, that given human greed, finite resources, and unchecked population growth, raised doubts about continued progress and even human survival.

Yet, as Alkon also notes, *The Last Man* is spiritual and theistic in tone as well, providing an "analogue" to the Book of Revelation. We find the familiar elements of God, Satan, Adam, the resurrection of the dead, the prophecy of the end of time and the world, and an eternal heaven in the novel. But Grainville's fantastical and spiritualist vision is in ways unique. There is no mention of Christ, Christian religion, or the Bible, and it is the "Terrestrial Genius" or "Spirit of the Earth"—a character not found in the Book of Revelation—that destroys the earth in the story's climax. At a supernatural or spiritual level, at least to a certain degree, Grainville creatively moves beyond orthodox religious doctrine and visions of the future, producing a new synthesis of novel elements and those of ancient eschatological myths.

As another important feature of the book, Alkon points out that *The Last Man* provides the first personalized narrative "phenomenology of the apocalypse." Through the characters of

Omegarus and Syderia, we vicariously experience the sequence of events leading to the end of the world and the characters' personal reactions. *The Last Man* is a story of how the final apocalypse would feel to someone living through it; all is not revealed at once, and we follow the characters and their inner consciousness as the catastrophe progressively unfolds. As Alkon argues, this personalized and sequential narrative form differs greatly from earlier religious revelations of the end of the world. In this respect, Grainville set the stage and fictional form for later novels of world catastrophe.

Alkon sees Grainville as part of the negative Romantic reaction to modern science's attempt to bring order and reason to the world. Science undercut the credibility and value of fantasy, but Grainville saw fantasy as a necessary and desirable component of the human experience. For him, fantasy kept mystery and wonder in the world. His inclusion of ghosts and spirits and a far future, both bleak and yet immensely imaginative, contributes into the fantastical and mystical quality of his story. If Romanticism, as a reaction to science and modern progress, took different forms, one form was to reassert what modernists were attempting to transcend, namely, the enigmatic and wondrous qualities of the spiritual and the supernatural.

But above and beyond the re-assertion of the supernatural, it is just as noteworthy that Grainville attempted to synthesize the scientific-naturalistic and spiritual-supernatural elements in his novel. In this regard he would influence later writers with similar integrative ways of thinking. Alkon contends that Camille Flammarion's apocalyptic *Omega: The End of the World* (1893/1894), which combined astronomy and environmental science with spiritualism, was inspired by Grainville. (Recall that Davy's combination of mysticism and science also may have influenced Flammarion.)

Nonetheless, the synthesis of the secular and the supernatural in *The Last Man* is uneasy and contentious. As introduced above,

The Last Man can be seen as a *reductio ad absurdum* of theistic doomsday visions of reality and humanity's fate in the future. As Alkon notes, *The Last Man* was paradoxically interpreted by some later writers in the nineteenth century as, in *actuality*, an assertion of the central importance of earthly human romantic love and hope for humanity in the future over theologically inspired doomsday thinking. In reading *The Last Man*, our sympathy is with Omegarus and especially Syderia, who are good people who have done no wrong and yet, due to the "higher" purposes of God, must suffer and forsake their personal hopes for an earthly future together. The ghost of Adam is a dismal and weak character, guiding Omegarus toward acquiescence and acceptance. The arguments for the necessity of the end of the world are not that convincing. Omegarus' surrender to cosmic fate equally seems unconvincing; Omegarus is infuriatingly passive. All told, both from an emotional and rational point of view, as Alkon argues, *The Last Man* calls into question the whole idea of a divinely inspired apocalypse and the values associated with it.

In the final analysis, we can ask, what is the nature of the mythic narrative embedded in *The Last Man*? From one perspective, it is the "hero's journey," in this case involving sacrifice and eventual enlightenment in the face of the forces and designs of the cosmos. Equally though, it is a raw and deeply depressing tragedy, negating the human spirit. It is a mythic nightmare justified (rather weakly) through supernatural ideology. Although an oxymoronic unity of contradictions — of earthly misery and the hope of eternal bliss, of sympathetic human characters and unconvincing spiritual personae — *The Last Man* stands at the negative extreme on the continuum of hope versus despair in our mythologies of the future. It is a haunting myth of transcendence that takes us through the deepest valleys of spiritual desolation.

And yet, *The Last Man* also expands futurist human

imagination; it journeys into the deep future time of humanity and the earth. It opens the door to many later narratives, such as Flammarion's *Omega* (1893/1894), Wells' *The Time Machine* (1895), Hodgson's *The Night Land* (1912), and Fowler Wright's *The Amphibians* (1924), stories that also venture out tens of thousands, if not millions, of years. *The Last Man* is a key starting point in the mythos of the far future, a future mysterious, bizarre, and almost unrecognizable.

Lastly, in spite of its promises of an eternal transcendent afterlife, the novel presents the tormenting possibility that perhaps there is no never-ending future. Who are we to know for sure? In the story's final paragraphs, we are blocked from any further understanding over what will come next. Is there an eternal realm at the end of time? Is there a heaven or not? We travel far out in time and are left hanging in the dark abyss of uncertainty and potential oblivion. In Grainville's *The Last Man* the Gothic-Romantic, spiritual-supernatural, and the futuristic-scientific are woven together into a creative whole, both uneasy and complex, in perhaps the quintessential prophetic narrative of "This is the way the world will end and how it will feel." But it is not clear whether this grand finale of humankind is good or bad, or if anything will follow afterward. After having been dragged through Hell, plagued with doubts and confusion, we are left with our questions unanswered. All we know is that none escape death, including the author.

* * *

... Frankenstein is the modern theme, touching not only science but man's dual nature, whose inherited ape curiosity has brought him both success and misery.
Brian Aldiss

The story behind the creation of Mary Shelley's novel

Frankenstein is almost as well known as the book itself. The events and characters involved in the novel's creation have the feel of a piece of Gothic literature. In the "summer of darkness" in 1816, Mary Shelley and her lover and soon-to-be-husband, Percy Shelley, met with Lord Byron, his physician and friend, John Polidori, and Mary's stepsister Claire Clairmont (who was pregnant with Byron's child) at the Villa Diodati near Lake Geneva, Switzerland. Due to incessant rain and inclement cold, they spent much of their time indoors reading and discussing ghost stories, including the famous horror anthology *Tales of the Dead* (1813). Byron proposed that they each attempt to write a ghost story that would provoke fear in the reader. Byron and Shelley never completed their stories, but Polidori eventually wrote and published *The Vampyre*, modeling his central character, Lord Ruthven, after Byron (the Byronic hero). Initially frustrated and emotionally stressed in meeting Byron's challenge, Mary Shelley later participated in a group discussion on the nature of life and the principle of "galvanism" — the animation of muscular movement through electricity. That night, she had a "waking dream," in which the imagery and inspiration for *Frankenstein* appeared to her.

Mary Shelley describes her dream in an introduction to *Frankenstein* added in 1831, years after the first release of the novel in 1818:

> I saw the pale student of unhallowed arts kneeling beside the thing he had put together. I saw the hideous phantasm of a man stretched out, and then, on the working of some powerful engine, show signs of life, and stir with an uneasy, half vital motion. Frightful must it be; for supremely frightful would be the effect of any human endeavor to mock the stupendous mechanism of the Creator of the world.

Although not a ghost story per se, Shelley's *Frankenstein* was written with the intent to evoke both horror and fear. But what is the source of the fear, if it is not the supernatural? The answer, as revealed in the above quote, is the vanity of human science, manifested in the "hideous phantasm" brought to life in the tale. It is the fear of "playing God."

To set the historical context, Clute (1995) has argued that futurist science fiction emerged when the hopes and predictions of secular progress were incorporated into popular storytelling about the future. The world of the future could be imagined as one very different from the present due to the ongoing advances in science; in particular, as Panshin and Panshin (1989) put it, the imagined future would be one in which through science and its applications we could realize transcendence over our present mentality and ways of life. Yet, futurist stories in science fiction could take either a positive view on the promises of science and secular progress or a negative one. Science, secular progress, and the growth of technology could lead to a heaven on earth or to our ruin.

Although as Holmes (2008) points out, the Romantic spirit of the early nineteenth century was not necessarily opposed to the growth of science, as described earlier, some Romanticists distrusted the optimistic promises of science, advancing technology, and modernity. They felt fear and apprehension over the possible future consequences of advancing science and technology. A science-inspired, technologically driven future may be more a Hell than a Heaven.

Frankenstein; or, the Modern Prometheus (1818) by Mary Shelley (1797-1851) is the *classic*—indeed archetypal—case of the Romantic fear over the dark future possibilities of modern science and technology. Indeed *Frankenstein* also presents the archetypal case of the "mad scientist" run amok, one driven by delusions of grandeur that eventually lead to misery and disaster. The main character in the story, Victor Frankenstein, is obsessed with scientifically discovering the secret of life and technologically creating life in his laboratory. Although his professed motivation is to bring great benefit and power to humankind, he is just as much—if not more so—driven by the desire for fame and personal power. He is flawed.

As he soon realizes, what Frankenstein achieves in his experiments is not a scientific miracle but a monster and abomination. After creating the "creature" by patching together human body parts and animating it (in a way never really explained), the creature comes alive. Frankenstein immediately flees from it, repulsed by its hideous appearance (symbolic of the sinful, ugly, and incompetent nature of his act), and abandons it. As the story unfolds, he tries to hide from it, suppress and ignore it in his mind, conceal its existence from others, placate it, and destroy it. The creator rejects the created, and the created haunts the creator till the story's end. (This drama reflects the psychodynamics of obsession: To energize and empower the unwanted thought through hatred of it.)

Significantly, throughout the whole novel, Frankenstein never gives his scientific creation a name (and hence personal identity), instead referring to it as a "creature," "wretch," "daemon," "devil," "fiend," and even a "vile insect." This negation of the creature's personhood ties in with attitudes of the time regarding the limits of science. Although galvanization and the possible animation of life through electricity were discussed on the night Shelley had her memorable dream, she was actually familiar with these ideas as early as 1812; she had attended Humphrey Davy's talks on the power and promises of science, in which he described galvanism. And one issue arising out of these talks was whether a reanimated human body could possess a soul. Perhaps only God could give a living body a soul; perhaps a body reanimated by science could not possess a personal identity. Frankenstein's depersonalization of his creation reflects this religious and spiritual concern. Frankenstein's abhorrence of his creation, seeing the creation as an "it," represents a visceral condemnation of humanity's aspiration to play God. The act of creation is hideous; the creature is hideous.

Throughout the bulk of the novel, Frankenstein obsesses on how horrible a person he is for having produced the creature. The human creator, through his own eyes, is condemned and judged to be just as wretched as his creation. Instead of creator and created mutually elevating each other—as for example, with an artist and a great work of art—each pole of the relationship reflects and reinforces the depravity and degradation of the other.

The creature, rejected by his maker, escapes from the laboratory, and in his subsequent wanderings encounters other humans who find him repugnant and terrifying as well. Embittered and with feelings of deep dejection, amplified by the desire for revenge on his creator, the creature commits a series of ghastly murders. At one point, Frankenstein reneges on creating a female companion for the creature—the creature had promised to leave civilization if he had a mate—and in retaliation the creature kills Frankenstein's newlywed bride. (In twentieth-century cinema, going beyond the original story, a "Bride of Frankenstein" is created.)

At the story's end, Frankenstein dies of exhaustion and hypothermia in pursuit of the creature near the North Pole, and the creature, despondent over his creator's death and vowing to commit suicide, disappears into the Arctic darkness, never to be seen again. The message: This is what happens when you vainly attempt to play God through the instruments of science; the world around you collapses and everyone you love dies. Clearly the story's end is a warning against ambition.

Frankenstein is fundamentally an introspective nightmare, more a critique of human nature than of science and technology. It was the egomania of Victor Frankenstein, coupled with his heartless abandonment of the creature, that is the real cause of the misery, tragedy, and suffering described in the novel.

Shelley does not discuss in any detail at all the technology of creating life. There is very little science in the story. Rather, as a true Romanticist, if not Gothic, in her writing she focuses on Frankenstein the man, his tormented psychology and emotional turmoil, and the haunting thoughts and feelings that literally destroy him as the novel progresses. In fact, the recurrent descriptions of Frankenstein's emotional consciousness seem excessive, and his reactions to events seem extreme, impulsive, and emotionally driven.

In total, the content of the novel is darkly Romantic, focusing as it does on human emotion—in particular tumultuous and distressed emotionality. It also has a decidedly manic-depressive quality, for it is the mania, with its associated delusions of grandeur that ignites the consequent mayhem and misery of the story. And there is a strong obsessive quality to both the elevated manic states and the subsequent depressive states of mind, of fanatically driven aspirations followed by incessant and torturous despair. It is the flaws and weaknesses of Frankenstein's character that the novel highlights, and it is these psychological factors that primarily lead to the tragic outcomes.

We actually feel more sympathy toward the creature than for the man; the creature is innocent, having been brought into the world and then hated and repulsed by all those around him. In learning how to speak, the creature becomes articulate and thoughtful, in ways appearing much more rational than his creator. He even promises to leave the civilized world and live the rest of his life far from humans, if Frankenstein will create a female companion for him. But as noted above, Frankenstein goes back on his promise to create a companion, out of fear that the creature and his mate will reproduce and multiply, posing a threat to humanity. To say the least, Frankenstein repeatedly behaves poorly against his creation.

Still, in spite of its excessive Romantic-emotional and introspective qualities and the dearth of scientific discussion in

310

the novel, *Frankenstein* has become strongly associated with the potential dangers of science and technology and is frequently identified as the first modern science fiction novel.

Indeed, the negative view of science became a stronger, more visible theme associated with the story as its notoriety grew. *Frankenstein* first achieved significant popularity in the 1820s with a number of stage productions, through which the story began to transform. The term "monster" became the principal name given to the creature, and instead of being articulate, as in the novel, the creation was presented as a dumb, hulking brute—hence, soulless. Frankenstein became more "evil" (rather than simply vain and emotionally neurotic), and the laboratory of mysterious gadgetry connected with reanimation appeared. By the time we arrive at movie versions in the twentieth century, we have bubbling gaseous beakers of chemicals and scintillating, gyrating arcs of electricity (the galvanism imagery) in Frankenstein's infamous, Gothic-infused laboratory. Holmes states that the new edition of the novel, published in 1831, much more explicitly demonized science. It is in Shelley's new introduction that she describes Frankenstein's scientific endeavor as "mocking the stupendous mechanism of the Creator of the World." Thus the root of evil lies in the mysterious gadgetry and possibilities of scientific technologies, not, as in the original story, within the character of Frankenstein.

One main reason for viewing *Frankenstein* as the first modern science fiction story can be summed up in Panshin's argument that the novel was the first story to describe plausible transcendence through science. In *Frankenstein*, we briefly glimpse "the world beyond the hill," realized through an imagined scientific experiment. Science produced the fantastical, of the resurrection of life from the dead. Even though there is so little real science or technology in the novel, as the Panshins state, Shelley does describe how Frankenstein pursued the study of science and in particular the science of life leading up to his infamous experiment. There is then, some degree of explanation of plausible transcendence through science in the novel.

But the Panshins go on to state that although the Romanticists were able to envision transcendence through science, they hid from it and were fearful of it. Frankenstein runs from his creation; Shelley destroys both creator and created in the story's conclusion. (We assume the creature dies in the Arctic.) As Shelley feared the power of science, correspondingly Frankenstein feared the creature. Although it is an exaggeration, given Holmes' (2008) documented analysis, that all Romanticists recoiled from the thought of transcendence through science, Shelley clearly fell in with this camp, envisioning such scientifically enabled transcendence as dreadful and appalling.

For the Panshins, although it poked its head out into the great and mysterious beyond, Romantic science fiction never journeyed beyond "the village." (The Panshins do not discuss Grainville's *The Last Man,* which clearly traveled to the "world beyond the hill.") The hideous hulk of a creature in *Frankenstein* talks like a "normal" educated Romantic character: it is neither transcendent nor alien-like (at least regarding its psychology and state of mind). Interestingly, the Panshins do contend that Shelley herself is the true new Prometheus referred to in the novel's title, rather than Frankenstein, since she challenged the gods in her imagination regarding the potential powers of science. But Shelley sees the creation of her imagination as a blasphemous nightmare; that is the point of the whole story. There is nothing Promethean in such a mindset.

Another writer who places Frankenstein in a seminal position in the emergence of modern science fiction is the science fiction author and historian Brian Aldiss. Aldiss (1973) identifies *Frankenstein* as "*the* modern theme" for it not only addresses the dual nature of humanity—of being an animal (severely limited in wisdom and foresight) yet God-like in the power to create—it also delves into the double-edged sword of humankind's superior scientific and technological powers. According to Aldiss, the power to create brings both "success and misery". Progress— technological and scientific—is a double-edged sword, and *Frankenstein* focuses upon the potential negative consequences of humanity's increasing scientific-technological power over nature and the world. Aldiss, in fact, sees *Frankenstein* as a "new myth," a modern myth for our times. This new myth can be described as the myth of failed transcendence through science, but this is not an uplifting myth; it is a bummer and a warning. Equally, we can see the scientist Frankenstein as a new archetypal character: the mad, socially isolated scientist obsessed with the power to both understand and create. In alignment with this new myth, the aspiring, adventuring scientist is not a hero but an anti-hero, and quite possibly evil at that.

This "new myth" and archetypal character raises a number of important questions: Through science and technology humanity may be growing more God-like with the power to create, but do we have the maturity and foresight to use this power wisely? *Frankenstein* answers in the negative. With science challenging if not replacing God, humankind has become empowered to remake the world, and even, perhaps, achieve transcendence in the future. But is this desirable? Victor Frankenstein though is a poor new God, a fearful and vainglorious God—invented by a fearful author—for he recoils from his own creation and dies a lonely death haunted by the reality of what he has brought upon the world.

The pessimistic "new myth" of *Frankenstein*, embedding humanity's enhanced power to create in a deeply flawed character that cannot wisely consider and nurture its creations, is a common theme repeated throughout later science fiction. This "new myth" is tragic and apprehensive over the future, over humanity's maturity and wisdom, and the promise of scientifically inspired secular progress. It is fearful of and repulsed over playing God through the instruments of science.

Although Shelley subtitled her novel *The Modern Prometheus*, this title is to a degree a misnomer (unless it is meant to be ironical). Prometheus, the Titan, is a heroic figure, especially as interpreted in more modern times by Mary's husband Percy Shelley. Prometheus suffers, but not because he develops, as Frankenstein does, an immediate guilt complex, spiraling into depression over his actions. Prometheus' intention is to benefit humanity, and he doesn't experience self-loathing over his actions. Frankenstein is not so much a "modern Prometheus," heroically bringing to humanity the beneficial powers of science, as he is a Faustian character selling his soul to the devil in the vainglorious pursuit of power and fame, and then realizing the magnitude of his sin, recoiling and obsessing over it. At best, symbolically we can see Frankenstein as Promethean in the sense that Prometheus suffered at the hands of God (Zeus) for bringing God-like power to humanity, while Frankenstein, as a mortal human, suffered for trying to achieve the God-like power to create life.

Whether it is science and technology, the vain human desire to gain control over reality, or the lack of wisdom regarding our scientific powers that produces the tragedy of *Frankenstein*, there is something actually anti-science fiction about the novel. So it is ironic that it is commonly identified as the first modern science fiction novel. The novel is a rejection of the scientific worldview, a reaffirmation that life and mind are seen (by Shelley) as phenomena only to be understood through God and spiritualism. The book is a rejection of the theory of progress and a transcendent future with its message that we should not try to fundamentally alter the nature of human reality through science, technology, and our own rational capacities. The new view of the universe that arose in modern times brought forth new values and new ways of thinking about the future, yet Shelley clung to the old assumptions. Shelley's *Frankenstein* expresses a fearful and reactive mindset, provoking further fictional nightmares to come, as well as out-and-out resistance against the imaginative possibilities of science fiction. If modern science fiction begins with *Frankenstein* it begins with a nightmare *about* what science fiction can imagine.

Yet we obsess on our nightmares and we are drawn toward the objects of our fears—as is evidenced in the long-standing popularity of Gothic horror—and by writing her nightmare down on paper and publishing it—though terrified and repulsed by it— Shelley provoked the literary creation of many further nightmares that adopted similar story lines and archetypal themes. Following Aldiss, there is a mythic narrative within the novel—the mad scientist creating the technological monster that destroys the scientist and possibly all of humanity—that would form the archetype of many science fiction stories and movies to come. In this regard, *Frankenstein*, in spite of its anti-science fiction qualities, has been highly influential in the evolution of science fiction.

As one final note connected with this last point, one version of the *Frankenstein* archetypal myth is that the created "monster" transcends humanity in power and/or intelligence. We may fear God, we may fear technology, we may fear ourselves, but perhaps what we most deeply fear is something more advanced than us that will replace us. Shelley's creature is a first clumsy step in this direction, and Frankenstein fears that if he creates a mate for his monster, they will reproduce and usurp humanity's dominion over the world. As contemporary tales and theoretical speculation about robots, AI, and genetically re-engineered humans highlight, our technological creations may beat us at our own game, and either wipe us out and put us into protective cages. In the future we may become lost in the evolutionary dust. This theme runs through a good deal of science fiction, both in recent times, as well as back into the nineteenth century. Our deepest fear is that Frankenstein could succeed.

The Double-Edged Sword of Science Fiction – Hope and Fear

Since man is above all future-making, he is, above all, a swarm of hopes and fears.
Ortega y Gasset

Because of the dual influences and complex and contradictory messages of the philosophies of Romanticism and the Enlightenment, modern science fiction in the nineteenth century expressed a fundamental ambivalence regarding the promises of science and technology, human nature, and the future in general. Change is both exhilarating and frightening; technology and science can be seen as either empowering or self-destructive. The aspirations of science and advancing technology can be seen as elevating or sacrilegious. Tomorrow holds possibilities of both great progress and good, as well as great disaster and evil. Modern science fiction combines the optimism of science and reason associated with the Enlightenment and the apprehensions of hi-tech modernity, scientific hubris, and change associated with Romanticism. It weaves together the embrace of change and human self-empowerment with the fear of change, of human self-determination and evolution, and of God. And on the fearful side of things, it may bring in the Gothic, with dark and terrifying settings, regressive mentalities, mysterious and perhaps even supernatural events, and combinations of madness and evil.

Two of the most fundamental human emotions are hope and fear, and science fiction creates stories that stimulate both types of feelings. Hope and fear are, in fact, the two primary *anticipatory* human emotions; both emotions have a future reference. The experience of hope involves an anticipation of something positive and rewarding in the future; the experience of fear involves the expectation of something dangerous or destructive (Lombardo, 2017).

Science fiction deals with the strange and the different—often arising in an imagined future—and the strange and the different can stimulate either positive or negative emotions in the reader. What is out of the ordinary can provoke awe, hope, and wonder, or anxiety, fear, and terror. Indeed, more often than not, in science fiction narratives we can expect both clusters of emotions, positive and negative, to arise within the same story, providing the dramatic energy and tension of the tale as events shift in a hopeful direction and then in a dangerous or frightening direction. In science fiction we are on an emotional roller coaster into the future, the unknown, and the fantastical.

It is also important to see in this contrast between hope, wonder, and optimism and fear, terror, and apprehension that science fiction is both a rational and thoughtful mode of consciousness and an expression of human emotion. Ideas about the future based on science, technological extrapolations, and reasoned predictions are expressions of the rationalist and cognitive dimension of science fiction—the future is imagined, conceptualized, and thought out. But science fiction as a literary and artistic form of expression attempts to stimulate emotional reactions in the reader regarding these rational predictions and the associated narratives created around the predictions. Inherent in the story is a cognitive dimension and an emotional dimension. This dual nature of science fiction reflects both its rational-cognitive (coming from the Enlightenment and modern scientific thinking) and its Romantic-Gothic formative tributaries—both of which in turn extend back to the Greeks with the Apollonian and the Dionysian modes of consciousness. (Indeed, the cognitive and the emotional are fundamental dimensions of the human mind to be traced back to our primordial beginnings.) As explained in the opening chapter, science fiction is psychologically holistic, embodying both thought and emotion.

* * *

... nightmares are dreams whose usefulness is to keep us on our toes.
J. T. Fraser

Although I am following a rough chronological sequence in describing the evolution of science fiction, at this point in order to further reinforce the bipolar dimension of hope and fear in science fiction, I want to highlight two contemporary movies that the reader is probably familiar with and that powerfully and graphically capture the double-edged sword of science fiction. These two movies are *2001* and *Alien*. Not only do both films powerfully illustrate, in striking visual form, the themes of hope and fear about the unknown and the future within science fiction, they also illustrate evolutionary trajectories that science fiction would take after the uplifting and hopeful visions of Herschel and Davy, and the fearful and depressing nightmares of Grainville and Mary Shelley.

2001: A Space Odyssey (created by Arthur C. Clarke and Stanley Kubrick in 1968) exemplifies a hopeful and elevating cosmical attitude toward the unknown, toward transformative human evolution in the future, and the wondrous possibilities of science and technology. As described earlier, the mythic archetypal narrative of *2001* is death and resurrection, of a lower form of intelligence and consciousness transforming and transcending to a higher form. The central protagonist, David Bowman, journeys into the unknown, into deep space, on the trail of an enigmatic signal coming from Jupiter (the movie version). The dark monoliths, the technological instruments (or perhaps embodiments) of a highly evolved alien intelligence first take Bowman on a phantasmagoric cosmic trip across the universe and then transform him into an ethereal Star Child.

The unknown—both deep space and the mysterious

alien monoliths—leads to both profound revelation and eventual evolutionary advancement. *2001* can be viewed as an "extraordinary adventure," where the journey into the unknown reveals fantastical sights and provokes wondrous enlightenment. Outer space—a frequent arena of exploration in science fiction and symbolic of the vast unknown—once traversed, leads to both great discoveries and personal growth. Further, the highly advanced alien technologies bring to humanity, and Dave Bowman in particular, a higher level of consciousness and a more advanced form of existence. Technology is a vehicle toward human evolution and self-empowerment. Although there is a deep personal transformation, to the point of the death of Dave Bowman's present body, the end result of the change is a more sublime form of personal identity. Although on the journey Bowman does show anxiety, shock, and befuddlement, in the final analysis the personal transformation he experiences, pointing toward a transcendence of humanity, is not something to fear but to embrace. As a story grounded in our past (the aliens have been guiding our evolution for millions of years) and looking toward our future, it is an uplifting and hopeful vision of what lies ahead for humanity.

Alien, on the other hand, goes in almost entirely the opposite direction. Set in the future, human travelers in a spaceship from the earth somewhere out in deep space detect a signal from an unexplored world. The humans follow the mysterious signal to its origin. So far, this is basically the same general scenario as in *2001*. *The unknown is calling to us and we are drawn toward it.*

But then, on arriving at the signal's source on the alien planet—a windy, dark, forbidding world—the humans find a strangely shaped derelict spaceship, with an interior that is decidedly Gothic, creepy, and foreboding in appearance. One of the humans becomes "impregnated" with an alien monster from an alien egg that eventually bursts forth out of the human's chest, killing the human host, and then speedily slithering away.

The monster, diminutive in size at its birth, quickly grows into a human-size creature that—slimy, hideous, and grotesque—is reptilian and dragon-like in appearance, with yellow acid for blood and a distending second set of sharp teeth that can rip through human flesh. All the crew members, but one (the woman Ripley), are eventually killed by this alien monster before Ripley is able to eject the creature into space, after the human spaceship takes off from the planet, presumably killing it.

The alien monster, based on the surrealist artwork of H. R. Giger, is the most nightmarish and frightening creature ever produced in science fiction cinema. Just like the alien spaceship, where the creature's progenitive egg was found, the monster is decidedly Gothic in appearance; with its elongated scale-like protuberances on its back and its serrated knife-like tail, it would not be out of place with the gargoyle statues on medieval Gothic cathedrals.

And just like the alien spaceship, the monster embodies a mixture of the organic, animal-like and the industrial machine-like in its steely structure and slimy appearance. The blending of the biological and the technological, of flesh and machine, produces a grotesque aberration. Its machine-like qualities (a metallic exoskeleton, hands and feet that look like jointed metal bars with talons on the ends, and a jaw that catapults out like a spring-loaded mechanism) can be seen as representing the evil, soul-consuming nature of machines. Symbolically, machines are going to eat us up, or perhaps transform us into monsters, a blending of the biological and the mechanical.

As was frequently inscribed on the outer borders of ancient navigation maps—"Here be dragons"—the alien monster is a concrete manifestation, carried to the extreme, of humanity's deepest fears of what may exist out in the unknown. The dragon is a mythic symbol, with both negative and positive meanings, and the reptile (or serpent), from which the image of the dragon is derived, represents the primordial sinister beast. Outer space replaces the unexplored seas as the deep and unfathomable realm of mystery and danger out beyond the horizon where all manner of dragons and monsters may lie in wait for us.

We can also view the alien monster as self-reflective and id-like, a psychological projection of the dark animal nature within us. The alien monster visualized on the screen symbolizes the deep fear of what lies lurking within the human soul that only needs some foolish or vainglorious act to trigger its release. Moreover, the alien is devil-like in appearance; symbolically, by invading and gestating within the human body, it is Satan assaulting and capturing the soul and the life of its human host. Following from a depth psychology analysis, the image of Satan (an archetype) is a psychological projection of what we most deeply fear and perceive as evil within us.

On a psychological level, it is Giger's amazing imaginative synthesis of the Gothic, mechanical-industrial, and biological, that, in his alien creature as a paradigm example, pulls us into the pathological, nightmarish, and surrealistic realm. Although perhaps only partly captured in the movie, much of his art produces a decidedly visceral reaction, often of repugnance, and yet his art powerfully pulls our attention toward its macabre imagery. It is hard not to *feel* in gazing upon his artistic creations. It is difficult not to be drawn into and fascinated with his visual nightmares.

In summary, the monster in the movie can be seen as representing various types of fears connected with the unknown (both within us and outside of us). And the vast and mysterious depths of outer space provide the ideal sphere—open to all possibilities—in which to project and envision all manner of bizarre beings and terrifying dangers. In the movie *Alien*, the unknown is to be feared; outer space as the blank canvas is filled with demons and monsters. Aliens are not beautiful and beneficent; they are ugly and ferocious fiends. We should not follow the mysterious beckoning trail. We will lose our souls to the Devil if we travel outward into the darkness and the abyss.

* * *

The eighteenth and early nineteenth centuries produced the Enlightenment, Romanticism, and the Gothic, and gave us scientific, techno-industrial, and social progress and transformation and provoked varied emotional reactions—of hope, fear, wonder, and terror—regarding these changes and where such developments may lead in the future. We find both futurist utopian dreams—fictional and theoretical—and narratives of the destruction of the world. We find elevated visions of a wondrous universe to be studied and explored and nightmares of the scientific impulse for power and understanding going too far. We see hopes for the positive transformation of human nature in the future versus apprehensions over deep flaws within the human psyche. We observe aspirations toward transcending God, eliminating God, or playing God, and admonitions that we must acquiesce to God's supremacy and His divine plan.

During this period, Western mythological themes both transformed, yet retained key features from the past. Spiritual beings, including God, continued to be significant if not central characters, but the ideas of science and secular progress became increasingly important in stories and visions of transcendence. The future of humanity on the earth became a critical issue and a major area of speculation. But as human imagination and thinking journeyed outward into new territories and possibilities, such adventures of the mind produced visions and narratives of both hope and fear.

As scientific and philosophical thinking in the nineteenth century continued to evolve, offering new discoveries and theories, not only did human consciousness expand (regarding cosmic reality, human nature, and the possibilities of the future), human emotional reactions evolved and intensified as well. It was in the nineteenth century that modern science fiction really blossomed, producing a huge array of new scenarios and narratives and highly original speculative ideas, as well as instigating an increasingly complex mixture of hopes, fears, feelings of wonder, and other human emotions. In the next few chapters this blossoming of science fiction in the nineteenth century is explored in depth.

Chapter 7

The Mysteries and Romances of Science

Futuristic Fiction and *The Mummy!*

... it is not in the nature of the human mind, to be contented: we must always either hope or fear ...
Jane Loudon

Moving into the nineteenth century, we find in science fiction writings and, more broadly in popular Western culture, both hope and fear in the face of the future. We find an ongoing debate about the possibilities of the future. On one hand we have the dark and foreboding imagery of Grainville and Mary Shelley, with their apprehensions over the "end of the world," as well as humanity's inability to direct technology toward positive ends. On the other hand, we find an increasing sense of enlightened and democratic self-empowerment, as witnessed in both the American and French Revolutions, although in the latter case reason quickly seemed to descend into conflict, madness, and violence. Equally we observe a growing popular sense of scientific, technological, and industrial transformation and progress, as new discoveries and mechanical inventions emerge in an accelerative fashion, affecting all aspects of everyday human life. The dual anticipatory emotions of hope and fear—as well as associated feelings and states of mind, such as wonder, awe, anxiety, dread, confusion, and enthusiasm—colored and energized human future consciousness throughout the coming century. The ideological and cultural struggle continued over whether change and scientific-technological progress should be embraced, or whether stasis, tradition, and a "natural" state of human existence were more healthy and sane. Mysticism, the supernatural, and the Gothic and Romantic would strongly influence the evolution of science fiction literature during the century, both competing against and striving for synthesis with the scientific and technological. In intellectual and popular culture, God would go to war with science over evolution. As a general trend, science fiction would undergo an explosive growth, especially in the second half of the nineteenth century. Before the century was over, "modern" science fiction fully spread its wings through the writings of Jules Verne and H. G. Wells, among others.

* * *

It was a dark and stormy night.
Edward Bulwer-Lytton

Written in roughly the same decade as Shelley's *Frankenstein*, three other noteworthy stories of the period important in the history of science fiction were: E. T. A. Hoffman's *The Sandman* (1816), *Symzonia* (1820) by John Symmes, and *The Mummy! A Tale of the 22nd Century* (1827) by Jane Loudon, this last directly inspired by Shelley's novel. Within these well-known tales we find a variety of popular narrative themes of science fiction: good versus evil; God versus science; mysterious and mad scientists; extraordinary adventures into the unknown; the possibilities of future human society; the reanimation of the dead; and even the challenges of romantic love.

Before describing the first of these tales, *The Sandman*, let's highlight some further historical context on automatons and robots. A female automaton is a main character in *The Sandman*, and animated mechanical "humans" would continue to pop up in science fiction throughout the nineteenth century.

To recall, the mythical, giant, human-like Talos, a construction of the god Hephaestus, is one historically famous ancient robot, among many animated mechanical automata supposedly created by Hephaestus. But numerous automata can be found, not only in ancient Greek tales but also in Egyptian, Jewish, Asian Indian, and Chinese legend and writings. These imaginary automata included both animal and human forms, and at least in the case of the ancient Chinese, were described as not only replicating realistic external living forms, but internal organs as well. Stories of automaton and robots go back to possibly pre-1000 BCE.

During the height of the Islamic empire (c. 800 to 1200 CE) a huge assortment of functional automata were actually built, powered by wind and water, both animal and human-like in appearance, including programmable musicians and devices that could play different pieces of music. Leonardo da Vinci designed and possibly constructed a mechanical robotic knight around 1495 that was capable of a variety of actions. In early modern times (the fifteenth through the eighteenth centuries), automata became increasingly popular and sophisticated, capable of intricate motions, including the abilities to draw, sing songs, and act in theatrical productions. Mechanical cuckoo clocks probably first appeared in the mid-seventeenth century. Such complex animate constructions inspired the scientist-philosopher Descartes, in the seventeenth century, to compare animals and animal behavior with automata, proposing that animals operate under mechanical forces like human constructed automata, just in a much more refined fashion. For Descartes, neither automata nor animals possess consciousness or souls.

By the beginning of the eighteenth century, when Hoffman wrote *The Sandman*, automata—now part of popular awareness—could mimic a diverse array of human and animal behaviors, so it was not that far-fetched to imagine a human automaton that could fool somebody into thinking it was alive and conscious. But, as was the case with *Frankenstein* (and consistent with Descartes' thinking), it was also generally believed that such devices could not possess an inner consciousness or soul, so any attempt to achieve a human level of awareness in the construction of an automaton was associated with the magical or the demonic.

Mentioned earlier as the author of *The Devil's Elixirs* (1815), Ernst Theodore Amadeus Hoffman (1776-1822) was a popular Romantic-Gothic writer of horror and fantasy. His short story, *The Sandman*, is a perverse and dark inversion of the fairy tale character, "The Sandman," who throws sand into the eyes of children to help them fall asleep. In Hoffman's tale, the reputed "Sandman" is incarnated in a nightmarish form as the evil Dr. Coppelius, who presumably throws sand into the eyes of children so that, after they fall asleep, he can steal their eyes and take them to the Moon, where he feeds them to his own children who reside there.

The central character of the story, Nathaniel, is haunted by the nightmarish vision of the "Sandman." Having heard the story of the evil Sandman from an old woman as a young child, he associates this sinister character with Dr. Coppelius, a menacing and hideous figure who regularly visits his father after Nathaniel goes to bed. Nathaniel finds these visits very disturbing. As Nathaniel discovers, Dr. Coppelius and his father are involved in some mysterious "work" in a dark, secret room in Nathaniel's house. (Science is connected with nefarious characters and clandestine activities.) One night, when Dr. Coppelius is visiting, there is an explosion in the house. Nathaniel's father is found dead, his body terribly burned and charred, and Dr. Coppelius has vanished from the scene. Nathaniel, of course, believes that Dr. Coppelius is responsible for his father's death but cannot prove it. As a true Romantic-Gothic character, Nathaniel becomes increasingly obsessed and depressed, if not psychotic-like, after his father's death, ruminating on the enigmatic Dr. Coppelius, who has now completely disappeared from the local area.

Nathaniel grows up to be a tormented soul. As a young adult, he attends a university to study science, and he comes to believe that an acquaintance of one of his professors, with the suggestive name Coppola, is Dr. Coppelius in disguise. Coppola sells barometers and what he refers to as pretty "eyes," which are various optical magnifying lenses. Nathaniel is decidedly spooked by Coppola but buys one of the "pretty eyes," a mini-telescope.

The university professor, Dr. Spalanzani, has a daughter, Olimpia. Upon first viewing Olimpia through his newly acquired magnifying instrument (which of course must be hexed), Nathaniel falls madly in love with the beautiful and yet notably mute young woman. Despite her inability to converse, Olimpia plays musical instruments, recites poetry, and dances quite gracefully (all forms of animated behaviors that had been produced in actual automata by that time). As their relationship develops, the two frequently meet, during which time Olimpia listens to Nathaniel for hours, apparently enthralled. Nathaniel barely notices that during their meetings she says very little to him.

But then, the universe falls apart again. Nathaniel observes Spalanzani and Coppola in an intense physical confrontation over Olimpia. They engage in a tug-of-war, one pulling her by the head and the other by the toe. Coppola wrenches Olimpia free of Spalanzani's hold and runs away with her over his shoulder. Nathaniel watches in horror. Olimpia looks like a "lifeless doll," wooden and dead, her eye sockets two black holes, and her dislodged eyes lying on the ground. Nathaniel realizes at last that Olimpia is an "automaton," something he should have clearly figured out before. Although throughout the story, Olimpia shows little outward affect or expressiveness and her spontaneous vocalizations are almost non-existent, Nathaniel, infatuated with her beauty and demure character, remains blind to her inner mechanical reality. As Nathaniel discovers, Olimpia was the dual creation of Spalanzani and Coppola/Dr. Coppelius and their confrontation is over who will possess her.

Nathaniel collapses over these revelations and descends into a hysterical state of mind. Happily, he is nursed back to physical and mental health by his friend and the friend's sister, Clara. Clara is a rational, calm, and pleasant individual who thinks that Nathaniel's obsessions and bizarre stories about his experiences are delusional; the "evil" visions he sees in the world are actually psychological projections of his own inner demons and fantasies. Having been betrothed before Nathaniel's obsession with Olimpia, the two lovers now resume their plans to marry after Nathaniel's recovery. But it is not to be. One day, when Nathaniel seems healthy and sane, he and Clara climb to the top of a high tower. Clara spots what looks like a "gray bush" coming toward them. Nathaniel pulls his optical "eyes" from his jacket pocket and, looking through the telescope, sees Coppola/ Dr. Coppelius approaching from off in the distance. It's too much. Nathaniel descends once again into fear, madness, and hysteria, and, after a dramatic struggle with Clara, he jumps to his death at the end of the story.

The Sandman was published two years before Frankenstein, and there are some similarities between the two tales. As much a vision of Gothic and horror literature as of science fiction, The Sandman offers us the archetypal figure of the solitary and mysterious scientist delving into a realm of inquiry and experimentation beyond normal human reality. The pursuit of power is part of the quest, but the figure of Dr. Coppelius also exhibits a decided malevolence in his actions and goals. There is a strong suggestion, too, of the occult connected with his personhood and his endeavors. Whereas Frankenstein is a victim of his actions, Dr. Coppelius is in control of events, remaining unscathed and apparently continuing to practice his nefarious arts at the story's end. As part of his malevolent powers, Coppelius also draws others (Nathaniel's father) into his dark pursuits; they suffer in the end for their complicity with the devil.

We also find, as in Frankenstein, the power to create artificial life, in the case of *The Sandman,* a mechanical robot. And the suggestion, similar to *Frankenstein,* is that the artificial creation possesses no soul, although the creature in *Frankenstein* (at least in the novel if not in the theatrical productions) possesses much more of a personality than Olimpia, who is "mechanical" in behavior.

Both stories feature a tormented soul, although in *Frankenstein* the tormented soul is the mad scientist, whereas in *The Sandman* the tormented soul is the victim of the evil scientist. Nathaniel is a frightened and foolish character, depressive and anxious in his childhood, who as a young adult falls in love with a mechanical creation (why can't he see that Olimpia possesses a vacuous personality?), only to suffer the consequences of his delusional obsession. Nathaniel is overpowered by his own fears (his inner demons) but also appears under the insidious influence of the Sandman. For example, Coppola sold Nathaniel the "pretty eyes" through which he was first drawn into his infatuation with Olimpia.

Sigmund Freud, the father of psychoanalysis and depth psychology, found *The Sandman* a provocative tale, suggestive and symbolic of the workings of the unconscious. The theme of psychological projection—of inner torments being projected into the outer world—is clearly present in the tale, but so is the psychotic/magical theme of introjection—of outside evil forces invading the inner conscious mind.

As tormented souls, a notable similarity between Frankenstein and Nathaniel can be found in the personal narrations of these two characters. Both are Romantic characters, describing their emotional states of consciousness and their tormented thinking in excessive and florid detail. They are obsessive personalities, who are very self-involved with their own miseries. The intensity of introspective description in Nathaniel's narration is, though, more convincing and realistic, since there is a well drawn and convincing nemesis provoking Nathaniel's highly agitated state of mind. The creature in *Frankenstein* does not initially appear inherently fearful or evil, whereas Dr. Coppola is insidious right from the beginning of the tale.

Hoffman does a very good job of blending together Nathaniel's psychopathological self-narrative with an ominous and malevolent ambience, where madness and evil complement and reinforce each other. Questions of fantasy and reality, of scientists and automata, of good and evil, and of love and madness, all get interwoven in this mysterious and dark tale. All in all, *The Sandman* is a highly effective and unnerving tale, weaving together horror, madness, evil, the supernatural, and science fiction.

Going in a much different direction, but still carrying forward another popular set of early themes in science fiction, we find John Symmes (1780-1829) who became well known in his time for championing the ever-provocative "hollow earth theory." Although there is some debate on this point (Roberts, 2005), Symmes — presumably writing under the pseudonym of Captain Adam Seaborn — is usually credited with authorship of *Symzonia* (1820), a tale in which human travelers journey below the surface of the earth, encountering a highly advanced civilization.

The idea of a hollow earth, or some type of subterranean immense cavernous realm, can be found in numerous ancient myths in diverse cultures across the globe; it is one of the many fantastical lands described in ancient adventure tales, and we find the idea, theologically embellished, in Dante's *Inferno*. In the Christian worldview, Hell exists deep under the surface of the earth, where Satan rules and evil souls are sent to endure eternal punishment. In general, the "Underworld," frequently associated with the abode of the dead (or dead souls), is a pervasive mythic idea found throughout the ancient world that continues into medieval times.

The popularity of the hollow earth theory extended into the modern era. Blurring the line between myth and fantasy on one hand, and modern science on the other, the famous modern astronomer Edmond Halley in 1692 proposed that the earth consisted of a set of inner rotating concentric shells, each with its own atmosphere and each possibly inhabited. To recall, from the last chapter, in the eighteenth century both Robert Paltock, in *The Life and Adventures of Peter Wilkins* (1750), and Ludvig Holberg in *Niels Klim's Underground Travels* (1741) wrote stories of journeys to the interior of the earth in which the protagonists find intelligent and yet strange subterranean inhabitants.

Continuing in this imaginative line of thought, Symmes gave popular lectures on his theory of a hollow earth throughout his life, describing four inner shells, each with openings onto the surface of the earth at the North and South poles. Due to his influence and notoriety, he almost convinced the United States government to fund an exploratory expedition to the North Pole to investigate the truth of his theory.

Symzonia describes just such an imagined journey. Identified as probably "the first American utopian science fiction novel," Captain Seaborn recounts traveling through a hole in the Antarctic, claiming the newly discovered land for the United States, and naming it "Symzonia." He finds a highly advanced society—one without social misfits—that possesses incredible technologies, including airships, jet propulsion devices, flame-proof clothing, and various advanced weapons of mass destruction. Seaborn and his crew are eventually expelled from this underground utopia, and through various misfortunes, Seaborn loses all material evidence for the existence of this subterranean civilization—hence, the suggestion (consistent with Symmes' theory) that in some manner or form the tale might contain an element of truth. It is also reasonable to think, if Symmes is the actual author, that a main purpose of the novel was to convince people of the validity and importance of his theory of the hollow earth. After all, one of the main functions of science fiction is not only to entertain but to influence people's beliefs and motivate their behavior.

Continuing and further developing the narrative theme of the hollow earth, later in the nineteenth century two very popular novels of journeys into the interior of the earth would be written: Jules Verne's *A Journey to the Center of the Earth* (1864) and Bulwer-Lytton's *Vril, The Power of the Coming Race* (1871). The latter tale, highly influential in its time, is especially noteworthy for having powerfully brought to public consciousness the idea of an underground, highly advanced civilization, provoking *both* great apprehension and fascination in its readers. Although from a contemporary perspective, a hollow earth or large subterranean cavernous realms seem excessively fanciful and scientifically implausible—not to mention underground civilizations—it is noteworthy that the line of writers who imagined these hollow earth stories did, at least, attempt to convey to their readers a strong sense of scientific credibility, if not motivate people into action. And this storyline would even continue into the twentieth century with Edgar Rice Burrough's *Pellucidar's* series "At the Earth's Core."

* * *

Although *The Last Man* is a futurist narrative set in a far distant time, the novel presents an end-of-the-world scenario of civilization's collapse, rather than one describing a developmental projection of contemporary social and technological trends and a transformed future human civilization. It is a narrative about the end of human society (and the earth), rather than a narrative about a future human society. To the best of my knowledge, the first noteworthy Western novel to envision a future human society based on developmental extrapolations from the present, both social and technological, as well as creating a narrative with colorful characters and dramatic action, is Jane Loudon's *The Mummy!* (1827). Although the popular contemporary image of a resurrected mummy—derived from numerous cinematic productions over the last century—is one of horror, ancient curses, and the supernatural, Loudon's original take on the theme is actually a key starting point for futuristic science fiction.

Before further discussing *The Mummy!,* another novel of roughly the same period should first be described. This book, *The Novel of the Future* by the French politician and writer Félix Bodin (1795-1837), was published somewhat later than *The Mummy!* in 1834. Bodin outlined in his novel a general theory of futuristic fiction—an abstract model of how to write a story about the future—that not only did Loudon successfully realize to a significant degree in her story, but more broadly anticipated and clarified a basic narrative framework for futuristic fiction to be found in numerous later stories as well.

After its publication Bodin's *The Novel of the Future* "descended into historical obscurity" and remained generally forgotten until its pivotal significance in the evolution of science fiction was brought to center stage by the science fiction historian Paul Alkon in his *Origins of Futuristic Fiction* (1987). According to Alkon, (and Clute and Roberts generally concur), what is so important about Bodin's novel is not so much the futurist narrative itself, which has numerous flaws, but the lengthy preface included in the book, which outlines a philosophical and literary theory of futurist fiction. According to Alkon, Bodin is the person who first articulated a theory of how to effectively write a futurist novel.

Bodin argued in his preface to his novel that prior to 1834, stories of the future, both utopian and disaster novels, did not reflect any realistic change in the world of the future, "giving neither relief nor movement to things or persons – without, in sum, getting to grips with the living creation of an ordinary world to come". In essence, according to him, stories of the future did not contain specific imagined events and realistic characters based on extrapolations from the present. Of special note, Bodin contends that "In times [past] dominated by belief in the progressive degeneration of humankind, imaginations only launched themselves into the future fearfully, painting it in the darkest colors. ... people dreamed about ends of the world and the last man." If specific changes were anticipated, it was regressive changes.

Bodin, who embraced the idea of progress, proposed that an "epic of the future" should attempt to portray the future as a world transformed by advances in science and technology. Within a futurist novel, we should "find a new world: a new milieu which is entirely fantastic, and yet not unbelievable ..." To bring in Panshin's terminology, the futurist novel should convey plausible or credible transcendence. In contrast to a regressive or static vision of the future, Bodin describes the successful futurist novel as one reflective of future advances:

> When progress towards improvement, the striking result of the comparison of several phases in our history, had been accepted in its turn ... the future offers itself to the imagination resplendent with light. Progress, conceived as a law of human life, became both a clear demonstration and a holy manifestation of providence.

Although Bodin includes in the above quote a reference to "holy providence," connecting secular progress with supernatural guidance, his overall argument assumes that through empirical observation and thoughtful considerations on historical change, we can extrapolate into the future to write a convincing and realistic novel about the future. As noted earlier, the concept of progress was embraced by secular and scientific thinkers as a "law of nature" from which predictions (and very positive ones at that) could be derived about the future (Nisbet, 1994). What Bodin is championing, in addition, is that specific detailed stories with imagined characters, particular events, and dramatic energy can be created within the context of general progressive predictions.

Illustrative of the overall exposition within Bodin's preface, there is a clear sense of a transformative, progressive, and even fantastical future. It is, of course, a challenge to the human imagination to write futurist fiction that transcends the mental constraints of the present; this has been an ongoing challenge up to the present in science fiction. Also, at an emotional level it is difficult to confront and transcend the fear of the different and the unknown, both factors clearly associated with the future. But Bodin gets the idea—the imaginative and literary challenge of futurist fiction and the importance of meeting it—if one is to successfully write engaging and consciously elevating stories about the future.

According to Clute and Roberts, Bodin's novel does not, however, succeed very well in carrying through on the vision. Although the story, which takes place in the second half of the twentieth century, does delve into the growing importance of steam power and aerial travel in the future, and anticipates the decline of monarchies and the growth of democracy, business corporations, and global politics, overall it does better at anticipating social-moral developments than technological ones.

Let's turn now to *The Mummy! A Tale of the 22nd Century* by Jane Loudon (1807-1858), which does succeed in creating a realistic story of the future based on progress. Loudon was not only familiar with Shelley's *Frankenstein*; Shelley's novel was a prime stimulus behind Loudon's writing *The Mummy!* There are some notably similar narrative themes in both works, including the idea of using modern science to create life, but there are also some significant differences, one of which is a strong supernatural dimension added onto the scientific in *The Mummy!* Loudon reconciles science and God, whereas Shelley does not.

The Mummy! takes place in the year 2126 with the action

centered in England. At the beginning of the novel we find one of the main characters, Edric, becoming increasingly obsessed over the idea of using scientific and technological knowledge to bring a dead corpse back to life. A deceptive and manipulative priest has helped to plant this obsession in Edric. Edric is both uncontrollably attracted and yet highly anxious and repulsed by this idea of the reanimation of the dead. In gaining knowledge and power over the mystery of life, he would become god-like and "attain immortality," but he fears the vengeance of God if he were to follow through and succeed in his obsessional goal and impious aspiration. All of this sounds very similar to the story of *Frankenstein*.

Although Edric suffers from this deep ambivalence and inner conflict, he is compelled to realize his scientific goal. With his scientific mentor, Dr. Entwerfen, he travels in a motorized balloon to the ancient pyramids of Egypt. Searching for a perfectly preserved corpse, the two of them enter one of the pyramids and find the royal tomb. Apparently through the power of special batteries and advanced electrical apparatus, they succeed in bringing the mummy of the dead ancient Egyptian Pharaoh Cheops back to life.

At this point the story goes in a decidedly different direction than the story of *Frankenstein*. Although fearful in appearance, the eyes and mesmerizing gaze of the Mummy capture and hold the attention of Edric. Psychologically overpowered by the presence of the Mummy, he loses consciousness. As soon becomes clear, the Mummy is not a demonic being, and neither does he behave like a disoriented and abandoned child. He is rational, reflective, and seems to possess psychic mental abilities and prescient knowledge. In fact, he is a being of deep moral purpose.

The Mummy leaves the pyramid before Edric and Dr. Entwerfen gather their wits and recover from the shock of the Mummy's resurrection. Upon their own departure, Edric and

Dr. Entwerfen are arrested and thrown in jail for desecrating the pyramid and ancient tomb. Meanwhile the Mummy journeys forth into the surrounding city, observing and contemplating the changes in the world since his entombment over three thousand years earlier. He gains passage on a balloon and travels to England, while Edric and Dr. Entwerfen are judged guilty for their illegal acts and remain imprisoned.

The bulk of the remaining novel recounts how the Mummy, amidst a variety of human dramas, political and romantic, involving an assortment of colorful characters, provides sage advice and assistance to these characters in their different struggles and challenges. The Mummy emerges as a force for good, helping deserving characters achieve just and ethical goals, while undermining the insidious purposes of various nefarious characters (including the earlier mentioned priest) and their evil aspirations. Part of the multi-faceted process of moral triumph within the novel is the eventual enlightenment of Edric—on the nature of his sacrilegious and foolish actions— which the Mummy plays a significant role in facilitating.

The overall content of the novel can be divided into two categories: a scientific-technological dimension and a moral-psychological-social dimension. These two dimensions come together at the novel's end. Consider first the scientific-technological dimension.

One of the distinctive features of *The Mummy!*—for which it was recognized in early reviews—was the great variety of futurist technological extrapolations in the story. Aside from dirigible-like global transportation in this future world, women wear hair ornaments of controlled flame; lawyers and surgeons are technological automata that can speak; air mail is achieved through cannon balls shot between villages into nets; houses and bridges can be mechanically moved about across the countryside; cities have temperature and air quality control; the weather and rainfall are modulated to serve agriculture; people travel about on aerial horses and sledges; soldiers wear armor made of flexible steel; and there is a global communication network.

Moreover, the advancement of scientific knowledge and technological invention—trends increasingly more powerful and visible in Loudon's time—are seen as beneficial to the improvement of the human condition. The novel conveys a clear optimism over the possibilities of science in the future, such as expressed in Humphrey Davy's intellectual lectures (Hopkins, 2003). Yet, there is still a strong cautionary note about science that is expressed at the end of the novel, very similar in ways to Frankenstein.

On the moral-psychological-social dimension of the book, the story has a decided soap opera quality, combining both comedic satire and political intrigue. A number of characters have romantic obsessions with each other—often not mutual— and they suffer various challenges in achieving their romantic aspirations. They also exhibit assorted neurotic and obsessive qualities, often attempting to meddle in each other's romantic affairs. Two women characters of very different temperaments— one bossy, obnoxious, and self-centered, the other inhibited, demure, and overly sensitive— engage in an intense competition over who will be the next queen of England, while royalty, the wealthy, politicians, and various vindictive figures try to steer events in opposing directions. There are traditional heroic warriors, including Edric's brother Edmund, leading armies that are engaged in various battles and military campaigns. On that note, however, the military dimension is more reflective of its time than it is of the future, glorifying the traditional values of courage, glory, honor, revenge, and conquest; armored horseman and infantry enter into bloody hand-to-hand conflict, their swords clashing and spears flying.

All in all, the novel overflows with mayhem, confusion, and tribulations, punctuated with good doses of human silliness. As one example, the lower working and servant classes have all been highly educated in linguistic communication skills—the servants are exceedingly verbose—but often seem incapable of efficiently executing their identified vocations. Through all of this emotionally agitated social interaction, filled with fools, star-crossed lovers, and unholy alliances, the Mummy repeatedly appears to move events in a positive and moral direction.

In general, Loudon describes human psychology and human behavior as basically unchanged in the future. All the individuals in the story, except perhaps the Mummy, are recognizable character types. Indeed, from the perspective of present times, the characters frequently sound like people from the past. (Anticipating future technology is sufficiently difficult; anticipating future psychology is even more challenging; we do not so readily assume that the human mind *will* change or evolve in the future.) Loudon does foresee a time when women could rule England—as virgin queens. The book, in fact, has been cited as an early example of feminist literature. Yet, on the other hand, Loudon envisions England in the twenty-second century as still ruled by a royal monarchy, reflective of a pre-modern system of government; in Loudon's mind people require a royal figurehead and a top-down controlled social order and unity of purpose that cannot be achieved through a pluralistic free-for-all democracy.

Even with its technological and futurist elements, the central message of the novel is moral and religious. Science can be of benefit to humanity, but our scientific aspirations, as well as our overall way of life, must be guided by a theistically grounded morality. Scientific and technological advancement are good, but must be kept in their place. Moreover, it is the variety of ethical character flaws in different characters in the story that drive most of the action and which, in the novel's conclusion, are rectified and addressed. People learn moral lessons; the evil and unjust are exposed and defeated; and the good triumphs in the end.

Of special note in this regard is the story's final revelation: Before passing back into unconsciousness and death, the Mummy explains to Edric, that it was not Edric's scientific-technological apparatus that brought the Mummy back to life; rather it was the power of the original Creator that reanimated him. There was no physical (or scientific) way to reanimate the Mummy's physical body, which had deteriorated across the millennia, much less bring consciousness back into his body. The reintroduction of the conscious mind or soul into the body was realized through an immaterial and transcendent force. And not only that; we learn that the Mummy's actions throughout the story were a form of atonement for the evil actions that had originally led to his death.

In acknowledging his reverence for and ultimate dependency upon the Creator, the Mummy sets a clear example of humility for humanity—and for Edric in particular, who has attempted to control and conquer the forces of nature through science and technology. Although we may aspire to God-like power, this is hubris and vanity. There are things outside the boundaries of science that humans should leave alone. This is the insight Edric realizes in the end. The supernatural trumps the scientific; God trumps man; the immaterial soul transcends the body. In this message, *The Mummy!* presents a stronger argument against the powers of science than *Frankenstein*, for in the latter novel it *appears* that Victor Frankenstein *was* able to reanimate the dead, whereas in *The Mummy!*, the technological resurrection of the dead is a complete illusion.

The Mummy! represents a philosophical and scientific evolution in narrative form on the issue of the relationship of mind and consciousness with the physical biological body. There is a variety of discussions within the book on how mind and body are possibly connected. In the beginning of the nineteenth century, the sciences of psychology and brain physiology were advancing, with ongoing philosophical debates on the relationship of consciousness and the physical world, including the physical body. Loudon explores these ideas, even if she eventually sides with the dualistic view that not only is self-consciousness distinct from the natural world studied in science, but it also has a supernatural and divine origin. We will come back to the issue of science, consciousness, and the supernatural in the next section when we turn to Edgar Allan Poe.

In later cinematic adaptations of *The Mummy!* the reanimation of the archetypal character and its various powers have been invariably connected to the supernatural, the occult, and the mysterious religious beliefs and powers of the ancient Egyptians. The character has become both a totally supernatural figure and a stock horror movie monster. The original benevolent Mummy has completely disappeared in modern consciousness. Indeed, as with the Creature in *Frankenstein*, he has become a sinister figure intended to repel and terrify rather than enlighten.

Horror, the Gothic, and Science Fiction:
Edger Allan Poe

During the time Shelley wrote *Frankenstein* and Loudon wrote *The Mummy!* the Industrial Revolution (1760-1820) was in full swing. Beginning in England and spreading across Europe, the United States, and eventually the entire globe, it was transforming the civilized world. With the advent of steam power and steam engines; the progressive shift from wood to coal as the main source of energy; iron and machine production; the first steam powered locomotives; and the rise of factories, the modern industrialized landscape and the emergence of industrial labor brought a new look and feel to human life. This mechanistic ambience—and all its inhuman associations—was a big part of what the Romanticists recoiled against in the rise of modern science and technology.

Moreover, as introduced in the previous chapter, a second wave of discovery and invention—a Second Scientific

Revolution—soon followed the First of the sixteenth and seventeenth centuries. As a significant part of this second revolution, in the beginning of the nineteenth century the scientific study of electricity and magnetism was reaching full stride. In 1791 Galvani had discovered that the nerves of an animal body operated on electrical impulses and could be technologically (artificially) stimulated; Volta invented the first battery in 1800; and magnetism and electricity were experimentally and theoretically connected in the 1820s, in great part due to the work of Michael Faraday, who also created the first electric motor during the same time. The telegraph, operating on electricity, was invented in the 1840s. These technological and scientific developments concerning electricity and magnetism, as part of the Second Scientific Revolution, would lay the seeds for the Second Industrial Revolution (1860-1910) that, among other things, would involve the electrification of everyday human life (electric lighting and telephones), including notably the beginnings of electrically powered personal and mass communication.

So, as industrialization spread and factories multiplied, electricity was in the philosophical and scientific air—foretelling what was to come later in the century. Moreover, the scientific study of the brain and nervous system, involving an early understanding of the electrical nature of neural tissue, was also emerging. The anatomically localized functions of the nervous system were being mapped (however crudely at first) and the body/brain system was progressively yielding to a scientific analysis in terms of electrical signals and chemical reactions. Electricity replaced "spirits" as the hypothesized medium of animation moving through the body (Boring, 1950; Lombardo, 1987).

It was in this historical and scientific context that Franz Anton Mesmer (1734-1815) proposed his theory of "animal magnetism," arguing that an energetic and magnetized fluid permeated the human body and could be controlled through various technological means, which included strategically placed magnets around a body. According to Mesmer, various disorders could be cured using his principles and techno-scientific apparatus. Eventually "animal magnetism" morphed into "mesmerism" and the use of magnets was dropped from the therapeutic setup. Although he believed his ideas and practices were scientifically credible, Mesmer and his theory of animal magnetism were increasingly viewed by the scientific establishment as highly suspect and scientifically implausible. The scientists' views seemed validated when the surgeon James Braid (1795-1860) reinterpreted Mesmer's work and developed the theory of "hypnotism," which did away with magnetic fields and fluids permeating the body. A hypnotic state of consciousness seemed to be a scientifically sound idea that could be elicited within realistically and scientifically grounded psychotherapy.

Still, hypnotism and its progenitor idea, mesmerism, became popularly associated with strange, mystical, and occult phenomena. In the nineteenth century, going into a hypnotic trance was frequently the starting point for a seance that presumably could lead to communication with spirits, and especially the spirits of the dead. Seances became exceedingly popular in the nineteenth century, as a wave of anti-scientific mysticism spread across parts of the Western world. Moreover, hypnotism appeared to be some type of altered state of normal waking consciousness, provoking all kinds of mystical speculation and transcendental thinking. Can we rise to "higher levels" of consciousness within hypnotic states, perhaps mentally journeying into "former lives"? Although Mesmer contended that his ideas were grounded in scientific concepts and empirical data, his heritage fed into and reinforced the opposite stream of human thinking: the spiritual, mystical, metaphysical, and occult.

We should particularly note that electricity and magnetism,

even if completely understandable within a scientific framework, can provoke in the human mind all kinds of mystical associations. Magnets are spooky: They seem to generate action at a distance. Electricity is ephemeral, brilliant, scintillating, and it comes out of the sky (the abode of the gods). Not a solid substance, electricity appeared to scientists and early psychologists somehow connected with the enigmatic and wondrous phenomena of life and consciousness. When Faraday first introduced the notion of "electro-magnetic" fields, the idea was rejected as unscientific (fields seem intangible), although it was later acknowledged as one of his greatest theoretical achievements. The idea of fields of energy or force would become a highly provocative notion at the boundaries of science, inspiring all kinds of pseudo-scientific analogies, including psychic energy and mental forces, auras, and fields.

All told, as the science of electricity and magnetism evolved in the nineteenth century, it carried with it a huge wave of psychic, mystical, and occult associations. And as science fiction developed in the nineteenth century, assimilating into its imagination the potential wonders of electromagnetic energy harnessed by futurist technologies, the genre also cultivated numerous ideas about higher states of consciousness, mental fields and forces, and mystical transcendent realities. The ongoing dialectic and ambiguous boundary of the scientific versus the mystical-spiritual in science fiction would continue through the nineteenth century, greatly stimulated by ideas associated with magnetism, electricity, states of consciousness, and force fields.

It is within this scientific-mystical context that we come to Edgar Allen Poe.

* * *

... a starving artist, a devious liar, a drunkard, a sexual reprobate,

and an all-around mad genius whom one could easily imagine inhabiting his own sensational fictions.
Thomas Disch on Edgar Allen Poe

The significance of Edgar Allen Poe in the history of science fiction has been a subject of great debate; see, for example, the contentious discussions on Poe in Aldiss (1973), Disch (1998), and Roberts (2005). In popular culture, Poe's tales of the macabre, the ghostly, and the occult are generally associated with Gothic horror and mystery so he might not seem to fall within science fiction proper, but rather within fantasy, horror, and the psychological thriller. But in a number of stories and essays he blended together the bizarre, gruesome, and mysterious with ideas about science, technology, cosmology, and the future of humanity. He was particularly interested in hypnotism and mesmerism, which, as scientifically "plausible" psychological phenomena, informed a number of his tales, providing a connecting link between the spooky and occult and the scientific and naturalistic.

Disagreeing with Aldiss's view that Shelley is the key starting point of modern science fiction not Poe, Thomas Disch argues that Poe holds that honor. According to Disch "Poe is the source." As noted earlier, there is very little science and technology in Shelley's *Frankenstein*. Indeed *The Mummy!* gives us a good deal more. *Frankenstein* is primarily a Romantic novel in that it is anti-scientific in philosophy and focuses on psychological content, in particular, Frankenstein's obsessive and neurotic ruminations. Poe, on the other hand, although definitely including the psychological, pathological, and mystical in his stories, also repeatedly delves into science and the possible future direction of both humanity and the universe as a whole. Poe was a strong critic of numerous features of modern industrialization and the secular theory of progress, creating dark and negative visions of where these modern trends were heading in the future; in a number of his works, he repeatedly discussed a host of scientific ideas and theorists, and in his lengthy essay "Eureka," he laid out a future cosmology of the universe that he believed had plausibility—and at the very least imaginative truth. In so far as he included mesmerism and hypnotic states of consciousness in his writings, he was engaging the cutting-edge psychological science of his time, albeit science with strong suggestions of the mysterious and supernatural. All told, Poe was much more engaged in his writings in current scientific and futurist thought than Shelley.

Disch describes a set of provocative and connected criteria for identifying the "science fiction" dimensions in Poe's writings. Using Poe's short story "Mesmeric Revelation" as a starting point, Disch argues that this one tale contains all the following features, and that numerous other tales by Poe contain one or more of these qualities as well:

- Mesmerism: (More generally, unusual and revelatory states of consciousness.)
- Dreams can come true: (As one example, the achievement of immortality, but more generally, the science fiction theme that what we hope for, with sufficient techno-scientific advances, may be realized in the future.)
- Chip-on-the-shoulder superiority: (The attitude of many science fiction readers and writers toward the limiting mindsets of popular culture; the arrogance associated with achieving transcendence beyond "village" mentality.)
- Genuine visionary power: (Poe realizes cosmic consciousness.)
- Great special effects: (Poe's tales are filled with fantastical, extremist, and often grotesque scenes and characters.)
- Sophomoric ("gross-out") humor: (The intent to generate shock, elicit terrified gasps, and outrage common sensibilities.)

- Vicarious participation in the "divine madness" of the characters: (Poe's characters often seem way out there, existing at the ambiguous borderland between profound insight and hallucinatory psychosis.)

I would suggest that what unites all these qualities is the effort to expand consciousness, and at emotional, sensory, imaginative, and philosophical levels to stretch the boundaries of the plausible to the breaking point. We enter into a strange, unsettling, uncertain, far-reaching, and hypnotic world in the writings of Poe.

Poe's writings with science fiction qualities—most of which are short stories and many of which can be found in the Penguin Classics *The Science Fiction of Edgar Allan Poe* (1976)—include:

- "Ms. Found in a Bottle" (1833)
- "The Unparalleled Adventure of One Hans Pfaall" (1835)
- *The Narrative of Arthur Gordon Pym of Nantucket* (1838)
- "The Conversation of Eiros and Charmion" (1839)
- "A Descent into the Maelström" (1841)
- "The Colloquy of Monos and Una" (1841)
- "A Tale of the Ragged Mountains" (1844)
- "Mesmeric Revelation" (1844)
- "Some Words with a Mummy" (1845)
- "The Facts of the Case of M. Valdemar" (1845)
- "Eureka: A Prose Poem" ("An Essay on the Material and Spiritual Universe") (1848)
- "Mellonta Tauta" (1849)
- "Von Kempelen and His Discovery" (1849)

In these stories and essays Poe blends Gothic atmosphere and themes—the bizarre, macabre, hideous, spooky, psychotic, and horrific—with futurist and, what he contends to be, scientifically plausible ideas. Moreover, he brings in strong suggestions and intimations of the supernatural blended with the Gothic; that is, he introjects the dark and ominous side of the supernatural into his writings. Further, there is a blurring of the distinction between the metaphysical and mystical and the scientific, giving his tales their unique quality; it is this exploration into "no man's land"—an obscure, shadowy, and pathological arena— that unnerves the reader and stretches the limits of the plausible.

In "The Conversation of Eiros and Charmion" and "The Colloquy of Monos and Una" we find spiritual beings who, having realized a form of elevated consciousness after their material-earthly death, discuss the future destruction of the earth due, respectively, to a comet and to the pollution and deterioration of the earth caused by giant industrialized cities in the future. Notably, Poe describes two of the most frequently identified causes of the end of the world: destruction through heavenly events or destruction through our technologies and disregard for the earth. Recall that Grainville combined both these destructive forces in his *The Last Man*.

In "Mesmeric Revelation" and "The Facts of the Case of M. Valdemar," the continuation of life and consciousness and consequent discoveries into the deeper dimensions of existence are accomplished through mesmerist states of dead or dying individuals. As a "plausible" scientific procedure—which Poe and many others in the early nineteenth century saw as provocative and deeply revealing about the nature of self and consciousness—mesmerism in these tales takes us into the netherworld of death and the afterlife. Both mesmerism and Poe's ongoing fascination with life after death provided a basis for exploring states of consciousness in considerable depth. In these two stories Poe delves not only into states of horror but also those of mystical and transcendental consciousness, where the boundaries of the self and the world evaporate after death into states of conscious "oneness" with the cosmos. Through the ideas of mesmeric transformation and life after death, Poe engages in serious and thoughtful reflection on the nature of consciousness and its relationship with ultimate reality, an age-old theme explored in both Eastern and Western philosophy.

The potential animating power of electricity (galvanism), seen in Shelley's *Frankenstein* and Loudon's *The Mummy!*, is invoked in "Some Words with a Mummy." In this tale an ancient Egyptian mummified corpse is "galvanized" into motion, self-consciousness, and intelligent speech. A debate ensues between the mummy and modern scientists and Egyptologists over whether the modern world has progressed since the incredible achievements realized in ancient Egypt. It is a rather comical tale, one in which the modern-day humans eventually win the argument with the mummy based on our invention of brand-name medical lozenges.

Representative examples of the genre of "extraordinary voyages" can be found in "Ms. Found in a Bottle"; *The Narrative of Arthur Gordon Pym of Nantucket* (Poe's only novel); "A Descent into the Maelström"; and "A Tale of the Ragged Mountains." The various journeys of the central characters lead to innumerable disasters and strange and inexplicable events and scenarios: characters stranded on a "ghost ship"; coming upon mysterious signs of a lost civilization around the South Pole and locating an opening into the interior of the earth (suggestive of Symmes's hollow earth theory that Poe presumably knew about); being sucked into a violent and bottomless whirlpool in the sea; and discovering a city of the past, which presumably has long since crumbled into dust, this last story intimating at both time travel and time loops of causality. In all these stories, Poe, as a true Gothic-Romanticist, engages in graphic, detailed, and evocative descriptions of the strange and often violent settings and conditions in which the protagonists find themselves; creating mysterious and psychologically unnerving scenes. We are immersed in the sensory richness of the macabre and fantastical.

Running through many of these stories, Poe also creates

characters, alive and dead, that viscerally jolt the reader: we find decaying flesh; rotten and discolored teeth; skewed and twisted body parts; bloodied and viscous eyes; revolting secretions oozing out of the skin and/or bodily orifices; and inhuman sounds emanating from the afflicted characters. The mysterious and aberrant gets coupled with the horrific and grotesque; the Romanticist focus on sensory color and imaginative power creates an unsettling experience of extreme realism of the grotesque in tales that journey beyond the commonplace.

"The Unparalleled Adventure of One Hans Pfaall," which can also be viewed as another "extraordinary voyage," involves a rather odd title character (it seems that all of Poe's characters are odd), who constructs a flying balloon with an attached large basket that allows him to travel from the earth to the moon. Although by the time the story was published in 1835, the idea of traveling through outer space in a balloon was losing credibility, Poe attempted to explain in considerable scientific and technological detail how such a balloon mechanism would work and how such an astral journey could be realistically achieved. The story is chock full of technological details and naturalistic observations.

It is, however, on the issue of scientific and technological credibility that we encounter an ambiguity in the story. As in many of his tales, Poe presents his reasoning and his theories of reality and consciousness—and indeed, his knowledge of science—to give plausibility to the strange events he describes. Although Poe was no scientist, he does regularly put forth the "scientific" considerations behind his flights of fantasy. What is plausible? Is it always so easy to determine? What is fantasy and what is science fiction? In Poe, the dividing line is not altogether clear. This ambiguity is part of the psychologically unsettling power of his stories: Could the events described really happen? Indeed, it is not always obvious whether Poe actually believed in the credibility of what he espoused in his writings. At the end of

"The Unparalleled Adventure" it is not clear whether the story was intended as a hoax or not.

In his essay "Eureka" and his story "Mellonta Tauta," Poe presents his ideas on the universe, the nature of knowledge, and the distant future. For Poe, neither deductive nor inductive logic—the pillars of modern science and philosophy—are sufficient or even helpful in finding the truth. Again, speaking as a Romanticist, Poe puts more value on insight, intuition, and imagination. The universe he describes in "Eureka" is a cosmos revealed through such faculties, and the future world he describes in "Mellonta Tauta" is one that has, at least to some degree, transcended logic and secular ideals and embraced imagination and intuition.

Although not a narrative but a lengthy philosophical essay, the theory of reality developed in "Eureka" informs many of Poe's stories, including his mesmerist tales describing mystical consciousness. For Poe, the universe (or God) is fundamentally a Oneness that exploded in the "Act of Creation" into a divergent and particularized many, and will eventually collapse and reintegrate back into the primordial Oneness. This cosmic theory sounds very similar to the modern ideas of a "Big Bang" and "Big Crunch" (Tipler, 1994; Lombardo, 2002b), although Poe's basis for proposing this theory is imagination, insight, and metaphor rather than astronomical evidence. The universe, balanced between forces of attraction and repulsion, is like a beating heart, a Romantic cosmic metaphor if ever there was one. Analogously, consciousness moves from an individuated, differentiated, and finite awareness realized at birth to a holistic and undifferentiated awareness after death. All in all, Poe's fascination with speculative cosmology and its influence on many of his stories places him within the cosmological thread that steadily evolved within modern science fiction. Ideas about the universe and its past and future evolution would inform numerous later cosmic science fiction writers, such as

Flammarion and Stapledon.

What is also noteworthy about the cosmic dimension in Poe is how this aspect of his writings is connected with the eerie and the horrific. We may feel awe and wonder in the face of the universe, but we also may experience "fear and trembling," for there may be forces at work in the great scheme of things that are deeply unnerving, if not insidious. Poe provides an important beginning point for "cosmic horror" literature, which was to flourish later in the writings of William Hope Hodgson and H. P. Lovecraft.

"Mellonta Tauta," which is probably the most futuristic science fiction story that Poe wrote, repeats various ideas from "Eureka," but sets the cosmic ideas in the form of a fictitious letter being written aboard a giant flying balloon (the "Skylark") approximately one thousand years in the future. It is written as a critique of the present from the point of view of the future. But the tale also spoofs the various errors that can occur if a civilization in one period of time (the distant future) attempts to make sense out of the ideas and practices of a time much earlier in history (our present time). Although complaining about the tedium and crowded conditions in extended aerial travel (there are too many people on the "Skylark" and too many other balloons simultaneously traveling in the sky), the narrator, in discussing Kepler, Newton, George Washington, Cornwallis, and other notable figures, muddles up almost everything in human history, reinforcing the protagonist's arrogance and sense of philosophical and scientific superiority over the primitive ideas of the ancients (Poe's contemporaries). He may live in a more advanced era, but he does not accurately grasp the parameters of progress.

One of Poe's central intellectual heroes was Kepler, whom he seemed to admire for his capacity to achieve profound cosmic truths through intuitive and mystical insight. Poe's "Unparalleled Adventure" is modeled on Kepler's *Somnium*, combining scientific and naturalistic detail with strange and imaginative realities that leave the question of "what is real" versus "what is fantasy" uncertain.

As a Gothic writer, Poe throws the psychologically haunting and the horrific into the equation of science fiction as well, reinforcing the legacy that goes back to *Frankenstein* and *The Sandman*—of science fiction often having a dimension of terror and things that "go bump in the night." Poe is equally Dionysian, creating exciting and heart-stopping scenarios, bombarding the senses with revolting and grotesque details. There is a hyper-sensory dimension to his horror.

Poe strongly engaged the philosophical and the scientific ideas of his time, and left a legacy that other writers would follow. *The Narrative of Arthur Gordon Pym* and other adventure stories would strongly influence Jules Verne in the creation of his "extraordinary voyages." There are fantastic adventures into the unknown, both physical and psychological, within Poe. And Poe's cosmic philosophy would impact Camille Flammarion when he created his mystical tales of the universe and the far distant future.

He was particularly drawn into the mysterious and provocative possibilities of mesmerism, which had captured contemporary public attention. Given these new psychological phenomena, what are the possibilities of mind and consciousness, now and into the future?

In spite of continued debate over his place in science fiction literature, Poe is unquestionably a significant figure in the history of science fiction. In stretching the territory of plausibility and imagination, at a sensory-emotional as well as a cognitive level, he compels the reader to deeply ponder the ambiguity of reality and the possibilities presented by psycho-pathological and transcendental states of consciousness.

As with myth in general, Poe's is a psychologically holistic experience, if one that delves into the dark and demented side of consciousness and the cosmos. His contribution into the evolving mythology of science fiction can be found in expanding and enriching the territory of the fantastical along the dimensions of the horrific, pathological, macabre, and eerie and viscerally engaging, unnerving, and even shocking the reader as part of the mythic experience.

The Extraordinary Voyages of Jules Verne

Every great genius is mad upon the subject in which he is greatest.
Fitz James O'Brien

The next significant figure in the evolution of science fiction is Jules Verne, who was greatly inspired by Poe. But before turning to Jules Verne, two notable stories, frequently cited in histories of science fiction and published around the same time as Verne's creative outpouring, should be described.

The first story is "The Diamond Lens" (1858) written by Fitz James O'Brien (1828-1862). In this story, O'Brien creates a speculative scientific-inspired scenario that would be frequently adopted and embellished upon in later science fiction tales: a world (or universe) existing at a microscopic or sub-microscopic level.

The protagonist of the story has been fascinated since early childhood with microscopes and the various living creatures and material forms that are too tiny to perceive with the naked eye. As he grows into an adult he becomes obsessed with building the ultimate microscope, but his experiments repeatedly fail in achieving this goal. Yet, one day he visits a strange old lady who is a spiritual medium and she puts him in touch with the ghost of the famous Antonie van Leeuwenhoek (1632-1723), the father of modern microscopy. In communicating with the spirit of van Leeuwenhoek, he learns how to build the ultimate microscope, which requires that he locate a giant diamond of a precise number of carats. Almost immediately afterwards, upon discovering that his friend possesses such a diamond, he murders his friend and steals the diamond.

Creating his "diamond lens" microscope and peering into it, he discovers in a drop of water a strange and cloud-like world of rainbow-colored trees. In this microscopic realm he observes a beautiful and enchanting woman-like creature who visits and drinks from a pond existing in her ultra-tiny world. He becomes obsessed with watching her and falls madly in love but feels forever separated from her because of the colossal difference in scale between his world and hers. Too late he realizes that the drop of water he had been observing day to day has almost completely evaporated, and he watches his beautiful microscopic woman and her entire world shrivel and die. In the end, he accidentally breaks his microscope beyond repair, and he becomes despondent, depressed, and ultimately mad when no one will believe his story.

"The Diamond Lens" is a short but very engaging tale of crime, mysticism, and obsession that creates a powerful sense of a strange other world (the microscopic) that exists unseen and unknown within our everyday reality. It is another tale of warning against scientific obsession (murder and madness follow) and it also mixes together a new idea of modern science (the microscopic world) with the mystical notion of communing with the spirits of the dead. O'Brien wrote other fantastical tales, such as "The Wonder Smith," (1859) a story about animated toys that become possessed by evil spirits and turn against their creators, but "The Diamond Lens" was his most famous story.

The second tale, a short novel titled *The Brick Moon*, was written by Edward Everett Hale (1822-1909) and first published in serial form from 1869 through 1870. Identified as the first story to include the ideas of an "artificial satellite" and a "space station" orbiting the earth, *The Brick Moon* is fascinating in several respects, including the window it provides into how the construction of a projectile into outer space would be envisioned, both from a scientific-engineering and a financial perspective, by someone writing immediately after the end of the American Civil War. (Confederate figures such as Jefferson Davis and General Pierre Beauregard appear in the novel.) The story also includes a model of a human utopia, one that is almost entirely disconnected from the frenzied pace of modern human civilization.

The story of the "Brick Moon" is told in "The Papers of Captain Frederic Ingham," one of the key characters involved in designing and creating the artificial moon. The chronicle begins by describing a scientific discussion among a group of college friends concerning the creation of an orbiting satellite that, moving in line with the Greenwich Meridian, would serve as a navigational guide (or visible marker in the night sky) for determining longitudinal position on the earth, just as the North Star provides a beacon for determining latitude. They come to the conclusion that this spherical structure should be made out of bricks and could be successfully launched with sufficient escape velocity using two giant spinning flywheels to achieve a permanent orbit around the earth. The cost, though, for the entire project would be exorbitant and out of reach for the college students, and so the "brick moon," for the time being, remains but a fantastic dream in their minds.

Yet years later, having achieved a level of financial and professional success, the former college friends are able to raise the money for the project. They purchase an appropriate area of land for building the moon, with running water to power the flywheels and available deposits of clay for making the bricks, and hire a team of workers for the project. They determine the moon will be two hundred feet in diameter (to make it visible in the night sky) and construct the sphere through juxtaposing and locking together an arrangement of smaller inner spheres. The giant flywheels are built next to running water. As the construction moves along, the workers, together with their families accompanying them on this extended project, temporarily take up residence in the inner spheres of the moon (which are more comfortable than camping outside). One night during an intense rainfall, the moon slips free of its mooring, slides down into the flywheel mechanism, and unbeknownst to the thirty-seven people asleep inside, is catapulted into the atmosphere. The brick moon disappears into the upper reaches of the sky.

After many months of worry by those on the earth, through the use of telescopes the new moon is discovered orbiting the earth. Miraculously, it is revealed that all the people on the artificial moon are still alive. Apparently the tiny moon has not only captured a surrounding atmosphere, but the outer temperature on the moon's surface is sufficiently temperate due to the illumination of the sun; there is adequate water on board; and the inhabitants have begun growing food for themselves. Indeed, when the moon is observed through telescopes on the earth, palm trees can be seen growing on the surface. Of course, all this sounds very implausible, given our contemporary understanding of space flight and the conditions in outer space surrounding an artificial satellite, but the description in the story of these strange events and circumstances is presented with an effort to sound scientific, plausible, and realistic.

The residents of the new moon and people on the earth figure out how to communicate with each other using Morse code, and the inhabitants of the moon describe how they were able to adapt to their new conditions and create a life for themselves. Stranded in outer space, they struggled at first but eventually achieved self-sufficiency. Interestingly, one of the moon inhabitants tells the people on the earth that he has been able to selectively breed and evolve plants, creating a new moon agriculture to feed the population and thus confirming "Mr. Darwin's" theory. (Darwin's *The Origin of Species* had only been published ten years before *The Brick Moon*.) In time, the "Brick Moon" inhabitants progressively develop a new routine of life revolving around social, religious, and educational activities. They seem content in this life, and happy to have achieved independence from the earth. They are a closely knit community with strong family bonds, providing love, friendship, and social support for each other, and they are no longer subjected to the fast-paced, complex, and competitive aspects of modern life. They have created a world of their own—a surprising utopian reality—perhaps a better world than the one they left behind.

Thus by the end of the 1860s, the imagined human colonization of outer space had begun with a tale of the launching of an artificial world of our own construction. Planting the seeds for many science fiction stories to come, the new world and social reality created in outer space, as described in *The Brick Moon*, is envisioned as superior to our earthly modern society. Utopia moved into outer space. As an evolved expression of the vision of a "New World" and a new form of human society that grew out of the Age of Exploration and the New Enlightenment, the idea of creating a better world for humanity in outer space—transcending the geographical and psycho-social boundaries of the earth—would become a powerful and influential mythic narrative in modern science fiction.

* * *

[His aim is] to outline all the geographical, geological, physical, and astronomical knowledge amassed by modern science and to recount, in an entertaining and picturesque format that is his own, the history of the universe.
Pierre-Jules Hetzel on Jules Verne's *Extraordinary Voyages*

I would hazard to guess that for a large percentage of science fiction fans the first author they read as a youth was Jules Verne.

As Ray Bradbury stated, "We are all, in one way or another, the children of Jules Verne." In my case, the first science fiction novel I ever read, soon after watching the movie in 1959, was Verne's *A Journey to the Center of the Earth*.

I distinctly remember though being disappointed with the book in one respect: Unlike the film adaptation, the explorers who journey to the interior of our world never reach the center of the earth. Regardless, I found the story of an extraordinary journey into a strange and fantastical realm amazing and captivating, with its array of wondrous scenarios: prehistoric beasts; a forest of giant mushrooms; strange and inexplicable giant humans; and an immense subterranean sea. Moreover, the book introduced me to my first heroic science fiction character, the mysterious Icelandic explorer Arne Saknussemm. In the beginning of the novel, a contemporary scientist discovers an old document—in code, written in Latin and Runic script, adding to the intrigue of the whole tale—with Saknusseemn's name on it. The document provides directions to the center of the earth; presumably, Saknusseman had traveled alone to the earth's deep interior. Saknussemm, a fictitious individual who hypothetically lived sometime in the distant past, was compellingly real to me—a ghost larger than life that went on a solitary journey into the abyss—and was for me as a youth, the true hero of the novel. I half-believed that Saknussemm actually had lived such was the realistic and provocative power of Verne's storytelling.

But of course, *A Journey to the Center of the Earth* (1864) was only one among many very popular novels written by Jules Verne (1828-1905) during the second half of the nineteenth century. Jules Verne, in fact, was the first modern science fiction writer to explode into popular consciousness and culture. A prolific and immensely successful writer, for several decades he published on average over two novels a year, among which were many of the most noteworthy early classics of science fiction. All told, he wrote over fifty "extraordinary voyage" novels between 1863 and 1905. Those novels and stories of particular significance in the history of science fiction — many of which have been turned into movies — include the following:

- *Five Weeks in a Balloon* (1863)
- *Paris in the Twentieth Century* (Written in 1863, but not published till 1994)
- *A Journey to the Center of the Earth* (1864)
- *From the Earth to the Moon* (1865)
- *Round the Moon* (1869)
- *20,000 Leagues Under the Sea* (1869)
- *Around the World in Eighty Days* (1872)
- *The Mysterious Island* (1874)
- *Off on a Comet* (1877)
- *The Begum's Fortune* (*The Begum's Millions*) (1879
- *Robur the Conqueror* (*The Clipper of the Clouds*) (1886)
- "In the Twenty-ninth Century: The Day of an American Journalist in 2889" (1889)
- *Master of the World* (1904)
- "The Eternal Adam" (c.1905)

From his early youth, Jules Verne was attracted to travel and adventure, the study of nature and science, and the vocation of writing. As a teenager and young adult he wrote poetry and plays, and early in his life he went on a number of sea voyages around Europe, which he found exhilarating and intellectually stimulating. As a young reader, he was drawn to and inspired by the tales of *Robinson Crusoe* (1719) and *The Swiss Family Robinson* (1812). Although his father, who was a lawyer, attempted to push him into law, Verne resisted, desiring instead to make a career as a writer. But he did not want to become just a common writer. From early in his life, Verne passionately studied geography, history, nature, and science, compiling an extensive system of notecards of important facts and ideas, and as he was engaging in this ongoing research, he began to formulate in his mind an idea for a new kind of novel, a "novel of science." By the early 1850s, he was writing and publishing adventure stories that were intended to be both entertaining and educational, incorporating into his stories information drawn from his ongoing scientific research.

While engaged in his studies, he discovered Edgar Allan Poe, whose stories he found fascinating. Although his assessment of Poe was mixed, Verne wrote and published a review of Poe in which he highlighted "the originality of his situations" that still possessed a "verisimilitude which grips the reader's credulity," due, at least in part, to the self-admitted "extreme sensitivity of his [Poe's] brain," perhaps creating a "new form of literature" in the process.

While Verne was working on his first novel of science in 1862, he met the publisher Pierre-Jules Hetzel, struck a deal on the book, and—collaborating with Hetzel—completed this first novel, *Five Weeks in a Balloon*, a tale of adventure across unknown areas of Africa. The novel appeared in Hetzel's "Magazine of Education and Recreation," a publication that Hetzel envisioned would provide its readers with educational adventure stories, the very kind of tales that Verne was attempting to create. The novel was a popular success, and Verne signed a long-term contract with Hetzel to produce a series of "extraordinary voyages" (as they would be advertised), beginning with *Five Weeks in a Balloon* (1863). Thereafter Verne had a steady income to support himself as he pursued a full-time career in writing. Most of the novels listed above were part of the "extraordinary voyage" series published through Hetzel.

Although *Five Weeks in a Balloon* was not in any obvious sense science fiction, a general narrative form would emerge in this novel that would continue through the bulk of his "extraordinary voyages" to follow. Verne's adventure stories, "written with style," encompassed both the far reaches of the earth (including its interior) as well as outer space. They invariably feature as central protagonists one or more scientists or educated individuals who witness and describe amazing sights; visit exotic lands; and suffer numerous challenges along the way. Of course, whatever the dangers encountered, they always return home alive in the end.

The scientist/protagonist is often a heroic figure who provides richly detailed, ongoing naturalistic and technological narratives of the various colorful and exciting journeys recounted in the novels. Although not always the case (see Robur and other examples below), frequently the scientist in Verne's novels combines deep knowledge with courage and a spirit of adventure, thus counter-acting the negative "deranged" image of the mad scientist to be found in Shelley's *Frankenstein*. This contrast of opposing character types provides a mythic tension found throughout the subsequent history of science fiction: the scientist as an archetype—viewed either in a positive or a negative light—exploring the universe and, through knowledge gained, attempting to harness its forces, either for good or for evil.

Roberts (2005) argues that Verne's novels are always "technologically enframed," with one or more technological devices as critical to the story, providing the means for travel, exploration, revelation, and sometimes even destructive violence. But Verne did not see himself as a scientific prophet; he asserted that he "invented nothing." All his imagined technologies, as well as his descriptions of exotic and strange realities, according to him were based on scrupulous research in science, nature, geography, history, and contemporary technological progress. Still, at the very least, Verne wrote at the cutting edge of science, naturalistic exploration, and advancing technology.

Yet, in spite of his imagined space guns, balloons, submarines, electrical motors, and flying airships, and all the dramatic forays into strange and unusual places that occur throughout his novels, in the end the hero (as Roberts argues) usually returns to the same commonplace world he started from, and not only physically. By and large, he remains psychologically the same as when he began the adventure—stable and anchored to the immediate here and now.

Moreover, even if Verne explored the technological cutting edge of things and filled his novels with the latest ideas in science, the bulk of his most popular novels convey no real sense of a future significantly transformed from the present. The majority of his most well-known tales stay locked in the relative "today" of his time.

Accordingly, there has been ongoing debate whether Verne should be classified as a science fiction writer at all (Roberts, 2005). Yet, Verne is *always* included—indeed given an essential niche—in any history of science fiction. His novels are considered required reading for anyone interested in science fiction; fans around the world are raised on Verne (and Wells); and Verne has been a great source of literary inspiration in the genre and even outside the genre in technological innovation. As noted earlier, the science fiction writer, Ray Bradbury stated, "We are all ... the children of Jules Verne." Moreover, even if Verne argued that he was not technologically inventive, it seems to me that he was and repeatedly so. As a final point, he did write about the future—with great prescience and philosophical depth—at least in a few of his tales, as we will see below.

The year after *Five Weeks in a Balloon*, Verne published one of his most famous novels, *A Journey to the Center of the Earth* (1864), a tale that clearly falls within the evolutionary history of science fiction. Following the directions of Arne Saknussemm, three explorers—Professor Lindenbrock, his assistant and nephew, Axel, and their Icelandic guide, Hans—descend into a dormant volcano in Iceland and journey deep down through descending caverns into the interior of the earth. Along the way, Axel, a student of science, describes in copious and frequently excruciating detail the geological, mineralogical, and fossilized wonders encountered on the journey. (What science fiction commentators would come to call "info-dumps.") Although filled with mystery, danger, and repeated mishaps, the story is also very funny, the reluctant and anxious Axel juxtaposed against the tenacious and obsessive Lindenbrock, who is bound and determined in his scientific quest to follow Saknussemm's lead and reach the center of the earth. Thus in the tale we have the fundamental emotional clash of fear versus hope regarding the unknown represented in two extreme character types, with the social dynamics of the two providing a humorous touch.

There is plenty of adventure throughout the novel: The explorers almost die of thirst; Axel gets separated and lost at one point, and before being rescued, resigns himself to death. They observe dangerously close-hand a battle to the death between a Plesiosaur and an Ichthyosaur; they are sucked into a mysterious electrical storm and giant whirlpool as they cross the subterranean sea; they quake with terror upon encountering giant primitive humans tending to equally giant mastodons in a prehistoric underground forest; and in the grand finale of the novel, the explorers, riding on a rising gushing flow of lava, are explosively shot back to the surface of the earth through the mouth of an erupting volcano in the Mediterranean Sea.

Now, Verne clearly was not the first writer to envision journeying into the interior of the earth and encountering strange and fantastical realities, living and dead, along the way. Recall the hollow earth theory and Holberg's, Symmes', and Poe's stories. But as demonstrated through various sections in the novel, Verne was very aware of the scientific theories, issues, and literature regarding the nature of the earth's interior, even if some of the elements in the story, such as the giant whirlpool, appear to be inspired by Poe.

Verne discusses at length the popular scientific view of the time that the earth was not hollow and was increasingly hotter the further you went into the interior. Obviously, this popular theory would not provide a scientifically plausible scenario for a journey to the "center of the earth." Yet, what Verne does, through the voice of Lindenbrock, is to critically examine and debate this theory from a scientific point of view, bringing to bear on the issue a wealth of scientific ideas. He considers from a variety of angles whether it is realistic that the earth's interior is not totally solid and extremely hot. Even though from our contemporary perspective, Lindenbrock's science (or scientific reasoning) seems totally off base, Verne did attempt to present a scientifically credible case for a vision of the earth's interior that would allow for a journey into its subterranean realms.

In any era, people can argue about the plausibility of an idea. Even with the emergence of modern science, the debates on numerous topics continue, perhaps even intensify. What may seem scientifically plausible during one period of time (or from the perspective of one or more scientific minds), may later be judged as scientifically implausible, or vice versa. And the pendulum may swing more than once.

All in all, not only did Jules Verne include a wealth of scientific and technological detail in his novels, he attempted repeatedly to reason out what was possible or not using this knowledge. And this empirically and scientifically informed foundation behind scenario building and technological inventiveness would become a recurrent feature in a good deal of subsequent science fiction. Verne set the tone. More than any science fiction writer before him, he achieved a soundly scientific and technologically astute voice in his novels and stories.

In Verne's two sequential novels on journeying to the moon, *From the Earth to the Moon* (1865) and *Round the Moon* (1869), he again attempts to scientifically support the plausibility of his hypothetical scenario. Both novels serve as scientific-technological "thought experiments": the stories were not only adventures but, textually, in-depth expositions exploring the implications of modern science and technology for realistic space travel. As such, they represent a colossal intellectual advance over anything anyone had written before on how to journey into outer space.

In the first novel, Verne gives a great deal of attention to the deliberations and the eventual construction of a giant gun and projectile that will propel the human travelers from the earth to the moon. The book appealed to many scientists and engineers in the decades to come, and can be considered a scientific and technological argument set in the form of a narrative for the feasibility of traveling to the moon. Although after the publication of the novel, scientists would argue that Verne's gun design wasn't feasible (it was much too small), and that he did not take into account key scientific and technological considerations (the effects of acceleration on human occupants), the book did inspire numerous later rocket scientists to work out better technological solutions that would realize successful human travel into outer space.

From the Earth to the Moon opens with members of the Baltimore Gun Club debating the possibility of building a giant cannon that would propel a projectile to the moon. A bitter confrontation soon develops between the president of the Gun Club and leading proponent of the cannon's construction, Impey Barbicane, and his longstanding engineering rival, Captain Nicholl, who believes the moon shot will end in disaster. Representative of a common theme found in both history and science fiction, the creation of the new and the innovative frequently provokes a strong opposing reaction; the philosophies of stability versus change, a fundamental polarity in the history of humanity, clash in this novel (Nisbet, 1994). Furthermore, as illustrated in this story, determining the course of the future often becomes a battleground of personal rivalries. After a series of difficulties and challenges for Barbicane and the Gun Club— including a duel to the death between him and Nicholl, which is averted at the last moment—the two rivals reach a peaceful understanding. With a third scientist, Michel Ardan, who has designed the projectile, they are launched with a great explosion into outer space. The novel ends in suspense, with the travelers in their projectile heading toward the moon.

In the second novel, *Round the Moon*, our travelers experience weightlessness on their journey; are almost destroyed by an asteroid; and finally achieve an orbit around the moon. They examine the surface of the moon through a telescope, debating whether there are any notable signs of life. But in attempting to land on the moon, their efforts backfire and the projectile heads back to earth. They plummet into the sea and are rescued; only partially realizing their dream of exploring the moon.

Taken together, these two books would form part of the basis of the first science fiction movie: George Méliès' *A Trip to the Moon* (1902). A half a century after that, the books—with the plot somewhat changed—were given cinematic form in the movie *From the Earth to the Moon* (1958). Moreover, the two-book saga would inspire various theme park rides in the century to come, again illustrating the pervasive and multi-faceted influence Jules Verne's visions would have on later generations. Although trips to the moon had been imagined before, Verne's novels are the inspirational starting point for modern efforts to realistically envision for entertainment, and even achieve this age-old dream.

Another book that inspired numerous cinematic adaptations and theme park rides in the century to come—and motivated many scientists and engineers in their research—was Verne's *20,000 Leagues Under the Sea* (1869). Probably his most critically acclaimed novel, *20,000 Leagues Under the Sea* introduces one of the most memorable and iconic characters in science fiction, the enigmatic genius and creator of the *Nautilus*, Captain Nemo, who unexpectedly appears, disappears, and then reappears throughout the story. Often secluded away in his private rooms aboard the *Nautilus*, engaged in secretive scientific study,

Nemo's past remains relatively obscure throughout the novel, as do the guiding purpose and goals of his maritime travels around the globe. Indeed, he conveys a clear sense of detachment and disconnection, if not aversion and alienation, from human society. He is a mysterious figure engaged in mysterious if not nefarious activities.

The *Nautilus* itself is the second famous character introduced in the novel. Following Roberts' view, *20,000 Leagues Under the Sea* is a clear example of a "technologically enframed story": Not only does the *Nautilus* provide the means for realizing the underwater adventure, but with its advanced technological capabilities and luxurious furnishings, it is also a magnificent source of wonder in itself. Powered by electricity, the *Nautilus* is a scientific marvel for its time, able to dive to unbelievable oceanic depths and outrun, destroy, and sink any other vessel on the sea. It is relatively self-sufficient, a perfect hideaway from the world for Captain Nemo, and houses an incredible library and huge assortment of aquatic specimens for scientific study. Although Verne did not invent the concept of a submarine—by his time, submarines had actually been built—he raised the machine to public consciousness with this story. The *Nautilus* would become the model, or "mythic archetype," for all later submarines, both real and imagined. In fact, the *Nautilus* emerged as a "technological icon" in the history of science fiction, taking its place beside Wells' time machine and Fritz Lang's female robot as a magnetic and influential technological object, one with great symbolic significance. Part of the archetypal evolutionary mythology of science fiction is the progressive emergence of such technological icons.

Even more so than *A Journey to the Center of the Earth*, *20,000 Leagues Under the Sea* saturates the reader with naturalistic facts and details, with its innumerable descriptions of underwater life, both plant and animal, as well as copious amounts of data on the geography of the earth, underwater environments, and geological structures. The number of fish identified and described in the story ascends from the mind-boggling to the mind numbing.

Aside from Captain Nemo, a second major human character is the narrator of the novel, a biological scientist named Pierre whom Nemo rescued and now holds captive on the *Nautilus*. Pierre serves as the mouthpiece for the incredibly lengthy naturalistic descriptions in the book, as well as for those of the technological wonders and luxuries of the *Nautilus*. Pierre is so enraptured with the wonders of nature and science revealed on the journey that, although he is forbidden to leave the *Nautilus*, he is highly ambivalent about escaping.

Pierre finds the experience of journeying across and underneath the world's oceans mesmerizing. He walks along the ocean bed with Nemo in an underwater breathing suit; he is shown the lost sunken city of Atlantis; he journeys under the ice to the South Pole; he watches and studies whales and sharks; and at one point, he is caught up in an attack on the *Nautilus* by a giant squid. But he is also sickened and appalled when he observes Nemo turn the powerful weapons aboard the *Nautilus* against a ship filled with humans, sinking the vessel and killing them all. Throughout, it is through the conscious mind of Pierre that we vicariously experience the astonishing and fantastical dimensions of Verne's updated "extraordinary voyage" and all its "wondrous technologies." And it is from his perspective that we see Nemo and the *Nautilus* disappear into the swirling depths of a giant whirlpool, his fate unknown.

That last scene is one of two in which, toward the end of the novel, Verne alludes to Edgar Allan Poe, the first occurring in the account of the journey of the *Nautilus* to the South Pole. (See Poe's *The Narrative of Arthur Gordon Pym of Nantucket*.) In the tumultuous conclusion of the tale Pierre and his fellow captives escape from the *Nautilus* just as Nemo dives his submarine into what deeply resembles the monstrous whirlpool described by

Poe in his short story "A Descent into the Maelström".

In *20,000 Leagues Under the Sea,* Verne once again attempts to realize scientific plausibility in both his descriptions of the natural world and his variety of technological inventions. One of his main goals as a writer was to educate the reader on the wonders of science and nature. In this regard, as exemplified in this novel, he set the standard for future science fiction tales with his depictions of newly explored environments (the ocean depths) and innovative and futuristic technologies (the *Nautilus*). Following his lead, future science fiction tales would often feature such naturalistic, scientific, and technological context. Indeed, with his "hi-tech," scientifically informed style, Verne was writing the equivalent of what in contemporary times has been described as "hard science fiction," with a heavy dose of exotic and fantastical natural phenomena thrown in as well.

Yet, what Verne is remembered for most is his supreme skill as a storyteller. *20,000 Leagues Under the Sea* exemplifies his capacity to create engaging, action-packed plots and colorfully memorable characters who "fly by the seat of their pants." That he was able to present his forays into science and technology, and realize an educational purpose, in such an entertaining way has secured his ongoing popularity.

Three years after completing *20,000 Leagues Under the Sea,* Verne published *Around the World in Eighty Days* (1872). Although not a science fiction novel, it was clearly another grand adventure tale—an "extraordinary voyage"—this time one inspired by Verne's ongoing study of recent developments in transportation technologies around the globe, in particular, the building of new railway lines and the opening of the Suez canal. Perhaps even more famous a novel than *20,000 Leagues Under the Sea, Around the World in Eighty Days* has inspired multiple cinematic adaptations (1919, 1956, 2004), radio shows, cartoons, TV series, and even musicals.

The plot begins with a wager: Phileas Fogg, the central

character of the story, makes a bet that, given the rapid advances in the construction of railroad lines around the globe, he can accomplish a complete journey around the world in eighty days. Again, we find the main character(s) traveling a circuitous route—from home into the unknown and back again—as in *20,000 Leagues Under the Sea*, the action involves circling the globe. And again, the characters confront an array of challenges. Mistaken for a wanted criminal, Fogg must contend with a detective from Scotland Yard in hot pursuit, adding to the tension and excitement of the tale. He travels through exotic lands; faces challenges and obstacles galore (drugs and American Indians, among others); and deals with an emerging love interest on the adventure. In the end, just when all seems lost, he of course emerges the victor.

Most of the travel in *Around the World in Eighty Days* is realized on the ground by railroad, but in *The Mysterious Island* (1874), Verne returns to the air and to balloons. Another novel that inspired numerous film adaptations (1929, 1961, 2005, 2012), *The Mysterious Island* comes close to being a science fiction story, especially with the various "bio-tech" embellishments (including bio-engineered giant bees, mollusks, and birds) created in the movie versions. Hypothetically taking place in the year 1865, five men escape in a balloon from Richmond, Virginia, then under siege by Union forces. They are first transported across the American continent and then out over the Pacific Ocean, eventually coming down on an unknown island somewhere in the South Pacific. There is something very "mysterious" about the island: when our travelers face challenges to their survival (such as an attack by pirates), some unseen benefactor provides the necessary help, weapons, or supplies. Eventually, it is revealed that the secretive benefactor is Captain Nemo, who has survived—along with the *Nautilus*—his descent into the maelstrom at the end of *20,000 Leagues Under the Sea*. Now older, Nemo is nearing death, and in telling his story to the men on the island, he reveals that he is a former (Asian) Indian prince. After this revelation, Nemo dies and is entombed in the *Nautilus*. The volcano on the island erupts; the men quickly escape; and Nemo and his *Nautilus* are swallowed up by the sea along with the entire island.

The next of Verne's novels significant in the history of science fiction was *Off on a Comet* (1877) (originally titled in French *Hector Servadac*). Here again Verne takes a flight of imagination into outer space, this time throughout the solar system. In this tale Verne really pushes the limits of scientific credibility. The story involves a comet striking the earth, with a collection of earth fragments adhering to the comet after the collision, and (incredibly) whisking away a number of humans as it returns to space. Surviving the cataclysm, the characters go on an adventure around the solar system. Yet in spite of such scientifically dubious events, Verne includes a great deal of astronomical detail (as well as geological and geographical), attempting to explain and give realistic plausibility and naturalistic color to the ongoing drama within the story.

In the beginning of the novel, two of the main characters, Hector Servadac and his orderly Ben Zoof, experience a "convulsion of nature." The ground quakes violently. The sky blazes. A sonic boom knocks Servadac unconscious. Once the convulsion subsides and the two gather their wits, they discover a host of perplexing phenomena. The air seems rarified; they can jump exceedingly high; the sun moves in the wrong direction across the sky; and the cycle of day and night has shortened considerably. Further, the star constellations are in the wrong locations; a strange bright new sphere glimmers in the sky; where before they were on the northern mainland coast of Africa, they now find themselves on an island. Finding no other humans, and after some initial reconnaissance, they discover that all the familiar towns and landmarks have disappeared. The complex and fascinating mystery of their predicament provides dramatic intrigue and a sense of wonder early in the story, and a good portion of the subsequent tale involves figuring out what has happened to the world. Indeed, *Off on a Comet* is a scientific mystery, the action revolving around its solution through the use of scientific observation, theory, and reasoning.

As the story progresses, Servadec and Ben meet other survivors of the cataclysm (thirty-seven in all). Exploring this new world — which they first take for a transformed earth — they discover that it is mostly sea with a scattering of islands, all of which is surrounded by huge rocky cliffs. Eventually, they ascertain that the total surface area is 1400 miles in diameter. Perhaps most unnerving is the steady rise in temperature; they appear to be coming ever closer to Venus and moving toward the sun. As these revelations emerge, the various characters engage in ongoing geographical and astronomical dialogues, trying to make sense out of what is happening. Fortunately, they swing by Venus without colliding, but then the land on which they ride changes course, sending them away from the sun. Their world grows progressively colder; eventually the sea freezes over.

As events proceed, they rescue a stranded astronomer, Professor Rosette, who, from some unknown location, had been sending them enigmatic messages filled with puzzling numbers. Rosette explains that they are on a comet traveling in an orbit around the solar system. He claims to have discovered the comet as it was first approaching the earth, and feeling a sense of ownership, has named it Gallia. A cantankerous character, Rosette provides some of the lengthiest astronomical expositions in the novel, both on the planets of the solar system as they travel out toward the Jupiter, as well as the stars beyond. He also expounds on his ongoing calculations regarding the orbit of the comet, predicting that after a two-year journey through the solar system, it will once again collide with the earth.

Our comet travelers take sled-rides and go ice skating on the frozen sea — the cover of the first issue of *Amazing Stories*

(April, 1926) features a colorful painting of this scene—before eventually having to move into deeper and deeper caverns near a volcano to avoid freezing to death. In the story's conclusion, as the comet approaches the earth once again, they construct a balloon, take off from the tiny world, and miraculously manage to land back on the earth unharmed. Once again, we come full circle, having ventured into the unknown, but—with human ingenuity, courage, solid scientific knowledge, and a good dose of luck—safely finding our way back home.

Again, although *Off on a Comet* sounds totally implausible scientifically, it is astronomically inspired and scientifically enframed. As always, Verne teaches while he entertains. And, as we've seen before, the novel is another highly engaging "extraordinary voyage," one of my favorite of all Verne's novels. Although exaggerated and stereotyped, the characters in the story are memorable and comical, adding to the quality of the tale. The exchanges between Servadec and Ben, his orderly, are especially funny as they try to make sense of their predicament; their relationship is suggestive of that between Don Quixote and Sancho Panza. The dialogues between Rosette and others, and the interactions with the British soldiers and Spanish sailors are equally hilarious.

Although not as well known as many of his other novels, Verne published *The Begum's Fortune* (also titled *The Begum's Millions*) in 1879, a story relevant to several important themes in Verne's writings as well as in the history of science fiction. The novel was probably based on a manuscript written by an exiled revolutionist, Paschal Grousset, which was purchased by Hetzel and significantly reworked by Verne. As was also the case in *Off on a Comet*, *The Begum's Fortune* is even more filled with racial and ethnic stereotyping, which in itself also has significance in the history of science fiction. Additionally, according to different reviews, the novel contains the first published examples in Verne's writings of cautionary thoughts on the social impact of advancing science and technology and of an "evil scientist" hell bent on using science for purposes of destruction and military conquest (illustrative of the negative stereotyping in the novel, this malevolent scientist is German). The novel also provides an interesting contrast between utopian and dystopian societies, both created through advanced science and technologies, but based upon entirely different ethical philosophies regarding the preferable uses of technology (Dirda, 2006; Kincaid, 2006; Morgan, 2006; *The Begum's Fortune*).

The plot involves two individuals: a good natured and morally admirable French physician named Dr. Sarrasin and a bombastic and arrogant German scientist named Professor Schultze, each of whom inherits half of a substantial monetary sum from a recently deceased "begum" (an Asian woman of royal and aristocratic status). With their large funds, the two individuals are both able to purchase areas of land in Oregon, where each sets about creating a new city and ideal society. But their visions are vastly different: Dr. Sarrasin creates a peaceful utopia dedicated toward the enhanced physical well-being and health of all its citizens based on cutting-edge scientific and medical innovations, whereas Professor Schultze creates "Steel City" — a mining and industrial complex focused on developing new forms of military weaponry — and assumes a dictatorship role within an authoritarian and repressive regime.

Schultze plans on wiping out the French settlement since he believes in the genetic superiority of the Germans over the French and everyone else. According to his vision of human progress, he believes the Germans are rightfully destined to rule the world. The eradication of the French city is an important first step in his grandiose plan of world domination. With great fervor and imposing highly regimented efficiency practices on his workers, Schultze constructs the most powerful cannon ever built as well as an incendiary bomb that could destroy a city (a premonition of an atomic bomb) and a chemical projectile able to suffocate and freeze everything alive wherever it hit (an anticipation of chemical warfare).

The good French and their utopian city seem doomed. But in firing its incendiary bomb at the French city, Schultze's cannon is severely damaged. The projectile sails over the city due to Schultze's miscalculations and achieves orbit around the earth (in effect producing a satellite such as in *The Brick Moon*). Moreover, one of the chemical bombs accidentally explodes in Schultze's office, bringing to a poetic end Professor Schultze, his mad plans of destruction and world conquest, and his militaristic Steel City. The surviving French take over operation of the military industry created by Schultze as a protective measure against possible new aggressors. Good health is not enough; in the modernized world it is paramount to be militarily prepared.

After the French defeat by the Germans in the Franco-Prussian War (1870-1871), the French became increasingly apprehensive over future German aggression and highly critical of German character. (To be described later, the English exhibited a similar reaction to the war and the Germans, as seen in Chesney's *The Battle of Dorking*, 1871.) The resultant negative stereotyping of German mentality and culture is very apparent in Verne's novel, especially insofar as Verne contrasts the Germans in this tale with the generally much more admirable French. Moreover, this novel not only reflects contemporary nationalistic tensions and cultural stereotyping, it has also been cited for its highly prescient anticipation of an obsessive and militaristic madman rising to absolute power in Germany, one who believes in the racial superiority of Germans (Saxons/Aryans) and their right to rule the world; that is, Schultze is a proto-Hitler. Not that Verne is totally innocent of cultural elitism himself since there are many expressions (or insinuations) in this novel of supposed ethnic/racial superiority of the French over the Chinese, Blacks and Jews.

According to McDougall (2001), "... after the Franco-Prussian

War of 1870–71, [Verne] began to invent mad scientists and evil geniuses." To be described next, one notable example is the scientist-inventor Robor who aspires to be the "master of the world." But the dividing lines between sanity and madness and good and evil are not always clear in Verne's novels—there are elements of moral and psychological ambiguity in Robor, as well as Nemo before him. Even regarding the nature of utopian versus dystopian societies and the anticipated benefits of science and technology in creating a better world, Verne frequently offers complex rather than simple answers. His utopian French city in *The Begum Fortune* is in many ways highly controlled (its citizens are going to be forced to be healthier whether they want to or not) and it is a rather boring place; Verne spends much more time describing the fascinating dystopian Steel City. And although it may seem obvious that weapons of mass destruction are a potential negative consequence of advancing science and technology, Verne also wrote about the many deeper if more subtle perils of science and technology at the social and psychological levels. Although he has been described as a science-technology enthusiast, other noteworthy publications such as *Paris in the Twentieth Century* and "In the Twenty-ninth Century: The Day of an American Journalist in 2889" (both described below), suggest that the promised scientific and high tech future utopia is at best ambiguous and even perhaps highly destructive to the human spirit.

Aside from his two novels chronicling a trip to the moon, Verne wrote another pair of connected tales important in the history of science fiction: *Robur the Conqueror* (*The Clipper of the Clouds*) (1886) and *Master of the World* (1904), in both of which we find the central character of Robur, another scientist-inventor who creates technologically advanced heavier-than-air ships and other amazing weaponized vehicles. In various ways (perhaps even more so than Nemo), Robur taunts and terrorizes the civilized world. As he describes himself in the first novel, "I have no fear of anything or anybody. I have a strength of will that never had to yield ... When I have an idea I allow no one to share it and I do not permit any contradiction." In essence, Robur believes he is indomitable and superior to all others. In the movie adaptation (1961), loosely combining the two novels and titled "Master of the World," the mad-eyed Vincent Price plays Robur, a fanatical, vainglorious, and decidedly crazed individual.

In the first novel, Robur has created a giant electrical-battery-powered air ship, the *Albatross*, which, with an assortment of huge propellers, is able to move swiftly both horizontally and vertically through the sky. A mysterious presence roaming the sky, the *Albatross* has been terrifying people across the globe. Early in the novel, Robur appears at a meeting of flight enthusiasts in Philadelphia that are designing lighter-than-air dirigible air ships, and debates with them the superiority of his craft, the *Albatross*, over their balloon ships. (A prophetic argument for the superiority of airplanes over balloons, repeated at the end of the novel as well.) The balloonists vehemently disagree with Robur, which infuriates him. After the meeting ends, Robur captures a group of the attendees and takes them on a journey across the globe in the *Albatross*, demonstrating the incredible powers of his airship. Thus, we go on another guided geographical tour, along the way also getting an education on both the history and present state of development of aerial technologies and the cutting edge innovations of the *Albatross*.

The captives eventually escape and get back to Philadelphia, after first severely damaging and then apparently destroying the *Albatross*, which sinks into the sea. But Robur builds a new *Albatross*, returns to Philadelphia, and challenges his former captives—who have just launched their new giant dirigible—to a confrontation in the sky. The *Albatross* literally runs circles around the dirigible, forcing it into higher and higher elevations until it collapses. Having demonstrated the superiority of his new *Albatross,* Robur exits the scene, vowing to return sometime in the future.

In *Master of the World*, Robur does return, but this time his motivation is not so much to enlighten the world with his advanced inventions, but rather to terrorize and subdue civilization through the use of his superior technology. He is now intent on being the "conqueror," signing his name on a couple of letters as "Master of the World." Robur has now created a new technological marvel, the *Terror*, a combination speedboat, submarine, automobile, and aircraft, all versions of which are capable of achieving unsurpassable speeds whether on land, in the sea, or in the air. Clearly possessing a huge ego and sense of superiority over normal humankind in the earlier novel, Robur has now "devolved" into the "mad scientist," an outsider from human civilization who, despite his scientific genius, lacks any moral scruples whatsoever. He is one who, as he states, "raises his arm toward heaven ... in defiance of God," an egomaniac whose pride increasingly leads him into insanity. A dark and mysterious figure—representing Verne's growing fears over tyranny and totalitarianism sweeping across the world and his apprehensions over the threats presented by advancing technology—Robur shares Nemo's fate at the end of *20,000 Leagues Under the Sea.* Upon diving into an electrical storm the *Terror* is struck by lightning and plummets into the sea. As with Nemo it is uncertain whether Robur lives or dies at the end of the tale.

The narrator of the story, a federal police inspector who is captured by Robur but eventually escapes, poses a thought-provoking theory at the end of the novel. It seemed to him "as if some irresistible force drew [Robur] toward those upper zones of the sky, that [Robur] belonged no more to the earth, that he was destined to live in space; a perpetual dweller in the clouds." Is it then that Robur has been pulled toward transcendence, but has gone mad and perhaps evil in the process? Certainly there are times when Verne's protagonists embrace the "world beyond the hill" to their own detriment. Having become separated from common humanity, they suffer for it, morally and psychologically. Robur is such a case. Yet, to introduce some ambiguity based on the rather sympathetic interpretation of the police inspector, perhaps Robur's arrogance is a defense against being repudiated by the scientific status quo and ostracized by society; perhaps he only appears mad and evil because he has transcended the commonplace into "the clouds"?

These stories illustrate how extensively Verne used archetypal central characters to explore the role of science in contemporary society: In Saknussemm; Lindenbrock; Nemo and Pierre; Barbicane and Ardan; Phileas Fogg; Rosette; and finally Robur; we find the scientist, inventor, explorer, and scholar—individuals who transcend conventional thinking and mores in their imagination, intellect, values, courage, and personal determination. (As a military figure, Servadec does not quite fit within this character type; at best he is an educated but reluctant explorer.) Unlike the "normal" and security-minded bulk of humanity, they venture into the unknown, both in body and in mind; they are visionary figures. But Verne does not ignore the dangers presented by such outliers. With Robur and perhaps also with Nemo, we find a dimension of madness emerging out of their unique personalities and disconnection from humanity; transcendence has a price. (With Schultze, his evil and vainglorious character is a product of cultural elitism.) Still, this character archetype—scientist, inventor, and courageous explorer—articulated and developed along both positive and negative lines in Verne's novels—would serve as a hugely inspirational source for later science fiction stories, even if such characters, often socially ostracized and solitary, would oscillate between sane and benevolent and mad and villainous.

On the technological dimension of his stories, although Verne stated that he never "invented," both the *Albatross* and the *Terror* are creations of scientific-technological intellect and imagination. What was noteworthy about Verne was how he conscientiously attempted to ground, in contemporary knowledge and research, all the technological, scientific, and naturalistic elements in his stories. He may not have invented *ex nihilo*, but he did extrapolate from a solid body of knowledge in envisioning his technological devices, as any good inventor would. The *Albatross*, the *Terror*, the *Nautilus*, and the weaponry of Steel City are marvels that surpassed the actual technologies of his day; in bringing them to life in his stories, he demonstrated the key elements of creativity, synthesizing existing ideas into novel visions and extrapolations (Lombardo, 2012c). Even if, as noted above, Verne's visions do not always sound scientifically plausible, he at least regularly attempted to explain his imaginative conjectures in terms of scientific principles. Combining his knowledge of science and technology with speculative extrapolation, his prescient visions were at the cutting-edge of scientific and technological consciousness.

It is a strange result of the twists and turns of history that the novel by Jules Verne that to my knowledge is most decidedly futuristic and science fiction was never published during Verne's lifetime. After *Five Weeks in a Balloon*, Verne submitted another novel to Hetzel in 1863: *Paris in the Twentieth Century*. Hetzel rejected it for publication, stating it was too bleak and pessimistic. As Hetzel put it to Verne, "No one today will believe your prophecy." Verne put the novel away, and it remained relatively forgotten until rediscovered by his great grandson. It was finally published in 1994.

In several important ways, *Paris in the Twentieth Century* is the antithesis of all Verne's extraordinary voyages. Beginning in 1960, the central character, Michel, a student of classic literature and a poet, has no personal or intellectual resonance with either science or technology. Indeed, he is repulsed by the technological mechanization of his world, as well as by the dominance of business and the motivation toward the acquisition of wealth which drives his society. (Obviously a very prescient future social scenario.) Michel is young, naïve, and an idealist, unskilled in any of the practical matters of his day, and he simply wants to study literature and write poetry—unfortunately both activities having fallen into disrepute and disregard in his world.

In fact, with Michel as an anchor point, this novel can be viewed as an expression of the clash between Romantic and Enlightenment philosophies; in many ways Michel embodies the former yet lives in a world dominated by the latter. Although Michel is an anti-hero—one who fails in the end to realize his romantic dreams—the picture of this future world controlled by science, mechanization, and business, with a corresponding decline in the arts, music, literature, and the creative human spirit, is highly dystopian. It is a world without color, passion, and romance, and in the end, it kills Michel. In this future world, women have been de-feminized, drained of Eros, lost in pursuit of careers; they've become functional and emotionally stiff cogs in the business world. Sure, this future world features many scientific and technological wonders, but the overall quality of life is decidedly empty and mechanical—a fulfillment of the deepest fears of the Romanticists regarding the future consequences of a world ruled by science and reason. If Verne was pro-science and technology in his extraordinary voyages, he stands at the other end of the continuum in this novel.

Yet, even if Verne expresses significant reservations about where science and technology—as well as other secular features of society—could be heading in the future, in this novel he engages in more futurist prediction and technological extrapolation (to my knowledge) than in any of his other stories. Aside from the anticipated general shift of emphasis toward science, engineering, and business and the abandonment of the humanities and arts, here Verne predicts automobiles; computer-like calculating machines; technological wiring and communication between these computer machines, forming something analogous to the Internet and Ethernet; fax machines; magnetically powered trains; skyscrapers; the "end of war"; the end of journalism (there is no news, everything having become so mechanized, peaceful, and orderly); the electric chair; automated security systems; and music and art created through the use of technologies, thus destroying the spontaneity and human element in such activities.

The central plot of the story involves Michel's attempts to secure a source of income through employment in the banking business. Failing at one job after another but meeting a fellow non-conformist—a musician and musical composer who also works in the banking industry—he and his friend become comrades in the fight for creativity, humanity, and the arts. Sadly, though, the two are fired from their jobs, and Michel's financial resources steadily diminish. Undeterred, he spends his time as a starving artist, writing a book of poetry that he can't get published. Along the way he meets and falls in love with a young lady, but he has no financial means to support her. Eventually, with his last few coins, he buys her some flowers, only to find that the lady's uncle and guardian—the last teacher of rhetoric at the local college—has been fired from his job, and that both of them, uncle and niece, have been evicted from their apartment for not paying the rent, leaving no forwarding address. He wanders through Paris searching for his lost love during a bitterly cold winter's day and night, suffering from psychotic thoughts and images that he is being pursued by the "Demon of Electricity"—a symbol of the oppressive and unemotional scientism and technologism of his time. In the novel's end, the frozen and starving Michel enters a cemetery and collapses in the snow, losing consciousness, and becoming one with the souls of the past buried around him.

A bleak tale indeed, but again, the most futuristic and visionary of all of Verne's novels. He peers outward one hundred years and writes a powerful critique not only of technological developments, but psychological, social, and even artistic possibilities in the future as well. His portrait of a world ruled by economics and business is especially prescient and thought provoking. With so many adaptations of Verne's adventure tales already brought to the screen, it would be a powerful and enlightening cinematic experience to see this novel turned into a movie as well.

Aside from *Paris in the Twentieth Century*, and although considerably shorter in length, Verne wrote other stories about the future. Two of his better-known futurist short stories are: "In the Twenty-ninth Century: The Day of an American Journalist in 2889" (1889/1890) and "The Eternal Adam" (c. 1905). The former of the two appeared in different versions, first in English and then in French, and Verne's son, Michel Verne (1861-1925), significantly contributed into the writing of the story (Evans, 1995). Along with "The Eternal Adam" this story of a journalist of the twenty-ninth century can be found reprinted in the collection of short stories by Verne titled *Yesterday and Tomorrow* (1965). Among other distinctive features, the tale probably contains the greatest concentration of futurist predictions per page of text than any other work by Verne.

The central character of the story is Francis Bennett, director of the newspaper/news company, the *Earth Herald*, located on the block of 16823rd Avenue in Centropolis, capital city of the seventy-five states of the Confederation of the Americas (which includes all of England). The main office building of the *Earth Herald* is colossal, measuring two miles across on each of its four sides. Bennett is super-rich, and the *Earth Herald* not only has a gigantic number of subscribers but in many respects controls the complex and multi-faceted operations of the world at large. Science, industry, government, entertainment, agriculture, popular literature, technological research and development, and the marketing industry all seem to answer to Bennett and the *Earth Herald*. (Only his wife seems to have a will of her own.)

Bennett manages tens of thousands of employees, which, aside from journalists, include research scientists and astronomers whose primary purpose seems to be to make new discoveries and create new inventions that are worth reporting in his newspaper. Media—the perceived newsworthiness of an item—controls the direction of science and technology. Bennett also oversees popular fictional literature, supervising the writing of numerous popular serial novels for publication. Essentially, the story follows Bennett through a typical busy day, as he manages not only the *Earth Herald* but to a great degree the world at large.

This plot device allows for an impressive range of conjectures on the future. Within the first twenty pages, we find futurist descriptions of the following: the universal channeling of all types of energy sources (wind, water, sunlight, etc.) into a common energy delivery system that can then be transformed into heat, electricity, light, or whatever other type of power needed; multi-media mass and personalized communication; computer calculators; moving roads and sidewalks; moving cities; music created by artificial intelligence; the mass delivery of meals through tubes; underground super-sonic transportation; airplanes, aero-cars, and aero-buses; nutritious air; the control of the weather; giant optical advertisements projected onto clouds; germ warfare through biological bombs; mechanical dressing rooms; something like holographic virtual reality; and astral communication with inhabitants of different planets.

Yet, all of these new technologies and associated transformations in ways of life are frequently described in a farcical fashion. Does human life have deeper meaning or purpose as a result of all these technological advancements? Does Bennett's life, as rich and powerful as he is, seem to have any real substance or values? As stated at the beginning of the story, "The men of the twenty-ninth century live in a perpetual fairyland, though they do not seem to realize it. Bored with wonders, they are cold towards everything that progress brings them ..." Through his busy day, Bennett discusses with one scientist the possible technological capacity to create any form of matter we wish (the alchemist dream); ponders a new drug that will deliver immortality; casually suggests rotating the moon to see if there are any lunar inhabitants on the backside; and observes, at the end of a long and highly profitable day, the failed effort to rejuvenate a one-hundred-year-old intentionally frozen human body, nonchalantly commenting after the experiment that it is back to the drawing board. The people of the twenty-ninth century are not omnipotent yet, but that is their aspiration for tomorrow. But is this imagined future reality something to be desired? Is this real progress in the quality of human life? That is the question Verne poses in this story. As with *Paris in the Twentieth Century*, Verne envisions a dystopia created through advancing technology and an economic-business-driven world.

"The Eternal Adam" moves outward much further into the future—many thousands of years—and, written at the end of his life, was also probably a collaboration with his son, Michel. Rather than describing a "progressive" vision of tomorrow, the story presents a cyclical theory of human history.

An archeologist in the far future, Zartog Sofr-Aï-Sran, has discovered and translated an ancient journal, which appears to describe the destruction of a previous, highly advanced civilization (which is our own). This civilization appears to have been obliterated in a great flood that inundated most of the world. The discovered journal describes the personal challenges of a small group of people who survived the flood and relates how they began to create a new life after the global deluge. In the journal, the lost civilization of the mythical Atlantis is discussed, alluding to the possibility that before the rise of their recently destroyed civilization, there had been a previous highly advanced society that had also been obliterated. As the journal comes to its end, the writer reflects on how all the knowledge and skills gained in his world are fading into oblivion, and the challenge the descendants of his small group of survivors face in starting all over again and having to climb once more out of barbarity. Perhaps the name "Adam" refers to an eternally recurrent forefather who, having survived the previous catastrophe, provides the historical marker and figurehead for the next rise of civilization. As such, the world of Zartog Sofr-Aï-Sran is doomed to collapse as well, repeating the unending cycle of the rise of order out of primordial beginnings and the eventual collapse of order back into chaos and death. Also of great interest in this story is the description of the adaptive evolution of life forms, woven together with the idea of mass extinctions. In later sections, I examine both evolution and the themes of order and chaos—key emerging ideas in mid-nineteenth century science—and explore the way new scientific concepts have impacted the development of science fiction. Clearly, evolution and the meaning of progress, coupled with the cyclic theory of time and apprehensions over the dire possibilities of tomorrow, were circulating around in Verne's mind toward the end of his life.

In conclusion, Jules Verne and his extraordinary tales of adventure, mysterious scientists, intrepid explorers of the unknown, and diverse technological inventions, all extensively grounded in scientific, naturalistic, and technological facts, reasoning, and theory, left an amazing and highly influential legacy for later writers. No one, to the best of my knowledge, had previously created such an immense body of imaginative novels that fall within the evolutionary development of science fiction. He is one of the few science fiction writers whose name is almost universally recognized in contemporary cultural consciousness. His literary creations and visions have morphed, across the globe, into numerous multi-media experiences and forms of entertainment. Although there was a "dark side" to Verne's imagination and his prognostications, which perhaps became more pronounced later in his life, his scientifically informed extraordinary adventures into the unknown and the intrepid explorers that peopled his tales contributed an uplifting and energizing core mythic narrative to the development of modern science fiction.

Chapter 8

Evolution and Science Fiction

The Theory of Evolution

There is nowhere anything lasting, neither outside me, nor within me, but only incessant change. I nowhere know of any being, not even my own. There is no being.
Johan Fichte

The First and Second Scientific Revolutions, with discoveries and theoretical advances in astronomy, physics, mechanics, optics, chemistry, geology, steam power, electricity, magnetism, biology, and the study of the brain and nervous system, provided modern science fiction with a host of inspirational ideas and principles in the creation of its fantastical and futurist narratives. Jules Verne, for one, incorporated into his stories a wealth of information and concepts from many of the above scientific disciplines. He may have invented and speculated, and at times even challenged the scientific consensus of his time, but he established a benchmark for later science fiction writers who conscientiously constructed their scenarios and narratives using the ever-growing wealth of new scientific ideas and discoveries.

Yet moving beyond the Second Scientific Revolution and the bulk of the writings of Jules Verne, in the second half of the nineteenth century, two new scientific theories would coalesce that would have a profound effect on subsequent thinking—both factual and fictional—regarding the direction of time within the universe, inclusive of life, the earth, and the history and future of humanity. These two theories, which would greatly inform and inspire science fiction in the later nineteenth century and thereafter, were evolution and the laws of thermodynamics.

On the surface, evolution and, particularly, the second law of thermodynamics (the law of increasing entropy or disorder in nature), appear to lead to opposite visions of natural change: In the former case the flow of time moves toward new creation and increasing order and complexity; in the latter case, the flow of time moves toward the reduction of order and complexity, and decline, decay, and death. Particularly regarding the anticipated future, we have two highly disparate theoretically based visions: The future is advancement; the future is disintegration. These two visions of the shape of things to come respectively provoke the opposite human emotions of hope and despair and lead to antithetical dramatic tones in narratives about the imagined future.

Although creations of the nineteenth century, these two theoretical ideas—of evolution and increasing entropy—have a long developmental history, running back to ancient times. In early Babylonia, for example, we find the idea that order and chaos compete with each other in nature, the creation of the former leading to the advancement of civilization, whereas the latter works against civilized order. In the ancient Greek philosopher Empedocles, we find the theory that love (creation) and hate (destruction) oscillate in dominance, producing a cyclic, up and down pattern to time. Even earlier, in Hindu philosophy, we find Shiva, the lord of creation and destruction, and the idea that temporal existence, as expressed in "the dance of Shiva," involves the oscillatory creation and destruction of one universe after another.

These ancient views on the coupling of creation and destruction, and order and chaos, were often connected with the cyclic theory of time, which in early human history (as previously noted) was the dominant vision of time. Time was a circle, a Yin and Yang, of birth and death, and birth again. The Greek philosopher Heraclitus, for example, saw change as pervasive throughout reality, and involving the oppositional qualities of "becoming and passing away." The universal flow, of creation and destruction, pulsates and circles around (Lombardo, 2006a).

In considering the mythic origins and archetypes in science fiction, this fundamental oppositional theme of creation and destruction, of becoming and passing away, and of order and chaos—with all its metaphorical and emotional associations— has significantly influenced modern narratives in science fiction. The coupling, the conflict, and the oscillation of these primordial forces, embedded within the narrative, brings dramatic energy and tension (with the necessary element of uncertainty) into science fiction stories. Part of the evolution of the mythology of science fiction has been the ongoing development of this fundamental archetypal theme.

As noted earlier, beginning with Zoroaster, and later with Democritus, Lucretius, and Augustinian Christianity, and in contrast with the cyclic theory of time, a linear and progressive vision of change emerged in human history. But even for a progressive vision of change, the oppositional qualities of creation and increasing order versus chaos and destruction were often seen as integral to the overall directional motion in nature (Lombardo, 2017). As Nisbet (1994) notes, many modern historians viewed civilization as moving forward through successive ups and downs. History is dialectical; history is filled with disruptive revolutions and oscillations. This thematic integration of creation and destruction within a progressive vision of the advancement of human civilization has also strongly influenced futurist narratives in science fiction. We will move forward in the future, but there will be great disasters— natural and manmade—along the way, repeatedly sending us backwards. This dramatic framework makes for a great story; it is a recurrent theme, as noted earlier, in the writings of H. G. Wells and Olaf Stapledon.

Still, at the beginning of the modern era, in a coupling of Christian religion and Newtonian physics, the idea of stability in the universe occupied center stage in Western scientific thinking. For Isaac Newton, the laws of the universe were stable, created at the beginning of time by God. Further, the universe was a predictable and regulated "clockwork" that ticked away, the heavenly bodies going through regularly repeating revolutions of motion (Goerner, 1999). Moreover, at the start of the modern era, Christianity still subscribed to the theory of "static creationism." The universe and all the creatures of the earth, including humankind, were created at the beginning of time in their present form. Natural forms did not change. And undergirding this whole static and harmonious natural system (as envisioned by Western scientists and philosophers) was the imagined Platonic realm of eternity—of God and heaven—the ultimate reality, unchanging, immutable, and perfectly ordered.

As noted earlier, not everyone bought into a static vision of the universe and humankind. In the philosophical, naturalistic lineage of Heraclitus and Lucretius, modern writers, such as Descartes and Leibnitz, suggested a dynamic and evolutionary history of the universe. And with the rise of the theory of secular progress in the eighteenth century, popular thinking was definitely shifting toward a more transformative (and in fact progressive) vision of both humanity's past and future. But it was the emergence of the sciences of evolution and thermodynamics, and especially the former, that colossally and definitively undercut both the theory of static creationism as well as the stable clockwork vision of the natural universe (Lombardo, 2002b, 2002c, 2006a). It should go without saying that such a monumental transformation in our understanding of the universe and humankind would dramatically influence subsequent scientifically inspired fiction.

* * *

Judging from the past, we may safely infer that not one living species will transmit its unaltered likeness to a distant futurity.

And of the species now living will transmit progeny of any kind to a far distant futurity ...

Charles Darwin

Let's first consider the theory of evolution and its modern historical development. When modern science emerged in the seventeenth century, writers such as John Ray (1627-1705) and Thomas Burnet (1635-1715) attempted to synthesize the new ideas of science with Christian doctrine regarding the history of life and the planet Earth. According to Watson (2005), until the end of the eighteenth century, the main concern of geologists and other investigators of natural history was to reconcile the Bible, and in particular Genesis, with the new findings and ideas of geological and natural science.(See also Green, 1959 and Gould, 1987.) This attempt toward integrative compatibility between science and religion pertaining to natural history paralleled a similar effort, described earlier, of attempts to reconcile post-Copernican astronomy with God-centered visions of the cosmos.

But from early in the modern scientific era, there was the problem of fossils. Robert Hooke (1635-1703), the famous contemporary of Newton, raised the issue that numerous discovered fossils of animal and plant life seemed to indicate that there were living creatures in the past that no longer existed in the present. The forms of life were not static. Moreover, in the next century, following the lead of Galileo, William Herschel (as described at length earlier) began to accumulate mounting evidence, based on improved telescopic devices, that there were fundamental changes occurring in the heavens as well. All in all, mounting evidence, geological, paleontological, and astronomical, seemed to indicate that nature was not stable; from the point of view of modern science, static creationism was becoming increasingly implausible.

In his book *Universal Natural History and Theory of the Heavens*

(1755), Immanuel Kant argued in a vein similar to Descartes and Leibniz that evolution was a general process occurring throughout the universe. Kant believed that through the influence of the laws of nature, order and structure emerged out of amorphous and chaotic beginnings—a physics of order arising out of chaos. Kant saw his explanation of cosmic order as following from Newtonian ideas, specifically invoking natural laws to explain natural phenomena, but Kant's vision of the heavens was decidedly anti-Newtonian in describing the cosmos as dynamical and evolutionary, rather than static and stable. Yet Kant still wanted to preserve a place for God in his system and argued that the evolutionary and creative effect of natural laws was evidence for a divine intelligence behind the creation of these natural laws. Kant saw cosmic evolution, as well as social-historical evolution, as teleological, being guided by the plans and purposes of God.

On the other hand, Pierre-Simon LaPlace found no evidence of God in the emerging sciences of astronomy and astrophysics. LaPlace adopted Herschel's idea of "nebular condensation" to explain the formation of the solar system and, in general, saw the heavens as undergoing change due to the inherent forces and laws of nature. No *telos*, purpose, or final causes were needed to explain the apparent directional flow of time within nature.

Critical to the theory of evolution was the discovery of "deep time." James Hutton (1726-1797), the father of modern scientific geology, published in 1795 his famous work *Theory of the Earth*, in which he argued that the earth was much older than traditional estimates based on biblical text. Hutton proposed that geological change involved two complementary processes, destructive deterioration and creative restoration. He viewed earthly time as an endless cycle of creation and decay, of becoming and passing away. Just as Copernican astronomy, followed by Herschel's monumental discoveries and insights, had dramatically expanded the vistas of space, Hutton (and

Herschel as well) greatly expanded the vistas of time, setting the stage for exploration of deep time, both past and future, in modern science fiction. Again, based upon scientific evidence and reasoning, the possibilities of existence were greatly expanded over the more limited imagination and thinking of previous religious doctrine.

Comte de Buffon (1707-1788) added into the scientific dialogue, arguing, just as had Hooke a century before, that fossils were evidence for extinction; thus the perfect and stable order of living forms, presumably created by God, was not so perfect or stable. Further, Buffon took a naturalist point of view regarding history and believed that natural forces, uniform throughout time, produced all the changes that had occurred throughout history; God was not directing the drama. Also, anticipating Darwin and contradicting Genesis, Buffon did not see the biological world as a set of clearly distinct and separate species. His fellow contemporary countryman, Restif de la Bretonne, (whom we examined earlier) would incorporate some of Buffon's biological ideas in *The Discovery of Australia by a Flying Man, or the French Dedalus* (1781), his story of primordial human-animal hybrids in which, contrary to the Bible, humankind and the animal kingdom were connected.

Further elaborating on the theme of creation and destruction within a scientific framework, the founder of modern paleontology, Georges Cuvier (1769-1832) proposed that the growing scientific evidence pointed to a series of pervasive or "catastrophic" upheavals in both biological and geological history. Catastrophic geological changes produced mass extinctions of innumerable life forms which, according to Cuvier, were followed by creative outbursts of new life forms.

As a significant prelude to Darwin's evolutionary theory, Jean de Lamarck (1744-1829) proposed that offspring inherit the survival-promoting "acquired characteristics" of their parents. Although Lamarck's theory of evolution was generally rejected by the scientific community in the decades to come, it was Lamarck who first articulated a comprehensive theory of how the evolution of all of life from simple beginnings could have occurred through entirely natural forces.

A fundamental idea in Lamarck's theory of evolution is that species are transformative rather than static or stable. For Lamarck, the fossil evidence indicated that there was an overall direction in nature from simpler life forms to more complex, organized, and intelligent life forms. When the environment undergoes changes, life is challenged to adapt to these changes, and living forms extend and further develop their capacities in order to survive. Biological change is generated through the challenge of survival.

So, during the time leading up to Darwin's publication of *On the Origin of Species*, numerous ideas connected with evolution were "in the air" as popular topics of scientific discussion and debate. Darwin's contemporary, the influential British philosopher Herbert Spencer (1820-1903), an advocate of the "law of progress" and originator of the phrase "survival of the fittest," was working out a theory of the evolution of everything (inclusive of physical, biological, and psycho-social realms), prior to the publication of the *On the Origin of Species*. As a general trend, the various pieces of evolutionary theory had been developing over the previous two centuries, involving a constant struggle of scientists trying to preserve the biblical theory of creation only to repeatedly relinquish elements of it in favor of more dynamic, naturalistic, and evolutionary ideas.

After decades of study and research, Charles Darwin (1809-1882) published *On the Origin of Species by Natural Selection, or the Preservation of Favoured Races in the Struggle for Life* in 1859. His theory of evolution by natural selection became the most influential scientific idea in the modern West, and—next to the Bible—*On the Origin of Species* emerged as the most influential book written in Western civilization. In the nineteenth and twentieth centuries, evolution was the pivotal theory that influenced the course of most of science, across numerous scientific disciplines. For scientists, philosophers, and social theorists, evolution came to provide a comprehensive scientific basis for understanding both the natural and civilized world (Phipps, 2012). Darwin and his theory of evolution transformed the basic picture of nature provided by science; redefined the nature of humanity; overturned almost all metaphysical views in traditional world religions regarding the mechanism of creation and the origins of order; and laid the groundwork for a new cosmic view of time and the future. After Darwin, speculation on the origin, development, and the future of the universe and humanity was cracked wide open to scientific study and debate.

Darwin's theory not only overturned static creationism as expressed in Christianity, as well as teleological and anthropocentric views that saw the universe as purposefully created for the benefit of man, it also, perhaps most fundamentally, overturned the Platonic-Newtonian static image of the universe. The concept of dynamic evolutionary change replaced Newton's stable and harmonious machine as the central idea in science. As a result of this revolution in thought, contemporary science has come to view reality, time, order, and the future in predominantly evolutionary and dynamic terms, and the entities and laws of nature no longer look so permanent (Lombardo, 2002b, 2017).

Looking more closely at his specific biological theory, Darwin's argument was that life forms exhibit (perhaps random) variation in offspring produced in each generation and that given the limited food and resources in the environment too many offspring are produced for all to survive. Darwin seems to have derived this second idea from Thomas Malthus and his book *An Essay on the Principle of Population* (1798), which argued that there is natural competition over resources among the members of a species. Because there is variability among the species, some members will possess greater abilities for finding resources and staying alive. Those members possessing favorable traits will survive and pass on those favorable traits or abilities to their offspring. Favorable adaptive traits steadily accrue and magnify over successive generations due to the ongoing process of natural selection of those members of a species better able to survive. Given sufficient time, this ongoing selective process produces the evolution of new species and eliminates various species that are not able to survive. Within this process there is no purposeful design directing the evolution of life; survival and reproductive success, as determined through natural selection, create the evolutionary pathway.

The argument is often made that Darwin's biological theory implies that evolution occurs by chance. Such an interpretation of Darwin is at best a half-truth and misleading. The more accurate and complete description of Darwin's theory of natural selection is that it combines chance and natural law, providing an alternative explanation for species to that of divine purposeful creation. The environment, in which life evolves, is a relatively lawful reality; reproductive success is a consequence of staying alive within the environment and not primarily due to chance. The transmission of traits from parent to offspring is far from totally willy-nilly; fish do not have feline offspring, and cows do not give birth to baby whales.

Darwin saw order and lawfulness in the evolution of life. What Darwin did not see was transcendent purpose or intelligent design. Evolution occurs through natural selection and there is no purposeful direction to this process; there is no need to postulate a guiding force or transcendent intelligence. There is no plan or goal to the evolution of life; natural selection explains why life evolves. (Darwin did not totally reject Lamarck's acquired characteristics, but Lamarck's theory was naturalistic as well, without purposeful divine guidance.)

Darwin applied his theory of evolution to humans in his book

The Descent of Man and Selection in Relation to Sex, published in 1871. Where Christianity saw humankind as a special creation of God, Darwin states, "The main conclusion here arrived at, and now held by many naturalists who are well competent to form a sound judgment, is that man is descended from some less highly organized form." Lamarck had already argued that humans were descended from apes and, as Darwin notes, many other contemporary scientists and philosophers also held such a view. What Darwin provides in *The Descent of Man* is an explanation of the origin and development of humanity in terms of his theory of evolution through natural selection: Humanity is part of nature and is connected with the rest of life through common descent and natural selection.

Although Darwin presents his theory of evolution as an explanation of the origin and development of biological forms, he also applied this framework of evolution beyond biology. For example, he believed that human civilization had gradually evolved from a state of primitive barbarism. He embraced this theory of cultural history and combined it with biological history into one grand scheme of human evolution. For Darwin, the entire bio-social history of humanity is one of steady progression upward from the simple and the primitive to the complex, intelligent, and increasingly civilized. Herbert Spencer took a similar view, and saw cultural development as a continuation and further elaboration of biological evolution. For Darwin and Spencer, as well as many other scientists and philosophers of the day whom they influenced, evolution became an all embracing theory which explained the entire history of humanity from our most primitive beginnings and provided a conceptual framework for understanding the future of humankind.

Moreover, as introduced above, evolution was applied to the universe at large and the history of the earth, the solar system, and the life of stars. By the time we come to Spencer, we find evolution applied to everything, from the physical to the psycho-social. As we move into the twentieth century, going beyond Spencer's more philosophical speculations, the physics of the universe and its formation—inclusive of atoms, complex chemical compounds, planetary geology, stars, and galaxies— was integrated into a comprehensive scientific evolutionary vision (Chaisson, 2005).

Because evolution provided a transformative description of the history of nature, with both drama and sense of direction, it offered a new all-encompassing narrative of humanity and nature, extending both into the distant past as well as reaching out into the far future. It is important to see that although evolution is a scientific theory, formulated as a set of abstract principles and laws, it generates a narrative or story, for it provides a historical-transformative description of natural reality. As Watson (2005) states, "Evolution is the *story* of us all." (My italics.)

As an alternative narrative derived from science, evolution contradicted the grand narrative of the cosmos and humanity provided by Western Christianity. The theory of secular progress articulated in the Age of Enlightenment had already challenged aspects of the Christian narrative of humanity, bringing self-empowerment, democracy, rationality, science, and technological-material growth into the forefront in envisioning the directionality of the future. But secular progress, although inspired by science and reason, was not strictly speaking a scientific theory, and it did not offer an all-encompassing new story of the universe and humanity. Evolution, on the other hand, was a scientific theory, pulling together ideas and empirical data from numerous scientific disciplines, and its scope extended to all of nature. In fact, evolution theoretically swallowed secular progress.

Evolution became the grand narrative informing and structuring science fiction, at least insofar as specific science fiction stories aspired toward scientific plausibility. As described in the opening chapters, one meaning behind the expression "evolutionary mythology of the future" is that contemporary science fiction narrative, informed by current scientific thinking, is framed within an evolutionary narrative of humanity and the cosmos.

The specific application of evolution to understanding the nature and history of humankind further exacerbated the growing rift between modern science and Western religion, and produced unsettling emotional reverberations regarding the future of humanity. In jettisoning the idea of purposeful divine direction, the future of humankind no longer seemed certain or secure. Within a Darwinian universe, the future was not being guided toward some divinely determined end. Hope for the future could not be guaranteed. Accordingly, evolution-framed science fiction could ensure neither a positive future for humankind nor even the continued existence of humanity. As a result, the possibilities of the future envisioned in post-evolutionary science fiction significantly expanded from what they had been before.

As Richard Tarnas (1991) notes in *The Passion of the Western Mind*, after evolution, humankind "... was not God's noble creation with a divine destiny, but nature's experiment with an uncertain destiny." *Homo sapiens* are simply "a highly successful animal." According to Tarnas, this evolutionary insight was both liberating and alienating, for divine purpose gave humans a sense of meaning and security, as well as a yoke on behavior and thinking. Although philosophers of progress embraced evolution as a naturalistic justification for their belief in increasing improvement in humankind and human society (Nisbet, 1994), Tarnas argues that Darwin's theory of evolution also undercut the absolute optimism of the Enlightenment. Not only did the theory of evolution seem to imply that Christianity, as well as other religious doctrines, was nothing but an "anthropocentric delusion," but given the dethronement of humanity from a special position within the cosmos, there was no longer any guarantee for the indefinite success of the species. In the ongoing competitive reality of nature, who is to say if humankind will survive? No god from above is watching out for us. Further, culture and ethics can no longer be seen as having some higher, divine origin or justification. Both civilization and morality are expressions of the evolutionary process, part of nature rather than being divinely ordained or created. It follows then that the ideal future (utopia) defined in terms of ethical standards—of what the good is—is a creation of the human mind and consequently open to both debate and ambiguity.

Still, even if Darwin introduces deep uncertainty regarding the future of humanity, he did subscribe to an optimistic and progressive vision of the future, which he grounded in his evolutionary theory. Although there has been ongoing debate on this point (Gould, 1989; Lombardo, 2002b), Darwin believed that evolution implied progress. He believed, as did many of his contemporaries, that evolution provided a scientifically grounded explanation for the modern Western theory of progress. As he states,

"There is grandeur in this view of life...from so simple a beginning endless forms most beautiful and most wonderful have been, and are being, evolved."

And further he proposes:

"As natural selection works solely by and for the good of each being, all corporeal and mental endowments will tend to progress towards perfection."

Darwin believed that evolution through natural selection led to improvement and progress. As Nisbet (1994) points out, Darwin often used the words "progress" and "evolution" interchangeably. Darwin spoke of "higher" and "lower" life forms, equating lower with simpler, older, and more primitive species. Higher life forms were more complex, and thus, in resonance with Lamarck, Darwin used increasing complexity as a criterion for defining evolutionary progress. Darwin also saw in animal and human evolution both increasing intelligence and moral capacity. He believed that future humanity would evolve further in both intelligence and morality. Although there was no purposeful direction to the evolution of life through a divine guidance system, there was for Darwin a naturalistic and progressive direction to evolution. In this linking together of evolution with progress, Darwin articulated a new "scientifically grounded" framework for imagining, at least potentially, a positive future for humanity.

But the coupling of evolution and progress had controversial implications and disquieting repercussions in the nineteenth century. With the emergence of Darwin's theory, many philosophers of progress, Spencer being one noteworthy example, embraced the evolutionary perspective as providing a scientific explanation for the inevitability of progress. But Spencer's particular interpretation of the connection between evolution and progress—which developed into what came to be called "Social Darwinism"—provoked significant criticism.

When Darwin published *On the Origin of Species*, to many readers he appeared to be arguing that competition was the primary force generating evolution. Since it was those members of a species best adapted to the environment that survived and reproduced, Spencer, on reading Darwin, suggested the phrase "survival of the fittest" to concisely describe the competitive dimension of the Darwinian principle of natural selection. In later editions of *On the Origin of Species,* Darwin included this phrase to describe his theory. "Fittest" is a relative term defined in terms of competitive advantage in securing resources to support continued existence and eventual reproduction.

Philosophers of progress, such as Spencer, viewed this competitive reading of Darwin as a naturalistic justification for the economic and social reality of competitiveness in the modern European world. Adam Smith identified competition as a central theme in his economic theory of capitalism: Competition was responsible for driving the advancement of productivity. Hence, defenders of capitalism embraced Darwin's theory as a justification for their competitive economic system, and in general, Darwin's theory of evolution seemed to vindicate competition in all aspects of life. Competition makes things get better; and what is better is determined in the arena of competition. This is the core belief underlying Social Darwinism. Competition is how nature works and competition produces progress; therefore competition is good.

But Social Darwinism provoked strong counter-reactions on both logical and moral grounds. For critics of Social Darwinism, the ethical implications drawn from a competitive model of human evolution seemed heartless and self-serving. Social Darwinism downplayed cooperation, nurturance, compassion, and community in favor of competition and self-centered individualism. It seemed to support a "law-of-the-jungle" morality and the idea that might makes right, an ethical view that was highly suspect.

Also Social Darwinism provided an ethically questionable justification for the authority and privileges of those who possessed social and economic power. Europeans could feel superior to other cultures and races based on the idea that they were more advanced on the evolutionary scale—having presumably outcompeted other cultures and races—and rich capitalists could feel morally exonerated and superior to the poor and the underclass because they had presumably earned their positions of power through the natural law of competition. Social Darwinism seemed to support the status quo, cultural elitism, and biological racism.

On logical grounds, Thomas Huxley (1825-1895), the great defender of Darwin's theory and later teacher of H. G. Wells, took issue with Spencer on whether evolution—a scientific theory—provided any kind of justification for a social or moral philosophy. How, Huxley argued, does one derive an ethics from statements of fact? As Huxley put it, "Let us understand, once for all, that the ethical progress of society depends, not on imitating the cosmic process, still less in running from it, but in combating it." As a basic point, theorists of progress often conflate the idea that there is a direction through history (however defined) with the idea that this direction is ethically a good thing. It can't be simply assumed that a long-term historical direction means things are getting better in some ethical sense. As John Green, in the *The Death of Adam* (1959), puts it, survival is "a brute fact, not a moral victory."

Yet Darwin's theory of evolution was not so simple. Social Darwinists embraced the idea of competition in Darwin's theory. But Darwin had other thoughts on evolution, especially as expressed in *The Descent of Man*, which highlighted such concepts as love, sympathy, mutuality, and cooperation. Darwin saw social institutions and morality in humans as a consequence of evolution though natural selection. He believed that integral to human morality and social organizations was a highly developed capacity for concern and caring among humans. Behaviors, feelings, and modes of thinking connected with cooperation and mutual affection would be highly advantageous for the survival of the group. A cooperative group is much more efficient in facing the challenges of life than a non-cooperative group. Consequently, groups of humans showing greater cooperation and caring would survive, passing on the traits connected with cooperative ethics in its individuals, whereas groups of humans not showing these traits as strongly would falter and fail. Those emotions and moral principles that bind humans together would be selected for within the evolutionary process. Beginning with Darwin but continuing to the present day, in writers such as E. O. Wilson (1998c) and Michael Shermer (2004), the argument has been developed that a cooperative and caring ethics in humans is a consequence of evolutionary forces at work in our history.

The evolutionary writer David Loye goes so far as to argue,

in his book *Darwin's Lost Theory* (2007) and other writings, that Darwin in *The Descent of Man* emphasized cooperation and caring much more than individual competition and survival of the fittest. Further, according to Loye, Darwin saw further moral development based on cooperation and caring, rather than cut-throat self-centered competition, as the central driving force in the future evolution of humans. Loye accuses earlier writers and thinkers, such as Social Darwinists, of over-emphasizing the competitive theme in evolutionary theory in order to scientifically justify the competitive and individualist behavior and philosophy of modern Western society.

As a general point, beginning with Darwin and Huxley—and through the latter's influence, finding another strong advocate in H. G. Wells—the argument developed that although competition and "survival of the fittest" might capture a central process going on in evolution, our future development as a species needs to be guided by moral principles that may contradict, transcend, or at the very least guide, the natural forces of change that created humans. For Wells (1934), nationalistic competition, which invariably provokes war, will lead to the downfall of humankind. Competitive nationalism needs to be transcended, replaced by a morality of cooperation among all of humankind. Wells wrote numerous stories and non-fictional futurist treatises warning of the dangers of excessive competition, offering in place visions of a preferable future of humanity built on a morality of global cooperation and unity of purpose.

After the debates on evolution and progress put forth by Darwin, Spencer, and Huxley, science fiction would grapple with such questions as: What are the potential negative consequences of a society that revolves around competition, including competitive capitalism? Can humanity transcend competition and the "laws of the jungle", through the further evolution of ethics and morality? What are the pros and cons of competition versus cooperation in the potential future evolution of human society? What are the pros and cons of individualism versus communalism? How does the ongoing development of science and technology fit into an evolutionary framework for understanding human progress in the future? Certainly other significant social and economic theories would influence the ongoing development of social science fiction, including utopias and dystopias—take, for example, Marxist communism and socialism (Lombardo, 2006a), which emerged in the nineteenth century—but the theory of evolution (and its connection with human progress) provided a major source of ideas in thinking through and creating *narratives* of future human society.

Indeed, Darwin's grand theory provided a new transformative vision encompassing humanity, nature, and the cosmos, inclusive of past history and future possibilities. Its complex and expansive new mind space informed and inspired science fiction narratives that went far beyond simply the future of human society, addressing such additional questions and issues as: How will humanity biologically, techno-biologically, and psychologically evolve in the future? Will humanity be replaced by something more evolved or better adapted to the earthly environment (or the cosmos)? Does evolution imply that humankind is a transient form, one that sometime in the future will be out-competed by some other form of life? Will humanity become extinct? Will we perhaps create our own evolutionary descendants? Will intelligence, technology, or civilization be preserved as advantageous to further human evolution? How will potential, perhaps catastrophic, changes in the environment impact the future evolution of humanity and other life forms? How does the future evolution of humanity fit within the more expansive evolutionary directionality of the universe as a whole? How might alien life forms have evolved in different ways as a consequence of natural selection and adaptation to other types of planetary conditions? How does evolution inform our understanding of the development of life and intelligence on other worlds? What are the evolutionary possibilities of life and intelligence at a cosmic level? How does evolution and both competition and cooperation play out at an interplanetary or interstellar level? If there is no over-arching purpose or design to the universe, will humanity (or other intelligent beings) in the future create a purpose for the cosmos? Can we still find a place for God within evolutionary scenarios and narratives of the future? Clearly the possibilities presented by evolution provided an immense territory of imaginative exploration for subsequent science fiction narratives.

One other offshoot of evolutionary thinking that would have great relevance to the further development of science fiction came from Darwin's half cousin, Francis Galton (1822-1911). Galton read Darwin's *On the Origin of Species* and was particularly struck by his extensive discussion of the selective breeding of animals and plants. Galton applied the idea of selective breeding to humans, coining the term "eugenics." For Galton, there is positive eugenics, which involves efforts to increase the reproductive rate of humans with desirable traits (such as physical strength and intelligence), and there is negative eugenics, which involves efforts to decrease or limit the reproductive rate of humans with undesirable traits. In essence, eugenics was conceptualized as the purposeful evolution of future humans, involving guided selection based on criteria defining standards of superior and inferior humans. Prior to Galton, humans had already engaged in various eugenic activities such as forced sterilization, forced abortions, and even genocide. (And is not "sexual selection" of preferable mates also a form of purposeful evolution and eugenics?) What Galton did was to suggest that we make the process systematic and scientifically informed. He believed that humans are not born equal, and that it clearly makes sense to speak of superior and inferior humans. He believed that we should work toward increasing and maximizing the former and decreasing and eliminating the latter. We should systematically evolve ourselves in a manner similar to how we have purposefully evolved domesticated animals and plants through selective breeding.

Although the eugenics movement became popular in the immediate decades after Galton presented his vision, in the long run it came under significant attack. Eugenics was eventually associated with the atrocities of German Nazism, in which systematic genocide was committed with the professed intent to eliminate "inferior" humans in order to make room for the "superior" Aryan race. But the Nazis' criteria for selection were psycho-pathologically determined, and the methods heinous, immoral, and vicious. Consequently, eugenics came to be seen as anathema to the basic rights and freedoms of human beings; it became associated with mass murder, unimaginable cruelty, and a total abandonment of morality and human sanity.

The shadow of negative eugenics would strongly influence dystopian science fiction in the twentieth century. Any narrative in which a tyrannical controlling elite attempts to "weed out" or extinguish particular humans based on some set of criteria regarding what constitutes acceptability or desirability is an expression of negative eugenics. The fear of such systematic and insidious forms of government and social control became an important theme in dystopian science fiction.

But the reverse side of the coin—positive eugenics—has evolved in twentieth- and early twenty-first-century science and technology (Lombardo, 2002c), becoming a central motivating idea in numerous science fiction visions of the future of humanity. Any imagined futurist scenario in which humans (or other animals), are selectively bred or, through biotechnology, genetically manipulated to generate more "advanced" or desirable humans (according to some set of standards of superiority), is an example of positive eugenics (as Galton broadly understood it).

To place positive eugenics in a historical context, humans have always aspired toward improvement and increasing excellence according to whatever standards they accepted at that time. The ideal of positive eugenics can be seen as an expression of this deep aspiration, applied to the biological foundations of the human species. Positive eugenics, and its more modern manifestations in genetic biotechnology, framed in terms of evolutionary theory, is an expression of the "purposeful evolution" of life by humans (Lombardo, 2017). Instead of allowing natural selection—blind in its consequences—to direct the future evolution of humans, we are now empowered with modern technologies and biological-evolutionary knowledge, and we can intentionally guide our own evolutionary process. There are literally thousands of science fiction stories that address the purposeful evolution of future humans through science and technology.

Of course, following this line of thought we are back to a variation on the *Frankenstein* scenario, in this case with humans attempting to guide or create their own biological future with the use of scientific knowledge and modern technologies. We fret whether such efforts are wise and moral, or whether we are asking for trouble in our attempts at self-determination and the control of our own nature. Genetic biotechnology has been repeatedly accused of "playing God," the very criticism raised by Shelley against Frankenstein in his creation of the Creature (Lombardo, 2002c). (See also Wells' *The Island of Dr. Moreau*, 1896, for another famous dark vision of this type of endeavor.) Who are we to determine what is best or most desirable? Who are we to believe we have the capacity to successfully carry out such purposes and goals? Isn't this all unnatural?

Yet, evolution and its transformative vision of nature rejected the notion that humankind is a static, once-and-for-all creation. We are part of the evolutionary flow, and from an enlightened post-evolutionary perspective, we should ask, whether it is better to simply "go with the flow," wherever it leads (and it will lead someplace different), or whether we should thoughtfully and ethically guide it (Lombardo, 2002b; 2017)? If we believe a divine entity guides nature, then it makes sense to adopt a position of non-interference. But obviously the scientific theory of evolution collides head on with this theological mindset. And where is the line to be drawn regarding interfering with nature?

To go back to a basic thesis in this book: Science fiction operates in a reality judged plausible relative to modern scientific views of reality (even if there is debate and ambiguity about the scientifically plausible). And one pivotal idea in modern science is that nature is a transformative reality and an evolutionary process propelled by natural laws and forces. Moreover, humans are participatory in this process, both shaping and being shaped by it. Within numerous science fiction stories, both prior to and after the emergence of modern genetic biotechnology, humans have actively engaged in the evolutionary process in a self-reflective and purposeful way, using science and technology to guide and improve upon our own nature and other forms of life as well. Such efforts may fail or backfire—or they may not—but such efforts make sense within a naturally evolving universe. (See Stapledon's *Last and First Men*.) This is a new fundamental narrative of human existence and our future. It is diametrically different from the pre-evolutionary vision of divine creation and control of nature that viewed such efforts at purposeful evolution as off limits to humans, as immoral and blasphemous, as unnatural and "playing God."

The theory of evolution, and in particular purposeful evolution facilitated by humans, provided a new central mythic narrative for modern science fiction: the purposeful effort to transform, evolve, and improve ourselves through the use of science and technology—often set in a future reality. What drives the dramatic tension in the narrative is the uncertainty of success, in part due to the uncertainty of our abilities, moral and intellectual, but also due to the uncertainty within all evolution and the flow of time. The central archetypal character is the individual (or social group), attempting to integrate science, technology, morality, and wisdom; aspiring to self-improvement and purposeful evolution; and having to muster the fortitude and courage to face the precarious nature and challenges inherent in the endeavor, often involving conservative forces who see the whole process as unnatural and sacrilegious. Further, this archetypal science fiction narrative of purposeful human evolution is often placed within the more general narrative of cosmic evolution: We are self-evolutionary beings in an evolutionary universe. Where is it all leading? Where do we want it to lead? Are there other intelligent beings involved in this process as well? If, as Watson notes, "Evolution is the story of us all," then, within modern post-evolutionary science fiction narratives, we have become prime authors, enthusiastic or reluctant, of the story.

In a Post-Darwinian universe, we come face-to-face with a new "brute fact," powerfully captured in the following statement by the evolutionary biologist Julian Huxley, the grandson of Thomas Huxley:

It is as if man had been suddenly appointed managing director of the biggest business of all, the business of evolution — appointed without being asked if he wanted it, and without proper warning and preparation. What is more, he can't refuse the job. Whether he wants to or not, whether he is conscious of what he is doing or not, he is in point of fact determining the future direction of evolution on this earth. That is his inescapable destiny, and the sooner he realizes it and starts believing in it, the better for all concerned ...

Entropy and the Heat Death of the Universe

Kipple is useless objects ... When nobody's around, kipple reproduces itself ... the entire universe is moving towards a final state of total,

absolute kippleization.
Philip K. Dick

Coming back to the big circle of order and chaos, of creation and destruction, of becoming and passing away—literally of life and death—we turn to the other half of the cosmic scientific vision that crystalized in the later nineteenth century: the inexorable flow of increasing entropy and the heat death of the universe. We have already seen in Grainville's *The Last Man* a vision of the end of things, of the collapse of humanity and the termination of time and the universe; in part inspired by the Christian vision in the Book of Revelation, this vision also derived from the idea of humankind's eventual exhaustion of earthly resources, a "scientific" idea Grainville apparently derived from Malthus. Just as in human history there have been countless narratives revolving around creation, birth, and becoming, there have also been myriad stories and images that focus on death, destruction, and passing away (Clute, 1999; Newman, 2010). But in the mid-nineteenth century, a connected set of ideas and experimental observations came together in the scientific study of energy and heat that coalesced into a quantitative and mathematically articulated argument that everything must eventually run down and fall apart. Death and dissipation is our ultimate destiny; through scientific reasoning we can demonstrate that it is the destiny of the universe. Within this scientifically inspired cosmic narrative, we have an all-encompassing and unavoidable tragedy, a bleak and depressing conclusion of the story of the universe.

Just as the theory of evolution was a sustained and collective achievement of numerous philosophers and scientists, the emergence of the laws of thermodynamics, including the concept of entropy, involved the contributions of many scientists and engineers. Spanning centuries, these thinkers worked in such diverse scientific fields as: the study of temperature and heat;

engines and machines; kinetic (mechanical energy); fluids and gases; friction; statistical mechanics; and the microscopic and molecular motion of particles in fluids. Again, just as with evolution, the laws and principles of thermodynamics integrated and explained a diverse and expansive array of phenomena in nature. It was another big picture theory, the modern beginnings of which go all the way back to Newton and Leibnitz.

The first law of thermodynamics is the thermodynamic statement of the conversation of energy principle: Within any physical system the amount of internal energy remains constant. Put in everyday language, energy can neither be created nor destroyed. The earliest clear formulation of the first law of thermodynamics (1850) came from Rudolf Clausius (1822-1888).

Although anticipated by Nicolas Sadi Carnot (1796-1832), the "father of thermodynamics," Clausius is also responsible for the first clear statement of the second law (also 1850), as well as the introduction of the concept of entropy into the second law in 1865. Indeed, with Clausius, the idea of entropy became an integral feature of the second law.

The first law states that energy in a closed system remains constant; the second law states that energy in a closed system moves in the inexorable direction of homogeneous or equilibrated distribution. Entropy is the term used to refer to the degree of homogeneity of energy distribution within a system. Hence, the second law states that the entropy of an isolated system never decreases (heterogeneity never increases), because isolated systems always evolve toward thermodynamic equilibrium, a state of maximum entropy. The second law can also be succinctly described by stating that heat never spontaneously moves from a colder object to a hotter one (thus increasing the heat or energy difference) but always the reverse, from the hotter to the colder object, thus leading to a state of equal distribution of heat. Things inexorably even out over time.

Entropy can also be understood as the degree of disorder

within a physical system, where order is understood as differentiation or structure. Hence, the degree of entropy equals the degree of homogeneity (or equilibrium) or lack of structure. Therefore, the second law implies that within any closed system, the amount of order, structure, or differentiation spontaneously breaks down. Metaphorically, things move toward chaos and away from order, order requiring (indeed being synonymous with) differentiation and structure.

The first and second laws of thermodynamics have direct implications regarding the nature of conceivable (or possible) machines in the universe, in particular entailing that perpetual motion machines are naturalistically impossible. Work performed by a machine requires a flow of energy within a machine, which requires a differential in energy distribution. If energy or heat is equally distributed within a system, there is no available energy or capacity for work. So, since all natural systems move in the direction of energetic homogeneity, we cannot have a self-sustaining machine that indefinitely maintains an energy differential to keep it operating. To keep operating (to keep doing work), all machines require a flow of energy from outside themselves. Interestingly though, creating a perpetual motion machine has been a long-standing quest in engineering and an often expressed aspiration described in science fiction stories; stating that something is scientifically impossible provokes in the human mind the desire to challenge and transcend the presumed impossibility, and find a way to show that it is naturalistically possible. This point explains, at least in many cases, why science fiction writers frequently push beyond the scientifically credible toward the scientifically implausible.

Given the second law of thermodynamics, the perplexity naturally arose regarding the apparent profusion of order and differentiation observed in the natural world. Of special note, there is a high level of structure and differentiation in the biological realm, life forms growing from relatively simple beginnings when they germinate into much more complex forms as they mature. Furthermore, evolution seems to generate increasing complexity and order over time; indeed, it seems to run in the opposite direction to the law of increasing entropy. How can this be?

The answer that developed to address this perplexity was relatively simple: Life is not a closed system. During the germination, growth, and ongoing maintenance of life, living systems draw energy from the environment to create and sustain structure. Evolution, as a process of increasing order and complexity, requires the infusion or input of an energy flow to keep it going. Neither life nor evolution is a perpetual motion machine. Through the radiation of the sun (as in plants), or through the ingestion of living material (as in animals), living forms draw in and replenish energy reserves to stay alive, grow, and evolve. Life is an "open system" (Goerner, 1999; Lombardo, 2002a).

Yet when all is said and done, this profusion and growth of life that we observe on the earth cannot continue indefinitely; if the universe is a closed system, then eventually all differences will be wiped out (for example, the sun and all other stars will burn out), and consequently all differential energy flow will evaporate into a state of maximum thermodynamic equilibrium. As Clausius put it, "The entropy of the universe tends toward a maximum." Inspired by the great nineteenth-century scientist William Thomson's (Lord Kelvin) paper "On a Universal Tendency in Nature to the Dissipation of Mechanical Energy" (1852), the equally illustrious scientist and philosopher Hermann von Helmholtz (1821-1894) put forth the idea of the "heat death of the universe" (1854). As Lord Kelvin argued, not even the sun (or any other stars) can keep radiating light and heat indefinitely; the sun must exhaust itself. With this insight, Helmholtz realized that all unequal distributions of energy and connected pockets of order across the universe would eventually disappear, with the universe as a whole, winding down.

Yet, though accepted by many scientists and philosophers as a necessary and realistic conclusion of the second law of thermodynamics, this dismal and bleak finale to the saga of the universe has not sat well with many scientists and writers, including science fiction writers. (With whom could it possibly sit well?) Even Kelvin (1824-1907), who inspired the idea, did not unequivocally accept it. Just as with the impossibility of a perpetual motion machine—which is actually the same idea— the inevitable death of the universe became a point of challenge in both scientific inquiry and science fiction visions of the far distant future. To quote from Kelvin in 1852:

> The result would inevitably be a state of universal rest and death, if the universe were finite and left to obey existing laws. But it is impossible to conceive a limit to the extent of matter in the universe; and therefore science points rather to an endless progress, through an endless space, of action involving the transformation of potential energy into palpable motion and hence into heat, than to a single finite mechanism, running down like a clock, and stopping for ever.

At one level, the question of the "heat death of the universe" is a scientific issue. There remains up until today debate over whether the universe is a closed system, and how to apply the concept of entropy to the universe as a whole (Adams and Laughlin, 1999). But at another level, the issue is highly emotional and personal, for if the grandest, most encompassing narrative of the universe is creation, growth, and evolution inexorably followed by the absolute decay and death of everything, then we live within a great cosmic tragedy, one that provokes questions such as, "What is the point of it all?" or "What is the point of our lives?" How do we find meaning and purpose in the face of inevitable oblivion?

Questions of scientific validity versus issues of personal preference can easily get mixed together in considering the law of increasing entropy and its cosmic implications. The possibility of the ultimate death of everything motivates the human mind into imagining all kinds of ways to circumvent it. Indeed, the issue of scientific plausibility becomes intensely debated in the context of "the heat death of the universe." Is there some scientific (or technological) avenue for avoiding or counter-acting this presumed all-enveloping cosmic direction and horrendous and dismal conclusion? Do we accept what appears inevitable, and simply fall into the ontological and emotional abyss, or do we personally and intellectually challenge the presumed necessity of this scientific conclusion? Science fiction writers in the coming century would in various ways address the issue of entropy and the heat death of the universe, often attempting to find some scientifically credible way to circumvent its ultimate pronouncement of decay and death for everything. Camille Flammarion, cosmic and metaphysical in his vision of things, found a "scientifically plausible" doorway through the end of the universe. The issue of the heat death of the universe is a very good example of how intense debate and alternative points of view regarding what is presumably scientifically plausible can enter into science fiction stories.

On the other hand, the idea of universal increasing entropy also provided, if one accepted the idea, a scientifically inspired archetypal narrative framework for creating multiple types of futurist scenarios involving the death and decay of both physical and social-technological systems. That is, entropy served as the archetypal foundation for futurist tragedy. Of course, prior to the nineteenth century, the archetypal themes of chaos, destruction, and death worked their way into world literature; in the eighteenth century, Gothic literature often revolved around such dark and dismal themes. Poe frequently delved into the themes of decay, destruction, and death. Yet, with the emergence of a grand scientific theory articulating and explaining the physics of death, we have a new, modern, scientifically grounded version of the ideas of chaos and the abyss to scientifically inform and inspire fictional writings. As Clute (1995) points out, especially after 1960, entropy and the death of the universe became increasingly popular themes in science fiction. But even before that we can see the idea taking form in Wells' dark and mesmerizing description of the far future earth and sun in the concluding sections of *The Time Machine*.

Evolution and entropy are the modern, scientific versions of the ancient themes of order and chaos, but now set in dynamic or temporal form, by which evolution is directionality toward increasing order and complexity, and the law of entropy is directionality toward increasing chaos and simplicity. As such, evolution and entropy and the relationship between the two forces provide one of the most fundamental narrative themes in modern science fiction literature. We can conceive of the relationship as a conflicting struggle; we can conceive of the relationship as some type of interdependent or reciprocal dance, life feeding off death and vice versa. The future becomes an arena in which the dual and oppositional forces of evolution and entropy work out their struggle and antagonism. Again, Clute (1995) notes that this modern conflictive/dialectical narrative framework, of evolution versus entropy, informs a great deal of modern science fiction. The belief in inevitable secular progress—sparked during the Enlightenment but counteracted by the apprehensive visions of Romantic-Gothic thinking on the future of technology and human civilization—evolved in the late nineteenth century into futurist narratives on the ongoing dramatic struggle of evolution versus entropy: of the hope for the continued growth of life, consciousness, and civilization versus the fear of death, decay, and destruction of all things, including humankind. Insofar as contemporary science fiction addresses this deep archetypal and cosmic theme it possesses a mythic quality, creating narratives that both inspire and frighten us at primordial levels of our consciousness, for indeed what is more existentially fundamental than the issue of life versus death in the future? We have created world religions—perhaps all world religions—around this conscious confrontation with the stark and unnerving reality of the end of our existence (Becker, 1973). And regarding the dimension of transcendence realized in the mythology of science fiction, no issue is more viscerally impactive and epistemically important than whether we will survive and indeed advance, or whether we will dissipate into the dust in journeying "beyond the hill." When we peer outward from "the village" and from where we stand today, this is the most critical and frightful question we can ask. Is what is transcendent, something or nothing?

Invasions and War—Evolution and Machines

Chesney's Battle of Dorking ... must be the most talked-about and imitated short story in the history of publishing.
I. F. Clarke

According to Clute it was the Enlightenment that planted the seeds of modern science fiction with its vision that through science, technology, and democratic self-empowerment the future could be imagined as dramatically different from the past. There is a degree of truth in this argument, but modern science fiction—with Verne as a clear exception—only really takes off after the publications of Darwin's *On the Origin of Species* (1859) and *The Descent of Man* (1871). Perhaps this is because evolution provided a scientific vision of the flow of time, of past and future, of naturalistic transformation, or perhaps because evolution (and its dark twin entropy) put drama, struggle, becoming and passing away, and uncertainty into the whole process of future change, fueling the narrative imagination. Would humanity survive in the future? For the Enlightenment the future was much more a confident pathway of smooth sailing forward. Whatever the case, the last few decades of the nineteenth century saw an outpouring of new science fiction novels, many of which became acknowledged classics of the genre. In the final decade of the century, this imaginative efflorescence reached its greatest and unparalleled creative expression in H. G. Wells, who was unequivocally informed and inspired by evolutionary thinking.

In this section we focus on the 1870s, in particular 1871-1872, which began with a notable publishing coincidence involving three well-known novels: George Chesney's *The Battle of Dorking* (1871), Samuel Butler's *Erewhon* (1872), and Sir Edward Bulwer-Lytton's *Vril, The Power of the Coming Race* (1871). All three novels address fundamental themes introduced in the last sections on evolution and entropy, including competition, destruction, and the evolutionary possibilities of humanity. The novels also consider from various perspectives the significance of technology, its rapid growth, and potential further developments in the future; indeed the themes of evolution and technology are woven together in two of these novels. It is an interesting historical fact that all three books are associated with a particular date, May 1st, 1871, which Jess Nevins identifies as "The Day Science Fiction was Invented." Chesney's and Bulwer-Lytton's books were published on that day, and the manuscript that evolved into *Erewhon* was first submitted for publication on the same date (Nevins, 2011).

Let's begin with *The Battle of Dorking* and the topic of future war. To set the context:

War, and even more specifically "future war," has been an archetypal theme from ancient mythologies up to the present. Zoroastrian in its origins, the mythic-religious vision of a cataclysmic final battle, Armageddon, pitting the forces of good against evil is perhaps the seminal future war narrative, providing an inspirational starting point for many later novels.

As a mythic-archetypal theme running through numerous sagas and tales in human history, images of war can be seen as a narrative and symbolic expression of the forces of chaos, destruction, and death, from deep within the workings of nature and the human mind, made manifest and conscious within human imagination.

War can also be viewed, as it often has been, as a confrontation of order and chaos. Order must confront and defeat chaos—which threatens it in the arena of human existence—but order and civilization can only maintain or advance itself within the destructive battlefield of the chaos of war itself. War can acquire, as it often has, a heroic and elevated dimension, although in a sense there is a deep contradiction within its purpose.

Both metaphorically and literally, war has also been seen throughout human history as a force of creativity—through turmoil and chaos, a new order will arise. Perhaps Heraclitus put it most simply: "War is the father of all things." For Howard Bloom (2000), war, and conquest in particular, is one of the two primary forces behind progress. The dialectical and oscillatory vision of human progress, as expounded in Wells' visions of the future, requires chaotic collapses involving war in order for civilization to recreate itself, rising upwards to a new level of intelligence and maturity. War has been envisioned as a great cleansing to make room for something better.

Yet because of the dramatic uncertainty of the future, visions of future war frequently create fear and apprehension over whether order and peace will prevail in the world (the hopeful and creative outcome), or whether the forces of chaos and destruction will bring an end to human civilization or some particular human society. The forces of evolution and entropy spiral around the existential possibility space of war, haunting our future.

In general, war, and especially future war, is a theme running back through the historical tributaries of science fiction. It is noteworthy that the "first" science fiction novel, Lucian's *True History*, included war as a main narrative thread—in this case one taking place in outer space and waged on a colossal scale. Lucian's was a prescient vision, for outer space would become a primary battleground for modern science fiction stories of future war, with popular action-packed scenarios bursting forth in great ferocity in the early twentieth century in the writings of Wells, Garrett Serviss, "Doc" Smith, Joseph Campbell, and Olaf Stapledon, among others.

To recall, one of the first modern futurist fictions to deal with war was the novel *Reign of King George VI, 1900-1925* (1763). But the vision of future war it presented did not anticipate any significant changes, tactical or technological. Loudon's *The Mummy!* (1827), written roughly sixty years later, also contains numerous episodes describing military leaders, battles, extended military campaigns, and armed sieges and bombardments of cities in an imagined twenty-second century, but again, the scenarios, characters, weapons, and values all sound very reflective of the past, rather than of anything really new and different being foreseen in the future.

All in all, from the seventeenth through the nineteenth centuries, many fiction and non-fiction writers (predominately the latter) did expound on the possibilities of future wars—as predictions, nationalistic exultations, "calls to arms," and warnings to provoke preparedness (Roberts, 2005). And even if the human imagination fell short in realizing the strange and different possibilities of future war, by the mid-nineteenth century apprehension over potential new threats posed by modern warfare had taken hold of human consciousness. Although the Enlightenment vision of secular progress viewed technological development as an instrument of human progress and benefit, the double-edged sword of technological evolution also brought with it the possibilities of more advanced and powerful weapons of destruction. The American Civil War, for example, saw the introduction of "iron clad" battleships (a technological jump), rendering all existing navies across the globe obsolete. As another ominous new technological development, the rapid fire Gatling Gun (the machine gun) was invented in 1861 and used, although sparingly, in the Civil War. The world of war was changing.

The fuse that ignited the explosive profusion of futurist war narratives toward the end of the nineteenth century was George Chesney's (1830-1895) *The Battle of Dorking*. A Captain in the Royal Engineers of the British Army, Chesney came at the topic of future war with the intent to create an effective warning scenario that would motivate the British Empire into action and greater military preparedness. After observing how quickly and decisively Prussia had defeated France in the Franco-Prussian War (1870-1871)—in great part due to Prussian superiority in the use of modern technology coupled with the effective and organized implementation of strategy and tactics—Chesney published a number of letters and articles arguing that Britain was ill-prepared for a possible conflict with Prussia. Hoping to galvanize the British government and military into action, the effect of these published warnings was nonetheless negligible. Undeterred, Chesney decided to change his approach and write a story, dramatically and concretely depicting Great Britain's devastating military defeat by invading foreign forces (not explicitly identified as Prussian but strongly implied).

Told from the perspective of a veteran of the battle fifty years after its occurrence, *The Battle of Dorking: Reminiscences of a Volunteer* (1871) was an immediate and stupendous success. As one reviewer stated, "We do not know that we ever saw anything better in any magazine ... it describes exactly what we all feel." Written first as a serial in a popular magazine but later published as a stand alone short novel, the narrator describes how invading forces from the European mainland first destroy the presumably invincible British Navy with mysterious technological weapons ("fatal engines") and then invade England, routing the ill-prepared and disorganized British forces at the Battle of Dorking; from there, they conquer all of Great Britain, breaking apart and destroying the British Empire.

The story shocked and outraged the British populace as well as the British government and military, becoming a bestseller and acquiring significant notoriety in other Western nations around the world. Was Great Britain (or any other established world power) prepared for cutting-edge modern warfare? Or was the country still living in the past? Although the novel does describe modern technologies of war, Chesney focuses on the arrogance, complacency, and foolishness of the British government and people, who assumed that because England had realized a position of great power in the modern world its future would naturally continue along similar lines. England, as Chesney states, had come to expect ongoing "wealth and prosperity" without thoughtfully considering other possibilities or dangers. By simply reveling in past glories and relaxing in the comforts of the present with no significant thought of the immense possibilities of change in the future, England was "ripe for the fall."

The Battle of Dorking is a clear effort to heighten future consciousness in both the public and the government, its primary intent to shake people out of complacency and false security. As the narrator states in the novel, "... the bitterest part of our reflection is that all this misery and decay might have been so easily prevented and that we brought it about ourselves by our own shortsighted recklessness." With the publication of the book, it became harder to envision future war primarily through a past or present perspective. Rather, *The Battle of Dorking* heightened readers' consciousness of the future, in particular of the potential transformations that could occur in future weaponry, military tactics, cultural values, and the new global politics.

Chesney's novel also played on modern Western concerns over the competitive balance of national powers, as well as the related issue of nationalistic pride. Although many nations were more prosperous and technologically advanced than in the past, and populations were better off with a seemingly never-ending flow of new gadgets and conveniences, basic human motivation still reflected fundamental insecurities connected with the "law of the jungle," "survival of the fittest" (the strongest), and fear of the "other." Paranoia and perceptions of threat did not diminish with secular progress. Nationalistic pride continued, if not intensified; wars continued across the globe. In fact, prosperity and technological advancement triggered greater competition. It seemed as if the primordial human mind became more emboldened through ongoing economic-technological development. Getting more did not satisfy; rather it provoked greater hunger. The ongoing wars among nations in the late nineteenth century were an evolutionary battlefield for survival and supremacy, facilitated by the advancing powers of modernity and technology. In this regard, Chesney's novel stoked the flames and passions of nationalistic competition.

More significantly regarding the evolution of science fiction, *The Battle of Dorking* not only motivated the British government, or other nations where the novel also became well known, to upgrade and transform their military capabilities, but it also ignited a huge outpouring of other future war novels. Indeed, in the decades to come, *The Battle of Dorking* spawned the creation of a literary genre, the "future invasion" narrative. According to some estimates, up to four hundred future war (or invasion) novels were published between 1871 and the outbreak of World War I in 1914. In fact, we can view this "literary craze," which was especially pronounced in Great Britain, as an ongoing prophetic litany that both anticipated and provoked the eventual worldwide military conflict to come. A reviewer of the novel, writing in 1914, saw very strong parallels between the state of international affairs in 1871 and 1914, reinforcing the novel's continued relevance to contemporary affairs and considerations regarding the threat of war. Starting with *The Battle of Dorking*, future war novels had a strong impact on the thinking, imagination, emotions, and even government policies concerning the possibilities of war and military development. Consciousness was heightened and agitated; trigger fingers became itchy; guns got bigger. Future war novels both reflected and amplified public consciousness and worry over potential invasion or war. Insofar as such "future war" novels fall within science fiction, they provide a dramatic example of how science fiction (and visions of the future) not only reflect but actually influence events in the world. Such impact can certainly be seen in what is probably the apotheosis of future war novels leading up to World War I, those of H. G. Wells: *The War of the Worlds* (1898), *The War in the Air* (1908), and *The World Set Free* (1914), the latter two novels anticipating mass aerial warfare and the use of atomic bombs leading to the destruction of much of human civilization.

Even granting the great abundance of future war novels during the period of 1871 to 1914, the narrative theme of "future war" in science fiction would even further evolve in intensity of imagination and graphic destruction. The space operas of John Campbell and "Doc" Smith, for example, in the 1930s reached gargantuan heights in techno-violence and world annihilation. Moreover in the last sixty years, we have witnessed another escalation in the imagination of destruction. Perhaps we could date this further jump in evolution from the cinematic production of *The War of the Worlds* (1953). With the emergence of modern cinematic special effects, the narrative theme of future war has increased in popularity over recent decades, now offering viewers mind-blowing, perceptually jolting, multi-sensory experiences of fantastically destructive weapons, massive conflicts, and colossal devastation.

Throughout history the human mind has obsessed over war, chaos, and destruction. And with modern science fiction's focus on the future and its imaginative visions of futurist weaponry carried to the extreme, one of the central mythic themes of contemporary science fiction has been the terrifying and colossal possibilities of future war, upon which the destiny and very survival of humankind hangs in the balance. Such scenarios hit us on the deepest existential level. They bring into question our continued existence, hyper-stimulating our senses and our emotions, and triggering our fundamental drive for survival. We are drawn to such images like a moth to the flame.

All in all, the power of the *The Battle of Dorking* and the influence it achieved seems to greatly derive from the graphic and gruesome sensory and psychological detail in the story. The protagonist of the tale observes and personally experiences the carnage and confusion, the suffering, the filth and chaos, and the bloody and deadly ugliness of the failed effort to defend England against the vastly superior, better organized invading forces. There is ongoing disarray and mismanagement of military maneuvers; supplies and food are often lacking; military communications break down. Our protagonist sees his friends suffer and die without proper medical attention. His fellow troops fall victim to exhaustion, anxiety, terror, and depression. Eventually they experience great humiliation over their defeat, the whole country spiraling into a state of psychological degradation. The whole experience is existentially horrendous and putrid; the disaster is *felt* through the raw senses of the narrator. Although based on a rational argument for preparedness in the face of the uncertainty and transformative nature of the future, the message is primarily conveyed at an emotional and sensory level, alarming people out of their closed-minded lethargy.

Recall that Chesney was unsuccessful in influencing public consciousness through his non-fiction essays and letters on the potential threats and dangers of future invasion and war. But with the publication of a fictional futurist story he had an immediate and significant effect on people's minds. As I stated early in this book, science fiction as futurist narrative is the most influential form of modern futurist thinking because of its narrative form and its capacity to stimulate holistic future consciousness. Describing in dramatic form, with all the blood and guts, violent confrontations, colorful heroes and villains, and accompanying stress and traumatic emotions, science fiction narratives of future war powerfully grab and move human consciousness at a personal level, much more so than non-fiction essays or books. The addition of modern special effects further magnifies the psychologically holistic effect. But this increased holistic power brings with it concerns over self-fulfilling prophecies and the "priming of the pump" of our aggressive impulses. In this regard, *The Battle of Dorking*, followed by the numerous other future war novels that culminated in Wells' powerful narrative visions, helped prepare and fortify, for better or worse, the modern mind for modern war.

* * *

The power of custom is enormous, and so gradual will be the change, that man's sense of what is due to himself will be at no time rudely shocked; our bondage will steal upon us noiselessly and by imperceptible approaches ...
Samuel Butler

The Romantic unease with secular progress, modernization, and industrial-technological growth continued throughout the nineteenth century. The Luddite movement (1811-1817), which emerged specifically in opposition to the introduction of new labor saving technologies within the textile industry, became symbolic of a general philosophical opposition toward any and all forms of new technology, automation, and industrialization in the modern world. And in contemporary times, the term "luddite" has come to mean an absolute antagonism toward technology or technological progress.

An influential movement to come out of this Romantic reaction against industrialized modernization was American transcendentalism. First articulated in the writings of Ralph Waldo Emerson (1802-1883) during the 1830s and 1840s, it advocated for a re-connection with nature and a more wholesome and simple life. Transcendentalism was a philosophy of individual freedom and self-sufficiency set in opposition to the perceived corrupting and repressive influences of modern society. (Contrary to the promises of the Enlightenment, modernity seemed to be generating increased regimentation taking away our freedom.) Supporting a spiritual life, grounded in individual intuition (a Romantic vision to be contrasted with the rationalism of the Enlightenment), transcendentalism contributed to the ongoing development of utopian thought in the nineteenth century, provoking the establishment of experimental communities following its principles, such as Brook Farm and Fruitlands (Lombardo, J. B., 2010).

Probably the most famous book inspired by transcendentalism was Henry David Thoreau's (1817-1862) *Walden; or, Life in the Woods* first published in 1854. A close friend of Emerson, Thoreau spent roughly two years living in a self-built cabin in the woodlands near Walden Pond. During his time there, Thoreau led a relatively solitary and contemplative existence, existing in resonance with and deep appreciation of nature. After returning to modern urban society, Thoreau wrote *Walden*, recounting his alternative way of life in the wild, and providing a thoughtful meditation on the benefits of a life of simplicity and self-sufficiency. Aside from praising the numerous benefits associated with this unencumbered way of life, *Walden* was also a damning critique of modernity, consumerism, materialism, and the Western obsession with progress. *Walden* describes an intentional "spiritual journey" of discovery and insight set in the context of the stark reality and beauty of physical nature, a reality, according to Thoreau, increasingly disconnected from modern Western consciousness.

Yet, from a philosophical and imaginative perspective, the most thought-provoking and engaging critique of technological growth in the later nineteenth century was Samuel Butler's *Erewhon: or, Over the Range* (1872). Often compared with Bulwer-Lytton's *Vril, The Power of the Coming Race* (1871) and William Morris' agrarian utopia *News from Nowhere* (1890), Butler's *Erewhon* describes an ambiguous utopian-dystopian society, where modern industry and technology have been outlawed. The title of the book, "Erewhon," is (with slight variation) "nowhere" spelled backwards. In the tradition of More's *Utopia* and Swift's *Gullivers' Travels*, the novel describes the protagonist's discovery of a hypothetical human society that exists in some far away and unknown land.

There are, at least, two noteworthy dimensions to *Erewhon* that are especially important in the history of science fiction. First, Butler connects the issue of increasing technological growth in the modern world with the theory of evolution. Butler read Darwin's *The Origin of Species* (1859), and finding Darwin's ideas highly significant, he himself wrote four books on evolution during his life. In *Erewhon*, Butler presents the argument that machines are evolving in ways analogous to the evolution of biological life, but—disconcertingly—much more quickly and effectively than humans. Modern machines (anything invented in roughly the last four hundred years) do not exist in the society of Erewhon because the population—inspired by a famous essay "The Book of the Machines" written by an Erewhonian scientist—believes that if technological evolution is left unchecked, machines will eventually develop the capacities of self-consciousness and super-human intelligence. In so doing they will become superior beings totally ruling over humanity, as masters to slaves, and replacing us as the dominant form of life on the earth.

Second, within this anti-machine framework, *Erewhon* presents an extremely bizarre human society, one in which, relative to the modern West, values, beliefs, and customs are turned upside-down. The strange psycho-social reality of the land provides the narrator with a host of unusual ideas to contemplate and puzzle over. *Erewhon*, indeed, is rich in philosophical reflection and speculative inquiry, provoked in the narrator by the exceedingly odd assortment of ideas, values, and customs within Erewhonian society—criminals, for example, are treated with sympathy and victims of disease are viewed with moral contempt. Our consciousness of psycho-social possibilities is expanded into the range of "hypothetics," a term found in the story that refers to the realm of the extraordinary beyond the commonplace. In fact, the beliefs and customs of Erewhon are so peculiar and fantastic that the novel simultaneously realizes great philosophical depth and perspective, and human comedy and perversion.

Erewhon tells the story of a young man, the narrator of the novel, who has emigrated from England to a far away, unspecified territory in the British Empire. This new land has been settled primarily by cattle and sheep farmers, but our narrator is drawn to the huge mountain range bordering the settled land, and one day sets out to see what may exist "over the range."

After crossing the mountain range, he comes upon a lovely pastoral land dotted with villages and towns and populated by stunningly handsome "dark-complected" humans who also appear radiantly healthy. The first inhabitants he meets in this new land, which they refer to as Erewhon, take him into one of the towns. There it's discovered that he is carrying a watch, which highly upsets the town's magistrate, and he is placed in prison. (It is unclear whether he is imprisoned for having the watch or for appearing poor.)

But after an extended stay in the prison, during which time he first observes and reflects upon the strange customs of his captors, he is released (apparently because he is light-complected). He is taken to live with a highly esteemed and wealthy citizen in another town, who is *recovering* from an act of embezzlement he perpetrated on a poor and unfortunate woman. Oddly, the wealthy citizen is not only receiving treatment by a "straightener" but also sympathy from his friends and neighbors, while the poor woman has been blamed and punished for her bad luck in falling victim to the embezzler.

As the story unfolds, our narrator explores various locations and different institutions in Erewhon, including the "Musical Banks" (where worthless money is religiously deposited) and "The College of Unreason," all the while observing and commenting on the odd beliefs and behaviors of Erewhonians. He also falls in love with the embezzler's younger daughter. In the story's conclusion, he convinces the king and queen of Erewhon to allow him to build a balloon, presumably to interview the "air-god"—the Erewhonians fanatically personify and deify all natural forces and qualities of human personality— and he escapes with the daughter, returning to his own land on the other side of the mountain range.

As just a sample of the strange customs of Erewhon encountered by our narrator: Physical illness is considered criminal and immoral and victims are imprisoned for it, with the greater the illness, the greater the punishment; the more the physical illness seems beyond the control of the person, the more the person is blamed for it; if a person is a victim of misfortune and bad luck, they are not given sympathy, but viewed as putting a "black mark" on society; immorality and criminal behavior, though, are viewed as forms of victimization, worthy of sympathy, hospitalization, and treatment by "straighteners"; people openly talk about their mental problems and immoral behaviors, but obsessively attempt to hide any physical problems or infirmities (which is one main reason why everyone in Erewhon looks so healthy); Erewhonians believe in the pre-existence of human souls before birth and think that the unborn haunt and hound their parents into birthing them; consequently parents who must suffer through the indignity of birth (especially the mother who is hidden away during her pregnancy) are exonerated of any blame or responsibility pertaining to the behavior and character of their children after they are born; at birth the child has to "sign" a "Birth Formulae" absolving his or her parents of any accountability for their behavior; and finally, in the College of Unreason, students are taught, among other things, how to evade and defend all errors and irrationalities in their thinking and to balance reason with unreason, while professors, some of whom have the title of "Professors of Inconsistency and Evasion," learn the art of sitting on the fence on all topics, so as never to be wrong about anything, and they frequently suffer from the "fear-of-giving-themselves-away-disease."

All in all, from the point of view of the narrator, the Erewhonian philosophy of life seems comically absurd, and the people mad in living this philosophy. Yet, many of the qualities of Erewhon perversely exaggerate negative features of contemporary Western society. For example, citizens of Erewhon suffer from deep hypocrisy, as do late nineteenth-century Europeans, ostensibly worshiping gods and idols that they actually put no practical faith in at all. (Musical Banks are like European churches.) Aside from providing an expanded mind space in which to consider outlandish possibilities of human mentality and society, *Erewhon* is in some ways a dystopian satire on the modern world.

During his time in Erewhon, the narrator learns that a great war took place four hundred years earlier in Erewhon between the machinists and the anti-machinists. Provoked by the publication of the essay "The Book of the Machines," half the citizens of Erewhon perished in this war. The anti-machinists emerged victorious, leading to the elimination of much of the technology in Erewhon. Our narrator obtains a copy of the famous essay and summarizes its content in three chapters toward the end of the novel.

These chapters, collectively titled "The Book of the Machines," were based on earlier essays Butler wrote titled "Darwin Among the Machines" and "The Mechanical Creation" (1863, 1865). In these chapters the argument is developed that the scientific principles of evolution and life apply to machines as well as biological life forms, and that given the ways that humans care for and interact with machines, it makes perfect evolutionary sense to predict that machines will continue to rapidly evolve in intelligence, complexity, and power, eventually usurping humankind's dominion on the earth. Machines are evolving much faster than any existing biological life form. And they exhibit most of the basic processes of biology (metabolism, digestion, and reproduction) even if these processes are recreated in a different fashion.

As stated in "The Book of the Machines":

What sort of creature man's next successor in the supremacy of the earth is likely to be. We have often heard this debated; but it appears to us that we are ourselves creating our own successors; we are daily adding to the beauty and delicacy of their physical organization; we are daily giving them greater power and supplying by all sorts of ingenious contrivances that self-regulating, self-acting power which will be to them what intellect has been to the human race. In the course of ages we shall find ourselves the inferior race ...

Moreover,

Day by day ... the machines are gaining ground upon us; day by day we are becoming more subservient to them; more men are daily bound down as slaves to tend them, more men are daily devoting the energies of their whole lives to the development of mechanical life. The upshot is simply a question of time, but that the time will come when the machines will hold the real supremacy over the world and its inhabitants is what no person of a truly philosophic mind can for a moment question.

In the above quotes, Butler proposes a theory of the *purposeful evolution* of technology, facilitated by humans, to explain the evolution of machines. Humans are intentionally improving and evolving machines, with great devotion and energy. But as described throughout the three chapters, in this process humans are progressively becoming parasites on the machines— dependent on them — even while providing for various biological functions in the machine population, such as reproduction (we keep making more and more improved copies of them) and resource/nourishment procurement (we fuel them).

Not only did Butler see the relevance of the process of evolution toward understanding the ongoing development of machines and technology, he also, as illustrated in the above quotes, taps into the human fear that we are becoming enslaved by our technologies, as opposed to our technologies serving us. The promise of the Enlightenment was the empowerment of humanity through science and technology; the promise was the betterment of the human condition. But in the nineteenth century there was the growing apprehension, fueled by Romanticism and reinforced by observations on the ongoing mechanization of human life, that the world of industry and machines was increasingly controlling us (a dystopian vision) rather than vice versa. Who is the master and who is the slave in all of this? "The Book of the Machines" clearly and powerfully explains that we are the slaves rather than the masters. Further, what we are doing is creating our successors and speeding our own demise. Applying the principles of evolution, Butler scientifically justifies humanity's apprehensions about technology.

Looking toward the future, Butler speculates that:

... there is reason to hope that the machines will use us kindly, for their existence will be in a great measure dependent upon ours; they will rule us with a rod of iron, but they will not eat us; they will not only require our services in the reproduction and education of their young, but also in waiting upon them as servants; in gathering food for them, and feeding them; in restoring them to health when they are sick; and in either burying their dead or working up their deceased members into new forms of mechanical existence.

The perceived threat of the ascendency and domination of machines leads to an inevitable conclusion: Before it is too late, death to the machines.

War to the death should be instantly proclaimed against them. Every machine of every sort should be destroyed by the well-wisher of his species. Let there be no exceptions made, no quarter shown; let us at once go back to the primeval condition of the race.

This call to war is what provoked the violent confrontation in Erewhon between the machinists — those who wished to preserve technology — and the anti-machinists — those who wished to destroy the machines and protect humanity before it was too late. Butler's idea of a "war" involving the destruction of machines (eliminating them before they get the upper hand) morphs in twentieth-century science fiction into the general narrative theme of a "war with intelligent technology" (including robots), such as envisioned in *Terminator* and *The Matrix*. If machines are gaining in power and intelligence through time, at what point will they develop the self-consciousness, intelligence, and capacity to resist and fight against any human efforts to eradicate them or "turn them off"? (Perhaps it is already too late to "pull the plug"?) At what point in time might the machines become the proactive aggressors, deciding that humans are a threat or encumbrance? And when will we need to be eliminated? Or will the machines perhaps impose some deeper form of enslavement on humanity in order to better realize their mechanistic purposes? In *Erewhon*, the machines need us to perpetuate their evolution; in *The Matrix* we are their power supply. In twentieth-century science fiction, we not only go to war with ourselves (nothing new), we go to war with the machines.

The war scenario of humans versus machines is part of the more general archetypal narrative in modern science fiction of the struggle to maintain our humanity in the context of the ubiquitous and accelerative development of technology. As envisioned in various science fiction tales, technological growth may destroy our humanity in many different ways aside from militant conquest or the elimination of the species; we may become more machine-like as technology increasingly infuses into human society, losing our soul, our creativity, our emotionality, our self-reliance, and our inner direction in the process. See for example, E. M. Forster's "The Machine Stops" (1909), Yevgeny Zamyatin's *We* (1921), and Jack Williamson's *The Humanoids* (1949). Yet, just to keep in mind, the issue of humanity and technology is a contentious area of debate. As an expression of the philosophy of the Enlightenment, we can view technology as facilitating the empowerment of humanity rather than our disempowerment or extinction (Kurzweil, 1999, 2005). Innumerable science fiction stories envision just this type of future scenario.

Butler's discussion of the ongoing evolution of machines also seriously considers the question of machine consciousness. Although machines, however complex, can be viewed as automata, possessing neither a will of their own nor self-awareness or consciousness, Butler asks whether there is any plausible scientific or philosophical reason for denying the possibility that machines may realize consciousness, volitional self-control, or creativity in the future. As least, as he states in "The Book of Machines," he does not see any convincing reason for rejecting these possibilities. In modern times, at least since Descartes and his dualistic theory of mind and body, machines have been viewed as mechanical contraptions powered by physical forces, without anything like a soul or inner consciousness. But as we move through the twentieth century, the question of machine consciousness has become an increasingly plausible possibility (Kurzweil, 1999, 2005). This question is addressed even in the late nineteenth century; see *The Future Eve* (1886), described in the next chapter, for a thoughtful consideration of a self-conscious robot that possesses more "inner humanity" than some human characters in the story. Science fiction in the twentieth century becomes populated with a host of different robots and forms of artificial intelligence that seem to evince such qualities as purpose, self-identity, emotion, moral conscience, creativity, and inner awareness. Can we so unequivocally reject as scientifically implausible such hypothetical future realities, of consciousness emerging in machines? Butler thinks not.

In summary, Samuel Butler presents in *Erewhon* a highly engaging, thought provoking, and comically entertaining narration of a strange human culture that expands our imagination of the possibilities of human societies. The novel provokes us into pondering the ambiguity surrounding utopian versus dystopian realities. Further, Butler offers a convincing exposition on the potential future evolution of machines and machine consciousness. Some reviewers saw "The Book of the Machines" and the envisioned Erewhonian society that outlawed technology as an attempt, on Butler's part, to reduce "Darwin's theory to an absurdity." Butler rejected this interpretation, though, stating that he had the "most profound admiration" for "Mr. Darwin's theory." Whatever his intentions, Butler's *Erewhon* should be remembered for realistically and thoughtfully describing how machines, through the evolutionary process and the purposeful and selective involvement of humans, could overtake and assimilate humanity, an idea that would haunt science fiction imagination in the century to come.

* * *

... the various forms under which the forces of matter are made manifest have one common origin; or, in other words, are so directly related and mutually dependent, that they are convertible, as it were, into one another, and possess equivalents of power in their action.

Sir Edward Bulwer-Lytton

Considering the multitude of further writings, philosophical speculations, social initiatives, esoteric and underground organizations, and even commercial products provoked and inspired by the book, Sir Edward Bulwer-Lytton's (1803-1873) *Vril, The Power of the Coming Race* (1871) was the most popular and influential science fiction novel of the 1870s. (Indeed, it was one of the most impactful science fiction books of the entire nineteenth century.) Although it can be argued that the novel is relatively weak on plot, the book addresses a vast and comprehensive array of topics, including: human evolution; advanced technologies; telepathy; religion and metaphysics; utopian social thought; gender roles and sex; art and the humanities; the connection of the mental and the physical; and just about every other aspect of human existence. As an adventure into the unknown, involving contact with a distinctive and different form of mentality and social order, and weaving together technological speculations with psychological and humanistic themes, it is true science fiction in scope and subject matter (at least as much so as anything published up to that point in time). In fact, *Vril, The Power of the Coming Race* is a highly philosophical science fiction novel, delving into the deep issues of existence and human reality. Moreover, adding to the aura and mystique of the book, its themes and ideas became strongly associated with mesmerism, spiritualism, and the occult; the novel bridges the divide between the scientific and the supernatural.

The plot of the novel is relatively simple and based on a recurrent story line in science fiction, similar in ways to *Erewhon*, but also *Niels Klim's Underground Travels* and *Symzonia*. The protagonist and narrator of the story journeys into the interior of the earth and comes upon an advanced civilization of human-like beings (the "Vril-ya") who live in numerous spacious caverns in the subterranean depths of our world. The protagonist is taken by the Vril-ya into one of their cities, and as becomes clear to him early in the story, is held against his will. The bulk of the novel involves the narrator interacting with the Vril-ya and describing at length various features of their underground civilization. Like *Erwehon*, the story serves as a commentary on an alternative society. As events unfold, one of the female inhabitants—a scientist and scholar who towers in height over the narrator—falls in love with him and wants to bond. Our protagonist is totally shocked by this overture, which contradicts his stereotypes on acceptable gender roles. More alarmingly, he discovers that he is going to be eliminated (due to the impure effects of his presence on this ideal society). With the help of a youth who has befriended him, he escapes back to the surface of the earth and sets out to warn humanity of the immense power and potential threat of this advanced underground civilization.

A key feature of this underground society is their capacity to control through technological instruments and devices the energetic power of "Vril," which they identify as the pervasive and fundamental form of energy that exists throughout all of nature. Given what is said in the book, as well as in other writings by Bulwer-Lytton, "Vril" seems to be basically equivalent to electrical energy. The Vril-ya, who have named themselves after their fundamental power source, have created all the various wonders of their civilization through harnessing the power of Vril; Vril is apparently an unlimited energy source. They have animated automata servants powered by Vril; they can heal themselves of disease, ill-health, or injury using Vril; they have colossally powerful destructive weapons energized through Vril; they have telepathic powers and flying apparatus (attachable/detachable wings) energized by Vril. Perhaps most significantly, they have created personalized wands that channel and direct the energy of Vril (of body and mind) and are under the individualized control of the will and desire of the users. Through Vril, this society has achieved incredible technological power over both the physical world and mental reality, one that the citizens can control with their conscious minds.

As our narrator learns, from early on in life the Vril-ya are educated to effectively and wisely use the powers of their personal technological wands. Undergirding this educational system, there is also a selective eugenic process to facilitate greater and greater resonance between the psycho-physiological make-up of newborn Vril-ya and their wands. The Vril-ya are guiding their own biological evolution to make themselves increasingly compatible with their central physical technology. Thus we have both an evolving bio-techno resonance occurring in the Vril-ya, as well as a guided psycho-educational development of young Vril-ya, as they learn to bring their minds into increasing attunement with their technology. In short, the Vril-ya are progressively developing an increasing intimacy of mind, body, and machine in their civilization. They are purposefully self-evolving cyborgs in the true sense of the word.

The Vril-ya believe that their highly advanced civilization only emerged from barbaric and primitive beginnings when they first learned to understand and utilize the power of Vril. As they describe their ancient history, the legends of their far past seem to indicate that they are descendants from surface humans (thus our genetic cousins) who, escaping a "great flood," ventured into the earth's subterranean caverns. After thousands of years of challenges and false starts—in many ways parallel to human history—the Vril-ya finally came into their own with the discovery of Vril. The message—one resonant with the Western Enlightenment—is that powerful technologies, if wisely used, will facilitate the emergence of a highly evolved society. The Vril-ya have created a utopia through the technological channeling and utilization of the primal forces of nature.

As introduced in previous chapters, different perspectives are taken on the relationship of advancing technology and its impact on human society. Bulwer-Lytton's novel depicts technology as something that can be effectively controlled—if we evolve our minds accordingly. Evolving technology will support human empowerment and facilitate an improved human society. How different from *Erewhon* (and many other science fiction novels and movies) that conversely taps into the fearful perspective that technology will undermine (conquer or repress) humanity.

Yet, the fearful mindset can engender another type of scenario in which, primed to be apprehensive about ever-evolving machines, humans may behave prejudicially and unethically toward future intelligent technologies. Such a plot device renders the machines more admirable and ethical than the paranoid fearful humans, as we will see in many science fiction stories to come. (See, for example, Isaac Asimov's *I, Robot* 1950 and his robot detective series, such as *The Caves of Steel* 1954.) If there is a good guy and a bad guy (humans versus machines) in the ongoing saga of future evolution, who is the good guy and who is the bad guy?

The extensive scope of topics covered in *Vril, The Power of the Coming Race* derives from observations provided by the narrator of the novel, on Vril-ya behavior, values, and beliefs, and the various organizational dimensions of their civilization. As other key features of Vril-ya society described by the narrator:

There is essentially no poetry, art, and or fictional literature because, according to the Vril-ya, all these pursuits are grounded in human pathos and struggle, which have by and large been eliminated. The pursuit of riches, political power, or fame offer little if any value either, and the philosophies of competitive individualism and democratic debate have been rejected (or transcended). There is both inner and collective harmony in Vril-ya society.

As one of the Vril-ya asserts, their civilization is based on "... the art of diffusing throughout a community the tranquil happiness which belongs to a virtuous and well-ordered household." In another passage, a proverb of the Vril-ya is quoted: "No happiness without order, no order without authority, no authority without unity." All is one. Their vision of the ideal society emphasizes communalism and social order over individualism.

Despite all this, the Vril-ya do not have a strong authoritarian top-down government; in fact, the system of government is marginal and weakly articulated. The Vril-ya believe in the good of the whole and by and large do not attempt to coerce each other to act in particular ways. There is a genuine (though not perfect) agreeableness among them.

At the core of their belief system is a universal acknowledgement of a Supreme Being, just, all-powerful, and beneficent. They also have faith in an afterlife. There are no atheists and they do not debate or discuss the nature of God or the afterlife, which they acknowledge is beyond their comprehension. There is no theology; there are no conflicting religions or religious wars. Further, their metaphysical beliefs are synthesized with their scientific beliefs, technology, and social system.

The Vril-ya have the ability to fly through the air with their Vril-empowered mechanical wings and, as the human protagonist discovers, they possess the capacity to control (to some degree at least) the mind of the narrator—and by implication other surface dwelling humans as well. This capacity is one of the most disturbing and yet amazing powers of the Vril-ya. Not only can they channel physical energy with their highly evolved minds, they can direct the flow of thoughts and feelings in the minds of others as well.

The underground world of the Vril-ya is an extensive and intricate network of cities; as their population increases, they simply create new cities, methodically planned out, in unsettled caverns underneath the earth. But their population keeps growing and the number of empty caverns for new cities is steadily diminishing.

There is a strong didactic quality to the extensive descriptions of all these features of the civilization of the Vril-ya, including those on their language, aesthetics, and architecture, all of which present philosophical and practical arguments for the value and superior functionality of their society. In this sense the novel is both philosophical and utopian, and more an argued treatise on an ideal society than a gripping and complex dramatic narrative.

Yet a key dramatic point emerges: Because of their amazing social cohesion, superior mental and physical capabilities, and incredibly powerful technology, the narrator realizes the extreme threat they present to human civilization on the surface of the earth. The Vril-ya are aware of the existence of surface humans and our unruly and barbaric ways (which they see as a threat to their ideally ordered society). Alas, we are not aware of them. Further, as mentioned above, their population keeps growing, pushing the limits of available space below the surface. In the near future they may be forced to emerge from below; they have seriously considered this possibility. And given the fact that they have no compunction about killing any living entity that disrupts their harmonious and intelligent way of life, our narrator concludes that surface humans are in great danger of being invaded in the near future by the Vril-ya.

One fascinating aspect of the social impact of this novel is that many people felt it might not be entirely fictitious but rather, in some manner, prescient and possible. At the very least, the novel provoked a level of anxiety over the potential invasion by some mysterious and superior form of intelligence living under the surface of the earth. So aside from the general apprehension over potential invasion by a neighboring nation—as provoked by *The Battle of Dorking* and other future war novels—the book seeded the additional fear of being invaded by some more mysterious force lying right beneath our feet. In the 1870s then, science fiction clearly amplified social paranoia along numerous dimensions: Machines may supplant and destroy us; other nations may invade and conquer us with better weaponry; or superior humans may come popping out of holes in the ground and wipe us out.

A second provocative development instigated by the publication of the novel was the recurrent associations it engendered with the occult, the supernatural, and mesmerism. Bulwer-Lytton had previously published several books dealing with these topics, and although he explicitly connects the concept of Vril with both electricity and some underlying unifying physical force that could be understood through science, many readers of *Vril, The Power of the Coming Race* connected this powerful hypothetical energetic force with some kind of supernatural or psychic power that permeates through nature. Numerous writers and esoteric mystical groups found inspiration in Bulwer-Lytton's novel. And as we will see, throughout the latter part of the nineteenth century, science fiction was often mixed up with spiritualist and mystical ideas, the latter mode of thinking being a strong feature of popular culture and consciousness during this time.

As chronicled throughout this history, science fiction has repeatedly influenced society in numerous ways. As with *The Battle of Dorking*, Bulwer-Lytton's novel is another good example of how science fiction writers observe, ponder, and extrapolate on ideas and possibilities that could impact the ongoing evolution of human reality—and then feed those ideas back to society.

Building upon a well-articulated and comprehensive utopian vision, the two key innovative themes developed in *Vril, The Power of the Coming Race* are: First, evolution is applied to all aspects of a civilization, inclusive of the technology, biology, and psychology of its inhabitants; and second, the book offers an insightful treatment of the purposeful co-evolution of minds and biological bodies coupled with technology. The power and future potential of mind and matter are brought together into an integrative evolutionary whole.

This being the case, *Vril, The Power of the Coming Race* provides a comprehensively developed vision of an evolutionary, advanced society of human-like beings that greatly surpasses that of present day humanity. Physically and biologically, the Vril-ya are healthier, bigger, and more robust than present humanity; the Vril-ya are a product of biological selective breeding and advanced medical technologies. And their minds and characters are more evolved as well, exhibiting mental powers and cognitive capacities beyond us, as well as personalities that seem happier and more self-fulfilled. Vril-ya education is focused on psychological development and psycho-techno synthesis. Although the narrator sees the Vril-ya in some ways as heartless, the Vril-ya perceive themselves as much more civilized and ethically advanced than us. The evolved quality of their utopian society is a reflection of the advanced level of the individual members. Reciprocally, the society collectively supports their evolved individual personalities. Moreover, as stated above, the human-techno cyborg synthesis has been significantly developed in the Vril-ya, vastly transcending any such melding in contemporary humans. The Vril-ya are in harmony with their machines and their underlying energy source. Their total being—biological, psychological, social, and ecological—is techno-empowered to the point of being almost god-like in nature.

Although the Vril-ya can engender uplifting and inspiring thoughts and feelings about the possibilities of the future evolution of intelligent life, they can equally provoke fear and apprehension. What is greater than us is to be feared as much as admired. This is a theme that future science fiction will address in considerable depth: If vastly superior humans emerge (and the Vril-ya are at one level just improved versions of ourselves) how will we react to them and how will they react to us? Is the evolutionary transcendence of humanity—a more evolved human—to be anticipated with hope or with fear? *Vril, The Power of the Coming Race* compels us to consider the dilemma; they may already be here, watching and waiting.

Vril, The Power of the Coming Race is one of the great classics of nineteenth-century science fiction.

Chapter 9

Utopias, Robots, and Cosmic Journeys

The Cosmic and Mystical: Camille Flammarion

Time lapses into eternity. But eternity remains and time is born again ... And these universes passed away in their turn. But infinite space remained, peopled with worlds, and stars, and souls, and suns; and time went on forever. For there can be neither end nor beginning.

Camille Flammarion

This chapter focuses primarily on the 1880s and 1890s, covering the further evolution of utopian-dystopian writings, tales of robots and "machine men," nightmares of the human mind, and visionary journeys into the outer reaches of the universe. The archetypal polarities of hope and fear, good and evil, nature and technology, science and spiritualism, and progress and collapse continue to manifest themselves in the science fiction tales of the time. And the science fiction character types of hero, anti-hero, and villain also continue to evolve in complexity and nuance.

Although ongoing advances in industry and technology supported the optimistic secular vision of continued progress, as Roberts (2005) notes there was also the contradictory theme of pessimism and decay running through the second half of the nineteenth century. The decay and pessimism thesis was a consequence of ongoing apprehensions over the ultimate benefit of science, technology, industry, and modernization—first expressed in the philosophy of Romanticism—as well as growing concerns over potential war and mayhem in the West (the proliferation of future war novels). The emerging cosmic-scientific vision of entropy and the heat death of the universe further fed into and reinforced the bleak and depressing visions of the ultimate future. All told, in the era science fiction was a platform for both hope and optimism, as well as fear, despair, and pessimism regarding the future.

As part of the negative reaction against the growth of science, technology, and secular thinking, mysticism, supernaturalism, and diverse forms of spiritualism (or "spiritism") were influential cultural movements throughout the nineteenth century. Even though the modern Western world was presumably moving away from superstition and metaphysics, the second half of the nineteenth century saw an upsurge in occult and spiritual practices and beliefs. Correspondingly, although modern science fiction was inspired by and anchored to new scientific discoveries and the new scientific vision of reality, mysticism and spiritual ideas repeatedly worked their way into nineteenth-century science fiction. As we've seen, Bulwer-Lytton's *Vril, The Power of the Coming Race* mixes together the potential wonders of electricity with mystical suggestions and speculations on psychic powers.

In the later nineteenth century, advances in astronomy further enriched the breadth and depth of space travel stories. And although without much scientific grounding, one popular theme involved anti-gravity devices and substances as a way to propel vehicles off the earth and into outer space. Roberts (2005) argues that, at the very least, the idea of anti-gravity substances propelling humans beyond the confines of the earth was a science fiction metaphor, symbolizing the sense of freedom of imagination produced by the scientific vision of reality and the feeling of unconstrained empowerment inspired by new scientific technologies. But as we will see, some writers did take the anti-gravity idea very seriously, treating the concept as scientifically credible.

Optimism and pessimism; evolution and the heat death of the universe; spiritualism and science; the wonders of astronomy and imaginary visitations to other worlds; and even Poe's oscillatory universe and Davy's ideas of astro-reincarnation: They all get woven together in the writings of Nicolas Camille Flammarion (1842-1925), the French astronomer and great popularizer of modern science. Flammarion is without question the most cosmic of all the science fiction writers described thus far, creating literary narratives that journeyed to the farthest reaches of space, time, and mind. His visions were ontologically expansive, drawing on the far distant future; reincarnation and the evolution of souls; alien worlds and life forms; disembodied spirits; the cosmology of good and evil; the revelatory nature of light; eternity and God; and more mathematical analysis and text than is found in any other science fiction writer up to that point in time.

Flammarion was a child prodigy, fascinated with astronomy from his early youth. By the age of sixteen he had written *A Visionary Journey to the Regions of the Moon, Related by an Adolescent Philosopher* and a huge philosophical-scientific treatise titled *Universal Cosmology*, later retitled and published as *The World Before the Creation of Humankind*. Aside from studying astronomy, he read and assimilated the evolutionary and scientific ideas of Davy, Lamarck, and Darwin.

As a young avid student, scholar, and devotee of astronomy, from his early twenties he began publishing both a regular scientific magazine on astronomy and an ongoing series of immensely popular science and astronomy books, doing "more than any other nineteenth-century writer to prepare the public for the cosmic perspective." Throughout his life he was a student of history as well, researching the historical development of ideas on the various scientific, philosophical, and cosmological themes he addressed in his books and articles.

Yet, along with his scientific studies, Flammarion also delved into the popular "spiritism" writings of his time, which, inspired by the influential visions of Emanuel Swedenborg (1688-1772), argued for such ideas as reincarnation and the progressive perfection of souls over successive lives. Flammarion was particularly impressed by Jean Reynaud (1806-1863), who believed that souls, released from the body after death, migrate from planet to planet, spiritually improving with each successive incarnation.

Reflecting these two seemingly polar fields of interest, he eventually created an astronomical observatory with a large telescope in his home and — on the other end of the philosophical spectrum — conducted seances there as well. Later in his life he focused on psychic and paranormal research, writing books on these areas of study as well. All told, he published over fifty books, ranging in topics from the solar system and the stars to disembodied spirits and life after death.

Flammarion can be placed in the line of thinking and cosmic visioning starting with Bruno, Kepler, de Fontenelle, and Huygens and continuing with Kant, Hershel, and Davy. Among Flammarion's many published books, those writings especially relevant to the evolution of science fiction include:

- *The Plurality of Habitable Worlds* (1862)
- *The Inhabitants of the Other World: Revelations of the After Life* (1862-1863)
- *Real and Imaginary Worlds* (1864)
- *Lumen* (1872 /Revision 1897)
- *Urania* (1889)
- *Omega: The End of the World* (1893-1894)
- *Popular Astronomy* (1894)

As a general theme running through many of Flammarion's books, John Clute (1995) describes Flammarion as "obsessed with life after death and life on other worlds." Given Flammarion's belief in the sequential reincarnation and evolution of souls occurring across diverse planets in the universe, the two central themes merge together, for life after death on the earth leads to life, reincarnated and progressively evolved, on other planets.

A recurrent theme in science fiction, the possibility of life on other planets can be seen as a scientifically legitimate area of inquiry. Influenced by evolutionary theory, Flammarion scientifically addressed this question in a number of his books: How would alien life adaptively and distinctively evolve, given the varied environmental conditions of different types of planets? He is, in fact, given credit for being the first writer to seriously address, from a scientific point of view, the potential wide diversity of alien life forms specific to different types of planetary environments. (To a great degree Huygens had considered this topic as well, but from a pre-evolutionary perspective.)

On the other hand, life after death is a theme associated with religious, spiritual, and mystical thought: What scientific evidence is there for immaterial souls continuing to exist after the death of the biological body? Almost all major world religions support some type of theory of a non-physical soul (or spirits) and some kind of afterlife. But such religious-spiritual ideas about the nature of reality were critically questioned, if not rejected and transcended, by modern science.

So, we could describe Flammarion as both a scientist and a mystic, attempting to reconcile two very different and seemingly incompatible visions of reality. As already noted on a number of occasions, combining these two perspectives is a recurrent phenomenon in science fiction, going all the way back to Kepler's mystical-scientific *Somnium*. Yet, what is noteworthy about Flammarion is that when he introduces spiritualist, religious, and metaphysical ideas, he repeatedly attempts to demonstrate the *scientific credibility* of such ideas; when Flammarion investigated psychic phenomena, he addressed the topic scientifically, subjecting apparent cases of psychic abilities to logical-empirical testing and analysis.

This point leads us back to another recurrent theme in the history of science fiction: What is scientifically plausible is open to debate and differences of opinion in science fiction (if not within science itself). We can view Flammarion as aspiring to a scientifically grounded spiritualism that extends into his grand cosmology, which is both evolutionary and theistic, uniting the mental and the physical, and the temporal and the eternal.

Moreover, in reading Flammarion we encounter another "union of opposites" for his commitment to science and astronomy had a distinctive "Romantic" dimension. He is a beautiful example of the "Romantic scientist" described by Holmes. As a great popularizer of science and scientific cosmology, Flammarion approached his subject matter with great passion, evincing a quality of spiritual elevation. For him, viewing the night sky evoked powerful emotions, brought deep pleasure, and engendered a great sense of wonder. His science fiction books, such as *Lumen* and *The End of the World*, have been described as "ecstatic voyages," frequently lyrical and poetic in tone and style. Flammarion is clearly enthralled as he describes the wonders of the universe. Writing in the "hybrid" fictional forms of the "philosophical dialogue" and the "dream journey" (the latter form used by Kepler as well), and with the intent to educate, Flammarion takes the reader on fantastical journeys intended to inspire and elevate the human spirit—doing so with a profuse use of metaphor and imagery and a reverie in the beautiful and sublime. This uniting of science with lyricism, art, and emotion can be seen as a key synthetic feature in many modern science fiction stories. Reason and emotion, science and art, and humanism and cosmology: Flammarion powerfully weaves them all together, contributing significantly into the evolving holistic quality of science fiction.

On this last feature, it is important to consider just how much Flammarion appreciated the power of the image and dramatic visualization. *Omega: The End of the World* brims with numerous paintings depicting different scenes and events described in the book. Many of the paintings, done by different artists, have an expressionistic, eerie, and ethereal quality, similar to the Romantic-spiritualist paintings of William Blake. A key dimension of the holistic and immersive quality of the science fiction experience has been the ever-evolving visual and multi-media elements that enrich and enliven the literary narratives. With its many cosmic and mystical visions of the far distant future, *Omega: The End of the World* is an evolutionary step in the development of science fiction art.

Flammarion is especially remembered in the history of fantastical art for the iconic "Flammarion Engraving," a picture that first appeared in *The Atmosphere* (1888). The picture presents two fields—the larger one depicting the earth with its blue-domed star-spangled vault of heaven dominated by the sun and its mountainous terrain below; the second in the upper left corner beyond the curved boundary of the earth and dome of the stars showing the "spheres," clouds, and clockwork mechanisms of the heavens. A cloaked figure sticks his head through the boundary separating these earthly and celestial realms, pondering, perhaps, the metaphysical underpinnings of existence that keep everything in nature moving in an orderly fashion. Perhaps a recreation of the Ptolemaic vision of the heavens, the "Flammarion Engraving" is provocative, and whatever interpretations we give it, it is just one among many arresting cosmic visualizations contained in Flammarion's books. The most famous of his illustrations, it frequently appears in various articles, books, and web pages dealing with cosmology, science, and the evolution of human consciousness (*Flammarion Engraving*).

Flammarion first attracted popular attention with *The Plurality of Habitable Worlds* (1862), described in its subtitle as "a study of the conditions of habitability of the planets in the solar system from the viewpoints of astronomy, physiology, and natural philosophy." This bestseller marked Flammarion's emergence not only as a popularizer of astronomy and science but also an influential voice in popular culture.

That same year, revealing his mystical and supernatural interests, he published *The Inhabitants of the Other World: Revelations of the After Life* (1862-1863), in which he describes a variety of revelations presumably transmitted by a medium from beyond the grave. After the book's publication he was informed that such writings on spiritualist topics would damage his credibility and career as a scientific astronomer, yet he was never able (or willing) to abandon this area of interest, and repeatedly professed that he always approached such mystical topics with the rationalism, empiricism, and skepticism of a scientist.

Building on the ideas introduced in *The Plurality of Habitable Worlds*, he published *Real and Imaginary Worlds* (1864). In this book Flammarion demonstrates his historical scholarship, including an exhaustive history of speculations on inhabitants of other planets and stars and covering ancient mythology, Christian ideas, Kepler, Godwin, Bruno, Wilkins, Fountenelle, Huygens, and the imaginary voyages and journeys of Swift, Voltaire, and Holberg, among many others. Along with this, he also includes a discussion of writers who believed that reincarnated souls live on other planets.

In this strange combination of aliens, spirits, and the afterlife, bringing together the scientific and the mystical—built on a scholarly review of both domains—Flammarion attempted to articulate a cosmic vision in which the spiritual could be credibly embedded within the astronomical and scientific. Moreover, as Roberts (2005) notes, in spite of the nineteenth-century intellectual rejection of the religious-spiritualist mindset in favor of the scientific-naturalistic perspective, many other authors also saw outer space (metaphorically "the Heavens") as the abode of spirits and higher beings. Thus the vast reaches of outer space, revealed through science, were now populated by similar kinds of beings to those that inhabited religiously informed higher realms of cosmic reality. The view that "in the heavens" there existed more advanced forms of intelligence and higher civilizations—an idea that Flammarion clearly championed and one that would become the stuff of so much modern science fiction—is rooted in the religious-mythological mode of thinking.

Although structured as a series of philosophical dialogues involving scientific arguments and expositions, Flammarion's *Lumen* (1872; Revised 1897) is generally considered a science fiction novel or narrative, for it features both characters in the dialogue and descriptions of various journeys across the universe. Lauded as a powerful and highly significant work of scientific imagination by the contemporary historian and writer of science fiction, Brian Stableford (2002), *Lumen* recounts the travels of a disembodied spirit of a person who has physically died. In the dialogues, this spirit, conversing with a living physically-embodied human, presents a philosophical theory of the subjective nature of human knowledge and perception, a scientific theory of the nature of life, and a dualistic theory of reality, involving both the physical and the spiritual.

In *Lumen*, the spirit explains in depth the nature and finite speed of light—an exposition critical to what comes later in the dialogues. As the spirit explains, reflected light from any and all events in the universe, from its beginnings on, is extending outward in all directions at a finite speed, carrying an optical representation through the cosmos of everything that has ever happened in the entire history of the universe. As the spirit contends, the universe is infinite in spatial expanse, so a record of all history is forever preserved. Moreover, the farther away from an event a potential observation point in the universe is, the longer it takes light reflected from that event to reach the observation point. Therefore, moving along a pathway of light, the farther out you go away from the source, the farther you see backward into the past for events that transpired at the originating source. The history of everyone's life is therefore observable in the optical pathways of traveling light. To wit— light contains a memory of the life of the universe.

Consequently, a cosmic record of everyone's good and bad deeds is written in the stars. Since Flammarion posits a God who watches over and governs the entire universe, nothing is hidden and nothing is forgotten; God sees it all as an eternal record in the emanating and boundless display of reflected light.

Since Flammarion provides his spirit narrator with the capacity to move instantaneously through the universe—being non-physical he is not constrained by physical laws—and the spirit is able to observe and chronicle from different spatial locations throughout the universe and via different trajectories of light the different lives he has lead on various planets. As the spirit relates, with each new incarnation, as his soul evolved, he was progressively embodied in more advanced physical forms on these different alien worlds, with different types of bodies adapted to different planetary environments. Alien life forms exist at various levels of physical and intellectual evolution across the universe, providing a diverse and progressive abode for evolving spirits. Just as our narrating spirit has evolved, the same will be true for everyone. When we physically die, our soul moves to a new physical body on a new world somewhere in the universe, advancing both spiritually and physically with each new reincarnation.

In introducing a variety of different alien worlds and compatible life forms through the spirit's account of his own former physical lives, Flammarion sets the stage for describing a huge array of worlds and forms of intelligence. This survey is presented in an evolutionary framework; given different habitats and environmental conditions on different worlds, what kinds of life would evolve? It is noteworthy that Flammarion's aliens are not always earth-like or humanlike in their qualities. At its time, this exposition was the most well-developed and imaginative descriptive survey of possible aliens grounded within a scientific framework; it is the first clear instance of applying biological evolution to understanding the possibilities of alien life.

In *Urania* (1889), Flammarion continues his imaginative exploration of other worlds and diverse alien forms of life. On one world we find androgynous humans existing in symbiosis with mobile planets. There is also a dialogue with Martians — six-limbed winged creatures — on the nature of war. And in *Popular Astronomy* (1894), he offers an extensive speculative discussion of extraterrestrial life, including in-depth treatments on the moon and Mars, the latter, in his opinion, probably having some type of intelligence superior to ours. All told, within these and other books, Flammarion laid the scientific and imaginative groundwork for numerous science fiction novels to come on alien life and intelligence.

Although *Lumen* realized a cosmic perspective on human reality and the saga of intelligent life, the novel that most clearly expresses the cosmic point of view — the big picture of things is his chronicle of the far future, *Omega: The End of the World* (1893-1894). As Flammarion stated, capturing the panoramic viewpoint realized in *Omega*, "The universe is so immense that it appears immutable, and that the duration of a planet such as that of the earth is only a chapter, less than that, a phrase, less still, only a word of the universe's history."

The novel has two distinctive parts to it. The first half describes a potential world calamity in the twenty-fifth century, when a giant comet approaches the earth, possibly on a collision course, sending the world population into great panic and distress. In this first half, Flammarion injects a series of scientifically and mathematically grounded discussions of the different possible ways that the world could end: for example, by heat and fire, cold and ice, and the exhaustion of water. Here, too, he again exhibits his depth of scholarship, providing an extensive factual history of different end-of-the-world theories and visions, scientific and religious.

Although there is great destruction produced by the comet, it does not strike the earth, and human civilization goes on, continuing to move forward and evolve through time. It is at this point, moving into the second half of the book that Flammarion jumps to a new level of perspective. The second half opens one hundred centuries in the future; humans have evolved new senses, acquired psychic powers, and biologically transcended their "monkey form."

Then, after describing this far future, Flammarion leaps forward in time again, now to several million years in the future. After immense and diverse human achievements, we find a future frozen earth under a dying sun on which only two humans remain alive: a male, Omegar, and a female, Eva. Amidst the colossal yet abandoned architectural structures of future humankind, our two lonely characters, at first separated, eventually find each other. But the imminent death of the earth, as well as their own demise, robs them of any enthusiasm or hope for their future. Into this bleak situation appears the spirit of Cheops, the ancient Egyptian pharaoh (previously encountered in *The Mummy!*), who reveals to them that on the planet Jupiter, a more spiritually evolved form of humans exist. Omegar and Eva are transported there, to participate in the next stage of human evolution.

But he does not stop there. Flammarion extends the saga still farther into the future. He describes the end of our solar system, and eventually the end of our universe, when all the stars die out and the cosmos devolves into amorphous chaos. This part of the story sounds very much like the predicted entropic collapse and heat death of the universe. But since Flammarion scientifically embraces the ideas of both infinite space and infinite time, in his final section of the novel, he describes the emergence of a new universe, to be populated with new solar systems, new civilizations, and new forms of intelligent life. In a cyclic vision of the cosmos and time, Flammarion envisions never-ending creation, evolution, and destruction, all enveloped within the realm of eternity and God. In a model of the cosmos that sounds similar to Poe, but also Hinduism, Flammarion integrates evolution and entropy as the two basic natural forces, coupled together in an oscillatory and cyclic never-ending pattern, of birth, growth, decay, death, and resurrection.

Just as Flammarion provided an imaginative foundation for the creation of aliens in future science fiction, in *Omega: The End of the World*, he anticipates — if not directly influences — both H. G. Wells in his creation of "The Star" (1897) and *The Time Machine*, and Olaf Stapledon in *Last and First Men*. Further, there are sections in both *Lumen* and *Omega* that also strongly resonate in spirit and vision with Stapledon's *Star Maker*. Without question, Flammarion's cosmic visions of infinite space and time set the stage for Stapledon, who in his evolutionary fiction written fifty years later would transcend even Flammarion's far-reaching speculations.

All told, Flammarion richly illustrates the mythological dimension of science fiction. Even more so, he demonstrates how the theme of evolution applies to this mythic dimension. As archetypal themes we find creation and destruction and resurrection; we see the ongoing and sequential transcendence of humanity and cosmic intelligence; we find the contrasting perspectives of the mental and the physical and the scientific and the mystical woven together into holistic, ecstatic visions of wonder; we see the journey of enlightenment and the guiding power of higher forms of mentality leading us forward on our adventure into the future. Contributing to a new emerging archetype, we find his amazing elaborations on alien minds and alien worlds, and everything that these core concepts in science fiction symbolize; as one key example, the alien representing the unknown. Given the diverse and significant contributions

Flammarion made to bringing the universe of astronomy more into popular consciousness, we see how he helped to facilitate the growth of scientific consciousness in human society, which was an important factor contributing to the receptivity of the general population to the literature of scientifically inspired fiction. Whether successful or plausible in his big picture thinking, he added to the ongoing dialectic and evolving dance within science fiction of modern science and ancient spiritualism, as well as the related themes of eternity and time. Perhaps most critically, he applied the evolutionary framework to alien worlds, alien intelligence, astronomy, humanity's own future—both social and biological—and to the future of the universe as a whole. He was a scientifically informed, mystically inspired, evolutionary mythologist of the farthest reaches of outer space and the future.

This cosmic perspective on space, time, and the possibilities of life and intelligence in the universe brings us to one last point on Flammarion. As a scholar, researching previous stories and theories concerning outer space travel, alien worlds and alien life, and the far distant future—all central narrative themes in modern science fiction—he was an important evolutionary stepping stone in the growing self-consciousness of science fiction. Describing and integrating the historical contributions to the above spheres of imagination he was articulating a heritage and adding to it, for some of the most basic narrative themes in science fiction. He was identifying and integrating numerous tributaries of thought in the history of science fiction and then building on them.

Visions of Future Utopian Societies: Morris, Bellamy, and Robida

Humanity has burst the chrysalis. The heavens are before it.
Edward Bellamy

Let us (momentarily at least) come back down to earth.

Along with its antithesis, the dystopia, a key narrative theme in the history of science fiction is the utopian tale. Although early utopias were more often hypothetically placed within distant or unknown lands, including Butler's ambiguous utopia *Erewhon* and Bulwer-Lytton's unnerving *Vril*, the modern science fiction utopia, inspired by the transformative and optimistic thinking of the Age of Enlightenment, was a tale of an ideal society usually placed in the future. Anticipated advances in either the scientific-technological or social-political spheres, or both, provided the substance and building blocks for many such futurist stories. In resonance with the plethora of ongoing changes in Western society and associated hopeful visions of tomorrow provoked by such changes, the popularity of futurist utopian stories grew in the latter part of the nineteenth century, as well as into the twentieth century with the writings of H. G. Wells. But reactions varied to the ongoing transformative flow of modern Western society; the reader is referred back to Jules Verne's *Paris in the Twentieth Century and* "In the Twenty-ninth Century." There was debate and dialogue on what constituted an ideal future human society, and whether the ideal future society should be envisioned as a simple extension and further development of the "progressive" trends of modern times.

This section primarily focuses on three important and influential futurist utopias published in the period of 1880 to 1890: William Morris' *News from Nowhere* (1890), Edward Bellamy's *Looking Backward 2000-1887* (1888), and Albert Robida's *The Twentieth Century* (1882). Each novel reacts differently to the Western vision of secular progress. Robida's novel feels most like a science fiction novel with its immense and colorful array of anticipated new technologies, reflecting both the progressive spirit of scientific-technological progress and positive visions of an ever-growing capitalist economy. Yet at the same time, it is the most ambiguous of the three utopias, repeatedly questioning whether a life of enhanced technological immersion and the proliferation of gadgets is an unequivocally good thing. Bellamy is wholeheartedly optimistic about secular-scientific progress though, even as he jettisons capitalism and commercialism as anathema to the human spirit in his idealist futurist vision. Morris' novel, which is also decidedly utopian, revels in a hypothetical ideal pastoral future human existence rejecting almost the entirety of Western modernity and the philosophy of secular progress. Finally, as a coda and counterpoint to all these futurist utopian visions, the section concludes with a discussion of John Ames Mitchell's short novel *The Last American* (1889), a poignant tale about the failure and collapse of modern Western civilization in the future.

* * *

... the huge mass of men are compelled by folly and greed to make harmful and useless things ... Friends, this earthly hell is not the ordinance of nature but the manufacture of man ... it is your business to destroy it ... so that no one henceforth can ever fall into it.
William Morris

In *News from Nowhere or An Epoch of Rest, Being Some Chapters from a Utopian Romance* (1890), William Morris (1834-1896) argued for a future socialist and agrarian form of human community. Reflecting the Romantic vision of a revitalized resonance with nature, which we saw expressed in American transcendentalism and Thoreau's *Walden*, Morris created a "medieval reverie," featuring a return to a medieval type of society in which life, art, and work formed a cohesive whole within a meaningful life. He was decidedly critical of modern manufacturing and capitalist and commercial trends and the increasingly fast paced and unsettled quality of human life in the modern world. Instead,

Morris advocated for a more static, if not regressive, society that cultivated leisure, beauty, and overall health and well-being.

Although published after Bellamy's and Robida's novels, Morris had formulated many of the main ideas that went into *News from Nowhere* over the previous couple of decades before the book's publication. He had spoken on the negative impact of industrial capitalism, especially on the arts in the 1870s, and he read Marx's socialist-communist ideas and joined the socialist movement in the early 1880s. In 1889 Morris had written a critical review of Bellamy's *Looking Backward*, which embraced industrialism and state controlled socialism, and *News from Nowhere*, with its individualist socialism and pastoralism, can be viewed as a literary critical reaction to Bellamy's novel. But Morris' vision in *News from Nowhere* had been crystalizing in his mind long before Bellamy's book. And his critique of the direction modernity was taking goes much deeper than simply a counter-proposal to Bellamy's views. What Morris and Bellamy shared in common was a sincere desire to influence and redirect the future evolution of Western human society, and in this regard, they both had a significant effect on human thinking and behavior.

Perhaps the central message and most distinctive idea in *News from Nowhere* is that work should be viewed as pleasurable and intrinsically rewarding, rather than being associated with drudgery and misery. In his envisioned future society people work because they find it enjoyable and self-fulfilling and because they are motivated to contribute into the well-being of others. Work is not experienced as a necessary evil and a type of enslavement in order to make money. For one thing there is no money in Morris' future society. Further, work is not seen as separate from either life or art; all three are ideally integrated into a whole. The fulfilling life is found within work, which should be an expression of personal artistic creation. Work (and life) should be personal and inventive, rather than dull and mechanical, which according to Morris, is often the case in our industrialized capitalist society of factories and mass production.

Other key ideas in the book include: heightened individual self determination and freedom, where centralized government and authoritarian top-down control (of all types) are eliminated, and out of which freedom comes a greater sense of communalism than within the competitive and dog-eat-dog modern world; equality rather than elitism with its hierarchy of social classes; a pastoral existence of small villages (rather than big cities) where people live much closer to nature and revel in its beauty; a significant reduction in machinery and industrialism, based on the thesis that in our modern world we have become slaves rather than masters to our machines (an idea very similar to Butler's *Erewhon*); and the cultivation of simple pleasures and a deep sense that life and nature are beautiful, without the need for excessive luxury or the sacred and transcendent. There are no rich or poor people, and no hint of religion or belief in an afterlife. Morris is clearly not an advocate of asceticism or worldly renunciation, instead presenting a sensual and hedonistic philosophy of life derived from nature and the unencumbered pursuit of our natural desires.

Morris presents his utopian ideals in the context of a rather simple story. The protagonist and narrator, William Guest, after an engaging discussion on how to transform human society for the better with fellow members of a "socialist league," returns home and falls into a deep sleep in his bed. When he awakens in the morning, he finds himself—although in the same location—in a world transformed. When he went to bed it was the winter, when he awakens it is the summer. He eventually discovers it is approximately one hundred years in the future. He meets various characters in this future world, begins to observe a host of differences in their customs, their buildings, and the general layout of the land—their clothing reminds him of the fourteenth century—and initiates a series of conversations with them about their way of life and their values. In particular he befriends a married couple and becomes deeply infatuated with a young single woman. Both the couple and the young woman embody new and different ideals, the married couple involved in an open partnership without a marital contract and the young beautiful woman exhibiting a much more emancipated spirit than women of his own time. Our protagonist asks a host of questions and engages in almost continuous dialogue with different individuals throughout the story. He eventually goes on a boat trip down the River Thames and meets with an older man who explains how this new world arose in a great collective and liberating socialist rebellion against the previous oppressive capitalist system. It was particularly important for Morris in presenting this ideal future society to not just describe it, but to explain how it could hypothetically emerge out of our present social system. How can we get from here to there? At the end of the novel, our enlightened and inspired protagonist "reawakens" in his own bed and own time, pondering whether it was all just a dream but hoping it was something more, a prophetic "vision" of what could emerge in the future.

Although in *News from Nowhere* Morris attempts to convey how it would "feel" to live in this ideal future, describing at length the psychology of individual characters; the normal, everyday activities of these people; the sensory beauty of the surrounding nature, farmlands, and villages; the peaceful idyllic ambience of the world; and the way all of these factors impact the thoughts, emotions, and overall mood of William Guest— who frequently compares this new reality with his own world— the novel is also highly didactic. The dialogues often turn into lectures presented by the imaginary characters on the rationale and logic behind all the important aspects of their new social reality.

Another important topic extensively examined in the novel is education. Again in the utopian spirit of increased freedom, children are not given any formal schooling. Instead it appears that children are encouraged to pursue their own interests as they naturally emerge. As Morris sees it, schools are a form of factory-like regimentation, a product of an industrialized society. In Morris' imagined world children learn through interacting with nature; books are no longer important.

The ongoing dialogues reveal other startling changes: There are no law courts or prisons; for Morris, such institutions are used to protect the rich from the poor and enforce social tyranny. There is no criminal class, which, according to the arguments in the book, arises from possessiveness and the accumulation of private property (the desire for money and riches). Instead of the negative cultural message that people shouldn't steal, the story conveys the message that work is not only necessary but joyful. There are no nations, forcing people into unnatural groups. There is no patriotism or politics. In general, all institutions and customs that force people into regimented and unjust situations have been eradicated.

All in all, Morris appears to believe that if people are encouraged to cultivate their own interests—with a certain amount of guidance—but without being subjected to authoritarian control and enslavement emblematic of our commercial-industrialized world they will form into harmonious social groups with individuals helping each other and contributing to the benefit of the social whole. As such, News from Nowhere is both individualistic and socialistic.

On the personal front, there are no divorces, since there are no legally binding marriage contracts. Again, as an advocate for increased individual freedom, Morris envisions a time when the tyranny of gender—of men over women and women over men— has been eliminated. (But he still sees women as the primary domestic caretakers since he believes that they are naturally inclined in this direction.) Possession of any form is anathema to freedom (a marriage contract is a form of possession), and consequently there is no private property or ownership of people or of things. Commercialism is dead.

The psychology and mode of consciousness of people in this utopia differs notably in other ways as well. History is not important and people tend to live primarily in the relative present; they thoroughly enjoy the here and now. Yet this presentism supports a rather static and timeless society with no invention or transformation. Indeed, reading *News from Nowhere* is not very exciting. There is no drama or discovery in the world of *News from Nowhere*. Nothing really happens.

Because the stress, frenzy, pressure, anxiety, possessiveness, jealousy, envy, and drudgery associated with modern human life are gone, people are much more relaxed, genuine, and sane, even if boringly so. Their minds are uncluttered by all the turmoil and drama of the modern urban psyche. Accordingly, "romantic novels" are no longer popular, since people in this utopian world do not identify or empathize with such emotionally tumultuous tales and characters. (Recall a similar theme in *Vril*.) By and large, among the characters in *News from Nowhere*—excepting perhaps the narrator—neurotics, romanticists, dreamers, psychotics, or manic-depressives are nowhere to be found.

When all is said and done, Morris resolutely rejects the value and vision of secular progress as a preferable direction for humanity's future. For Morris, the ideal future is a personal work of art, rather than a driven work of progress. He saw many of the features of modern Western progress, especially its capitalistic, industrialized, and commercialized dimensions, as generating increasing human misery and emptiness in life. All that is of value in human life gets corrupted and perverted in such a reality, one in which work loses its personal meaning and intrinsic reward, and art and design get degraded in the name of economic progress and the mass production of "harmful and useless things." In a true Romantic vein, Morris envisions a society in which art is the center of gravity in human society, rather than science, technology, or commerce.

News from Nowhere is a significant counterpoint to the evolution of techno-inspired science fiction utopias, providing a classic, inspirational vision of a return to nature and timeless simplicity in a society that elevates the pursuit of beauty and serenity as the ideal future direction for humanity. Highly influential in its time, as well as in decades to come, many features of Morris' pastoral-agrarian, freedom-embracing regressive-futurist vision show up in later science fiction stories that recoil against the negative trends associated with urbanized, high-tech, industrialized, fast paced and stressful modern life. (Adding to the above, for a somewhat different interpretation of *News from Nowhere* and a comparison to B. F. Skinner's *Walden Two*, see "Medieval Reverie versus Behaviorist's Experiment: The Utopias of William Morris and B. F. Skinner." J. Lombardo, 2004.)

* * *

... buying and selling is essentially anti-social in all its tendencies. It is an education in self-seeking at the expense of others, and no society whose citizens are trained in such a school can possibly rise above a very low grade of civilization.
Edward Bellamy

Although not to minimize the influence of Morris' *News from Nowhere*, the most popular futurist utopia of the late nineteenth century was Edward Bellamy's (1850-1898) *Looking Backward 2000-1887* (1888). One of the best-selling books of its time—selling millions of copies—it provoked the emergence of numerous groups and "clubs," and even some experimental communities, dedicated to the ideas and philosophy expressed in the novel. Within ten years of its publication, *Looking Backward* had instigated a huge wave of other books, both fiction and nonfiction, either defending and further developing its controversial themes or critiquing its ideas (including Morris' book). Although some of its critics argued that Bellamy's book was primarily derivative, based on the ideas of other social and philosophical writers—thus reflecting the culture of its time—Looking Backward provides an excellent example of how science fiction can strongly impact human culture and society.

What is most striking about the book is its straightforward, unremitting, and tenacious optimism about the future. From the skeptical and cautious perspective of contemporary times, the book generates a great deal of cognitive dissonance and unease, for we expect to find some flaw or uncertainty in any vision of an ideal human society. Yet Bellamy never wavers in presenting a rational and positive futurist vision. At one level, Looking Backward is a sustained social-philosophical argument, set in the form of a dialogue (almost like Plato), for an orderly, humane, and positive vision of the future. The dialogue raises questions regarding the feasibility and plausibility of the futurist vision, but Bellamy responds, within the ongoing dialogue, to each of these supposed challenges and potential problems. The book repeatedly provokes such questions as: What is the matter with us? With our attitudes? Why can't we simply embrace the good life and live the way people do in this book? Our tainted post-modern skeptical side keeps thinking this vision, this logic for tomorrow, is too good and too simple to be true. We keep looking for the flaws in the system, as does the character of the visitor from the past. Yet, through the ongoing contentious dialogue, Bellamy doggedly and resolutely reasserts his theses and with great conviction and clarity explains how we can create the good future envisioned in this book.

The basic plot of the novel concerns a central male character who lives in Boston in the year 1887. One night, put into a hypnotic state, he falls into a deep sleep in his secret and private below-ground sleeping quarters and wakes to find himself, without having aged, in the year 2000. Upon awakening, he is cared for by a family—father, mother, and a daughter, the latter a strangely familiar young adult woman. The family lives in a house built upon the former location of his own home, which, except for his secret sleeping room below the surface, had been burned to the ground many years earlier. The father engages the man from the nineteenth century in a series of debates and discussions regarding the social and technological order of the world of 2000, while the daughter shows our central character some of the sights and wonders of the city, during which time a romantic resonance emerges between the two. Love bursts forth. A mystery emerges, however, involving a type of romantic destiny facilitated by time travel that I won't divulge, but it generates an interesting romantic twist to the whole utopian tale. Toward the end of the book, our central character experiences a "nightmare" in which he travels back to his own time—which explains the odd fact that although the tale recounts a "looking forward" a hundred years plus into the future, the novel is titled *Looking Backward*.

The bulk of the book concerns the nature and the philosophical justification behind Bellamy's vision of the ideal society of the future in which our central character finds himself. The society centers around a collaborative and cooperative effort for mutual benefit, rather than competitive and self-centered behavior, the latter presumably characterizing the world of the late nineteenth century. Using the fictional futurist society to illustrate its major philosophical points, the book serves (as most utopias do) as a critique of present society. For Bellamy, individualism, competition, capitalism, material and financial greed, self-aggrandizement, and social-political hierarchies—all qualities of the late nineteenth-century Western world—have negative and destructive effects upon the realization of human happiness and the good society. In contrast, the future society described in this book—being grounded in the humanistic principles of human equality, social community, and mutual concern and care for everyone—is happy, sane, ethical, and prosperous.

To get more specific, Bellamy builds his utopia on the concept of a national government-controlled "industrial army," which is responsible for all production and distribution of goods. The "industrial army" is an orderly, top-down system that eliminates waste, competitive frenzy, and strife. There are no privately owned factories or companies locked in competition with each other. Moreover, everyone serves in this industrial army, with the youth apprenticing in more rudimentary or "menial" jobs, thereby distributing equally among all members of society those tasks usually associated with the lower class. There is no lower or upper class in this world. Expressing a socialist vision of an ideal society, everyone receives a yearly allowance of "credit" sufficient to purchase those goods necessary for a comfortable life. There is no money in this world. Furthermore, there are no uneducated or unemployed; everyone receives a mandatory level of education and everyone has a job. People can retire by the time they reach the age of 45 in order to pursue their particular individual interests, cultivated in the first part of their lives.

Bellamy imagines an impressive array of technological advances in *Looking Backward*. Smoke and air pollution have been eliminated, with electricity now the central power source for commercial, manufacturing, and domestic needs. The cities are clean, orderly, and well maintained. Music and other forms of entertainment and education are transmitted into individual households through a type of cable telephone system. Sidewalks, highway systems, and transportation vehicles are all technologically advanced. Food and all other commercial products are purchased and ordered within huge "stores" (more like warehouses) that serve as hubs for the production system.

The main emphasis, though, of this utopian vision is economic, social, ethical, and psychological rather than technological. Extended discussions deal with how criminal, mentally ill, and maladapted people are "treated" in this society. As with utopias before, *Looking Backward* offers both a critique of contemporary society and a "solution" to the various diagnosed ills of our way of life. Bellamy describes the modern world in which he lived as an unhappy, messy, dysfunctional, and irrational reality, grounded in the most unethical and lowest human needs and values. His idealized world is built on what is best, most rational, and most humanistic of personal traits and values set in critical opposition to our contemporary world. How can we possibly want to keep going in the same direction that we presently are?

If we were to criticize Bellamy's vision—and one should read the book first to appreciate the clarity and force of his arguments—it would be along similar lines to other critiques of previous idealized societies: Everybody is good; peace, order, and prosperity prevail; and as a result, the whole thing feels boring, monotonous, and uninteresting. (The same criticism was raised against Morris' vision, or More's for that matter.) In spite of all the great changes realized, Bellamy's society feels static. And yet he believes that it is through such a well-ordered system that progress into the future is most effectively realized; the chaos and drama of our world is wasteful and ugly and is holding us back, severely retarding our development. As Bellamy states,

"With a tear for the dark past, turn we then to the dazzling future, and, veiling our eyes, press forward. The long and weary winter of the race is ended. Its summer has begun."

Both Morris and Bellamy embraced socialism and opposed capitalism. But whereas Morris advocated for a communal socialism in which neighbors provide for each other, while maintaining a strong sense of individual freedom, in Bellamy, all individuals are expected to participate and serve in a centralized social system that provides for all. Morris' society is organized from the bottom-up and Bellamy's from the top-down. Moreover, Bellamy sees great value in technological advancement, whereas Morris recoils against it. Bellamy believes in the vision of progress; Morris believes in the enjoyment and immersion in the here and now. Indeed, Morris looks to the distant past (the medieval era) for inspiration, while Bellamy sees the past as "dark" and the future as "dazzling." Put most simply, Bellamy's world is highly urbanized and technological while Morris' ideal social reality is pastoral and agrarian.

Yet, as one final point where they resonate, both writers saw our contemporary world filled with too much "sound and fury," neuroses and emotional chaos, and distress and psychological dysfunction. Both writers connected these negative features of the contemporary human mind with competitive capitalism (among other things), and both based their futurist socialist visions on changes that would bring human happiness and psychological well-being. The achievement of this goal, however, produces distinctly different societies: In Morris' vision full sanity leads to tranquility, stasis, and a loss of motivation to pursue progress, whereas in Bellamy, sanity facilitates more efficient progress.

In the end, we can argue that both of them got it wrong. Craziness and chaos did not disappear, but if anything intensified. And the very craziness of the human condition— at odds with both the envisioned rational orderliness of the New Enlightenment and the idealized idyllic return to nature in Romanticism—is perhaps integral to human nature and necessary for progress. The writer who seems to have most realistically and presciently foreseen the shape of things to come was Morris' and Bellamy's contemporary, Albert Robida.

* * *

A perpetual chiming has replaced the deafening racket of yesteryear's earthbound vehicles. Electricity circulates everywhere, facilitating all social interactions with its motive force and light. Thousands of musical chimes and bell sounds coming from the sky, from homes, and even from the ground, merge into one vibrant, merry, metallic melody that Beethoven, could he have heard it, would have named

the great symphony of electricity.
Albert Robida

In so many ways at the opposite end of the stylistic and philosophical continuum from Bellamy's *Looking Backward* and Morris' *News from Nowhere*, the literary works and visions of Albert Robida (1848-1926) immerse the reader in a multi-media, holistically-realized, fantastical future. An artist as well as a writer, Robida drew roughly one thousand striking illustrations for his books, showing as well as describing life in the future; some even identify him as the first true science fiction artist. Thus illuminated by his artwork, his depictions of the particularities of life and the entertaining escapades of his characters serve to reflect not only a host of hypothetical technological changes in the future but social and psychological changes as well. In Robida's books, we participate in the richness and dynamism of future life. His stories abound with color, perpetual and unbounded inventiveness, and endless action, with "one damn thing after another." We are right there along with the characters, engulfed in all the concrete richness, craziness, and nuances of human existence: we go to the theater; shop for new clothes; watch the world news on giant video screens; turn Italy into a theme park; and vicariously travel to the beaches of France on a flying yacht. Bellamy is didactic, abstract, and serious; Morris is almost equally didactic and serious. In both their novels, there is not much of a story. Robida presents a slice of life with complex storylines—comedic, animated, and electrical.

Robida wrote at least a dozen science fiction novels between 1879 and 1919, including a satirical series on the "extraordinary voyages" of Jules Verne, *The Very Extraordinary Adventures of Saturnin Farandoul,* 1879-1883; time travel stories; end of the world scenarios; and outer space journeys into the solar system. Aside from illustrating his own books, Robida also created hundreds of illustrations in collaboration with other authors, including one magazine series *The Infernal War* (1908) in which Germany attacks London and the United States goes to war with Japan. Three of Robida's best known science fiction novels form a trilogy on the near future of humanity in the twentieth century: *The Twentieth Century* (1882); *War in the Twentieth Century* (1887); and *Electric Life* (1890). By far his most famous work, *The Twentieth Century* has amazingly only been translated from the French into English in the last decade (Willems, 2004).

The main setting for the novel is Paris in 1952, although as the story progresses some of the characters go on various adventures, including a journey across the Pacific Ocean. The central character is a young woman and recently graduated high school student named Hélène. Other central characters include Hélène's guardian—a billionaire banker and corporate magnate, Raphaël Ponto; Ponto's two daughters—friends and co-graduates of Hélène; Ponto's wife—a feminist and political leader who, like her husband, is always busy and on the go; and Ponto's son—a dreamy and impractical character who, in the novel's finale, paradoxically becomes the hero of the story.

The central plot of the novel is a madcap romp through love, war, and politics: Having graduated, Hélène is expected to pursue a professional vocation (women have moved beyond the roles of housewife and mother). Under pressure from Ponto, but stymied in her efforts at various professions including journalism and law, Hélène finds herself dissatisfied and frustrated. As this main storyline unfolds, with one mishap and comedic blunder after another, Hélène is challenged to a duel; the French populace stage a choreographed political revolution; the French President is replaced with an automaton; Ponto's son is rescued from the polygamous Mormons who now rule England; and Hélène, instead of finding a suitable profession for an emancipated woman, finds her "Prince Charming," Ponto's son, and has a newly constructed continent in the Pacific Ocean named after her.

Along with the main characters—and to use a cinematic expression—the novel features a huge cast of supporting characters as well as thousands of extras; these we observe participating in the staged revolution; watching giant-screen news shows in public spaces; and busily shopping in city streets. But despite the rich characterization, Robida places his characters and their actions in a richly envisioned futurist environment, which becomes the real focus of the novel. Indeed, the central function of the story is to depict the imagined ecology of life in the twentieth century.

At a technological level, the book focuses on two main areas of futurist extrapolation: advanced telecommunications and rapid transit. Air cars, air taxis, air buses, and transatlantic airships clog the skies, while pneumatically powered "trains" barrel through huge tubes under the ground. We also find video enhanced telephones and big screen cinema (TV) with multiple channels, as well as music and news feeds delivered into the home. There are giant outdoor movie screens and electrically powered advertising signs (billboards) and displays everywhere in the city. On top of that, a network of secret cameras located throughout the city and its buildings surreptitiously spy on people everywhere.

Other technological developments include the mass production and pumped delivery (through a network of tubes) of full course meals into the homes; burglar prevention systems that include electrified floors; the mass production of classical art through photographic technologies; floating casinos and rotating buildings; and—the epitome of self-indulgent extravagance—a space project by which the moon has been towed appreciably closer to the earth to allow for more illuminated and romantic evenings for lovers. All of this technology lends the story a hyper-stimulating, media-saturated, and fast paced ambience. From our present perspective, it accurately foresees and captures the frenzied, information-glutted, image-engulfed, pervasively commercialized reality of our contemporary times.

Underneath it all is the ubiquitous presence of electricity permeating through everything, empowering new technological conveniences, yet generating an overall sense of galvanized agitation throughout the society. As noted earlier, the scientific and technological possibilities of electricity became an increasingly important topic of speculation in the nineteenth century, and *The Twentieth Century* (as well as *Electric Life*) reflects this cultural fascination with the possibilities of electrical power. Robida invents a host of new electrical technologies, transforming human society and giving this futurist world a heightened level of dynamism, stimulation, and animation.

All the above is not to say that Robida did not provide a rich, fully developed social dimension to the novel as well. This future world is ruled by capitalism and big business. New technologies are products, mass produced and distributed to a consumerist culture. Multi-national corporations are so powerful in fact that a business conglomerate directed by Ponto purchases the country of Italy and turns it into a colossal theme park. Ponto also develops a plan for selling France back to its citizens by making everyone a shareholder in the country. It is under Ponto's leadership and huge financial investment that, in order to provide new land and living space for the growing global population, a new continent is constructed in the Pacific Ocean. Although he may not get all the details right, it is with great prescience that Robida anticipates the rise and eventual domination of business and economic concerns in the modern world. And although presented in comedic form, from the pastoral perspective of Morris, Robida's vision for a future world is one of a Dionysian, hedonistic hell and a *reductio ad absurdum* of the philosophy and aspirations of modernity.

In connection with the spreading power of multi-national corporations and big business, Robida envisions a future global society in which cultural differences blend together (facilitated by high tech mass communication and travel). Everyone is being assimilated into a worldwide capitalist, consumerist culture— even the American Indians. Once more, Robida seems on the mark in his predictions.

Another important social theme in *The Twentieth Century* is the emancipation of women. Ponto's wife, forever rushing from one meeting to another, is a powerful political activist, championing the rights and involvement of women in the running of society. And as we've seen, after graduating Hélène is expected to find a professional vocation. This right to achieve success in the public sphere is not only a freedom but equally a responsibility. Hélène does, in fact, do quite well as a lawyer-apprentice; in Robida's future, women dominate the legal and many other socially elevated professions. And yet this freedom opens women to the same cutthroat competition men have faced. When Hélène finds law unfulfilling and eventually tries journalism, she finds herself challenged by another emancipated woman to a duel (with sword, gun, or other weapon of choice). The cause? Hélène's antagonist has taken umbrage over one of Hélène's news reports. Still, despite the heavy dose of comedy and satire, as well as Robida's mixed messages on female empowerment, he does address an important area of futurist speculation that other futurist science fiction writers had largely underplayed or ignored: How might women's social role, identity, and power change and expand in the years to come?

As one last important social element in the novel, Robida envisions a French government that orchestrates regular "staged revolutions," complete with mock battles, the overthrow of the ruling government by younger politicians, and a giant celebration once the whole affair comes to a close. These revolutions are funded by a planned government budget surplus, and prizes are given out for the best "performances." Serving as intentionally generated "escape valves" for the tensions and frustrations that build up over successive administrations (as purposefully created pockets of chaos amidst the order of things), they allow all citizens to actively participate in the rejection of the old and stale and the establishment of the new and liberating. And yet, under the ultimate management of the corporate world, the staged revolutions allow for a continuation, if not further development, of the capitalist, high-tech, and consumerist way of life. The more things change, the more they stay the same, and freedom is nothing but an illusion.

The theatrical quality of the political revolutions reflects a general dimension of human society highlighted in the entire novel. The world described by Robida is a world of ubiquitous advertisement, commercialized art, mass entertainment, and resplendent architectural displays. News has become an intentionally orchestrated cinematic production. The world is one great big multi-media show, an entertaining interactive theater in which the population fully participates. In this regard, *The Twentieth Century* is not simply a projection into the future; the novel itself is a fantastical display and exhibition, a work of art and entertainment. Without question, Robida realizes, more so than anyone before him, the artistic and entertainment dimensions of science fiction. He equally foresees the blurring of reality and theater, of fact and fiction. The news of the world, to a degree at least, is being created for the purpose of entertainment.

A big part of the entertainment value of *The Twentieth Century* stems from its comedy and satire, for although the positive and liberating effects of advancing technologies and progressive social thinking are repeatedly applauded throughout the novel, Robida highlights the potential downside and ridiculous consequences of these modern ideas and gadgets as well. In one case, one of the food tubes leading into a house malfunctions and a whole room fills up with lobster bisque. Freedom of speech repeatedly turns into shouting matches. At the beginning of the novel, Hélène is repeatedly awoken by incessant news feeds broadcast into her bedroom. Hélène starts off looking for a career but ends up tickled pink with a husband and a baby. How desirable is the emancipation of women? And in one comical episode at a university, an ego-inflated professor, in arguing for the rejection of absolutist authoritarian history, spirals out of control into a fully revisionist and relativist theory of history: The past is no longer a firm ground on which to stand, but rather a totally ambiguous no man's land where anything about the past might have been true. (A comical anticipatory spoof on postmodernism, presaging George Orwell's *1984*.) The ground is gone; the bedrock of truth and the good has evaporated in the future. Indeed, almost everything in *The Twentieth Century* oscillates and buzzes around, appearing one way and then some other way: Is all this progress good or bad, foolish or sane, right or wrong? Although on one hand the novel repeatedly celebrates the idea of social and technological progress, on the other it repeatedly questions the benefits of embracing this modernist philosophy.

As Robida states in one of his other futurist novels, *Electric Life*,

Overwrought, wired up, frightfully busy and nervous, life in the electrical age, we must admit, has overtaxed the human race and brought about a kind of universal degeneration...

Perhaps the ultimate comedy and irony in the story is its finale. Having married Hélène, Ponto's son, the impractical dreamer, goes on his honeymoon with her, part of which involves traveling in a submarine. But they become stranded in the Pacific Ocean. Arriving at a group of small islands near Tahiti, he gets the fanciful idea that the islands could all be connected to serve as scaffolding for the creation of a new continent. Loving the idea, Ponto funds the colossal endeavor, uniting the capitalist drive toward ever-increasing wealth with the high-tech engineering capabilities of the modern world. The son decides to name the continent Helenia after his new wife. Ironically, Hélène, who in no way resonates with the progressive, capitalist, emancipated, high tech world she lives in, will become the "queen" of this new land.

In the final analysis, we are left with a question: Is *The Twentieth Century* a utopia, grounded in the philosophy of secular progress and envisioning a future of wonder and liberation? Or is it a dystopia, making a farce of commercialism, capitalism, and hi-tech run wild? Reflecting a deep ambiguity regarding the direction of the modern world, it seems to be both. And that, in a large part, is what makes the book so intelligent, thought provoking, and funny.

With the comedy and satire, the animated illustrations, the two sides to every coin, the colorful personalities, the crazy customs, gadgets, and behaviors, and the cast of thousands, *The Twentieth Century*, though narrative in form, is a complex and scintillating collage, a fireworks display of the future. As an array of sights, sounds, inventions, and ideas, it all hangs together, but without any simple and singular message or philosophy. It is a holistic Gestalt of an experience, though not a logical and consistent whole. The intricate and multi-dimensional vision created anticipates later comprehensive scenarios of future human societies. Its level of energy and information overload resonates with more contemporary hi-tech dystopias. Unquestionably one of the greatest achievements, along with Wells' *The Time Machine* and *The War of the Worlds*, of nineteenth-century science fiction, it is the most fully fleshed out narrative vision of future human society written in the nineteenth century, surpassing everything that came before.

* * *

In what sense do visions of future human society such as *News from Nowhere*, *Looking Backward*, and *The Twentieth Century* contribute into the evolving mythology of the future in science fiction? For one thing, because of their disparate visions, they complicate our sense of our future, regarding both what to expect (or predict) and what to hope for. Although Bellamy's and Robida's novels based their respective narratives of the future on the secular theory of progress, they offer very different extrapolations of where secular progress could take us in the future. At a general level, the former vision is orderly, Apollonian, peaceful, and unequivocal in its statement of things; the latter is more chaotic, Dionysian, agitated, and ambiguous in its judgment. Although clearly aspiring toward the ideal of secular progress, Bellamy's vision feels lifeless, while Robida's is much more concrete, messy, and full of life.

Bringing Morris into the picture of possible preferable futures, he provides an alternative to the Western vision of secular progress, turning to nature, art, freedom, mental health, and tranquility as desirable ideals. Although Morris' utopia presents an idealized past, it is one that never really existed. His philosophical integration of communalism with independence, and work with art and personal expression, is very different in spirit from the unsanitary, deprived, and controlled life of the common peasant in feudalist Europe.

Hence, all three novels are forms of transcendence relative to the present, as imaginative visions to inspire us regarding the possibilities of tomorrow. They provide a complex array of mythologies of our collective future. In terms of fundamental archetypal themes, these narratives address the questions: What is the good life? How do we realize it? What basic conditions generate meaning, purpose, and happiness in human life?

One point that is particularly fascinating in comparing *Looking Backward* and *The Twentieth Century* is that the rational and orderly ideals presented in the former novel, although intended to describe a preferable social future for humanity, will in the decades ahead often come to signify a very undesirable and dystopian type of future. Bellamy's top-down utopia seems to rob us of our freedom. Yet, Robida's high-tech, corporate-dominant, frenzied world would also come to be seen as dystopian, equally robbing us of control and freedom in our lives. Given this Scylla and Charybdis of opposites leading to a loss of freedom on both counts, it is understandable that Morris' vision of the future— where we can at least breathe—seems desirable to many people in our contemporary world—consider the whole "simplify" movement of recent decades.

Lastly, the beautifully orchestrated society in *Looking Backward* has come to be seen as unrealistic. The "happening" world of *The Twentieth Century*, filled as it is with ambiguity, agitation, and misfortunes, seems much more in tune with our actual society and where it seems to be heading (or has already arrived). Everything in contemporary times has become more complicated, in flux, moving and shifting around too fast, including our assessments of things and our fundamental ideals (Toffler, 1971; Gleick, 1999). Our social reality and social mythos has become noisy, contentious, and fluctuating (Best and Kellner, 1997). Hence, the continued mythic appeal of visions like Morris' utopia with its return to a simpler and more pleasant life uncomplicated by the complexity, ambiguity, and dynamism of modernism. But is Morris' ideal any more realistic than Bellamy's? The extreme orderliness, uniformity, and harmony found in *Looking Backward* simply take a different form in Morris' *News from Nowhere*. In the former case reason and science create order; in the latter case, nature, art, and fulfilling work produce order and tranquility. Although in both cases, the chaos and conflict of human existence have been eliminated, it is Robida's vision that seems much more realistic.

* * *

To those thoughtful Persians who can read a warning in the sudden rise and swift extinction of a foolish people this volume is dedicated. Hedful "The Axis of Wisdom," Curator of the Imperial Museum at Shiraz

Although it's just possible that modern Western civilization will end as it does in *News from Nowhere,* with a great social revolution and the transformation of society into a pastoral and agrarian utopia, a darker view is at least equally plausible: In the future the whole modern edifice could collapse due to its inherent flaws and excesses, ushering in a new Dark Ages. That is just the scenario presented in *The Last American* (1889) by John Ames Mitchell (1845-1918), the founder and publisher of *Life* magazine. Written about the same time as *News from Nowhere,* this global-disaster novel is a thoughtful counterpoint to the futurist utopias described above.

The Last American begins with a short introduction by "The Axis of Wisdom," author of "The Celestial Conquest of Kaly-phorn-ya," which includes commentary on Noz-yt-ahl's "History of the Mehrikans" to help orient the reader. The bulk of the story, however, chronicles the adventurous exploits of the Persian admiral Khan-li of Dimph-yoo-chur who, sailing across the Atlantic Ocean in his ship, the Zlotuhb, rediscovers the continent of North America in the year 2951. Although aware of the ancient country of "Mehrika," which, according to their historical records, was founded by George-wash-yn-tun, the Persians have only a vague and incomplete understanding of the ancient Mehrikans. What *is* clear in this tale of the future is that the United States of America no longer exists in 2951, and hasn't for roughly the last one thousand years. Merika presumably fell into ruin in the twentieth century, plunging into another Dark Ages that appears to have swept across Europe as well. A new Persian civilization has arisen, and Khan-li and his crew have set out across the ocean to conduct archeological and geographical research, hoping to locate and explore the mysterious and intriguing land of Mehrika.

When the Persians reach North America, they sail into a gargantuan abandoned city of giant towers, which they eventually realize is the famous ancient city of "Nhu-Yok." In awe over the immensity of this empty and decaying metropolis, they wander about exploring areas of the city and venturing into various buildings—at one point climbing up through the interior of the Statue of Liberty. Everywhere they observe a corroding and crumbling opulence. In the houses of the rich, they find luxurious furniture, rugs, and sculptures, all covered in dust and rotting away; they find a corpse of a young women still in her bed, preserved for one thousand years. They encounter various wooden Indian statues, which the Persians take to be statues of nobles. For some reason—perhaps due to the severe climate changes the Mehrikans presumably instigated across the country a thousand years earlier—the city is suffocatingly hot and humid.

As they walk about through "Nhu-Yok," pondering what they see, they discuss what the Mehrikans must have been like and what caused their extinction. The evidence they see around them confirms their belief that the Mehrikans were a "mongrel race," shallow, nervous, imitative (borrowing everything from other cultures), extravagant, and with few redeeming virtues. They were a "greedy race, given body and soul to the gathering of riches ... their chiefest passion was to buy and sell." The Mehrikan women seem to have spent all their time and energy shopping. Moreover, these ancient people voraciously read highly popular printed chronicles of "scandals and horrors ... of crime and filth" (our newspapers). Their one redeeming trait was their great mechanical ingenuity. The Persians marvel that their own civilization in the year 2951 has not achieved anything equivalent to the "noisy industries," mysterious locomotive powers, and advanced technologies of the twentieth century. Yet, Mehrika collapsed under the weight of its immorality.

Although the reasons for this collapse are not altogether clear to the Persian explorers, a few things seem evident: the Mehrikans were "drunk with money." And the poor, afflicted with the disease of greed and envy, rose up in rebellion. This lust for money, along with the "frightful climate changes" the Mehrikans somehow produced, had doomed their civilization.

The Persians eventually leave "Nhu-Yok" in search of the supposed capital city of Washington. Following ancient maps, they sail south and observe under the water the wreckage of a large number of metal ships, presumably the remains of the greatest navy in human history, sunk in a colossal sea battle between Mehrika and all of Europe. According to Persian history, Europe was provoked into a massive naval attack on Mehrika because the greedy Mehrikans were appropriating too much of the world's economic profits. The Mehrikan fleet, although significantly outnumbered by the Europeans, emerged victorious, sinking the European fleet.

When the Persians arrive in Washington, they find fresh human footprints. Following these they encounter a young couple and an old man living in the capitol building. They are apparently the last surviving humans in the city. Although communication is difficult, this first meeting between the Persians and the last Mehrikans begins peacefully. But a violent brawl erupts when one of the Persians attempts to kiss the young woman. The old man is killed first, then the young woman, and although several Persians also perish in the fracas, the young man, a ferocious fighter, is also finally killed. After this unnerving altercation— which occurs on the fourth of July—the Persians set sail back across the Atlantic, carrying with them the skull of the "last American."

The Last American is a poignant and highly effective critique of Western-American culture. In ways a comical tale about the murky quality of human history, the story helps us appreciate how all that now exists can be rendered obscure. Resonant with the anti-capitalist philosophies of Morris and Bellamy, this story jolts the reader into vicariously experiencing a future world in which our present modern society—built upon the pursuit of money, greed, and consumption—vanishes into oblivion, leaving only a bleak and decaying record of its presence. The modern West will not be saved. And not because of our advancing technologies: they are neither the key threat to humanity nor our saving grace. It is the shallowness of our collective character that will destroy us, however mechanically ingenious we are. In the end we die from our sins and are reduced to a skull as a museum exhibit in a future civilization.

Steam Men, Robots, Fiends, and Thomas Edison

... the Edisonades were among the most morally reprehensible works of fiction of the 19th century, on a par with the dime novels the Confederacy published to glorify slavery.
John Clute

While Flammarion, Bellamy, Robida, and other writers were traveling through the universe on the wings of cosmic inspiration, as well as thoughtfully contemplating the complex future possibilities of technology and human society, a different stream of writing—more crass, superficial, and sensationalistic—was achieving great popularity in the United States. This wave of lowbrow, action-packed popular stories and short novels both reflected a new social phenomenon in the latter part of the nineteenth century and greatly influenced the future evolution of science fiction.

As a consequence of ongoing secular progress with improved economic conditions and educational opportunities, mass literacy was spreading across the Western world. Specifically in the United States, this increasing literacy fueled the emergence and growth of popular culture, the most far-reaching expressions including serial magazines and the "dime novel." It was within these types of mass produced publications—which included westerns, crime stories, and human interest pieces—that science fiction found a new niche, one that especially reflected the more immature and prejudicial attitudes and sensationalistic tastes of the reading public.

Because almost all of the dime novel science fiction stories—of which there were a huge number published between 1870 and 1910—were geared to a young male readership, science fiction literature, at least as it was realized within such publications, became popularly associated with a juvenile mentality. The stories were, by and large, filled with action and adventure; highly aggressive "Damn the torpedoes, full speed ahead" plot lines; amazing weapons and "gee-whiz" technologies; and a lot of violence and killing, all high energy, high wallop thematic elements that appealed to the young male mind.

Moreover, these stories reflected the rugged individualist, good-guys-versus-bad-guys, and "Manifest Destiny" conquest-of-the-West mentality of nineteenth-century America. As such, they reinforced a simplistic—indeed deeply prejudicial and hypocritical—set of ethical values, strongly contributing to the vulgar public image of early American science fiction. Coinciding with the brutal campaign to dislodge the American Indians from their lands, the novels both fed on the romanticized and highly distorted, self-serving vision of the American expansion westward and conquest of the native Indians; and reflected the ethnocentric mentality that fueled it. In line with popular white American culture, they portrayed the American Indians as dangerous and inferior savages that needed to be contained and taught, if possible, the enlightened principles of modern civilization. The white American hero of the Wild West was Buffalo Bill; the American martyr was General Custer. No matter that the European colonies, and eventually the United States, were the actual aggressors, invading the lands of indigenous populations and taking away their freedom, livelihood, and resources. The science fiction dime novel reflected a dishonest, self-elevating, racist, and culturally biased vision of white American heroic explorers versus the barbaric Indians and any other "primitive" people in need of civilization.

As Clute and Nicholls (1995) observe, almost all dime novel science fiction fell into one of three general categories: invention; a lost race; and marvel stories. The first of these, invention, was instigated by a real technological creation, the "Newark Steam Man" constructed in 1868. Intended to be a commercial product, used to pull carts or wagons, it never realized success, but it probably did inspire the first dime novel science fiction story, *The Steam Man of the Prairies* by Edward Ellis in 1868. Modeled on the human anatomy and powered by steam, the "steam man" has a head, torso, arms, and legs, all built out of metal parts—it is essentially a steam-powered robot. As described in the novel, the steam man of the prairies is a "high tech" transportation machine that pulls a wagon and takes its passengers on adventures out west.

This single novel would ignite an avalanche of imitative science fiction stories in the coming decades, beginning with the dime novel *Frank Reade and his Steam Man of the Plains, or, The Terror of the West* (1876), probably written by Harold Cohen. The author identified in the issue is "Noname," a frequently used pseudonym in subsequent *Frank Reade* stories.

Although all the Frank Reade stories catered to a juvenile mentality and philosophy, they did convey a redeeming message of technological empowerment, igniting the scientific imagination of the typical young reader. For example, from the *Steam Man* (1876):

Charley Gorse beheld a metallic imitation of a man. The figure was about twelve feet high from the bottom of the huge feet to the top of the plug hat which adorned the steam-man's head.

An enormous belly was required to accommodate the boiler and steam chest, and this corpulency agreed well with the height of the metallic steam chap. To give full working room to the very delicate machinery in the interior, the old giant was made to convey a sort of knapsack upon his shoulders. The machine held in its arms in the position taken by a man when he is drawing a carriage.

Charlie glanced up at the face of the monster and beheld a huge pair of glass eyes and an enormous mouth.

"Now then," said Frank, "the lamp will be in his head, and his eyes will be the headlights. His mouth holds the steam whistle. Here, in his belly, we open a door and put in fuel, and the ashes drop down into his legs and are emptied from the moveable kneepan, and without injury to the oiled leg-shafts, for they are inclosed in a tube. That is why the fellow's limbs are so large. These wire cords increase the power in one leg, and cause that leg to go much faster, and in that manner we get a side movement and can turn around" (*Cyberneticzoo.*)

The Frank Reade and Frank Reade, Jr. stories, collected together in the *Frank Reade Library* (1892-1898, 1902-1904), constituted the first serial publication devoted entirely to science fiction. All told, 191 issues were published, exceeding in number all the science fiction magazine issues later published by Hugo Gernsback. The first four volumes chronicled the adventures of the fictitious central character, Frank Reade, and all the remaining ones featured Frank Reade, Jr. As representative titles, after Frank Reade and his steam man, we find *Frank Reade and his Steam Horse* (1882) and *Frank Reade and his Steam Tally Ho* (1893). As the first Frank Reade, Jr. novel, we are introduced to *Frank Reade, Jr., and his Steam Wonder* (1879). Later there is *The Electric Man, or Frank Reade, Jr. in Australia* (1893) and *Lost in the Land of Fire; or, Across the Pampas in the Electric Turret* (1893), among many other rousing tales into wild and uncivilized lands.

In these adventure stories the protagonists travel, at one time or another, across the continental United States and the Wild West; to Mexico and Central America; to the Andes, Ecuador, and the Amazon; to Africa and around the globe; and under the seas and through the clouds above (*Comicbook+.com*). Yet after its long and popular run, the Frank Reade and Frank Reade, Jr. series were discontinued because of its "offensive and morally impoverished content."

Luis Senarens (1863-1939), the "American Jules Verne," writing under the pseudonym of "Noname," wrote most of the Frank Reade, Jr. stories. Altogether, Senerens wrote over three hundred dime novels and up to two thousand stories (Clute and Nicholls, 1995). His prolific and sustained outpouring of Frank Reade, Jr. stories was produced quickly, one right after another, without much editorial polishing or complex plot or character development. His stories were filled with racist and white supremacist thinking, Western imperialist and Manifest Destiny themes, and visions of war and conquest, often involving the slaughter of indigenous peoples living in the wild lands being explored by the stories' protagonists. The central protagonists— presumably exploring but to a significant degree actually invading a land and its people—frequently had to defend themselves against "uncivilized," non-white, non-European inhabitants who, in reality, were the ones being persecuted in defending their own land. The stories mirror the romanticized tales of the glorified American Wild West, only with new and more powerful technologies thrown in to make the confrontations between the natives and the "civilized" protagonists even more lopsided and horrendous.

In highlighting central thematic elements of the classic American western, often taken to exaggerated and morally reprehensible extremes, the Frank Reade stories provided an American western narrative template that many American science fiction adventure stories would adopt in later decades.

The nineteenth-century science fiction dime novels were the direct antecedents of twentieth-century American science fiction "pulp" (cheap paper) magazines, which came into their own under the direction and guidance of Hugo Gernsback and a bit later, John Campbell, in the 1920s and 1930s. In many ways the science fiction pulp magazines inherited the mentality and values of the earlier dime novels. The American mythos of the tough and heroic individual, exploring and conquering new lands, with good guys confronting bad guys while fighting off hostile and primitive natives, in later years was often transformed into outer space settings and unexplored alien worlds, with stupendous battles involving good guys and bad guys and confrontations with hostile aliens that are eventually conquered, if not totally exterminated or destroyed.

According to Clute and Nicholls (1995), after the Frank Reade, Jr. series, Senarens took the same prejudicial and violent thematic elements to even greater extremes in his Jack Wright series (121 stories published from 1891 to 1896), including, for example, *Jack Wright and his Electric Turtle* (1891); *Jack Wright and his Electric Air Rocket* (1894); *The Boy Lion Fighter; or, Jack Wright in the Swamps of Africa* (1895); and *Jack Wright and Frank Reade, Jr, the Two Young Inventors; Or, Brains against Brains: A Thrilling Story of a Race around the World for $10,000* (1896).

In commercial competition with Senarens and the Frank Reade, Jr. series, a second series of science fiction dime novels appeared in the early 1890s. The central character in these novels was Tom Edison, Jr., a fictitious person with no relationship to Thomas Edison, the famous real-life inventor. But the imaginary Tom Edison, Jr. undoubtedly evoked, intentionally so, various positive associations with his namesake. Again, readers thrilled to an assortment of technological inventions (advanced weapons, aircraft, flying suits, and super-submarines), adventure tales to unexplored lands, and many battles and violent conflicts, reflecting similar themes and values as those in the Frank Reade,

Jr. stories. Nine stories were written in the series, including what was probably the best known tale of the collection, *Tom Edison Jr.'s The Electric Sea Spider, or the Wizard of the Submarine World* (1891-1892), in which two hi-tech submarines do battle with each other.

One noteworthy dimension in this story and other novels in the series was the depiction of Germans or Asians as evil and aggressive adversaries that must be defeated in battle. As a plug for the novel put it, *"The Electric Sea Spider* features Kiang-Ho, the first modern "Yellow Peril,"... [an] intelligent, evil Asian mastermind devoted to the goal of the conquest of the West." (*JessNevins.com*). Just as the indigenous people of a territory being explored were often portrayed as the aggressive "bad guys," people of different cultures and "races" — relative to white Americans — were also seen as covetous "bad guys" plotting to invade and conquer our own country and rob us of our freedom. Of course, no one considered the obvious parallels between what these "bad guys" were doing and what we ourselves were doing in exploring and colonizing "uncivilized" lands.

While ostensibly not a literary incarnation within the stories bearing his name, the real-life figure of Thomas Edison and his public image as the greatest inventor of his time had considerable influence on the evolution of science fiction that extended far beyond this one series. Considering that the protagonist of the series, Tom Edison, Jr., is an inventor who creates new technologies — and that this same character-type appears in many other dime novels — it can be argued that whether the actual name of Thomas Edison is used or not, many of the dime novel science fiction stories modeled their central protagonist, in some idealized fashion, on Thomas Edison, the real creative technological genius. We can view an idealized Thomas Edison as providing the realistic inspiration for a central archetypal protagonist in American science fiction during this period, the inventor-hero-explorer who combines scientific-technological knowledge and creativity with a courageous and adventuresome character.

Clute (Clute and Nichols, 1995; *Encyclopedia of Science Fiction*) contends that much of the whole dime novel science fiction phenomenon can be accurately conceptualized and described as "Edisonade," where the central character is, in fact, modeled on Thomas Edison. As Clute describes him, Thomas Alva Edison (1847-1931), especially from the 1880s on, actively worked at promoting a grandiose public image of himself as a unique, unparalleled genius who, through his amazing and numerous inventions, was in the process of transforming the world for the better. (Edison was a science fiction character living in the real world.) This larger-than-life public image took on "mythic" qualities, becoming a powerful icon of the modern technological world. Edison was the great heroic figure of his era, both in his own opinion and that of the public, and for Clute, this idealized image became the inspirational basis—the heroic archetype— behind dime novel science fiction.

As I see it, the elevated image Edison cultivated replaced (or at least vied with) the infamous image of Frankenstein as the archetypal scientist-inventor in science fiction. Not only does the idealized Edison character succeed in his scientific endeavor where Frankenstein fails, he embodies the courage, confidence, and conviction that Frankenstein so tragically lacks. Edison is not afraid to play God.

Including the stories of Frank Reade, Frank Reade, Jr., Jack Wright, and Tom Edison, Jr. in this category, Clute provides the following descriptions of Edisonade:

... any story dating from the late nineteenth century onward and featuring a young US male inventor hero who ingeniously extricates himself from tight spots and who, by so doing, saves himself from defeat and corruption, and his friends and nation from foreign oppressors.

... a brave young inventor creates a tool or a weapon (or both) that enables him to save the girl and his nation (America) and the world from some menace, whether it be foreigners or evil scientists or aliens; and gets the girl; and gets rich.

Clute highlights that the various inventions imagined in the Edisonade books were not simply advanced forms of weaponry but primarily new types of transportation mechanisms. These devices might eventually be used as weapons as well, but their primary function was to facilitate the journey into the unknown and make possible the adventure in the story. Indeed, the machine as a mode of advanced transportation served as a technological icon for the narrative of adventure. As noted earlier, tales of adventure—of extraordinary voyages—are one of the main historical tributaries that fed into the evolution of science fiction. As technology advanced, adventures into the unknown were connected with ever more wondrous vehicles of transportation, empowering ever more extraordinary and amazing journeys into mysterious lands. The machine, ever evolving, was the means and consequently the inspirational symbol for the ever-evolving experience of adventure.

Moreover, going back to the Age of Exploration, we also find a strong association between the exploration of a new land and the acquisition of new knowledge (for example, in *The New Atlantis*). The unknown that is explored and revealed is both a geographical territory and an epistemic wonderland of new discoveries and insights; this was the experience of Banks in his south sea adventures. We see this connection between geographical adventure and increased enlightenment highlighted in the novels of Jules Verne, in which, facilitated through new technologies, we encounter new geographical locales and also achieve new insights and a deeper understanding of humanity, nature, and reality. The adventure is both physical and psycho-philosophical.

As we move into the twentieth century, the rocket or spaceship, as the new icon of transportation technology, takes us not only to unknown alien worlds but to new levels of understanding and knowledge about the universe. From a technological mindset, in which technology is seen as a central facilitator of human progress, the imagined new forms of space transportation symbolized our ascent into new spheres of reality. Through such machines we were elevated both physically and mentally. Indeed, in high tech science fiction, but equally within our high tech culture as a whole, we project our ideologies, beliefs, aspirations, and values onto our machines; they become meaningful symbols of not only who we are but also of our purpose and direction in life. The imagined future of transportation technologies symbolized the courageous and empowered spirit of adventure into the unknown and the never-ending quest for and realization of new knowledge about the cosmos.

A fundamental mythic narrative emerges from the above considerations on Edisonade, transportation technologies, and adventure, one that is emblematic of the high-tech, secular-progress mindset of the modern world: A scientist-technologist hero creates some new device that empowers (usually) him to travel into and explore the unknown. There he encounters obstacles, including dangerous and/or primitive beings, but eventually realizes success, which includes new discoveries and perhaps the opening of new lands to colonize and settle.

Following Stapledon's description of myth as expressing the highest values of a culture, Panshin's concept of transcendence, and Joseph Campbell's theory that myths provoke wonder, awe, and the rapture of being alive, the stories that fall within this deep and pervasive narrative structure are clearly mythic in nature. The empowering technology is fused with a protagonist of brains and courageous spirit; the techno-enhanced hero goes on a journey of discovery and enlightenment, of transcending the commonplace and the immediate here and now, realizing conquest and dominion through his advanced technologies. Although some parts of this mythic narrative extend back to the Age of Exploration and more recently the American Western, the evolving narrative structure, now expanded and amplified with futurist techno-marvels, would continue forward and further develop in twentieth-century science fiction involving the exploration and "conquest" of outer space.

This evolving mythic narrative provided the general plot line behind a good deal of science fiction space opera in the 1930s and 1940s, such as in the writings of "Doc" Smith and John Campbell. In "Doc" Smith's *Skylark* series, for example, we find the young inventor hero, now in the vastly more expansive unknown realm of outer space, exploring the universe with more mind-boggling technologies of transportation and combating aliens with even more stupendous weapons of destruction, in various good-guy-versus-bad guy scenarios.

Clute argues that as Edison became more enraptured in his own myth-making, he became more of a charlatan, announcing new secretive projects that would revolutionize war and give the United States an invincible edge over all other countries in the world. In a sense, Thomas Edison became his own science fiction character in imagined science fiction scenarios in the creation of his titanic public self-image, propelling all of us into an amazing, technologically empowered vision of the future with him leading the way.

Yet, as Clute notes, Edison never delivered on many of his promises. Although the heroes of nineteenth-century Edisonade stories were often portrayed as great inventors and innocent victims defending themselves against outside aggression (resonating with the American self-image that the outside world was filled with tyrants and America was a defender of freedom), Clute contends that Edison, the man, is perhaps best reflected by the fictional inventor in "The Wizard of Oz": a fraud, lost in his own light show.

When the hero of the story moves from a defender of freedom only drawn into the battle due to outside aggression, to a character who sees himself on a mission of facilitating progress and enlightenment in opposition to belligerent or deluded minds, we have a different kind of protagonist. The protagonist moves from defense to offense. Perhaps the aliens or the indigenous population need saving. Perhaps the answer is to be found within our "light show" of techno-marvels and elevated consciousness. The protagonist becomes a colonist in the name of what is true and good.

Considering that many Edisonade storylines involved characters that intentionally journey into other lands with their machines and visions of cultural superiority, Clute's above criteria for the sub-genre omit the "offensive" dimension of many of these stories. Edisonade heroes are enraptured by the self-conceit of the light show they take out West and into other distant lands, forcing it on the natives whether they want to partake in it or not. Edisonade reflects an American offensive philosophy of Manifest Destiny and the racial-cultural superiority of "White America." These heroes are neither innocent nor honest about their ostensible purpose to preserve and defend freedom; they are instead flawed characters infatuated with their own powers, and ethnocentric vision, mission, or values.

Reflecting on the Edisonade phenomenon and the American Western narrative form in much of dime novel science fiction, we are provoked into asking a set of important questions regarding the heroes and protagonists in current scientifically informed mythologies of the future:

- Who is our modern hero in the scientific age? What are the traits and powers of this hero? What are our new morality and ethics as expressed and symbolized in this hero?
- Can ethical character and the aspiration toward scientific-technological knowledge and power be synthesized into a

credible hero?

- What is the hero's journey in science fiction adventure? What is accomplished or realized? What are the central themes of this mythic narrative?
- What is learned on the journey? How is the hero transformed?
- How are we inspired, enlightened, and transformed by vicariously experiencing the recounted journey?
- To what degree do the themes and values of early Edisonade stories continue into the present time? It is highly instructive to look at contemporary science fiction cinema, which seems to be overly populated with versions, or at least key elements, of the narrative plot line of Edisonade and its representative heroes.

* * *

Demonstrating the world-wide fame and influence of Thomas Edison, it is noteworthy that the first science fiction novel in which Edison actually appears as a central character is *Tomorrow's Eve* (or *The Future Eve*) (1886) by the French author Auguste Villiers de l'Isle-Adam (1838-1889). A strange and memorable tale, in which the word "android" appears for the first time in science fiction literature, the novel weaves together the scientific and the mystical, the mental and the physical, technology and philosophy, and sexuality, love, and madness— all these themes spiraling around a fictional version of Thomas Edison, the "Wizard of Menlo Park."

As an integral part of his self-orchestrated larger-than-life public image, Edison enthusiastically embraced the title "Wizard of Menlo Park," one originally given to him by a news reporter. This self-promoted public image—of being a wizard, possessing great powers of invention, creativity, and quasi-magical influence over the forces of nature—is especially significant when we consider how Edison, as a fictional character, was portrayed in stories like *The Future Eve*.

In ancient and medieval mythological tales, the wizard was an archetypal character who possessed both wisdom and magical and mysterious powers. With the rise of the modern scientific framework, such mystical figures became increasingly non-credible and suspicious. Still, the general character type of the wizard persisted in the new archetype of the wise scientist and technologist who, using his scientific knowledge and technological abilities, could effect amazing and seemingly magical acts for the benefit of all. The supernatural wizard of ancient times became the scientific wizard of modern times. Modern science fiction followed suit, retaining the knowledge and mysterious powers of the wizard archetype but now anchoring them to the scientific as opposed to the supernatural. The question is whether this modern wizard also possesses the wisdom of the ancient archetypal character.

The fictional Edison character in *The Future Eve* realizes this synthesis of power and wisdom. He is not a young and innocent inventor hero, as typical of Edisonade stories, but an older, more experienced individual who understands life (he is wise at least in some ways). He possesses great scientific and technological powers (often mysterious in their nature) that he uses to realize wise and ethically elevated ends. He demonstrates both humility and benevolence. Again, he is the ancient wizard, made over, in scientific-technological clothing.

But in this novel the transformation from the supernatural wizard to the scientific wizard is not absolute or complete. As already frequently illustrated, the shift from a metaphysical or supernatural ontology in ancient myth and fantasy to a scientific ontology in modern science fiction has not been absolute, for many religious and mystical elements and themes have carried through to modern science fiction. Such that Edison, the fictionalized, technological wizard in *The Future Eve*, not only engages and manipulates forces within the scientific realm but also dives into the mystical and the spiritual realm as well.

The plot of *The Future Eve* is as follows: A young and wealthy Englishman falls in love with a beautiful young woman—a Venus—whom the young man soon realizes is totally shallow without any depth of character. But the young man is obsessed and unable to break free of the spell cast by this woman. Feeling totally depressed, he decides to commit suicide. He tells his story to his friend, Thomas Edison, who proposes a scheme to help him. Edison will build an exact replica of the woman—an android—that will possess all the outward beauty of the woman but also a "greater profundity of soul." This new Eve—that in many ways can be programmed to do whatever the young man desires—will free the man of his fixation on the beautiful but vacuous young woman. The young man agrees to the proposal and the new Eve is built. True to the plan, she is both completely realistic in appearance and behavior and utterly amazing in the quality of her character. She does seem better than the original. After his initial shock wears off, the young man finds himself totally enraptured by the new Eve and freed from the spell of his previous fixation.

The Future Eve explores many important themes. First, what is real and what is artificial? When Edison first proposes the creation of the new Eve, the young man argues at length that he could not possibly find an "artificial" woman romantically satisfying. But Edison repeatedly points out that at present the young man is obsessed with a flesh-and-blood woman who is totally artificial in her mannerisms and personality; she is a calculated mask presented to the world. What, indeed, is real, and what is simply a simulation? Secondly, related to this first theme, Edison and the young man engage in an extended and complex dialogue on how modern humans are increasingly overpowered and controlled by the growing artificiality in modern society, in particular, the way many young men fall victim to pretty yet superficial, calculating, and "artificial" women. All of this dialogue serves to explore the nature of love and romance between men and women. And here Edison, the technological genius, has a lot to stay about the humanistic and emotional sides of life. Can science solve the problems and challenges of love?

But besides his humanistic wisdom, Edison is portrayed most emphatically throughout the book as an unparalleled technological wizard. His laboratory holds many mysterious and wondrous inventions, electrical, mechanical, and chemical. Most of these devices and strange new materials far surpass anything that actually existed in Edison's day. For example, when Edison shows the young man the still inanimate new Eve—opening up her encasing—there ensues an exceedingly detailed description of the various internal mechanical and electrical devices and chemical substances inside her, including what sounds like a central information processing device similar to that of a computer. Through recording technologies, the android has been programmed with a huge variety of behaviors, mannerisms, and linguistic expressions. Edison also describes, in a poetic and artistic fashion, the subtle and complex external features of the android: the exquisitely realistic and soft skin; the radiant eyes; the ruby lips; the lustrous hair; the delicate fingernails; and the complex array of perfumes and scents Eve can emit. At one level, the new Eve is a miracle of scientific engineering, aesthetic design, and human reason. For its time, the detailed and exhaustive description of the workings and behaviors of the android, even if based on engineering and scientific concepts that are fuzzy or somewhat lacking in modern credibility, is one of the most noteworthy and creative dimensions of the novel. What would it mean to create an artificial human?

But, as the young man repeatedly brings up in the tale, this mechanistic miracle cannot possibly possess a soul or an inner realm of personal experience, or so he believes. It is empty inside, without consciousness, he argues. And yet, as one of the more interesting turn of events in the novel, the young man is unwittingly drawn into a "Turing Test." The Turing Test, derived from the twentieth-century computer theorist, Alan Turing, is a thought experiment for determining if an artificial intelligence machine is actually thinking (Lombardo, 2002b). The Turing Test could also be seen as a way to assess whether or not a machine (for all practical purposes) captures the essence of being human. In *The Future Eve*, the android, in a romantic, intimate, and ingenious version of the Turing Test, actually passes the test. Eve's apparent compassion, sensitivity, and emotional expressiveness (and not just simply her intellect) seem totally human, in fact, realizing a sublime level of feeling and empathic understanding.

And yet, there is a twist. As the novel nears the end, Edison reveals that he has been assisted in the creation of this android by a mysterious woman who, under a mesmeric spell that Edison produced in her (he is a wizard in many diverse ways), is able to telepathically communicate her thoughts and feelings to others. This female assistant has invested the android with her own feelings, thoughts, and even personal identity: she has in essence conducted a mind transfer of sorts. Eve, then, is not simply a product of physical science and engineering, but also one of the assistant's enigmatic and mystical powers.

The Future Eve is a highly philosophical novel, delving into the nature of reality and the nature of consciousness and the soul. Through the characters' back-and-forth debate, Villiers de l'Isle-Adam explores the relationship between science and spiritualism; between the mental and the physical; and the eternal and the temporal. The human soul is described as an eternal reality whereas the body, whether biologically or technologically produced, is depicted as a temporal reality, with no inner substance or consciousness. And although the story generally seems to support a scientific vision of the nature of humankind — such that it could be engineered through the appropriate technologies — by its end the story supports a dualistic vision of physical reality and the conscious mind. If the android possesses consciousness, she has realized awareness and an inner personal self through means other than those of physical science. In the novel's conclusion, Edison, the wizard of the scientific age, reveals himself as a bit of a mystic, pondering the limitations of his own powers not only in creating a truly technological conscious human but also in addressing the agonies associated with romantic love.

In the final analysis, we are left with such questions as: Why does it seem plausible to believe that a self-conscious mind can be realized in a physical body through obscure and mysterious mystical means, but not through clearly defined and understood scientific methods? And also, must we still accept Frankenstein's (Shelley's) view that only God can give the physical human form a conscious soul?

* * *

I thus drew steadily nearer to that truth, by whose partial discovery I have been doomed to such a dreadful shipwreck: that man is not truly one, but truly two.
Robert Louis Stevenson

As explained in the opening chapters and illustrated throughout the book, science fiction delves into the possibilities of all aspects of reality. Although the popular stereotype of science fiction emphasizes the physical sciences and the future potential of physical technologies, science does include the study of the psychological as well. Certainly stories can be written that are grounded in psychology and explore the strange and extraordinary powers of the human mind — as we've seen with Mary Shelley and Poe. Transcendence may be realized in literary speculations on the possibilities of consciousness. Such psychological science fiction often brings in philosophical and even spiritual-religious considerations, as well as bio-physical ideas. Such weaving together of the scientific with more abstract and metaphysical ideas is not unusual, even when the focus of the story is on physical science (including astronomy) and the possibilities of physical technologies. Indeed, the psychological and its diverse, often interweaving perspectives—scientific, philosophical, spiritual, and even the occult and Gothic—has been a common feature of science fiction at least since Kepler speculated on the different psychologies of lunar inhabitants based on whether the earth was present or absent in the sky.

Frankenstein raised the question of whether a body constructed out of dead parts and reanimated through electricity could possess a mind, a self, or a soul. *The Future Eve*, as well as *The Sandman*, presented a similar set of questions regarding a robot. Both today's science fiction and computer technology communities continue this debate: Can machines of sufficient complexity achieve a conscious mind (Kurzweil, 1999, 2005)? Of course, answering this question requires an understanding of the nature of the conscious mind and its possibilities. Both Mary Shelley and Auguste Villiers de l'Isle-Adam suggested through their stories that the mind required the spiritual or supernatural, although the latter examined this issue in much more philosophical depth than the former. And clearly this debate in science fiction (and science) over whether a conscious mind can be realized or constructed based upon advanced scientific knowledge and technologies has stimulated an almost continual outpouring of provocative books and films.

The scientific study of the conscious human mind was a rapidly developing discipline of thinking and research in the latter half of the nineteenth century, inspired and informed by Darwin's evolutionary theory of humans; physiological inquiry into the brain and its connection with consciousness and various psychological capacities; and other diverse scientific arenas, including even physics and chemistry (Boring, 1950; Lombardo, 1987). We have already explored the rise of mesmerism and the study of hypnosis that influenced both psychological thinking and more esoteric speculation in the nineteenth century. As the complex and evolving arena of the psychological sciences developed and achieved increasing public visibility, they would similarly influence and inspire new themes in literature, including science fiction. To recall from Chapter Two, a key theme in twentieth-century science fiction would be the possibilities of the future evolution of humans, biologically, psychologically, and socially, and in particular, how the sciences of mind, body, and brain might inform and guide this process.

In the last decades of the nineteenth century the scientific study of psychopathology was gaining momentum, informed by naturalistic science rather than superstition and the occult. (Madness in ancient times had been seen a product of demonic possession.) Depth psychology—delving below the surface of consciousness—was an area of increasing interest and inquiry; pathology, in fact, was connected with the strange and mysterious undercurrents of the human mind. By the turn of the century, Freudian psychoanalysis would pull together madness with the unconscious into an extremely influential and comprehensive vision of the workings of the human mind. But even before Freud, in the 1870s and 1880s, a particular idea within depth psychology and the study of pathology (that Freud would later embrace) was being widely written about and discussed. This idea—which actually has very ancient origins—was that within the human mind there exist multiple selves (or personalities), one or more existing below the surface of consciousness. Of special note, this plurality of selves could be conceptualized as a fundamental duality in a state of inner conflict—of a "good self" (civilized) and an "evil self" (animal-like) that struggled for dominion over a person's mind. This was the theme that would carry the plot of one of the most famous literary creations of the 1880s, (the) *Strange Case of Dr Jekyll and Mr Hyde* (1886) by Robert Louis Stevenson.

It might seem odd to include the story of Dr. Jekyll and Mr. Hyde in a study of science fiction, but in several respects this short novel warrants inclusion. First, as explained above, it is informed by psychological science—indeed contemporary psychological thinking at its time. Second, it is a tale of intended psychological evolution, of an effort to transcend the inner conflict of the normal human mind. Third, the protagonist, Dr. Jekyll, is a man of science, a medical doctor, who concocts a chemical potion to bring about the psychological transformation. Science is the means to transcendence. Fourth, the story has a definite Gothic and horror feel to it; we have a "monster" invented by science haunting the dark and mysterious city streets of London. In fact, in some ways the story has a *Frankenstein* feel, for in tampering with nature, the scientist not only brings suffering to people around him but in the end is destroyed for his secretive research into the workings of human nature and the human mind. Finally, the central theme of the duality of human consciousness, and in particular the idea of a "dark self" inhabiting the deeper stratum of the human mind, would be a recurrent theme in subsequent science fiction. *Dr. Jekyll and Mr. Hyde* is the archetypal modern narrative dealing with the theme of the duality of human nature, a duality that we will struggle with in imagining and guiding our future evolution.

Robert Louis Stevenson (1850-1894) achieved great fame in his lifetime above and beyond the writing of this ominous tale, being the author of *Treasure Island* (1883), *Kidnapped* (1886), and numerous other works. But the story of Jekyll and Hyde reflects a deep personal dimension that sheds light on how the author saw himself; his personality, so he believed, possessed its own Jekyll and Hyde. In this sense, *Dr. Jekyll and Mr. Hyde* reveals the inner dynamics of Stevenson's mind and life struggles.

The idea that the human mind contains both a good side and an evil side—an ethical duality—has ancient roots that can be traced back to Zoroastrian and Judeo-Christian thinking. Yet, as psychologists and historians might argue, the ancient theme of a battle between a powerful good spirit and an opposing evil spirit in a war over control of humanity is a psychological projection of our perceived inner duality of moral versus immoral personalities. Stevenson was raised in a strict Calvinist home environment, one he found exceedingly repressive. As a young adult he reacted against this rigid moral-religious framework, adopting a bohemian lifestyle and partaking, as he states it, in "precocious depravity." Writing during the Victorian era of repressive sexual and moral codes, Stevenson saw within himself the conflict and tension between a strict religious and moral mode of thinking and unconstrained passion and uninhibited pleasure. (It was a battle of order versus chaos.) He suffered from nightmares of hell and damnation, the moral and punitive conscience within punishing him in his dreams for his disbelief, transgressions, and hedonistic lifestyle. As early as 1876 he expressed the belief that there was a dual dimension to the human mind, further stating that this duality was not a good thing, for the human mind strives for unity and wholeness rather than conflict and division. He strove for unity in his life but what he experienced was duality (Luckhurst, 2006).

Referring back to the above comments on late nineteenth-century depth psychology and the study of psychopathology, and in line with Stevenson's own thoughts, a number of cases of multiple or dual personalities were documented in the 1870s and 1880s. The idea was "in the air." Indeed, after the publication of *Jekyll and Hyde*, Stevenson engaged in written correspondence with psychologists on the duality theme of the story and its connection with contemporary psychology. The story was later described as "foreshadowing ... the most startling scientific discovery" that the disintegration of the human personality is a constant occurrence (Luckhurst, 2006).

Along with the contemporary psychological writings, then, the tale of Jekyll and Hyde found its stimulus in the turbulence and self-reflection of Stevenson's own mind. Further, consider that the main storyline came to Stevenson in a dream (Freud's window into the unconscious) while the author was sick and bedridden, after which he wrote the story in what could be described as a "feverish frenzy." After creating the first draft, he showed it to his wife Fanny, who critiqued it. This provoked him into tossing it into the fire and completely rewriting it. Conflagration, figurative and literal, is part of its genesis.

Not only is *Dr. Jekyll and Mr. Hyde* Gothic in tone, with dark and spooky elements and settings, it reveals its Romantic roots as well, exploring human emotions and the psychological turmoil associated with our passions, revulsions, and fears. It brings to the forefront the idea that we are a mystery to ourselves, one that we hide and run from but which nevertheless haunts the corridors and recesses of our mind. The psychological becomes a tangible element projected into the mood and setting of the story—and what is fearful within us is painted onto the world around us.

The story of *Dr. Jekyll and Mr. Hyde* is not written in the chronological order of events recounted in the tale; time to some degree jumps around. We only learn that Dr. Jekyll and Mr. Hyde are the "same" person at the end of the story, which is initially presented as a mystery—the mystery of Hyde.

But following the chronological order of events covered in the story, the starting point is Dr. Jekyll's realization that despite the upstanding moral rectitude he has maintained throughout his life, he cannot completely control himself. He has struggled to hold in check various unspecified immoral and depraved impulses, but at times he has given in and acted upon these desires. (It always remains a mystery what these depravities are.) Jekyll is concerned that his social reputation may suffer if these transgressions ever become publicly known. Provoked by these concerns, Dr. Jekyll creates a chemical potion that he believes will release the evil side within, bringing it to the surface and allowing it to manifest as a distinct and separate person, unrecognizable as Dr. Jekyll. This alter-ego can then engage in immoral actions, unbeknownst even to him. In essence, instead of struggling against his dark side, he creates a way to let the dark side run free and have its due, without troubling or implicating the good side. Rather than fight against and attempt to contain the devil within, he lets the devil loose. This evil personality is of course Mr. Hyde. And this act of emancipation will be Dr. Jekyll's undoing.

Mr. Hyde is the repugnant and mysterious presence that haunts the story, repeatedly appearing and then disappearing throughout the tale. He is observed in different actions and encounters by other characters in the story, who are suspicious of him and wonder who he is, believing he is a nefarious and sinister person. Who is this strange individual, this enigmatic Mr. Hyde? One character in the story observes Mr. Hyde trample a young girl. Another person comes to the conclusion that Hyde is blackmailing Dr. Jekyll, for Dr. Jekyll (for reasons unknown) seems to be protecting him. It is discovered that Dr. Jekyll has made Mr. Hyde the sole beneficiary of his will. A third character (the maid) is convinced that Hyde is responsible for the murder of an older gentleman, found bludgeoned to death in the streets. (The murder weapon puzzlingly turns out to be Dr. Jekyll's cane.) Hyde is described, by one of the above characters as possessing "Satan's signature upon his face." Hyde is "troglodytic." Smaller in stature than Jekyll, Hyde appears to another person in the story as having "something wrong with his appearance," though he is unable to precisely define what that "something" is: How do you describe "the appearance of evil"?

The truth is finally revealed in two letters that appear in the last section of the story. The first is written by a medical colleague of Dr. Jekyll who has witnessed Hyde transform back into the doctor, and was thus the first person to discover the true connection between the characters. After witnessing the transformation, he goes into shock and dies within a week. The second letter—apparently a suicide note found next to the dead body of Mr. Hyde (but in Jekyll's oversized clothes)—is from Dr. Jekyll himself. This second letter explains Jekyll's experiments leading to the release of Mr. Hyde, and all the troubles that followed, culminating in Jekyll's decision to kill himself and necessarily Hyde as well. As Jekyll recounts in his letter, once released through the ingestion of the potion, Mr. Hyde became an increasingly powerful force, vying for supremacy in Jekyll's life. Jekyll was steadily drawn into the evil vortex, vicariously reveling in Mr. Hyde's immoral escapades. Jekyll was losing control to Hyde. Jekyll attempted to put a stop to things by not ingesting the potion, but it got to the point where Mr. Hyde would "come out" on his own without Jekyll taking the drug. Becoming increasingly reclusive, Jekyll decided that the only solution was suicide, an act that would serve as both punishment and atonement for what he had done. It was also the only way to put an end to the soul-destroying Mr. Hyde. In order to kill Hyde, he had to kill himself, for the devil within him only lived through him, a parasite on his soul.

As Roger Luckhurst (2006) explains, Stevenson's *Dr. Jekyll and Mr. Hyde* has been the subject of many diverse interpretations, from the psychological and social (including Freudian analyses) to the theological and philosophical. Due to its immense success and notoriety, the tale has become both archetypal and mythic within popular culture, resonating so deeply with the dark corners of the human psyche that the expression "Jekyll and Hyde" has become part of the popular idiom. *Dr. Jekyll and Mr. Hyde* symbolizes the deep and uneasy duality within our minds, between the good and the bad, and the dangers and struggles associated with this moral and personal bifurcation. After great sales in its first year of publication, the first stage production opened in London in 1888. Unfortunately, soon thereafter the first of the "Jack the Ripper" murders occurred, forcing the closing of the show—the popular view being that the show somehow provoked the murders. Yet Jekyll and Hyde would not stay out of public consciousness, and many cinematic adaptations would be produced in the decades to follow, including the most famous ones: the 1920 production starring John Barrymore, Jr.; the 1931 film with Fredric March (who won the best actor Academy Award for his role); and the 1941 adaptation with Spencer Tracy, Ingrid Bergman, and Lana Turner. In true Hollywood fashion, these movie versions introduced a romantic element, something totally absent in the original story, but this device—involving two women, good and evil, vying for the love of Jekyll and Hyde—would also symbolize and further reinforce the dual nature of the human soul.

Although the moral duality of good versus evil is an ancient archetypal theme in human consciousness, informing and structuring numerous myths and tales running back through the entirety of human history, the story of Jekyll and Hyde, as personifications of this duality, resonates deeply with the modern mind. The tale can be interpreted as a clash between the Apollonian and the Dionysian, of civilization versus barbarity, or of Freud's super-ego (the bastion of the moral conscience) versus the primitive, lustful, and unconstrained id. It is a tale of the modern, civilized man of science who cannot control his darker, more primordial self. Can science and conscious reason lead us to wisdom and human progress? Can we transcend our primordial passions?

Not that Jekyll is completely wise or unified in purpose: Does he release Hyde to bring peace to his troubled and conflicted mind, or does he release Hyde in order to revel more completely in his own lusts and desires? Is the experiment ruled by reason or by passion? Following the dualism of the story, as well as the dualism in Stevenson's own mind, the answers to all these polar questions are "both." Although we could view Jekyll as engaging in the purposeful evolution of the human mind through science—in allowing (as an enlightened modern mind) increasing freedom for his primitive appetites and passions—it is also a story of regression, as well as the fear of regression. At any rate, Jekyll does not reflect or realize Stevenson's own expressed insight that the mind strives toward unity. Rather, Jekyll unleashes an uncontrollable duality. In the end, it's an unworkable solution: Having released the monster within, the monster destroys him.

Chapter 10

Adventures into the Solar System and Encounters with the Martians

Across the Zodiac and the Canali of Mars

There is life on the planet Mars ... Professor Percival Lowell, the recognized greatest authority on the subject, declares there can be no doubt that living beings inhabit our neighbor world.
Lilian Whiting

The Italian astronomer Giovanni Schiaparelli (1835-1910) reported in 1877 that through his telescope he could see various *canali* on the surface of Mars. The Italian word *canali* can be translated into English as either "channels" or "canals," but by far the more favored translation in the popular news covering his discovery was "canals." Inspired by Schiaparelli's discovery of *canali* on Mars, many people in the late nineteenth and early twentieth century believed that there were artificially constructed canals of water on Mars, indicating some kind of highly developed Martian civilization. Schiaparelli's *canali* aligned with the common belief, at least among the scientifically educated, that there were numerous other civilized worlds in outer space and that Mars was a very likely candidate as a habitat for an advanced alien "race" and civilization.

The writer and astronomer, Percival Lowell (1855-1916), inspired in mid-life by reading both Schiaparelli and Flammarion, thereafter devoted himself to the study of Mars, writing three books on the planet, and becoming the strongest and most visible advocate for the theory that there were canals on Mars. In fact, through his own telescopic observations, Lowell not only reported that he could see them, he created numerous drawings and illustrations depicting in considerable detail the network of Martian "canals" and identifiable "oases" at convergent points along them. (We see what we believe.) In his books *Mars* (1895), *Mars and its Canals* (1906), and *Mars as the Abode of Life* (1908), Lowell hypothesized that Mars was an old planet and drying up; that it was the home to intelligent life; that the Martian civilization was very ancient; and that the Martians had constructed the canals as a way to channel water from the Martian polar ice caps in order to irrigate its vast deserts. It all made perfect sense.

A world-renowned writer, scholar, and scientist, and founder of the Lowell Observatory in Flagstaff, Arizona, Lowell saw himself as a courageous and imaginative leader in new scientific discoveries about the universe, combating the closed-mindedness and egocentricity of traditional, conservative thinking. As he argued, at first new scientific discoveries and innovative ideas often seem implausible, if not ridiculous. He firmly believed that his own scientific work and various mind-expanding hypotheses on the Martian canals and Martian civilization created such conservative counter-reactions. But in his mind he was bravely and creatively expanding the sphere of human knowledge and in the end he would be vindicated.

Although Lowell believed he was a scientific visionary, he was also well respected within the scientific community. Lowell was a highly credible authority on what was scientifically plausible. Yet, after Lowell presented his theory and diagrams of the Martian canals, what was progressively and definitively revealed in subsequent years, with increasingly more powerful and detailed telescopic observations of the Martian surface, was that contrary to Lowell's views there were no canals on Mars. Was Lowell hallucinating? How was it possible that a scientific authority could misperceive and misrepresent reality? There were detailed diagrams of the canals that he drew of what *he believed he saw* on the Martian surface. In his mind, his scientific ideas were based on observable facts; facts that it turned out did not really exist.

What Lowell's scientific writings and telescopic observations of Mars most importantly illustrate are two related points: What is observed is strongly influenced by theory, beliefs, and attitude, hence the "theoretical nature of facts" (Feyerabend, 1965, 1969; Lombardo, 2017). Lowell believed in the existence of the canals and therefore "saw" them in great profusion across the Martian surface. Critics of Lowell's ideas progressively invalidated his observations, arguing that his viewings suffered from "optical illusion" effects. But Lowell's beliefs and theories locked him into perceiving reality a certain way. As a second point, what is considered scientifically plausible versus implausible is to some significant degree a shifting and ambiguous reality. For a few decades the idea of canals on Mars did seem scientifically plausible, grounded in a number of independent telescopic observations reporting the canals and bolstered by Lowell's scientific reputation. But the scientifically plausible, specifically regarding the surface of Mars, changed over time, and Lowell's factually observable canals became illusions and expressions of his wishful thinking.

Yet once an idea catches on, especially if it stimulates provocative and dramatic associations, it may take decades (if not centuries) for the idea to lose popular credibility. In the 1880s and 1890s we find a number of science fiction novels focusing on the Martians and the planet Mars. Stimulated by popular astronomy publications such as those of Flammarion and others, Mars was a hot topic within public consciousness, and numerous speculative writers created stories about Mars and the Martians. In one of these novels, Thomas Edison appears again in a fictionalized version as the scientist hero. In two novels—*Two Planets* (1897) by Kurd Lasswitz and *Edison's Conquest of Mars* (1898) by Garrett Serviss—the Martian canals are central fixtures of the Martian surface. And both of these tales, as well as Percy Greg's *Across the Zodiac* (1880) and H. G. Wells' *The War of the Worlds* (1898) adopted the view that Martian civilization was much older and more advanced than human civilization. Indeed, the idea of canals on Mars created by some ancient Martian civilization would continue in science fiction into the twentieth century, from Edgar Rice Burroughs' amazing adventures on Mars — the *Barsoom* series — written from the 1910s through the 1940s, and up to the 1950s in Ray Bradbury's classic and compelling *The Martian Chronicles* (1950), long after the ideas of Martian canals and ancient Martian civilization lost any scientific plausibility.

In this final chapter of volume one, I describe a noteworthy set of science fiction novels in the 1880s and 1890s about Mars and the Martians, up to and including Wells' *The War of the Worlds*. I also include a couple of other important novels published in the same period that take us to other planets and encounters with other aliens within our solar system, including one novel where the human explorers meet and converse with the ghosts of the dead. Fascinatingly, these novels say as much about our own values and beliefs as they do about the imagined aliens encountered in the stories.

* * *

Peace be yours no force can break, Peace not Death hath power to shake;
Peace from peril, fear, and pain; Peace — until we meet again!
Not before the sculptured stone, But the All-Commander's Throne.
Percy Greg

Frequently cited in histories of science fiction, *Across the Zodiac: The Story of a Wrecked Record* (1880) is described on the title page of the original edition as "Deciphered, Translated, and Edited" by Percy Greg, as if Greg, the identified author, were publishing a document written by someone else. In the first part of the novel the "translator" of the document explains how he came into possession of this strange tale—presumably originally written in Latin—through an acquaintance of his who first found the book. Supposedly the book was discovered in the wreckage of some kind of aerial object that had plummeted to the earth. Adding to the intrigue of it all, in the wreckage were the remains of a human body, obliterated beyond recognition. Was this the corpse of the actual author of the tale? Was this the corpse of the adventurer described in the manuscript?

The extraordinary tale recounted in *Across the Zodiac* concerns a man who travels to Mars in a spaceship that he has designed. Upon landing on Mars he encounters human-like Martians who are members of an ancient civilization with highly advanced technologies, but governed by social customs and values that the earthman finds ethically and spiritually repugnant. The "translated" document, which makes up the bulk of the book, describes the earthman's experiences on Mars.

In spite of the effort to create a sense of mystery regarding the provenance of the Martian adventure tale, it makes perfect sense that Percy Gregg (1836-1889) was the actual author of the tale of the journey to Mars. Greg was a political and historical writer, and this novel about the Martians and their civilization is strongly informed and inspired by Greg's views on human progress and the nature of the good society. Indeed, the book is primarily a dystopian novel and a predictive warning concerning the future of human civilization. The novel presents an excessively detailed and comprehensive critique of a highly advanced Martian civilization on moral and spiritual grounds. Related from the characters' points of view, the implication, which is fairly explicit, is that modern human society, with its obsession on science, materialism, and technological growth, could sadly end up the same way.

The novel begins with a dialogue between the presumed

translator of the adventure tale and the man who supposedly discovered the manuscript in the wreckage of the spaceship. They comment on how modern positivist science is dogmatic in its doctrines, and in particular, how science has a strong bias against religious beliefs in miracles that from the scientific point of view seem highly improbable, if not impossible. Moreover, the two characters foresee that science in the future, with its absolutist truth claims, may come to completely dominate human society, and traditional religious thinking may become outlawed. Science is the enemy of freedom of thought. In this opening dialogue Greg lays his philosophical cards on the table. He is throwing back at science the very argument that science leveled against religion: that the latter constrained and repressed human thought and imagination.

After recounting how he came into possession of the mysterious manuscript and his efforts to decipher the meaning of its contents, the translator presents his edited version of the manuscript, which is as follows:

The protagonist of the adventure story has discovered how to contain and channel the anti-gravitational force of "APERGY" — as noted earlier, a popular speculative scientific idea in late nineteenth-century science fiction — and he constructs a spaceship the "Astronaut" (the first time this word is used), which is powered by this force. He intends to travel to Mars in this ship, since popular opinion is that Mars contains water, an atmosphere with clouds, and a reasonably temperate climate.

In a preview of the literary style throughout the whole tale, the construction and operation of the spaceship and the journey through outer space from the earth to Mars are both described in excruciating and pedantic detail. The obsessively precise and elaborate descriptions of *everything* encountered and experienced within the Martian adventure greatly enhance the realism of the story — the challenges of traveling through outer space are particularly prescient and insightful — but this style of writing also makes the novel laborious and difficult to read. The book is a compendium of a million hypothetical facts, rivaling the info-dumps of Verne.

Landing on Mars, the protagonist almost immediately encounters its inhabitants, whom he refers to as the "Martials" (not Martians). The Martials are human in appearance, but notably smaller and frailer than earth humans, the tallest ones being barely five feet in height. The Martials seem agitated by his presence and even hostile, but they take him to the home of one of the Martials, an older and impressive looking male who appears more calm and receptive to his presence. This Martial allows the earth man to stay in his home and, with the help of his family, starts to teach him about Mars, Martial customs, and most importantly Martial language. *Across the Zodiac* is often cited as presenting the first fully developed treatment in science fiction of an alien language, and as with other aspects of the Martial world, in this section the structure and nuances of the Martial language are described in intricate and precise detail.

In this early part of the story, the Martial home is also described—including rooms, walls, floors, decorations, and furniture—in great detail. With almost a psychedelic flair, the Martial home is alive with bright colors; in fact, the Martial culture appears to be highly engaged in decorating and embellishing almost everything with brilliant, super-saturated colors. They also maintain exquisite and lush gardens in and around the home, with an immense variety of beautiful and strange flowers, which are meticulously and artistically arranged in pleasing and dramatic patterns. (Our protagonist had first noticed in landing that the Martials' agricultural fields were very orderly and well manicured.) Through this initial tour, our protagonist observes a highly refined and pronounced aesthetics, domestically as well as in the Martial civilization as a whole.

Underneath this precise order and vivid color, our protagonist also soon discovers that Martial society is much more scientifically and technologically advanced then earthly human society. As the Martial who took him into his home explains, the official Martial philosophy is to conceptualize everything completely in physical scientific terms. The Martials are forbidden to believe in anything that goes against the "laws of nature" (as they understand such laws). The first Martials he encountered were hostile toward him because he seemed to contradict their sense of what was scientifically possible. As the senior Martial explains, in the ancient past the Martials had believed in a non-corporeal realm, but they now completely and officially reject miracles, God, or an afterlife as unscientific and impossible. The Martials are pure secularists and absolutely authoritarian about it.

Presumably connected with this scientific and materialist theory of reality, the Martials subscribe to a self-serving philosophy of life. The "sole motive" driving Martial behavior is the personal enjoyment of the longest life possible. Selfishness is the central principle in their lives, and the ideals of both love and affection have been abandoned. Marital relationships are grounded in business-like contracts, similar to the sale and purchasing of goods, and parental affection has disappeared, with children primarily raised in nurseries, divorced from parental involvement. Offspring that are born deformed (as well as lunatics) are eliminated.

As the story unfolds, the argument emerges that the selfishness and "moral degradation" of the Martials stems from their absolute scientism and abandonment of any belief in God and an afterlife. It is strongly implied that morality is only possible if grounded in a belief in a Supreme Being. Science may empower the material world (science being connected in this book with physicalism), but it impoverishes the soul. This kind of argument reflects the reactionary and traditionalist fear that in abandoning God and religion, modern Western science was creating a moral vacuum with no transcendent principle for ethical guidance.

But we also learn that all is not lost. The male Martial who has befriended our protagonist also reveals the existence of a secret society on Mars—a small minority of the population— that still embraces beliefs in a Supreme Being, an immortal soul, and an afterlife. Practicing a philosophy of care and love, the members of this underground movement believe that the individual mind, educated and trained in their secret principles and practices, can both learn to control matter and communicate with other minds through thought. (They seem to believe they can even kill people through thought.) The older Martial is an important leader in this clandestine society, and he has educated all his family members (wife and children who live with him) in this rebellious underground philosophy. This conflict in Martial society between the spiritual-caring and the materialist-selfish philosophies of life creates the dramatic tension and much of the consequent action within the story.

This duality of ways of life, hypothetically represented in this imaginary Martian world, represents two alternative social directions and possible utopian visions for humanity in the future. Do we go toward the scientific or the spiritual? Through the voice of his protagonist, Greg clearly holds the spiritualist vision as the more preferable of the two. Again, his critical representation of the Martial scientific-secular society is intended as an ominous warning regarding the negative direction in which he sees contemporary Western society heading. *Across the Zodiac* is a combination utopian and dystopian novel, using Mars as a canvas on which to paint and compare both these visions. We can also view this contrast of perspectives as between striving toward greater physical powers versus striving toward greater mental powers in our future evolution.

An early turn of events in the story both underscores the value of love and caring and sheds light on the role of women in Martial society: In a courageous and unselfish act (demonstrating his belief in a philosophy of caring), our protagonist saves the life of one of the daughters of the elder Martial. Since the daughter, Eveena, now owes her life to the earthman, she is offered to him in marriage by the father. Delicate and demur, Eveena is both totally baffled and elated at being rescued from certain death.

Although in many respects a sharp contrast is drawn between the scientific and spiritual Martials, when it comes to Martial women, it seems that on both sides of the divide they are conceptualized, socialized, and treated as subservient individuals. Wives are cloistered in the home and wear veils (as do all females) whenever they leave. The husband is the master of the household and owns the wife by contract. The primary roles for almost all women in Martial society are "marriage and maternity"; they raise children and serve their husbands. In turn, they are protected and cared for by the male.

But Eveena's character departs from this traditional stereotype. Although raised in this sharp and lop-sided division of the sexes, and shy and diffident at first toward the earthman, she transcends the constraints placed upon her sex and as the story unfolds becomes a heroic, tenaciously assertive, and admirable character. She explains to our protagonist that while she repeatedly grapples with misunderstandings between the two of them, she wants to be his true companion and partner in all his adventures and challenges in life, not simply a pampered and protected wife behind the scenes. In the story's finale, in an act of love and courage, she repays her debt to him.

Eveena especially demonstrates her wisdom and character when she is put in the position of being the "first wife" in the earth man's "harem." When our protagonist eventually meets the "Prince"—the supreme sovereign of Mars—the Prince is so elated to meet a visitor from another world that he bestows upon the earth man a host of gifts, including a mansion with both human and animal servants, an agricultural plot sufficient to provide both ample food and a wealthy income, and six more wives. As the first wife Eveena must manage all the other wives, who are often petty, childish, competitive, and envious of her privileged status.

While descriptions of the earth man's travels across different regions of Mars—often including Eveena—allow for copious detail in his observations and reflections on Martial society the deeper plot involves his induction into the secret spiritualist society—"The Children of the Silver Star"—with its accompanying elaborate rituals, recitations, incantations, and mystical apparitions. Our protagonist and his fellow spiritualists must contend with the nefarious schemes plotted by a group of Martials (the selfish scientific kind) who wish to steal the secret of APERGY from the earthman and expose and destroy the society of "The Children of the Silver Star."

As these plot elements unfold, the novel serves as an exemplar early case of "world building," a vision of an alternative reality covering the physical-ecological, social-psychological, ethical-philosophical, and scientific-technological dimensions of an alien world, civilization, and species. As just a sample of elements included, the novel describes: Martial homes, gardens, and agriculture; transportation vehicles (aerial, ground surface, aquatic, and submarine mechanisms); giant factories and immense engineering structures; Martial language, culture, art, literature, theater, music, and poetry; the extensive and almost complete automation of all production and distribution of goods; selective breeding and domestication of animals, including intelligent servant animals who cultivate and gather agricultural products and do numerous household chores, as well as giant birds ridden by the Martials during hunting; a recycling system for waste and the complete hygienic purification of water; the medical elimination of all infectious microbes and diseases and the cessation of aging (when the Martials die it is because of a lack of "will to live"); the electrification of all machinery and all devices, with electricity as the central and apparently unlimited power source for Martial civilization; the design of cities, including streets and buildings; Martian geography and climate, including depictions of the wild and untamed areas of Mars; and finally, even a social-political-economic history of Martial society extending back thousands of years. Notably though, and probably reflective of the repressive Victorian morality of Greg's time, there is absolutely no mention of Martial sex in the novel. All in all, in spite of the critical depiction of the scientific-secular philosophy of Martial civilization, there is clearly a host of positive features in this superior, advanced, scientifically based Martial civilization.

One especially revealing and mystical aspect of the Martials appears during the section describing the initiation rites into the secret spiritualist society, alternatively referred to as the "Children of the Silver Star" or the "Children of Light." Included in the rites are numerous chants, prayer-like recitations, and lyrical and poetic aphorisms, all filled with symbolic and metaphorical meaning. Our earthman witnesses some kind of cosmic light show (is it technologically or spiritually created?) depicting the evolution of life and consciousness in the universe and in our solar system. In an optical display that has the qualities of virtual reality, he observes cosmic evolution being directed by some kind of divine will and intelligence. (Greg seems to believe in teleological evolution.) A luminous image of "The Founder" appears during the ceremonies, a sage who, although having died thousands of years ago, seems conscious of the present reality, including the presence of the earthman. (The Founder's mind seems able to transcend time.) As is revealed through this mystical ceremony, the Martials have a highly lyrical and metaphorically rich heritage of poetical proverbs and philosophical sayings.

But all extraordinary tales must come to an end, and *Across the Zodiac* follows suit with an action-packed conclusion and a return to the commonplace world. When a traitor among the harem wives attempts to poison the earthman, it is decided that he must leave Mars to protect himself and the secret of APERGY. He and Eveena—who is going to accompany him back to the earth—head for the Astronaut with their enemies in hot pursuit. A violent confrontation ensues in which both Eveena and her father are killed, Eveena sacrificing herself to protect the earth man. As he safely escapes in the Astronaut, the earthman affirms his belief in "Allah" and his conviction that he and Eveena will eventually be reunited in heaven—a destiny seemingly confirmed by a disembodied voice asserting that "vengeance is mine."

Across the Zodiac is the first of several novels in the 1880s and 1890s that, in dealing with Martians and the exploration of the solar system, also actively pursues utopian and dystopian speculations on what constitutes an advanced society. The two themes are connected together. Of particular note, *Across the Zodiac* addresses the tension, if not clash, between the alternative mindsets and conflicting preferable realities of the spiritual and the religious versus the scientific, technological, and materialistic. The uneasy relationship between these two modes of consciousness and theories of reality would also be explored, from different angles, in other novels of the period. The themes of outer space and the Martians seemed to provoke theological reflection and ideological debate. Even more broadly, since science fiction derives from a framework of reality that challenged traditional Western religion, almost all science fiction grapples in one manner or form with the relationship between science and religion. If science fiction is the mythology of the future, promising transcendence to a new level of reality and consciousness, then the centrality of this issue makes perfect sense. It is clear that Greg in *Across the Zodiac* finds the scientific worldview as a pathway to advancement and transcendence very disturbing, undermining in his view the validity and value of religious and spiritual beliefs, as well as the foundations for human morality.

The Great Romance and *A Journey in Other Worlds*

I saw, as in a dream through the countless ages, the eternal warfare
of matter with spirit, the intensity of impossibility, and again I
wished I had never awakened.
The Inhabitant

The Great Romance (1881) was originally published in New
Zealand as two novelettes under the pseudonym of the
"Inhabitant," and although there are various speculations
regarding the true identity of the author, according to Dominic
Alessio (2008), who has published extensively on this strange
and mystical story, there is no definitive answer to this mystery.
Nonetheless, the novel is frequently mentioned in histories of
late nineteenth-century science fiction, and in several regards it
is a highly distinctive, innovative, and fascinating story of the
future. Although the plot is relatively simple—a man awakens
in the future and subsequently travels in a spaceship with two
comrades to the planet Venus—the novel, according to Alessio,
is filled with creative and original ideas, anticipating many
popular themes in later science fiction. Moreover, in the annuals
of science fiction, its style is unique for its time; lyrical, dreamlike,
and impressionistic, it is totally different in tone and structure
from, for example, Greg's complex and dense language. It *sounds*
like a novel of the future. As stated at the beginning of the book,
the story is "Stranger than the vision of the maddest prophet."

The story begins with a flow of fragmented thoughts and
fleeting impressions of a man awakening from a deep sleep
in the year 2143. The main character of the story, John Hope,
had been placed in a chemically induced unconscious state in
1950, and when he wakes up, it is almost 200 years into the
future. According to Alessio, this is the first instance in science

fiction of an extended purposefully induced "sleep," bringing a character from the past into the future using scientifically guided procedures.

Upon awakening, Hope meets a number of people in this future society—in particular two male inventors and the sister of one of them, who is named Edith. As he is shown the incredible wonders of this future human society and converses with his new friends, he finds himself falling deeply in love with Edith. Sound familiar? As Alessio points out, there is a strong possibility that Bellamy modeled his opening scenario in *Looking Backward* (1888) on *The Great Romance*. In both cases a man from the present awakens from a deep sleep in a future utopia; the time-traveler falls in love with a woman of the future; and the woman's name is Edith.

In the first novelette—part one of *The Great Romance*—Hope observes and contemplates the utopian reality of 2143. In many ways it is a "perfect" and utterly transformed society, both technologically and socially. Hope is shown many technological wonders, including amazing flying machines. His new friends seem to possess the power to control the movements of physical objects through some type of synthetic coupling of their minds with electromagnetic energy. (This capacity, as Alessio points out, sounds very similar to the techno-mental abilities of the Vril-ya in Bulwer-Lytton's *Vril, The Power of the Coming Race*.)

Hope is informed that the key factor instigating the profound changes he observes in this futurist society is that most humans have developed, indeed evolved, the power of telepathy (again sounding similar to the Vril-ya). This capacity to read each other's minds and know each other's thoughts has brought an enhanced level of peace and social order to their world. Instead of some type of social revolution or scientific-technological development instigating a jump forward to a utopian society, it is a psychological evolution, presumably a consequence of natural processes without intentional design that has transformed the world of humans. Hope has awakened into a telepathic utopia. He also discovers that an ongoing scientific research initiative addressing human mortality has already led to significant life extension with the intent to eventually realize immortality. The humans in this future world use the term "perfect" in describing their reality. Hope sees them as "godlike."

Hope also learns that the men and women practice free love. Humans no longer attempt to suppress their passions, but rather cultivate a heightened emotional awareness and a constructive channeling of their feelings. Possessing these evolved qualities, Edith is an emancipated woman, and Hope is powerfully drawn toward her.

In coming to the end of part one, Hope and his two male comrades agree to go on an expedition to Venus in order to ascertain if the planet possesses environmental conditions sufficiently hospitable to support human colonization. Although there are practical reasons for this journey—to relieve population pressures on the earth—there are deeper reasons for making the trip and opening up outer space to human exploration. As one of the future men states, the journey and eventual colonization would provide a sense of expanded purpose and meaning for the human species, an adventure to stimulate and further advance human consciousness. Moreover, in spite of the level of perfection realized in their utopian reality, there continues to exist within the human spirit in this future world a dissatisfaction and yearning for something more. In short, these evolved future humans realize that there is no ultimate perfect state for humanity. However far we evolve, the human spirit, due to its very nature, will always feel a need to advance further. There is no end to the journey, no quiescent state of total satisfaction and achievement. The exploration and colonization of outer space will address this relentless aspiration and unquenchable desire.

In connecting themes from part one with the outer space adventure described in part two, *The Great Romance* achieves a synthesis of two basic narrative structures within science fiction: the future utopian novel and the space travel scenario. The journey into outer space is described as a natural, if not inevitable, consequence of realizing a highly advanced utopian society. We will see the thematic connection of outer space and utopia repeatedly in novels of the period; as we've already seen it in *Across the Zodiac,* where outer space is *the setting* for a utopia, albeit an ambiguous one. But even more significant, as Alessio argues, *The Great Romance* presents the first-ever scientifically grounded vision of the human colonization of other worlds, in which humanity, empowered by advanced technologies and evolved modes of mentality, attempts to spread its advanced civilization outward to other planets — to take its utopia to other worlds.

Yet to complicate the picture the novel introduces uncertainty in the face of our advances:

Should we go wandering on in the pathless places of eternity? Should we meet the God of the Universe as we went out between the planets? ... Suppose we find the angels there?

Indeed. Yes, perhaps we will find angels; but we may just find devils instead.

Part two, which recounts Hope and his comrades' outer space adventure to Venus aboard the spaceship, *The Star Climber,* presents a number of innovative scientific and technological ideas. We find the first-ever description of a spacesuit, in either fiction or non-fiction. Also included are: descriptions of airlocks on spaceships; shuttle craft; space walks; the effects of weightlessness in outer space; the dangers of encountering meteors; and the effects of planetary atmospheres on the take-off and landing of space craft. There is even a brief mention of eventually traveling beyond the solar system and finding a scientifically based technological means for exceeding the speed of light. All these ideas would become central fixtures in outer space science fiction in the coming decades.

Upon landing on Venus, Hope and his comrades discover a wet tropical world containing various alien life forms, both animal and vegetable. After exploring the planet, they decide that it is sufficiently hospitable for mass colonization. Hope agrees to set up camp on the planet, while his two comrades return to earth to lead the first mass wave of colonists (including Edith) to Venus in a newly constructed space fleet.

Left alone on Venus, Hope becomes increasingly introspective—immersed in his inner flow of consciousness—contemplating how strange his life has become, first journeying into the future, and then into outer space, and now finding himself alone on an alien world. Having found love with Edith, he left her, and now he hopes to soon be reunited with her.

But he is soon startled into something even stranger: Awakening from sleep he sees before him two alien beings—what he takes to be a male and female couple. Perplexed by the meaning and intent of their various actions, he struggles to communicate with them and achieves some level of success. Though definitely appearing intelligent these aliens (the Venuses) are not humanoid in form. Covered in a soft down, their limbs are suggestive of prehistoric elephants. Yet the exact physical qualities of the aliens are never precisely described; they remain mysterious and enigmatic, part of the dreamlike reality of Venus—and of the whole novel. In his interactions with the aliens, Hope observes how affectionate they are toward each other, a plot element that allows the author to strike out into a new area of speculative fiction: Hope contemplates the nature of alien sex and even sexual relations between himself and the aliens.

The final chapters of the novel leave Hope traveling with the alien couple on his shuttlecraft in search of other Venuses. What other wonders will he encounter? We are left with a mystery. As for his comrades, on their journey back to earth, the *Star Climber* is caught in the orbit around a giant meteor and land on it. Leaving the ship to explore the meteor, one of them slips off a cliff-like edge of the meteor and falls, perhaps forever, into the infinite blackness of outer space. Thus ends *The Great Romance,* a poetic, mystical, and highly imaginative novel, one that leaves the reader with a sense of awe and wonder regarding human existence and the cosmos. Of course it is no accident that the central character is named Hope, a personification and symbol of this fundamental human emotion in the face of the uncertainty of the future, the immense possibilities of evolution and transformation, and the mystery and ultimate strangeness of the beyond.

* * *

This period—A. D. 2000—is by far the most wonderful the world has yet seen ... Free to delve in the allurement and fascination of science, emancipated man goes on subduing Nature, as his Maker said he should, and turning her giant forces to his service in his constant struggle to rise and become more like Him who gave the commandments and showed him how to go.
Professor Henry Courtland (John Jacob Astor IV)

Another well-known novel of the period involving travel into the solar system is *A Journey in Other Worlds: A Romance of the Future* (1894) by Colonel John Jacob Astor IV (1864-1912).

Astor was a real estate tycoon and one of the wealthiest men in the world in his time, but he also was a veteran of the Spanish-American War and an accomplished inventor. He is perhaps best remembered for building the luxurious Astoria Hotel in New York and heroically dying on the *Titanic*.

His novel, which strongly expresses a philosophy of human empowerment and unending progress, is an impressive work of intellectual synthesis. He weaves together diverse disciplines of naturalistic science; numerous technological and industrial predictions for the future; global economic-political theory; an "African safari" adventure on Jupiter; a futuristic cosmic synthesis of astronomy, evolution, and Biblical spiritualism; and a love element to provide some personal poignancy and sentimentality. Moreover, it is the first American science fiction novel to achieve bestseller status. The book shows strong affinities with Flammarion's cosmological speculations and Robida's hi-tech utopia, and notable thematic anticipations of both Edgar Rice Burroughs and Olaf Stapledon. *A Journey in Other Worlds* is a grand, comprehensive, and vainglorious vision of humanity's future and our place in the big scheme of things—and one of the greatest works of science fiction of the 1890s.

The basic plot of the story involves an initial and very extensive review, provided by Professor Courtland (one of the main characters of the novel), of world-wide human progress in the year 2000. This scenario-setting introduction leads into a meeting between Courtland; a young heroic-type character Dick Ayrault; and Colonel Bearwarden, President of the Terrestrial Axis Straightening Company, where it is decided that "for the future glory of the human race" a spaceship will be built to enable a tour of the solar system. The spaceship, the Callisto, is powered (as was the case in *Across the Zodiac*) by APERGY—the anti-gravitational force. Once it is constructed, our three main characters take off on the Callisto to visit Jupiter and Saturn, before returning to the earth, philosophically, personally, and spiritually transformed. The exploration of space turns into a religious experience.

A preview of the "African safari" episode appears in the opening of the book, grabbing the reader's immediate attention with some drama and action. Landing on Jupiter, the characters explore the landscape, observe the interesting flora and fauna, and shoot a giant flying reptile-like creature.

But after this quick teaser of what is to come later in the tale, the bulk of the first part of the novel focuses on describing the incredible developments in the future world of 2000. For one thing, in an engineering project that sounds like something from a Robida novel, humanity is attempting to straighten the axis of rotation of the earth so that it is perpetual springtime all over the globe. Also described are electric (battery-powered) cars; TVs; magnetic levitation trains; world-wide communication (telephone) networks; aeroplanes; "marine spider" transports (which skim across the surfaces of water); the cessation of pollution, with electrical batteries and geothermal and solar energy technologies having replaced coal; and the elimination of most diseases and the almost complete eradication of poverty. Numerous other techno-industrial advances involve medicine, biology, transportation, chemistry, and metallurgy. Indeed, one character makes the prophetic comment (anticipating Kurzweil's 2005 "Law of Accelerative Returns") that invention builds on itself, producing a geometrical rate of progress.

Moreover, the opening exposition on the year 2000 integrates technology and industry with economics, politics, business, and demographics. The population of the world has continued to increase, and New York has become a giant megalopolis, but there are no problems associated with overpopulation; the masses are provided for better than ever. A business dominated global system has emerged, controlling world affairs. The United States has assimilated Canada, Mexico, and large areas of South America. After a great arms race through the 1920s, the world collectively turned away from military and nationalistic competition and achieved global peace, averting the anticipated "Great War," for it became apparent that modern hi-tech warfare would probably lead to the destruction of human civilization. Military spending was consequently re-channeled into human welfare. All in all, humanity in 2000 A.D. has realized a heightened sense of empowerment, progress, plentitude, and increasing health and wealth for almost everyone.

And yet, in spite of all the material and scientific advancement, as Professor Courtland notes, it is clear that there is something missing that is essential for human happiness and self-fulfillment in life. This overall assessment on the state of the world in 2000—that material plenty and technological-industrial empowerment isn't enough—points toward the spiritualistic philosophy developed in the last part of the novel when our travelers reach Saturn. This view on human nature and happiness also provides connecting thematic links to both *The Great Romance* and *Across the Zodiac*. Will we ever be satisfied? In particular, are material wealth and technological advancement ever enough?

After the complex and comprehensive array of predictions on human progress that Astor presents in the first part of the novel (through the voice of Courtland), impressively integrating so many different areas of human life, we move into an equally well-informed description of the planning and construction of the Callisto, one that explains both the engineering and financing of the spaceship. There is again a clear sense, through the exposition on the design of the spaceship, that Astor has a deep fascination and significant level of understanding of science and technology. There is, for example, considerable discussion regarding how the concept of "APERGY" fits into a scientific understanding of the basic forces of nature, with the argument being made that forces in nature balance each other, and thus there must exist a force that is in oppositional balance to gravity. Indeed, throughout the book, Astor frequently engages in speculative scientific theorizing, repeatedly attempting to establish the plausibility and reasonableness of his cutting-edge ideas. The author's enthusiasm and knowledge of science is further demonstrated when Astor describes, through the voices of his characters, the journey of the Callisto through outer space, which includes numerous commentaries on Jupiter, Saturn, the other planets of the solar system, comets and asteroids, and the physical universe at large.

When our three explorers land on Jupiter, they find a

planet lush with vegetation and wildlife, in many ways similar to prehistoric earth, perhaps comparable in evolutionary development to the Carboniferous or Devonian Age. But Astor also includes an imaginative mixture of animals suggestive of different earth periods, including creatures like wooly mammoths and rhinos, and dinosaurs and giant snakes and turtles. There are also colossal predator ants that attack and eat a mammoth and other creatively envisioned types of life, including flowers that attract birds for cross pollination through captivating harmonic sounds.

The section detailing our explorers' adventures on Jupiter reads like a combination of a naturalistic narrative, describing and explaining the strange and numerous sights and wonders of this incredible world (including a Jupiter-size Niagara Falls), and an African safari tale, describing the stalking and killing of various ferocious and dangerous animals (to secure meat to eat). During one episode the explorers shoot dinosaurs with their hunting rifles while riding on a giant turtle. In this synthesis of adventure and action with scientific exposition, our characters discuss the ecology of life on Jupiter, its evolution and possible future directions of development, including the emergence of higher forms of intelligence, and the geology and transformative geography of land and sea on the planet, articulating in the process a grand philosophical theory of the evolutionary nature of life. Moreover, our characters attempt to pull together science, ecology, and evolution with philosophical metaphysics.

In this part of the book, Astor repeatedly moves from the concrete, practical, and blood-and-guts action-adventure of things to the abstract, ethereal, and cosmic, and then back again. He engages in scientific theorizing, disputing the popular view of his time that only the upper atmosphere of Jupiter is visible from the earth. As he speculates in this story, Jupiter has a solid surface; the visible bands encircling it are varied chemical streams in the oceans of the planet; and the giant red spot is really a landmass with brilliant scarlet vegetation. Of course, he was wrong on all of this, but in the tradition of Jules Verne, he was attempting to scientifically justify his innovative ideas regarding either the make-up of nature or future technological advances.

Rising like a grand conclusion out of this synthesis of hunting adventure, nature tour, scientific cogitation, and philosophical extrapolation, clearly expressing Astor's self-empowering vision of human progress, one of the characters enthusiastically pronounces that, "Man is really lord of creation." They decide that Jupiter, with its immense areas of land and its colossal resources, is an ideal planet for human colonization. Their vision sounds similar to the romanticized story of the European settlement of America, replayed and multiplied a thousandfold in scale.

After our characters have explored Jupiter, flying over large regions of the planet in the Callisto, they take off for Saturn. Again engaging in speculative science with the clear intent to sound plausible and convincing, Courtland proposes that the rings of Saturn are due to the counter-balancing force of APERGY.

When our characters land on Saturn, which also has a solid surface, they again find vegetation and animal life, and once more engage in hunting, shooting Saturnian birds for food. They also have to fight off and kill giant "flying dragons" that attack them. But Saturn has a different ambience than Jupiter, more like a "dreamland" than a primordial jungle, and the key discovery on Saturn is not naturalistic but supernatural and spiritualistic. On Saturn our characters are visited by spirits (and angels) who are souls of the dead.

The essence of this last part of the novel is an elucidation of a philosophy of reality that integrates the scientific-naturalistic-evolutionary vision of the universe (as described during their time on Jupiter) with a spiritual and theistic metaphysics that significantly derives from Biblical theology. Whereas the adventure on Jupiter is similar to an Edgar Rice Burroughs' jungle tale with strange beasts and lots of violence and action, the tale on Saturn is highly resonant with Flammarion's vision of the evolutionary journey of disembodied spirits into outer space, as well as Stapledon's grand cosmology of the ultimate future and fate of the universe.

The main spiritual character encountered on Saturn is a translucent, white-bearded, old man who is the soul of a dead bishop from the earth—specifically the United States—who has now ascended in non-material form to the planet Saturn. This spirit explains to our characters the meaning and purpose of human life and human love; the nature of spirits and how the spiritual universe is connected with the physical universe; the nature of good and evil; and how the spiritual and the physical realms synthesize in determining the future of the cosmos. In this exposition on cosmic enlightenment, Astor clearly intends to demonstrate with reason and evidence that there exists a spiritual reality that can be credibly and plausibly integrated with our scientific understanding of the universe.

The spirit explains that people possess immortal souls which are liberated from the body at death. Moreover, within the spiritual realm there exist unknown forces and laws yet to be discovered by flesh-and-blood humanity, over which spirits, on leaving the body, acquire knowledge and control. The conscious faculties of spirits are heightened relative to their mental capacities when contained in mortal physical bodies. Because spirits possess no physical bodies (dragging them down) they can ascend into outer space. This process of ascension into outer space after death is a new evolutionary stage in human consciousness. Spirits can also see into the future, as well as instantaneously visit distal locations in space. (Courtland is allowed to see his own funeral in the future and Ayrault to consciously visit his fiancée back on earth.)

Spirits released from the bodies of people who led evil lives eventually drift outward into the farther reaches of the solar system, where there exists a giant planet named Cassandra beyond the orbit of Neptune. Cassandra is the abode of Hell, where misery and unhappiness intensify in all those souls who are sent there. Just as good souls are progressively drawn closer and closer to the presence of God, evil souls residing on Cassandra progressively move further and further away from God. There are plenty of quotes from the Bible through all of this discussion, as well as extensive explanations regarding how these supernatural and theological ideas about spirits make scientific sense.

According to the spirit of the bishop, the next evolutionary stage in humanity will be the collective movement from the physical to the higher plane of the spiritual. (This sounds somewhat like St. Augustine.) As the spirit explains, in the higher level of existence imagined in this futuristic prophesy, humanity will presumably realize many new powers. The spirit suggests that humanity will eventually find the "Fountain of Youth" and will be able to routinely communicate with the dead.

This idea of transforming from a physical to a spiritual being has been pervasive throughout ancient religions and mythologies. And re-conceptualized, it has been a dominant theme in modern science fiction, in which the concept of a "spirit" is replaced with the analogous idea of a disembodied mind or consciousness (perhaps instantiated within an energy field, virtual reality, or matrix of information). In the scientific vision, humanity evolves, perhaps facilitated through technology, from a physical plane to a mental plane of existence. In either case, there is an anticipated transition or jump from the crude and primordial (a body of physical matter) to the ethereal and enlightened (a being of pure consciousness).

All in all, this transformational-evolutionary theory of the future expresses a key mythic narrative contained in many stories of modern science fiction, derived from ancient dualistic thinking (moving from the physical to the spiritual) but in modern scientific times, re-imagined and made plausible through some kind of scientific-technological means, in which consciousness is transferred (or moves) into an immaterial form. There are advanced robots that even do this in futuristic science fiction.

The spirit of the bishop also explains to our explorers the general evolutionary dynamics of the universe. He states that existing in the center of the universe is a gargantuan star named "Cosmos" around which everything in the universe—all the myriad stars—revolve and to which they are steadily drawn. In conjunction with this stupendous process of cosmic accretion into the star Cosmos, there will be a corresponding and ongoing evolution of spirits throughout the universe riding on the ripples of this physical convergence. The spirit reveals that there are innumerable forms of intelligent life throughout the universe and that there are also "dark stars" which germinate in their system's bizarre forms of life. Whatever their nature, all forms of life and intelligence are moving toward the spiritual, drawn forward on the overall evolutionary thrust spiraling toward the star Cosmos. In this philosophy of convergent cosmic evolution, Astor strikes a resonant chord with later "Omega Point" theorists, such as Teilhard de Chardin (1959) and Frank Tipler (1994).

Courtland and Ayrault, both deeply moved by their respective spiritually facilitated personal visitations—Courtland to his own death and Ayrault into the heart and consciousness of his loved one—return to earth with their comrade, Bearwarden, renewed and enlightened, with a heightened sense of future consciousness and cosmic understanding. They are ready to further help humanity move forward, while clearly honoring the central importance of leading a good life and finding love and personal meaning in their existence. Although it may seem totally incongruous to weave together engineering, industry, and science with ethics, spirituality, and cosmology, Astor in *A Journey to Other Worlds* attempts to articulate an inspiring futuristic utopian vision that unites matter and spirit into a grand evolutionary tale of the near and far future. In so doing, he paints his vision of an idealized form of human existence upon the vast spatial expanse and evolutionary dynamics of the universe. Astor creates a cosmic utopia.

Once again, then, we see that although modern science provided an alternative theory of reality to the supernatural spiritualism of Western religion, writers of science fiction such as Astor continued to strive to integrate both worldviews in their writings. (Astor, notably bringing evolutionary science into this synthesis.) In so doing, writers such as Astor, and Flammarion before him were motivated to explain how their spiritualistic ideas were scientifically credible, consequently keeping the issue open to debate regarding what is and what is not scientifically plausible. It is also clear in Astor's case that although he wholeheartedly embraced the modern secular theory of human progress, which implied a transformed and improved future, he attempted to integrate this modern view of the future of humanity with a religious and spiritual philosophy that also supported progress and, in fact, evolution. Indeed, human progress and evolution, which in his mind included humanity's increasing dominion over nature, seemed directed and mandated by God.

Two Planets and *Edison's Conquest of Mars*

Although Astor thought that Mars would not be a very interesting place to visit, or a hospitable place to settle, as noted earlier, the public in his time was highly enthralled with Mars and the possibilities of intelligent life on the planet. There were indeed a number of notable novels written in the 1890s, reflective of this public fascination with the red planet that delved into Mars and the Martians and had very provocative things to say, not only about the Martians, but also about humanity, our limitations, and our species-centric prejudices regarding other forms of intelligent life. One of these novels was *Two Planets*.

From our contemporary perspective, the vision of Mars presented in *Two Planets* (1897) by Kurd Lasswitz (1848-1910), as well as many aspects of the advanced Martian technologies described in the book, seems scientifically implausible. Yet, one of the central features of the novel is the unparalleled depth, breadth, and inventiveness of its scientifically informed technological extrapolations and speculations—as scientific knowledge was formulated and understood at the time—regarding Martian civilization. Lasswitz clearly surpasses Greg in this regard.

In *Two Planets*, Lasswitz, a German philosopher and historian of science, describes in depth a host of advanced Martian technologies, including diverse transportation vehicles and communication systems; new types of architecture and movable habitats; different types of space ships; an economy built on solar energy; gravity neutralization devices; hovering space stations; food generated from inorganic materials; advanced weaponry; long range monitoring systems; and even forms of mind reading and telepathic control. Lasswitz repeatedly attempted to articulate in scientific detail how all of these hypothetical technologies and advanced capabilities would operate. His expositions on advanced hypothetical technologies equal if not exceed those of Astor.

Indeed, Lasswitz would inspire a whole generation of young scientists and rocket engineers in early twentieth-century Germany. He may not have gotten all the theory and technology right, but as a science fiction writer, he lit the inspirational fuse for the science and technology of rocketry in Germany. So much so that, after World War II, with the emigration of German scientists, his writings inspired further advances in space technology around the world in the second half of the twentieth century. Lasswitz and his *Two Planets* is a paragon example of science fiction stimulating the actual growth of science and technology.

Moreover, Lasswitz strongly influenced Hugo Gernsback, in providing him with a powerful illustration of how to teach science and technology through science fiction. Gernsback's vision for a new type of fiction, which he eventually labeled as "science fiction," was futurist narrative that both entertained and educated readers on the possibilities of scientific and technological development. Lasswitz provided an exemplary case of science and technology education, seeding human imagination and stimulating the human intellect within the context of an engaging story.

But *Two Planets* is not simply a high-tech science fiction novel. It is equally a philosophical and political study on the evolution of intelligence, ethics, and civilization. These humanistic themes propel the basic plot of the novel. Lasswitz creates Martians who are both scientifically advanced and mentally evolved, pulling together the two opposing sides of the ontological and moral schism described in Greg's Martial society.

At the beginning of the story, three German scientist-explorers travel in a balloon to the North Pole and, upon arriving, discover a hidden Martian base. Two of the three scientists are taken into the Martian base, where they meet and begin to communicate with the Martians. The Martians are human in appearance, although somewhat taller, thinner, and with captivatingly bigger eyes. The scientists learn that in the very near future the Martians intend to establish peaceful global contact with all of humanity, and bring to humanity all the benefits of their highly advanced civilization. They also begin to learn about the Martians' many incredible technologies and abilities, including the Martian space station positioned above the North Pole, which is able to modulate gravitational forces and serves as a way station for Martian ships traveling back and forth between the Earth and

Mars. In essence, our human protagonists have stumbled upon the earth-shaking realization that we are being watched by a form of life that is vastly more intelligent and superior than our own.

One of the two scientists eventually travels to Mars on a Martian ship where he marvels at all the wondrous technologies, architectural structures, and massive environmental engineering projects across the surface of the planet, including the amazing canals (Lasswitz believed Lowell). And, following the earlier model, our human scientist also finds himself falling in love with a Martian woman who seems drawn to him as well. Yet he is hesitant and uncertain: He is wary of the Martians and can't shake the sense of inferiority he feels in their presence. The Martians themselves manifest a clear sense of both technological and moral superiority relative to humans, and they do not hide their intent to educate and guide us, not just scientifically and technologically, but mentally, ethically, and socially. They see themselves as our benefactors and teachers.

Back on earth, after a violent initial encounter between the Martians and a British Navy vessel near the North Pole—where the Martians easily incapacitate the British ship—the collective Martian opinion of humans goes downhill. And when the Martians first publicly appear across the globe, one thing leads to another, and the Martians, using the threat of their superior weapons, establish a benevolent dictatorship over humans, at least across Europe.

Our benefactors bring to the earth many new technological wonders, which greatly benefit the world economy—humanity enters a time of material plenty—but the Martians also establish a compulsory education regime in their attempt to evolve humans to a higher level of ethical character. In essence, the Martians try to force humanity through the threat of military might to improve, psychologically and morally, as a species.

As to be expected, many humans become resentful and

rebellious, leading to the deterioration of interplanetary relations. To make things worse, a number of governing Martian officials placed on earth develop "earth fever," a corrupting of their superior character through the infestation and growth in their minds of various human vices. Becoming increasingly obsessed with greed and power, the infected Martians become more aggressive and cruel to humans, which only intensify the interplanetary hostility.

Lasswitz peoples his tale with a variety of interesting characters—human, Martian, and even one adult half-breed (how this happens is explained in the novel), and presents numerous twists and turns along the way as the Martians and humans struggle to work out a mutually satisfactory and respectful relationship with each other. Eventually a number of humans rebel against the prejudicial Martian system of control, and the Martian woman, who is in love with the German scientist, helps to unsettle things even further. After the humans capture the Martian North Pole base and the space station, a negotiated peace is finally achieved. As an inspirational symbol of this inter-species reconciliation, the Martian woman and the German scientist profess their love in a Martian bonding ceremony at the end of the story.

Two Planets addresses the question of what would constitute, relative to present day humanity, an ethically and psychologically higher form of mentality and social order. This question is one important piece of the broader issue of envisioning a utopian reality. Even if we are not trying to realize perfection—whatever that would mean—how would we at least conceptualize a distinctively more advanced society and more advanced individual minds within that society? Lasswitz provides a model for such a scenario in *Two Planets*; rather than envisioning a hypothetical higher level of human reality, his utopian ideal takes the form of an alien civilization and alien minds more advanced than present day humanity.

Although what may first impress the reader in *Two Planets* is the superior science and physical technology of the Martians, as the story unfolds it becomes clear that the Martians have both a much more cooperative society than humans and a much more evolved sense at an individual level of mental self-control. They seem to have created a society in which social cohesion and individual self-determination necessarily coexist, supporting each other. It is this psycho-social dimension of the Martians that makes possible their scientific and technological achievements.

Critical to their psychology is the principle of self-responsibility; the Martians have developed a high level of autonomy and internal locus of control, where external environmental factors or internal fluctuating emotional states do not strongly influence the direction of their thinking or their actions. They are masters of their own minds and own fate, having a deep sense of individual empowerment and individual freedom. As repeatedly highlighted in the story, the Martians are much more capable of controlling their conscious minds than are humans.

This enhanced mental control is a consequence of their early education (as described in the novel), which is focused upon developing their capacities of mental self-determination and self-actualization. Education is not so much an institution for exerting control over the youth; it is an institution for teaching the youth how to control themselves and fully develop their psychological powers. Education is not grounded in rote learning the sciences, but rather in heightened self-awareness and the internal development of the Martian mind. Their psychological development brings in emotion as well as thought and self-discipline; for example, one of the key areas their education focuses on is the nature and cultivation of the capacity for love.

It is worth further emphasizing that the Martians' high level of social cohesion is necessarily coupled with their individual self-control. Social order does not preclude individual freedom but requires it. Their well-ordered society, involving a deep sense of duty to the whole, would fall apart without individual self-control. The social cohesion is built on choice and the internal discipline of the individual. As described earlier, visions of utopias and human progress in modern times have highlighted either individual freedom or social order (Lombardo, 2006a); the hypothetical Martians of Lasswitz's novel synthesize these two fundamental qualities of psycho-social existence.

In Lasswitz's hypothetical Martian civilization, technological evolution comes together with psychological evolution. Advances in the physical sciences and the application of this knowledge are a natural expression of their mental evolution. It is not an either/or situation, of choosing between psychological excellence or material power, as for example, in *Across the Zodiac*. A wise society of psychological and ethically evolved individuals generates technological advances. Complementarily, science and technology are not seen as anathema to an evolved consciousness. But it does appear that it is the mental sphere and the ethics of the Martians that is their center of gravity, directing the evolution of the physical and technological spheres of their civilization.

Another major issue explored in the novel is how a superior civilization should behave toward a more primitive one. The Martians engage humanity in a spirit of benevolence, but also from a standpoint of self-conscious superiority. Yet the issue emerges in the interactions of the Martians and the earth humans whether progress can or should be forced upon the more primitive society by the more advanced one. How should one go about helping to liberate and empower the mind of another? What the Martians eventually realize is that although they are cautious and thoughtful in their approach to humans, they cannot presumptuously direct humans toward a higher level of existence. Even if humans, from the perspective of the Martians, do not do a very good job of managing their minds, lives, and society, humans need to feel in control of their destiny; at least there needs to be a sense of mutual determination and cooperation between humans and the Martians.

The question of how a more evolved society should behave with respect to a lesser evolved society presupposes that we can determine which society is more evolved. Utopian writers and philosophers of progress have repeatedly attempted to identify standards of excellence or superiority for determining the level of development (or evolution) of a society or individuals within that society. But can such standards be convincingly demonstrated? Are there universal (trans-cultural or trans-world) standards of excellence?

In twentieth-century Western philosophy, postmodern relativism has argued that Western visions of ethics and ideal societies are cultural-centric and elitist, and that within the history of Western modernity, the West has repeatedly attempted, with extreme prejudice and bias, to impose its values and visions upon non-Western cultures, the former invariably and unjustifiably judging the latter as more primitive and less developed (Lombardo, 2006b). Moreover, using Astor's novel as an illustrative expression of this philosophy and approach to life, Western modernity has aspired to transform indigenous populations and the entirety of nature into Western visions of an ideal world. In Astor's novel, Jupiter is going to be conquered and colonized and turned into a new America, only on a much vaster scale. At a cruder level, the same mindset and logic of plot appeared in the dime novel Edisonade stories of the same period.

The twist in Lasswitz's novel is that although he takes the view that principles defining higher levels of mind and society can be objectively articulated and rationally justified—he is not a philosophical or cultural relativist—he turns the tables on Western modernity, with a "superior" alien civilization attempting to enlighten and transform the modern West (indeed all of humanity) to align with their principles and values. And the indigenous population—we humans—has to submit to this facilitated evolution because it is good for us, even if we believe we have the right to make up our own minds and define our own culture. In *Two Planets,* Western imperialists are given a taste of their own bitter medicine.

If science fiction expands the imagination, we are faced with two connected challenges: On one hand, can we envision more advanced or evolved minds or societies, either in the future of humans or in alien form? On what principles or values do we determine this? In this case, Lasswitz does present a well-articulated and holistic psycho-physical vision of an advanced form of intelligence and society relative to contemporary humanity. But on the other hand, can we envision exceedingly strange and distinctly different types of minds, life forms, or societies, by which it may not be so simple—indeed may not make any sense—to compare the level of evolution or advancement relative to contemporary humans? Such imaginative visions of alien life (which will emerge in science fiction to come) may stretch the boundaries of our egocentricity (or species-centricity) and may push us into expanding, adjusting, or even jettisoning our standards and values—perhaps even pushing us to abandon the whole comparative notion of advanced versus primitive forms of intelligence?

In conclusion, Lasswitz's *Two Planets* is a highly impressive science fiction achievement, especially for its time, synthesizing into a comprehensive whole highly inventive and intelligent scientific and technological speculation, and in-depth philosophical, psychological, and social analyses of the nature of mental evolution. The novel provokes us into thinking about ourselves—our capacities, values, and limitations. Lasswitz, who has been identified as the "father of German science fiction," inspired the *Kurd Lasswitz Award,* given out every year since 1981 for the best science fiction written in German (Wuckel and

Cassiday, 1989).

* * *

Other popular visions of the Martians emerged around the same time as Lasswitz's novel, ones that took very different approaches in describing our closest hypothetical neighbors in our solar system. In many ways at the opposite end of the philosophical continuum, *Edison's Conquest of Mars* (1898) by the astronomer Garrett Serviss (1851-1929) tells the story of how a space fleet of electronically powered ships, created by a fictionalized Thomas Edison, journeys to Mars and thoroughly destroys the entire Martian civilization, killing the King of Mars and millions of other Martians in the process. The novel is a strange and arresting combination of fact and fiction; of reality and myth making; of reason, passion, and violence. It is one, too, that well illustrates the interactive nature of science fiction and the cultural setting in which it is published and read.

Serviss was provoked into writing his novel in response to H. G. Wells' *The War of the Worlds*. When *The War of the Worlds* was published in England (serialized in magazine form in 1897 and released as a hardcover book in 1898) it created a public sensation—amplified when two altered and unauthorized American versions of it (titled *Fighters from Mars, or the War of the Worlds*) were serially published in American magazines in 1897-1898. (In one of the American versions of the tale, Boston, not London, was destroyed in the Martian attack.) But in all these versions, original and derived, humanity was militarily overpowered by the Martians—a powerful insult to humanity's ego and pride—and Serviss took it upon himself to retaliate against the Martians, albeit in fictional form.

With the personal approval and input of Thomas Edison, Seriviss quickly wrote and published his sequel to *The War of the Worlds*, in which the nations of the earth come together in a political and financial partnership to build and launch an attack fleet of spaceships to destroy the Martian military before the Martians can launch a new attack on the Earth. (Wells brings up this possibility at the end of his novel.) At one level, *Edison's Conquest of Mars* can be read as a fight for the survival of humanity, a chronicle of a courageous and justified military counter-attack against an outside evil aggressor. On a deeper level, it worked as a salve to the bruised vanity of Western/American civilization, so severely damaged in Wells' novel with its scenes of the obliteration of Western military defenses and the chaotic panic that ensues. In Serviss' novel, humanity (and the West especially) regains its dignity and sense of superiority in the cosmos by attacking Mars and destroying the Martian civilization.

Although written after *The War of the Worlds*, for a couple of reasons I want to first focus on Serviss' tale before examining Wells' novel in any further depth. *The War of the Worlds* — the most famous of the turn-of-the-century novels about the Martians — provides a more fitting and appropriate text to conclude this first volume and transition into the next one. The emergence of H. G. Wells and his numerous science fiction stories is the best historical marker for the passage from nineteenth-century to twentieth-century science fiction.

In *Edison's Conquest of Mars*, the unquestionable hero is a fictionalized version of Thomas Edison. As described earlier, although the real Edison may have been a vain and enthusiastic self-promoter of his image as the "Wizard of Menlo Park," the characfer in the novel — his alter-ego — is a taciturn practical man of action, neither pretentious nor theatrical. The fictional Edison is the kind of male ideal to be admired; he is not out for fame or recognition; he just wants to get things done, defeat the enemy, and save the earth and humankind. This fictional Edison, pure of heart and dedicated to the survival of humanity, served to bolster the idealized if not accurate image of the real Edison, the self-proclaimed benefactor of humanity.

This imaginary Edison and his exploits in Serviss' novel align well with Clute's definition of Edisonade: The inventor-genius creates some amazing new technologies (including transportation technologies), journeys to a far off land, and conquers the bad guys—although at the end of this novel, the hero Edison gets neither the girl nor gains great fortune. He does, however, achieve even greater fame and public appreciation around the world, saving humanity from the scourge of the Martians. Edison is the scientific genius as courageous hero. Moreover, the evil that Edison confronts and defeats is understood as a calculating force whose aim is the subjection and enslavement of humanity. This conception of evil derives from the American-Western ideal of freedom as a central or pivotal value to be cherished and defended; evil is that which attempts to deprive us of our most valued possession.

The story opens immediately following the Martian attack on the United States and the subsequent defeat of the Martians brought about by their vulnerability to the infectious microbes of the earth. Having gained access to information on the Martian war machines, the fictional Edison fears another attack on the earth. Applying his miraculous scientific genius, he quickly builds both an electronically powered spaceship and "disintegrator" guns, which vaporize solid matter through the breaking of the molecular bonds between atoms—the latter device, notably, the original prototype "ray guns" that would appear again and again in many later science fiction novels.

The countries of the world come together under the leadership of the United States and agree to fund Edison's construction of a fleet of one hundred spaceships, as well as the manufacture of thousands of disintegrator guns. Edison recruits an army to man the spaceships, which includes a large number of real-life famous scientists, engineers, world leaders, and military men, including Lord Kelvin.

As can be seen, the boundary between fiction and reality gets blurred in the novel. Serviss writes the story using real-life characters. One of them, Edison, examines the fictional Martian machines. Further, the earth's fictionalized counter-attack is marshaled against a fictionalized invasion that *in reality* undercut our pride and sense of security and power. In a sense the Martians did invade us, assaulting our imagination and violating our perceived sovereignty, and Serviss' fictionalized retaliation is intended to beat back the Martian insult and intrusion into our consciousness.

After the fleet is built, the ships take off into space, journey to the moon to test their equipment, run into various problems, end up back on earth, take off again, and finally travel out first to the asteroids, and then to the moons of Mars. The heroes engage the Martians in perhaps the first modern fictionalized interplanetary battle of spaceships, ray guns, and death rays. Along the way, they capture a Martian who, though humanoid in appearance is roughly fifteen feet in height. (The Martians in Serviss' novel are different in appearance from Wells' Martians, who resemble octopuses.) Although the disintegrator guns are effective against the Martians, in their initial encounters with the Martians, the humans realize that they are woefully out-numbered by the Martian military forces. How can a fleet of merely one hundred ships, now appreciably dwindling in number, possibly defeat a whole world so much more technologically advanced?

The humans finally hit upon an idea that could just lead to victory. With the courageous Edison at the lead, a small group sneaks into one of the giant irrigation dams on Mars and opens the gates flooding not only the Martian canals but the flat plains of Mars and all its major cities as well, drowning the majority of the Martians. A final aerial battle takes place between the earth ships and the remnants of the Martian air force. The humans emerge victorious. Eventually the King of Mars is captured and forced to agree to a permanent peace with Earth. But the King, as indicated by swellings in his skull around the brain centers for aggression and violence, proves to be a hostile and dishonest individual, and is soon thereafter killed. (Serviss invoked the later discredited "science" of phrenology, explaining that the Martian males are selectively bred and nurtured for warlike behavior, their brains consequently enlarged in the appropriate areas for these aggressive capacities, producing bulges in the cranium.) With most of Martian civilization now destroyed and the threat to earth eliminated, Edison and his fleet of ships return home, where he is greeted as the savior of humanity.

Edison's Conquest of Mars has been described as a "cornucopia of technical ingenuity" for its inclusion of the first phaser gun; the first functional spacesuit; a description of asteroid mining; and the first modern space battle. But another noteworthy feature of the novel is that it was accompanied by a whole set of fascinating illustrations: of the spaceships and outer space battles; the Martians and the Martian surface; and—mixing fact with fiction where the author steps into his own novel— even a picture of Serviss conferring with Edison "on the best means of repaying the damage wrought upon this planet by the Martians." Although not as flamboyant and playful as Robida's drawings the illustrations do possess a raw power, energy, and dynamism. Dark and expressionistic, they are another important evolutionary step in the development of science fiction art.

Indeed, beginning with Flammarion but most dramatically with Robida, science fiction novels in the 1880s and 1890s now frequently included illustrations, mostly black on white drawings. Verne commissioned a variety of compelling and imaginative pictures (sometimes in color) for both the inside and the covers of his novels (Holland, 2009); Mitchell himself illustrated *The Last American*; Astor had numerous penned drawings throughout *A Journey in Other Worlds*; and the Edisonade dime novels (c. 1880 to 1900) had either black and white or action-packed color illustrations on their covers. In the original and the republished

1906 version of Wells' *The War of the Worlds*, two different sets of illustrations graphically depicting the Martians, their machines, and their assault on the earth were included. Having achieved a high level of pop recognition and fame, many of these pictures can be viewed on the Web. Clearly, by the turn of the century, science fiction art was gaining considerable momentum as a distinctive and popular art form.

Serviss went on to write other well-known science fiction novels, including *A Columbus in Space* (1909) and *The Second Deluge* (1911), both engaging tales; these novels are described in the next volume. Serviss, in fact, became one of the most popular science fiction writers in the early twentieth century. But the writer who was unequivocally the most significant science fiction author at the turn of the century — the man who provoked Serviss into writing *Edison's Conquest of Mars* — was H. G. Wells, the truly heroic figure and architect of modern science fiction.

The War of the Worlds

In skipping over an analysis of Wells' *The War of the Worlds* and focusing first on *Edison's Conquest of Mars*, I have departed a bit from the chronological order of this history. I did so, as mentioned above, because *The War of the Worlds* serves as an ideal point for concluding this first volume and transitioning into the next. In examining this novel I come full circle from where I began: watching the movie version in 1953. After describing in the previous pages the evolution of science fiction from the Greeks to the time of Wells, my youthful thoughts and reactions to the movie can now be placed in historical context. Moreover, *The War of the Worlds* serves as an excellent anchor point for summarizing a number of key themes in this first volume, in particular those covered in this last section on Martians and journeys into outer space. As a point of transition, *The War of the Worlds* provides an introductory teaser to the next volume, which opens with an entire chapter devoted to H. G. Wells, covering all his many highly influential science fiction novels.

The War of the Worlds presents a "bolt out of the blue" scenario, where the everyday world is abruptly upset and plunged into chaos by a totally unexpected and unthinkable event. Building upon ideas Wells developed early in his writing career on the evolution of life and intelligence, as well as the history of human civilization (Wells, 1934; Wagar, 2004), *The War of the Worlds* is perhaps the best example of Wells' repeated narrative strategy of the extraordinary breaking through the commonplace to shake humans out of their complacency. The novel shocks us into a highly disquieting transcendence; instead of journeying to far off places in search of the transcendent, the transcendent thrusts itself into our everyday world. While we go about our mundane business, safe in our unreflective bubble and secure in our sense of rightful dominion over nature, some unknown but vastly superior and intelligent force comes shooting out of the sky, totally overpowering us and almost destroying all of human civilization. *The War of the Worlds* is a wallop to the mind. The sudden and deep shock it delivers to normal consciousness is exactly what I experienced as a youth in watching the movie.

Moreover, similar to Lasswitz's *Two Planets*, *The War of the Worlds* turns the tables on Western imperialism. (Indeed, Wells' novel very emphatically turns the tables on Edisonade, which, in its crass form, derived its inspiration from techno-enthusiastic American-Western imperialism.) Just as Western civilization, in its self-conceited drive toward exploration and conquest, had swept aside less technologically developed societies around the world, the Martians now do the same to us. *The War of the Worlds* is an allegory on Western imperialism and expansionism turned in reverse. The science fiction narrative of humanity spreading outward and exploring and colonizing new worlds — the Western vision of progress placed within the science fiction setting of outer space — is flipped over, with humanity becoming the primitive indigenous species ("... like the transient creatures that swarm and multiply in a drop of water") conquered by a more advanced race of beings ("... intellects vast and cool and unsympathetic"). Wells' Martians though, unlike Lasswitz's Martians, are not benevolent dictators or colonialists; they intend to annihilate us. In *The War of the Worlds*, the mindset we had projected outward into the unknown cosmos, of conquering explorers armed with advanced technology and weaponry, comes flying back at us.

The heavens may contain beings more biologically evolved and more technologically advanced than we are—a visionary idea that emerged in modern astronomy—but they may very well be the opposite of angelic or beneficent. They may be hostile and ruthless. As noted earlier, extraterrestrial aliens as imagined through the eyes of modern astronomical science are a historically evolved version of earlier mythological gods and goddesses. Only now the gods bearing the secret of fire may be intent on torching us out of existence. Sadly, the priest in the 1953 movie version fails to consider this possibility when he says, "If they are more advanced than us they must be closer to the Creator." On what grounds can we assume that such alien minds, higher up in the great evolutionary chain of being, will look upon us with love and concern rather than brutal disregard? Isn't this just an anthropomorphic view of a benevolent God? We should rather expect the latter attitude of callous indifference; it is, ironically after all more in line with our own murderous imperialist drive toward conquest. Why shouldn't advanced aliens see the demise of such an un-evolved and primitive species as of little consequence?

Wells also achieved in *The War of the Worlds* a jolting and realistic vision of "alienness" that goes beyond most other previous conceptions of beings from outer space. In his earlier speculative essays, Wells had envisioned the evolution of intelligent life as leading to larger and larger brains and more atrophied bodies (Wells, 1893). The Martians in *The War of* the Worlds, hideous and frightening to the human eye, have bulky heads, combined with octopus-like bodies and multiple slithering tentacles. They are evolved—indeed informed by Wells' evolutionary thinking—but relative to our species-centric point of view they are inhuman and monstrous. In previous stories of intelligent aliens, including Martians, such as in the novels of Greg and Lasswitz, the "other" was frequently human in form. (The Venuses in *The Great Romance* were one exception.)

The war machines in *The War of the Worlds* are just as strange, terrifying, and other-worldly, giant tripods towering into the sky with long legs and "heads" that shoot death rays and poisonous gases, vaporizing or asphyxiating everything in their path. The Martians and their machines—nightmares of the imagination—set the standard for later stories of ghastly warlike aliens. (Pal's cinematic re-creations of the Martians and their machines, different in ways than Wells' versions, also seemed eerie and other-worldly to my six-year-old mind; their grotesque appearance frightened the hell out of me.) The "other," both intelligent and utterly strange, becomes an object of terror—a form of transcendence which shocks the emotions, disturbs our aesthetics, and dis-equilibrates the mind. Moreover, set in the context of evolutionary thinking, by which humanity is no longer God's special creature, heir to all creation, the Martians and their machines explode our self-centered conceit and narrow state of consciousness.

The plot of *The War of the Worlds* begins from the premise that the earth, with all its bounty and natural resources, has been coveted by the Martians with "envious eyes." They are an aging species living on an aging world. This conception of the Martians reflects the popular view, as expressed for example by Lowell, that the Martians are an ancient civilization. Leaving their dying world and in need of new lands, they send a wave of meteor-like projectiles that land at different locations on the earth. Inside are the Martians and the equipment needed for constructing their various war machines.

The story of their initial landing, their emergence from their projectiles, and their attack on humanity is related through the eyes of a central male character who lives through and barely survives the catastrophe of the Martian invasion. His narrative primarily describes events that take place in and around London, where a number of the Martian projectiles have landed, but there is also news that Martians have landed throughout other parts of the world, causing great carnage and disaster across the globe. Suffering only a few losses, the Martian war machines are almost totally invincible and the bulk of the novel describes with great emotional force and riveting detail the collective panic, misery, and mayhem caused by the Martian attack. The reader is thrust into a whirl of chaos and uncertainty. People flee their homes by the hundreds of thousands; towns and cities, including London, go up in flames. The narrator is caught up in the panic and disaster, part of the thousands running away from the Martians, but at times wandering alone through desolate landscapes and abandoned towns. At one point he is trapped in a half-collapsed home, where, terrified and repelled, he observes the Martians close at hand. (There is a famous illustration in the novel of this encounter.)

In the end, when humanity seems doomed to total annihilation, the Martians succumb to earthly microbes that infect and kill them. Where humanity fails, the earth—perhaps, as suggested in the novel, orchestrated by God—defends itself against the alien invaders. As stated in the opening chapter, after some reflection, this resolution (in both the novel and the movie) seems unconvincing to me; if the Martians were so scientifically advanced, shouldn't they have been aware of this potential danger?

Yet, although Wells does invoke the God's design in bringing about the Martian defeat—implying that God, a supernatural reality, is superior in foresight and power to the corporeal

Martians and humans—as a philosopher and futurist he was openly antagonistic toward religious visions of reality. If science provided an alternative framework for understanding reality, one both distinct from and opposed to religious supernaturalism and spiritualism, it was one that Wells clearly understood and embraced (Wells, 1934). I've noted that many science fiction writers managed to embrace science without necessarily abandoning religious and supernatural ideas in the process. And certainly *The War of the Worlds* does contain a "theological" intrusion. But by and large Wells led the way in the twentieth century toward a purely secularized and naturalistic approach to science fiction and the possibilities of human progress in the future without the need for divine guidance. He may have momentarily backed off in *The War of the Worlds* from the great uncertainty of existence, in a universe of science and evolution without an omnipotent and supernatural Creator, but the overall thrust of his futurist thinking and writing would reject this spiritual cosmological comfort.

Moreover, even if God is brought into play at the end of the story to rescue humanity from disaster, *The War of the Worlds* highlights the sense of the deep and terrifying mystery of the vast universe that had opened up through the revelations of modern science and astronomy. As stated earlier, science colossally expanded and deepened humanity's understanding of the universe and existence; within this heightened consciousness there are many more uncertainties and possibilities of terror. Even if God is still somehow mysteriously "up there," the vastly enlarged cosmos of Herschel, Flammarion, and modern astronomy afforded an almost unfathomable array of new and strange "bolts out of the blue."

At the time of its release, *The War of the Worlds* created a public sensation, a warning shot similar to *The Battle of Dorking*. It reinforced human paranoia and assaulted human arrogance, just as did Chesney's novel. There was the strong emotional reaction in the United States, as evidenced by *Edison's Conquest of Mars*; the vivid and disturbing depiction of the defeat of civilized humanity was too unsettling to go unanswered. More generally, Wells' novel heightened and agitated human consciousness on the disastrous possibilities of any kind of future hi-tech war, whether with aliens or among humans. Wells' novel—his first among many tales of colossally devastating world wars—provided a connecting thematic link between the earlier "future war" and "invasion" novels (such as Chesney's) and Wells' own later global war novels, such as *The War in the Air* (1908) and *The World Set Free* (1914). Also, connecting with the previous history of science fiction, *The War of the Worlds* offered a vivid illustration of the warning contained within *Vril, The Power of the Coming Race*: A superior intelligence and civilization could invade and conquer humanity and we might be powerless to stop it.

Decades later in the late 1930s, feeding on the paranoia preceding World War II, Orson Welles' radio broadcast of the story would generate real terror in the hearts of many American listeners, who took the radio broadcast as real news. Whatever the version, the story seems to have resonated with something deep within the human psyche. The other-worldly alien is an archetypal symbol of the invasive "other." The tale of the Martian attack on the earth, although fiction, has repeatedly reverberated with reality and fact. It has both informed and expressed the undercurrents of (modern) human consciousness.

Indeed, even later in the twentieth century, the novel maintained its immense influence on science fiction. For example, beginning in the 1950s, there were numerous alien invasion movies inspired by this story, including George Pal's version of Wells' novel. Pal's cinematic creation is set in contemporary times with redesigned Martian war machines floating in the air and transformed Martians, still hideous but with suction-cup fingertips and lacking the octopus tentacles.

There was also *Invaders from Mars* (1953), which I also watched as a youth. Here the ghastly Martians are again somewhat differently conceived, although the human-faced Martian leader has a giant bald head with octopus-like tentacles coming out of its atrophied body. Once more, they are aggressive and intent on conquest. In *Invaders from Mars*, dream and reality get mixed together—adding to its disquieting effect—and a psychological element is added: The Martians now take over people's minds. I was decidedly spooked by the whole movie experience. Suggestive of medieval superstitions regarding evil spirits and demons, aliens can invade our consciousness and rob us of our personal identity and self-control.

The wave of alien visitation and invasion movies produced in the 1950s included two other movies: *The Thing from Another World* (1951) and *Earth versus the Flying Saucers* (1956). The former movie with its scenario of an alien crash-landing near an isolated human outpost in the dark, frigid arctic was particularly spine tingling for me as a youth; how many different ways can an alien presence unsettle the human psyche? My early consciousness of the imaginative possibilities of science fiction—of getting frightened out of my wits (and I am sure for many other youthful fans of the day)—evolved on the cinematic ripples and reverberations of Wells' original vision written over half a century earlier.

As a youth, I was also not aware that the alien invasion movies of the time (and perhaps also the flying saucer craze of the 1950s) was simply the latest expression of generalized human paranoia, this time stoked by fear of invasion by belligerent forces in other parts of the world. Of course, the 1950s saw the escalation of the "Cold War" between the United States and the Soviet Union, provoking considerable public worry over the threat of atomic warfare. As I have suggested, imagined aliens are psychological projections of both our hopes and fears. And just as *The War of the Worlds* tapped into our fear of the "other" however conceived, the 1950s cinematic explosion of alien invasion movies—which

Wells' story provided the seminal inspiration for—reflected our fear of the Russians and atomic warfare. Such was the psychological undercurrent that fueled the popular fascination in the 1950s with such science fiction cinematic productions.

Continuing forward in time, there have been many further variations on this basic science fiction theme up to contemporary times—of monstrous and ruthless aliens with superior technologies of war, attacking and devastating the world. (The first part of the movie *Independence Day* (1996) took this scenario to an orgy of destruction.) The archetype of the alien invasion scenario with its nightmarish imagery and associated feelings of terror and panic has continued to maintain its psychological force. It is a mythic narrative that expresses a deep sense of fear and horror in the face of a mysterious and intimidating cosmos or other enigmatic and malevolent forces—human or otherwise. It is a psychological projection of that evil generic "other" forever intent on enslaving or destroying us.

The two scenarios presented in *The War of the Worlds* and *Edison's Conquest of Mars* have also frequently been blended together in various ways in science fiction literature and cinema. The resulting storyline, though still hair-raising, is more uplifting, providing another influential mythic narrative. Technologically superior aliens attack the earth, and although at first all seems lost, through human ingenuity and tenacity—and perhaps some luck—humans rise up out of the ashes of defeat. Invariably led by one or more courageous self-sacrificing heroes, they defeat the evil, seemingly invincible invading aliens. (This is the complete scenario of *Independence Day*.) The message: Humans do not give up when their back is against the wall. We defiantly reassert our sovereignty and freedom in the face of impossible odds—mythically speaking, in the face of the gods. Although perhaps egocentric and naïve, and grounded in human hubris, it is a hopeful and inspiring myth, even if it is fueled by paranoia, and punctuated by terror, chaos, and colossal destruction. Only with evil and death staring us in the face do we achieve our best.

The theme of alien encounters also unites two fundamental lines of thought running through the evolution of science fiction: First, what will be discovered or revealed in the vast expanses of outer space? And second, what constitutes an advanced society, or a more evolved form of life and intelligence? Some far away and isolated land on the earth may be the location for an advanced society and higher form of mentality, as in Bacon's *New Atlantis*; or, assuming the theory of secular and scientific progress, the future may provide the setting for imagining an advanced society, and even perhaps a more evolved form of mentality, as with Astor, Bellamy, or *The Great Romance*. But we can also imagine a superior mentality and civilization existing somewhere out in the vast expanse of our physical universe. In all these cases the imagined superior form of mentality and civilization is transcendent to contemporary human society and the present capacities of the human mind.

Visions of advanced forms of mentality existing in outer space go back at least as far as Voltaire's *Micromegas*. But with the rise of modern astronomy, as expressed and popularized in the writings of Bruno, de Fontenelle, and Huygens, and later Hershel and Flammarion, the idea of a plurality of inhabited worlds in outer space, perhaps supporting "higher" and different forms of mentality, became a popular speculation.

In fact, outer space offered a blank canvas on which to create all manner and form of more highly evolved societies and types of minds. Indeed, with the scientific theory of evolution informing and inspiring writers from Flammarion to Wells, it made perfect sense to suppose that evolution was at work on a cosmic scale and that somewhere out there lay something much more evolved than — and different from — us. Although Wells' Martians are the most famous case in the nineteenth century of more advanced aliens, Lasswitz's more complex (though more anthropomorphic) vision of the Martians and Martian civilization was the most elaborate, comprehensive, and scientifically informed vision of superior alien minds and a more advance society up to that point in time. Lasswitz offered a powerfully and thoughtfully drawn vision, integrating the themes of utopia, evolved minds, and the mysteries and possibilities of outer space. He united the mental, social, scientific, and technological in his alien vision. There will be many more depictions of advanced aliens to come in the twentieth century.

In considering how humans would react to superior beings and how superior beings would react to us, many different scenarios can be envisioned. The advanced aliens may wish to enlighten us, or they may wish to conquer and enslave us. Humans, on the other hand, might enthusiastically embrace the insights and achievements of the alien society, or humans might feel threatened and try to destroy the aliens. We humans have a hard time with the idea of something more evolved or "better than" us. We could argue that advanced aliens are often depicted as aggressive simply because humans need to feel justified in fighting against them. Their superiority is threatening to us, so we had better make them "bad guys" if we want to attack them.

When we gaze into the unknown, whether the future or outer space, we experience either hope and wonder, or fear and revulsion. The possibilities may inspire or terrify us. What is more advanced may either elevate or frighten us. As explained earlier, science fiction is a double-edged sword, affecting our emotional consciousness, depending on the story, in diametrically opposite ways. Confronting the "evolved other" is one basic science fiction scenario in which these contrasting feelings can emerge.

As one concluding point on Wells and *The War of the Worlds*, he created a host of very engaging fictional narratives—as exemplified in this novel—with color and drama and human pathos, that not only provoked strong emotional reactions, but more broadly impacted the full psychological breadth of holistic consciousness. Science fiction, as argued, is so popular because it engages the total human psyche through its narrative form, and Wells excelled in this regard; he was the greatest storyteller in science fiction up to that point in time. He was an evolution on what came before, and *The War of the Worlds* was one of his most memorable narrative creations, taking the reader on a captivating, dramatic, cognitively jolting, and visceral journey into the realm of the possible.

Indeed, in *The War of the Worlds* Wells powerfully synthesized the scientific and the romantic. As he would demonstrate in other novels, the connected emotional elements of fear, tension, and horror (or wonder) could be realized within a scientifically informed and inspired scenario, perhaps even more effectively and imaginatively than within a supernatural or Gothic setting. Science opened up human consciousness to a universe much more expansive, strange, wondrous—and unnerving—than anything previously envisioned in religious, spiritual, or supernatural narratives. Both the conscious mind and the human heart can ascend to new heights (and descend to new depths) in the fantastical settings of science fiction narratives. Somehow, at the age of six I grasped this cosmic and psychological revelation in first watching the movie *The War of the Worlds*. It was a terrifying enlightenment.

Summary and Conclusion

In the opening chapters of this volume I outlined and explained my over-arching hypothesis that science fiction—informed and inspired by modern science and contemporary thought—is the evolutionary mythology of the future. Key concepts in this hypothesis include myth (and the mythic narrative), the future, evolution, and science.

Thus far, I have described a variety of mythic themes, archetypes, and narratives expressed in early writings of science fiction. Notable mythic narratives in science fiction described thus far include: The "Playing God" warning narrative in

Frankenstein; the scientist as the courageous hero and wise wizard, as in *The Future Eve* and *Edison's Conquest of Mars*; the cosmic ascension narrative in Davy, Flammarion, and Astor; the extraordinary adventure with accompanying enlightenment, as in Kepler, Holberg, Verne, and Greg; a global and perhaps cataclysmic future war, which goes back to the religious prophecy of Armageddon; the alien invasion (with possible defense and counter-attack) in *The War of the Worlds* and *Edison's Conquest of Mars*; and the transcendence of humanity, for better or worse, expressed in numerous novels, such as Bulwer-Lytton's *Vril* and Lasswitz's *Two Planets*.

Insofar as the mythic adopts a narrative form, and mythic narrative engages both intellect and emotion, part of the history in this present volume concerned itself with the evolving dance and complex synthesis, realized in science fiction, between the Dionysian and the Apollonian and the Rationalistic and the Romantic. The polarity of reason versus emotion and sensation, and its integration, goes back to the ancient Greeks. From the modern scientific end of things, the spirit of Romanticism strongly manifested itself in the scientific work and writings of Hershel, Davy, and Flammarion, among others. For such individuals, science (an intellectual endeavor) and emotion were not diametrically at odds with each other. But it was Verne and Robida who first brought science and the intellect into the emotionally engaging narrative form, with Wells dramatically and powerfully achieving this synthesis after them. In such modern tales, the Romantic and the Dionysian—emotion and intense sensation—became informed by and facilitated through science. The long and the short of it: By the end of the nineteenth century, we have the "scientific romance" in which the mythic narrative with its emotional and sensory wallop is combined with the imaginative ideas of science and the intellect.

The issue of the future—and particularly of a future that is distinctly different from the present—has been addressed on numerous occasions in this book, beginning with St. Augustine and his Zoroastrian and Platonic ideas, but most importantly coming to center stage with the Age of Western Enlightenment and the secular theory of progress. Such imagined futures, however, veer off in two directions, toward utopian and dystopian realities—with ambiguous and mixed cases in between. Bacon, Campanella, Mercier, Bellamy, Morris, and Astor are clearly utopian, although in different ways, embodying different values; Robida and Butler are comically ambiguous, and *The Great Romance* brings a mystical uncertainty into the utopian scheme; and Jules Verne, in spite of the scientific-techno enthusiasm in many of his novels, is clearly dystopian in his *Paris in the Twentieth Century*. Grainville is flat-out abysmal and depressing, while Mitchell in *The Last American* is both insightfully comical and unequivocally negative in his assessment of the Western utopian vision of future progress. There will be many more novels to come in the twentieth century, covered in subsequent volumes, on this dialectical futurist theme, with Wells contributing significantly to this area of speculative writing. The twentieth century will especially see a proliferation of dystopian novels.

I also examined the theory of evolution—going all the way back to Democritus and Lucretius—and described the impact of evolution on Western intellectual thought, as well as the creation of notable fictional works, such as *Vril*, *Erewhon*, *Lumen*, and *Journey in Other Worlds*. Although the theory of secular progress through science and advancing technology provided a framework for extrapolative and positive prediction on the future, it is only after the *Origin of Species* and *The Descent of Man* that science fiction literature experiences its most profuse flowering. Modern science fiction was "born" or "invented" almost immediately after Darwin's publications. By the end of the nineteenth century, the evolutionary perspective achieves astronomic cosmic proportions, in both space and time—multiverses and the far future—in Flammarion's *Omega: The Last Days of the World* and

Astor's Journey in Other Worlds. As mentioned earlier, Stapledon will expand further the evolutionary vision of the cosmos in the twentieth century.

The theory of evolution is central to modern science (Lombardo, 2002b, 2002c, 2017). On the broad question of how science fiction has been informed and inspired by modern science, the historical reality has been complex. Although modern scientific astronomy opened up the universe to a naturalistic understanding of reality, in many ways totally at odds with ancient theories and supernatural interpretations— Galileo, Kepler, de Fontanelle, Herschel, and others leading the way—writers such as Flammarion and Astor continued to populate the modern heavens with supernatural spirits and ghosts. God was still out there somewhere in a scientifically informed cosmos. The spiritual and the supernatural also haunt narratives involving high-tech and futurist extrapolations, such as in *The Mummy!* and *The Future Eve,* in which the non-corporeal sneaks into the workings of machines and reanimated corpses.

Further, within the history of science fiction (as described thus far), there have been been anti-scientific and reactionary philosophical and literary movements that have nonetheless strongly influenced the evolution of science fiction. As mentioned, there was a powerful anti-scientific dimension to Romanticism, one that clearly influenced both Shelley in *Frankenstein* and Morris in *News from Nowhere*—albeit in very different ways. (It is fascinatingly ironic that *Frankenstein,* frequently identified as the first modern science fiction novel, is really an anti-science fiction novel, a nightmare and a warning against science inspired speculative fiction.) Also, as a distinctive outgrowth of the Romantic Movement, the Gothic (which also influenced Shelley) was an intentional turning away from modernity and a re-embrace of the ghostly and supernatural. Yet, the Gothic influenced the growth of science fiction (and continues to do so in the present). Consider the synthesis of the Gothic and the scientific in Poe and in Stevenson's *Dr. Jekyll and Mr. Hyde*. Key features of the Gothic, with its mystery and horror, became infused into science fiction, through elements such as the mad scientist, outer space, and the alien, all evoking the dark and terrifying dimensions of human experience. Looking ahead to the early twentieth century, we will encounter Hodgson and Lovecraft, powerfully pulling together the cosmic-scientific with the horrific and mysterious.

Moreover, although writers such as Verne, Flammarion, and Astor enthusiastically embraced modern science and technology, what was considered scientifically plausible continued to be an arena of contention throughout the nineteenth century; for example, the hollow earth theory found advocates in Holberg, Symmes, and Verne; the idea of an anti-gravity force was proposed by Greg and Astor; psychic powers appear in Bulwer-Lytton, Greg, and Astor; and the illusory Martian canals, observed and graphically pictured by Lowell, would simply not go away. Yet all in all, "scientific" theories and technological extrapolations, even if haunted by ghosts and hallucinations and open to various interpretations, became a central and essential feature in eighteenth- and nineteenth-century science fiction. Science (and the scientifically informed future) provided a new, more expansive and imaginative arena in which to experience mythic transcendence.

Evolution and science, the future, utopian-dystopian thought, and Romanticism swirl around and interconnect on the issue of a more advanced form of life and mentality than presently exists in the human arena. Perhaps this issue is the most emotionally charged and personally engaging theme in our evolving mythology of the future.

It is within the context of this issue that we grapple with the mythic theme of "Playing God," as, for example, in Shelley's *Frankenstein*. Can we create a superior being? What would it be like? Should we attempt this? If we are creations of God, then are we engaging in the most rebellious and blasphemous of all acts by taking control of ourselves and our destiny? Is it a sin to embrace the myth of the "modern Prometheus"? Is it a sin to aspire toward self-determination, self-control, and mastery over ourselves and nature? Or are these aspirations expressive of our most empowering and important human dimension (Lombardo, 2017)?

Perhaps our creations will not, strictly speaking, be human; perhaps they will be robots? Maybe they will turn on us? Or worse yet, maybe we will lose our self-respect and decline into existential depression and eventual extinction. In the eighteenth and nineteenth centuries, robots (or artificially constructed animate beings) were beginning to populate science fiction, such as in *The Sandman, The Future Eve*, and the plethora of Edisonade stories. In the twentieth century they would become much more visible (especially after Isaac Asimov's robot stories and novels), presenting a clear threat to our sovereignty and pride.

On the other hand, maybe the superior minds will come knocking on our door, having descended from the skies or ascended out of the bowels of the earth (as in *Vril, the Power of the Coming Race*). Perhaps this is what looking into the face of God (or the devil) feels like. We may be annihilated; we may fall into self-dejection; or perhaps (as envisioned by Lasswitz) we will be "uplifted," against our will, transforming into something better than we presently are. Key to the nature and power of myth is the facilitation of transcendence, but transcendence can provoke both ecstasy and recoil. Do we want to be uplifted? Do we want to transcend our present state?

Metaphorically, if not literally, transcendence can involve devastation and death (the resurrection theme). Cutting across many of the above themes, the forces of chaos, entropy, and destruction flow alongside those of evolution on the journey into the future, at times facilitating, at times upsetting human progress and the realization of our utopian dreams. From our earliest myths — such as the defeat of the Titans by the Olympian gods and the battle of Armageddon — war and catastrophe have been an integral part of our mythic consciousness. The ancient theory of order versus chaos (and its modern version of evolution versus entropy) has influenced the development of science fiction from its beginnings up to contemporary times. In the next volume we will see how this archetypal theme was a central idea in the writings of Wells, "Doc" Smith, and Olaf Stapledon, among others.

Instead of thinking of human transcendence primarily from a techno-physical or biological point of view, alternatively we can consider how we might dramatically alter the nature of our conscious minds. I see this question raised in *Dr. Jekyll and Mr. Hyde*, but I also see it circulating around in the writings of Edgar Allan Poe, combining scientific and mystical means of transcendence. Such speculative writings are eerily disquieting, for what is perhaps most mysterious and unnerving is the depth and possibilities of consciousness and the mind. In the coming century, the science fiction of both Wells and Stapledon will delve deeply into the possibilities of advanced minds.

And that, my friends, is our next destination. If we take evolution and science; the future; both dystopian and utopian thought; chaos and war; and visions of superior minds and forms of life, and weave it all together into engaging emotionally charged narratives, pregnant with multiple mythic themes, what we arrive at is H. G. Wells, the father of modern science fiction, as well as modern futures studies, and the subject of the first chapter in the next volume of this historical study.

My intent in this first volume has been to demonstrate that science fiction has a deep history threaded with countless tributaries of thought, encompassing myth and mysticism; religion; philosophy; science; psychology; social-political thinking; art; technology; and the exploratory-naturalistic spirit. Science fiction is an ongoing evolution in consciousness — in particular, fantastical and future consciousness—that, integrative and cosmic, extends back to ancient times and has built upon itself over the centuries. As I have stated, science fiction is both an expression of the evolution of the human mind and a powerful stimulus to further self-evolution and transcendence. In this regard, Wells is a fitting place to start the next volume, for he reflects a deep understanding of history and the development of life, mind, and society while attempting to *anticipate* and *guide* the further evolution of humanity in the future.

From Wells we will journey to the equally colossal mind of Olaf Stapledon in the concluding chapter of volume two. Also integrating diverse historical streams of human thought in his works, Stapledon applied his synthetic knowledge to envisioning the deep future of humans—and diverse forms of alien intelligence throughout the universe—with the intent to inform and inspire our future evolution. Wells and Stapledon are the two great pillars of thought framing the saga of narrative speculation in the early decades of the twentieth century. It's going to be a cosmic ride from Wells' *The Time Machine* (1895) to Stapledon's *Star Maker* (1937) on the continuing and extraordinary voyage of science fiction.

Preview of Volume Two:

The Time Machine to Star Maker

Chapter 1: H. G. Wells
Thinking Out Evolution, Ethics, and the Future of Humanity
The Science Fiction of H. G. Wells
Futures Studies and Utopian Thought

Chapter 2: The Early Twentieth Century
Disturbing the Peace: Turn of the Century Revolutions in Vision
    and Thought
Visions of a "Glowing Future"—Méliès and the Cinema
A Transforming and Expanding Universe: Physics, the Big Bang,
    Rocketry, and Russian Cosmism
A Bright and Terrible New Century: A Cornucopia of Science
    Fiction

Chapter 3: The Efflorescence of Imagination
The Fantastic Adventures of Edgar Rice Burroughs and its
    Accompaniments
Cummings, Wright, and the Phantasmagorias of Abraham
    Merritt
Early Twentieth Century Utopias and Dystopias: *We*, *The Iron
Heel*, *Herland*, and *City of Endless Night*

Chapter 4: Science Fiction Becomes Visible and Self-Conscious
The Amazing and the Wondrous: Gernsback, Paul, and Fandom
The Emergence of Comics and Super-Heros: *Flash Gordon*, *Buck
Rogers*, *Gladiator*, and *Superman*
The Cinema: *Aelita*, *The Lost World*, *Metropolis*, and Adventures
    in Horror, Sight, and Sound

Non-Fiction Bibliography

(Including Websites and Cited Collections)

Adams, F. and Laughlin, G. (1999) *The Five Ages of the Universe: Inside the Physics of Eternity*, New York: The Free Press.

Aldiss, B. (1973) *Billion Year Spree: The True History of Science Fiction*, New York: Schocken Books.

Aldiss, B. and Wingrove, D. (1986) *Trillion Year Spree: The History of Science Fiction*, North Yorkshire, UK: House of Stratus.

Alessio, D. (2008) "Introduction," in Alessio, D. (ed.) *The Great Romance: A Rediscovered Utopian Adventure*, Lincoln, NB: University of Nebraska Press, pp. xi-lx.

Alkon, P. (1987) *Origins of Futuristic Fiction*, Athens, Georgia: University of Georgia Press.

al-Nafis [Online]. Available at https://en.wikipedia.org/wiki/Ibn_al-Nafis (Accessed 1 April 2017).

Amazing Illustrations [Online]. Available at http://www.artistsandart.org/2009/06/amazing-illustrations-for-ancient-proto.html (Accessed 1 April 2017).

Ancient History [Online]. Available at http://www.ancienthistorylists.com/greek-history/top-10-inventions-discoveries-ancient-greece-remarkably-used-today/; http://ancienthistory.about.com/od/sciencemedicine/tp/042810GreekScientificInventions.htm (Accessed 1 April 2017).

Apollonian and Dionysian [Online]. Available at https://en.wikipedia.org/wiki/Apollonian_and_Dionysian (Accessed 1 April 2017).

Argonautica [Online]. Available at https://en.wikipedia.org/wiki/Argonautica (Accessed 1 April 2017).

Armstrong, K. (1994) *A History of God: The Four Thousand Year Quest of Judaism, Christianity, and Islam*, New York: Alfred Knopf.

Ash, B. (ed.) (1977) *The Visual Encyclopedia of Science Fiction*, New York: Harmony Books.

Asimov's Science Fiction [Online]. Available at http://www.asimovs.com/ (Accessed 1 April 2017).

Bailey, J. O. (1947) *Pilgrims through Space and Time: A History and Analysis of Scientific Fiction*, New York: Argus Books.

Barbour, I. (1997) *Religion and Science: Historical and Contemporary Issues*, New York: HarperCollins.

Becker, E. (1973) *The Denial of Death*, New York: Free Press.

The Begum's Fortune, Wikipedia [Online]. Available at: https://en.wikipedia.org/wiki/The_Begum's_Fortune.   (Accessed: August 25, 2017).

Bell, W. (1997) *Foundations of Future Studies: Human Science for a New Era*, New Brunswick, NJ: Transaction.

Berman, M. (1981) *The Reenchantment of the World*, New York: Bantam.

Best, S. and Kellner, D. (1997) *The Postmodern Turn*, New York: Guilford Press.

Bleiler, E. (1991) *Science-Fiction: The Early Years,* Kent, OH: Kent State University Press.

Bloom, H. (2000) *Global Brain: The Evolution of Mass Mind from the Big Bang to the 21st Century*, New York: John Wiley and Sons, Inc.

Bloom, J. (2010) *Fantastic Voyages: By Ship to Nowhereland and Back Again* [Online]. Available at http://www.cabinetdesfees.com/2010/fantastic-voyages-part-1/ (Accessed 1 April 2017).

Borges, J. (1969) *The Book of Imaginary Beings*. New York: Avon Books.

Boring, E. (1950) *A History of Experimental Psychology*, 2nd edn, New York: Appleton-Century-Crofts.

Bova, B. (ed) (1973a) *The Science Fiction Hall of Fame Vol. IIA*, New York: Avon Books.

Bova, B. (ed) (1973b) *The Science Fiction Hall of Fame Vol. IIB*, New York: Avon Books.

British Science Fiction Awards [Online]. Available at http://www.bsfa.co.uk/ (Accessed 1 April 2017).

Broderick, D., and DiFilippo, P. (2012) *Science Fiction: The 101 Best Novels 1985-2010*, New York: Nonstop Press.

Brown, D. (1991) *Human Universals*, New York: McGraw-Hill.

Bulfinch, T. (1855/1962) *Bulfinch's Mythology: The Age of Fable*, New York: The New American Library.

Buxton, R. (2004) *The Complete World of Greek Mythology*, United Kingdom: Thames and Hudson, Ltd.

John W. Campbell Award (Gunn Center for the Study of Science Fiction) [Online]. Available at http://www.sfcenter.ku.edu/campbell.htm (Accessed 1 April 2017).

Campbell, J. (1949) *The Hero with a Thousand Faces*, New York: Pantheon Books.

Campbell, J. (1988) *The Power of Myth*, New York: Doubleday.

Center for Future Consciousness [Online]. Available at http://www.centerforfutureconsciousness.com/ (Accessed 1 April 2017).

Chaisson, E. (2005) *Epic of Evolution: Seven Ages of the Cosmos*, New York: Columbia University Press.

Chaisson, E. (2009) "Cosmic evolution: state of the science" in Dick, S. and Lupisella, M. (eds.) *Cosmos and Culture: Cultural Evolution in a Cosmic Context*, Washington, D. C.: NASA, pp. 3-23.

Chardin, T. de (1959) *The Phenomenon of Man*, New York: Harper.

Arthur C. Clarke Award [Online]. Available at http://www.clarkeaward.com/ (Accessed 1 April 2017).

Clute, J. (1995) *Science Fiction: The Illustrated Encyclopedia*, London: Doarling Kindersley.

Clute, J. (1999) *The Book of End Times: Grappling with the Millennium*, New York: HarperPrism.

Clute, J. and Nicholls, P. (1995) *The Encyclopedia of Science Fiction*, New York: St. Martin's Press.

Comicbook+.com [Online]. Available at http://comicbookplus.com/?cid=2283 (Accessed 1 April 2017).

Crossley, R. (1994) *Olaf Stapledon: Speaking for the Future*, Syracuse, NY: Syracuse University Press.

Cyberneticzoo [Online]. Available at http://cyberneticzoo.com/; http://cyberneticzoo.com/steammen/1868-1904-fictional-steam-man-steam-horse-electric-man-electric-horse-american/ (Accessed 1 April 2017).

Damasio, A. (1999) *The Feeling of What Happens: Body and Emotion in the Making of Consciousness*, New York: Harcourt Brace.

Damasio, A. (2010) *Self Comes to Mind: Constructing the Conscious Brain*, New York: Random House.

Davies, P. (2001) *How to Build a Time Machine*, New York: Viking.

Diamandis, P. and Kotler, S. (2012) *Abundance: The Future is Better than You Think*, New York: Free Press.

Philip K. Dick Award [Online]. Available at http://www.philip kdickaward.org/ (Accessed 1 April 2017).

Dirda, Michael (2006) "Review of *The Begum's Millions*", *Washington Post*, March 5, 2006 [Online]. Available at: http://www.washingtonpost.com/wp-dyn/content/article/2006/03/02/AR2006030201547.html. (Accessed: August 25, 2017).

Disch, T. (1998) *The Dreams Our Stuff is Made of: How Science Fiction Conquered the World*, New York: The Free Press.

Dawkins, R. (2006) *The God Delusion*, Boston: Houghton-Mifflin.

Dictionary.com [Online]. Available at http://www.dictionary.com/browse/fantastic (Accessed 1 April 2017).

Donald, M. (1991) *Origins of the Modern Mind: Three Stages in the Evolution of Culture and Cognition*, Cambridge, Massachusetts: Harvard University Press.

Encyclopedia of Science Fiction [Online]. Available at http://www.sf-encyclopedia.com/about-us (Accessed 1 April 2017).

Evans, A. (1995) "The 'New' Jules Verne", *Science Fiction Studies*, vol 22, part 1[Online]. Available at http://www.depauw.edu/sfs/backissues/65/evans65art.htm (Accessed 1 April 2017).

Fantasy [Online]. Available at https://en.wikipedia.org/wiki/

Fantasy (Accessed 1 April 2017).

Feyerabend, P. (1965) "Problems of empiricism", in Colodny, R. (ed.) *Beyond the Edge of Certainty*, Englewood Cliffs, NJ.: Prentice-Hall, pp. 145-260.

Feyerabend, P. (1969) "Problems of empiricism II", in Colodny, R. (ed.) *The Nature and Function of Scientific Theory*, London: University of Pittsburgh Press, pp. 275-353.

Feyerabend, P. (1970) "Against method: Outline of an anarchistic theory of knowledge", in Radner, M. and Winokur, S. (eds.) *Minnesota Studies in the Philosophy of Science, vol. 4*, Minneapolis, MN: University of Minnesota Press, pp. 17-130.

Flammarion Engraving [Online]. Available at https://en.wikipedia.org/wiki/Flammarion_engraving (Accessed 1 April 2017).

Franz, M. von (1978) *Time: Rhythm and Repose*, New York: Thames and Hudson.

The Free Dictionary [Online]. Available at (http://www.thefreedictionary.com/myth); http://www.thefreedictionary.com/fantasy; http://www.thefreedictionary.com/myth) (Accessed 1 April 2017).

Gleick, J. (1999) *Faster: The Acceleration of Just About Everything*, New York: Pantheon Books.

Greek Astronomy; Ancient Greek Astronomy [Online]. Available at (https://explorable.com/greek-astronomy; https://en.wikipedia.org/wiki/Ancient_Greek_astronomy) (Accessed 1 April 2017).

Goerner, S. (1999) *After the Clockwork Universe: The Emerging Science and Culture of Integral Society*, Norwich, Great Britain: Floris Books.

Gould, S. (1987) *Time's Arrow Time's Cycle: Myth and Metaphor in the Discovery of Geological Time*, Cambridge: Harvard University Press.

Gould, S. (1989) *Wonderful Life: The Burgess Shale and the Nature of History*, New York: W. W. Norton.

Green, J. (1959) *The Death of Adam: Evolution and Its Impact on*

Western Thought, Ames, Iowa: Iowa State University Press.

Gunn Center for the Study of Science Fiction (University of Kansas) [Online]. Available at http://www.sfcenter.ku.edu/index. html (Accessed 1 April 2017).

Gunn, J. (1975) *Alternate Worlds: An Illustrated History of Science Fiction*, Englewood Cliffs, NJ: Prentice-Hall, Inc.

Gunn, J. (ed.) (1977) *The Road to Science Fiction: From Gilgamesh to Wells*, New York: New American Library.

Gunn, J. and Candelaria, M. (eds.) (2005) *Speculations on Speculation: Theories of Science Fiction*, Lanham, MD: The Scarecrow Press, Inc.

Hamilton, E. (1942) *Mythology*, Boston: Little, Brown, and Co.

Hephaestus [Online]. Available at https://en.wikipedia.org/wiki/ Hephaestus) (Accessed 1 April 2017).

Hesiod [Online]. Available at https://en.wikipedia.org/wiki/ Hesiod) (Accessed 1 April 2017).

Hitchens, C. (2007) *God is Not Great: How Religion Poisons Everything*, New York: Twelve.

Holland, S. (2009) *Sci-Fi Art: A Graphic History*, New York: Collins Design.

Holmes, R. (2008) *The Age of Wonder*, New York: Vintage Books.

Hopkins, L. (2003) "Jane C. Loudon's *The Mummy!*: Mary Shelley meets George Orwell, and they go in a balloon to Egypt" [Online]. Available at http://shura.shu.ac.uk/8710/ (Accessed 1 April 2017).

Hugo Awards [Online]. Available at http://www.thehugoawards. org/; *Hugo Awards – Best Novels and Nominees*: http:// en.wikipedia.org/wiki/Hugo_Award_for_Best_Novel (Accessed 1 April 2017).

Internet Speculative Fiction Data Base [Online]. Available at http:// www.isfdb.org/cgi-bin/index.cgi (Accessed 1 April 2017).

Jaynes, J. (1976) *The Origin of Consciousness in the Breakdown of the Bicameral Mind*, Boston: Houghton Mifflin.

JessNevins.com [Online]. Available at http://jessnevins.com/

edisonade/electricseaspider.html (Accessed 1 April 2017).

Jung, C. (ed.) (1964) *Man and his Symbols*, Garden City, New York: Doubleday and Company.

Kelly, K. (2010) *What Technology Wants*, New York: Viking.

Kincaid, P. (2006) "Review of *The Begum's Millions*", *SF Site* [Online]. Available at: https://www.sfsite.com/03a/bm219.htm. (Accessed: August 25, 2017).

Kirk, G.S. and Raven, J.E. (1966) *The Presocratic Philosophers*, Cambridge: Cambridge University Press.

Koestler, A. (1964) *The Act of Creation*, New York: Dell.

Korshak, S. (ed.) (2010) *Frank R. Paul: Father of Science Fiction Art*, New York: Castle Books.

Krippner, S., Mortifee, A., and Feinstein, D. (1998) "New myths for the new millennium", *The Futurist*, vol. 32, no. 2, pp. 30-34.

Kuhn, T. (1962) *The Structure of Scientific Revolutions*, Chicago: University of Chicago Press.

Kurzweil, R. (1999) *The Age of Spiritual Machines: When Computers Exceed Human Intelligence*, New York: Penguin Books.

Kurzweil, R. (2005) *The Singularity is Near: When Humans Transcend Biology*, New York: Viking Press.

Leonardo da Vinci (1956) New York: Reynal and Company.

Locus Awards and Comprehensive Listing of Awards [Online]. Available at http://www.sfadb.com/Awards_Directory (Accessed 1 April 2017).

Lombardo, J. B. (2004) "Medieval Reverie versus Behaviorist's Experiment: The Utopias of William Morris and B. F. Skinner" [Online], *Center for Future Consciousness*. Available at http://www.centerforfutureconsciousness.com/pdf_files/2008_Essays/Medieval%20Reverie%20Versus%20Behaviorist%20s%20Experiment-The%20Utopias%20of%20William%20Morris%20and%20B.%20F.%20Skinner.pdf (Accessed 1 April 2017).

Lombardo, J. B. (2010) "The ontological underpinnings of the modern utopia" [Online], *Center for Future Consciousness*. Available at http://www.centerforfutureconsciousness.com/ pdf_files/Readings/Jeanne's%20thesis.pdf (Accessed 1 April 2017).

Lombardo, T. (1987) *The Reciprocity of Perceiver and Environment: The Evolution of James J. Gibson's Ecological Psychology*, Hillsdale, NJ: Lawrence Erlbaum Associates.

Lombardo, T. (2002a) *The Future of Science, Technology, and the Cosmos*, [Online], *Center for Future Consciousness*. Available at http://www.centerforfutureconsciousness.com/ST_Readings. htm (Accessed 1 April 2017).

Lombardo, T. (2002b) "Science and the technological vision of the future" [Online], *Center for Future Consciousness*. Available at http://www.centerforfutureconsciousness.com/pdf_files/ Readings/ReadingSciTech.pdf (Accessed 1 April 2017).

Lombardo, T. (2002c) "Life, biotechnology, and purposeful biological evolution" [Online], *Center for Future Consciousness*. Available at http://www.centerforfutureconsciousness.com/ pdf_files/Readings/ReadingLifeBiotech.pdf (Accessed 1 April 2017).

Lombardo, T. (2002d) "Ecological evolution" [Online], *Center for Future Consciousness*. Available at http://www.cen terforfutureconsciousness.com/pdf_files/Readings/Read ingEcoEvolution.pdf (Accessed 1 April 2017).

Lombardo, T. (2002e) "Space exploration and cosmic evolution" [Online], *Center for Future Consciousness*. Available at http:// www.centerforfutureconsciousness.com/pdf_files/Readings/ ReadingSpaceExploration.pdf (Accessed 1 April 2017).

Lombardo, T. (2006a) *The Evolution of Future Consciousness: The Nature and Historical Development of the Human Capacity to Think about the Future*, Bloomington, IN: AuthorHouse.

Lombardo, T. (2006b) *Contemporary Futurist Thought: Science Fiction, Future Studies, and Theories and Visions of the Future in the Last Century*, Bloomington, IN: AuthorHouse.

Lombardo, T. (2006c) "Science fiction as the mythology of the future" [Online], *Center for Future Consciousness*. Available at: http://www.centerforfutureconsciousness.com/pdf_files/Readings/ScienceFictionLongArticle.pdf (Accessed 1 April 2017).

Lombardo, T. (2009) "The future evolution of the ecology of mind", World Future Review, vol.1, no. 1, pp. 39-56.

Lombardo, T. (2011a) *Wisdom, Consciousness, and the Future: Selected Essays*. Bloomington, IN: Xlibris.

Lombardo, T. (with Lombardo, J. B.) (2011b) *MInd Flight: A Journey into the Future*. Bloomington, IN: Xlibris.

Lombardo, T. (2011c) "Creativity, wisdom, and our evolutionary future", *Journal of Futures Studies*, vol. 16, no. 1, pp. 19-46.

Lombardo, T. (2014a) "Science fiction: The mythology of the future (Three Part Video)" [Online], *Center for Future Consciousness*. Available at http://www.centerforfutureconsciousness.com/science_fiction_video.htm (Accessed 1 April 2017).

Lombardo, T. (2014b) "The future evolution of consciousness", *World Future Review*, vol. 6, no. 3, pp. 322-335.

Lombardo, T. (2015a) "Science fiction: The evolutionary mythology of the future", *Journal of Futures Studies*, vol. 20, no. 2, pp. 5-24.

Lombardo, T. (2015b) "Contemporary trends and paradigms and theories of the future (Three Part Video)" [Online], *Center for Future Consciousness*. Available at http://www.centerforfutureconsciousness.com/cont_trends_video.htm (Accessed 1 April 2017).

Lombardo, T. (2016a). "Tom Lombardo's Evolving List of All-Time Best Science Fiction Novels" [Online], *Center for Future Consciousness*. Available at http://www.centerforfutureconsciousness.com/sf_novels.htm (Accessed 1 April 2017).

Lombardo, T. (2016b) "Tom Lombardo's Evolving List of All-Time Best Science Fiction Movies" [Online], *Center for Future Consciousness.* Available at http://www. centerforfutureconsciousness.com/sf_movies.htm (Accessed 1 April 2017).

Lombardo, T. (2016c) "Historical evolution of consciousness and human understanding" [Online], *Center for Future Consciousness.* Available at http://centerforfutureconsciousness. com/pdf_files/Readings/Historical%20Evolution%20of%20 Consciousness%20and%20Human%20Understanding.pdf (Accessed 1 April 2017).

Lombardo, T. (2017) *Future Consciousness: The Path to Purposeful Evolution,* Winchester, UK: Changemakers Books.

Loye, D. (2007) *Darwin's Lost Theory: Who We Really Are and Where We're Going,* Carmel, CA: Benjamin Franklin Press.

Luckhorst, R. (2006) "Introduction" in Stevenson, Robert Louis *Strange Case of Dr. Jekyll and Mr. Hyde and Other Tales,* Oxford: Oxford University Press, pp. vii-xxxii.

Lundwall, S. (1971) *Science Fiction: What It's All About,* New York: Ace Books.

Mallory, M. (2012) *The Science Fiction Universe ... and Beyond: Syfy Channel Book on Sci-Fi,* New York: Universe Publishing.

Manuel, F. and Manuel, F. (1979) *Utopian Thought in the Western World,* Cambridge, MA: Harvard University Press.

McDougall, W. (2001) "Journey to the Center of Jules Verne ... and Us," *Foreign Policy Research Institute,* Sept.1, 2001 [Online]. Available at: https://www.fpri.org/article/2001/09/journey-to-the-center-of-jules-verne-and-us/. (Accessed: August 25, 2017).

Montague, C. (2015) *H. P. Lovecraft: The Mysterious Man Behind the Darkness,* New York: Chartwell Books.

Morgan, C. (2006) "Verne the Unknown", *Emerald City: Fantasy and Science Fiction* [Online]. Available at: http://www.emcit. com/emcit125.php?a=20. (Accessed: August 25, 2017).

Moskowitz, S. (1954) *The Immortal Storm: A History of Science Fiction Fandom,* Westport, CT: Hyperion Press.

Moskowitz, S. (1963) *Explorers of the Infinite: Shapers of Science Fiction*, Cleveland, OH: World Publishing Co.

Moskowitz, S.(1966) *Seekers of Tomorrow*, Westport, CT: Hyperion Press, 1966.

Nebula Awards [Online]. Available at: http://www.sfwa.org/nebula-awards/; *Nebula Awards – Best Novel and Nominees*: https://en.wikipedia.org/wiki/Nebula_Award_for_Best_Novel (Accessed 1 April 2017).

Nevins, J. (2011) "May Day: The day 'science fiction' was invented" [Online], *Gizmodo*. Available at: http://io9.gizmodo.com/5796919/may-day-1871-the-day-science-fiction-was-invented (Accessed 1 April 2017).

Newman, S. (2010) *The Real History of the End of the World*, New York: Berkley Books.

Nietzsche, F. (1872/2006) *The Birth of Tragedy*, New York: Barnes and Noble.

Nisbet, R. (1994) *History of the Idea of Progress*, New Brunswick: Transaction Publishers.

Noss, D. (1999) *A History of the World's Religions*, 10th edn., Upper Saddle River, NJ.: Prentice Hall.

Oxford Dictionaries [Online]. Available at: http://www.oxforddictionaries.com/us/definition/american_english/myth (Accessed 1 April 2017).

Panshin, A. and Panshin, C. (1989) *The World Beyond the Hill: Science Fiction and the Quest for Transcendence*, Los Angeles: Jeremy Tarcher, Inc.

Panshin, A. and Panshin, C. (2005). "Science fiction and the dimension of myth", in Gunn, J. and Candelaria, M. (eds.) *Speculations on Speculation: Theories of Science Fiction*, Lanham, MD: The Scarecrow Press, Inc., pp. 219-234.

Phipps, C. (2012) *Evolutionaries: Unlocking the Spiritual and Cultural Potential of Science's Greatest Idea*, New York: Harper Perennial.

Pinker, S. (2002) *The Blank Slate: The Modern Denial of Human*

Nature, New York: Penguin Books.

Pirsig, R. (1974) *Zen and the Art of Motorcycle Maintenance*, New York: Bantam.

Poe, E. A. (1976) *The Science Fiction of Edgar Allan Poe*, London: Penguin Books.

Pohl, F. (1978) *The Way the Future Was: A Memoir*, New York: Ballantine Books.

Pohl, F. (1996) "Thinking about the future", *The Futurist*, vol. 30, no. 5, pp. 8-12.

Polak, F. (1973) *The Image of the Future*, Abridged edition by Boulding, E., Amsterdam: Elsevier Scientific Publishing Company.

Pringle, David (1985) *Science Fiction: The 100 Best Novels*, New York: Carroll and Graf Publishers, Inc.

Randall, J. (1960) *Aristotle*, New York: Columbia University Press.

Robb, B. (2012) *Steampunk: An Illustrated History of Fantastical Fiction, Fanciful Film, and Other Victorian Visions*, London: Voyageur Press.

Roberts, A. (2005) *The History of Science Fiction*, New York: Palgrave Macmillan.

Robinson, F. (1999) *Science Fiction in the 20th Century: An Illustrated History*, New York: Barnes and Noble Books.

Romanticism [Online]. Available at: https://en.wikipedia.org/wiki/Romanticism (Accessed 1 April 2017).

Science Fiction [Online]. Available at: http://en.wikipedia.org/wiki/Science_fiction; *Timeline*: http://en.wikipedia.org/wiki/Timeline_of_science_fiction; *Science Fiction Studies*: http://en.wikipedia.org/wiki/Science_fiction_studies (Accessed 1 April 2017).

Science Fiction and Fantasy Hall of Fame [Online]. Available at: http://www.empmuseum.org/at-the-museum/museum-features/science-fiction-and-fantasy-hall-of-fame.aspx (Accessed 1 April 2017).

Science Fiction and Fantasy Writers of America [Online]. Available at: http://www.sfwa.org/ (Accessed 1 April 2017).

Science Fiction.com [Online]. Available at: http://sciencefiction.com/ (Accessed 1 April 2017).

Science Fiction Hub [Online]. Available at: http://www.thescifihub.com/ (Accessed 1 April 2017).

Science Fiction Research Association [Online]. Available at: http://www.sfra.org/ (Accessed 1 April 2017).

SCIFI at Dark Roasted Blend [Online]. Available at: http://www.scifi.darkroastedblend.com/ (Accessed 1 April 2017).

Shelley, W. (2011) "The history of science fiction" [Online]. Available at: http://www.wardshelley.com/paintings/pages/HistoryofScienceFiction.html (Accessed 1 April 2017).

Shermer, M. (2004) *The Science of Good and Evil*, New York: Times Books.

Siegel, N. (2016) "From hell to heaven in the hometown of Bosch" [Online], *New York Times*. Available at: http://www.nytimes.com/2016/05/01/travel/hieronymus-bosch-netherlands.html?emc=eta1&_r=1 (Accessed 1 April 2017).

Silverberg, R. (ed.) (1970) *The Science Fiction Hall of Fame Vol. I*, New York: Avon Books.

Smolin, L. (1997) *The Life of the Cosmos*, Oxford: Oxford University Press.

Stableford, B. (ed.) (2002) *Lumen: Camille Flammarion*, Middletown, CT: Wesleyan University Press.

Stableford, B. (2016) *New Atlantis: A Narrative History of Scientific Romance Vol. 1-4*, San Bernardino, CA: Wildside Press.

Suvin, D. (1988) *Positions and Presuppositions in Science Fiction*, Kent, OH: The Kent State University Press.

Talos [Online]. Available at: https://en.wikipedia.org/wiki/Talos; http://www.wondersandmarvels.com/2012/03/the-worlds-first-robot-talos.html) (Accessed 1 April 2017).

Tarnas, R. (1991) *The Passion of the Western Mind: Understanding the Ideas that have Shaped Our World View*, New York: Ballantine.

Theologus Autodidactus [Online]. Available at: https://en.wikipedia.org/wiki/Theologus_Autodidactus) (Accessed 1 April 2017).

Tipler, F. (1994) *The Physics of Immortality: Modern Cosmology, God, and the Resurrection of the Dead*, New York: Doubleday.

Toffler, A. (1971) *Future Shock*, New York: Bantam.

Verne, J. (1965) *Yesterday and Tomorrow*, New York: Ace Books.

Wachhorst, W. (2000) *The Dream of Spaceflight: Essays on the Near Edge of Infinity*, New York: Basic Books.

Wagar, W. W. (2004) *H. G. Wells: Traversing Time*, Middletown, CT: Wesleyan University Press.

Watson, P. (2001) *The Modern Mind: An Intellectual History of the 20th Century*, New York: HarperCollins Perennial.

Watson, P. (2005) *Ideas: A History of Thought and Invention from Fire to Freud*, New York: HarperCollins Publishers.

Watson, R. (1971) *The Great Psychologists*, 3rd edn, Philadelphia: J.P. Lippincott Company.

Wells, H. G. (1893/2005) "The man of the year one million", in Wells, H.G. *Certain Personal Matters*, San Bernardino, CA: Wildside Press, pp. 75-79.

Wells, H. G. (1934) *Experiment in Autobiography*. New York: The Macmillan Company.

White, R. (2003) *Prehistoric Art: The Symbolic Journey of Humankind*, New York: Harry N. Abrams.

Whitehead, A. N. (1925) *Science and the Modern World*, New York: The Free Press.

Willems, P. (2004) "Introduction" in Robida, Albert *The Twentieth Century*, Middletown, CT: Wesleyan University Press, pp. xiii-lxiii.

Wilson, E. O. (1998a) *Consilience: The Unity of Knowledge*, New York: Alfred A. Knopf.

Wilson, E. O. (1998b) "Back from chaos" [Online], *The Atlantic Monthly*. Available at http://www.theatlantic.com/magazine/archive/1998/03/back-from-chaos/308700/ (Accessed 1 April

2017).

Wilson, E. O. (1998c) "The biological basis of morality" [Online], *The Atlantic Monthly*. Available at http://www.theatlantic.com/magazine/archive/1998/04/the-biological-basis-of-morality/377087/ (Accessed 1 April 2017).

Wilson, T. (2011) *Redirect: The Surprising New Science of Psychological Change*, New York: Little, Brown, and Company.

Worlds Without End [Online]. Available at: https://www.worldswithoutend.com/; *Classics (Books) of Science Fiction*: https://www.worldswithoutend.com/lists_classics_of_sf.asp (Accessed 1 April 2017).

Wright, R. (2009) *The Evolution of God*, New York: Little, Brown, and Company.

Wuckel, D. and Cassiday, B. (1989) *The Illustrated History of Science Fiction*, New York: Ungar.

Index

Changemakers Books
TRANSFORMATION

Transform your life, transform your world - Changemakers
Books publishes for individuals committed to transforming their
lives and transforming the world. Our readers seek to become
positive, powerful agents of change. Changemakers Books
inform, inspire, and provide practical wisdom and skills to
empower us to write the next chapter of humanity's future.
If you have enjoyed this book, why not tell other readers by
posting a review on your preferred book site.
Recent bestsellers from Changemakers Books are:

Integration
The Power of Being Co-Active in Work and Life
Ann Betz, Karen Kimsey-House
Integration examines how we came to be polarized in our dealing
with self and other, and what we can do to move from an either/
or state to a more effective and fulfilling way of being.
Paperback: 978-1-78279-865-1 ebook: 978-1-78279-866-8

Bleating Hearts
The Hidden World of Animal Suffering
Mark Hawthorne
An investigation of how animals are exploited for
entertainment, apparel, research, military weapons, sport, art,
religion, food, and more.
Paperback: 978-1-78099-851-0 ebook: 978-1-78099-850-3

Lead Yourself First!
Indispensable Lessons in Business and in Life
Michelle Ray
Are you ready to become the leader of your own life? Apply simple, powerful strategies to take charge of yourself, your career, your destiny.
Paperback: 978-1-78279-703-6 ebook: 978-1-78279-702-9

Burnout to Brilliance
Strategies for Sustainable Success
Jayne Morris
Routinely running on reserves? This book helps you transform your life from burnout to brilliance with strategies for sustainable success.
Paperback: 978-1-78279-439-4 ebook: 978-1-78279-438-7

Goddess Calling
Inspirational Messages & Meditations of Sacred Feminine Liberation Thealogy
Rev. Dr. Karen Tate
A book of messages and meditations using Goddess archetypes and mythologies, aimed at educating and inspiring those with the desire to incorporate a feminine face of God into their spirituality.
Paperback: 978-1-78279-442-4 ebook: 978-1-78279-441-7

The Master Communicator's Handbook
Teresa Erickson, Tim Ward
Discover how to have the most communicative impact in this guide by professional communicators with over 30 years of experience advising leaders of global organizations.
Paperback: 978-1-78535-153-2 ebook: 978-1-78535-154-9

Meditation in the Wild
Buddhism's Origin in the Heart of Nature
Charles S. Fisher Ph.D.
A history of Raw Nature as the Buddha's first teacher, inspiring some followers to retreat there in search of truth.
Paperback: 978-1-78099-692-9 ebook: 978-1-78099-691-2

Ripening Time
Inside Stories for Aging with Grace
Sherry Ruth Anderson
Ripening Time gives us an indispensable guidebook for growing into the deep places of wisdom as we age.
Paperback: 978-1-78099-963-0 ebook: 978-1-78099-962-3

Striking at the Roots
A Practical Guide to Animal Activism
Mark Hawthorne
A manual for successful animal activism from an author with first-hand experience speaking out on behalf of animals.
Paperback: 978-1-84694-091-0 ebook: 978-1-84694-653-0

Readers of ebooks can buy or view any of these bestsellers by clicking on the live link in the title. Most titles are published in paperback and as an ebook. Paperbacks are available in traditional bookshops. Both print and ebook formats are available online.

Find more titles and sign up to our readers' newsletter at
http://www.johnhuntpublishing.com/transformation
Follow us on Facebook at
https://www.facebook.com/Changemakersbooks